D1440853

The Genesis of Neo-Kantianism, 1796–1880

The Genesis of
Neo-Kantianism,
1796–1880

Frederick C. Beiser

OXFORD
UNIVERSITY PRESS

OXFORD

UNIVERSITY PRESS

Great Clarendon Street, Oxford, OX2 6DP,
United Kingdom

Oxford University Press is a department of the University of Oxford.
It furthers the University's objective of excellence in research, scholarship,
and education by publishing worldwide. Oxford is a registered trade mark of
Oxford University Press in the UK and in certain other countries

Published in the United States of America by Oxford University Press
198 Madison Avenue, New York, NY 10016, United States of America

British Library Cataloguing in Publication Data
Data available

Library of Congress Control Number: 2014941600

ISBN 978-0-19-872220-5

Printed and bound by
CPI Group (UK) Ltd, Croydon, CR0 4YY

*In Memory of All Those Beisers who
Perished, 1941–1945, Victims of National-
Socialist Persecution*

Preface

This book is the product of a renewed interest in neo-Kantianism in the Anglophone world, an interest that grew out of the long overdue realization that one of the most influential philosophical movements of the late 19th and early 20th centuries had been badly neglected. This interest has been evident in four recent anthologies: *The Kantian Legacy in Nineteenth-Century Science,* edited by Michael Friedman and Alfred Nordmann (Cambridge, MA: MIT Press, 2006); *Back to Kant: Neo-Kantianism and its Relevance Today,* edited by Andrew Chignell, Terence Irwin and Thomas Teufel (*The Philosophical Forum,* Summer 2008); *Neo-Kantianism in Contemporary Philosophy,* edited by Rudolf Makkreel and Sebastian Luft (Bloomington, IN: Indiana University Press, 2010); and, last but not least, *The Impact of Idealism: The Legacy of Post-Kantian German Thought,* eds Nicholas Boyle, Liz Disley and Ian Cooper (Cambridge: Cambridge University Press, 2013), 4 vols. This interest has been the motivation for three academic conferences: the first one at the Dibner Institute for the History of Science and Technology at MIT in November 2000; another at Cornell University in Ithaca, New York, in September 2007; and the final one in Cambridge, England, in May 2008. I was fortunate enough to attend the conferences at MIT and Cornell; but because of family circumstances, I had to cancel plans to attend that in Cambridge, England. The stimulus I received from these conferences, either in attending or helping to plan them, was the main source of the present book.

The aim of this book, though intended as an introduction, is ambitious: to provide an account of the main ideas of the leading neo-Kantians from the 1790s to 1880s, the period before the institutionalization of the movement in the late 19th century. My subject is therefore the neo-Kantians before neo-Kantianism, the chief figures of the movement before its formation and division into distinct "schools". This is a study in the origins of neo-Kantianism, how and why it arose as a reaction against speculative idealism in the late 18th century, and as a response to the great cultural crises of the mid-19th century.

My approach to this subject is old-fashioned: I focus on the main writings of major authors, attempting to understand their chief ideas in historical context. I have not attempted to write an institutional history of the neo-Kantian schools, or to trace the social and political factors behind the rise of neo-Kantianism as a whole. While I find all these alternative approaches admirable, they should not replace the more basic knowledge of the *philosophy* of the neo-Kantians. We are far from such a basic knowledge, especially in the Anglophone world. The leading neo-Kantians and their main writings are still largely untreated in English. My main focus has therefore been upon them, and I have given philosophical content priority over social and political context.

Though my chief focus has been content, I do not ignore context. Since my main theme has been the origins and genesis of neo-Kantianism, it has been necessary to study the intellectual development of the major neo-Kantians. It is only through the study of the intellectual development of particular figures that we gain insight into the origins of neo-Kantianism, especially the goals and motivations behind the movement.

The study of neo-Kantianism is still in its infancy. It has taken two great strides forward in the work of Klaus Christian Köhnke, *Entstehung und Aufstieg des Neukantianismus* (Frankfurt: Suhrkamp, 1986) and Ulrich Sieg, *Aufstieg und Niedergang des Marburger Neukantianismus* (Würzburg: Königshausen & Neumann, 1994). Yet what Köhnke has done so brilliantly for the origins of the movement should be done for its establishment and fall; and what Sieg has done so well for the Marburg school should be done for the Southwestern and Göttingen schools. Not much will be known about neo-Kantianism unless and until we can recover the correspondence of its many participants. Though much has been destroyed, some has been preserved, though it lies mouldering in archives. Fortunately, we have much of the correspondence of the early neo-Kantians (Fries, Herbart and Beneke). It is a sad truth, however, that the only published correspondence we have of the later neo-Kantians is that of Hermann Cohen, which is lamentably brief because of the destruction of the Cohen family archives. Let me declare my hope here that future German scholars will make up for this terrible deficiency in the preservation of their cultural inheritance.

My debts to previous scholars are evident throughout, in the various footnotes in the fourteen chapters. I have been especially indebted to the work of Klaus Christian Köhnke, who has done more than anyone else to place neo-Kantian scholarship on a sound footing. I have honoured Köhnke, however, more by my many disagreements with him, which appear in the many footnotes in various chapters.

I have also great debts to many colleagues with whom, over the years, I have discussed various aspects of neo-Kantianism: Michael Friedman, Paul Guyer, Paul Franks, Gideon Freudenthal, Reinier Munk, Ingo Farin, Sebastian Luft, Michael Zank and Daniel Dahlstrom. In more ways than I can count or recall, their thinking about neo-Kantianism has been a major stimulus for this book.

Just as I was putting the finishing touches on this manuscript, I received the fruits of the Cambridge conference: *The Impact of Idealism: The Legacy of Post-Kantian German Thought*, eds Nicholas Boyle, Liz Disley and Ian Cooper (Cambridge: Cambridge University Press, 2013), 4 vols. These volumes have a much wider scope than the present book, which is confined to neo-Kantianism in the more narrow scholastic sense. The present book can be considered an addendum or supplement to these splendid volumes.

Syracuse, New York
December 2013

Contents

General Introduction
Defining and Re-Examining Neo-Kantianism

1. Chronology and Topography

Simply defined, neo-Kantianism, in a historical sense, was the movement in 19th-century Germany to rehabilitate Kant's philosophy. Neo-Kantianism was the predominant philosophical movement in Germany in the final decades of the 19th century, and its influence spread far and wide, to Italy, France, England and Russia. The golden age of neo-Kantianism was from 1860 to 1914. During these decades, to be at the cutting edge of philosophy, to have a rigorous training in the discipline, meant studying Kant. In 1875, Johannes Volkelt, an up-and-coming neo-Kantian, gave witness to this new *Zeitgeist*: "With few negligible exceptions, all philosophers agree in the high estimation of Kant; all attempt to orient themselves around Kant, and all see in his philosophy more or less explicit indications of their own position."[1]

Some hard statistical facts confirm the Kantian hegemony of these decades.[2] From 1862 to 1881 the number of lecture courses on Kant trebled, and there were more lectures on Kant than all modern philosophers combined. Bibliographies show that, after 1860, the number of works on Kant increased geometrically every year. And, by 1870, every major German university had at least one neo-Kantian professor on its philosophy faculty, which was better representation than any other philosophical standpoint or tendency. Because of facts like these, Klaus Christian Köhnke, doyen of neo-Kantian scholars, has called these decades "the neo-Kantian period of German university philosophy".[3]

Customarily, neo-Kantianism is divided into three main schools or groups: the Marburg school, whose chief protagonists were Hermann Cohen (1842–1918), Paul Natorp (1854–1924) and Ernst Cassirer (1874–1945); the Southwestern, Baden or Heidelberg school, whose major representatives were Wilhelm Windelband

---

[1] Johannes Volkelt, *Kant's Kategorischer Imperativ und die Gegenwart* (Vienna: Selbstverlag des Lesevereins der deutschen Studenten Wiens, 1875), p. 5.
[2] These facts are taken from Klaus Christian Köhnke's seminal study, *Entstehung und Aufstieg des Neukantianismus* (Frankfurt: Suhrkamp, 1986), pp. 314–317, 381–385.
[3] Köhnke, *Entstehung und Aufstieg*, p. 385.

(1848–1915), Heinrich Rickert (1863–1936) and Emil Lask (1875–1915); and the neo-Friesian school in Göttingen under the leadership of Leonard Nelson (1882–1927).[4] The dominant neo-Kantian universities were Marburg, Göttingen, Strassburg and Heidelberg; Berlin too eventually became a centre of neo-Kantianism later in the 19th and early 20th centuries, when Friedrich Paulsen (1896–1901), Alois Riehl (1844–1924) and Benno Erdmann (1851–1924) held chairs there.[5]

It is necessary to emphasize that these three schools do not define or exhaust neo-Kantianism. If one reads every article and every book by every member of all these groups, one would still be far from having an adequate knowledge of the movement. These groups came into being relatively late, between 1880 and 1904, decades after the core of the movement had been formed. All the founding figures of neo-Kantianism preceded them; and even later neo-Kantians fell outside their orbits. Among these "outsiders" were the Berliners Riehl, Paulsen and Erdmann, but also Johannes Volkelt (1848–1930), Hans Vaihinger (1852–1933), Erich Adickes (1866–1928), Arthur Liebert (1878–1946), Emil Arnoldt (1828–1905), and last, but certainly not least, Hermann Helmholtz (1821–1894). We too easily ignore these thinkers, some of whom played a crucial role in the movement, if we think of neo-Kantianism strictly in terms of schools.

The crucial formative decade for neo-Kantianism was the 1860s. Although there had been several neo-Kantian manifestos in earlier decades,[6] they grew in number and coalesced into a single force only in the 1860s. It was in this decade that some of the most dynamic young philosophers in Germany wrote articles, essays and even whole books, championing the cause of Kant's philosophy. There were five major figures who helped to re-establish Kant in this decade: Kuno Fischer (1824–1907), Eduard Zeller (1814–1908), Otto Liebmann (1840–1912), Jürgen Bona Meyer (1829–1897) and Friedrich Albert Lange (1828–1875). Part II will examine each in some detail.

---

[4] On the Marburg school, see Ulrich Sieg, *Aufstieg und Niedergang des Marburger Neukantianismus* (Würzburg: Königshausen & Neumann, 1994). Unfortunately, there is no counterpart history for the Southwestern school. On the neo-Friesian school, see Arthur Kronfeld, 'Geleitworte zum zehnjährigen Bestehen der neue Friesischen Schule', in *Das Wesen der psychiatrischen Erkenntnis* (Berlin: Springer, 1920), pp. 46–65; and Erna Blencke, 'Zur Geschichte der neuen Fries'schen Schule', *Archiv für Geschichte der Philosophie* 60 (1978), 199–208. Though neglected by standard histories, the group surrounding Nelson was especially eminent. Among its members were the theologian Rudolf Otto (1869–1937), the psychiatrist Arthur Kronfeld (1886–1941) and the Nobel prizewinner Otto Meyerhoff (1884–1951). The group published their own journal, *Abhandlungen der Fries'schen Schule, Neue Folge*, ed. Leonard Nelson (Göttingen: Vandenhoeck & Ruprecht, 1907–1937), 6 vols. Histories of the Southwestern and neo-Friesian schools are desiderata of future research.

[5] On neo-Kantianism in Berlin, see Volkert Gerhardt, Reinhard Mehring and Jana Rindert, *Berliner Geist: Eine Geschichte der Berliner Universitätsphilosophie bis 1946* (Berlin: Akademie Verlag, 1999), pp. 179–193.

[6] Among these earlier manifestos were Friedrich Beneke, *Kant und die philosophische Aufgabe unserer Zeit* (Berlin: Mittler, 1832); Christian Hermann Weiße, *In welchem Sinn die deutsche Philosophie jetzt wieder an Kant sich zu orientiren hat* (Leipzig: Dycke, 1847); and Carl Fortlage, 'Die Stellung Kants zur Philosophie vor ihm und nach ihm', *Deutsche Vierteljahrsschrift*, Heft IV (1838), 91–123.

It has been a commonplace of older scholarship that neo-Kantianism *began* in the 1860s. The starting point of the movement has been seen as Otto Liebmann's famous polemic *Kant und die Epigonen*, with its alleged mantra *"Zurück zu Kant!".*[7] But this commonplace, strictly speaking, is false. As Köhnke has argued, Liebmann's book came at the end, not the beginning, of a series of neo-Kantian manifestos.[8] Even Liebmann's mantra, which never appeared in such a punchy and pithy form, had its precedents in earlier works. Still, there is some merit to the old commonplace: though not the beginnings of neo-Kantianism, the 1860s were a crucial formative decade.

It is a central thesis of the present work that the origins of neo-Kantianism go back to the 1790s, even before Kant's death (1804).[9] The founding fathers of the movement were Jakob Friedrich Fries (1773–1843), Johann Friedrich Herbart (1776–1841) and Friedrich Eduard Beneke (1798–1854). All defined themselves as Kantians, and all called for a return to the spirit of Kant's teachings. They anticipated, and laid down the foundation for, defining doctrines of later neo-Kantianism: the importance of the Kantian dualisms between essence and existence, understanding and sensibility; the limitation of all knowledge to experience; the leading role of a critical and analytical method in philosophy; and the need for philosophy to follow rather than lead the natural sciences. The crucial role of Fries, Herbart and Beneke in founding neo-Kantianism, though ignored in recent neo-Kantian scholarship,[10] cannot be underestimated, especially in view of the enduring and widespread influence of Fries and Herbart. Part I will be devoted to a close study of the intellectual development and major writings of these early neo-Kantians.

It might seem absurd to trace neo-Kantianism back to the 18th century. Neo-Kantianism by its very name, someone will protest, implies *re-newal, re-habilitation*, so that it can begin only *after* a period when Kant's philosophy was in decline. Since that decline came during the era of German idealism—so the argument goes—neo-Kantianism could arise only at the end of that era, which came, at the earliest, with Hegel's death in 1831. However widespread and plausible, this reasoning passes over two central facts. First, Kant's reputation was already in decline in the early 1790s with the advent of Reinhold's *Elementarphilosophie* and Fichte's *Wissenschaftslehre*. For the young Romantic generation, Kant's philosophy seemed to have been surpassed and was considered obsolete. The more orthodox defenders and expositors of Kantian doctrine—Ludwig Jakob (1759–1827), C.G. Schütz (1747–1832), Carl Christian Schmid (1761–1812) and Johann Schultz (1739–1805)—appeared to belong to an older

---

[7] Otto Liebmann, *Kant und die Epigonen: Eine Kritische Abhandlung* (Stuttgart: Carl Schober, 1865). Liebmann concluded several chapters with the declaration *"Also muß auf Kant zurückgegangen werden."* He never used the more brief and punchy slogan.

[8] Köhnke, *Entstehung und Aufstieg*, p. 264.

[9] The reaction against speculative idealism began in the late 1790s. In the winter of 1796 the young Fries retired into his garret and sketched his programme for a revision of Kant's philosophy. In the same year Herbart wrote several short essays critical of Schelling. See Chapter 1, Section 3 and Chapter 2, Section 2.

[10] For this literature, see Part I Introduction, Section 3, note 7.

generation, and they were duly pushed aside in the path of philosophical progress. Second, the reaction against Reinhold's, Fichte's and Schelling's methods, and against speculative idealism in general, came later in the 1790s, in the fragments and notebooks of Hölderlin, Novalis and Friedrich Schlegel,[11] and not least in the early writings of Fries and Herbart.[12] The most compelling critique of Reinhold, Fichte and Schelling came with Fries 1803 *Reinhold, Fichte und Schelling*, which is really the source book for neo-Kantianism. All this will happen before the rise in Hegel's reputation; the neo-Kantian battle against Hegelianism will begin only in the 1820s, though it will largely reprise what had been said decades earlier during the campaign against Reinhold, Fichte and Schelling.

2. The Rise of Neo-Kantianism

How do we explain the rise of neo-Kantianism? What made this movement such a powerful one in the second half of the 19th century?

There were two cultural forces, already apparent in the 18th century, that had a powerful influence on the emergence of neo-Kantianism. The first was German nationalism, that is, the belief and pride in a single German nation, which was still not a political reality in the 1860s and would become so only in 1871. Kant, it was generally recognized, was a major inspiration for the German cultural revival at the end of the 18th century. The Germans were proud of Kant because he was a thinker of international stature, the first German philosopher to have achieved such status since Leibniz. This nationalism took visible form in 1854 when the city of Königsberg erected a statue to commemorate its most famous resident. The second was German historicism, which encouraged reflection on, and recollection of, historical roots. For the historicist, self-awareness is a matter of knowing one's origins, of retracing the past that made oneself. It was clear to all historically-minded philosophers in the early 19th century that Kant was the great revolutionary thinker dividing them from the intellectual life of the 18th century, and that he was the starting point of all modern German philosophy. Self-awareness therefore demanded understanding Kant, tracing the development of his views and seeing how his influence gave rise to contemporary philosophy. Such was the motivation behind much history of philosophy in the 1840s and 1850s, which gave pride of place to Kant.[13] It was in this spirit that Karl

---

[11] On the Romantic reaction against the foundationalism of Reinhold and Fichte, see Manfred Frank, *»Unendliche Annäherung«, Die Anfänge der philosophischen Frühromantik* (Frankfurt: Suhrkamp, 1997). Frank finds a tendency towards "rekantianization" already in the early 1790s in the writings of Herbert, Erhard, Feuerbach and Forberg (pp. 502, 617, 705). They too could be regarded, then, as precursors of neo-Kantianism.

[12] See Chapter 1, Section 3 and Chapter 2, Section 2.

[13] See Ernst Sigismund Mirbt, *Kant und seine Nachfolger oder Geschichte des Ursprungs und der Fortbildung der neueren deutschen Philosophie* (Jena: Hochhausen, 1841); Carl Fortlage, *Genetische Geschichte der Philosophie seit Kant* (Leipzig: Brockhaus, 1852); and Karl Rosenkranz, *Geschichte der kantischen Philosophie* (Leipzig: Voß, 1840).

Rosenkranz and Friedrich Wilhelm Schubert published the first collected edition of Kant's works, which was finished in 1842.[14]

These were only general cultural forces behind the rise of neo-Kantianism. They explain why it became *one* intellectual current, but not why it became the *predominant* one. For an intellectual movement to gain hegemony, it has to justify itself philosophically, to legitimate itself with reasons or arguments, and it has to defeat its competitors in the intellectual market place. What, then, was the philosophical rationale or justification of neo-Kantianism?

Part of that rationale was purely negative, deriving from the misfortunes and inherent flaws of its competitors. First and foremost among these competitors was speculative idealism. But speculative idealism had collapsed by the middle of the 19th century, independent of any neo-Kantian attacks upon it. The demise of speculative idealism left an enormous vacuum in the German intellectual scene, leaving neo-Kantianism as a viable contender to fill it. The decline of speculative idealism began with Hegel's death in 1831, but, because his spirit lived on through his many disciples, it would not dissolve until the end of the 1840s. There were two developments in the 1840s that doomed the Hegelian movement. First, the accession to the throne in 1840 of Friedrich Wilhelm IV, whose reactionary policies spelled the end of the Prussian Reform Movement, which had for decades sustained the political hopes and dreams of the young Hegelians. Second, on a purely intellectual level, the combined effect of the many assaults on Hegel's philosophy. Though Hegel's philosophy was already heavily criticized in the late 1820s and 1830s,[15] the 1840s saw a much higher calibre of criticism. In his *Logische Untersuchungen* (1840) Trendelenburg launched a powerful attack on Hegel's dialectic, whose devastating effect was conceded even by leading Hegelians.[16] In his *Metaphysik* (1841), Lotze exposed relentlessly the hypostases and weak transitions of Hegel's logic.[17] And, finally, in *Das Wesen des Christentums* (1841) Feuerbach convinced many neo-Hegelians of the need to go beyond Hegel, whose philosophy now seemed to be an obsolete metaphysics, the last

---

[14] Karl Rosenkranz and Friedrich Wilhelm Schubert, eds *Immanuel Kant's Sämtliche Werke* (Leipzig: Voß, 1838–1842), 12 vols.

[15] Among these were Carl Fortlage, *Die Lücken des Hegelschen Systems der Philosophie. Nebst Andeutung der Mittel, wodurch eine Ausfüllung derselben möglich ist.* (Heidelberg: Karl Groos, 1832); Otto Friedrich Gruppe, *Antäus. Ein Briefwechsel über speculative Philosophie in ihrem Conflict mit Wissenschaft und Sprache* (Berlin: Nancke, 1831); and Christian Hermann Weiße, *Ueber den Gegenwärtigen Standpunct der philosophischen Wissenschaft: In Besonderer Beziehung auf das System Hegels* (Leipzig: Barth, 1829). Fortlage, Gruppe and Weiße, as we shall see below, will later play an important role in preparing the neo-Kantian revival.

[16] Adolf Trendelenburg, *Logische Untersuchungen* (Berlin: Bethge, 1840), I, 23–99. On the effect of Trendelenburg's criticisms, see Karl Rosenkranz, *Die Modifikation der Logik abgeleitet aus dem Begriff des Denkens* (Berlin: Jonas, 1846), p. 250; Karl von Prantl, *Gedächtnisrede auf Friedrich Adolf Trendelenburg* (Munich: Akademie der Wissenschaften, 1873), pp. 10–11; and Hermann Bonitz, *Erinnerung an Friedrich Adolf Trendelenburg* (Berlin: Dümmler, 1873), pp. 22–23.

[17] Hermann Lotze, *Metaphysik* (Leipzig: Weidmann, 1841).

desperate stage of Christian apologetics.[18] The net result of all these criticisms was to re-affirm the Kantian limitations upon knowledge, the inescapability of the dualisms between form and content, essence and existence, understanding and sensibility.

The other part of the rationale is more positive. Neo-Kantianism became so popular and prevalent in the 1860s because Kant's philosophy, or at least some revised version of it, was widely seen as the only attractive solution to two major intellectual controversies of the mid-19th century. One of these controversies was the so-called "identity crisis of philosophy"; the other was the "materialism controversy".[19]

The identity crisis of philosophy, which began in the 1840s, was the result of two factors: the decline of speculative idealism and the rise of the empirical sciences. Now that the empirical sciences covered every sphere of reality, and now that the old a priori methods of speculative idealism had proven themselves bankrupt, it seemed as if there was no place anymore for philosophy in the *globus intellectualis*. What, then, should philosophy be? What could it do? To many, it seemed as if philosophy were obsolete, as if it had nothing more to offer than the hocus-pocus of metaphysics. The neo-Kantians appeared to rescue philosophy from this imminent obsolescence and to give it a new mission and identity. Their solution to the crisis, which we will examine in more detail below,[20] went by the name of "theory of knowledge" *(Erkenntnistheorie)*, what we now call "epistemology". It was a central and defining thesis of neo-Kantianism in the 1860s that philosophy could resurrect itself, and that it could find a definite place within the division of sciences, only as epistemology. The neo-Kantians had in mind a very specific conception of epistemology: the examination of the methods, standards and presuppositions of the empirical sciences. Though this conception would ultimately prove too narrow, it was very strategic when it was first advanced. For it not only aligned philosophy with the new natural sciences, whose dazzling success set the intellectual standards of the age, but it also gave philosophy a distinctive and definite task independent of them. Understood as epistemology, philosophy is no longer in danger of obsolescence because it determines "the logic of the sciences", a logic that the sciences use and apply but never examine and discuss. What the sciences presuppose that philosophy brings to self-consciousness, so that science becomes self-critical.

The materialism controversy began in 1854 and raged for decades thereafter. The central question posed by that controversy was whether science is leading inevitably to materialism. The advance of the natural sciences in the first half of the century seemed to make the old beliefs in a personal God, immortality and freedom, which were so important for Christian dogma, into so much mythology. Like the famous

---

[18] Ludwig Feuerbach, *Das Wesen des Christenthums* (Leipzig: Wigand, 1841). On the influence of Feuerbach's work on the young Hegelians, see Friedrich Engels classic statement in *Ludwig Feuerbach und der Ausgang der klassischen deutschen Philosophie* (Stuttgart: Dietz, 1888), p. 13.

[19] I have provided a more detailed account of both controversies in *After Hegel: German Philosophy from 1840 to 1900* (Princeton, NJ: Princeton University Press, 2014), Chapters 1 and 2.

[20] See Chapter 6, Sections 2, 3 and 5; and Chapter 12, Sections 2 and 3.

pantheism controversy of the late 18th century, the materialism controversy confronted the philosopher with a dramatic and drastic dilemma: choose between either a rational materialism or an irrational leap of faith. The critical philosophy seemed to rescue philosophers from this dire dilemma, providing the true *via media* between its horns: the critical philosophy showed how it is possible to have *both* natural science *and* moral or religious faith. While it championed freedom of enquiry for the natural sciences, the right to investigate without limiting the causes of phenomena, it also stood for the autonomy and rationality of the moral and religious sphere. Kant's famous statement that he had to deny knowledge for the sake of faith resonated as much in the 19th century as it did for the 18th. While neo-Kantian philosophers were highly critical of Kant's doctrine of practical faith—his attempt to justify the beliefs in God, providence and immortality on the basis of morality—they still believed in the necessity of a moral or normative sphere above and beyond nature.

The triumph of the neo-Kantian philosophers in the materialism controversy went hand in hand with their victory over another major competitor in the 1860s: the materialists. Materialism had become a powerful intellectual force in Germany during the 1850s in the wake of the materialism controversy. The writings of Ludwig Büchner (1824–1899), Heinrich Czolbe (1819–1873), Karl Vogt (1817–1895) and Jakob Moleschott (1822–1893) had become popular,[21] spreading the message far and wide that materialism is the new philosophy of the natural sciences. The Kantian counter-attack against materialism, which began in the 1860s in the works of Jürgen Bona Meyer and Friedrich Lange,[22] effectively blocked the materialist advance. The neo-Kantians put forward two powerful arguments against the materialists: first, they could never bridge the chasm between matter and consciousness; and second, they were naive and dogmatic, simply assuming the reality of matter, as if it were a pure given, completely ignoring the physiological and intellectual conditions of knowledge of the world.

And so, by the 1870s, neo-Kantianism had seemingly triumphed. It had not only provided plausible solutions to the main controversies of its age, but it had also defeated two of its main rivals, speculative idealism and materialism. But intellectual hegemony never lasts long and it is always quickly contested. There was another major rival to neo-Kantianism in the 1860s, and its challenge would only grow in the decades thereafter. This was the strange rise of Arthur Schopenhauer, who, after being ignored for decades, had become the most famous philosopher in Germany during the 1860s. Schopenhauer was something of a neo-Kantian himself, given his great debts to Kant, and he had even claimed to be Kant's sole legitimate heir. But he was still a potent challenge to the neo-Kantians because he had a competing solution to the identity crisis of philosophy. For Schopenhauer, philosophy is first and

---

[21] On these figures, see Frederick Gregory, *Scientific Materialism in Nineteenth Century Germany* (Dordrecht: Reidel, 1977).
[22] See Chapters 8 and 9.

foremost reflection on "the puzzle of existence", which for him meant the Hamlet question: "To be or not to be?". The importance of this question, and its sheer popularity among the public, forced the neo-Kantians to redefine their own conception of philosophy in the late 1870s and 1880s, so that it is not only epistemology but also ethics, not only a science but also a worldview. Despite this redefinition, Schopenhauer, and the *Lebensphilosophie* he inspired, would continue to challenge the neo-Kantians until the beginning of World War I.[23]

3. Removing Preconceptions and Prejudices

Like any major intellectual movement, neo-Kantianism has been the subject of misleading preconceptions and prejudices. We do well to remove them here. Some of these preconceptions are popular, others more esoteric or scholarly.

One popular preconception is that neo-Kantianism was an essentially scholarly movement, an attempt to revive the historical study of Kant's philosophy. Certainly, there is some truth to this view. The movement did give rise to new editions of his writings, to studies of his intellectual development as well as interpretations of his major ideas. The Akademie edition of Kant's writings, still the authoritative edition today, is very much the product of the neo-Kantian movement.[24] There was also a period of Kant philology at the turn of the century, in the works of Benno Erdmann, Erich Adickes and Emil Arnoldt, which gave rise to some of the best historical scholarship on Kant. Still, neo-Kantianism was more a philosophical than scholarly movement. It was the attempt to reaffirm the validity of Kant's philosophy, and more specifically one crucial aspect of it: his conception of philosophy and its method. The neo-Kantians believed that Kant's critical conception of philosophy, and his transcendental method for determining the necessary conditions of experience, are of enduring value, and that it is only by reviving them that philosophy can become a science.

Another popular misconception is that the neo-Kantians were epigoni, faithful disciples who would have to go without truth for a week if the mail coach from Königsberg broke down.[25] Nothing could be further from the truth. Though all neo-Kantians were intent, in one way or another, on the rehabilitation of Kant's philosophy, none were strict disciples of Kant. All were severely critical of Kant, and all used him for their own ends. Often they would appeal to a distinction between the "spirit" and "letter" of Kant's philosophy; but the spirit "blew where it listeth", taking on all shapes and forms depending on the philosopher.

[23] On Schopenhauer's challenge to and influence upon the neo-Kantians, see Part II Introduction, Section 4, and Chapter 10.
[24] *Kants gesammelte Schriften*, ed. Königlich Preußischen Akademie der Wissenschaften (Berlin: de Gruyter, 1902f). This edition is still in progress. Among the neo-Kantians who worked upon it were Erich Adickes, Benno Erdmann, Paul Natorp, Karl Vorländer, Bruno Bauch and Wilhelm Windelband.
[25] As Friedrich Schlegel once said. See his 'Fragmente', *Athenaeum* I (1798), 202.

One of the most prominent scholarly prejudices originated with Karl Löwith's influential book on 19th-century philosophy, *Von Hegel zu Nietzsche*.[26] Löwith saw neo-Kantianism as a scholastic academic philosophy, and attributed the real source of revolutionary thinking in the 19th century to the great outsiders, Marx, Kierkegaard and Nietzsche. It was these thinkers who were concerned with questions of existence and the meaning of life, whereas the neo-Kantians, ensconced in their ivory towers, had become entangled in abstruse questions about the logic of the sciences. Löwith's image of 19th-century philosophy has been a remarkably persistent one, captivating scholars even in the 21st century. What Löwith fails to see, however, is that the neo-Kantians were themselves outsiders for a long time, and that most of them, unlike Kierkegaard and Nietzsche, were persecuted for their heterodox moral and religious doctrines. He also does not recognize that the neo-Kantians, beginning in the late 1870s and early 1880s, were concerned to overcome their own narrow epistemological conception of philosophy, and that they shifted their interest towards moral, political and aesthetic questions. Löwith tends to identify neo-Kantianism with the arid positivism that it repudiated.

Another more recent but no less powerful source of prejudice was Richard Rorty's influential *Philosophy and the Mirror of Nature*.[27] Though Rorty wrote with an air of authority about neo-Kantianism, almost everything he said about it is false, confused or misleading. Neo-Kantianism played a crucial role in his narrative about modern philosophy and how it went astray. The neo-Kantians were for him the source of the modern conception of philosophy as a science and as a profession distinct from the positive sciences.[28] While Rorty is certainly correct to ascribe a crucial role to neo-Kantianism in forming much 20th-century philosophy, he ascribes doctrines to the movement that reveal ignorance of its intentions and origins. He maintains that the neo-Kantian conception of epistemology went hand in hand with the theory of the mind as a mirror of nature[29]—though even a partial familiarity with neo-Kantian thinking shows that they decisively rejected that theory. He also states that the neo-Kantian conception of philosophy as epistemology is essentially foundationalist, that it is based on the idea that philosophy can provide grounds for the positive sciences.[30] But the neo-Kantians, virtually without exception, rejected foundationalism. Their movement began with a reaction against the foundationalist tradition in epistemology, and it contested the idea that philosophy could provide a grounding for the empirical sciences. In the neo-Kantian view, the positive sciences are autonomous, and they no longer require, as the speculative idealists once held, a foundation from philosophy. We will see, in the following chapters, this anti-foundationalist stance appear again and again in the history of the movement.

---

[26] Karl Löwith, *Von Hegel zu Nietzsche, Der revolutionäre Bruch im Denken des 19. Jahrhunderts* (Zurich: Europa Verlag, 1941), pp. 135–136.
[27] Richard Rorty, *Philosophy and the Mirror of Nature* (Oxford: Blackwell, 1980).
[28] Rorty, *Philosophy*, pp. 131–136.
[29] On the neo-Kantians as purveyors of the mirror metaphor, see Rorty, *Philosophy*, pp. 12, 163, 393.
[30] See Rorty, *Philosophy*, pp. 4, 131–132.

PART I

Introduction

The Lost Tradition

1. Unearthing the Lost Tradition

The origins of neo-Kantianism are shrouded in mystery. Neo-Kantianism arose from a tradition of philosophy that has been almost entirely forgotten.[1] At the very end of the 18th century and the very beginning of the 19th century, a distinctive idealist tradition was formed in Germany by three young philosophers: Jakob Friedrich Fries (1773–1843), Johann Friedrich Herbart (1776–1841) and Friedrich Eduard Beneke (1798–1854). Though idealist themselves, they stood in self-conscious opposition to the idealist tradition of Fichte, Schelling and Hegel. Their tradition has been "lost", however, because it was overshadowed by the speculative idealism of Fichte, Schelling and Hegel, which is normally regarded as the sole form of idealism in this period. Yet it was from this lost tradition that neo-Kantianism arose. The neo-Kantian movement, which became fully visible and established only in the 1860s, has its *fons et origo* in the lost tradition.

Fries, Herbart and Beneke were separate, isolated spirits, working independently of one another. Although they knew one another, sometimes even met, and on one occasion even attempted to collaborate, they did not form an organized and self-conscious movement; there were also many important intellectual differences between them. Still, they had so many attitudes, values and beliefs in common that

---

[1] The only scholar who came close to recognizing the existence of an antithetical idealist tradition was Kuno Fischer in his *Die beiden kantische Schulen in Jena* (Stuttgart: Cotta, 1862). Fischer's argument is that there were two traditions active in Jena in the late 18th and early 19th centuries, the "metaphysical" tradition of Reinhold, Fichte, Schelling and Hegel and the "anthropological" tradition of Fries. However, Fischer does not mention Beneke, and he places Herbart in the "metaphysical" tradition. The anthropological tradition, on his reckoning, consists only in Fries and his followers. We will see below that there are strong reasons for placing Herbart in the opposing tradition and for questioning his so-called "realism".

one is justified in regarding them as a distinct tradition. They shared an allegiance to transcendental idealism, a programme for reforming epistemology through psychology, a mistrust of rationalism and speculative metaphysics, a deep belief in the reliability of the methods of the exact sciences, an ethics based on aesthetics, and an antipathy to the speculative idealism of Fichte, Schelling and Hegel.

The reason this tradition has been lost has much to do with how the history of philosophy has been written since the early 19th century. We are often told that the history of philosophy after Kant consists chiefly in the emergence of an idealist tradition that begins with Reinhold, continues with Fichte and Schelling, and then culminates in Hegel. The source of this simple but powerful narrative was Hegel himself,[2] who saw his own system as the *telos* of post-Kantian philosophy. His narrative was re-affirmed later in the 19th century by two neo-Hegelians: Johann Erdmann and Kuno Fischer;[3] it was then revived in the 20th century by Richard Kroner and Frederick Copleston.[4] What this history so tendentiously leaves out is its competition, the tradition of Fries, Herbart and Beneke. For self-serving reasons, Hegel had virtually written his opponents out of history, and his disciples gladly followed him.

The general fact obscured by Hegel's history of philosophy is that there were two opposing idealist traditions in Germany in the late 18th and early 19th centuries. There was the rationalist-speculative tradition of Reinhold, Fichte, Schelling and Hegel, *and* the empiricist-psychological tradition of Fries, Herbart and Beneke. These traditions were opposed in five fundamental ways.

– The rationalist-speculative tradition rejected, while the empiricist-psychological tradition accepted, Kant's transcendental idealism in its original intended sense, that is, the limitation of knowledge to appearances and the distinction between appearances and the thing-in-itself. Rather than decrying the thing-in-itself as the great weakness of the Kantian system, as Fichte, Schelling and Hegel had done, Fries, Herbart and Beneke regarded it as its great strength.
– The rationalist-speculative tradition employed a deductive or dialectical method, believing in the powers of pure thought or a priori reasoning to reach substantive conclusions; the empiricist-psychological tradition, however, stressed the importance of an empirical method, insisting that pure thinking alone could reach no substantial conclusions and that knowledge must receive its content from experience.

[2] G.W.F. Hegel, 'Neueste deutsche Philosophie', in volume III of his *Vorlesungen über die Geschichte der Philosophie*, in *Werke in zwanzig Bänden*, eds E. Moldenhauer and K. Michel (Frankfurt: Suhrkamp, 1971), XX, 314–462.
[3] Johann Erdmann, *Die Entwicklung der deutschen Spekulation seit Kant*, volume 5 of *Versuch einer wissenschaftlichen Darstellung der Geschichte der Philosophie* (Stuttgart: Frommann, 1977), first published 1834; and Kuno Fischer, Vols V–VIII of his *Geschichte der neueren Philosophie* (Heidelberg: Winter, 1872–1877).
[4] Chapter 1, Sections 3 and 7.

- In Schelling and Hegel, the rationalist-speculative tradition developed into an "objective" or "absolute idealism", according to which all reality is the manifestation of the ideal, where these ideals are forms or archetypes existing independent of human consciousness; the empiricist-psychological tradition stuck to "subjective idealism", protesting that there are no such ideals and that all knowledge is relative to human consciousness.
- The rationalist-speculative tradition attempted to surmount Kant's dualisms between understanding and sensibility, essence and existence, form and content, through an organic concept of nature; the empiricist-psychological tradition, however, wanted to retain these dualisms, and disputed the constitutive validity of that organic concept.
- The rationalist-speculative tradition believed in the unity of reason, that is, that there is a single source of theoretical and practical reason; the empiricist-psychological tradition disputed that there is any such unity and stressed the fundamental divide between theoretical and practical reason.

Some of these conflicts are clear to us now only with the benefit of hindsight. But it would be wrong to assume that the existence of these two traditions is a mere *post facto* reconstruction, the product of the historian's abstraction. For sometimes these differences became all too plain to these thinkers themselves. Fries, Herbart and Beneke were aware of their common opposition to the speculative-rationalist tradition; on these grounds, Beneke proposed collaboration with Herbart, and Herbart hoped for an accord with Fries. For their part, Reinhold, Fichte and Schelling were well aware of their differences with Fries, Herbart and Beneke, though they did not deign to write polemics against them. In the case of Hegel, however, opposition to Fries and Beneke became hostile, even political. He condemned Fries in the preface to his *Philosophie des Rechts*, and he has been accused of using his influence on the Prussian government to place a rescript against Beneke's lectures in Berlin.[5]

2. Two Conflicting Kantian Traditions

It is a striking and perplexing fact that both these traditions, despite all the conflicts between them, would invoke the name and authority of Kant to justify themselves. Both claimed to represent "the spirit of the Kantian philosophy", which pushed them in opposing directions. The source of all the conflicts between them lay indeed in their conflicting interpretations of Kant's main project.

Reinhold, Fichte, Schelling and Hegel read Kant's philosophy as a foundationalist enterprise along Cartesian lines, that is, its aim is to provide a self-evident basis for knowledge, one completely immune from sceptical doubt. They maintained that

---

[5] See Chapter 3, Section 2.

Kant's philosophy contains self-evident first principles—namely, the possibility of experience, the unity of apperception, the facts of consciousness, the concept of representation, subject–object identity—from which it could derive deductively all its central conclusions about the structure of human knowledge. It was often admitted that Kant did not provide a straightforward exposition of this foundationalist project, though it was still held to be implicit in his texts and his ultimate design. Formulating that exposition, realizing the true foundationalism inherent in Kant's project, was the aim of Reinhold's *Elementarphilosophie*, Fichte's *Wissenschaftslehre* and Schelling's *Vom Ich als Prinzip der Philosophie*.

The philosophers in the empiricist-psychological tradition, however, read Kant's philosophy in a completely different light, though one that seemed no less sanctioned by Kant's texts. For Fries, Herbart and Beneke, Kant's transcendental philosophy was not a foundationalist but a psychological or anthropological project whose chief task was to describe human psychology and the basic workings of the human mind. Kant's aim was to realize the old Enlightenment project for a science of human nature or anthropology. Although they conceded that Kant had not given a perfect exposition of that project, they still insisted that it was implicit in his texts. It would be their aim to make this project clear and explicit. No less than their rationalist-speculative counterparts, Fries, Herbart and Beneke wanted to put Kant's philosophy on a solid foundation; but for them that foundation would lie not in deductive or dialectical reasoning but in the observation and experiment of the empirical sciences. Kant's philosophy was to be placed on a sound *empirical* foundation, its psychology based upon solid "facts of experience".

Now, with the benefit of hindsight, we can see that each tradition had stretched one aspect of Kant at the expense of the other. They had pitted his rationalist and empiricist sides against one another. Reinhold, Fichte, Schelling and Hegel had taken hold of Kant's rationalist side, namely, the value he placed on systematic unity, on a dogmatic method of demonstration, on a priori principles and reasoning. Fries, Herbart and Beneke, however, had grasped the empiricist side, namely, his insistence that the content of knowledge be given by the senses, that metaphysics should not transcend the limits of experience, that analysis of concepts cannot provide substantive knowledge. Both traditions knew that Kant's intention was to synthesize empiricism and rationalism; but they could not bring both sides together. Thus Reinhold, Fichte, Schelling and Hegel complained about Kant's empiricism, which appeared in his lack of systematic rigour in deriving the categories. But Fries, Herbart and Beneke would grumble about the "remnants of scholasticism" in Kant's philosophy, that is, his too rigid systematic sense, his artificial conceptual distinctions, his old-fashioned dogmatic method of analysis and demonstration. *Summa summarum*, for the rationalist-speculative tradition, Kant was too much of an empiricist; but for the empirical-psychological tradition, he was too much of a rationalist. For both traditions, Kant's grand attempt to synthesize rationalism and empiricism seemed a hopeless delusion.

In the battle over Kant's legacy, both traditions could put forward a strong case for why they alone were the true heirs. Fries, Herbart and Beneke could give several reasons. First, they advocated Kant's transcendental idealism in its original form, especially its limitation of knowledge to appearances and its postulate of the thing-in-itself. Second, they upheld Kant's regulative constraints upon teleology, which had been violated by Schelling and Hegel. Third, they banished appeals to intellectual intuition, which Kant had proscribed but which had been re-invoked by Fichte, Schelling and the young Hegel. Fourth, they dwelled in "the bathos of experience", insisting that all knowledge be limited to experience. Fifth, they re-affirmed Kant's dualisms, more specifically, those between understanding and sensibility, essence and existence, practical and theoretical reason, all of which are central to his critical teachings. For all these reasons, Fries, Herbart and Beneke believed they represented the true Kant, the spirit of his teachings. They called for a return to Kant in the early 1800s, decades before that refrain became widespread in the 1860s.

The rationalist-speculative tradition could also muster a strong case. In stressing the foundationalist side of Kant's philosophy they were attempting to show how it could be a response to scepticism, which had been Kant's intention all along. Had not Kant said that he was aroused from his "dogmatic slumbers" by Hume? And had he not made it plain that it was his intention to reply to the Scotsman's scepticism? It was in Kant's transcendental deduction, Fichte, Schelling and Hegel claimed, that one could find the true "spirit of the Kantian philosophy", because the plain purpose of that deduction was to legitimate synthetic a priori knowledge against scepticism. Their demands for rigorous deductive or dialectical reasoning, for strict systemic form, and for a priori science, also seemed sanctioned by Kant himself. For Kant had often insisted that reason is by its very nature systematic, that a system should be organized around a single idea, and that all science involves a priori principles and reasoning.[6] Fichte, Schelling and Hegel were well aware that, in some respects, they were revising Kant, namely, they were abolishing the thing-in-itself, postulating an intellectual intuition, and casting aside regulative constraints upon teleology. But they insisted that in doing so they were violating only "the letter" of Kant's philosophy, and that for all these "infractions" of the letter they could find reason enough in the Kantian spirit. After all, they were only trying to make Kant's philosophy consistent, to help Kant solve his own problems according to his own principles. Since it transcends the limits of possible experience, the thing-in-itself is an untenable postulate according to Kant's own standard of knowledge. The concept of intellectual intuition, though contrary to the Kantian letter, seemed to be strongly suggested by Kant's teaching in several places: it was implicit in his theory of mathematical construction, in his conception of the self-awareness of our own cognitive activity, and in the "fact of reason". And as for the regulative constraints upon teleology, Schelling and Hegel insisted that

---

[6] Kant, KrV, B 502, 673, 708, 862.

Kant himself had to infract them, for it is only by giving constitutive status to the idea of the organism that it is possible to overcome the Kantian dualisms, which otherwise pose an insuperable obstacle to explaining synthetic a priori knowledge.

3. Neo-Kantianism and the Lost Tradition

Fortunately, we need not decide here who were the rightful heirs of Kant's legacy. The question is perhaps irresolvable. Both traditions had crucial texts in their favour, and both could claim that in dropping some aspects of Kant's teaching they were only making it consistent. Both traditions could describe themselves therefore as "neo-Kantian".

Yet, as history would have it, we now regard only one of these traditions as neo-Kantian. The battle to represent Kant's legacy was won—whether rightly or wrongly—by the thinkers of the empiricist-psychological tradition. They won the battle simply because their arguments were later adopted by a slew of thinkers whom we now happen to call, for purely customary reasons, "neo-Kantians". After the 1840s and the decline of neo-Hegelianism, the arguments of the rationalist-speculative tradition had lost their power to persuade. The first generation of neo-Kantians in the 1860s—Kuno Fischer, Eduard Zeller, Otto Liebmann, Jürgen Bona Meyer and Friedrich Albert Lange—reacted against the neo-rationalism of Schelling's and Hegel's metaphysics, much as Fries, Herbart and Beneke did decades earlier. These "neo-Kantians" were writing in an age even more dominated by the empirical sciences, and to them it seemed all the more necessary that philosophy give up its pretensions to legislate for the sciences; its only feasible task seemed to be the examination of their underlying logic. The position of the empiricist-psychological tradition seemed prescient, then, the best advice for philosophy to go forward in a more scientific age. These neo-Kantians also adopted other basic contentions of the empiricist-psychological tradition: that Kant's philosophy should be interpreted in psychological terms; that philosophy should remain within the limits of experience; that Kant's concept of teleology should remain regulative; that it is necessary to accept Kant's dualisms between understanding and sensibility, essence and existence, form and content, as inherent limits of the human understanding. So, for better or worse, it was the empiricist-psychological tradition that triumphed in history, and that won out over its rationalist-speculative rival.

It is all the more surprising, therefore, that the empiricist-psychological tradition has been forgotten, slipping away into the mists of the past. Though it had paved the way for early neo-Kantianism, its powerful influence has been scarcely recognized. Some neo-Kantians acknowledged the importance of Fries, Herbart or Beneke, but later scholars of neo-Kantianism have virtually ignored them. Most of the standard works on the history of neo-Kantianism do not discuss them.[7]

---

[7] Among these works are Hans-Ludwig Ollig, *Der Neukantianismus* (Stuttgart: Metzler, 1979); Thomas E. Willey, *Back to Kant* (Detroit, MI: Wayne State University Press, 1978); Gerhard Lehmann,

There are several reasons for such neglect. First, there was the reaction against the psychological interpretation of Kant in the 1870s and 1880s by the later neo-Kantians, especially by Windelband and Cohen. The argument that Kant's transcendental philosophy is epistemology and not psychology made it seem legitimate to leave out of account a tradition of interpretation that had stressed the psychological aspect of Kant's project. For this reason, it is common to limit neo-Kantianism to the Southwestern and Marburg schools alone. Second, some scholarship remains fixed on the idea that the neo-Kantian tradition begins only when epistemology is made a *sui generis* discipline distinct from the empirical sciences, not least among them psychology. Third, though many scholars assume, correctly, that neo-Kantianism arose from a rejection of the methods and metaphysics of absolute idealism, they date that reaction much too late, placing it in the 1840s after the collapse of Hegel's metaphysics. It is important to realize, however, that the reaction against speculative idealism took place much earlier, and indeed for very Kantian reasons. It arose in the early 1800s when Fries and Herbart criticized the methods and metaphysics of Fichte's and Schelling's idealism. If "neo-Kantianism" means a revival of Kant after his decline, then it is necessary to recall that Kant's reputation fell into decline even before his death; he had lost his stature as a major innovator by 1800 in the eyes of the early Romantics and metaphysical idealists. The protest against his decline, the case for his rehabilitation, was made by Fries in the early 1800s in his *Reinhold, Fichte und Schelling*. This brilliant but much neglected book, as we shall soon see, was the first statement of the neo-Kantian programme.

By far the most important factor working against the rehabilitation of the empiricist-psychological tradition has been its association with "psychologism". Since the work of Husserl and Frege at the beginning of the 20th century, "psychologism" has been regarded as a basic fallacy, the simple conflation of logical rules of inference with natural laws of thought.[8] Because of their advocacy of empirical psychology, Fries, Herbart and Beneke were associated with this fallacy, and so they became widely discredited.[9] Beneke's work, especially, was regarded as "the most radical form of psychologism".[10] It is important to realize, however, that neither Fries nor Herbart nor Beneke are guilty of the fallacy of psychologism in the simple sense attributed to

---

Geschichte der nachkantischen Philosophie (Berlin: Junker und Dünnhaupt, 1931); Klaus Christian Köhnke, *Entstehung und Aufstieg des Neukantianismus* (Frankfurt: Suhrkamp, 1986); Ulrich Sieg, *Aufstieg und Niedergang des Marburger Neukantianismus* (Würzburg: Königshausen & Neumann, 1994); L.W. Beck, 'Neo-Kantianism', in *The Encyclopedia of Philosophy* (New York: Macmillan, 1967), V, 468–473; and H. Holzhey, 'Neukantianismus', in *Historisches Wörterbuch der Philosophie* (Basel: Schwabe, 1984), VI, 747–754. Of all these authors only Lehmann gives some importance to Fries and Herbart; and only Köhnke recognizes Beneke.

[8] On the charge of psychologism and its many meanings and associations, see Martin Kusch, *Psychologism* (London: Routledge, 1995), pp. 95–121.

[9] For how many times exactly, see Kusch, *Psychologism*, who documents all the instances, p. 97.

[10] Wilhelm Windelband, *Die Geschichte der neueren Philosophie*, sixth edition (Leipzig: Breitkopf & Härtel, 1919), II, p. 423.

them. We will see in later chapters that they carefully made the distinction between the normative and the factual, between rules of inference and laws of thought. It was, however, an important question among them, given such a distinction, how far psychology is still relevant to epistemological and logical questions. On the whole, the tradition saw psychological and epistemological questions as distinct yet complementary. They believed that it is still necessary and important to have both perspectives while distinguishing between them. The blanket charge of psychologism simply begs questions against the subtle discussions of the interrelationship between epistemology and psychology that took place in the empiricist-psychological tradition.

Though Fries, Herbart and Beneke understood Kant's project in psychological terms, it would be a mistake to think—as many neo-Kantians later did—that their intent was to read all epistemology out of Kant's project. They did not reduce the *quid juris?* to the *quid facti?*, as Cassirer was later to complain; and they were perfectly aware of, and indeed insisted upon, the distinction between these kinds of questions. Rather than ignoring or abolishing epistemology, they understood it in very different terms from the rationalist-speculative tradition. Fries, Herbart and Beneke wanted to steer epistemology away from an ambitious foundationalism and towards a more modest examination of the logic of the sciences. They rejected the old conception of philosophy as a *philosophia prima,* whose aim is to provide a foundation for all the sciences, and they advocated instead a new conception of philosophy as the "underlabourer" of the empirical sciences, whose task is to investigate their methods and presuppositions. For Fries, Herbart and Beneke, empirical science is an autonomous activity that has already established its legitimacy and that stands in no need of a higher philosophical foundation; the philosopher need not, and should not, interfere with the sciences, attempt to anticipate their results or justify them from first principles. Since science is a fact, a fait accompli, the task of philosophy is to understand it and explain how this fact is possible. Fries, Herbart and Beneke were all critical, therefore, of the *Naturphilosophie* of Schelling and Hegel, which they regarded as an illegitimate intrusion of philosophy upon the domain of empirical science. The famous reorientation of philosophy around the empirical sciences, which is supposed to be a legacy of positivism or Trendelenburg, was really the work of Fries, Herbart and Beneke in the early decades of the 19th century.

4. Origins and Context

The origins of the empiricist-psychological tradition lie in the early 18th century, in the project for "a science of human nature" that came originally from the Scottish Enlightenment. This new science, which was advocated by Hume, Smith, Home, Ferguson and Millar, was modelled on the methods of the new natural sciences. It would be, in Hume's memorable phrase, "An Attempt to introduce the experimental

Method of Reasoning into Moral Subjects."[11] What Newton had done for the physical cosmos, the Scottish philosophers intended to do for "the moral realm". Their aim was to formulate precise laws about human nature based on natural history, whose facts were to be collected from introspection, observation, travel narratives and histories.[12] Beginning in the middle of the 18th century, this project was imported into Germany through translations of the Scottish philosophers,[13] and it soon found many devotees, among them Karl Friedrich Flögel, Ernst Platner, Jakob Friedrich Abel, Johann Georg Feder, Christoph Meiners, and, last but not least, the young Herder.[14] The Germans word for this new science of human nature was *"Anthropologie"*, which was defined in a broad sense: "The doctrine of man, his parts and relations, in a theological as well as a physical and moral sense."[15] There was a naturalistic perspective behind anthropology, which saw human beings as parts of nature as a whole and therefore as subject to her laws. Following this perspective, anthropology would stress the interaction between the mind and nature (viz. geography and climate) and between the mental and physical aspects of a human being, striving to grasp man as a unity and whole. The old metaphysical mind–body problem, which had so troubled the great minds of the 17th century, was simply laid aside in favour of a kind of empirical interactionism. The aim was to show the intimate interaction between mind and body, regardless of the metaphysical basis for that fact.

There are some direct links between the anthropological and empirical-psychological traditions. It is no accident that Fries sometimes called his "new critique of reason" an "anthropological critique", and that he had made anthropology into the basis of philosophy in his early *System der Philosophie*. As a student in Leipzig in 1796, Fries had attended the lectures of Ernst Platner, who was the foremost spokesman for anthropology in Germany; he later acknowledged Platner's great importance for his own philosophy.[16] The young Beneke called his psychology *Erfahrungsseelenkunde*,

[11] From the subtitle of the first edition of *A Treatise of Human Nature* (London: John Noon, 1739).

[12] On the methods of Scottish anthropology, see Aaron Garrett, 'Anthropology: the 'original' of human nature', in *The Cambridge Companion to the Scottish Enlightenment*, ed. Alexander Broadie (Cambridge: Cambridge University Press, 2003), pp. 79–93.

[13] On the dates of these translations, see Max Wundt, *Die deutsche Schulphilosophie im Zeitalter der Aufklärung* (Tübingen: Mohr, 1945), pp. 270–271, n.1.

[14] Eighteenth-century German anthropology has recently become the subject of intensive investigation. See especially the recent studies by John Zammito, *Kant, Herder & the Birth of Anthropology* (Chicago, IL: University of Chicago Press, 2002), pp. 221–254; and Michael Carhart, *The Science of Culture in Enlightenment Germany* (Cambridge, MA: Harvard University Press, 2007), pp. 222–247. See also Mareta Linden, *Untersuchungen zum Anthropologiebegriff des 18. Jahrhunderts* (Frankfurt: Lang, 1976); and Karl Fink, 'Storm and Stress Anthropology', *History of the Human Sciences* 6 (1993), 51–71. See also these anthologies: *Der ganze Mensch: Anthropologie und Literatur im 18. Jahrhundert*, ed. Hans-Jürgen Schings (Stuttgart: Metzler, 1992); *Anthropologie und Literatur um 1800*, eds Jürgen Barkhoff and Eda Sagarra (Munich: Iudicium Verlag, 1992); and *Anthropology and the German Enlightenment*, ed. Katherine M. Faull (Lewisburg, PA: Bucknell, 1995).

[15] See Johann Christian Adelung, *Grammatisch-Kritische Wörterbuch der hochdeutschen Mundart* (Vienna: Bauer, 1811), p. 392.

[16] See Jakob Friedrich Fries, *Handbuch der Psychischen Anthropologie* (Jena: Cröker, 1820), I, 'Vorrede' (unpaginated).

a very revealing term in pinning down his intellectual roots. *Erfahrungsseelenkunde* was an immediate offshoot of the anthropological tradition, whose precedent was Karl Phillip Moritz's *Erfahrungsseelenkunde,* a project of the Berlin *Aufklärung* that flourished at the end of the 18th century.[17] This project was pursued by two Kantian philosophers in Halle, J.C. Hoffbauer and L.H. Jakob, whose lectures Beneke attended when he was a student there.[18]

The triumph of Kant's philosophy in the 1790s thwarted and interrupted the tradition of anthropology. Though Kant himself was an anthropologist in his pre-critical years, he had turned away from anthropology on the road to transcendental philosophy.[19] Kant's critique of the empiricist tradition, and his sharp separation between the *quid juris?* and *quid facti?,* meant a turning away from the empirical methods of anthropology. Kant had located the problem of knowledge in a place where it could not be solved by empirical methods; indeed, he had shown that following those methods to their ultimate conclusion, in the manner of Hume, could end only in scepticism. Accordingly, for the critical Kant, the method of philosophy is no longer empirical but transcendental, that is, it determines through logical analysis of concepts and discursive reasoning the necessary conditions of knowledge.[20] The method of philosophy, Kant now taught, essentially consists in "rational cognition in concepts", which involves discursive proofs.[21] It is no wonder, then, that the champions of anthropology saw Kant's methodology as a relapse into the old scholasticism, a vice for which their empirical methods were a remedy. It is also no surprise that they were more impressed by the "analytic method" of the young Kant's *Prize Essay,* which they believed to be more in accord with the empirical sciences.

Despite this friction between transcendental philosophy and anthropology, there was still, in one important respect, a confluence of these traditions. Despite their naturalism, the anthropologists still had an anthropocentric view of the world. They would often stress how what we know depends on our powers of perception and organs of sense, so that the object of knowledge is not simply given to us; and they would often emphasize how what we value depends on our desires and emotions, so that the good does not exist in a Platonic realm beyond us. Since what we know and value depends crucially on our human powers and needs, the anthropologists made anthropology

---

[17] See Karl Phillip Moritz, *Gnothi sauton oder Magazin zur Erfahrungsseelenlehre als ein Lesebuch für Gelehrte und Ungelehrte* (Berlin: Mylius, 1783–1793), 10 vols. There is a large literature surrounding Moritz's *Erfahrungsseelenkunde.* Two good introductory accounts: Hans Joachim Schrimpf, 'Das Magazin zur Erfahrungsseelenkunde und sein Herausgeber', *Zeitschrift für deutsche Philologie* 99 (1980), 161–187; and Martin Davies, 'Erfahrungsseelenkunde: Its social and intellectual origins', *Oxford German Studies* 16 (1985), 13–35.

[18] This is pointed out by Otto Gramzow, *Friedrich Eduard Benekes Leben und Philosophie* (Bern: Steiger, 1899), p. 15. See, for example, Johann Christoph Hoffbauer, *Allgemeine Betrachtungen über die Seelenkrankheiten und eine Klassification derselben* (Halle: Hahn, 1802) and *Naturlehre der Seele* (Halle: Renger, 1796). See also, Ludwig Heinrich Jakob, *Grundriß der Erfahrungs-Seelenlehre* (Halle: Hemmerde und Schwetschke, 1791).

[19] On that story, see Zammito, *Kant, Herder & the Birth of Anthropology,* pp. 255–307.

[20] KrV, B 750, 762. [21] KrV, B 741, 762.

into their master science, the basis of, or key to, all the other sciences. Following Pope's famous adage, they believed that "the proper study of mankind is man." This anthropocentric tendency was an important shift in priorities away from the old Wolffian school philosophy, which had made ontology into *philosophia prima*. Rather than beginning with being in general, the anthropologists believed that we must first look at the man who knows being, given that all knowledge of being depends on him. It was this anthropocentric tendency of the anthropological tradition that eventually merged with the Kantian tradition, for it expressed the same direction of thought as Kant's Copernican Revolution. Kant's philosophy had given a powerful new rationale and epistemology to support the anthropocentric direction of anthropology. Hence, in this important respect, the critical philosophy was not a turn away from anthropology but a vindication of it. We can now understand why Beneke could claim that anthropocentrism was "the proper critical spirit of the Kantian philosophy."[22]

Once we place Fries, Herbart and Beneke in the context of the anthropological tradition, we can begin to understand their early reaction to Kant. They were very ready to embrace the Copernican Revolution, which to them established in subtle and sophisticated ways the fundamental anthropological truth that all knowledge is conditioned by human psychology. Fries, Herbart and Beneke very much celebrated the Kantian critical enterprise, which they saw as a breakthrough for philosophy and as the final turning point against the old rationalist metaphysics that had dominated Germany in the past. Their task was now to carry through with that Revolution, though by using the modern tools and methods that they had learned in anthropology. They believed that Kantian epistemology had to be based on a new empirical psychology, one whose methods were akin to those of the natural sciences. They could not accept, therefore, Kant's scholastic or rationalist methodology, which they saw as a relapse into the old scholastic methods. Still less were they ready to adopt Kant's psychology, whose archaic doctrine of faculties seemed to come straight out of Wolff's *Psychologia empirica*. All that would be done away with in making the critical philosophy a new kind of anthropology.

It should be plain by now that the thinkers of the lost tradition are of the first importance for understanding the genesis of neo-Kantianism. For that reason we will now embark upon a examination of the early writings of Fries, Herbart and Beneke, the writings that established them as major thinkers in the neo-Kantian movement. Since these writings have been largely forgotten, we will introduce and expound their basic doctrines, all the while setting them in their original context. I follow their intellectual development only up to their discovery of Kant and the first formulation of their neo-Kantian doctrines. I make no attempt here to provide a complete account of the philosophy or intellectual development of these thinkers. That goes far beyond our business here: the story of the genesis of neo-Kantianism.

---

[22] See F.E. Beneke, *Das Verhältniß von Seele und Leib* (Göttingen: Vandenhoeck & Ruprecht, 1826), p. vii.

1

Jakob Friedrich Fries and the Birth of Psychologism

1. Place in History

Recent histories of neo-Kantianism give little place to Jakob Friedrich Fries (1773–1843).[1] This is a grave omission, because Fries should be regarded, along with Herbart and Beneke, as a founding father of neo-Kantianism. Though now almost forgotten, he is as important to the history of neo-Kantianism as Windelband and Cohen. Just as Windelband was the leader of the Southwestern school, and Cohen the founder of the Marburg school, Fries was the guiding spirit behind the neo-Friesian school, which was of no less stature and influence than its Southwestern and Marburgian counterparts.

There are compelling reasons to regard Fries as a founder of neo-Kantianism. First, when it was very unpopular to do so, and decades before the later neo-Kantians, Fries declared himself a Kantian, often referring to his "*Kantianismus*". In the early 1800s, before anyone else, he called for a return to Kant's teachings. The aim of his central work, *Neue Kritik der Vernunft*, was to defend and preserve the Kantian legacy. Second, Fries was the leader of the reaction against speculative idealism, a reaction crucial to the very identity of neo-Kantianism. His 1803 *Reinhold, Fichte und Schelling* was the first systematic critique of speculative idealism, making its mark even before Hegel's rise to fame in the 1820s. Third, Fries was a closer follower of Kant than any of the speculative idealists. While Fichte, Schelling and Hegel rejected or transformed Kant's transcendental idealism, Fries remained loyal to its original form, defending some of Kant's most controversial ideas, namely, the existence of the thing-in-itself, the noumenal-phenomenal dualism, the distinction between understanding and sensibility, the tripartite division of the mind into cognition, volition and feeling, the

---

[1] Köhnke, Wiley, Ollig and Beck say little or nothing about Fries. He is given his due only by Gerhard Lehmann, *Geschichte der Nachkantischen Philosophie* (Berlin: Junker und Dünnhaupt, 1931), pp. 118–125. Writing in the 1840s, Karl Rosenkranz devoted several pages to Fries in his *Geschichte der kant'schen Philosophie* (Leipzig: Voß, 1840), pp. 430–436. But, as a loyal Hegelian, Rosenkranz gave Fries shortshrift. He described his *Neue Kritik der Vernunft* as "*eine langweilige Verwässerung des spekulativen Kerns der Kant'schen*" (p. 431). The first scholar to recognize fully Fries' importance was Kuno Fischer in his *Die beiden kantischen Schulen in Jena* (Stuttgart: Cotta, 1862).

metaphysical deduction and table of categories. Fries' chief departure from Kant was more methodological than substantive. The aim of his *Neue Kritik* was to place the critical philosophy on a new foundation, not to change the doctrines themselves.

For all these reasons, by the early 1800s, Fries was seen as the foremost Kantian philosopher in Germany. All those who cited Kant's critical spirit against the new rationalist metaphysics and romantic *Naturphilosophie* were, in one form or another, allies of Fries. This reputation alone should be sufficient to ensure Fries a small place in the history of neo-Kantianism. There is, however, good reason to give Fries a larger place: his influence extended well beyond the early 1800s and his lifetime. Few philosophers, especially neo-Kantian ones, can claim two revivals in their name. But such is the case with Fries. In 1847, four years after his death, a Friesian school was formed in Jena under the leadership of Ernst Friedrich Apelt (1815–1859), who had been a student of Fries. Among the members of the school were prominent scientists, namely, the mathematician Oskar Schlömilch (1823–1901), the zoologist Heinrich Schmid (1799–1836), the botanist Matthias Schleiden (1804–1881), and the mathematician Karl Friederich Gauss (1777–1855). The group formed a common journal, *Abhandlungen der Fries'schen Schule*, whose express purpose was to keep alive the spirit of the critical philosophy "as founded by Kant and developed by Fries."[2] Though the first Friesian school soon dispersed, a neo-Friesian school was formed in 1903 in Göttingen under the direction of Leonard Nelson (1882–1927). The group surrounding Nelson was equally distinguished, counting among its members the theologian Rudolf Otto (1869–1937), the psychiatrist Arthur Kronfeld (1886–1941), and the Nobel prizewinner Otto Meyerhoff (1884–1951).[3] In 1904 Nelson restarted the Friesian journal, re-dedicating it to philosophy in the spirit of Kant as formulated by Fries.[4]

Fries played three prominent roles in the history of neo-Kantianism. First, he was the founder of the psychological approach to Kant, which interpreted his epistemology as an empirical theory of mental activities.[5] This became the dominant interpretation for decades—it was adopted by Beneke, Zeller, Meyer, Lange and Helmholtz—and it would not be questioned until the 1870s with the advent of the Marburg school. Second, Fries was the first spokesman for the scientific wing of

[2] *Abhandlungen der Fries'schen Schule,* eds E.F. Apelt, Heinrich Schmid and Oskar Schlömilch (Leipzig: Engelmann, 1847–1849). 2 vols.
[3] On the history of the neo-Friesian school, see Arthur Kronfeld, 'Geleitworte zum zehnjährigen Bestehn der neue Friesschen Schule', in *Das Wesen der psychiatrischen Erkenntnis* (Berlin: Springer, 1920), pp. 46–65; and Erna Blencke, 'Zur Geschichte der neuen Fries'schen Schule und der Jakob Friedrich Fries-Gesellschaft', *Archiv für Geschichte der Philosophie* 60 (1978), 199–208.
[4] *Abhandlungen der Fries'schen Schule, Neue Folge,* eds Leonard Nelson, Gerhard Hessenberg and Karl Kaiser (Göttingen: Vandenhoeck & Ruprecht, 1907–1937). 6 vols. On the purpose of the *Neue Folge,* see 'Vorwort der alten Folge zugleich als Vorwort der neuen Folge' in Volume I, vii–xii.
[5] It is a mistake to attribute this approach to Reinhold. His *Elementarphilosophie* is based on a phenomenological rather than psychological approach to Kant. Though Reinhold appeals to facts of consciousness, he intends to exclude speculation about the psychological origins of knowledge, and he has no interest in an "internal physics". On Reinhold's intentions, see my *The Fate of Reason* (Cambridge, MA: Harvard University Press, 1987), pp. 247–252.

neo-Kantian philosophy, which rejected speculative *Naturphilosophie,* and which stressed the fundamental importance of mathematical method for science.[6] Long before Trendelenburg and Cohen, Fries saw the critical philosophy essentially as the *aide-de-camp* of the empirical sciences, a footman whose chief task is to explain their methods and logic. Third, Fries was the chief apostle of the anthropological interpretation of Kant's transcendental idealism, according to which the cognitive subject is irreplaceable and the ultimate basis of cognition lies in human nature rather than reason.[7]

Fries' importance in all these respects became fully apparent only after his death. The first role became clear with the reaction against psychologistic interpretations of Kant, which began with Hermann Cohen's *Kants Theorie der Erfahrung* in 1871. Cohen explicitly acknowledged Fries' importance in developing the psychological interpretation.[8] The second role became plain only with the formation of the Friesian schools. When, in 1847, Apelt and his fellow editors founded the *Abhandlungen der Fries'schen Schule,* they declared the importance of Fries' legacy to consist in his opposition to "Schellingian Neo-Platonism" and "Hegelian scholasticism", and in his attempt to found philosophy on the methodology of the empirical sciences.[9] And when, in 1909, Nelson and his followers restarted the Friesian school, they reaffirmed that legacy, declaring that their enduring faith in Fries' philosophy was based on the scientific method.[10] It is striking that Fries' historical significance in this respect was acknowledged by two of his severest critics, Hermann Cohen and Ernst Cassirer.[11] For all the differences between the Marburg and neo-Friesian schools, they shared a common belief that philosophy should find its inspiration in mathematics and the empirical sciences. The third role became evident only in the early twentieth century in the dispute between the Marburgians and Friesians about the foundations of Kant's philosophy. Nelson's harsh review of Cohen's *Logik der reinen Erkenntnis,*[12]

---

[6] On Fries' philosophy of mathematics and relation to the natural sciences of his day, see Kay Hermann, *Mathematische Naturphilosophie in der Grundlagendiskussion: Jakob Fries und die Wissenschaften* (Göttingen: Vandenhoeck & Ruprecht, 2000), pp. 97–140; and Wolfgang Bonsiepen, *Die Begründung einer Naturphilosophie bei Kant, Schelling, Fries und Hegel* (Frankfurt: Klostermann, 1997), pp. 255–453, esp. 414–453.

[7] The anthropological and psychological interpretations are closely connected, of course, and sometimes indistinguishable. A psychological interpretation need not involve, however, the two characteristic claims of the anthropological one: that the cognitive subject is indispensable, and that psychological faculties are limited to human nature alone rather than reason.

[8] Hermann Cohen, *Kants Theorie der Erfahrung,* 1st edition (Berlin: Dümmler, 1871), p. 125.

[9] See the preface to the first volume of *Abhandlungen der Fries'schen Schule* (Leipzig: Engelmann, 1847), pp. 4–5.

[10] See the preface to the first volume of Leonard Nelson, ed. *Abhandlungen der Fries'schen Schule, Neue Folge* (Göttingen: Vandenhoeck & Ruprecht, 1904), p. viii.

[11] See Hermann Cohen, *Kants Theorie der Erfahrung,* 2nd edition (Berlin: Dümmler, 1885), pp. 296–297, 579–580; and Ernst Cassirer, *Das Erkenntnisproblem in der Philosophie und Wissenschaft der neueren Zeit,* 2nd edition (Berlin: Cassirer, 1923), III, 482–483.

[12] See Leonard Nelson, 'Hermann Cohen, System der Philosophie. Erster Teil: Logik der reinen Erkenntnis', *Göttingen gelehrte Anzeige* 1905, pp. 610–630; reprinted in Leonard Nelson, *Geschichte und Kritik der Erkenntnistheorie* (Hamburg: Meiner, 1973), pp. 1–27.

and Cassirer's polemical reply to Nelson,[13] brought out the clash between these rival interpretations of Kant: the Marburgers' rationalist and objective idealist interpretation versus the Friesians' anthropological and subjectivist interpretation. Every Kant scholar has to find his way between these rival interpretations. It is a struggle that ultimately goes back to Fries and the merits of his anthropological interpretation.

Given Fries' founding role and great importance in the history of neo-Kantianism, an investigation into his intellectual origins and development promises to shed some light on the genesis of neo-Kantianism itself. In Section 2 we will investigate Fries intellectual development from his early years in the Moravian seminary in Niesky (1792–95) until the publication of his *Neue Kritik der Vernunft* in 1807. We will examine all Fries' major writings during these years with a view to understanding his relationship to Kant.[14] Though we will consider only slightly more than two decades of Fries' development, that is, the years from 1797 to 1807, these were his formative years, and especially so for his interpretation of Kant, which came to its completion in the three volumes of his *Neue Kritik der Vernunft*. Our chief task here will be to understand Fries in his historical context and through his intellectual development. Taking this historical approach will make it necessary to reassess Fries' rather ragged reputation.[15] For we will find that Fries was a much more subtle and careful thinker than his critics gave him credit for; that most of the objections against his anthropological and psychological approach to Kant are misconceived; that he had interesting solutions to problems of transcendental philosophy; and that his interpretation of Kant is more accurate than the competing interpretations of the Marburg school.

2. Discovery of Kant

To understand Fries' intellectual origins, we need to raise two questions: "Why did Fries become a Kantian?", and "How did he learn about Kant?" The answer to them lies in Fries' youth, especially in the years 1792–1795 when he was a student at the Moravian seminary in Niesky. Fries received his education there at the hands of the Moravian brotherhood in the expectation that he would become a teacher or pastor in

---

[13]   See Ernst Cassirer, *Der kritische Idealismus und die Philosophie des "gesunden Menschenverstandes"* (Giessen: Töpelmann, 1906). On the circumstances behind this dispute, see Ulrich Sieg, *Aufstieg und Niedergang des Marburger Neukantianismus* (Würzburg: Königshausen & Neumann, 1994), pp. 241–242.

[14]   This genetic or historical approach to Fries has not been practised by his main expositors, who begin their treatment of Fries with his mature works, as if they sprang fully formed out of the head of Medusa. The paradigm of this ahistorical approach is Theodor Elsenhans' *Fries und Kant, ein Beitrag zur Geschichte und zur systematischen Grundlegung der Erkenntnistheorie* (Giessen: Töpelmann, 1906). 2 vols. Elsenhans rarely considers Fries' early work and begins his exposition with the second edition of Fries' *Neue Kritik der Vernunft*.

[15]   Personally, it gives me no satisfaction to defend or rehabilitate Fries, whose political views and anti-semitism I find abhorrent. However, one must take his philosophy on its own terms, independent of his politics. It was in this spirit that the neo-Friesian school, almost all of whose members were Jewish, rehabilitated Fries in the beginning of the 20th century. I follow their example.

their church. He was preceded in this path by no less than Schleiermacher, who, from 1785–1787, had also studied at the Moravian seminary (then at Barby). Like his illustrious predecessor, Fries rebelled against the narrow religious orthodoxy imposed upon him; but he too was deeply influenced by his education there. Fries later wrote of his time in Niesky: "In the three years in the seminary, under the influence of all that I was taught, my whole view of the world and life was formed in all its individuality."[16] The education at the seminary was based primarily upon the Bible and theology, but students also received a training in classical languages as well as a general education in history, mathematics and the natural sciences. Fries summarized his education at Niesky in these terms: "In three years I went through the whole course of theological studies, as far as was demanded of us . . . Along with that we learned the elements of applied mathematics and physics with some chemistry; we were led further into history and received lively instruction for an encyclopedic knowledge of all the sciences."[17] This education in the sciences, and a proficiency at mathematics, were decisive for Fries later intellectual development: it was the foundation for his interest in the scientific side of Kant's philosophy.

Though Fries, on his own testimony, received a good general education at Niesky, the study of the latest philosophy was discouraged there. Fearing the damaging effect of philosophical criticism upon the faith of their charges, the Moravian brethren carefully monitored their reading. Books deemed damaging to the souls of the young were prohibited and, if found, confiscated. But these were trying times for "the inspectors", as the censors were called at Niesky. The early 1790s were very exciting years intellectually, culturally and philosophically, and it was inevitable that some of this excitement would seep and creep into the seminary. It was during these years that Germany witnessed the pantheism controversy, the effects of the French Revolution and the rise of Kant's philosophy. Fries was introduced to this intoxicating new world by one of his teachers at the seminary, Karl Bernhard Garve (1763–1841), who made it his mission to educate the young about the latest issues in philosophy and theology. As one might expect, Garve's endeavours were not smiled upon by the elders at Niesky, who eventually relieved him of his duties. But Garve's efforts had their intended effect: his students made it their business to read the original works of the latest philosophers. At the top of their reading list was, of course, Immanuel Kant.

In some later autobiographical fragments Fries described his attempt to read Kant at the seminary.[18] At first the only books he could obtain were the *Prolegomena* and the so-called *Prize Essay*, that is, Kant's 1764 pre-critical work *Untersuchung über die Deutlichkeit der Grundsätze der natürlichen Theologie und der Moral*. Fries was greatly impressed with both works, which, he said, taught him a completely new method of doing philosophy. But how was Fries to get Kant's masterwork, his *Kritik*

[16] Ernst Ludwig Theodor Henke, *Jakob Friedrich Fries: Aus seinem handschriftlichen Nachlasse dargestellt* (Leipzig: Brockhaus, 1867), p. 27.
[17] Henke, *Fries*, p. 23.   [18] Henke, *Fries*, p. 26.

der reinen Vernunft? Only with great stealth. Against regulations, Fries sneaked out of the seminary and walked to a bookdealer in neighbouring Görlitz. There he bought only parts of the book, some printed sheets; he dared not buy a whole bound copy, because this would have attracted the suspicion of the inspectors. When the seminary's doctor visited the bookshop in Görlitz, the bookdealer praised the youth's intellectual curiosity; the doctor raised the alarm, and the inspectors duly confiscated the sheets. Fries managed to get them back by convincing the inspectors that he would do it again anyway.

It is clear that Kant had become "forbidden fruit" for students at the seminary. The temptation of reading him was all the greater precisely because it had been prohibited. The seminarians were attracted to Kant, however, not simply because of his heterodoxy. Kant was for them first and foremost a liberator. He stood for the power to think critically about religion, the right to think for oneself and not to be bound by dogmas and rituals simply because they were a hallowed tradition or sanctioned by authority. That, at any rate, was the effect that Kant had upon Fries, who later wrote that he studied Kant not just to learn his doctrines but to stimulate his thinking.[19] It is indeed noteworthy that Fries' early reception of Kant was sometimes critical. Although he was deeply impressed by the first *Kritik,* and especially the *Prize Essay,* he had doubts about the second *Kritik* and *Die Religion.* Unfortunately, he tells us very little about these doubts, only that his first philosophical essay took issue with Kant's claim that all principles of conduct falling outside morality are based on self-love.[20]

Two events were especially fateful for Fries' early reception of Kant: first, that he was introduced to Kant through Reinhold; and, second, that he read the *Prolegomena* and *Prize Essay* before the first *Kritik.* In introducing his students to Kant, Garve followed the exposition of Reinhold's *Elementarphilosophie,* which attempted to derive all the results of the critical philosophy from a single first principle. The young Fries enjoyed showing his intellectual mettle and nettle by finding fault with Reinhold's reasoning. Like many in the early 1790s, he detected gaps in Reinhold's deductions and flaws in his entire programme. It was only after finding these problems that he resolved to read Kant's own writings. He wanted to see for himself whether Kant's method and reasoning were prone to the same difficulties as Reinhold's. He quickly came to the conclusion that Kant's method was very different from Reinhold's and that it was completely immune to its difficulties. It was significant that, in reaching this conclusion, Fries kept in mind the *Prolegomena* and the *Prize Essay,* for the methods advocated and practised in these works are indeed very different from Reinhold's. In the *Prize Essay* Kant championed an "analytic" method that began with the analysis

---

[19] Henke, *Fries*, p. 27. For this reason it would be wrong to assume that Kant's *Kritik* was a kind of surrogate Bible for Fries, who had already discarded revealed religion. A new Bible would only replace one kind of authority with another; but Fries was really converted to Kant because he stood for the cause of *Selbstdenken,* that is, thinking for oneself.

[20] Henke, *Fries*, p. 27.

of concepts in ordinary experience and then proceeded to their general definitions; and in the *Prolegomena* he followed a similar "analytic" method by beginning with mathematics and the natural sciences and regressing to their necessary conditions.[21] In either case, the method used in these works stood in stark contrast to the "synthetic" method employed by Reinhold, which began from general principles and then derived more specific conclusions from them. Had Fries read the first *Kritik* before these works, he would have discovered that Kant is closer to Reinhold after all, for here Kant had also employed a "synthetic" method. But the die had been cast. The discovery of problems with Reinhold's synthetic method, and the belief that Kant followed a very different analytic method, which is not prone to the same problems, led Fries to the conviction that Kant had a more tenable philosophy than his successor. Thus was born Fries' "Kantianism".

As this early episode illustrates, Fries' "Kantianism" was based on his belief that the proper critical method is analytic, and that Reinhold had betrayed the critical philosophy by following a synthetic method. From his earliest days, a powerful contrast was forged in Fries' mind between Kant's reliable analytic method and Reinhold's unreliable synthetic one. Since Fichte and Schelling had followed Reinhold's methodology, the original contrast between Kant and Reinhold grew into a larger one between Kant and his idealist progeny.

We can see already, then, the motive for Fries' later agenda: restore the original analytic method of the critical philosophy against Reinhold and the idealists, and show that it is not prone to all the problems of their synthetic method. Fries' early intellectual career will be devoted to this goal, which will reach its fruition in his 1803 *Reinhold, Fichte und Schelling*, one of the foundational works of neo-Kantianism.

Fries later wrote about his early study of Kant in Niesky that the more he read the first two *Kritiken*, the more he became convinced that they lacked "a general psychological foundation".[22] Such a foundation would explain the meaning of Kant's various faculties, namely, transcendental imagination, the understanding, judgement and reason, and then determine the evidence on which they are based. Although the third *Kritik* was suggestive about where this foundation should lie, it too did not answer all his questions. And so Fries resolved to provide such a foundation himself. He called the kind of investigation he had in mind the "Propadeutic of General Psychology". This was the very name he gave to his early philosophical programme, which would bear its final fruit in the *Neue Kritik der Vernunft*. So it was already in Niesky, then, that Fries had formulated his psychological programme for the reformation of Kant's philosophy.

Why did Fries think that the critical philosophy required a psychological foundation? And where did he get the idea for such a foundation? Who and what were

---

[21] On the analytic method of the *Prolegomena*, see Kant, *Schriften* IV, 263, 275, 276n, 279, 365, 368; and on the analytic method of the *Prize Essay*, see Kant, *Schriften* II, 285–286, 289.

[22] Henke, *Fries*, p. 27.

its sources? *Prima facie* one might think that Fries is voicing the same complaints as Reinhold, Fichte and Schelling once did: that Kant had not provided sufficient systematic unity to his discussion of the faculties; that he only picked them up as he found them with no explanation of why there are just these and no others; and that he had failed to explain how they interrelate to one another as powers of a single mind. Though Fries shared these objections against Kant, removing them was not the chief purpose of his propadeutic. Its primary mission was not to restore systematic unity to Kant's haphazard discussion of the powers of the mind, still less to derive all these powers from a single first principle. Rather, its aim was to put the critical philosophy on a sound empirical foundation, to make sure that its results were based on the same solid procedures as the empirical sciences. The propadeutic would not provide a more cogent *proof* of the Kantian faculties but a more adequate *analysis* and *inventory* of them. It would begin from our ordinary experience, analyse the different powers of the mind, making sure each is basic and not composed of more elemental factors; and from this it would ascend to broader generalizations and definitions. In other words, the propadeutic would apply to the critical philosophy, in a rigorous and self-conscious manner, the analytic method Kant had already advocated in the *Prize Essay*. It was the Kant of the *Prize Essay*, then, who was behind Fries' programme for a general propadeutic. Ironically, the early pre-critical Kant was being used to correct the later critical Kant!

3. Justifying Psychology

After three years in the Moravian seminary, Fries went to the University of Leipzig to study law in the autumn of 1795. A self-confessed "rebel" in the seminary, Fries longed for freedom in the wider world, refusing the religious vocation imposed upon him. A training in law, he hoped, would give him the opportunity for a career in the secular world. But Fries was never very serious about jurisprudence, which he pursued only in a desultory and dispirited fashion. His heart and soul lay with philosophy, to which he devoted almost all his studies in Leipzig. He went to the lectures of K.H. Heydenreich (1764–1801), a celebrated aesthetician, and Ernst Platner (1744–1818), a critic of Kant and champion of anthropology. Fries read the works of Reinhold and Fichte, and he followed closely the intense debates in Jena about the foundations of philosophy. More important than his lectures or reading, however, were his efforts to write his own philosophy. In the winter of 1796 he withdrew into his garret and began to work on his propadeutic, his programme for the psychological reformation of Kant's philosophy. There he wrote the drafts for several articles, which he later revised and published in 1798 in C.C.E. Schmid's *Psychologisches Magazin*.[23]

---

[23] The five articles by Fries were published in volume III (1798) of the *Psychologisches Magazin*. They are 'Ueber das Verhältniß der empirischen Psychologie zur Metaphysik', pp. 156–202; 'Propadeutik einer allgemeinen empirischen Psychologie', pp. 203–267; 'Von der rationellen Seelenlehre', pp. 268–293; 'Abriß

The germ of Fries' later philosophy lies in these early articles, which have been much neglected. They reveal the motivation for Fries' psychologism, for his interpretation of Kant, and for his critical reaction against Reinhold, Fichte and Schelling. To no small degree, his later writings are the elaboration and execution of the line of thought developed in them. We will therefore examine them closely, in this and the next section.

The first of these articles, 'Ueber das Verhältniß der empirischen Psychologie zur Metaphysik', is the most important, because it sets forth the rationale for Fries' "psychologism".[24] Fries begins with a simple statement of his psychologism, one that makes it seem the natural interpretation of Kant, and indeed any epistemology:

Each cognition belongs as such to a state of mind (*Gemüthszustand*) and each individual cognition is an activity of the mind, namely, an activity (and this is its essential characteristic) by which an object is represented. Cognition, and so cognitions, are therefore objects of inner experience, and thus of psychology, especially its empirical part . . . I can, and must, therefore . . . consider all cognitions from a psychological standpoint, insofar as they are subjective and belong to states of the mind. (158–159)

With this simple statement, the whole matter already seems settled. Starting from the natural premise that cognitions are states or activities of the mind, Fries draws the inference that epistemology must be empirical psychology, which is the study of such states and activities. In appearing to come so quickly to that conclusion, Fries seems to ride roughshod over some basic distinctions, namely, that between mental activities and their content, that between *quid juris?* and *quid facti?*, and that between *ratio cognoscendi* and *ratio essendi*. Since Cohen and Windelband,[25] this has been the chief criticism of Fries, whose project has been dismissed as crude and naive. But any patient reader of Fries' articles soon finds that he is fully aware of these distinctions. Indeed, one of his central themes is that Fichte and Reinhold, and even Kant himself, are guilty of ignoring them. This should be enough to alert us to an important point: that Fries was neither crude nor naive, that the rationale for his psychologism goes much deeper than his critics were willing to admit.

One of Fries' central contentions in this article is that it is necessary to distinguish between the *metaphysical* knowledge involved in the first principles of transcendental philosophy and the *empirical* knowledge by which these principles are discovered, observed, identified and distinguished. These first principles are *first-order*, providing us with knowledge of the structure of experience; but the empirical knowledge

der Metaphysik der inneren Natur', pp. 294–353; 'Allgemeine Uebersicht der empirischen Erkenntnisse des Gemüths', pp. 354–402.

[24] Here I use the term "psychologism" in a very broad sense to designate the view that epistemology should be psychology. The various senses of the term, and which is applicable to Fries, we will investigate in Section 11.

[25] See Hermann Cohen, *Kants Theorie der Erfahrung*, second edition (Berlin: Dümmler, 1885), pp. 579–580; and Wilhelm Windelband, 'Kritische und genetische Methode?', *Präludien*, Neunte Auflage (Tübingen: Mohr, 1929), II, 100.

of psychology is *second-order*, giving us a knowledge of the principles of knowledge (178). While these principles themselves are universal and necessary, having an apodictic certainty, the empirical knowledge by which we discover, observe and analyse them is particular and contingent, having only an assertoric or probable certainty (181–182). Fries is careful to explain that the empirical knowledge of psychology does *not* provide a logical foundation or justification for these metaphysical principles (171, 182–183). He is very aware that we cannot derive from empirical premises, which are particular and contingent, synthetic a priori principles, which are universal and necessary. For just this reason he maintains that empirical psychology is meant to be only a *propadeutic* for philosophy, for the system of metaphysical principles. The task of the propadeutic is to discover the principles that we have, to determine how they differ from one another, how many there are, and their interrelationships in the general economy of the mind. But it is not intended to be a metaphysical foundation for the principles themselves.

Fries' firm distinction between propadeutic and system, between the empirical discovery and justification of transcendental principles, disarms the standard objection against his psychologism. It was held that his entire project cannot get off the ground and is misconceived because "What is a priori cannot be known a posteriori."[26] This objection of Fischer, which was reaffirmed by Liebmann and Zeller, simply confuses the distinction Fries was so intent on making. Fortunately, Meyer, Lange and Cohen were eager to uphold it.

Fries does admit, though, that there is something paradoxical about having an *empirical* knowledge of transcendental principles which are not empirical themselves. He even notes that such knowledge is circular, presupposing the very principles that it attempts to know (182). Since transcendental principles are conditions of any possible experience, they are also the conditions of the empirical knowledge of psychology too. This circularity is often held to be a fatal difficulty for any attempt to put transcendental philosophy on an empirical foundation. But Fries insists that the circularity is not vicious at all, for the simple reason that the empirical knowledge of psychology does not intend to provide a demonstration of the validity of these principles (183). A psychological propadeutic shows these principles to be "states within the mind", but it does not attempt to prove them.

On a more general level, Fries makes a distinction between the "subjective" method by which we know the principles of knowledge and the "objective" method by which we justify or demonstrate them (172). The subjective method consists in the *ratio cognoscendi* or in the order of discovery, the order in which we get *to know* these principles. It is a regressive method that begins from the particular and moves towards the universal. The objective method, however, concerns the *ratio essendi*, the order of the thing itself. It is progressive, moving from the universal to the particular. Fries

---

[26] Fischer, *Die beiden kantischen Schulen in Jena*, p. 99.

illustrates this difference with a helpful example (172). Before we know anything about the law of gravity, we see stones fall and the moon revolving around the earth; and it is only by accumulating particular facts like these that we eventually discover the law of gravity. Here, in the order of our knowledge, these particulars precede the universal. But, in the objective order of things themselves, the law of gravity determines these events, so here the universal precedes the particular. Fries makes this distinction precisely so that the method of psychology will not be confused with that of metaphysics. The method of empirical psychology is regressive or analytic, proceeding from the particular data of experience and moving towards broader generalizations. Just for this reason, though, it does not attempt to provide an objective justification for the metaphysical first principles of transcendental philosophy.

So we can now see that Fries makes, very explicitly and emphatically, the very distinctions that he is accused of confusing. Those who have conflated these distinctions, he argues, are Reinhold and Fichte. They make a fatal assumption, one which ultimately goes back to Kant himself: that because the principles of transcendental philosophy are metaphysical, they must be known by a metaphysical method.[27] In other words, it seems to them that the only means of knowing the synthetic a priori is through the synthetic a priori. So rather than beginning with a careful inductive survey of the mind before arriving at their first principles, Reinhold and Fichte begin with their intuitions about these principles themselves. Hence Fichte began straightaway with his "*Ich=Ich*" and Reinhold with his "*Satz des Bewußtseins*", and from these alleged first principles they attempted to derive all the doctrines of transcendental philosophy.

What seems to have been decisive in turning Fries towards his psychological approach was G.E. Schulze's celebrated attack on Kant and Reinhold in his 1792 *Aenesidemus*.[28] One of Schulze's fundamental objections concerns how the critical philosophy can justify its transcendental discourse in the light of its standard of knowledge.[29] That discourse is supposed to give synthetic a priori conclusions about the powers and limits of knowledge; but Kant also insists that all knowledge should be limited to possible experience. Such conclusions can never be justified by possible experience, however, given that they claim universality and necessity, whereas experience consists in only particular and contingent facts. Fries' response to Schulze's objection is to make the method of the critical philosophy empirical, so that its discourse conforms to its own standards of knowledge.

One basic question remains: How do we justify the principles of transcendental philosophy? Fries does not address this question in detail in his early essays, though

---

[27] Fries defines the term "metaphysics" in a special sense: "all cognition a priori from concepts in synthetic judgments" (164).

[28] Fries duly makes note of Schulze's critique and its validity against Reinhold (188).

[29] G.E. Schulze, *Aenesidemus, oder über die Fundamente der von dem Herrn Professor Reinhold in Jena gelieferten Elementarphilosophie*, ed. A. Liebert (Berlin: Reuther & Reichard, 1912), pp. 309–312.

he does suggest an answer to it. Of the difficulty of the problem, he is fully aware. These principles cannot be logically demonstrated by some other science, he points out, because they are already the most fundamental principles, those presupposed by all the sciences (170). They also cannot be justified by some regressive method that begins with experience, because the analysis of what is in experience will never end, and in any case it cannot provide a universal and necessary conclusion (171). Since they are demonstrable by neither a higher principle nor experience, it seems they cannot be justified at all. But Fries resists this conclusion. It is precisely here, he suggests, that the psychological approach shows its greatest value. Though it cannot prove (*beweisen*) these principles logically, it can still show (*ausweisen*) that they have a psychological necessity, that our human nature cannot sense or think without them.[30] We show their necessity psychologically, Fries suggests, when we explain how they are ultimate or basic powers, how they perform a necessary role according to "the basic constitution of the mind" (175). If we can only determine the "basic rule" behind the various functions of the mind, then we can identify all its different principles and order them into a system (176). Unfortunately, Fries provides little more explanation of what this rule might be, and he does little more than suggest how his proposed justification works. We shall soon see, however, that Fries eventually did provide a much more explicit account of this method of justification, which will prove to be one of his most controversial contributions to transcendental philosophy.[31]

4. Early Psychological Programme

Fries conceived his chief philosophical project as an introduction or "propadeutic" to empirical psychology. What, exactly, did he mean by such a "propadeutic"? And how, precisely, did he understand empirical psychology? Fries answers both questions in his second major article for the *Psychologisches Magazin*, 'Propädeutik einer allgemeinen empirischen Psychologie'.[32]

A propadeutic, as Fries understands it, performs the preliminary work for a science. Before one brings a manifold of cognitions into the systematic order of a science, he explains, one needs to conduct an investigation into these cognitions themselves (205). One needs to discover and distinguish the different kinds of

---

[30] Though he makes no explicit reference to it, Fries seems inspired by Kant's suggestion in the first *Kritik* that, though they are logically indemonstrable, a priori principles can still have some proof "from the subjective sources of the possibility of a cognition of an object in general" (KrV, B 188). Also important for Fries is Kant's account of his "subjective deduction" of the principles of the understanding. In the preface to the first edition of the *Kritik* Kant distinguished an "objective deduction", which demonstrates the "objective validity" of the concepts of the understanding, from a "subjective deduction", which concerns "the powers of cognition" on which these concepts rest (A xvi–xvii). Kant does not explain what this subjective proof would be; Fries work can be understood as an attempt to explain and develop it.

[31] See Section 10.

[32] Jakob Friedrich Fries, 'Propadeutik einer allgemeinen empirischen Psychologie', *Psychologisches Magazin* III (1798), 203–267.

cognition, to determine whence they originate, to which faculty they belong, and the relations between them. That preliminary work is the chief task of the propaedeutic. Since it examines cognition and not its objects, a propaedeutic is a second-order discipline, one that makes cognition an object of cognition. Given its preliminary role and second-order status, the propaedeutic seems to be conceived along the lines of Kantian critique. Sure enough, Fries calls it "transcendental critique" (208). Just like Kant's critique, Fries' propaedeutic contains a doctrine of method (*Methodenlehre*) and a doctrine of elements (*Elementarlehre*) (206). While the former examines the method of the science, the latter determines the kinds of cognition, their principles, the completeness of the principles, the sphere and limits of the science (206). Following the argument of his earlier article, Fries maintains that there is a basic difference between the method of science and the method of propaedeutic itself. While the method of science is progressive, moving from the universal to the particular, the propaedeutic employs a strictly regressive method, moving from particulars to universals (209).

As defined so far, the concept of a propaedeutic is very general. There can be a propaedeutic for each and every kind of science. Fries' concern now, however, is to create the propaedeutic for one particular science: "universal empirical psychology". What does he mean by psychology? What makes it empirical? And in what sense is it universal? Fries defines psychology in terms of its subject matter, which is "the mind" (*Gemüth*), a term he prefers to the older word "soul" (*Seele*), which has too many metaphysical associations (217). The mind is simply the subject of inner experience, whereas the soul has connotations of an enduring substance beyond experience. A psychology is *universal* when it deals with what appears in *all* human minds, that is, when it concerns the mind's "basic constitution" (*Grundbeschaffenheit*) as opposed to its contingent features in specific circumstances (213). And it is *empirical* when it is based upon experience, and indeed upon *inner* experience alone (213). Empirical psychology does not concern *outer* experience, that is, the content of what we perceive in the external world.

Fries is explicit that empirical psychology does not deal with the connection between mind and body. This is a metaphysical question beyond the ken of empirical psychology, which limits itself to the realm of inner experience. In this respect, Fries says, empirical psychology differs from anthropology, whose proper concern is just that connection (214). The exclusion of anthropology from the domain of psychology in this early essay is one respect in which Fries' early views differ from his later ones. By 1804 Fries will define anthropology differently, so that one form of it, philosophical anthropology, has the same concern as psychology, the realm of inner experience.[33]

Fries conceives of his psychology as a natural science, referring to it as a "doctrine of nature" (*Naturlehre*) (217). He states that, like any theory of nature, its treatment

---

[33] Fries, *System der Philosophie als evidente Wissenschaft* (Leipzig: Johann Conrad Hinrichs, 1804), §22, p. 33. Here philosophical anthropology now means "*die Wissenschaft vom Innern des Menschen*".

should be "physical-theoretical" (213). He does not mean by "physical", however, the material, as if he intended his theory to be materialistic. The word "physical" is used in the older Greek sense of *phýsis,* according to which it means simply the nature of something, implying no further assumption that such a nature is material (209). As if to ward off any suspicion of materialism, Fries makes a clear distinction between inner and outer *Naturlehre,* where the inner concerns the mind and the outer physical nature (219). Though not materialistic, Fries' psychology is naturalistic in the sense that it intends to employ the same form of explanation as the other natural sciences. In other words, it explains the mind according to general causal laws (224). Insofar as it attributes faculties and powers to the mind, it understands these in terms of "laws of causal efficacy" (224).

Although Fries wants his propaedeutic to have scientific status, he realizes this is difficult to achieve. Empirical psychology, he admits, cannot make a claim to be a strict science (236). It is impossible for it to make experiments as in physics or chemistry; and, as Kant warned, its objects are not readily capable of mathematical treatment (225). The prospect of applying mathematics to psychology will improve in the 1830s, after the appearance of Herbart's psychology and the experiments on visual perception by Alfred Volkmann (1801–1877), Ernst Heinrich Weber (1795–1878) and Eduard Friedrich Weber (1806–1871). But in the early 1800s Fries saw little hope for it. He does little more than envisage "a law of continuity in the flow of inner changes" (258).

As much as Fries insists that transcendental philosophy should be based on empirical psychology, it is important not to conflate his programme with empiricism. Fries was highly critical of empiricism for the standard Kantian reason: that the mind is in possession of a priori principles, whose claims to universal and necessary validity cannot be justified by any experience. For just this reason he did not think that empiricism alone could provide a sufficient foundation for the principles of transcendental philosophy. All the empirical evidence in the world about how people actually think, he stressed, is contingent and particular, whereas the metaphysical principles of transcendental philosophy are universal and necessary.

Why does Fries think that empirical psychology is the basis for transcendental philosophy? Empirical psychology is the basis for transcendental philosophy not in the logical or formal sense that it provides the first principles for the deduction of its elements, but only in the empirical or material sense that it supplies it with its materials. But why is even this necessary? The question arises because it seems that the essentially epistemological concerns of transcendental philosophy, which are about the validity or legitimacy of knowledge, are not about psychology at all. After all, Kant had distinguished firmly between the *quid juris?* and *quid facti?* Aware of this very objection, Fries is ready with an answer to it. Transcendental philosophy has its foundation in psychology, he explains, for the simple reason that its central theses are, on at least one important level, psychological, having as their subject matter the basic structure of the human mind. When Kant argues in the *Kritik* that the universal and necessary concepts of the understanding are subjective in origin—that they arise from the spontaneous activity of the mind—it is clear that he understands them to be laws of the mind, and that he intends them to have no validity apart from the subject itself (215, 240, 243). Since his synthetic a priori principles are necessary conditions of the possible experience of a human being, and since that experience cannot exist without a human being, it is legitimate to conclude that they are based upon faculties of that being (248). If these principles were somehow different, Fries argues, then the human mind too would be different (248). As Fries conceives synthetic a priori principles, then, they are essentially about human forms of conception and perception, and so deal specifically with human nature. Their status is not strictly logical or rational, as if they could exist in some realm of being independent of our human nature; rather, they are simply deep facts about human nature itself.

Fries' other articles for the *Psychologisches Magazin*, though much longer, are less original and important than the first two. Two of the articles—'Von der rationellen Seelenlehre' and 'Abriß der Metaphysik der innern Natur'[34]—sketch the foundations for a "metaphysics of inner nature" (269). A metaphysics of inner nature will determine the most universal principles of the soul, and it will do so a priori. *Prima facie* it is surprising to find Fries, who has insisted so much on the importance of an empirical foundation for transcendental philosophy, now laying down an a priori foundation for psychology. But Fries never maintained that psychology should be only or completely empirical, and he never laid down an embargo on metaphysics, which he still regards as the foundational part of any discipline. There are still fundamental a priori or metaphysical principles of psychology, just as there are such for physics.

Fries intends his "metaphysics of inner nature" to be the counterpart to Kant's metaphysical principles of natural science, which was a metaphysics of outer nature. It goes almost without saying, however, that, as a good Kantian, he places severe restrictions on the metaphysics of inner nature. The entire content of a metaphysics of inner nature turns out to be provided by the unity of apperception, by the "I think" that accompanies all representations (270). Mindful of Kant's Paralogisms, Fries then insists that we cannot derive any substantial knowledge at all from the "I think". It is the mere form that accompanies all our representations, and to give it any determinate content we need particular empirical intuitions (274, 278, 306). Fries is careful to say that nothing of metaphysical significance follows from the unity of apperception. From it we cannot infer that either materialism or spiritualism are true (283, 311, 321–323). We do not know whether the "I" is an ultimate subject or whether it is simply the property of some other deeper substance, whether material or spiritual (311, 364). The only value of the idea of a single enduring subject is strictly regulative (282, 331). Its use consists in providing systematic unity to the study of the mind, in reducing all activities down to a few basic ones, and then showing these basic ones to be derived from a single principle.

[34] Jakob Friedrich Fries, 'Von der rationellen Seelenlehre', *Psychologisches Magazin* III (1798), 268–293; and 'Abriß der Metaphysik der innern Natur', *Psychologisches Magazin* III, 294–353.

Fries' final article for the *Psychologisches Magazin*—'Allgemeine Uebersicht der empirischen Erkenntnisse des Gemüths'[35]—attempts to provide a general overview of empirical psychology, one that will serve as a guide for more special investigations (354). The task now is to find the basic faculties of the mind, and to do so Fries advises following the guiding thread provided by its a priori principles. For each fundamental kind of a priori principle he assumes that there is a basic faculty. Since Fries, following Kant, thinks that there are three basic kinds of a priori principles, he adopts Kant's tripartite division of the mind into three faculties: cognition, feeling and desire (368). "I know", "I feel" and "I desire" designate three fundamental forms of experience, which are completely distinct from one another and which cannot be further explained (370). Fries is again very careful in refusing to draw metaphysical conclusions from his psychology. He is agnostic about which position to take regarding mental-physical relations, and so he adopts the thesis of interaction only as a hypothesis (360, 364). But on one point he seems to infract his own embargo on metaphysics: namely, in assuming the existence of freedom. Since the spontaneous activities of reason and understanding do not depend on external causes, we have reason to believe in the existence of freedom, he argues (359). But here Fries was forgetting his own cautions elsewhere, namely, that the "I" can be the property of some other substance, which is the source of all its actions. To be consistent, Fries had to hold that freedom too, no less than the beliefs in God and mortality, is only a matter of faith.

5. Encounters in Jena

Fries' stay in Leipzig lasted only one year. Though he had made great progress in writing down his philosophy in the winter semester of 1796–1797, he paid a heavy price for it: isolation and loneliness. Still suffering from the confinement of his seminary life in Niesky, Fries had had enough; he now resolved to enjoy the world. With a group of friends he joined in the gay social scene of Leipzig. His life in the spring semester of 1797 became one merry round of "theatre, cafes and beer halls". "Never have I done so many stupid things as in my time in Leipzig", he later wrote.[36] Here too he had to pay the price: in a few months he squandered most of his modest means. Seeing that he could not last long in Leipzig, either financially or spiritually, Fries resolved to go somewhere less expensive and more congenial to his interests. And so, in the autumn of 1797, he went to Jena.

In 1797 Jena was in the very midst of its *Wunderjahre*. It had become the heart and soul of German cultural life. Reinhold, Fichte, Schiller and Schelling gave lectures there; Novalis, Hölderlin, the Schlegel and Humboldt brothers had foregathered there; and presiding over it all was *Geheimrat* Goethe himself. Though still too shy

[35] Fries, 'Allgemeine Uebersicht der empirischen Erkenntnisse des Gemüths', *Psychologisches Magazin* III, 354–402.
[36] Henke, *Fries*, p. 43.

and young to cavort with these titans, Fries quickly entered into the lively intellectual scene. Among his favourite subjects of discussion were "natural law, Brownianism, the new anti-phlogistic chemistry and especially aesthetics". One of the initial attractions of going to Jena was to hear Fichte's lectures. But he was quickly disappointed. "With Fichte", he later wrote, "I was finished after a few hours, because I saw through his unmethodical reasoning, his conflation of analytic and synthetic approaches, and the confusion in the abstraction and artificiality of his empty formulae."[37] After hearing Fichte's lectures, Fries would go home and write down refutations, which became the basis for his later polemics.

It was significant for Fries' philosophical development, and for the origins of neo-Kantianism in general, that he met in 1797 Carl Christian Erhard Schmid (1761–1812). Schmid had quickly established himself as one of the first Kantians in Germany. Arriving in Jena in 1785, he gave lectures on Kant there even before Reinhold, who would not arrive until 1787. He was the author of several compendia on Kant's philosophy, and of a very popular dictionary of Kantian terms, which is still used today.[38] Along with Friedrich Niethammer he founded the *Philosophisches Journal*, a vital journal for contemporary philosophical discussions. Schmid also played a central role in the disputes concerning the foundation of philosophy in Jena.[39] He was a respected critic of Reinhold's *Elementarphilosophie*,[40] and he had a bitter dispute with Fichte, which notoriously ended with Fichte, in his usual imperious manner, declaring Schmid "non-existent as a philosopher."[41]

Finding that they held common views, Fries and Schmid formed an intellectual alliance. They shared a sympathy for the spirit of Kantian doctrine, and an antipathy against the innovations of Reinhold and Fichte, which to them seemed to violate that spirit. Not the least of their common interests was their devotion to empirical psychology, which both saw as the proper foundation for the critical philosophy. As early as 1791 Schmid published his *Empirische Psychologie*,[42] which in many respects

---

[37] Henke, *Fries*, pp. 47–48.

[38] The compendia are *Critik der reinen Vernunft im Grundrisse* (Jena: Cröker, 1794); *Grundriß einer Moralphilosophie für Vorlesungen* (Jena: Cröker, 1793); and *Grundriß des Naturrechts* (Jena: Gabler, 1795). The dictionary is *Wörterbuch zum leichtern Gebrauch der kantischen Schriften* (Jena: Cröker, 1795). It has been edited by Norbert Hinske and reprinted twice, 1983, 1989, by the Wissenschaftlichen Buchgesellschaft, Darmstadt.

[39] For an account of Schmid's role in these discussions, see Manfred Frank, *Unendliche Annäherung: Die Anfänge der philosophischen Romantik* (Frankfurt: Suhrkamp, 1998), pp. 31, 743, 754, 783, 824–825, 851, 855–856.

[40] Schmid wrote a well-known review of Reinhold's *Fundament des philosophischen Wissens*, which appeared in *Allgemeine Literatur Zeitung*, Nr. 92–93, April 9–10, 1792, pp. 49–60.

[41] On that dispute, see Daniel Breazeale's editorial introductions to *Fichte: Early Philosophical Writings* (Ithaca, NY: Cornell University Press, 1988), pp. 307–315.

[42] Carl Christian Erhard Schmid, *Empirische Psychologie* (Jena: Cröker, 1791). How much Fries was influenced by this work is unclear. They are many similarities in approach and vocabulary. Fries, however, claims to have developed his position already in Niesky, when he probably would not yet have read Schmid. In any case, Fries was no special admirer of Schmid's writings, which he found boring. See Henke, *Fries*, p. 48.

anticipates Fries' later work. Their alliance bore its first fruit in 1797 when Fries published his first articles in Schmid's *Psychologisches Magazin*. Already in the late 1790s, then, the programme for a psychological re-interpretation of Kant, which will be a leitmotif of neo-Kantianism until the 1870s, had begun under Schmid's and Fries' stewardship.

Another important encounter for Fries' philosophical development was that with Alexander Nicholaus Scherer (1771–1824), the leading champion of anti-phlogistic chemistry in Germany.[43] When the major journal of chemistry, *Chemische Annalen*, had continued to propound phlogiston theory, Scherer in indignation founded his own anti-phlogistic journal, *Allgemeines Journal der Chemie*, which eventually became the leading chemistry journal in Germany. It so happened that the young Fries was greatly interested in chemistry, which initially attracted him as much as philosophy. He therefore regarded his meeting with Scherer as a great stroke of good fortune. He attended Scherer's lectures faithfully, went around with him on a daily basis, and virtually became a disciple. With Scherer's encouragment, Fries published two articles on chemistry, one a critique of Richter's chemistry and another on light and heat.[44]

It was Fries' alliance with Scherer that created his first significant rupture with Kant. Fries' early ambition was to develop a mathematical chemistry, one that could bring quantitative measurement and precision to the explanation of chemical interactions. He accepted Kant's famous dictum, in the preface to his *Metaphysische Anfangsgründe der Naturwissenshaft,* that there is only as much science in a discipline as there is mathematics in it.[45] But he then had to take issue with Kant's remark that chemistry, because it eludes mathematical treatment, is at best an art rather than a science.[46] In trying to apply mathematics to chemistry Fries knew all too well that he was bumping against the Kantian limits. As he later wrote: "Despite the warnings Kant gave in the preface to his *Metaphysischen Anfangsgründe der Naturphilosophie* [*sic*], I still hoped to apply the mathematical-natural philosophical doctrine of his dynamics to chemical forces."[47]

Though his first year in Jena had proved rich and rewarding, Fries found himself unable to stay there. Having gone through almost all his savings, he now had to make a living. The most expedient and comfortable means of doing so, he believed, was as a *Hauslehrer*, as a tutor to the children of some well-to-do-family. This had been the fate of a host of others of his generation, of Herbart, Hölderlin and Hegel; and now it was time for Fries to join their ranks. After arranging a position in Switzerland, he

---

[43] On Scherer, see Karl Hufbauer, *The Formation of the German Chemical Community (1720–1795)* (Berkeley, CA: University of California Press, 1982), pp. 140–142, 220–221.

[44] 'Versuch einer Kritik der Richterischen Stöchymetrie', in *Archiv für theoretische Chemie* I (1800), 315–446; and 'Versuch einer neuen Darstellung der Theorie des Lichts und der Wärme', *Archiv für theoretische Chemie* II, (1802), 25–96. Fries later disowned the second article.

[45] Kant, *Metaphysische Anfangsgründe der Naturwissenschaften*, IV, 470.

[46] Kant, *Metaphysische Anfangsgründe*, IV, 468, 471.   [47] Henke, *Fries*, p. 49.

travelled there in November 1798. In the little town of Zofingen he would remain for the next two and a half years. Isolated from the intellectual and political world, he continued to work on his philosophy, especially his psychology and critique of Fichte. His work grew in maturity and depth, and would soon bear fruit.

6. Foray into Medicine

After his stint as a house tutor in Switzerland, Fries returned to Germany in the summer of 1800. His first plans were to go to Halle to help Scherer edit his new journal of chemistry. But upon his arrival there he was greatly disappointed. Scherer had left academia to direct a pottery workshop in Berlin![48] With that, Fries' plans for a career in chemistry came to an abrupt end. He would now have to try his hand at a much more uncertain and quixotic business: philosophy.

Of all places to go for Fries in 1800, the most attractive was, again, Jena. Halle proved unappealing: "a maze of narrow, crooked and stinking alleys", barren of intellectual life. Jena was, by comparison, Athens. Though its intellectual life was no longer that of the 1790s—Fichte, Schiller and the Humboldt brothers had all left—it was still very active, providing the opportunity for all kinds of stimulation, contacts and discussion. More importantly, it was also a city where an aspiring young academic might make a living. Fries hoped to earn his subsistence there as a *Privatdozent* at the university, which involved offering lectures and collecting money from the few students able to pay him. With all these thoughts in mind, Fries returned to Jena in September 1800.

To have the right to lecture at the university, Fries first needed to receive a doctorate, which in those days was a purely formal affair. It required little more than writing a short dissertation, defending it, and, of course, paying a sizeable fee. Fries' dissertation was a critical examination of the idea of intellectual intuition,[49] a topical and controversial theme, given that Fichte and Schelling appealed to this magical and mysterious power all the time. Since he viewed it as an utter formality, Fries put little of himself into the dissertation, letting it be published without even proofreading it. He later dismissed it as the hasty product of audacity and poor Latin.[50]

Fries' experiment in earning his living as a lecturer proved to be a failure. He partly blamed himself for the fiasco. His voice was very weak, his delivery dull, and his exposition obscure—a fatal concoction, enough to scare off all but the most devoted students. But he alone was not to blame, because even if he had better rhetorical and pedagogical skills, there were still not enough students in Jena to support him. All the professors in Jena were having difficulty in attacting students—all but one, namely, Friedrich Wilhelm Joseph Schelling, whose full lecture halls were the envy of his

[48] Henke, *Fries*, p. 70.
[49] J.F. Fries, *Dissertatio philosophica de intuitu intellectuali* (Jena: Praeger, 1801).
[50] Henke, *Fries*, p. 77.

older colleagues. Fries smarted under Schelling's success, whose talent he fully recognized but whose popularity he also resented.[51] His own lectures either had to be
cancelled for lack of interest or they were poorly attended, with the students drifting
away as the semester went on. Already by Easter 1801 Fries declared: "With so meagre
fare I will not be able to last in the service of the goddess of wisdom."[52]

In despair about his prospects in philosophy, Fries decided around Christmas 1802
to try his hand at another career. His friend Schmid had suggested that he join him
and go to Braunschweig to study medicine. Though Fries remained in Jena, he did
begin to turn to medicine. He was so serious about the subject that he even wrote a little treatise about it, his *Regulative für die Therapeutik nach heuristischen Grundsätzen
der Naturphilosophie*, which he published in 1803.[53]

While one might think a treatise on medicine was of little relevance for philosophy, the very opposite is the case. The foundation of medicine was a hot topic in the
early 1800s, and it had indeed become a philosophical battleground. The aim of Fries'
foray into medicine was to lay down Kantian guidelines for medicine and to combat
the growing influence of Schelling's philosophy. In his later years Fries downplayed
the value of the work, regretting his own youthful foolhardiness in writing about
a subject about which he knew too little.[54] Still, his treatise is very important in his
philosophical development, for it lays down his general philosophy of science and his
views on the explanation of life.

The foundation for any philosophy of science lies in its paradigm of explanation.
Fortunately, Fries is perfectly straightforward in telling us about his paradigm, which
comes directly from the explanation of physical nature. He writes: "We understand
the changeable phenomena of external nature through concepts of physical processes" (19). Behind his physicalist paradigm was his adherence to the Kantian dictum that there is as much science in a discipline as there is mathematics in it. If we
are to explain everything in mathematical terms, we must also explain it in physical
ones, because it is only the physical phenomena of nature that are measurable. Fries
would stick to this physicalist paradigm in all his writings about the philosophy of
science, and it is basic to his general outlook. It is the most important respect in which
his philosophy differs from that of Schelling and Hegel, who attempt to break away
from the physicalist paradigm and advocate an organic or teleological model. This is
one place where Fries breaks dramatically from the speculative tradition.

If we adopt this mathematical paradigm, Fries realizes, then the prospects for
a scientific physiology look bleak. For none of its phenomena seem capable of

---

[51] Henke, *Fries*, p. 49.   [52] Henke, *Fries*, p. 76.

[53] Jacob Fries, *Regulative für die Therapeutik nach heuristischen Grundsätzen der Naturphilosophie*
(Leipzig: J.C. Hinrichs, 1803). All references in parentheses are to this edition. For other studies of this
work, see Bonsiepen, *Begründung*, pp. 416–426; and Frederick Gregory, 'Regulative Therapeutics in the
German Romantic Era: The Contribution of Jakob Friedrich Fries (1773–1843)', *Clio Medica* XVIII (1983)
179–189.

[54] Henke, *Fries*, p. 78.

mathematical treatment. Fries draws just this conclusion, insisting that contemporary physiology is far from having scientific status. We cannot develop a physiological theory of animal or vegetable organisms along mathematical lines, he argues,
for the simple reason that these organisms have such a complicated structure that it
eludes mathematical reconstruction (23). All physiological explanation is "a miserable thing", he says, because we cannot explain even the most basic activities of life,
that is, those in terms of which everything else is to be explained (127). We do not
know what a nerve is and how it works, or how muscles contract, or the mechanism
behind secretion and absorption (127). We know that life consists in self-motion, the
power of an organism to move itself; but we do not have any explanation for how it
can do this (109). Although Fries is convinced that the organic process is physical, he
also insists that it is a peculiar kind of physical process, one unlike the more simple
processes of inorganic nature (103). Life has its own special principle of motion, which
we designate with the term "irritability"; but this concept has little explanatory value
in itself, serving only to designate the characteristic phenomena of life, namely, the
chemical processes of absorption and secretion, the movement of fluids, the contrac-
tion of fibres, the law of reproduction through the sexes (107). For all these characteristic phenomena, we have no explanation at all.

Though Fries thinks physiology is far from the status of a science, he does not rule
out that possibility in principle. Despite the drastic limits of our knowledge of basic
organic processes, Fries still thinks that there could be, logically speaking, a physiology based on strictly physical laws. This point is not so explicit in the *Regulative* itself,
where Fries wants to limit premature theorizing in physiology; but it is stated clearly
in other works of the early 1800s. In his *System der Philosophie*, which Fries was writing at the same time as the *Regulative*, we learn that all qualities in the physical world
are resolvable in principle into quantitative relationships (§305; 258–259). And in his
Wissen, Glauben und Ahndung, also written around the same time, we are told explicitly that "all physiology of the organism falls under physical and mathematical laws"
(92). It is in this respect that Fries departs from Kant, at least in some of his moods,
who had sometimes insisted that organisms cannot be explained mechanically.[55]

Although the goal of a scientific physiology is a distant goal, Fries insists that this
should have no damaging consequences for the practice of medicine. Because we do
not have a scientific physiology, we cannot fully understand health and disease; but,
fortunately, we do not need a complete understanding of them to practise medicine
(27). The doctor proceeds from a pragmatic knowledge about what works and does
not work, even if he does not know why it works; and he needs to know only about

---

[55] Kant's position is ambivalent and unresolved. He sometimes writes that purposive explanation is
necessary in physiology, and that it cannot be reduced to mechanism. See *Kritik der Urteilskraft* §64, V,
369–370; and §68, V, 384. But he also writes that if we had more insight into the nature of things, we might
be able to find mechanical causes for all organic activity. See *Kritik der Urteilskraft*, §71, V, 388–389; and
§75, V, 400. It is the latter position that Fries adopts. It is unclear whether Fries thinks he is following Kant
or not, because he does not mention him explicitly in this context.

his individual patient, and what works for his or her particular case (28). "The need of the doctor is not really for a nosology [science of illness] but only a therapeutic diagnostics, which one could calls a nosognomy [practical knowledge of illness]." (28) Practical medicine can make great progress, Fries argues, if it simply sticks to observations, notes the general correlations between phenomena, and organizes them according to heuristic maxims (30). It should not attempt to provide, however, deeper explanations for these correlations. Medicine will progress if it avoids all more general theorizing, and does not attempt to mix general philosophical principles and mathematical models with observations of particular phenomena. For all these general theories are only so many wobbly hypotheses, whose application to experience is completely indeterminate (28–29).

Fries insists that it is of the utmost importance, in *Naturphilosophie* in general and in medicine in particular, to distinguish between two levels of theory (8–9). There is the philosophical-mathematical level, which is a priori and very general; and there is the empirical level, where we deal with all the particularities of experience. We must keep these levels distinct because there is no ready and obvious application of these general a priori principles to experience. They are compatible with all kinds of different empirical states of affairs; and we must not think that the necessities that hold on the a priori level also hold on the empirical one. On the empirical level we have nothing to guide us but observation and heuristic maxims for correlating and unifying phenomena (12). Though basic and simple, these levels are constantly confused by philosophers, who treat empirical matters of fact as if they could be determined a priori. The worst culprit in this respect is Schelling, who applies general metaphysical principles to empirical matters of fact, as if they were determinable a priori (13–14). Rather than examining matters of fact for their own sake, Schelling applies general concepts to them and thinks that he has sufficient knowledge of them. When applied to particular cases, this hasty and sloppy methodology can actually be dangerous, Fries warns (14). A doctor confident in the power of general principles will approach a particular case and presume a priori that he knows what must work, only for experience to defy him.

Fries' critique of Schelling contained a cruel *ad hominem* point.[56] The comment about the dangers of applying general theory too quickly to a particular case was a reference to the recent death of Auguste Böhmer, the sixteen-year-old daughter of Karoline Schlegel, a woman who now happened to be Schelling's lover. Allegedly, Schelling had applied his medical theory to cure Auguste. And with fatal results! Her death thus seemed to be a dramatic case of the dangers of the hasty and sloppy methods of Schellingian *Naturphilosophie*. A scandal soon erupted. There had been rumors in Jena of Schelling's role in Auguste's death, and there was even a reference in the *Allgemeine Literatur Zeitung* to the effect that Schelling had the misfortune of

---

[56] The context of Fries' critique of Schelling is made clear by Gregory, 'Regulative Therapeutics', p. 181.

killing someone he attempted to cure on idealist principles.[57] Fries himself makes a tacit but unmistakable allusion to the episode in the following passage:

Gradually this firm conviction [that one knows everything a priori], when applied in misfortunate moments to dietetics and therapeutics, can have very bad consequences, in that one pretends to treat a priori and through philosophical reasoning a hitherto unknown illness, or to know the effect of a medicine on an organism when it has still not been observed. This is in fact the dangerous side of the delusion involved in natural philosophical constructions of illnesses. (14).

Having chided Schelling for confusing pure theory with experience, Fries proceeds to set forth his own theory, which he claims is based on experience and heuristic maxims alone. The proper method to form a physiology, he advises, is to make careful observations, to abstract from inexplicable or irrelevant details, and to focus on the most general relations between phenomena (36). It is important to determine the quantitative relationships between these phenomena and to refrain from using qualitative concepts (37). We must aim for "the purely quantitative relationship between relations of the organisms with avoidance of everything qualitative" (37). This mandate to focus on quantitative relationships seems preparatory for determining mathematical constructions of the phenomena; but Fries, following his general distinction in levels of physiological theory, refrains from applying mathematics.

Fries thinks that medicine is fortunately already in possession of a physiology of this kind, and that it is only a matter of formulating its principles with sufficient precision. This is the physiology of John Brown, the Scottish doctor, whose theories were in great vogue in Germany at the end of the 18th and beginning of the 19th centuries.[58] The great merit of Brown's theory, Fries explains, is that it is based on solid observations, and that it has avoided the a priori constructions characteristic of *Naturphilosophie* (31). What Smith is for politics, and what Lavoisier is for chemistry, that Brown is for medicine (1). What has made all these thinkers so successful is that they have followed a method whereby theory follows experience rather than anticipates it (4–5). Schelling too was an advocate of Brown's theory, though he attempted to base it on general a priori principles of organic nature. One aim of Fries' tract was

---

[57] See anonymous review of 'Lob der allerneuesten Philosophie', *Allgemeine Literatur Zeitung* No. 225, August 10, 1802, p. 329. The work under review was a pamphlet by Franz Berg, a conservative theologian, who had reported that a medical student, Joseph Reuchlin, had written a Schellingian thesis to the effect that death could be overcome. The offending passage is very sly in its insinuation: *"Nur verhüte es der Himmel, daß ihn [Reuchlin] nicht der Unfall treffe, diejenigen, welche er idealisch heilte, reell zu todten, ein Unglück, das Schelling dem Einzigen zu Bocklet in Franken an M.B. [Mademoiselle Böhmer], wie böse Leute sagen, begegnete."* The phrase *"wie böse Leute sagen"* attempts to spread rumour yet avoid libel by attributing it to others. Schelling wanted to press charges for libel against the journal, which defended itself on the grounds that the article was only reporting the views of others. For a detailed treatment of the whole affair, see Robert Richards, *The Romantic Conception of Life* (Chicago, IL: University of Chicago Press, 2002), pp. 171–176.

[58] On the reception of Brown's theory in Germany, see John Neubauer, 'Dr. John Brown (1735–1788) and Early German Romanticism', *Journal of the History of Ideas* 28 (1967), 367–382.

to wrest Brown's theory from the Schellingians, and to show that the theory could and should be formulated without his a priori principles.

The fundamental concept behind Brown's theory is that of "excitability" (*Erregbarkeit*), which is the power of an organism to react to stimuli from its environment. Fries thinks that this concept designates the inner cause of the whole complex of powers making up the organism (39). Life just is the power to be excited and to respond to stimuli. Every part of the organism should then be understood as a moment or function of its excitability. The crucial factors to take into account in determining excitability are the organisms' degree of receptivity for external stimuli, and the energy of its response to these stimuli (50). We can assume that each particular organism is born with a definite quantity of excitability (43). There is a norm for each person, which expresses the proper relationship between these factors, that is, how much it should react to a definite degree of stimulus. That norm, which determines a person's health, consists in the proper balance between internal energy and external stimulus. With deviations from that norm, there is illness (57). Deviation arises from either too much or too little stimulus, so that all diseases are cases of either *asthenie* (i.e. too little stimulus) or *hyperasthenie* (i.e. too much stimulus). Treatment therefore consists in either increasing or decreasing the stimulus on the organism to restore balance (46–48).

Such are the crude outlines of the Brownian theory, at least as Fries understands it. We will leave aside here the question of the accuracy of his interpretation. Of greater philosophical interest is Fries' clash with Schelling in the *Regulative*. Though only a skirmish, it was the prelude for a much broader offensive, which was soon to come.

7. Critique of Reinhold, Fichte and Schelling

Shortly after his arrival in Jena, Fries met Christian Gottfried Schütz, a friend of Schmid who was the editor of the *Allgemeine Literatur Zeitung*, the most popular literary journal of the day. A fellow Kantian, Schütz encouraged Fries to publish his "*Antifichteana*", that is, the polemical notes he had been writing against Fichte's philosophy.[59] Schütz had promised to arrange a publisher and a review in his journal. Here was an opportunity that Fries could not miss. He had been writing about Fichte's philosophy ever since his student days in Leipzig, and he continued to do so in Jena and Zofingen. Now he had the chance to get his own views out in public. And so, from September 1800 until October 1803, Fries worked on a manuscript that eventually became his first book, his *Reinhold, Fichte und Schelling*, which appeared in November 1803.[60]

---

[59] Henke, *Fries*, p. 73.
[60] Jakob Fries, *Reinhold, Fichte und Schelling* (Leipzig: August Lebrecht Reineicke, 1803). All references in parentheses are to this, the only edition.

Fries' book was not only his literary debut, it was also an important event in the history of neo-Kantianism. *Reinhold, Fichte und Schelling* is significant because it inaugurates the Kantian reaction against the speculative idealism of Fichte and Schelling. That reaction was crucial for the development of neo-Kantianism; and it appears in its first systematic form in Fries' first book. Fries calls explicitly and repeatedly for a return to Kant's *Kritik*. "For us, the true art of philosophizing consists in going back to pure Kantianism." (198) That sentence is not as catchy as "Back to Kant!", but its meaning is the same.

Fries' book has been called "a polemic", and so to an extent it is. Its first half is devoted to a detailed critical scrutiny of Fichte's and Schelling's lastest writings. But the book is also much more than a polemic. It is primarily a discourse on method. Its entire second half contains a general discussion of philosophical method. Fries' main quarrel with Reinhold, Fichte and Schelling concerns less the results of their philosophy than their method for arriving at them.

When Fries wrote his book in the early 1800s the debate about philosophical method in Jena had already grown old. Starting in the early 1790s there had been an intense discussion about Reinhold's *Elementarphilosophie*, which attempted to derive all the results of the Kantian critique by beginning from a single self-evident first principle. Severe doubt had been cast upon the feasibility of Reinhold's project, which seemed dead in the water even before Fichte attempted to radicalize it with his *Wissenschaftslehre*. In his book Fries took note of this fact, declaring that the dispute about Reinhold's *Elementarphilosophie* was now "a finished business" (181, 214). And he added that even the latest speculative idealist on the scene in Jena— one "Dr. Hegel" in his book on the difference between Fichte's and Schelling's systems of philosophy—had brusquely rejected the attempt to begin philosophy with a single first principle (11–12).[61] Still, though the debate had grown stale, Reinhold's *Elementarphilosophie* had cast a long shadow, and even the more recent writings of Fichte and Schelling had yet to come out from under it. Indeed, Fichte and Schelling were still dominating figures on the Jena literary scene. So there was good reason yet for writing a critique against them. Fries knew well that by taking issue with these popular figures he would be drawing attention to himself. If his criticisms were compelling, he would establish himself as the chief spokesman for a new philosophical force: a resurgent Kantianism.

Though it was quickly forgotten, *Reinhold, Fichte und Schelling* did not fail to make a strong impression. Jacobi so loved the book that he resolved to meet its author.[62] Though one of its targets, Reinhold too admired it, not least because it confirmed his wisdom in having abandoned speculative idealism.[63] And Herbart regarded

---

[61] Georg Wilhelm Friedrich Hegel, der Weltweisheit Doktor, *Differenz des Fichte'schen und Schelling'schen Systems der Philosophie* (Jena: Seidler, 1801), pp. 42–50.

[62] Henke, *Fries*, p. 106. Jacobi went to Heidelberg to meet Fries in the summer of 1805, beginning their friendship and correspondence.

[63] Henke, *Fries*, p. 107.

its critique of Schelling as so thorough and convincing that he saw no point in any further refutation.[64] An anonymous reviewer in the *Allgemeine Literatur Zeitung* (A.L.Z.) had this to say about the book:

The philosophers named in the title have already found many opponents; but surely none that have penetrated so deeply into the spirit of the critical philosophy and their systems, and none that have so matched these three philosophers in acuity and learning . . . This writing deserves one of the first places in the history of the latest philosophy and it is very important for it.[65]

Predictable praise, perhaps, given that Schütz, the editor of the A.L.Z., had virtually commissioned the work. Still, coming from such a prominent journal, such an encomium could not be ignored or belittled. For better or worse, Fries had now arrived. Neo-Kantianism had gained its first spokesman against speculative neo-rationalism.

Fries' critique examines all Fichte's major writings from 1794 to 1800, which comprise *Über den Begriff der Wissenschaftslehre, Grundlage der gesamten Wissenschaftslehre, Bestimmung des Menschen* and the *Sonnenklarer Bericht*. Since it is so detailed and wide-ranging, Fries' critique resists easy summary. Here we note only his most important objections against Fichte's methodology.[66]

According to Fries' interpretation, Fichte's *Wissenschaftslehre* was meant to be a more plausible form of Reinhold's *Elementarphilosophie*. It endorsed the basic idea behind Reinhold's programme: that philosophy should begin from a single self-evident first principle and from it derive in a chain of reasoning all the basic propositions of the system of philosophy. Though Fichte never questioned Reinhold's methodology, Fries maintains, he did object to his first principle. Reinhold's first principle, the *Satz des Bewußtseins*—"In consciousness the subject relates the representation to itself and the object"—proved to be ambiguous and vulnerable to skeptical objections. Fichte therefore proposed replacing Reinhold's principle with a more self-evident one: "*Ich bin*", which refers to the immediate knowledge of our own existence, or "*Ich=Ich*", which designates the unity of self-consciousness. From such scanty and bare first principles Fichte proposed to derive all the basic results of the critical philosophy.

Granted this is Fichte's project, Fries is ruthless in pointing out the insurmountable logical difficulties in executing it. Whatever the merits of Fichte's first principle, it still cannot by itself establish the entire system of philosophy. The attempt to build a system on a *single* first principle does not work, because all reasoning requires at least *two* premises (12). There must be, therefore, not one but at least two first principles. Furthermore, since two premises give only one conclusion, to get further conclusions one would need more premises, which cannot be justified by the first principles (12). For the deductive programme to work, then, one must keep adding premises from

[64] J.F. Herbart, *Ueber die Unangreifbarkeit der Schellingschen Lehre* (Königsberg: Degen, 1813), p. 13.
[65] *Allgemeine Literatur Zeitung* Nr. 320–321, November 22–23, 1803, pp. 353–364.
[66] For a different and more extensive summary, see Bonsiepen, *Begründung*, pp. 332–344.

the outside which are not derived from the first principle. In other words, the pro-gramme does not really work at all.

Fries also notes a curious tension between the claims Fichte makes for his first principle and his method of deduction. Fichte maintains that his first principle is unconditioned, so that its certainty does not depend on the truth of any other propo-sition. But then the method of deduction consists in showing that the first principle A depends on another proposition B, and that B depends on proposition C, and so on. Such a deduction shows that the first principle is conditioned after all, because each proposition derived from it amounts to one of its presuppositions (62). Rather than the unconditioned principle, it is the most conditioned, having a long train of propo-sitions for its consequences.

Fries thinks that the chief fallacy behind Fichte's methodology is that he confuses "the mere logical form" of a system with the "synthetic form of knowledge" (179; cf. 8). What he means by this is that Fichte assumes that the certainty we acquire from a logical deduction from a first principle gives certainty to the principle itself. Fichte thinks that the principle will be valid if it agrees with experience, and if it is a suffi-cient basis to ground the entire system of philosophy. But this is a fallacy, Fries argues, for the simple reason that deduction from a first principle, no matter how rigorous, does not mean that the principle itself is true. Fichte would reply, of course, that his first principle is immediate and self-evident, requiring no further support from logi-cal deduction. But Fries questions the immediacy of all claims to self-knowledge. All self-knowledge is for him based on empirical intuition; and even the self-knowledge that I exist would be for him "an indeterminate empirical intuition" (37, 227).[67] Alluding to Kant's Refutation of Idealism in the second edition of the *Kritik*, Fries insists that all self-knowledge is mediated through knowledge of the world outside me (177). Fichte, he maintains, was stuck in the old Cartesian dualism, which opposes my immediate self-consciousness to the doubtful awareness of a world outside me.

Apart from the logical difficulties in his Reinholdian programme, Fries finds problems in Fichte's conception of the *Wissenschaftslehre*. He notes that Fichte often writes as if the *Wissenschaftslehre* were a science of the mind, as if it determines the laws of our mental activities which exist independent of the philosopher's attempt to systematize them (22–23). But in that case, he asks, why is it not a psychology proper, one which deals with causes and effects rather than premises and conclusions? The truth of the matter is the *Wissenschaftslehre* is a hotchpotch, a confused mixture of psychology and epistemology (23–24). The whole deductive methodology that Fichte outlines is irrelevant to psychology, and it belongs to the completely different enter-prise of constructing a system of philosophy. Fichte does not distinguish the system of laws or structure inherent in the mind itself from the philosopher's attempt to reconstruct that system in a second-order system of philosophy (24–25). Whatever

---

[67] Cf. KrV B 422–423n.

the merits of this criticism, it shows clearly how Fries separates logical and psychological questions and charges his contemporaries with having confused them.

Fries' examination of Schelling covers only his latest writings, especially his 1801
Darstellung meines Systems and his most recent writings on *Naturphilosophie, Von
der Weltseele* (1798) and *Erster Entwurf eines Systems der Naturphilosophie* (1799).[68]
His treatment of Schelling is no less exacting and severe than his handling of Fichte.
It is noteworthy, however, that Fries does give credit where he thinks it is due. Amid
all his criticisms of Schelling we find him expressing deep admiration for Schelling's
organic conception of nature. "Schellings *Naturphilosophie* or speculative physics is
the single, original great idea, which has showed itself in Germany since the publication of Kant's main writings." (101) Fries praises Schelling's organic conception
because, on his interpretation, it shows how everything in nature can be explained
according to natural laws so that it does not require any special teleology (101–102). It
is as if Schelling's achievement were in obviating the need to postulate teleology and
in laying down the basis for a completely mechanical explanation of life! This is not,
however, a correct account of Schelling's intentions and it reveals more about Fries,
who was reading his own mechanistic views into Schelling's writings.

While Fries admires the content of Schelling's writings, he takes exception to their
form or methodology. He notes that Schelling's methodology is not as indebted to
the Reinholdian programme as Fichte's (181). Rather than attempting to derive everything from a single first principle, Schelling attempts to reduce the variety of phenomena down to a few first principles by applying an a priori conceptual scheme to
them. Thus, he attempts to "construct nature a priori" by showing how its basic phenomena arise from the interworkings of a few basic forces. Nevertheless, even though
he drops the most problematic aspects of the Reinholdian programme, Schelling's
method is still a priori and deductive, beginning from first principles and then
imposing them upon the multitude of phenomena.

Fries' main objection to Schelling's method is that he does not really construct the
phenomena of nature from his first principles but simply redescribes them in philosophical jargon (108). He begins from the postulate of the absolute productivity of
nature; but because this productivity would not result in any finite products by itself,
he simply postulates the existence of something that serves as a primal limit on its
activity (109). Rather than examining the phenomena of nature for their own sake,
Schelling simply forces them to fit his own preconceptions. His concepts are so general and abstract that they seem to explain everything–but only because they really
explain nothing at all (136–137).

The chief problem with the Schellingian system, Fries argues, is that there is an
insurmountable gap between its first principle, A=A, the standpoint of absolute

---

[68] For a more extensive account of Fries' critique of Schelling, see Bonsiepen, *Begründung*, pp. 345–353;
and Frederick Gregory, 'Die Kritik von Fries an Schellings Naturphilosophie', in *Sudhoffs Archiv für
Geschichte der Medizin* 67 (1983), 145–157.

identity, and the multiplicity and variety of the finite empirical world. From the infinite, absolute or self-identical it is impossible to derive the finite, temporal and the different (183). Fries notes that Schelling is aware of this formidable problem, and he duly cites passages from *Bruno* where Schelling tries to respond to it (181–185). But he insists that Schelling has not really addressed the basic question: "how can I from the standpoint of the eternal, and without presupposing anything beyond the absolute idea, arrive at division and separation . . . ?" (185) In the end, then, Schelling leaves us with a complete dualism between the infinite and finite, the self-identical and different, the eternal and the temporal. Hegel, in his *Differenzschrift*, had charged Fichte with just such a failing; but Fries cannot see how Hegel can defend Schelling against the very charge he lays against Fichte (183).

After his separate critiques of Fichte and Schelling, Fries went on to provide a general diagnosis of their common errors and failings. Fichte's and Schelling's systems both represent, in his view, a relapse into "dogmatic rationalism". He sees the history of philosophy since Kant as one long struggle of rationalism to free itself from the limits of critique (199). Reinhold's foundationalism is little more than an attempt to rehabilitate the old methods of Wolffian rationalism, which proposed to prove everything in philosophy *more geometrico* (211). Although Schelling's methodology is less true to the Reinholdian paradigm, it still followed assumptions that are characteristic of classical rationalism. When Schelling declared his first principle A=A to be the standpoint of reason, and when he went on to claim that it is the basis for all knowledge, he had virtually assumed that "pure reason is enough for knowledge itself, and in its purity, independent of the senses, the single source of all reality" (192).

The fatal error of classical rationalism, Fries maintains, is that it begins right away with the synthetic or progressive method rather than waiting for the results of the analytic or regressive. The synthetic method begins with the universal and proceeds to the particular; the analytic method starts from the particular and proceeds to the general. Both methods have their place and worth, Fries believes. The synthetic method is best for systematic exposition, for showing the basic order of nature itself; the analytic method is best for discovery, for revealing the proper order in which we know things. The best method to *begin* enquiry, however, is the analytic or regressive, for the simple reason that we cannot know *ab initio* what is the first principle of the system of reason or the basic law of nature itself. We can determine that principle or law only by first undertaking an analytic investigation of our ordinary experience, by showing its necessary conditions, and then by ascending to first principles. This means that the first principles of reason, the basic laws of nature, are determined not at the beginning but only at the end of enquiry. The problem with Fichte and Schelling is that they presume to know, all too dogmatically, those principles and laws from the beginning.

One of Fries' favourite formulations for the failures of neo-rationalism is that it confuses critique with the system of philosophy. The business of critique is to determine through analysis the necessary conditions of experience; the system of philosophy, however, consists in an organic whole organized according to a single idea of reason (206–207). Reinhold, Fichte and Schelling believed that they could circumvent the whole business of critique simply by constructing the system of philosophy. Fries thinks that some of the blame for this error falls on Kant's own shoulders (199). Although Kant did distinguish between critique and system, he did not make it sufficiently clear that the critique follows a very different method than the system. Critique employs a method of observation and analysis in determining the basic facts of our ordinary experience and their necessary conditions. Reinhold, Fichte and Schelling reasoned that because these necessary conditions are a priori, then the method by which we discover them should be also a priori; but this confuses the object of critique (the a priori) with its method, as if the only means of knowing a priori knowledge has to be a priori itself (202–203).

Against the revival of rationalism, Fries pits the spirit of Kantian criticism. As the Marburg school would do more than a century later, Fries locates that spirit in Kant's methodology. "The single essential point about the Kantian philosophy is the Kantian method" (199). That method Fries finds not in the *Kritik der reinen Vernunft* but in the *Prize Essay*, for it was here that Kant stated so clearly that the method of philosophy should be that of empirical science, that philosophy should begin with the analysis of concepts of ordinary experience, and that definitions should be the result rather than starting point of investigation (198, 260). In the *Prize Essay* Kant had already determined the fundamental difference between the methods of mathematics and philosophy: that mathematics proceeds according to a synthetic method because it has a priori intuitions, whereas philosophy has to proceed with an analytic method because it is limited to concepts given in ordinary discourse. Though Kant reaffirmed this distinction in the *Kritik*, Fichte and Schelling ignored it, because they assumed we have an intellectual intuition in philosophy itself.

Faith in intellectual intuition, Fries maintained, is another common illusion of Fichte's and Schelling's neo-rationalism. They had taken the Kantian method of construction, which Kant had limited to mathematics, as the paradigm for philosophical method, as if the philosopher too has the power to grasp through intuition the universal in the particular. If, however, we follow the critical method, Fries argues, we quickly cure ourselves of this illusion. Rather than beginning with the presumption of intellectual intuition, the critical method demands that we begin with "the organization of reason itself", that is, the power of reason as it belongs to us as living human beings. The more we examine that organization, the more we see that, like all forms of organization, it is moved into action and functions only because of an outside stimulus (193). A close examination of the organism of human reason shows that it consists in two sources of knowledge, one of which is the form of reason itself, the other of which is the senses, which receive stimuli from external sources (193). This dualism of function within the organization of our reason, Fries contends, is

another distinguishing feature of criticism, which he distinguishes from both empiricism and rationalism (193). The rationalists overlook sensibility by reducing cognition down to its form, whereas the empiricists neglect reason by reducing cognition
down to its content. The critical philosopher, however, gives each power of the mind
its due, noting that form and content have completely distinct sources, that the senses
can no more think than the understanding can sense. Accepting this dualism is for
Fries basic to recognizing the finitude of our human reason, the fact that the world
we know cannot be created by us and has to be given to us. The postulate of intellectual intuition, which assumes that we somehow create the object of knowledge, steps
beyond these limits.

Besides its analytic methodology and its dualism of form and content, Fries finds
another central and distinguishing feature of criticism. Namely, it differs from both
rationalism and empiricism in giving a strictly regulative status to the ideal of a system of philosophy (194–195). While the rationalists believe that we are already in possession of the first principles of such a system and that it is only a matter of deducing
their results, and while the empiricists think that we can reach them through a more
exhaustive induction, the critical philosopher realizes that the ideal of a system of
pure reason is ultimately only a goal that we can approach but never attain. The critical philosopher understands through his analysis of the concepts given in ordinary
experience that there is no stopping point to such an analysis, and that it can continue
forever. Any attempt to impose a limit on analysis would be artificial and arbitrary,
a dogmatic fiat. And so, in the end, the ideas behind Fichte's *Wissenschaftslehre* and
Schelling's *Naturphilosophie* have their value after all–but only if we accept them as
having a regulative rather than constitutive status.

By now it should be clear how *Reinhold, Fichte und Schelling* is a founding text
of neo-Kantianism. On point after point, Fries attempts to reinstate the contemporary relevance and abiding validity of Kant's critical doctrines against
the neo-rationalism of Reinhold, Fichte and Schelling. This critique of that
neo-rationalism will later become a *leitmotif* of neo-Kantianism, a common theme
of the movement down to the Marburg and Southwestern schools. It is one of the
ironies of history that Fries' contribution in this regard went unrecognized by both
these schools, who became blinded by their stereotype of Fries as a purveyor of
psychologism.

Fries' book anticipates virtually every point made in the later neo-Kantian critique
of rationalism. It is missing, however, only one of its elements: Hegel. Eventually,
Hegel's reputation would grow so large that, instead of Fichte and Schelling, he would
come to symbolize neo-rationalism and turn into the *bête noir* of neo-Kantianism.
When Fries was writing in the early 1800s, however, Hegel had still not established
himself. He was little more than "the spear carrier" of Schelling, the author of an
obscure tract on the difference between Fichte's and Schelling's systems of philosophy. On several occasions Fries would refer to that tract (11–12, 181, 183), little knowing
what its author would later become and what bitter rivals they would soon be.

8. Early Political Philosophy

During his second period in Jena from 1800–1805, his so-called "*akademische Hungerjahre*", Fries wrote much in his struggle for recognition and survival. What money he could not get from his lectures he hoped to get from his writings. No sooner had he finished *Reinhold, Fichte und Schelling* than he wrote two more works. One was his *Philosophische Rechtslehre*,[69] which appeared in 1803; the other was his *System der Philosophie*,[70] which was published in 1804. The later work is a compendium, a guidebook for lectures. While it explores some new territory, it is chiefly a summary of Fries' thought so far. It is not as important as the earlier work, which demands careful scrutiny. The *Rechtslehre* laid down the foundation for Fries' political thought. What Fries later wrote and did as a leader of the liberal national movement, though it goes beyond this early work, is still largely based upon it.[71]

The deepest influence on Fries' *Rechtslehre* is, of course, Kant, who supplies its basic principles and values. Still, the *Rechtslehre* can hardly be described as a Kantian work. Fries is highly critical of Kant, departing from him on many basic points. While he follows Kant closely on most epistemological issues, he does not hesitate to criticise him on ethical and political ones.[72] The *Rechtslehre* was a profound critique and reformulation of Kant's ethical and political doctrines, one which no history of neo-Kantianism can afford to ignore.

Seen from a broad perspective of the early 1800s, Fries' *Rechtslehre* is a typical work of nascent German liberalism. Like later liberals, Fries advocates laissez faire, a written constitution, basic human rights, and the distinction between law and morality. There is still little trace of the communitarianism of Herder, Fichte and the Romantics, which will surface in his later political writings.[73] There is also no hint of the nationalism, intolerance and anti-semitism that will later mar Fries' reputation.[74]

---

[69] Jakob Fries, *Philosophische Rechtslehre und Kritik aller positiven Gesetzgebung* (Jena: Johann Michael Mauke, 1803). All references in parentheses are to this work. For another summary of this work, complementary to my own, see the article by the young Kurt Hiller. 'Die Philosophische Rechtslehre des Jakob Friedrich Fries', *Archiv für Geschichte der Philosophie* XXX (1917), 251–269.

[70] Jacob Fries, *System der Philosophie als evidente Wissenschaft* (Leipzig: Johann Conrad Hinrichs, 1804). All references to this work will be to paragraph and page number.

[71] On Fries' role in the liberal national movement, see Gerald Hubmann, *Ethische Überzeugung und politisches Handeln: Jakob Friedrich Fries und die deutsche Tradition der Gesinnungsethik* (Heidelberg: Winter, 1997).

[72] Friedrich Ueberweg is completely mistaken when he writes that Fries was closer to Kant in his moral and legal philosophy. See his *Die deutsche Philosophie des XIX Jahrhunderts und der Gegenwart*, Part IV of *Grundriss der Geschichte der Philosophie* (Basel: Schwabe & Co., 1951), IV, 152. Ueberweg does not consider Fries' *Rechtslehre*.

[73] The communitarian and nationalist element of Fries first becomes apparent in his *Von deutschen Bund und deutscher Staatsverfassung. Allgemeine staatsrechtlichen Ansichten* (Heidelberg: Mohr und Winter, 1816).

[74] Fries' anti-semitism emerges in his 'Über die Gefährdung des Wohlstandes und Charakters der deutschen durch die Juden', *Heidelberger Jahrbücher* 16–17 (1816), 241–264. Though contemptible by basic liberal standards, Fries' anti-semitism should not be understood anachronistically in national-socialist terms. This is a flaw in Shlomo Avineri's discussion of Fries in *Hegel's Theory of the Modern State* (Cambridge: Cambridge University Press, 1972), pp. 119–120. Fries' anti-semitism has no racial basis and

The *Rechtslehre* is Fries at his most liberal, the decade when his political views are still close to those of Kant, Humboldt and Jacobi.

Rechtslehre, which means literally doctrine of right or law, has a technical meaning for Fries. He conceives it to be part of ethics or morality. The sphere of right is formed by the application of moral laws to society. Like Kant, Fries insists that morality should be sovereign in the realm of politics, so that moral principles take precedence over political expediency. While moral principles are not a *sufficient* guide for all that we do in politics—they leave open to the statesman exactly how they are to be applied—they are still a *necessary* one. No state can plead *Realpolitik* to exempt itself from the authority of moral principle. Ultimately, then, right should rule over might.

Though the doctrine of right presupposes the basic principles of morality, it is not the task of the political philosopher to determine these principles. He must accept them as given, as already worked out by the moral philosopher, and then attempt to apply them to the social and political world (6). The task of working out these principles, Fries maintains, falls to "a universal practical philosophy", which he sketches in a few paragraphs of his *System der Philosophie*.[75]

Though based on ethics, the doctrine of right is not co-extensive with it. It deals with only one part of ethics, with one kind of duties. Which part? Which kind of duties? Ethics, Fries explains, consists of duties of virtue (*Tugendpflichten*) and those of right (*Rechtspflichten*). Duties of virtue are those that hold only for myself, or for my inner disposition, whereas duties of right are those that hold for my relations to others, or for my external actions (9–10). The doctrine of right is that part of ethics that deals with duties of right; hence it concerns solely my external actions, or how I ought to act with regard to others in society.

Fries' distinction between duties of right and virtue, which is of Kantian provenance,[76] seems banal and humdrum. Yet it had become very controversial by the early 1800s. The Romantics had criticized the separation of right and virtue on the grounds that the ancient republics were based upon virtue or the moral character of their citizens. Friedrich Schlegel and Novalis, for example, wanted the modern state to be founded upon the Christian ethic of love, which would provide a bond of loyalty and patriotism.[77] Fries, however, explicitly and emphatically distanced himself from the Romantics, dismissing their rhetoric of love and friendship as "the fantasy of a shallow novel" because it is useless in politics. (29)

We do well to note Fries' disagreement with the Romantics if only because his political philosophy has so often been lumped together with theirs. Ever since Hegel

---

its intent was forcible assimilation rather than extermination. The best discussion of the complex and delicate topic is Hubmann, *Ethische Überzeugung und politisches Handeln*, pp. 176–191.

[75] Fries, *System der Philosophie*, §§ 330–337 (264–270), and §§ 414–431 (323–337).

[76] Kant, *Metaphysik der Sitten*, VI, 219–220, 225.

[77] See, for example, Friedrich Schlegel's 1800–1801 lectures on *Transcendentalphilosophie* in *Friedrich Schlegel Kritische Ausgabe*, ed. Ernst Behler (Munich: Schöningh, 1958), XII, 137–139, 151–180; and Novalis, *Glauben und Liebe*, in *Novalis Schriften*, ed. Richard Samuel (Stuttgart: Kohlhammer, 1960), II, 485–498.

denounced Fries for his "subjectivism" and "sentimentalism" in the preface to his
Philosophie des Rechts, his political philosophy has been cast in that light.[78] Fries has
been taken to be a sentimentalist and subjectivist, partly because his own philosophy
has been conflated with Jacobi's,[79] and partly because he appealed to feeling and conscience in his political speeches. But Fries' ethical views were far from Jacobi's, and
the rhetoric of a political speech scarcely qualifies as the exposition of a philosophical position. There are indeed profound affinities between Fries and the Romantics,
which will become more evident in his later work, especially his *Julius und Evagoras*.[80]
Regarding the foundation of right, however, Fries' position is essentially Kantian, at
least no less rationalist than Hegel's. Fries maintains that the principles of morality
are founded in practical reason, which expresses itself not in feeling or conscience but
in universal and necessary laws.[81]

At the basis of Fries' political philosophy lies another Kantian distinction: that
between the realms of morality and nature. Fries lays down this distinction at the
very beginning of his *Rechtslehre*. The moral realm is that of reason, which gives laws
about what ought to be, while the natural realm is that apparent to the senses, which
consists in laws about what is and must be (2). Reason determines the laws of freedom,
whereas nature determines the laws of necessity. The laws of freedom hold for our
inner self, the laws of necessity for our outer being. This distinction between morality
and nature runs parallel to another: that between morality and history. Our moral
ideals have no necessary validity for the historical world, Fries maintains, because
whether they apply to it depends on our will, which might or might not act on them
(7). This distinction between morality and history—and not any "irrational romanticism"—was the real philosophical sticking point between Fries and Hegel.

Following his distinction between morality and nature, Fries makes yet another
basic distinction, now one between *pure* and *positive* doctrine of right. Pure doctrine
of right concerns those laws regulating conduct in society that *ought to hold* according to the moral law, whereas positive right concerns those laws that *hold as a matter*

---

[78] See the 'Vorrede' to Hegel's *Grundlinien der Philosophie des Rechts, Werkausgabe* VII, 18–19. Hegel
portrays Fries as an irrationalist who appeals to immediate feeling as the basis for his political doctrines.
Hegel's description of Fries' philosophy has been simply taken for granted in Hegel scholarship. Thus
Jacques D'Hondt, one of the most eminent scholars of Hegel's political thought, regards the main philosophical difference between Hegel and Fries as one between rationalism and "sentimentalism" and char-
acterizes Fries' view as "the philosophy of sentiment and intuition". See Jacques D'Hondt's *Hegel in his
Time* (Lewiston, NY: Broadview Press, 1988), pp. 84, 86, 97. Avineri, another prominent Hegel scholar,
writes of Fries' "subjectivist philosophy", which, he claims, leads to "romantic political terrorism"
because it undermines "any rational criterion for the discussion of public and social life." See Avineri,
Hegel's Theory of the Modern State, p. 119.

[79] Fries met Jacobi in the summer of 1805 and formed a close friendship. Rightly, Fries maintained that
he was never a disciple of Jacobi, and noted that his philosophy was far too Kantian for Jacobi. See the
manuscript cited by Henke, *Fries*, p. 107.

[80] See *Julius und Evagoras oder Die neue Republik* (Heidelberg: Mohr und Zimmer, 1814). The work
appeared anonymously. For a conspectus of the work, see Hubmann, *Ethische Überzeugung und
politisches Handeln*, pp. 136–141.

[81] See Fries, *System der Philosophie* § 330, pp. 264–265

of fact, whether they are morally correct or not (18–19). Fries special concern in his *Rechtslehre* is with the *pure* doctrine of right, not with *positive* right (19). A pure doctrine of right deals with two questions: 1) What is right? What does the moral law command regarding the interaction of people in society? and 2) How is right to be realized in society? The first question is the concern of legislation, whereas the second is that of politics (19). Politics is the art of determining the most effective means for the ends of action laid down by reason. While the question of right is practical or normative, the question of politics is entirely theoretical or factual (19).

Granted that right is based on the moral law, what is that law? How should we formulate it? Here Fries follows Kant very closely, paraphrasing Kant's formula of humanity as an end in itself. The moral law thus states: "Every person by his dignity has an absolute worth; he exists as an end absolutely; and dignity gives each person the same absolute worth as everyone else." (7). Or more simply: "Humanity in each person should be treated as an end in itself." (32). Fries emphasizes the equality implicit in this formula: everyone has the *same* absolute worth, no one more than another. Hence he states that the law of right means "equality of personal worth" (3). More explicitly: "The *highest* law for the freedom of a rational will is the equality of persons" (4). Of the three Kantian principles of right—equality, freedom and independence—Fries sees the first alone as fundamental, the other two as derivative. This emphasis on equality will play, as we shall soon see, a fateful role in Fries' later political thought.

Fries' formulation of the moral law, his distinction between morality and legality, and his contrast between morality and nature, show his great debts to Kant. The more we read into his *Rechtslehre*, however, the more we find him taking issue with Kant. Indeed, his *Rechtslehre* involves a complete redrawing of the conceptual terrain of the doctrine of right. Fries explicitly disagrees with Kant in two basic ways. First, he denies Kant's claim that right entails the authority to apply coercion against anyone who infringes it.[82] Right and coercion are completely opposed to one another, Fries insists (26, 172). The realm of right holds within the state of society, where it always depends on the obligations of others; the realm of coercion is that of force, which holds only for the state of nature (27). Second, he denies that the doctrine of right primarily concerns freedom, or that there is an original or natural right to freedom. Freedom for Fries is not, properly speaking, a right at all, but a precondition of right, a property presupposed by all rights (24). The source of this error, he maintains, is in thinking of rights in terms of permissions, as if they are whatever we are allowed to do.[83] But if we think of rights in this way, he argues, then it becomes impossible to base them upon morality (24). A right follows from a prior obligation—the obligation to treat human beings as ends in themselves—and does not consist in the *absence* of an obligation, as if it were definable where the realm of law ceases. A right is always

---

[82] Kant, *Metaphysik der Sitten*, VI, 231–232.
[83] Fries clearly attributes this view to Kant (26), though it is not clear that Kant holds it.

co-relative to a duty: it is essentially the claim I have against someone because he has an obligation to me (8–9, 23). If we make freedom an original right, as Kant does, we end out with complete license: everyone should have the right to do whatever he wants without the interference of others (25).[84]

As if these disagreements were not enough, there was another even more profound one, though it is not explicit in the text of the *Rechtslehre* itself. We know about it from a letter Fries sent to his friend Christlieb Reichel in August 1800.[85] While riding in a wagon during one starry summer night, Fries had an epiphany: that the Kantian account of the moral law was a mistake! Exactly what was wrong with it he does not explain. But another slightly later letter advises Reichel: "Do not recoil in horror! Kant's great 'Act as though thou could will … [a maxim as a universal law of nature] is completely false in my opinion; one's own dignity, the dignity of humanity, is that from which one should begin." As these lines reveal, Fries was advocating replacing Kant's universal law formula with the end-in-itself formula. What was wrong with the universal law formula? We do not know from Henke's extracts of the letters, but one hint is given in *Reinhold, Fichte und Schelling*, where Fries maintains that Gustav Hugo was right to expose the barrenness and emptiness of the universal law formula.[86] Thus Fries' call to replace the universal law formula with the end-in-itself formula was probably based on the realization that the end-in-itself formula secures more content and better results in justifying specific moral maxims. Later Kant scholars have come to a similar conclusion.[87] What Fries does not explain, however, is precisely how the end-in-itself formula is based on reason, that is, why reason commands that we treat each person as an end-in-itself.

The first theoretical part of Fries' *Rechtslehre*, 'Allgemeine Gesetzgebung', which treats the general principles of legislation, has a triparitite structure corresponding to the two premises and conclusion of the practical syllogism (16–21). The first section treats the major premise: the fundamental idea or principle of morality, the categorical imperative that we treat humanity as an end-in-itself (31–36). The second section expounds the minor premise, which determines the means for the realization of this moral principle in the political world (37–42). And the third and final section states the conclusion: specific laws about how to act in the political world so that this moral principle is realized (43–66). Fries follows the same structure in the second part of the *Rechtslehre*, 'Die Politik', and in the third, 'Kritik aller positiven Gesetzgebung'.

---

[84] In his *Neue Kritik der Vernunft*, III, 223–224, §214, Fries complains that understanding right in terms of permissions leads to an atomistic conception of society where everyone has the right to do whatever they want as long as they do not interfere with similar rights of others.

[85] Henke, *Fries*, p. 71.

[86] Fries, *Neue Kritik der Vernunft*, p. 319, writes of "*die Leerheit des Kantischen kategorischen Imperativs*". He cites §48 of Hugo's "*Philosophie des Rechts*". This is a reference to the second edition of Hugo's *Lehrbuch des Naturrechts als Philosophie des positiven Rechts* (Berlin: Mylius, 1799).

[87] See, for example, Allen Wood, *Kant's Ethical Thought* (Cambridge: Cambridge University Press, 1999), pp. 147–150.

Thus, not only each part, but the relations between the parts are meant to have the same syllogistic structure (99). While Fries only loosely follows this scheme, it does reveal one of his deepest convictions: that the realm of politics should be subject to the mandates of reason. He developed this scheme because he believes that the practical syllogism reflects the structure of reason itself (16). Hardly the *credo* of the romantic "sentimentalist"!

After expounding his ideal of morality in the first section of Part I, Fries proceeds to discuss the conditions for its realization in the second. He maintains that the chief precondition for the realization of his ideal—the kingdom of ends where everyone is treated as an end in himself—is that people *recognize* one another as rational beings (37). Recognition involves respecting the rights of everyone to be treated as an end in himself. There are two more specific physical conditions involved in achieving such recognition, Fries explains. First, that people have property, the exclusive use of certain goods, which are necessary for their survival and well-being (39–40). Second, that they have a common language, so that they can declare their intentions with regard to others (40–41). From this moral ideal and these conditions, Fries then deduces five laws for the realization of his ideal: 1) that promises be kept (1st law); 2) that property should be distributed according to the principle of equality (2nd law); 3) that there should be a civil constitution under public laws and courts (3rd law); 4) that there should be a public code of law whose chief principles should be the validity of contracts and equality in the distribution of property (4th law); and 5) that there should be a system of penal law based on retribution (5th law). Regarding these laws, Fries again takes issue with Kant when he contends that it is wrong to hold that honesty, telling the truth, is only a *moral* duty (46). It is also a *legal* duty because the realization of the kingdom of ends requires that people form a contract where they keep their promises to one another.

Having laid down the laws of right in Part I, Fries proceeds to consider the problem of politics in Part II. While Part I considered the *social* conditions for the realization of the moral ideal, Part II treats specifically the *political* conditions. In other words, Part II deals with the state.

The crucial question before politics, Fries explains, is how the individual can be forced to comply with the law (69), or how public right can be joined with power (72)? The idea of a social order based on principles of right, and enforced by a common power, Fries calls a "republic" (*Republik*) (72). He uses the term in the old Latin sense, that is, *res publica*, to signify any public body. The term does not have special political connotations for him. It does not imply a reference to, or preference for, any specific form of government. Which form of government is best Fries does not regard as a theoretical question at all. He maintains that it is best answered by experience, by determining what is best for a people according to its traditions and under its specific historical circumstances (88). Accordingly, the Friesian republic can be a monarchy, democracy or aristocracy.

Whatever the form of government, Fries insists that the ruler should have complete sovereignty. He rejects flatly the traditional doctrine of the separation of powers on the grounds that it leads to irresolvable conflict within government (90–91). While any government must have distinct executive, legislative and judicial powers, these should be ultimately united in the will of a single ruler, who not only makes the laws but also enforces and interprets them (75). For what if the legislative finds its laws unenforced by the executive? It must then force the executive to enforce them, so that it is really the highest executive power. And what if the judiciary interprets the laws in a manner completely unintended by the legislative? In that case the legislative must correct the judiciary and interpret the law for itself, so that it is the highest judicial power (75). In insisting on indivisible sovereignty Fries, yet again, put himself at odds with Kant. For in *Zum ewigen Frieden*, Kant had defined republicanism as that political principle where the executive power is distinguished from the legislative, and he had rejected as despotism the doctrine that one and the same power both makes and executes the laws.[88]

Having already given the ruler complete sovereignty, Fries goes on to increase his authority and power by insisting that there is no contract between people and government. While people contract among themselves to enter into society, they do not make a contract to form the state itself (76–78). A contract between people and government makes government impossible, Fries argues, because it allows people to withdraw from the state whenever laws are enforced against them (78). The lack of a contract between government and people implies that the ruler is not accountable to the people. But this is a conclusion that Fries is happy to draw. Indeed, he insists that because the ruler has sovereign power, he cannot be compelled by anyone (94). Individuals have rights against one another in civil society by virtue of the contract between them; but against the government they have no rights at all (94). This means—and here Fries silently endorses one of Kant's most controversial doctrines—that the people have no right to revolt against their government (96–97). What happens after an insurrection, Fries maintains, is not a question of right but only one of might (95).

Fries has now given his ruler such power—indivisible sovereignty and unaccountability—that he appears to sanction utter absolutism. Yet this impression he was very eager to correct. He insists that the highest power in the state comes from not the ruler but the people (*das Volk*), which consists in the will of the majority (80). Though the *Volk* does not have the right to make the law, it does have the power to control government. How? Through its opinion alone (80). Public opinion turns out to be the main check against absolutism in the Friesian state. While the ruler makes the people conform to the law through his sovereign power, the people make the ruler conform to the law by virtue of their opinion (81). "Public opinion is the actual active general will; through it . . . speaks the spirit of the people." (89). The maxim "*vox populi, vox dei*" is true in virtue of public opinion, which is not subject to the will of any political

---

[88] Kant, *Schriften* VIII, 352.

power (85–86). Public opinion is the result of not any express agreement among the people, still less any organization or institution, but the interaction between people at a specific time (83). Because its formation depends on particular circumstances at a particular time, public opinion is essentially an accidental historical phenomenon (87). In making public opinion the ultimate power in the state, and in making it depend on historical circumstances, Fries came his closest to the budding historicist doctrine of the *Volksgeist*.[89]

The state has for Fries three fundamental goals: distribution of property according to the principle of equality; the promotion of the physical welfare of the people; and the spiritual education of the nation (108). Of these three goals only the first, Fries insists, is legally binding on the state. The other two are only physically or politically necessary, that is, while the state has no moral obligation to realize them, it is prudent that it do so. How should the state strive to realize these goals? Fries' liberal convictions permit only a laissez faire approach. The best the state can do is to interfere as little as possible with the activities of its citizens (115). Each individual is the best judge of his physical and moral well-being, and the state should not command or forbid measures regarding it. The only task of the state is to serve as a watchguard, making sure that individuals do not trample over one another's rights in the scramble for material and spiritual well-being (115). The attempt to improve morality by external sanctions, Fries maintains, leads only to hypocrisy or deception (118). His mistrust of public institutions to secure morality extends especially to the church, which he finds a source of paternalism and heteronomy (118–19). Fries, in a final act of rebellion against the seminary at Niesky, looks forward to a "withering away" of the church, whose metaphysics and morality he finds unsuitable for the modern world.

Like Locke and Kant, Fries made protecting property the *raison d'être* of the modern state. Unlike them, however, he made its chief goal the *equal* distribution of property. The fundamental legal obligation of the state, he often declares, is to ensure distribution of property according to the principle of equality (42, 50, 106, 108, 135). Upon first reading, this pronouncement sounds extremely radical, indeed downright levelling, something like the proto-communism of Babeuf or the proto-socialism of Fichte. But the reader's suspicions or expectations are soon dashed. For when Fries

---

[89] The affinity with historicist doctrine is probably accidental. It is noteworthy that in early 1802, just when Fries was writing his *Rechtslehre*, Friedrich Savigny, later leader of the historical school of law and future champion of the *Volksgeist*, began a correspondence with him. See Savigny's February 3, April 3 and May 9, 1802, letters to Fries in Henke, *Fries*, pp. 293–298. Having been told by his brother-in-law, Clemens Brentano, that Fries shared his interest in the foundation of the law, Savigny decided to write Fries. This was also right around the time that Savigny began to develop his own theory of the historical foundation of law in his 1802–1803 lectures on jurisprudence. See Friedrich Savigny, *Vorlesungen über juristische Methodologie*, ed. Aldo Mazzacane (Frankfurt: Klostermann, 1993), pp. 139–144. Though Savigny respected Fries, and even helped to secure him a post at Heidelberg, he quickly realized there were irreconcilable differences between them. By the summer of 1800 Savigny had already repudiated the basic principles of Kant's moral philosophy. Savigny challenged the rationalism that Fries had simply assumed. See his April 3 letter in Henke, *Fries*, p. 296.

finally explains what he means by equal distribution of property in Part III of his *Rechtslehre* it becomes clear that it is nothing like communism or socialism. He repudiates Plato's theory of communal property as well as Fichte's closed commerical state (128). Both of them he finds oppressive, destructive of individual liberty. It is the central goal of the state, he insists, to protect the right to *private* property, that is, each individual having exclusive rights to dispose of certain possessions (39–40, 128).[90]

All this raises the question: What does *equal* distribution of property mean for Fries? He goes to some pains and lengths to explain himself in the first section of Part III. It turns out that it does not mean something as strong as everyone should have the same *amount* of property; but it also does not mean something as weak as everyone's right to property should be *equally* protected. Fries explains that we should equalize the right to property in two senses: first, there should be equal satisfaction of needs; and, second, everyone should enjoy the fruits of their labor (121, 123). Equal satisfaction means people should have enough for their basic needs so that they can be content with their situation in life (121–122). Because some people are content with a little and others are discontented with a lot, it is not necessary that everyone should have the same (121). And enjoyment of the fruits of one's labour means no one should work for the profit of another (123–124). Because people place very different values upon the very different products of labour, it is not possible that everyone should receive the same reward (125).

These are admirable goals, one might think, but the crucial question is how the state should realize them. And here Fries has very little to say. He suffers from the classic liberal dilemma: he sees the terrible injustices of the market economy; but he is hamstrung in his ability to address them because of his commitment to liberty and his fear of the state. Thus he notes that poverty and inequality are often the result of market mechanisms (124); he insists that the government enact measures to ensure that workers are not cast into poverty; and he even recommends that the government ensure some minimal standard of living (125). But his only specific proposal to deal with these issues consists in the provision of poor houses (*Armenanstalten*) (135). On the whole Fries was very thin on recommending specific policies for how the government should achieve his ideals of equal distribution. He claims that his task is only to lay down ideals, leaving it to governments to decide how to realize them in specific circumstances (126–127). But that seems disingenuous. For there was a deeper reason for his lack of recommendations: his liberal convictions were decidedly against the state taking any active role in governing the economy.

For all its emphasis on economic equality, the Friesian republic was not especially egalitarian. It had a class structure, a social hierarchy all its own. Fries never wanted to universalize the middle class, making it the sole estate in society. In one place he lays down a three-fold division of labour: the intellectuals, who work with

---

[90] In his *Neue Kritik der Vernunft* III, 224–226, §214, Fries went out of his way to deny that his doctrine of equality of property meant the abolition of differences in wealth and class.

their intellect; the professionals, who have some skill or trade; and the workers, who labour with their bodies and who use physical force (136). In another place he envisages two basic estates: one is physical, because its members labour with the body; and the other is spiritual, because its members work with the mind (111). He warns, however, against making these estates into a caste system, as if people were assigned their estate by heredity. Through their abilities and talent people should be able to rise in estate; and there should be social mingling between them (111). Though Fries was not without sympathy for the plight of the labouring poor, he never envisages or encourages changing their basic condition. He thinks that workers and peasants, if their wages are only secure, are happy with their lot in life, and they are content if others think for them (122). Of all the social classes Fries is especially concerned with his own, the intellectuals; and here he is not lacking in proposing specific policies and laws for the government. Fries was an advocate *avant la lettre* of intellectual property rights (109, 112). The government should ensure that writers can make a living by giving them copyright protections. After all, ideas are just as much a commodity as fruit or furniture.

Such was, in crude outline, Fries' early political philosophy. Its basic principles will be the foundation for Fries' later works in political philosophy, especially his *Von deutschen Bund und deutscher Staatsverfassung*. In one important respect, though, this later work will take these principles in a direction not apparent from the beginning: Fries will make the principle of equality the basis for a doctrine of ethnic homogeneity and communal solidarity. The principle that we should treat all people equally became the principle that all people in a nation should be equal, having the same language, religion, ethnic origin.[91] This understanding of equality, combined with a lack of tolerance for those who do not meet its requirements, was the basis for Fries' later anti-semitism, which remains an inexpungible stain on his reputation.

9. Philosophy of Religion

Nothing so focuses the mind, and so summons the energies, of a young man than the prospect of poverty. This alone explains Fries' extraordinary productivity during his *Hungerjahre* in Jena. For he wrote from 1801 to 1804 not only his *Rechtslehre* and his *System der Philosophie*, but also his *Wissen, Glauben und Ahndung*, which appeared in Spring 1805.[92] *Wissen, Glauben und Ahndung* is Fries' major work on the philosophy of religion, and one of his most important. This book also proved to be one of Fries' most popular and influential. His concept of *Ahndung*, of feeling or presentiment, attracted discussion well into the 20th century.[93]

---

[91] See Fries, *Vom deutschen Bund und deutscher Staatsverfassung*, p. 58.
[92] Jakob Friedrich Fries, *Wissen, Glaube und Ahndung* (Jena: J.C.G. Göpferdt, 1805). All references in parentheses are to this edition.
[93] In the beginning of the 20th century Rudolf Otto (1869–1937) gave Fries' concept of *Ahndung* a central place in his theology. See his *Das Heilige: Ueber das Irrationale in der Idee des Göttlichen und sein*

Prima facie it is odd to find Fries writing about the philosophy of religion at all. For it did not seem, after his experience at Niesky, that there was much religion left in the man. Religion, and especially Christianity, was something he wanted to liberate himself from, a dank and dark tomb from which he had happily escaped into the sunny and bright secular world. Fries later wrote about "the destruction of my Christianity", and even his "contempt for Christianity" in his early years at Niesky. As a self-described "rebel", it was inevitable that he would doubt all the orthodox beliefs that his elders had taught him. And, sure enough, by the end of his training there, he had rejected all the standard doctrines of revealed religion, namely, miracles, the trinity, incarnation and atonement. "With respect to religion", he later wrote of his time in Niesky, "I was a born deist and Lessingian fragmentist".[94] Fries also questioned the Bible as a rule of faith, because it was based on questionable history, and because people read into it whatever they liked. He took his doubts about Christianity far enough to question even its ethics, which he found fanatical, impractical and crude. The basic ideas behind its morality, which consisted in "love of one's enemy, forgiveness, suffering, repentance, castration and passive martyrdom", were either impractical or degrading (130).

Yet for all his doubts about Christianity, Fries did not discard religion entirely. On the contrary, he still clung to the beliefs in God and immortality. "I never doubted God and eternal life", he later wrote as an old man (28; cf. 23). Since he was so convinced of these beliefs, he never underwent "the anxiety of doubt" that afflicted so many of the faithful. The ideas of God, immortality and freedom were simply too deeply rooted in the human mind, he believed, for them to be cast aside or eradicated by doubt. Respect for religion remained for Fries one of the enduring legacies of the Moravian brotherhood. Despite his early scepticism about Christianity, he later wrote that his early years at the seminary had taught him a valuable lesson: "the experience of Moravian life showed me so clearly the great meaning of religion that I always recognized its importance." (28)

Exactly how to describe Fries' early faith is no easy matter. It resists simple classification. Though he labelled himself a "deist", this term is hardly accurate. While he endorsed the deist's natural religion and critique of revelation, he never accepted his confidence in the powers of reason to prove the existence of God and immortality. What the deist attempted to prove through reason, he regarded as a matter of faith alone. Fries also gave a much greater importance to religious sentiment than any deist. True to the pietism of the Moravian brotherhood, he held that the real meaning of faith consists not in assent to dogmas but in personal devotion, commitment and

---

Verhältniß zum Rationalen (Breslau: Trewandt und Granier, 1917). Otto even made Fries a central figure for his introduction to theology. See his *Kant'isch-Fries'sche Religionsphilosophie und ihre Anwendung auf die Theologie* (Tübingen: Mohr, 1909). In the 1920s Albert Görland, the Marburg neo-Kantian, also attempted to revive the concept of *Ahndung*. See his *Religionsphilosophie als Wissenschaft aus dem Systemgeiste des kritische Idealismus* (Berlin: de Gruyter, 1922).

[94] Henke, *Fries*, p. 28. All references in parentheses to Fries' early religious views are to this work.

action. Since Fries had doubted the atonement, the basis for pietist devotion, it would seem as if he had deprived religious feeling of its very meaning and rationale. But Fries had a substitute for the inspiration of the atonement: aesthetic experience. The basis for religious feeling, the source and stimulus for religious devotion, he held, should be the experience of the sublime and beautiful. In attempting to replace dogma with aesthetic experience, Fries seems to walk down the romantic road, like so many of his contemporaries in the 1790s. Yet Fries was never much of a romantic either: he had little time for myth, which was crucial for the romantic attempt to revive religion. So Fries was deist, pietist and romantic all in one, yet none of them completely.

What role did Kant play in the formation of Fries' religious views? *Prima facie* only a small role, because Fries informs us that he was reserved in his first reception of Kant's moral and religious doctrines (27). Kant's second *Kritik* and his *Religion* made little impression on him. Fries' critical reaction to Kant will grow and deepen in later years, so that eventually he will be more critical of Kant's philosophy of religion than any other part of his philosophy. Nevertheless, Kant was still a decisive influence, and in two crucial respects. First, Kant taught him to be sceptical about the traditional proofs for the existence of God and immortality. Though Fries would later question Kant's own *practical* proofs, Kant at least taught him the problems with the *theoretical* ones. Second, Kant's noumenal-phenomenal dualism provided the essential structure for his philosophy of religion, the basis for his reconciliation of the conflicting claims of reason and faith. For Fries, the Kantian dualisms are the solution, not the problem. It was only by upholding them, he believed, that he could resolve the perennial conflict between reason and faith.

Fries would probably never have written his philosophy of religion if it were not for a new disturbing development on the philosophical scene in Jena. Despite all his efforts in *Reinhold, Fichte and Schelling,* speculative idealism was not retreating but regrouping, even preparing for a new offensive. Since 1801, Schelling and Hegel had formed an alliance, co-editing the *Kritisches Journal der Philosophie.* The aim of their journal was to combat "the philosophy of subjectivity" in all its forms, not the least of which was the Kantian philosophy of religion. They were indeed intent on destroying the very aspects of the Kantian legacy that Fries wanted to preserve. Through the postulate of intellectual intuition, Schelling and Hegel believed they could provide a theoretical basis for the belief in God; and through their organic concept of nature, they were confident that they could overcome the noumenal-phenomenal dualism.

Fries could have perceived the Schelling-Hegel alliance only as a threat. It was probably the need to defend the Kantian legacy against it that moved him to write about the philosophy of religion. A critique of Schelling and Hegel would check the new offensive of speculative idealism, and it would be the natural sequel to his *Reinhold, Fichte und Schelling.* And so, sometime in the autumn of 1804, in the midst of preparing lectures, Fries set to work on *Wissen, Glauben und Ahndung.*

Fries reveals the aim of his tract when he writes that the business of philosophy is to protect faith and to separate it from knowledge (118). Philosophy can do this in two ways. First, by showing that knowledge has a subjective origin and validity, so that it cannot claim to be any more objective than faith. Second, by demonstrating that knowledge is limited to the sphere of nature alone. Fries follows both strategies in *Wissen, Glauben und Ahndung.* He does so by defending and re-interpreting Kant's dualism between appearances and things-in-themselves. It was only by defending this dualism, Fries believed, that he could protect faith and separate it from knowledge.

Defending this dualism was no small task in the early 1800s, given that Fichte, Schelling and Hegel had all subjected it to such severe criticism. Fries went to great lengths and pains to vindicate it in one long chapter of his book.[95] The best argument for Kant's distinction, he maintains, comes from the Third Antinomy (46–47). If we assume that appearances are things-in-themselves according to transcendental realism, then we get caught in the contradiction of having to assume that the world is both infinite and finite. If, however, we distinguish between appearances and things-in-themselves according to transcendental idealism, we avoid this contradiction. Fries stresses the argument from the Third Antinomy because he finds Kant's argument in the Transcendental Aesthetic wanting. Like Trendelenburg decades later, he points out that just because space and time arise a priori in the mind, it does not follow that they cannot correspond with things-in-themselves. Kant's arguments show only that we cannot *know* that our representations correspond with things-in-themselves; this does not exclude the possibility that they do so in fact (36, 44).

One respect in which Fries defends the Kantian dualism against Schelling and Hegel is by attacking their organic concept of nature, which was intended to overcome that dualism. Though Fries very much admired that concept, he does not think that it has the anti-mechanistic implications that Schelling and Hegel read into it. He maintains that physiology belongs to the realm of the physically and mathematically explicable no less than physics (92). The organic is simply a higher degree of organization of the material forces of nature and does not differ in kind from them. There is no need to postulate, then, the existence of an extra *sui generis* teleological concept to explain the functioning of organisms. In making this point against Schelling and Hegel, Fries ensured that the concepts of life and organism are not bridges crossing the phenomenal into the noumenal but simply part of the phenomenal itself.

How are we to interpret the distinction between phenomena and noumena, appearances and things-in-themselves? Fries maintains that appearances or phenomena are not simply representations within us, having no connection with things-in-themselves, but that they are aspects or relative properties of things-in-themselves, that is, they are how they appear to a human being with its characteristic cognitive capacities (32, 61). The distinction between appearance and thing-in-itself is also for Fries a distinction between finite and infinite, temporal and eternal, being. Schelling

[95] Fries, 'Die Natur ist blosse Erscheinung', pp. 31–60.

has performed a great service, he writes uncharacteristically, by formulating Kant's distinction between appearance and thing-in-itself as one between finite and eternal being (4). This formulation has the advantage of connecting the old religious ideas about the infinite and finite, the eternal and temporal, with Kant's "great discovery" that space and time are only forms of sensibility.

Whatever the merits of his defence and interpretation of Kant's dualism, Fries believed that he was justified in maintaining it and applying it to the philosophy of religion. The distinction between thing-in-itself and appearance now demarcates the spheres of knowledge and faith. Knowledge (*Wissen*) holds for the realm of appearances, nature or finitude, the world of space and time, whereas faith (*Glaube*) holds for the thing-in-itself, the infinite or eternal, the world beyond space and time (61–62, 173).

For Fries, the distinction between knowledge and faith is not only in their subject matter or domain but also in their epistemic status. To define that status, he carefully analyses the meaning of each concept, knowledge and faith. Of course, this was old conceptual territory, once fought over by Kant, Jacobi and Mendelssohn in the 1780s. Fries now revisits it, often taking issue with his predecessors. For him, the basic difference between knowledge and faith is essentially that between belief (*Fürwahrhalten*) that *can* be, and belief that *cannot* be, verified by experience. Knowledge (*Wissen*) means a belief whose objects *can* be known through sense intuition, whereas faith (*Glaube*) means a belief whose objects *cannot* be known through such an intuition (64, 74, 120). This distinction reflects Fries' allegiance to the Kantian principle that the limits of knowledge are determined by possible experience. In other words, if we are *to know* that something exists, as opposed to *just believing* that it exists, we must be able to confirm that belief through sense intuition. This principle is fundamental for Fries, the basis for his assigning knowledge and faith to distinct realms, for it implies that we can know only appearances or phenomena, that we cannot know things-in-themselves or noumena. Since appearances belong to the realm of experience, we can have a sensible intuition of them, and therefore we can know that they exist and how they do so. Since, however, things-in-themselves transcend experience, we cannot have a sensible intuition of them, and therefore have no means of knowing whether and how they exist (61–62). They are therefore solely the objects of faith.

In making his distinction between knowledge and faith Fries takes issue with Jacobi's famous competing account in his *David Hume*.[96] There Jacobi had maintained that the realm of reason is that of the demonstrable, that for which we can give reasons, whereas the realm of faith is the indemonstrable, that for which we cannot give reasons. This left him with a very broad concept of faith, however, so that whatever is indemonstrable falls *within* the realm of faith. This means that even self-evident intuitions, which are also indemonstrable, fall within the realm of faith.

---

[96] Jacobi, *David Hume*, in *Werke* (Leipzig: Fleischer, 1815), II, 144–146.

So, on Jacobi's reckoning, even the mathematician, who has to appeal to self-evident but indemonstrable intuitions or axioms, has to believe as much as the Christian! Fries does not accept Jacobi's distinction, however, on the grounds that it runs counter to ordinary usage; thus he points out that we call immediate or self-evident intuitions knowledge, not faith (71). While Fries disagrees with Jacobi that all indemonstrable belief amounts to faith, he does agree with him that all faith is indemonstrable.

Crucial to, and characteristic of, Fries' distinction between knowledge and faith is his denial of any *intellectual* intuition of things-in-themselves (57–58, 75, 250, 252). Fries stresses the necessity of *sense* intuition in distinguishing knowledge and faith precisely to exclude the intellectual intuition advanced by Fichte, Schelling and Hegel. Fries rejects intellectual intuition chiefly because he accepts the Kantian view that the human intellect is discursive and finite: discursive, in operating with concepts, judgements and syllogisms; and finite, in not having the power to create its object and requiring a given one.

So far we have seen how Fries defends an essentially Kantian position in his philosophy of religion. But there is another side of this philosophy that is very critical of Kant. *Wissen, Glauben und Ahndung* is filled with objections against virtually every aspect of Kant's philosophy of religion. One of the most important concerns Kant's distinction between reason and faith. Though intent on preserving that distinction, at least in a general sense, Fries sometimes formulates it in very different terms from Kant, and indeed by taking issue with him. He criticizes Kant for blurring the distinction by attempting to find a form of rational justification for belief in the noumenal world of freedom, God and immortality. For Fries, belief in that world is entirely a matter of faith, and there cannot be *any* rational proof for it, whether theoretical or practical (157, 165).[97] Thus he thinks that Kant is mistaken in assuming that we have through the moral law some kind of insight into our own freedom (164–165); and he maintains that it is also an error to assume that practical reason can provide a proof for our beliefs in God and immortality (68–69, 73). So, while Fries agrees with Kant that there cannot be any *theoretical* proof for these beliefs—that all the arguments for the existence of God and immortality collapse—he disagrees with him that there can be a *practical* proof for them through morality.

Fries rejects much of the reasoning by which Kant attempts to establish his doctrine of practical faith. In the second *Kritik* Kant had argued that our obligation to strive towards the highest good (i.e. the perfect correspondence between happiness

---

[97] Though Fries criticized Kant for blurring the distinction between faith and knowledge, this was a case of the pot calling the kettle black. For Fries too proves guilty of this sin. In later passages of *Wissen, Glauben und Ahndung* he maintains that there is a kind of knowledge involved in faith after all. Though he does not think that this knowledge amounts to a form of intellectual intuition, as Schelling and Hegel hold, he does say that faith amounts to a sort knowledge all the same. Thus he makes a distinction between *Wissen* and *Erkennen*, where *Wissen* is some form of demonstrable knowledge and *Erkennen* a form of indemonstrable knowledge. Faith involves for Fries the indemonstrable knowledge of *Erkennen* (176, 178, 250). Because faith involves *Erkennen*, Fries explains, it is closer to knowledge than to feeling (236).

and morality) justifies us in believing in the existence of God.[98] If we are to promote the highest good—so the argument goes—we need to believe in the existence
of a cosmic creator and governer who guarantees that moral effort is rewarded with
personal happiness. Without that belief, I will have no incentive or motivation to
strive for the highest good, for it could be that all my efforts to create a better world
are utterly in vain. But Fries objects that there is no necessary connection—either
logical or psychological—between the moral law and belief in the existence of God
(68–69). A morally good agent acts for the sake of the moral law alone, and for him
virtue is its own reward, even if he does not believe in the existence of God (158–159).
Furthermore, Fries finds Kant's whole argument for belief in the existence of God circular: we assume the existence of the highest good because we believe in the existence
of God, who alone has the power to create the harmony of morality and happiness;
and we believe in the existence of God because we assume that there is a highest good
(69–70; cf. 156–157).

Another central target of Fries' criticism is Kant's idea of the highest good. Kant
understood the highest good as the perfect harmony between morality and happiness, where virtue is rewarded and vice punished according to principles of justice.
Fries, however, thinks that this ideal only makes sense within the realm of appearances or the finite world (150). The concept of happiness involves those of need and
pleasure, which have meaning only for beings with our physical constitution (149–
150). In the eternal realm there will be no happiness whatsoever because there will
be no need or pleasure (159). Fries agrees with Kant that we must think of the divine
in connection with the moral world order, and indeed as the cosmic guarantee of the
highest good (148, 309). The very essence of religion involves, he insists, the idea of
a moral world order, that is, a world created and governed for the sake of the good.
Still, he maintains that we should explain the highest good not in terms of the harmony between morality and happiness but in terms of another Kantian ideal: the
kingdom of ends (148–149, 160, 166). That is a more suitable account of the highest
good, he argues, because the kingdom of ends exists in the eternal and noumenal
realm alone. The kingdom of ends is that ideal realm where everyone is autonomous
and a co-legislator, and where everyone is treated with respect and as an end in itself.
We should then conceive of God as the sovereign who governs all finite beings in this
kingdom, that is, the eternal ruler who ensures that all are treated as ends and never
as means and that all achieve their ends as autonomous agents (160).

Whatever the merits of Fries' defence and critique of Kant, the thrust of his book
lies elsewhere. Its chief contribution lies with Fries' introduction of a new concept,
a third concept that he distinguishes from knowledge and faith. This is the concept
that appears in the last word of his title: *Ahndung*. Fries gives great importance to this

---

[98] Kant, *Schriften* V, 124–132. For a more detailed account of Kant's reasoning, see my 'Moral Faith
and the Highest Good', in *The Cambridge Companion to Kant and Modern Philosophy*, ed. Paul Guyer
(Cambridge: Cambridge University Press, 2006), pp. 588–629.

concept, which he saw as his original contribution (64).[99] Following his tripartite title, virtually a third of the book is devoted to this concept, which receives equal treatment along with faith and knowledge.

Unfortunately, *"Ahndung"* is virtually intranslatable. It derives from the German verb *"ahnen"*, which means to suspect something, or to have a vague idea about something. It also has connotations of prophecy, foreboding or premonition. Perhaps the closest translation would be "presentiment" because the German word was the intended substitute for the Latin *"praesensio"*. J.G. Walch, in his famous *Philosophisches Lexicon*, defined *"Andungen"* [sic] as "such feelings that put us in an inner melancholy and dread because they indicate some future but unknown misfortune".[100] Kant in his *Anthropologie* defined it as "the hidden sense of that which is not yet present".[101] It was in this sense that Kant had banished the concept from philosophy: for how, he asked, could one feel what did not yet exist? Fries, however, did not have to worry about Kant's ban. Leaving aside all connotations of prophecy or premonition, he uses the term in a more technical sense. He defines *Ahndung* as "a feeling of the recognition of the eternal in the finite" (176).

In Fries' system, *Ahndung,* like knowledge and faith, has its own ontological domain. While faith deals with the infinite, and while knowledge concerns the finite, *Ahndung* deals with the *intersection* or *connection* between these realms, namely, the presence of the infinite in the finite (177). Fries reminds us that there is *one* truth in the infinite and finite—that the finite is the appearance of the infinite, that appearances are not subjective entities (i.e. representations) but how things-in-themselves appear to us. This one truth should have its own proper epistemic attitude, then, because faith and knowledge deal with only isolated aspects of it (173, 261).

Fries consistently calls *Ahndung* a feeling (*Gefühl*). What kind of feeling? That is the crucial question. As a feeling about the mysterious, *Ahndung* seems rather mysterious itself. Fries thinks of this feeling not only as an emotional but also as a cognitive state. Feeling involves a kind of knowledge, which is "the recognition" of the presence of the infinite in the finite. His term for "recognition" is *"Anerkennen"*, a variant of *Erkennen*, the form of cognition indemonstrable or inexplicable by concepts. By making *Ahndung* a form of knowledge Fries seems to come close to the position of Schelling and Hegel, who were bent on demolishing the distinction between knowledge and faith with intellectual intuition. But Fries could still point out that there is an importance difference between his position and theirs: while *Ahndung* is a feeling inexpressible in discursive form, intellectual intuition is an insight or perception intended for later conceptual elaboration in a philosophical system. He insisted that

---

[99] Jacobi wrote about it in his March 3, 1799 letter to Fichte, though he uses it in a different sense that virtually equates it with reason. See Fichte, *Briefwechsel*, ed. Hans Schulz (Leipzig: Haessel, 1930), II, 38.

[100] Johann Georg Walch, *Philosophisches Lexikon* (Leipzig: Gleditsch, 1775), I, 59.

[101] Kant, *Anthropologie* §35, VII, 187.

this feeling is irresolvable into distinct cognition (253), and that what we recognize through it is only a mystery (251).

Though Fries insisted that the content of feeling on any specific occasion is a mystery, he went on to provide a general account of the experience of *Ahndung*. It is here that we see the romantic or aesthetic dimension of his philosophy of religion. We recognize the eternal in the finite, he explained, through our feeling for the beauty and sublimity of nature (177). We feel the beautiful and sublime when we sense that nature forms an organic whole, that it is a system of ends or a purposive whole (181). This organic whole or system of ends is structured like a work of art, and so the experience of it is aesthetic. Following Kant, Fries states that the feeling of *Ahndung* involves "reflective judgment" (175, 182). Reflective judgement in Kant both expresses the feeling involved in aesthetic experience, and it involves the idea of a systematic whole that perceives nature as if it were a work of art.

The main reason Fries introduces the concept of *Ahndung* is to define the mental state characteristic of religion. Religion, he insists, should not be reduced to metaphysics or ethics. Rather, its distinctive characteristic is a kind of attitude or mental state towards life and existence. This mental state consists not in knowledge, still less in action, but in a kind of feeling, a responsiveness or sensitivity to the world (239). What is characteristic of religious life is devotion, which involves a feeling or mood (*Gefühlsstimmung*) (236).

Fries' definition of religion resembles no one more than his fellow Moravian, Schleiermacher, who had made a similar argument in his famous 1799 *Über Religion*. Nowhere does Fries cite Schleiermacher, but the affinity is unmistakeable. Fries' repudiation of intuition seems to put him at odds with Schleiermacher, who makes "intuition of the universe" the defining characteristic of religion. But this is more a difference in name than concept: Fries' *Ahndung* and Schleiermacher's *Anschauen* both involve the recognition of the infinite in the finite, and both resist conceptual or systematic articulation.

Seen as a whole, Fries' book was an original synthesis of Kantian and Romantic themes. Its Kantian themes are its dualisms between appearance and thing-in-itself, knowledge and faith; its Romantic themes are its aesthetic atitude towards the world and making feeling characteristic of religion. Like all syncretic works, it was doomed to dissatisfy the extremes it hoped to reconcile. No Kantian could stomach the abandonment of practical faith for aesthetic feeling; and no Romantic could suffer the re-introduction of the Kantian dualisms, which would violate his sense for the unity of things, his feeling for the "one and all". Still, the work held its own, attracting interest and commentary long after its author's death.[102]

---

[102] In the 1980s Fries' philosophy of religion was the object of interest among "the Swansea school" of neo-Wittengeinsteinian philosophers, especially Rush Rhees and D.Z. Phillips. Phillips translated one of Fries' later works under the title *Dialogues on Morality and Religion* (Oxford: Blackwell, 1982).

10. New Critique of Reason

All those writings during the *Hungerjahre* eventually had their effect. Fries was gain-
ing recognition and with that came opportunity. In February 1805, thanks in part to
the mediation of Clemens Brentano and Friedrich Savigny, Fries received the offer of a
full professorship at the University of Heidelberg. The offer was attractive: 900 florins,
9 measures of grain as well as repayment of travel and transport costs. How could he
refuse? Fries saw the offer as virtual deliverance. It hardly mattered to him that it was
first made to Herbart, who had declined. Ever since his return from Zofingen, Fries had
become alienated from the intellectual scene in Jena, which had become dominated
by the Romantics. He felt the lone sober Kantian amid a bunch of Romantic drunks.
His economic situation too remained precarious. Although it had improved somewhat
when he, along with Hegel, had been promoted to extraordinary professor in January
1805, his salary was still not enough. He could not supplement it with lecture fees, since
his lectures were not that popular. After all, who wanted to hear old Kantian stuff when
they could hear the latest exciting ideas from Romantic hotheads like Friedrich Schlegel
and Friedrich Schelling? And so, for philosophical and economic reasons, Fries gladly
accepted the offer from Heidelberg. He moved there in May 1805.

Fries would remain in Heidelberg for the next ten years, 1805–1816, which were the
culminating years of his academic career. All seemed promising when he first came
there. The University was going through a period of revival and growth. There were
many new students, many new faculty and several new departments. In the early
1800s Heidelberg had become a centre of the new Romantic movement, with Clemens
Brentano (1778–1842), Joseph Görres (1776–1848), Achim von Arnim (1781–1831) and
Joseph Eichendorff (1788–1857) all assembled there. But Fries soon discovered that
the Heidelberg Romantics were no better than their Jena counterparts; they too were
mystical, obscurantist and self-indulgent. Least of all could he stomach their sanc-
timony: "their mouths drip with the fat of the sacred, as if they had just eaten pork
roast." After only a year in Heidelberg, Fries felt isolated there too. Once again, it
was his "Kantianism" that had made him the outcast.[103] His letters to friends during the Heidelberg years are filled with complaints about the lack of "philosophical friendship". His feelings of isolation become fully apparent from an 1807 letter
to Beaulieu: "If one requested the rigour of science, I would be the only person in
Germany to answer."[104]

As if to console himself for his intellectual isolation, Fries turned inwards and
focused on his own writing. His first years in Heidelberg were devoted to finishing
his major work on Kant and anthropology. This was his *Neue Kritik der Vernunft*,
which appeared in three volumes in 1807.[105] This work was the fruition of all Fries'

---

[103] See Henke, *Fries*, p. 105.   [104] Henke, *Fries*, p. 119.
[105] Jacob Friedrich Fries, *Neue Kritik der Vernunft* (Heidelberg: Mohr und Zimmer, 1807), 3 vols. All
references in parentheses are to this edition, both to its paragraph number (§) and its page number.

thinking about epistemology since his seminary days in Niesky. He had already conceived the main doctrines of Volume I while a student in Leipzig;[106] and in Zofingen he had already worked out the outlines of Volumes II and III.[107] The early conception and composition of the work is testimony to the great continuity of Fries' philosophical development.

Our goal here is not to produce a conspectus of the three volumes of Fries' work. This would be not only an enormous task but also a tedious and superfluous one. For the originality and importance of Fries' work lies not in its content, which closely follows Kantian doctrine, but in how Fries attempts to justify that content, that is, in his methodology. The chief contribution of *Neue Kritik* consists in Fries' new conception of a transcendental deduction, that is, in his account of the justification of synthetic a priori principles. We have already seen how Fries was moving towards a new methodology in his early psychology essays and in the second half of *Reinhold, Fichte und Schelling*. In the first two volumes of the *Neue Kritik* Fries finally gives that methodology a rigorous and systematic exposition. Our sole task in this section will be to explain that new methodology.

The main problem Fries addresses in his *Neue Kritik* is the same question that had once troubled Kant in his old *Kritik*: namely, how are synthetic a priori judgements possible?[108] The justification of these judgements posed a severe problem for Kant, partly because they cannot be verified in experience (due to their a priori status), and partly because they cannot be justified by the principle of contradiction (due to their synthetic status). Since the fundamental principles of knowledge are synthetic a priori judgements, the justification of such judgements is an important task. The possibility of all knowledge hangs in the balance.

Though Fries faced in the 1790s the same problem Kant posed in the 1770s, the solution to it had become more pressing and difficult. The sceptical attacks on Kant, and then on the post-Kantian systems, seemed to reveal the weakness of every proposed solution to the problem. All paths had been tried; but all led only to the abyss of doubt. The result of this scepticism, as Fries later summarized the situation, is that philosophers had still not answered Maimon's nagging question: *quid juris?* (§54; I, 204). In other words, what is the justification of synthetic a priori judgements?

Why had past solutions failed? According to Fries' diagnosis, they all suffered from a common problem: "the rationalist prejudice". This prejudice assumes that

Volume numbers are indicated with capital Roman numerals. The second edition appeared under a new title, *Neue oder anthropologische Kritik der Vernunft* (Heidelberg: Winter, 1828–1831).

[106] Henke, *Fries*, p. 45.   [107] Henke, *Fries*, p. 61.

[108] The fact that Fries begins with the same problem as Kant shows how misleading it is to claim, with Nelson, that Fries' work proves the impossibility of epistemology. See Nelson, *Jakob Friedrich Fries und seine jüngsten Kritiker* (Göttingen: Dieterich, 1909), pp. 80–81. Fries himself would have found this a startling conclusion. Though Nelson is correct that Fries did not intend to provide an *objective* justification for the validity of knowledge, it hardly follows from this that he showed the impossibility of epistemology. Fries did intend to provide a *subjective* justification of synthetic a priori principles, which surely falls within the purview of epistemology.

to justify a judgement is to prove it, to show how it follows from self-evident premises. Reinhold, Fichte and Schelling all revealed this prejudice when they attempted
to prove the results of the critical philosophy from a single self-evident first principle. Their paradigm of knowledge was the classical rationalist one: a geometric system with definitions, axioms and theorems (xxix). But their programme collapsed
because they placed too much weight on their first principle. Such a principle must be
very abstract and general if it applies to all kinds of content; but for just that reason it
cannot derive concrete and specific results. We can derive content only if we smug-
gle in additional premises which do not follow from the first principle itself (§73; I,
305–306).

Fries thinks that Kant himself, despite his penetrating criticisms of rationalism,
still failed to break with the rationalist prejudice, and so he set a poor example for his
successors (xxvi–xxvii). In the first *Kritik* he attempts to provide a proof of synthetic
a priori principles by showing how they are necessary conditions of the possibility
of experience. He understood his transcendental deduction to be a kind of proof,
which would prove such principles from some higher self-evident fact in reason
(xxxvi). But Kant's transcendental deduction failed, Fries maintains, because the
sceptic need not accept the premise of the possibility of experience. Experience for
Kant consists in the conformity of perceptions to universal and necessary laws; but
it is just this conformity that is questioned by Hume and Maimon, who insist that
the given consists in nothing more than constant conjunctions of discrete impressions (xxxiv).

So if we are to justify synthetic a priori principles, Fries argues, we must free ourselves from the rationalist prejudice. To expose the problem behind that prejudice,
Fries analyses the reasoning behind it (xxx–xxi). We assume that: 1) all beliefs need
some justification; and that 2) to give a reason is to provide a proof, that is, premises
from which the belief follows of necessity. It then seems to follow from 1) and 2) that
3): all knowledge should be proven. That belief was the central prejudice behind
Leibniz's and Wolff's rationalism, which Kant and his progeny continued to uphold
(xxvii). Fries thinks that there is nothing wrong with premise 1). The basis for this
premise is nothing less than the principle of sufficient reason, which makes the rightful demand that we justify all our beliefs. No less than Leibniz and Wolff, Fries reaffirms this principle, which he calls the "catharticon of all knowledge" (§70; I, 280). We
must recognize, he insists, the right of the sceptic to ask the *"quid juris?"*, a question
that stems from his strict and proper adherence to the principle of sufficient reason.
The problem with this reasoning comes with the second premise, the conflation of
justification with proof or syllogistic reasoning. This premise cannot be upheld, Fries
argues, for the simple reason that all justification has to come to an end with premises
that have an immediate certainty and that cannot be proven (§70; I, 280–281). The
demand for proof cannot go on ad infinitum. We are now left with the question: How
are we to justify principles if not through a proof? We need to re-think, Fries insists,
the whole question of justification.

To sort out these issues, Fries makes two sets of strategic distinctions. The first set is between *proof, demonstration* and *deduction* (§§70–71; I, 278–286, 292–293). A *proof* consists in standard syllogistic reasoning, the attempt to derive a valid conclusion from true premises. *Demonstration* exhibits the content of a concept or judgement in intuition. It can be a priori in the case of mathematics, where we construct a concept in intuition; or it can be a posteriori in the case of an empirical concept, where we show how it derives from sense intuitions. Finally, there is *deduction*, which shows how a principle presupposes "the law of our immediate knowledge" or how it "originates in the essence of reason" (§70; 284). Rather than attempting to prove a proposition from self-evident premises, a deduction attempts to show how it plays a necessary role within the general structure of our reason. The second set of distinctions is between *objective* and *subjective* justification and *transcendental* and *empirical* truth (§71; 286–295). *Objective* justification attempts to prove *transcendental* truth, that is, that a judgement corresponds to being in itself, which is the nature of things independent of how we perceive it. *Subjective* justification attempts to show only *empirical* truth, that is, that a judgement conforms to other more basic or immediate principles of reason, which are true for only how we experience the world.

Fries' central contention in *Neue Kritik* is that synthetic a priori principles can have neither a proof nor a demonstration but only a deduction. They cannot have a proof because they are themselves fundamental principles of knowledge, so that there are no higher principles from which they can be derived. They also cannot have a demonstration, because they are not mathematical principles that are constructible a priori in intuition, and because they are not empirical principles derived from sense perception. The only possibility for their justification, then, consists in providing them with a deduction. A deduction will show how these principles are integral to or constitutive of our most basic ways of perceiving and understanding the world, how they play a necessary role in the workings of our most fundamental faculties.

Such a deduction, Fries is at pains to stress, cannot provide an objective justification. It cannot show the transcendental truth of these principles, for even if we show that the principle is essential to our faculty of knowledge, the fact remains that we cannot get outside this faculty to see whether it corresponds to things-in-themselves (§71; I, 287, 289). We cannot know whether our basic ways of conceiving and perceiving the world do conform to things-in-themselves. While it is possible that they do, it is also possible they do not, and we simply have to resign ourselves to ignorance. A deduction does provide, however, a *subjective* justification for these principles, because it shows how they are part of our basic mental economy, our fundamental ways of perceiving and conceiving the world, without which we would understand nothing at all. In this way we establish at least the *empirical* truth of these principles, that is, that they are part of our web of belief and basic ways of experiencing the world. Whether these basic ways of understanding the world have a transcendental truth is, however, a question that we cannot answer.

The great advantage of deduction, Fries believes, is that it satisfies the principle of sufficient reason without making unrealistic claims to transcendental truth. We satisfy the principle of sufficient reason by a special kind of justification: by analysing a proposition and showing how it it is necessary for our cognitive functioning. Yet, having done that, we do not make the additional impossible claim that the proposition is somehow true of things themselves. We recognize that we have to resign ourselves to a subjective standpoint, which denies us access to things-in-themselves. But learning to accept that truth, Fries thinks, is the basic lesson of Kant's Copernican Revolution. Agnosticism about transcendental truth, and the restriction of all knowledge to empirical truth, is for him the very spirit of the critical philosophy, the essential meaning behind "the idealistic turn in speculation" (§71; I, 295).

How, exactly, does deduction differ from proof? This is the crucial question regarding Fries' concept of deduction.[109] As Fries sometimes explains it, a deduction shows how a putative principle presupposes the more basic or immediate knowledge of reason (Cf. §70; 283, 284). This makes a deduction sound like a regressive argument, which through the analysis of a proposition shows how it presupposes more basic propositions. A proof would then be a progressive argument, which begins from self-evident premises and then derives the proposition as its conclusion. It is striking, however, that Fries rejects this interpretation. Both progressive and regressive arguments are for him kinds of proof (§71; I, 286–287).

If we take Fries at his word here, we must avoid conflating deduction with some form of regressive argument. What he means by a deduction is indeed very different from any logical argument, whether progressive or regressive. That this is so follows from his frequent insistence that he is not doing metaphysics or logic but anthropology, which attempts to provide an *empirical* account of facts derived from human experience. Understood as an empirical theory, a deduction attempts to describe a specific kind of fact: namely, a necessity of human nature. In other words, its concern is not with *logical* but with *natural* necessity. It attempts to show how a principle plays a necessary role in our cognitive constitution, a vital role in our mental economy, such that without the principle we will not be able to perceive or conceive the world. The ultimate justification of the principle against a sceptic would then be that the principle is *naturally* necessary, such that without it we human beings cannot perceive or conceive the world. Though it might not correspond to reality, we still cannot do without it, so that there is no point in demanding that we abandon it or replace it with some other principle.

---

[109] Most accounts of Fries' theory (Mechler, Grapengiesser, Nelson, Bonsiepen) do not explain this point very clearly, and largely content themselves with reproducing verbally Fries' explanations, which are exactly what stand in need of explanation. They state that the deduction of a proposition shows its necessity within a general theory of reason; but that statement is so vague that it does not exclude logical argument or proof. The account I offer here attempts to avoid this vagueness.

On the reading proposed here, Fries' deduction is a kind of *functional* explanation, which provides a kind of pragmatic justification for a principle. In other words, it explains and justifies a principle by showing how it performs a specific function.[110] Like all functional explanations, Fries' deduction has both a normative and descriptive component: a normative component, because a function involves a norm or lays down an end, something that it *should* achieve; a descriptive component, because a function also states what a thing actually does. This normative component serves as a kind of *justification* of the principle, because it implies that it is a necessary or efficient means for its ends, or that it conforms to the norms laid down for it. Understood in this way, Fries' deduction justifies a principle in *pragmatic* terms. It raises the questions: What use does a principle have? What function does it perform? And does it perform this function well or efficiently? The ultimate justification of the principle would then involve showing two things: that it performs a necessary function and that it performs it well.

The question still remains how we actually produce such a transcendental deduction? How does the transcendental philosophy go about making one? Fries spent much effort in answering these questions in the *Neue Kritik*, and it is to his explanation that we must now turn.

A deduction of a synthetic a priori principle is supposed to show its dependence on the most basic laws of the mind, its place within the systematic structure of our cognitive faculties. It succeeds, therefore, only if there are such laws, only if there is such a structure. Since, however, these laws and this structure are not immediately apparent to consciousness, since they are not evident as soon as we think about them, the Friesian transcendental philosopher has to postulate their existence. It is necessary to assume, therefore, that the systematic structure of reason, which is the basis of all our knowledge and the source of all certainty, lies beneath consciousness. Fries makes this presupposition very explicit when he insists on distinguishing between the reflective powers of the mind, whose employment depends on our voluntary activity, and the spontaneous activity of reason itself (§§43, 54; 159–60,198). It is the spontaneous activity of reason itself that posits these laws, that creates this systematic structure, and that contains the immediate truths in terms of which all others are justified; but its activity is not immediately evident to consciousness, which rather presupposes its workings. Fries would insist, therefore, that the transcendental philosopher does not himself create the justification of his principles; what justifies them is something he discovers within consciousness itself.

To be aware of the spontaneous activity of reason, then, the Friesian transcendental philosopher has *to reconstruct* it. He does so through what Fries calls "reflection",

[110] This would bring Fries close to what Kant, at least on one influential reading, meant by a transcendental deduction. See Dieter Henrich, 'Kant's Notion of a Deduction and the Methodological Background of the First *Critique*', in Ekhart Förster ed., *Kant's Transcendental Deductions* (Stanford, CA: Stanford University Press, 1989), pp. 29–46, esp. pp. 43–44.

that is, the discursive faculty that consists in concepts, judgements and inference. We must understand reflection, Fries insists, as a purely *re-productive* faculty, which *re-creates* the original productive and creative activities of reason itself. By using piecemeal methods of abstraction, comparison, analysis and systematization, the transcendental philosopher makes clear and distinct the obscure activities of reason which lie below the threshold of consciousness. The ultimate goal of the transcendental philosopher is to create "a theory of reason" that shows how its activities form a systematic whole. A deduction works by showing how a synthetic a priori principle then fits into such a theory (§70; 284).

The theory behind Fries' method does not bode well for its success. His insistence that the transcendental philosopher engage in the labour of reflection to create "a theory of reason" shows that he has to do much more than simply observe the facts of consciousness. The Friesian transcendental philosopher does not simply provide a phenomenological description of what appears to his consciousness, because he has to reproduce what goes on deep within the subconscious. But then a difficult question arises: How does the transcendental philosopher know that his reflection, his theory of reason, is an accurate account of the original activities of reason? All the problems of the correspondence theory of knowledge—that we can never really know that a representation corresponds with its object—now seems to arise within the mind for the transcendental philosopher himself.[111] The reason that Fries gets into this difficulty is because he insists on making a distinction between reflection and its object; but this is a distinction he cannot easily avoid, because, as a good Kantian, he does not think that the intellect has the power to create its own object. The opposite assumption, that the intellect does have such a power, is that of intellectual intuition, a position that Fries utterly and unequivocably repudiates. Whatever its intrinsic difficulties, we can now see the attraction of Fichte's intellectual intuition: it obviates the recurrance of the correspondence problem.

There are other paradoxes involved in Fries' theory of reflection, which he neither avoids nor addresses.[112] He maintains that the original activities of reason consist in immediate truths—truths that are self-evident and need no further proof—and that these provide the warrant for the synthetic a priori principles of a deduction. Yet it is odd to write about immediate certainties that are obscure and hidden. If these certainties are indeed immediate, they should be self-evident and apparent as soon as we think of them. The transcendental philosopher should be able to recreate them easily; and if he has done so, there is no need to hypostasize some other certainty lying deep within the mind. Fries also writes about reflection as if it were almost a passive power of observation, a faculty that mirrors the object given to it. But this is no genuine Kantian assumption. As all students of Kant know, the understanding is

---

[111] As Cassirer points out in his chapter on Fries in *Das Erkenntnisproblem* III, 473–474.
[112] For an incisive and thorough critique of Fries' theory, see Walter Mechler, *Die Erkenntnislehre bei Fries* (Berlin: Reuther & Reichard, 1911) (*Kant-Studien Ergänzungsheft* Nr. 22), pp. 39–86.

an active, spontaneous power, which as such alters, mediates and transforms what it knows, which is therefore only an appearance. We are then led straight to the Kantian distinction between the self-in-itself and the self as appearance, which means that the Friesian transcendental philosopher, restricted to the forms of reflection, should know even the creative activity of reason itself only as an appearance. Here again Fichte's intellectual intuition, however extravagant, seems the more attractive position. Since intellectual intuition creates its object in the act of knowing it, it knows that object in itself, which is only the product of its activity. The object of intellectual intuition is the creative activity of reason, which is realized in the act of intellectual intuition itself.

11. Psychologism?

We are still left with the controversial question of Fries' "psychologism". Beginning in the 1870s,[113] Fries acquired the reputation among some neo-Kantians (viz. Cohen and Windelband) as a founder of psychologism because he had made psychology the central concern of transcendental philosophy. "Psychologism" had become a term of abuse, associated with a welter of simple logical confusions, namely, conflating *quid facti?* with *quid juris?*, logical validity with laws of thought, *ratio essendi* and *ratio cognoscendi*. As a founder of psychologism, Fries seemed guilty of making these simple mistakes. In 1904 Leonard Nelson came to Fries' defence, protesting that Fries was not only innocent of the charge of psychologism but that he had even intended to refute the doctrine.[114] The debate between Nelson and the neo-Kantians was continued by Ernst Cassirer in 1906,[115] who reaffirmed the charge of psychologism against Fries. After Cassirer's contributions, the debate came to an end (though no resolution). In this section we will revisit this old dispute and see if we can sort out its insights and illusions.

We have already seen from Fries' early psychological essays that he is indeed *not* guilty of these fallacies, and that he did expressly warn against them.[116] To this extent, it is necessary to agree with Nelson's defence of Fries, even though, remarkably, he does not consider the early psychological essays, which are the strongest evidence for his case.

The question of Fries' psychologism is not, however, simply whether he is guilty of some basic fallacies. The more substantial issue concerns the meaning of his doctrines, and whether they can be regarded, in some meaningful sense, as amounting to

---

[113] The reaction against Fries and psychologism began with the first edition of Hermann Cohen's *Kants Theorie der Erfahrung* (Berlin: Dümmler, 1871), pp. 124–27. Cohen's judgement on Fries will become definitive for the Marburg school. Windelband too regarded Fries, along with Beneke, as a proponent of "psychologism". See his 'Kritische oder genetische Methode?', in *Präludien*, Ninth edition (Tübingen: Mohr, 1924), II, 100.

[114] See Leonard Nelson, *Jakob Friedrich Fries und seine jüngsten Kritiker* (Göttingen: Dieterich, 1904).

[115] Ernst Cassirer, *Der kritische Idealismus.*   [116] See Section 3 in this chapter.

"psychologism". Much here depends, of course, on the precise meaning that we give this notorious term.[117]

One common definition of "psychologism" specifically concerns logic. It is defined as the doctrine that logic is based on "laws of thought", where these laws are determined by human nature and valid only for it.[118] In this sense Fries definitely should *not* be charged with psychologism. For he insists explicitly in his *Neue Kritik* that logic, understood as the formal study of the rules of thinking, concerns not only the laws of how our intellect conceives, judges and infers but also the structure or essence of things in general (§66; 263). Fries regards the rules of formal logic as not merely subjective laws about how we happen to think but as objective laws about being itself. A proof, understood as a purely formal structure, gives us "transcendental knowledge" (in the sense defined in section 10) because it is true of all possible things. Hence we can say of any three things A, B and C, that if A is B, and if B is C, then A is C. On these grounds Fries states that proof is an *objective* method to justify knowledge (§71; 294–295).

Fries' later *System der Logik* shows how far he is from reducing logic to psychology. Here he is careful to distinguish *demonstrative* from *anthropological* logic, where demonstrative logic concerns the formal laws of inference and anthropological logic inference as an activity of the human mind.[119] Fries notes that it would be absurd to prove the laws of demonstrative logic on the basis of empirical psychology.[120] In this sense too, then, it is necessary to clear Fries of the charge of psychologism.

There is another sense of "psychologism", however, in which it concerns not formal logic but mathematics and the basic principles of our knowledge of the world, that is, in more Kantian terms, synthetic a priori principles. In this sense "psychologism" is the doctrine that these principles and mathematics are based upon laws of human nature and that they are valid only for it. If human nature somehow changed, or if we were born with a completely different constitution, these principles and mathematics would no longer be valid for us. This doctrine is opposed to the view that these principles and mathematics have a more general validity, that they are like laws of logic and so valid for any rational being and the world as such.

There can be no question that in this sense Fries is committed to psychologism. He is very explicit in spelling out the subjective implications and limitations of his method of deduction. The highest justification for our knowledge is ultimately "only subjective", he declares, because it determines only the laws of our human nature, the laws by which we sense, conceive and understand the world. After expounding his method, he writes in an italicized passage: "*Even for the ideal of a perfect scientific*

---

[117]   On the plethora of meanings from 1866–1930, see Martin Kusch *Psychologism* (London: Routledge, 1995), pp. 95–121.

[118]   This is the standard sense. See Simon Blackburn, *The Oxford Dictionary of Philosophy* (Oxford: Oxford University Press, 1994), p. 309, 'psychologism'.

[119]   See Jakob Friedrich Fries, *System der Logik* (Heidelberg: Winter, 1837), pp. 1–3.

[120]   Fries, *System der Logik*, p. 5.

form of our knowledge, the highest possible justification is only a subjective one which relates to merely the inner laws of the activity of our reason. It is always only a question of what human reason knows and recognizes, and never immediately about how things are in themselves." (§71; I, 295) For Fries, the guiding theme of anthropology is Protagoras' old dictum that man is the measure of all things. Anthropomorphism and anthropocentrism are not its vices but its virtues.

What is decisive in making Fries a psychologicist in this sense is his committment to the Kantian theory of mathematics.[121] Fries never questioned the Kantian doctrine that mathematics concerns the forms of human sensibility, space and time, and that it is therefore valid only for them. Mathematics gives us no insight, then, into some Platonic realm of being or nature as such. It is a common mistake, Fries cautions in his *Neue Kritik*, to think that demonstration provides us with objective justification, as if we knew reality in itself simply by showing how principles are grounded in intuition (§71; 293–294). All that demonstration ever gives us is knowledge relative to our way of perceiving the world. Proof is therefore for Fries the *only* objective method to justify knowledge (§71; 294–295).

With the rise of Marburg neo-Kantianism in the 1880s, Friesian-style anthropology and psychology had fallen out of favour. Cohen explicitly criticized Fries' anthropology in the first and second edition of his *Kants Theorie der Erfahrung*.[122] The ground was thus set for a conflict between Cohen and the neo-Friesians. Sure enough, Nelson and Cohen tussled in the early 1900s when Nelson rebutted Cohen's criticisms of Fries and wrote his damning review of Cohen's *Logik der reinen Erkenntnis*.[123] Ernst Cassirer rushed to Cohen's defence in a sarcastic polemic, *Der kritische Idealismus und die Philosophie des "gesunden Menschenverstandes"*.[124] The more substantive and extensive critique of Fries, however, would come only in 1920 when Cassirer devoted a substantial chapter to Fries in his study of the post-Kantian systems, what eventually became Volume III of his magisterial *Das Erkenntnisproblem*.[125] This chapter was meant to drive a stake, once and for all, through the monstrous heart of neo-Friesianism. It is a penetrating critique, showing a broad and deep knowledge of Fries' writings. It is here that Cassirer explicitly charges Fries with psychologism. Though he recognized that Fries did not espouse the doctrine *expressis verbis*, he insisted that Fries had supplied all the premises for it insofar as he held that "the last ground for the validity of necessary truth lies in the existence of the mind and its factual constitution".[126] Cassirer complained that Fries' method of

---

[121] On Fries' relation to Kant's theory of mathematics, see Hermann, *Mathematische Naturphilosophie*, pp. 97–139.

[122] See the first edition, *Kants Theorie der Erfahrung* (Berlin: Dümmler, 1871), pp. 124–127; and in the second edition (Berlin: Dümmler, 1885), pp. 296–299, 373–379, 601–602.

[123] The review appeared originally in *Göttingische gelehrte Anzeigen* 1905, Nr. VIII, pp. 610–630. It is reprinted in Leonard Nelson, *Gesammelte Schriften in neun Bänden* (Hamburg: Meiner, 1970), II, 3–27.

[124] Ernst Cassirer, *Der kritische Idealismus*.

[125] Ernst Cassirer, *Das Erkenntnisproblem*, III, 447–483. First published in 1920 under the title *Die nachkantische Systeme* (Berlin: Cassirer, 1920). All parenthetical references are to the second edition.

[126] Cassirer, *Das Erkenntnisproblem* III, 477.

deduction dissolved the *quid juris?* into the *quid facti?*, and that it recognized no distinction between questions of truth and existence. Fries could justify a principle, Cassirer contended, only by showing that it is based on a fact of human nature: "In the end basic metaphysical cognitions are called 'true' only because they are actual in us."[127] It was a form of justification, Cassirer pointed out, that ultimately went back to Thomas Reid and the philosophy of common sense.[128] According to that philosophy, there can be no further justification of our highest principles other than the hard fact that we are forced to think that way by "the constitution of our mind".[129]

Cassirer's critique, though often insightful, is somewhat simplistic. It not only ignores those passages of Fries' *Neue Kritik* where he refuses to treat logic psychologistically, but it also fails to recognize the normative and pragmatic dimension of Fries' method of deduction, which we have explained above (Section 10). Insofar as it provides a functional explanation of a principle, which involves taking account of its use and purpose, Fries' deduction does serve as a normative justification. To an important extent, though, Cassirer is correct. Leaving aside formal logic and considering synthetic a priori principles alone, Fries, like Reid, does leave us with nothing more than an appeal to natural necessity or "the constitution of the human mind". In that regard the normative question ultimately does come down to a factual one. "We ought to think this way", Fries is saying, "because we *must* think this way, and that is the end of the matter." Cassirer thinks that this is to surrender to the sceptic, who doubts whether our necessary forms of mental functioning are true.[130] But, doubtless, Fries would respond to Cassirer: there cannot be any higher justification than showing the limits of our human nature; we cannot transcend these limits by *leaping* outside our faculty of knowledge to see if it conforms to being itself.

For his part, Cassirer is happy to accept Fries' point against transcendental realism. He too readily admits that we cannot claim transcendental truth for our faculty of knowledge.[131] The source of his resistance to Fries' anthropology resides elsewhere: not in any lingering transcendental realism but in Cassirer's adherence to a quasi-Platonic theory of truth, whose sources came from Cohen and Lotze in the 1870s.[132] According to this theory, whether or not a proposition is true is independent

---

[127] Cassirer, *Das Erkenntnisproblem* III, 476.

[128] Cassirer, *Der kritische Idealismus*, p. 14. It is impossible to determine what influence Reid had on the young Fries. There is no mention of Reid in Henke. Certainly, Reid had a major influence on German philosophy in the late 18th century. See Manfred Kuehn, *Scottish Common Sense in Germany, 1768–1800* (Kingston, ON: McGill-Queen's University Press, 1987). As Kuehn points out, p. 223 n. 43, Fries had a high opinion of Reid.

[129] Cassirer cites the second edition of *An Inquiry into the Human Mind on the Principles of Common Sense* (Edinburgh: A. Kincaid and J. Bell, 1765), pp. 89ff, 111ff, 346ff. I have not been able to obtain this edition and so I cannot confirm Cassirer's citations or correlate them with other more accessible editions.

[130] Cf. Cassirer, *Das Erkenntnisproblem* III, 476–477; Cassirer, *Der kritische Idealismus*, pp. 29–30.

[131] Cassirer, *Der kritische Idealismus*, pp. 27–29.

[132] The *locus classicus* for this distinction is in the third book of Lotze's 1874 *Logik*. See Hermann Lotze, *System der Philosophie: Erster Theil: Drei Bücher der Logik* (Leipzig: Hirzel, 1874), I, 465–497. Cohen develops an analogous distinction, apparently independently. See Cohen's 'Friedrich Albert Lange',

of human psychology and even whether human beings know it at all. It is just a basic fact, for example, that $2 + 2 = 4$ is valid whether I think of it at all, and indeed even if there were no human beings whatsoever. This does not mean, however, that $2 + 2 = 4$ subsists somewhere or has a special kind of existence or being. On the contrary, the theory states that we must distinguish firmly and clearly between *all* questions of existence or fact on the one hand, and questions of truth or validity on the other hand. The distinction is intended in a broad sense, so that it holds for *all forms or kinds* of existence or fact. In other words, $2 + 2 = 4$ is still true or valid even if there is no mysterious realm of numbers (hence the *quasi*-Platonism), or even if there are no special kinds of facts; indeed, it would still be true even if nothing existed at all. This theory of truth is therefore very different from transcendental realism, which does require the existence of an object, and indeed a thing-in-itself like the representation which corresponds to it. From the perspective of this theory, the problem with Fries' anthropology is that it makes mathematical truths depend on human nature. For Cohen and Cassirer, the great value of transcendental idealism is that it distinguishes sharply between the *quid juris?* and *quid facti?*, where that distinction is co-extensive with that between truth and existence, validity and fact. Fries' anthropological or psychological brand of transcendental idealism has to be rejected because it confuses these questions entirely.

As we have seen, Fries understood fully well the importance of the distinction between the *quid juris?* and *quid facti?*. In his *Neue Kritik* he is explicit about the need for separating these questions in formal logic (§66; 263). Where Fries differs from the Marburg school is in insisting that synthetic a priori principles and mathematics are valid only for our human nature. His argument for this position is all too Kantian: that synthetic a priori principles derive their content from experience, which depends on our human sensibility, our characteristic human way of perceiving the world according to space and time. Similarly, according to Kant, mathematical propositions have to be constructed in intuition, which again depends on our human sensibility. Thus the ultimate foundation for Fries' anthropocentrism, for his restriction of knowledge to our human nature and way of perceiving the word, is his strict adherence to Kant's Transcendental Aesthetic.

No one saw these limitations of the Kantian Transcendental Aesthetic more clearly than the mature Hermann Cohen, who, beginning in 1896, took issue with Kant's theory of sensibility for just these reasons.[133] Concerned to maintain the objective validity of mathematics against Friesian psychologism and anthropologism, Cohen developed a bold objective idealism in his *Logik der reinen Erkenntnis*, according to

---

Preussische Jahrbücher 37 (1876), 353–378; and his *Platos Ideenlehre und die Mathematik* (Marburg: Elwert, 1879).

[133] Most notably and clearly in Cohen's 1896 'Einleitung mit kritischem Nachtrag zur neunten Auflage des *Geschichtes des Materialismus*' (Leipzig: Baedeker, 1896).

which the object of knowledge is entirely the product of pure thinking alone. Cohen readily admitted that his objective idealism was a revision of Kant, and he straight-forwardly criticized Kant for clinging to his theory of sensibility, which would make mathematics a mere human construction.[134]

Whatever the value of Cohen's objective idealism, his critique of Kant's Transcendental Aesthetic shows that, in the end, Fries was the more faithful Kantian. For Kant, mathematical truth is valid only for our human sensibility, our character-istic human way of perceiving the world. It was this all too Kantian point that Fries, a loyal Kantian, was insistent on upholding, and that Cohen, a not so loyal Kantian, was intent on contesting.

12. Wrestling the Thing-in-Itself

One overdue topic in Fries' discussion of the foundations of transcendental philoso-phy was the thing-in-itself. In his earlier expositions of his philosophy he had left this topic largely unexplored, contenting himself with simply repeating the standard Kantian position. This was a serious omission, however, because the difficulties with the thing-in-itself were legendary, and indeed fateful for the reception of Kant's phi-losophy. It was not least because they could not solve these difficulties within Kantian parameters that Fichte and Schelling turned to more speculative forms of idealism. Jacobi had perfectly summarized the predicament of the thing-in-itself with his famous dictum: "that *without* that presupposition [of things-in-themselves] I cannot enter the Kantian system; but *with* it I cannot remain inside it."[135] That raises the ques-tion: How did Fries try to stay inside the Kantian system *with* that assumption?

Fries finally engaged in a systematic discussion of this topic in a series of para-graphs in the second volume of his *Neue Kritik der Vernunft* (§§122–131). Here Fries takes on two extreme positions: the transcendental realist, who maintains that the objects of our experience are things-in-themselves; and the sceptic, who holds that the objects of our experience are only illusions. He attempts to defend the middle path: that what we know in experience are neither things-in-themselves nor illusions; rather, they are appearances, which are how things-in-themselves appear to someone with our sensibility.

Against the transcendental realist Fries marshals two arguments. First, he notes that it is impossible for us to get outside our faculty of knowledge to compare it with thing-in-themselves (§127; 178–179). He pushes this point very far. Even in the case of self-consciousness, the mere self-awareness of my existence, I cannot get outside my consciousness of myself to compare that consciousness with my self-in-itself;

[134] Hermann Cohen, *System der Philosophie. Erster Teil: Logik der reinen Erkenntnis* (Berlin: Cassirer, 1902), p. 11. Cf. *Einleitung mit kritischem Nachtrag* in *Hermann Cohen Werke*, ed. Helmut Holzhey (Hildesheim: Olms, 2005), V, 65–66.

[135] Jacobi, 'Beylage' to *David Hume*, in *Werke* II, 304.

and even a divine intuitive intelligence cannot get outside its intuitions to know if they correspond with things-in-themselves, because it too is limited by the laws of its own cognitive organization (179). Second, sensibility transforms the given matter of sensation according to the a priori forms of inner and outer sense, so that we know the something only as it conforms to these forms but not as it exists in itself, apart from and prior to the application of these forms (§128; 185). Fries thinks that both these arguments count against the transcendental realist's thesis that the objects of our experience are things-in-themselves; but they are actually weaker than that: they show only that we cannot *know* whether the objects of experience are things-in-themselves. Remarkably, this is a point that Fries admits elsewhere.[136]

Whatever their merits, Fries' arguments against transcendental realism still leave open the sceptical possibility that the objects of experience are mere illusions. Granted that these objects are not things-in-themselves, what prevents them from being entirely illusory? Fries contends that, normally, we determine whether a belief is true by comparing it with other beliefs in our whole system of belief. We determine truth *inside* our system of belief, and we do not go outside the system as a whole to see whether it is true (§126; 175). Nevertheless, he admits that it makes sense to ask whether the system as a whole is true in the transcendental sense, that is, whether it corresponds with reality in itself (§126; 174–176). The sceptic's argument is that if the system as a whole does not have such transcendental truth, then all our knowledge is an illusion (*Schein*). The sceptic thus reveals himself to be a transcendental realist in disguise, who assumes that truth consists in the correspondence of a representation with things-in-themselves. He differs from the naive transcendental realist only in one respect: he thinks that this standard of knowledge cannot be satisfied.

Although Fries agrees with the sceptic that the transcendental realist's standard of knowledge cannot be fulfilled, he still thinks that it is a *non sequitur* to infer from this point that human experience is an illusion (§129; 189). He insists that we must distinguish sharply, as Kant failed to do, illusion (*Schein*), which is only a representation in the subject reflecting nothing in reality, from appearance (*Erscheinung*), which represents reality as it appears or relative to beings with our cognitive constitution. We can determine whether something is illusion by determining whether it conforms to our general system of belief.

Fries' point that the sceptical argument is a *non sequitur* is well taken, though it still does not establish that the objects of experience are appearances. For Fries wants them to be appearances not just in the weak sense that they are only representations conforming to the general laws of consciousness, but in the much stronger sense that they are also appearances of things-in-themselves, which are objects existing independently of our consciousness. To establish this stronger sense, he needs to provide some independent argument for the existence of things-in-themselves. He attempts

---

[136] Most notably in Fries, *Wissen, Glauben und Ahndung*, pp. 36, 44.

to supply just such an argument when he writes: "Where there is appearance there must be something that appears" (§129; 189). But that old question-begging clunker from Kant, which Fries is desperate enough to repeat, works only if we have a right to assume the existence of appearances in the first place, which is the very point in question. Fries does provide more of an argument when he points out that we human beings, as finite creatures, do not have the power to create the object of our cognition (§122; 163). We have a passive sensibility, which has to be excited into activity by some external cause. But this argument too is hardly compelling: perhaps we have within ourselves a hidden power to create the world that we know? Descartes was troubled by that possibility in his *Meditations*.[137] Fries, however, does not take this doubt seriously, and casts it aside on "metaphysical" grounds: that we finite human beings are not complete and independent substances but are dependent upon other things outside ourselves to know something. Our innate cognitive powers are only formal; and to have content, they must receive material from some external source. This is just the problem with intellectual intuition, Fries argues. Appeals to it fail to respect the "rights of finitude", because they assume that we have the power to create the object of knowledge (§129; 188). Finitude means, however, that we human beings do not have such a power, that the object of knowledge is only given to us, and that it depends on external sources. It has "rights" because, though it gives us no knowledge of things-in-themselves, it does give us knowledge of how they appear to us. All that we can know about things-in-themselves, Fries contends, is *that* they exist; we cannot know *how* they exist in any positive sense; all our knowledge of how they exist is negative, that is, that they do *not* have the properties our human sensibility makes them appear to have (§128; 185).

Besides his claim that the sceptic's case is a *non sequitur*, Fries makes another parenthetical argument against the sceptic, which turns out to be very revealing for his entire position (§128; 185–186).[138] While he previously seemed to concede the meaningfulness of the sceptic's doubts about our whole system of knowledge (§126; 174–176), he now seems to bring that point into question. The sceptic contends that because we cannot *prove* a priori in any particular case that we are awake and not dreaming, we cannot *disprove* a priori that our entire system of knowledge is illusory (186). While these points are true, they seem problematic, Fries replies, only because they confuse error with irrationality (*Unvernunft*). Error is when we fail to operate correctly according to our faculty of reason; irrationality is when we assume that the whole faculty of reason is in error. The business of philosophy is to secure reason from error; but it cannot go on to found reason itself because to do so would be question begging; it would be to apply the faculty of reason itself. To doubt the entire faculty of reason itself is what Fries calls "folly" (*Narrheit*). And he then reminds us: it is not the

---

[137] See Descartes, Meditation VI, *Oeuvres de Descartes* eds C. Adam and P. Tannery (Paris: Vrin, 1964–1976), VII, 77.

[138] The argument, some two pages and three paragraphs long, literally appears in parentheses.

task of philosophy to attempt to transform "an insane asylum (*Narrenhaus*) into an academy of sciences" (185). The sceptic's folly takes us to the very limits of philosophy, Fries says, and in doing so it teaches us an important lesson: that no philosophy can achieve complete certainty through a priori means if it is not based on an anthropological investigation (186). Unfortunately, Fries does not explain his meaning here, leaving it a tantalizing *obiter dicta*. What he seems to suggest is this: that the a priori arguments against the sceptic, which presuppose our faculties of reasoning, work only if we also add the anthropological point that these faculties are naturally necessary, crucial to the functioning and operation of our cognitive organization. In other words, the ultimate response to the sceptic is that we cannot do otherwise according to our human nature; and it is pointless trying to imagine us having completely different faculties that might give us the truth.

It is just by appreciating this point about the limits of our powers, Fries thinks, that permits us to provide the only possible rationale for belief in the existence of the thing-in-itself. Although we cannot provide a proof for the existence of the thing-in-itself, we can supply a deduction of that belief. Such a deduction shows that the belief in the existence of the thing-in-itself is a necessity of our nature as rational beings (§130; 190). Just as we deduce the categories by showing them to be a necessity of our cognitive constitution, so we do the same for the ideas of reason, of which the first and foremost is the idea of absolute existence. The idea of the thing-in-itself is for Fries essentially the idea of substance, which is the notion of independent existence or self-sufficient being, that is, something that does not depend on anything else in order to exist.

How, then, can there be a deduction of such an idea? Why must reason presuppose the idea of substance? Fries argues that our perfect cognitive functioning demands that we seek systematic unity and necessity in all our knowledge (§130; 192). Answering to that ideal of systematic unity is the assumption that every experience is one appearance of a single absolute substance. In other words, we assume that each and every experience is an appearance of the thing-in-itself.

Fries' deduction of the thing-in-itself makes the belief in its existence into a Kantian practical postulate, that is, a belief that is justified on practical rather than theoretical grounds.[139] He makes this strategy perfectly explicit when he states that the proposition "Appearance presupposes being-in-itself" is a principle of practical faith (§131; 196). We can *know* what is an object of sense intuition; but we must *believe* in the existence of something that cannot be such an object (cf. §101; 82–83). The great advantage of such a deduction, Fries believes, is that it recognizes the limits of theoretical knowledge. It involves a principle of our ignorance because it admits that we cannot prove the existence of the thing-in-itself, and that we are limited to only a *belief* in its existence. Still, this belief is justified insofar as we have shown that it is

---

[139] Fries was not justifying it on *moral* grounds, however, and so his justification is consistent with his critique of the Kantian doctrine of practical faith. See Chapter 1, Section 9.

subjectively necessary for the functioning of our reason. In thus justifying the belief in the thing-in-itself, Fries was only complying with his general teaching that the basic presuppositions of reason are not capable of proof but only a deduction.

It is just at this point that Fries connects faith in the existence of the thing-in-itself with his philosophy of religion. The connection becomes clear as soon as we see that for Fries the assumption of the existence of the thing-in-itself is one and the same as that of the existence of substance. The idea of substance, of absolute independent being, is for him, just as it was for Spinoza, Schleiermacher and all the Romantics, the same as that of the divine or eternal. Belief in the existence of the thing-in-itself is then the same as belief in the existence of God itself. Fries then goes a step further in connecting this belief with his philosophy of religion by saying that the existence of the thing-in-itself is an object of *Ahndung* or feeling.

Whatever one makes of the connection between thing-in-itself and eternal substance, the essential point to see now is that Fries places belief in the existence of the thing-in-itself in the practical realm. With that manoeuvre he was confident that he had pulled off the apparently impossible: he managed to maintain belief in the existence of the thing-in-itself without having to transcend the limits of knowledge. Justified as an article of practical faith, he could now squarely meet Jacobi's challenge: he did not have to step outside the Kantian system at all. Whatever its merits, it was an ingenious solution to an apparently intractable problem. It is just another example of the many interesting ideas contained in Fries' much too maligned and neglected transcendental philosophy.

2

Johann Friedrich Herbart, Neo-Kantian Metaphysician

1. Herbart as Kantian

Of all the early neo-Kantians, Herbart has seemed the least Kantian. He appears in histories of neo-Kantianism even less than Fries and Beneke.[1] And few historians of philosophy today regard Herbart as a Kantian at all. This is partly because Herbart is usually portrayed as a realist who is implacably opposed to all forms of idealism.[2] But it is also partly because he is most famous for his empirical psychology, the empiricist and naturalist premises of which are completely antithetical to Kant's transcendental psychology. For these reasons, the inclusion of Herbart in the history of neo-Kantianism might seem strange and implausible.

Yet Herbart's non-Kantian reputation is strikingly at odds with his own self-conception. Herbart began his philosophical career as a Fichtean. But the more his philosophy moved in an independent direction, the more he began to identify with Kant, so that by the end of his career he regarded himself as a Kantian. In the preface to his 1828 *Allgemeine Metaphysik* he attempts to locate his philosophy in the chaos of contemporary views, and then bluntly declares: *"Der Verfasser ist Kantianer."*[3] And in his inaugural speech as ordinary professor in Göttingen, delivered in 1833, he makes a candid personal confession before the public: *"Kantianum ipse me professus sum, atque etiam nunc profitior."*[4]

---

[1] Here again the exception is Gerhard Lehmann, who devotes a chapter to Herbart in his *Geschichte der nachkantischen Philosophie* (Berlin: Junker und Dünnhaupt, 1931), pp. 163–170.

[2] The standard reading of Herbart is that he is a realist in a sense opposed to all idealism. Otto Flügel articulates this view when he writes in the very beginning of his book on Herbart: "Whoever knows only very little about Herbart still knows that he was a realist while his age mostly thought idealistically." See his *Herbarts Lehren und Leben*, Zweite Auflage (Leipzig: Teubner, 1912), p. 1. For a similar reading, see Walter Asmus, *Herbart in seiner und in unserer Zeit* (Essen: Neue deutsche Schule Verlagsgesellschaft, 1972), pp. 11–15. We will examine this interpretation in Sections 6 and 9 of this chapter; also see note 7 this Section.

[3] *Allgemeine Metaphysik* (Königsberg: A.W. Unzer, 1828), p. xxvi. This work is reproduced in Volumes VII and VIII of the *Sämtliche Werke*, ed. Karl Kehrbach and Otto Flügel (Langensalza: Hermann Beyer & Söhne, 1887–1912). All references to Herbart's writings are to this edition, which is abbreviated as SW.

[4] *Oratio ad capessendam in academia georgia augusta professionem philosophiae ordinariam habita*, SW X, 53–64. Cited p. 63.

As sincere, blunt and open as these professions might be, they are hard to understand given Herbart's general attitude towards Kant's philosophy. He had been
highly critical of Kant throughout his career, disputing many of Kant's signature doctrines. When we add together these spurned doctrines, there seems little
left to profess of Kant's philosophy. Herbart had rejected these central Kantian
themes: that space and time are a priori intuitions; that acts of synthesis are the
origin of the unity of the manifold; that the mind is divisible into cognition, desire
and taste; that there are mental faculties; that there are a priori concepts and intuitions; that reason is the source of moral obligation. And so on. If someone denies
all these doctrines, someone might well ask, how can they be, in any straightforward sense, Kantian at all? Suspicions about Herbart's Kantian declarations only
grow once we note that he considered his greatest debts to be to Kant's moral philosophy. It is difficult to understand what these debts could be, however, given that
Herbart not only denies the basic premises of Kant's moral philosophy, but that he
also attempts to base ethics on aesthetics, an endeavour that Kant had famously
condemned.[5]

Given Herbart's highly critical attitude, and given his rejection of such central
Kantian doctrines, what are we to make of his Kantian professions? We do well to let
Herbart speak for himself. He provides an interesting explanation in the form of the
long historical disquisition making up the first volume of his *Allgemeine Metaphysik*.
In the preface to that work Herbart describes himself as a "*Kantianer vom Jahre 1828*",
meaning, in part, that he wants to keep Kantian doctrine only to the extent that it is
in accord with the latest developments in the sciences. This does not mean, however,
that Herbart intends to engage in a wholesale revision and modernization of Kant's
philosophy. If that were so, we would have all the more reason to be suspicious of his
Kantianism. When we place Herbart's remark in the context of his historical survey,
we see that a "Kantian of 1828" means someone who continues to uphold defining
Kantian doctrines *against* contemporary trends. This is to keep Kant abreast of the
modern age because these contemporary trends happen to be, in his view, not progressive but regressive. Herbart wants to maintain these doctrines against a resurgent rationalism, which would take philosophy back to the early 18th century, back to
the age of pre-critical dogmatic rationalism, which is contrary to the spirit of modern
science.

There are two signature Kantian doctrines in particular that Herbart is especially
eager to uphold, both of them distinctions blurred by past and present rationalism.
One is the Kantian distinction between essence and existence. Kant had argued in
the first *Kritik* that however determinate and exact our concept of a thing, we still
must go beyond and outside it to know that it refers to something that exists. This
distinction played a fundamental role in his critique of the rationalist tradition,

---

[5] Most notably in his critique of Schiller's *Anmut und Würde* in *Die Religion innerhalb der Grenzen der bloßen Vernunft, Schriften* VI, 23–24n.

Herbart notes, because it shows that reason, whose stock-in-trade is concepts, cannot demonstrate existence. Herbart then tells a long story about the history of pre-Kantian metaphysics, a story which stresses the revolutionary significance of Kant's critique of that tradition, and which emphasizes the fundamental role of the distinction between essence and existence in that critique. Herbart very much identifies his philosophy with the Kantian Revolution, whose legacy he wants to continue. He stresses that his metaphysics upholds the crucial distinction between essence and existence, which has been blurred by the neo-rationalist metaphysics of Schelling and Hegel as much as the old rationalist metaphysics of Leibniz and Wolff. Since Herbart regards the distinction between essence and existence as Kant's great contribution and revolutionary feat, and since he appropriates it as the distinguishing feature of his own metaphysics, he thinks he is fully justified in regarding himself as a Kantian. He sees himself as the heir and torchbearer of the critical Kantian tradition, which must now continue its work into the first decades of the 19th century.

The other Kantian doctrine Herbart is so keen to uphold is the distinction between the normative and natural, between "ought" and "is" (77; Erste Anm).[6] He saw this distinction as no less fundamental to Kant's philosophy, for it was a major ambition of Kant to separate ethics from metaphysics, so that the purity and integrity of ethics would not become mired in and compromised by the dangers and disputes of metaphysics. The failure to observe this distinction, Herbart was convinced, was one of the main problems of speculative idealism. Fichte had blurred it when he made the moral law into the basic condition of the possibility of experience (167; §96); and Schelling and Hegel had confused it when they made teleology into a fundamental speculative principle of nature (80; Erste Anm). Though the normative/natural distinction was vital to Kant, Herbart believed that Kant himself was responsible for blurring it (68, 77; Erste Anm). The concept of an organism in the *Kritik der Urteilskraft* seemed to provide a connecting bridge between the normative and natural, the practical and theoretical. Of course, Kant had placed regulative constraints on this concept, so that we should treat nature only *as if* it were an organism, only *as if* it were purposive. But these regulative constraints were ignored by Kant's successors, who in their reckless enthusiasm made the concept of an organism into a constitutive metaphysical principle. A true Kantian of 1828 is for Herbart someone who keeps his distance from the *Kritik der Urteilskraft,* and who embraces the more critical doctrines of the *Kritik der reinen Vernunft* (73; Erste Anm). He is above all someone who refuses to revive teleology, which amounts to a relapse into the old scholastic view of nature.

Whatever the precise role of the normative/natural distinction in Kant, Herbart thought it was a crucial part of Kant's legacy, and he made it central to

---

[6] All references in parentheses are to SW VII, first the page number, then the paragraph number (designated by the "§" sign). "Anm" indicates "Anmerkung" or remark.

his own philosophy. All the more reason, then, for regarding himself as a Kantian. Herbart's emphasis on the Kantian distinction is indeed one of the most salient and pervasive features of his thought. He insisted on following the distinction so completely and consistently that he firmly separated metaphysics from ethics, banished teleology from his concept of nature, and denied the sacred post-Kantian tenet of the unity of theoretical and practical reason. This set Herbart apart not only from his idealist contemporaries, but also from his idealist successors, most notably Trendelenburg and Lotze, who were intent on restoring teleology. For just this reason Herbart became a formidable challenge for both those philosophers in the 1830s and 1840s.

We have now heard Herbart's case, at least as he puts it forward in his *Allgemeine Metaphysik*. It should be clear that his Kantianism is a very serious declaration of allegiance to some very basic Kantian doctrines, and that it is not based on a tendentious revisionist reading of Kant, but upon a well-grounded view of Kant's place in the history of philosophy. But it is worth noting that there was much more to Herbart's Kantianism than his adherence to these two Kantian distinctions. His Kantianism went much deeper: it involved nothing less than his conception of philosophy itself. Herbart believed in the great importance of metaphysics to philosophy because it alone could tackle basic questions and investigate central concepts; yet he saw metaphysics as essentially a transcendental enterprise, "a science of the conceivability of experience", "*ars experientiam recti intelligendi*". Metaphysics should have nothing to do with knowledge of the absolute, as Schelling and Hegel understood it, because it should limit itself to the modest task of investigating the basic concepts and presuppositions of our experience. No less than Fries, therefore, Herbart insisted on the importance of the Kantian limitation of knowledge to experience. Metaphysics, as he understood it, should not transcend experience but investigate the conditions of its possibility.

No less decisive for Herbart's Kantianism was his adherence to transcendental idealism.[7] Admittedly, it was a somewhat revised transcendental idealism, permitting a greater degree of realism than Kant's empirical realism. Herbart disputed the Kantian theory of space and time as a priori intuitions, and he insisted that particular spatial forms (viz. sizes and shapes) are simply given to us in experience. Nevertheless, like a good Kantian, he still maintained that the immediate objects of

---

[7] In attributing transcendental idealism to Herbart I am going against the standard interpretation of his philosophy, which regards it as a realism opposed to all forms of idealism. See note 2 in this chapter. According to Otto Flügel, *Herbarts Lehren und Leben*, p. 1, Herbart rejected idealism, where "idealism" means the "denial or doubt of the reality of the external world". Though Flügel is correct that Herbart disputes idealism in this sense, it is noteworthy that Kant himself does the same. Denial and doubt about the external world refer (respectively) to what Kant called dogmatic and sceptical idealism, both doctrines that he explicitly rejected in the first *Kritik*. On Kant's criticisms of these doctrines, see my *German Idealism* (Cambridge, MA: Harvard, 2002), pp. 75–131.

knowledge are representations, and that our consciousness of the world is limited to appearances. Though on different grounds than Kant, he upheld the distinction between things-in-themselves and appearances, which is so vital to transcendental idealism. Decades before Lange, Cohen or Windelband, Herbart advocated transcendental idealism as a bulwark against materialism, whose doctrines he saw as a threat to moral and religious values.

It was no accident for Herbart's Kantian affiliations that, from 1809 to 1833, he was professor of philosophy in Königsberg. For this meant that Herbart had ascended to Kant's throne. He would lecture in the very same buildings as Kant, using the very same lectern, and he would pass on his daily walks the very houses where Kant once lived and wrote. From this distant Prussian province Herbart, much like his great predecessor, viewed the intellectual life on the mainland with a mixture of estrangement and envy. He felt alienated from the current trends of his day, which were dominated by Schelling, Hegel and the Romantics. Like all aging philosophers, Herbart needed to define his place in history, to see where he belonged. Who better to identify with than the old sage of Königsberg himself? He lived in his city, taught in his classrooms, and occupied his chair. And so the older he became, the more Herbart saw himself as Kant's legitimate heir, as the very incarnation of the Kantian spirit. He believed that his mission was to be a torchbearer for Kant, to preserve what was still of value for his contemporaries in the Kantian legacy. Such was the context behind his famous declaration that he was a *"Kantianer von 1828"*.

Our task now is a very limited one: to examine how Herbart became this Kantian.[8] Alas, this is no easy task. For, unlike Fries, Herbart's intellectual development was not stable and continuous but tumultuous and fragmented. Before he became that Kantian, he first had to settle his accounts with Fichte, and then he had to contend with the Romantic ideas of his circle of friends. By all accounts, the young Herbart was a prodigy, and everyone during his student years, including Fichte himself, saw him as the new up-and-coming star. But to realize his gifts, to get them down on paper, Herbart had to wrestle with internal monsters; he had to go through personal struggles which threatened not only his health but also his sanity. Herbart had arrived by 1809, by the time of his appointment as ordinary professor in Königsberg. But before that triumph there lay a troubled and twisted tale, which we must now proceed to tell.[9]

---

[8] My aim here is not to provide a general introduction to Herbart's philosophy, though one in English is sorely needed. I will not attempt to explain Herbart's general metaphysics as it emerges from his *Allgemeine Metaphysik*, nor to explain his psychology as expounded in his 1824 *Psychologie als Wissenschaft*. Indisputably, these are Herbart's chief works. However, any adequate study of them would take me far beyond my task here, the study of the origins of neo-Kantianism.

[9] The chief study of Herbart's intellectual development is that by Walter Asmus, *Johann Friedrich Herbart. Eine pädagogische Biographie* (Heidelberg: Quelle & Meyer, 1968–70), 2 volumes. As the subtitle indicates, Asmus focuses upon the pedagogical aspects of Herbart's thought and does not treat the development of his philosophy, which is our main concern here.

2. A Troubled Fichtean

Johann Friedrich Herbart was born May 4, 1776, in Oldenburg, a prosperous town in Westphalia, near the Danish border. His social roots were upper-middle class. His grandfather, Johann Michael Herbart, worked his way up from poverty to become the headmaster of the Gymnasium in Oldenburg. His father, Thomas Gerhard Herbart, was a privy councillor and secretary to the municipal government. Because of his delicate constitution, Johann Friedrich could not withstand the rigours of the public schools, so that he had to be tutored at home. His tutor was Hermann Wilhelm Ültzen (1759–1808), a notable poet and theologian in his own right.[10] It was Ültzen who first introduced Herbart to philosophy, and for whom he wrote his first philosophical essays. Ültzen was Herbart's tutor from 1783 to 1788, after which he attended the Oldenburg Gymnasium. Philosophy was a regular part of Herbart's early education. As some early fragments attest,[11] he could write sophisticated philosophical essays even by his early teens. Among the first philosophers Herbart studied was, of course, Kant, whom, it seems, the boy took in with his mother's milk. A *curriculum vitae* he wrote in 1801 tells us how "almost as a boy" (*paene puer*) he had "pre-tasted Wolff and Kant" (*Wolfiana et Kantiana ratione praegustata*).[12] His valedictorian speech to his classmates, which he gave in 1793, shows a mastery of Kant's moral philosophy.[13] We know something about Herbart's early reaction to Kant, for in 1822, he recalled the impression reading Kant's *Grundlegung zur Metaphysik der Sitten* had upon him some thirty years earlier.[14] It was Kant, he said, who freed him from the errors of eudamonism, who taught him the value of human autonomy, and who showed him how morality is an end in itself.

After graduating from the Oldenburg *Gymnasium* in 1793, Herbart went to study law at the University of Jena. Like Fries, he was fortunate to be in Jena during its *Wunderjahre*. But, as fate would have it, he never met Fries there. Herbart was a student at Jena from October 1794 to March 1797, having left the town just before Fries' arrival that May. His reaction to Fichte was the very opposite of Fries'. Herbart did not rush home to write refutations of Fichte's lectures but studied his writings with religious devotion.[15] Herbart knew Fichte personally, became one of his inner circle, and was a frequent guest at the Fichte household.[16] He soon acquired a reputation as

---

[10] On Ültzen, see Asmus, *Herbart*, I, 307–308.

[11] See the 1790 fragment 'Etwas über die Lehre von der menschlichen Freiheit', SW I, 359; and the 1789 fragment 'Beweis für die Existenz eines ewigen Gottes', SW XIX, 58–59.

[12] SW I, 366.

[13] 'Etwas über die allgemeinsten Ursachen, welche in den Staaten den Wachstum und den Verfall der Moralität bewirken', SW I, 351–361. This essay was Herbart's first publication. It was published by his family friend G.A. von Halem in *Blätter vermischten Inhalts* (Oldenburg: J.F. Thiele, 1787), VI, 60–79.

[14] In a review of F.E. Beneke's *Grundlegung zur Physik der Sitten* in the *Jenaer Literatur-Zeitung* 1822, Nr. 211–213. SW XII, 172.

[15] See Herbart to Gerhard Anton von Halem, August 28, 1796: '*Die Wissenschaftslehre machte, um für ihr unendliches Ich Platz zu gewinnen, eine unendliche Leere in Meinem Kopfe.*' SW XVI, 9.

[16] See Herbart an Johann Smidt, January 23, 1796, SW XVI, 12; and Lantsch an Smidt, SW XVI, 22.

Fichte's best student. We know from the testimony of Georg Rist, a close friend of Herbart, that, by the autumn of 1795, Herbart was a convinced Fichtean, and so much so that he would try to convert friends to the new gospel. Rist describes how, one fine afternoon that autumn, he had a long conversation with Herbart, who persuaded him that his own pantheistic fatalism was untenable because the entire natural world was only "a dream in his own soul".[17] Since Rist found this conclusion disturbing, Herbart tried to reassure him by providing daily tutorials on Fichte's *Wissenschaftslehre*.

Shortly after his arrival in Jena, Herbart became a member of the *Gesellschaft der freien Männer*,[18] the fraternity of Fichte students who banded together to discuss philosophy and literature. It was the custom of this society to hold fortnightly meetings to discuss members' philosophical essays.[19] Herbart's comments on one of Rist's papers in the autumn of 1796 reveal his Fichtean ruminations.[20] Kant's great question "How are synthetic a priori judgments possible?" expresses, Herbart writes, "the need of reason for synthesis". All our attempts to acquire knowledge, and all our goals for action, involve the striving for synthesis. "What is the purest concept of synthesis?", Herbart asks. His answer is pure Fichte: the ego (6). The ego is an act of self-knowledge, which consists in pure synthesis because it involves a moment of both identity and difference: identity, insofar as the subject and object of self-knowledge are one and the same; and difference, insofar as there is a distinction between the self as knowing subject and the self as knowing object. The question then arises: How this synthesis is possible? Or, more specifically, how is self-knowledge possible? There is an infinite regress in self-knowledge, Herbart argues, because the self-knowing subject cannot know itself as subject but only as object; every attempt to know itself as subject makes it into an object, so that the subject remains forever out of view. It is the task of science, Herbart says, to resolve this problem and to explain the possibility of self-knowledge (7–8). Much of Herbart's early reflections on the *Wissenschaftslehre* will be preoccupied with this issue.

Though he much admired Fichte, Herbart's devotion to him was never unconditional or uncritical. Even before the autumn of 1796 doubts emerge. On July 1 he wrote his friend Johann Smidt that he would have to write his own *Wissenschaftslehre* because not a single page of Fichte's book was "a pure gain for truth."[21] Then, on July 30, he told Smidt that his philosophy was now moving in an independent direction,

[17] See Johann Georg Rist, *Lebenserinnerungen*, ed. G. Poel (Gotha: Perthes, 1880), I, 63. Also cited in SW XVI, 7.
[18] On the *Gesellschaft der freien Männer,* see Asmus, *Herbart*, I, 75–87; and Willy Flitner, *August Ludwig Hülsen und der Bund der freien Männer* (Jena: Diedrich, 1913), pp. 1–18.
[19] For a fascinating glimpse into these meetings, see Erich Fuchs, 'Aus dem Tagebuch von Johann Smidt (1794/95)', *Fichte-Studien*, VII (1995), 173–192.
[20] See Herbart's 'Einige Bemerkungen über den Begriff des Ideals, in Rücksicht auf Rist's Aufsatz über moralische und aesthetische Ideale', SW I, 5–8; the Rist essay, 'Über moralische und aesthetische Ideale', appears in SW I, 362–365.
[21] See Herbart to Johann Smidt, July 1, 1796, SW XVI, 28. Herbart was referring to Fichte's *Grundlage des gesamten Wissenschaftslehre* (Leipzig: Gabler, 1794).

and that he had misgivings about Fichte's philosophy of freedom.[22] As the months passed, so his qualms grew. In September 1796 he informed Smidt that he was now formulating his own theory of space because Fichte's deduction of it was too abstract.[23] And in December he revealed that his departures from Fichte's exposition of the *Wissenschaftslehre* were significant because Fichte's version was so vague and unmethodological.[24] Although he felt that Fichte had many good ideas in his *Naturrecht*, he was also convinced that his deductions of these ideas are false.

Unfortunately, Herbart does not go into detail in these letters, so we do not know much about the precise reasons for his growing doubts. For his Jena years there are only two surviving manuscripts about Fichte,[25] and only one of them sheds some light on his critical reaction to his master's teaching. This manuscript, dating from 1794, consists of some questions about Fichte's *Grundlage der gesamten Wissenschaftslehre.*[26] The questions are of the greatest importance, however, because they concern the viability of Fichte's foundationalist programme. It was Fichte's great ambition to base transcendental philosophy on a single first principle, namely, the principle that "the ego posits absolutely its own being."[27] Herbart asks the difficult and important question: How can Fichte's self-positing ego posit the non-ego if that non-ego is something opposed to itself? If it is the nature of the ego to be purely *self*-positing, as Fichte so often insists, how does it negate itself and limit itself by something that it is not? In short: How from something purely self-positing and self-affirming do we get something self-opposing and self-negating? The *Wissenschaftslehre* thus begins with an irresolvable paradox. At the very least it seems as if Fichte's first principle cannot explain the opposition between subject and object, the most basic structural feature of ordinary experience.

We know about Herbart's early critical reaction to speculative idealism more from his response to some of Schelling's first writings. Starting in 1796 Herbart began to read and comment critically on Schelling's early works, specifically his *Über die Möglichkeit einer Form der Philosophie überhaupt* (1794) and *Vom Ich als Prinzip der Philosophie* (1795). Why the focus on Schelling rather than Fichte? Herbart told Smidt that he discussed Schelling's philosophy because it is the most consistent form of Fichte's idealism.[28] Perhaps too Herbart did not want to criticize his teacher directly? And perhaps he saw Schelling as a rival within Fichte's inner circle? In any case, he took Schelling very seriously and examined his work with great care and precision. There are three essays on Schelling, none of which were published, all of which are

[22] See Herbart to Smidt, July 30, 1796, SW XVI, 31.
[23] See Herbart to Smidt, September 1796, SW XVI, 37.
[24] See Herbart to Smidt, December 1796, SW XVI, 42.
[25] One manuscript, probably from 1794, attempts to answer Fichte's question whether the concept of straightness is already involved in that of a line. See 'Antwort auf des Herrn Professors Fichte Frage an die Mathematiker, die Natur der geraden und krummen Linie betreffend', SW XIX, 65–68.
[26] 'Bemerkungen zu Fichte's Grundlage der gesamten Wissenschaftslehre', SW I, 3–4.
[27] Johann Gottlieb Fichte, *Grundlage der gesamten Wissenschaftslehre* (Leipzig: Gabler, 1794), p. 13.
[28] Herbart to Smidt, December 1796, SW XVI, 9–11.

dense, crude and fragmentary. Still, they deserve scrutiny because they are revealing documents about Herbart's early attitude towards speculative idealism, and because they laid the ground for his later reaction against it.

The first essay is a brief comparison of Schelling with Spinoza.[29] It is very complimentary to Schelling, whose work is regarded as the idealist antithesis to Spinoza's realism and naturalism. Yet Herbart cannot resist raising two critical questions about Schelling's system. The first is the same he had once posed against Fichte: How does the absolute ego oppose itself to a non-ego? This struggle seems to be an imaginary one with a "self-created enemy". The second poses a new problem: How can Schelling have an intellectual intuition of the absolute ego when he admits that it is not his own personal empirical ego? How does he raise himself above his empirical and personal limitations to grasp an ego that is neither empirical nor personal? Both questions went to the heart of the foundationalist programme. The first asks whether the idealist's deduction is coherent, and whether it has any real explanatory value at all. The second asks for the epistemic warrant for such a first principle. No less than Fries, Herbart was sceptical of the claims made on behalf of intellectual intuition, which he likens to a mystical experience.

The second essay is a critical commentary on Schelling's *Über die Möglichkeit einer Form der Philosophie überhaupt*.[30] Schelling's tract was a manifesto for Fichte's foundationalist programme, an argument for the necessity of founding philosophy on the basis of a single self-evident first principle.[31] There must be one first principle, Schelling argued, because if there were two such principles, there would have to be some higher synthesis of them, which would then be the first principle. But Herbart could see no a priori reason for assuming that there is a higher principle, for what if the principles have very distinct content? (13). Schelling had placed a very high demand upon his first principle, which should provide not only the form but also the content of his system. Yet such a demand, Herbart argues, simply cannot be fulfilled. If the first principle cannot derive the existence of the non-ego, it has even less power to deduce the variety of the content of sensation (14). The main problem with Schelling's programme, Herbart explains, is that he confuses "the concept of the absolute" with "the infinite" (14). Though his language is obscure, Herbart's main point seems compelling. While the concept of the absolute is the idea of the whole, the infinite consists in its many distinct parts. Just having the *concept* of the whole, Herbart is saying, does not by itself give us all its parts. This concept abstracts from the individual characters of the many parts, and for just this reason cannot deduce them.

[29] Herbart, 'Spinoza und Schelling: eine Skizze', SW I, 9–11.
[30] Herbart, 'Versuch einer Beurtheilung von Schelling's Schrift: Ueber die Möglichkeit einer Form der Philosophie überhaupt', SW I, 12–16.
[31] F.W.J. Schelling, *Über die Möglichkeit einer Form der Philosophie überhaupt* (Tübingen: Heerbrandt, 1795). In Schelling, *Sämtliche Werke*, ed. K.F.A. Schelling (Stuttgart: Cotta, 1856–1861), I, 85–112.

Herbart's final essay is a detailed examination of Schelling's *Vom Ich als Prinzip der Philosophie*.[32] Its central critical theme is Schelling's problematic inference from the first grounds of human knowledge to the first grounds of being itself. Schelling finds the first ground of human knowledge, its unconditional first principle, in the ego, and more specifically in the principle "I am". This principle is unconditional in the sense that it is self-evident and does not presuppose any higher principle. Thus "I am" is true whenever I affirm it; and even if I were to deny it I would still affirm it, because I have to be to deny it. Granting this point, however, gives us no reason to infer that the "I" is the first principle of being itself. Just because the proposition "I am" is unconditioned in an *epistemic* sense, does not mean that the "I" to which it refers, the ego itself, is unconditioned in an *ontological* sense, that is, that it is *causi sui* and depends on nothing else to exist. Schelling makes a leap from the *ratio cognoscendi* to the *ratio essendi*, from the grounds of our knowing something to the grounds of its being, confusing the unconditionality of thinking about an object with the unconditionality of the object itself (20). Although there is perhaps a deeper philosophical reason for assuming that thinking and being are ultimately the same, Schelling does not provide such a reason and seems simply to confuse them (18). For Herbart, it seems more plausible to assume that there is a basic distinction between the ego and reality:

Absolute being is pure rest; it is the silence over the surface of the sea completely at rest; no one should dare to disturb this surface with the smallest circles. The ego is exactly the opposite: a vortex striving outward and inward. Rest would be the death of the ego, activity is its only being. (23)

Herbart finds another glaring fault with Schelling's work: it is dogmatic, transcending the limits of possible experience. While Schelling abjures traditional metaphysics because it transcends these limits, he is guilty of the same sin. For his absolute ego, as the condition of all empirical consciousness, does not fall within empirical consciousness itself (26). The more we reflect on the status of Schelling's absolute ego, the more it becomes clear that it is beyond all finite experience, and that it is nothing less than Spinoza's single infinite substance, the first principle of all dogmatism (27).

Though Herbart never refers to Kant in these early essays, he might as well have done so, because there are Kantian leitmotifs throughout. All the problems that Kant found with dogmatic metaphysics in the 1760s Herbart now discovers in speculative idealism in the 1790s. Fichte and Schelling, despite their pretensions to criticism, lapse into the same old fallacies as Leibniz and Wolff. Again and again in these early essays, Herbart applies the lessons of Kant's "Transcendental Dialectic": that we must stay within the limits of possible experience; that we should not hypostasize thinking about being; that we must not search for a material criterion of truth; that a priori

---

[32] Herbart, 'Ueber Schelling's Schrift: Vom Ich, oder dem Unbedingten im menschlichen Wissen', SW I, 17–33.

principles are entirely formal; that we human beings do not possess an intellectual intuition.

Already in Jena, almost simultaneously with Fries, Herbart had discovered some of the same problems with speculative idealism and its foundationalist programme. However, his reaction to these problems was very different from Fries. While Fries regarded these problems as fatal, as reason for rejecting Fichte's philosophy and programme, Herbart believed that they were reason for revising that philosophy and placing it on a better foundation. Just what that new foundation and exposition should be Herbart still did not know; it would be the object of intensive search in the years to come. While Fries was hostile to Fichte from the start, Herbart had to contend with a man who had been his teacher and benefactor. Gratitude alone would make his reckoning with Fichte more difficult. It was only after a much longer inner struggle that Herbart would finally be able to liberate himself from Fichte's influence. We will now consider the crucial episodes in that struggle.

3. Swiss Years

The young men who formed *Die Gesellschaft der freien Männer* saw themselves as leaders in the new order of things, as foreseen by Fichte. It was their goal to move mankind forward towards a new state and society founded on the ideals of liberty and equality. The task of the Fichtean intellectual was to explain these ideals to the people and to show them how they should be realized.[33] The path forward did not lie with revolution, however, but through gradual reform, especially through the education of the people. The people would be able to understand and appreciate the ideals of liberty and equality, and they would be willing and able to act on them, only if they were properly prepared through education. So, before the new social and political order, there had to be the new man, which could be created only through education. With such reasoning in mind, many of the "free men" resolved to be *Hauslehrer*, which was not only the most practical means to realize their ideals but also the best way for them to earn a living.

The young Fichteans decided that the best place to realize their ideals was in Switzerland, the land of Jean Jacques Rousseau and Johann Pestalozzi, the greatest educational theorists of the 18th century. They were probably encouraged to go there by Fichte, who had lived in Switzerland in the early 1790s, and who had met Pestalozzi, whose educational experiments profoundly impressed him.[34] Two of the free men, Johann Rudolf Steck and Johann Rudolf Fischer, were already from Switzerland and

[33] See the fourth lecture of Fichte's 1794 *Einige Vorlesungen über die Bestimmung des Gelehrten*, in *Werke* VI, 323–334.
[34] On Fichte's encounters with Pestalozzi, see Xavier Léon, *Fichte et son temps* (Paris: Armand Colin, 1954), I, 211–214. Fichte met Pestalozzi in July 1793 through his wife Johanne Rahn, who was a friend of Pestalozzi's wife.

so could help organize affairs there. In 1796 two more Fichteans, August Ludwig Hülsen and Johann Erich von Berger, went to Switzerland to scout and assess the situation there. They began to encourage others to come, so that by the summer of 1797 twelve members of the society had emigrated to Helvetia. Not the least among them was Herbart himself, who travelled in a "caravan" with five other Fichteans to Berne in March 1796.

The night before the caravan embarked, they were to be fêted by Fichte and his wife.[35] The excited travellers were expecting to be sent off with a bash, a hearty celebration; but they were terribly disappointed when Fichte greeted them with reserve and served them "sour punch". Surely, this was no way to say goodbye to his dearest students! But a closer knowledge of the circumstances allows us to excuse Fichte's glumness: having already enjoyed an earlier bash, his guests arrived at midnight and left at four in the morning! In the final moment he did muster the energy to rise to the occasion: he become emotional, sorry to see the departure of his devoted students.

While still in Jena, Herbart had entered a contract with an aristocratic family in Berne to serve as a tutor to their three children. The head of the family, C.F. von Steiger, was the governor of the province of Interlaken. As fate would have it, Herbart's predecessor in this role was no less than Hegel, who had been tutor to the von Steiger family from 1793 to 1796.[36] While Hegel's time with the von Steiger family had been fraught with tension and mistrust, Herbart had a more rewarding experience. On the whole, he felt at home there, enjoying the confidence of von Steiger and the affection of his children.[37] Wisely, Herbart had negotiated that the position would leave him sufficient leisure to pursue his own studies. One of the reasons he chose to be a house tutor is that he believed it offered him more independence than other careers. Such independence, he believed, would give him the time necessary to prepare for an academic career.

The most important event in Herbart's intellectual development in his Swiss years (1796–1800) was his encounter with Pestalozzi, who became the most powerful influence on his philosophy of education. The first meeting was probably arranged through Fichte, who would have recommended Herbart to Pestalozzi. Apparently, Pestalozzi was as impressed with Herbart as he was with Pestalozzi. A series of mutual visits took place. Pestalozzi would come to Berne to see Herbart, and Herbart would go to Burgdorf to see Pestalozzi. It is not difficult to understand the attraction Pestalozzi's ideas would have for a young Fichtean philosopher. Pestalozzi's method of education

[35] See Steck an seine Mutter, March 28, 1797, SW I, 54–55.
[36] On Hegel's experience with the von Steiger family, see Terry Pinkard, *Hegel: A Biography* (Cambridge: Cambridge University Press, 2000), pp. 45–58.
[37] In a letter to an unknown addressee, written in Berne in September 4, 1799, Herbart lists among his reasons for leaving Berne that von Steiger has not given all that he has promised, and that he has asked more than the contract stipulates. See SW XIX, 116. On the whole, however, his experience seems to have been very positive, since he did not lose his respect for von Steiger and his affection for the children, to whom he wrote for many years thereafter.

stressed the natural development and independence of the child, which seemed the best means of creating the new Fichtean man, whose ideal was complete autonomy. Pestalozzi's method would attempt to awaken the senses and feelings of the child, letting it discover things for itself through its own experience and reflection rather than relying on abstract lessons prepared for it. It discouraged the rote learning, emphasis on languages and severe discipline of traditional education, which seemed to place so many constraints on the child's natural development and autonomy. Thanks to the inspiration of Pestalozzi, Herbart would devote much of his career to the philosophy of education and he would eventually engage in several educational experiments of his own. He became the chief spokesman for Pestalozzis' ideas in Germany. It was in this role that Herbart first became known in his homeland.

Although educational theory and practice was a major concern of Herbart in his Swiss years, he continued to think about philosophy. He wrote his family friend Gerhard Anton von Halem in January 1798 that, despite the distractions of nature and work, his need for doing philosophy remained as pressing as ever.[38] There are, however, only two short philosophical fragments from the Berne period, 'Über philosophisches Wissen und philosophisches Studium' and 'Erster problematischer Entwurf der Wissenslehre', which were both written in 1798.[39] It is often said that Herbart conceived his later system of philosophy during his Swiss years.[40] But there is little in these fragments that indicates the direction of his future philosophy. The first, which was probably written for *Die Gesellschaft der freien Männer*, provides some general advice for pursuing philosophy. Herbart recommends thinking for oneself, avoiding eclecticism and reliance on authority; he also encourages thinking experimentally and rigorously, following an idea to its end wherever it might lead, and not letting a train of thought be interrupted by pet ideas. The second fragment contains Fichtean reflections on the theme of self-consciousness. It continues Herbart's earlier reflections on synthetic unity, the problem of how self-consciousness is possible if the subject and object must be the same and different. Herbart now ponders the conditions of the unity of apperception, that is, how there can be a single self-consciousness throughout a manifold of distinct perceptions. Nowhere in this fragment, however, do we find Herbart taking issue with Fichte. Indeed, Herbart's argument is very similar to

---

[38] See Herbart an v. Halem, January 28, 1798, SW XVI, 77.   [39] See SW I, 84–95, 96–110.

[40] See, for example, Georg Weiß, *Herbart und seine Schule* (Munich: Reinhardt, 1928), p. 14. See also Howard Dunkel's article on Herbart in the *Encyclopedia of Philosophy* (New York: MacMillan 1963), III, 481, which states that in his Swiss years Herbart had "worked out to a large extent the views which he was to refine and elaborate for the rest of his life". Asmus' position on this important point is not coherent. Without citing sufficient evidence, he maintains that Herbart had already achieved an independent standpoint from Fichte, in both principle and method, at the end of the Jena years. See *Herbart* I, 107. But he later states that Herbart had developed only "a few points" of his own philosophy at Enggistein (I, 132). Unfortunately, Asmus does not specify what these points are; nor does he discuss the Enggistein fragment in any detail. He cites a passage (I, 132) to show Herbart's independence from Fichte's *Wissenschaftslehre*, which is really only a citation from Reinhold. See SW I, 95. In the very text that Asmus cites, Herbart declares his *dependence* on Fichte's method. See SW I, 94.

that of Fichte in the third part of his *Grundlage der gesamten Wissenschaftslehre*. Like Fichte, Herbart finds the solution to the problem of synthetic unity in the concept of an infinite striving. Despite his many doubts about Fichte, this fragment shows that Herbart was still following a Fichtean agenda, that he was still thinking about Fichtean problems, and that he was still trying to solve them according to a Fichtean method. His aim is still that of the Jena years: to rewrite the *Wissenschaftslehre*, not to overthrow it.

The thesis that Herbart developed, the germ of his later philosophy in Switzerland, ultimately goes back to Herbart himself. In 1798 he was confident that his thinking was moving in a new direction, and that some of his ideas would prove fruitful. This is clear from his January letter to von Halem:

Neither nature nor the work that I have found here silence the need for the philosophy I seek, and for which I believe I have found a starting point . . . I fancy it is a good omen for my idea of the science of knowledge that in every way it continues to urge itself upon me. I confess that Fichte's previous performances are conspicuous only by their contrast with the ideal.[41]

He was even more self-confident when he wrote his parents six months later:

The wealth of my present thoughts consists in some that seem to contain the germ of many others. I acquired them in the past two and a half years . . . But thoughts either produce new ones or they grow old and disappear. Now an inner certainty elevates me above the systems of our time, the Kantian and Fichtean not excepted; and even if I should be in error, I hold it to be a great fortune, without fear or the need for a leader, to be able to wander through a field that appears to grow larger with every step.[42]

But what were these ideas that Herbart was forging, the thoughts that gave him such confidence that he stood above the systems of his age? Unfortunately, Herbart does not explain and reveals nothing. Perhaps he had only vague intuitions, which he still had not been able to work out in any detail? Perhaps, after writing these letters, he tried to develop them but rejected them on further reflection? A remarkable letter from October 1798 to his friend Friedrich Muhrbeck in Paris shows that he was still not ready to write a system and that he was only collecting the materials for one:

Had I known six years ago what I now know, a philosophical system would have grown from it in a few months–at least as an experiment (*Probe*). Now I only look around for the tools to lift the heavy stones, [viz.] analysis of the infinite, experience with people and children, and that kind of thing.[43]

This tentative attitude appears more explicitly and emphatically only a month later in a letter to Rist,[44] in which Herbart responds to the rumour among his friends that he had created his own system of philosophy. In November 1798 Johann von Böhlendorff,

---

[41] An von Halem, January 1798, SW XVI, 77.   [42] An meine Eltern, June 1798, SW XVI, 84.
[43] An Muhrbeck, October 28, 1798, XVI, 96.
[44] SW XVI, 99. The letter is undated, though it must have been written in November 1798, after Böhlendorff's letter to Rist on November 10.

a friend of the society, wrote a letter to Rist with the exciting news: "Herbart has now found his own system."[45] Böhlendorff said that Herbart had gone into isolation in the forest near Engisstein for several weeks, and that he came out of it with a draft for his own system. It was a new kind of system, Böhlendorff said, one going beyond anything in Reinhold, Kant, Fichte and Schelling. Böhlendorff was probably referring to the manuscript 'Erster problematischer Entwurf der Wissenslehre', which was indeed written in Engisstein in 1798. But that fragment, as we have seen, contains nothing new and is only an exploration and reformulation of standard Fichtean themes. More tellingly, Herbart himself felt obliged to correct Böhlendorff's enthusiasm. In his letter to Rist he declared that he had no such system, and that he only had some provisional ideas for one. All he would claim for his ideas is that they seemed worth considering, or at least that he had still not found out what is wrong with them; but he told Rist that he did not regard them as important enough to bother explaining them.

The tentative attitude apparent from the letters to Muhrbeck and Rist show that Herbart was still far from having worked out his own system of philosophy during his Swiss years. Rather than breaking with the Fichtean *Wissenschaftslehre*, Herbart was still thinking in its shadow. He wanted a new exposition of the *Wissenschaftslehre*, one that would make clear its real foundation, but not a new philosophy or doctrine. As we have seen, this was a project he had already conceived in his Jena years. In the final analysis, then, the Swiss years were a period of consolidation, not even one of transition, let alone gestation.

Yet in one important respect Herbart was moving in an independent direction during the Swiss years: namely, in his personal attitude towards Fichte. Though he was still thinking with Fichtean methods and on Fichtean problems, Herbart felt himself less and less bound to the sway of his former teacher. Thus he told Muhrbeck in his October letter that "Fichte's fairy palace" was no longer habitable for him.[46] A spat with Fichte in early 1799 had also hastened the unravelling of their relationship. Apparently, Herbart wrote to Fichte that he wished to take issue with his latest work, his *Appellation an das Publikum*,[47] and that Fichte had taken offense, scolding Herbart like a schoolmaster.[48] Herbart in turn was offended by Fichte's attitude.[49] This step towards *personal* independence will ultimately lead to a much greater *intellectual* independence, whose results we will soon see.

[45] See Böhlendorff an Rist, November 10, 1798, SW XVI, 97–98.

[46] An Muhrbeck, October 28, 1798, SW XVI, 95.

[47] This writing was Fichte's defence against the charge of atheism. See *Appellation an das Publicum gegen die Anklage des Atheismus*, in Fichte, *Sämtliche Werke* V, 193–238. I have not been able to determine from Herbart's correspondence what were his objections against Fichte's book.

[48] This is the upshot of a letter of Horn to Smidt, March 31, 1799, SW XVI, 102. The first exchange of letters between Herbart and Fichte on this episode is apparently lost. See also Böhlendorff to Herbart, July 30, 1799, XIX, 115–116.

[49] See Herbart to Fichte, March 24, 1799, SW XVI, 101.

4. Years of Work and Sorrow

The most formidable force in Herbart's intellectual development was neither Pestalozzi nor Fichte, not even Kant. It was his mother. Lucie Margarete Herbart (née Schütte) was a well-educated and, by all accounts, formidable woman. She directed Herbart's education at every stage, from infancy to adulthood, from cradle to university. His education was her life's purpose. She had become alienated from her husband from the early days of their marriage, and she feared losing the affection of her only child. And so after his *Gymnasium* years Lucie Margarete followed her son to Jena, where she lived by his side for years and joined in university life. 'Madame Herbart' became part of the circle of Herbart's friends, some of whom she enlisted to serve as spies on the activities of her son. She was also a common guest in the Fichte household, where, on one memorable occasion, she cornered Fichte on his views about woman and marriage.[50] She eventually made Fichte her confidant, revealing to him her deepest feelings of despair before her divorce.[51]

Lucie Margarete gave her blessings to her son's journey to Switzerland. She very much liked the idea that her son would be teaching the children of a Swiss aristocrat. She did not share, however, her son's plans for a long stay there, least of all his hopes to prepare for a professorship. Convinced that philosophy is no career prospect, she had better ideas for her son. He was to accompany a prince from Oldenburg on his journey around Germany, and for his services he would receive a position in the local government. Herbart firmly resisted his mother's plans,[52] though only for a while. She later claimed to be so ill that she needed her son to care for her and the family business in Oldenburg.[53] With reluctance, Herbart resigned his post in Berne and returned to Germany in early 1800. Upon his arrival in Oldenburg he made a dramatic and traumatic discovery: that his mother was not so ill after all, and that she had called him home partly to realize her plans for him, and partly to use him in messy divorce proceedings.[54] Not surprisingly, this turn of events led to a breach in relations. Having overstepped her limits, Lucie Margarete had achieved what she most feared: the alienation of her only child.

Herbart now found himself back in Germany, estranged from mother and family, with neither work nor income. Having resigned his post in Berne, there was no going back to Switzerland, though he felt he really belonged there. In despair and distress he fell back on the one source of support that he had cultivated over the years: his circle of close friends. For the next two years Herbart lived with friends in Bremen and in Smidt's estate outside the city. Though the breach with his mother had ruined his nerves and sapped his health, Herbart continued to work on philosophy, classical

[50] See Herbart to Smidt, Early December, 1796, SW XVI, 43.
[51] See her remarkably candid letter to Fichte written in the night of October 12/13, 1797, in Asmus, *Herbart* I, 147–148.
[52] See his letter to his parents, June 1798, SW I, 82–91.
[53] See L. Otth an Herbart, June 10, 1799, SW XIX, 113–115.   [54] See Weiß, *Herbart*, p. 15.

scholarship and mathematics. He later described his Bremen years as "*voll Arbeit und Schmerz.*" Yet his pains were worth it. They bore great fruit. For the Bremen years mark the onset of Herbart's intellectual independence.

This new independence manifests itself in a more critical attitude towards Fichte, which first appears in a short manuscript that Herbart wrote in Lilienthal at the end of May 1800, 'Zur Kritik der Ichvorstellung'.[55] Herbart now begins to question Fichte's central and characteristic concept, the ego or self. He raises the question: What have we gained with all Fichte's reasoning about the ego? Was it only so much vain and delusory labour? And the answer now, of course, is a firm "yes". Herbart is now telling himself that he was wasting his energy in Enggistein in trying to think through the logic of this concept. What is wrong with it? Simply put, it is self-contradictory. Fichte maintains that the ego is pure subject–object identity, that in the ego being and thinking are one and the same. But the trouble is that Fichte also concedes that thinking *in actu* cannot be thought through this very act. So he is therefore saying both that: 1) thinking of being and being are one and the same; and 2) thinking of being cannot be the being thought of, because it cannot be thought through this very act (114). Herbart summarizes the absurdity of the idea: "The being of thinking is the reality of thinking—real thinking, the act of thinking. But it is just that which cannot be thought.—Therefore, an intelligence [i.e. a rational being or person] thinks of a thinking, it thinks of exactly that of which it cannot think-[which is to say] that it thinks nonsense." (114). With that, Herbart discards the concept that had troubled him since the mid-1790s. It is striking, however, that in this fragment he discovers no new problem in Fichte's concept, none that he had not already articulated in Jena and Berne. But now the problem is no longer a challenge to be solved; it has turned into an overwhelming objection. Herbart had simply decided not to try to save Fichte any longer.

Another sign of an important change in the Bremen years appears in some popular lectures Herbart gave in the Bremen Museum in 1800.[56] Nowhere in these lectures does Herbart explicitly take issue with Fichte; but his treatment of his main theme implies a break with Fichte's ethical idealism. Herbart's theme is the relationship between morality and religion. What role does each play in our lives? And what are the boundaries between them? Herbart draws a simple and basic distinction between morality and religion, so that one does not trespass into the realm of the other. Morality deals with human actions and decisions, with the world insofar as we can change it according to our will. Religion, however, concerns human feelings, involving an awareness of the world as it is given to us and lies beyond our control. While morality considers the human being in activity, insofar as it strives to change its world, religion treats the human being at rest, insofar as it is at peace with its world. In these lectures Herbart's

---

[55] Herbart, SW I, 113–114.
[56] Herbart, 'Über das Bedürfnis der Sittenlehre und Religion in ihrem Verhältnis zur Philosophie', SW I, 116–126.

conception of morality is decidedly Fichtean: that we create ourselves through an act of will. As he puts it: "everyone must posit himself, not as he finds himself but in what he demands of himself" (118). But the striking point is that Herbart sets limits to the realm of morality. Moral striving should not be so consuming that we lose ourselves in our actions, that we fail to see the world around us (120). There cannot be a morality for the human being at peace, Herbart argues, because peace deals with feelings, which cannot be created or commanded (123). In setting these boundaries to the realm of morality, Herbart was taking silent issue with Fichte's ethical idealism. For it was a central doctrine of that idealism, as Fichte expounded it in his *Grundlage der gesamten Wissenschaftslehre* and in his *Bestimmung des Gelehrten*, that there should be no limit to the striving of the human will, that the will should forever struggle and aspire to subdue all of nature, so that it is the product of its activity alone. Although Fichte believed that this striving would be infinite, that it could at best only approximate its goal, the ideal was still to overcome completely the otherness of the realm of nature, to break down even our physical and sensible natures, so that, in the end, all human beings would become a single infinite rational being, namely, God. Rather than striving to become the divine, Herbart is recommending that we rest and try to find it in the realm of nature outside us.

This shift in attitude away from Fichte's ethical idealism also appears in Herbart's pedagogical writings from the Bremen years. These writings, some of Herbart's first publications, were attempts to introduce Pestalozzi's ideas into Germany.[57] We learn right away from the first of them, 'Über Pestalozzi's neueste Schrift: Wie Gertrud ihre Kinder Lehrte', that the central point of education is to teach the child how to be aware of the world around it. We should not cultivate the child's imagination, nor train its intellect, to the point where it ceases to be sensitive and responsive to the world. Before we fantasize about *another* world, and before we *talk* about this one, we must first learn to see things. We must learn to develop what Herbart calls our power of intuition (*Anschauung*), that is, the capacity to perceive things accurately, just as they are given to us, and without trying to control them. The ultimate goal of Pestalozzi's education, as Herbart puts it, is to develop "aesthetic perception" (139, 150). It is only when we develop this capacity, he argues, that we acquire "subtlety of feeling, a wider field of vision, a richer fantasy and deeper investigative insight" (150). In another writing, the treatise *Pestalozzis Idee eines ABC der Anschauung*, Herbart further explains that seeing is an art, and that like all art, it has to go through a series of exercises to be developed (155). We can divide the powers of the child into

---

[57] These writings comprise essays, lectures and a book. The essays are 'Ideen zu einem pädagogischen Lehrplan für höhere Studien' (SW I, 129–135), which appeared in 1801, and 'Über Pestalozzi's neueste Schrift: Wie Gertrud Ihre Kinder Lehrte' (SW I, 137–150), which was published in 1802. The lectures are 'Zwei Vorlesungen über Pädagogik' (SW I, 279–290), and 'Über den Standpunkt der Beurteilung der Pestalozzischen Unterrichtsmethode' (SW I, 301–309), both delivered in 1804, and therefore after the Bremen years. The book is *Pestalozzis Idee eines ABC der Anschauung* (SW I, 151–274), which first appeared in 1802.

desire, fantasy and observation, and that to which we should give the greatest weight in education is observation. Why? Because cultivating desire and fantasy gives way to moods and whims, as Rousseau warned, while only observation teaches us a more realistic attitude, how things are and why they must be that way. Fantasy needs direction, desire needs a counterweight, and both are found in the power of observation, which shows us how things must be.

We need not go into further detail here about Herbart's ideal of education, which has been discussed extensively by others.[58] The point worth stressing here is that Herbart's ideal demands developing a completely different side of human nature than that stressed by Fichte. The goal of education is not to develop the titanic Fichtean will, which knows no limits and which would make all the world obey its commands; rather, it is to cultivate a capacity of aesthetic perception that recognizes our limits and grasps the necessity inherent in things. Rather than attempting to make nature bow to our rational commands, we now learn to see that it has its own inherent value and order. Applying Herbart's earlier distinction between morality and religion to his pedagogical views, it should be clear that his ideal of education attempts to develop the religious side of our nature, our capacity for feeling rather than for acting.

Herbart's move away from Fichte's ethical idealism in Bremen is not surprising or mysterious but only in keeping with the spirit of his age. Already in the late 1790s several members of the Romantic circle in Jena (Schlegel, Novalis, Schelling, Hölderlin), and several friends of the *Gesellschaft der freien Männer* in Switzerland (von Berger, Hülsen), had begun to react against Fichte's ethical idealism and to move towards an organic naturalism.[59] Rather than seeing nature in negative terms, as the *non*-ego, as an obstacle to be overcome in the infinite ethical striving of the ego, they saw it in more positive terms as an organic whole, as a living being in its own right. They ceased to regard the ego as a purely intellectual being independent of nature and having the power and mission to dominate it; instead, they now viewed the ego as only one being in nature, as a product and expression of its laws. This organic naturalism went hand-in-hand with an aesthetic vision of the world: the whole of nature, as an organic unity, is akin to a work of art. Rather than striving to make it conform to our ends, the vocation of man is now to understand nature in her own terms, to treat her as an end in herself and to grasp her as if she were a work of art by a cosmic creator. To understand nature in her own terms is to perceive her as a work of art. This new emphasis on aesthetic perception was often expressed in terms of a power of intuition or feeling.[60]

---

[58] For introductions in English, see Charles de Garmo, *Herbart and the Herbartians* (New York: Scribner, 1896), and Ossian Lang, *Outlines of Herbart's Pedagogics* (Chicago, IL: Kellogg & Co., 1894).

[59] This important generational shift was first thematized by Dilthey. See his *Die Jugendgeschichte Hegels*, in *Gesammelte Schriften* (Leipzig: Tuebner, 1921), IV, 43–60.

[60] This theme of Herbart's appears in the circle of his friends by 1797. See Erich von Berger and Hülsen to Herbart, January 11, 1797: "Alle Philosophie als Thätigkeit des Geistes betrachtet ... ist Versuch die Welt anzuschauen." SW XIX, 86.

All these ideas begin to appear in the early 1800s in some of Herbart's Bremen writings. Not surprisingly, Herbart was moving in the direction of his fellow friends and Romantic contemporaries. In short, he was a Johnnie-come-lately to the Romantic movement, and it had only been his extraordinarily close relationship with Fichte that had kept him from jumping into the Romantic stream earlier. Now that he had liberated himself from Fichte in his final Berne days, he was now ready to test the Romantic waters.

In Bremen Herbart sometimes did more than test the waters: he dived into them. He not only voiced Romantic themes but he embraced the Romantic worldview. Such is the upshot of an extraordinary essay that Herbart wrote probably in his Bremen days, 'Ueber die ästhetische Darstellung der Welt, als das Hauptgeschäfft der Erziehung', which he appended to the second edition of his *Pestalozzis Idee einer ABC der Anschauung*.[61] Here we find Herbart, flatly contrary to Fichtean dogma, embracing two central Romantic themes: the primacy of the aesthetic dimension of life and organic naturalism. The first theme emerges in the course of defending his thesis that the chief business of education is the cultivation of aesthetic sensibility. The question arises of the place of morality in this conception of education. Surely, a chief purpose of education is to develop moral character; but the cultivation of aesthetic powers seems to have only an accidental connection with that morality. Herbart's response to this difficulty is remarkable: he argues that morality, properly seen, is an aesthetic capacity, that moral judgement is ultimately subordinate to aesthetic judgement. He comes to this conclusion through an analysis of the concept of morality itself. Herbart maintains that the fundamental characteristic of morality consists in obedience, the acceptance of an obligation that binds the will. The source of obligation cannot lie in a *practical* capacity, the power of the will, because the will is bound by the law and has no power to change it. It also cannot lie in a *theoretical* capacity, because it is the business of theoretical reason to determine laws about what *must* be the case, whereas the will is bound by an *ought*, not a *must*. What, then, can be the source of obligation if it is not practical or theoretical? It can only be aesthetic. The source of moral obligation ultimately arises from a capacity of *aesthetic* judgement, which consists in perceiving the proper relations between things and judging their worth or value. Herbart sees aesthetic judgement as a power of reason, which is for him less a power of reasoning or inference than one of perceiving and judging. He calls it *Vernehmen*, an intranslatable term, which has connotations of perception and judgement, both of which are fully intended.

The second Romantic theme, organic naturalism, surfaces when Herbart questions the concept of the freedom of the will in "the latest moral system", an unmistakable

---

[61] Herbart, SW I, 259–274. Though the second edition appeared in 1804, Herbart described the essay as *"ein Fragment aus einem älteren Aufsatze, der ursprünglich zur Verständigung mit einem Freund geschrieben wurde"*, SW I, 256. Since the friend was probably Smidt, and since Herbart stood in closest contact with him in Bremen, it is safe to attribute the essay to the Bremen years.

allusion to Fichte's ethics. If we assume that the purpose of education is to foster morality, he argues, this concept undermines that purpose. According to this system, freedom is a purely intellectual or noumenal power, which is independent of the sensible and phenomenal world. This power therefore becomes inaccessible to the educator, whose means and influence fall entirely into the sensible and phenomenal world. For the educator, morality is an event, a natural occurrence, which takes place in the mind of the pupil; it is for this reason alone that he thinks that he has the power to stimulate and encourage morality in the young. All that takes place according to education happens of necessity, Herbart insists. The realistic standpoint of the educator does not permit, therefore, any interference from the idealistic standpoint: "Not the softest wind of transcendental freedom, not through the slightest crack, can blow into the domain of the educator." (261). Herbart notes that the advocate of this moral system will try to explain away the educator's influence over his pupil by dismissing it as just another event in the empirical world (260–261). But Herbart does not to give any weight to this attempt to escape the objection. His general view is that each person, though unique and individual, is still only one part of nature, whose necessity expresses itself through him (272).

By 1802, then, at the end of his Bremen days, Herbart had made enormous strides in escaping from his Fichtean heritage. He no longer accepted Fichte's ethical idealism, his concept of the ego, his view of nature, or his idea of transcendental freedom. In rejecting these Fichtean doctrines Herbart drew sustenance and spirit from the budding Romantic movement. Herbart the Fichtean had now become Herbart the Romantic. Yet, as we shall soon see, Herbart's Romantic days were very brief. There were weighty forces within him restraining his Romantic tendencies, forces that came from one powerful source and influence: Immanuel Kant.

5. Young Academic

In May 1802 Herbart found himself in Göttingen. His immediate reason for being there was to be a *Hauslehrer* for the son of a Hannoverian minister, Graf von Grote; but moving there also brought him closer to his ultimate goal: a post in a university.[62] Shortly after his arrival in Göttingen, Herbart registered to undergo the necessary examinations for both his doctorate and habilitation.[63] For these, he had to undertake two public disputations, one for the doctorate and another for the habilitation. The disputations, which took place on two consecutive days, October 22 and 23, 1802, required that he defend ten or twelve theses.[64] We know little or nothing about the reasoning behind these theses, still less what Herbart actually said during the

[62]   See Herbart an Gries, end of July 1802, SW XVI, 253–254.
[63]   See Herbart's 'Meldeschreiben zur Promotion und Habilitation', SW I, 366. This is undated, but would have been submitted no later than the theses, which were submitted July 1802, SW I, 275.
[64]   See Herbart, 'Thesen zur Promotion und Habilitation', SW I, 275–278.

disputation. The theses are simple Latin sentences that baldly state the proposition to be discussed.[65] They are remarkable, however, for revealing the sceptical and critical direction of Herbart's thinking at this time. Some of the theses target traditional metaphysics. The doctoral theses state that metaphysics cannot form a complete whole (III), and that it is doubtful whether there is a single first principle to derive all metaphysical truths (IV), while the habilitation theses declare that the concepts of absolute necessity and perfection of traditional theology are absurd or empty (I, II). This sceptical spirit also applies against ethics and practical philosophy. For one doctoral thesis maintains that natural law, separated from ethics and politics, is a nullity (X), whereas two habilitation theses proclaim that there is no general theory of the ideal state (VIII) and that a theory of punishment is impossible (IX). More significantly, Herbart is very critical of transcendental philosophy, in both its Kantian and Fichtean versions. Three doctoral theses blast transcendental freedom, declaring that the very concept is void (VII), that it is not necessary for ethics (VIII), and that even if it existed we could never be aware of it (IX). Another habilitation thesis disputes Kant's argument in the Transcendental Aesthetic: simply because space and time are necessary for our knowledge does not prove that they are innate (V). Two more habilitation theses attack Fichte's idealism: one declares intellectual intuition a nullity (VI), while another pronounces the ego to be self-contradictory (VII).

The disputation theses show how far Herbart had moved away from the Kantian-Fichtean idealism of his youth. Now he had greater critical distance than ever before on central doctrines of transcendental idealism. For some scholars, the theses show that Herbart now had his own independent philosophy that he conceived in opposition to transcendental philosophy.[66] We must be careful, however, to put the disputation theses in proper perspective. While Herbart will continue to be critical of all these aspects of transcendental philosophy—Fichte's concepts of freedom, the ego and intellectual intuition, and Kant's reasoning in the Transcendental Aesthetic—he does not reject transcendental idealism entirely. Indeed, he refuses to abandon it for the sake of empiricism, naturalism and realism. In the following Göttingen years he will develop his own metaphysics, some of whose central tenets he will describe as transcendental idealism. True to that doctrine, Herbart will maintain that the immediate objects of cognition are only representations, and that all that we know through them are appearances.

Herbart passed his doctoral and habilitation exams with flying colours. He was indeed the first candidate to satisfy the university's new stringent requirements, which stipulated that a *Dozent* should supply not only a dissertation but also take both doctoral and habilitation exams.[67] Since Herbart had the reputation of being

---

[65] For a German translation of the theses, see Asmus, *Herbart*, I, 345, 346–347.

[66] Asmus, *Herbart* I, 206.

[67] For his dissertation Herbart submitted his first book, *Pestalozzis Idee eines ABC der Anschauung*, which appeared in 1802, shortly after the disputation. See Asmus, *Herbart* I, 209.

a Fichtean, some of the old guard at Göttingen were wary of admitting an idealist in their ranks; but Herbart's criticisms of idealism would surely have dispelled their doubts on that score. For the next two years, 1802–1804, Herbart lectured as a *Privatdozent* on metaphysics, introduction to philosophy and pedagogics. He was by all accounts a popular and effective lecturer, enjoying close rapport with his students.

Such was Herbart's reputation that in 1804 the University of Heidelberg contacted him to see if he had any interest in a new philosophy position there. The Heidelberg authorities had already considered Fries with regard to the same position, though they soon lost interest when they heard about his teaching record. In February 1805 Herbart duly received an attractive offer from Heidelberg: a full ordinary professorship and 1000 Gulden salary. He declined, however, after Göttingen made an attractive counter-offer. Herbart felt at home in Göttingen, having acquired a good reputation there and a close circle of students. The position in Heidelberg eventually went to Fries after all.

Having been promoted to professor in Göttingen, Herbart, following academic custom, was obliged to give an inaugural lecture. His lecture, entitled *De platonici systematis fundamentio commentatio*,[68] concerns a classical problem in Plato's philosophy: the place of the good in the world of ideas. Herbart published the lecture in 1805, adding an appendix or 'Beylage' which explains his argument and translates some of the Greek passages.[69]

Prima facie it is surprising to find Herbart lecturing on classical philosophy, a subject that scarcely surfaces in his earlier writings and correspondence. Yet Herbart, like all *Gymnasia* students of his day, was thoroughly trained in classical Greek, and he loved classical philosophy, especially Plato. In his 'Beylage' he stresses the relevance of classical philosophy to contemporary thought (331). There is no better introduction to philosophy, we are told, than the great classical thinkers, because they engage with problems in a more simple and straightforward way than moderns, who indulge in needless technicalities and subtleties. Many modern thinkers believe that they surpass the ancients, only to lapse into errors the ancients already foresaw. Furthermore, the basic concepts of Heraclitus, Parmenides and Plato reappear in the latest systems of today, which are often an inconsistent mixture of them. Pointedly, Herbart notes that this is especially the case with Fichtean idealism. Herbart's emphasis on the contemporary relevance of classical philosophy is the key to understanding the motivation behind his dissertation, which is really a parable about the errors of contemporary philosophy, especially Fichte's and Schelling's idealism, which were moving in an increasingly Platonic direction around 1802.[70]

---

[68] Ioanne Friderico Herbart, *De platonici systematis fundamento commentatio* (Göttingen: Roewer, 1805). The text is reprinted in SW I, 311–332.

[69] The appendix or 'Beylage' appears in SW I, 327–332. Böckh, who reviewed the dissertation, called the 'Beylage' "a dangling rag" (*ein angeflickter Lappen*), though it is crucial for understanding Herbart's intentions.

[70] See Fichte's 1800 *Bestimmung des Menschen, Werke* II, 299–319; and Schelling's 1802 *Bruno, Werke* I/4, 226–230.

In his lecture Herbart locates the core of Plato's philosophy in his theory of ideas.[71] He maintains that this theory grew out of Plato's attempt to answer the question: What is the object of knowledge? Plato could not find this object in the sensible world, because he discovered contradictions within it. One and the same thing could be both heavy and light, small and large, beautiful and ugly, depending on its specific relations to other things. The object of knowledge, therefore, would have to be something whose being does not depend on its relations to other things, something that has independent being or being as such. This object is, of course, the idea. Although Herbart insists that Plato's ideas are not substances, that they are not things that exist in some mysterious place (323–4), he does maintain that they alone have being or reality in the full sense of the word. According to his interpretation, Plato holds that everything in the sensible world, because it is subject to change and contradiction, lacks true being or reality, and so is only an illusion. Plato accepted Parmenides' critique of Heraclitus: that we cannot ascribe change to being because this introduces negation into it; but since we see change in the sensible world, it follows that the sensible world cannot have true being, which we can find with the ideas alone.

The crucial question here concerns not the accuracy of Herbart's interpretation of Plato, which we can well leave to classical scholars, but its philosophical meaning and his attitude towards it. It is striking, and not accidental, that Herbart's interpretation is very Kantian: that Plato's idealism consists in ascribing reality to the ideas alone, and in maintaining that everything in the sensible world is only an illusion.[72] Herbart's attitude towards such a theory is also very Kantian. He makes it very clear in his 'Beylage' that he does not accept such idealism: "Plato's system is not my own." (330). Rather than trying to destroy the reality of the sensible world to prove the sole reality of the ideas, Herbart, like Kant, wants to preserve that reality to prevent us from fleeing into the intelligible world. He too wants to affirm "the bathos of experience". The challenge of Plato's system for Herbart then consists in showing that the alleged contradictions in the sensible world are not really contradictions at all. In the 'Beylage' Herbart announces that he has a method for dissolving these contradictions, one that can save the reality of the sensible world. He calls it "the method of relations" or "the doctrine of the completion of concepts". Yet he offers no explanation at all of this method, leaving us only with a name and a promissory note.

Fortunately, however, Herbart does provide an explanation elsewhere, though in an unlikely place, namely, the introduction to Pestalozzi's *Idee eines ABC der Anschauung* (168–169). There we are told that it is the very nature of philosophy to

---

[71] My task here is not to summarize the central theses of Herbart's lecture but only to focus on those aspects relevant to his critique of contemporary philosophy. Herbart provided his own summary in his 'Selbstanzeige', which appears in SW I, 333–334. The lecture was reviewed by no less than August Böckh in the *Jenaischen Allgemeinen Literatur-Zeitung* 1808, pp. 561–571, reprinted in SW I, 334–342. Herbart replied to Böckh's review in the *Neuen Leipziger Literatur-Zeitung* 1808, No. 43, pp. 673ff, also reprinted in SW I, 342–348.

[72] See Kant, *Prolegomena*, IV, 374.

isolate concepts, to strip them of their accidental associations, and to focus on them alone, as if they were independent entities. But in doing so philosophy removes concepts from their legitimate sphere of application; it treats them as if they have an unconditional validity on their own, quite apart from the specific conditions that give them their real sense and reference. The result of this feat of abstraction is that the use of these concepts gets caught in contradictions. We make general claims about the concepts, failing to see that they are true only in a specific sense and in a specific context. These contradictions serve as a stimulus to the philosopher to return the concepts to their original contexts, to show how their meaning depends on other concepts with which they stand in close necessary connections. Now "the chief purpose" of all philosophy, Herbart declares, consists in showing "the connections in the given", in restoring the interconnections and context that have been lost by the isolation and abstraction of concepts. Though Herbart does not mention his "method of relations" in this passage, it is clear that he understands its purpose along the lines stated here. The task of the method of relations is to restore context and connection, and thus to remove contradictions that are involved in the hypostasization of concepts.

There is another short writing from Herbart's early Göttingen years that is very revealing about his intellectual development, especially his evolving conception of philosophy. This is his *Kurze Darstellung eines Plans zu philosophischen Vorlesungen*, which appeared in 1804.[73] Written with a student audience in mind, this piece is simple description of Herbart's plans for his lectures on logic and metaphysics in 1804. Herbart defines philosophy as little more than the attempt to think about ultimate questions about the world and life. Philosophy has no definite a priori form, and its method is only that way of thinking that has become habitual because it has proven useful (294). More an activity than a system, philosophy is the activity of thinking for oneself. The best teacher of philosophy is one that encourages and cultivates this activity in his students, and not one who tries to indoctrinate them with his system. Some fifty years earlier Kant had given a very similar account of the purpose of philosophy in his plan for his lectures,[74] and it would not be at all surprising if Herbart was thinking of the sage of Königsberg. For towards the close of the piece he notes the power of the Kantian Revolution upon his generation, and he declares that the leading thinkers of his day have not really moved far beyond it (298).

All in all, the theses and lecture plans of the early Göttingen years show much about what Herbart is moving away from but very little about where he is going to. We learn something about his negative attitude towards speculative idealism, traditional metaphysics, and the natural law tradition, but next to nothing about what is to replace them. It is noteworthy that Herbart is also sceptical about the Romantic

---

[73] Herbart, *Kurze Darstellung eines Plans zu philosophischen Vorlesungen* (Göttingen: Röwer, 1804). SW I, 291–299.

[74] Kant, *Nachricht von der Einrichtung seiner Vorlesungen in dem Winterhalbjahre von 1765–1766* (Königsberg: Kanter, 1765). *Schriften* II, 303–313.

worldview that had once seduced him in Bremen. Thus he flatly dismisses the intellectual intuition that played such a prominent role in Romantic thinking; and he even warns against a too Romantic interpretation of his aesthetic account of moral judgement. This interpretation, he declares pointedly, should not be confused with "a certain pretentious aesthetic that talks about the beautiful as the highest" (298). That was a clear jab against the Romantics and even some of his friends from the *Gesellschaft der freien Männer*.

The general picture that emerges from the early Göttingen years is of a young thinker refusing to define himself—hence he hates all systems—and who wants to be nothing more than a free spirit in philosophy. This was Herbart enjoying and asserting his independence. After years of struggle against the dominance of Fichte, and after flirting with Romantic ideas, Herbart had finally come into his own. Now that he had wiped the slate clean, he was ready, finally, to begin writing his own philosophy. We must now consider the first fruits of his newly-found independence.

6. Main Points of Metaphysics

In 1806 Herbart published his *Hauptpuncte der Metaphysik*,[75] which he had composed in the summer of that year.[76] This was a breakthrough work for him, which finally lays down the foundation for his own philosophy. His 1828 *Allgemeine Metaphysik*, which is his central work on metaphysics, was largely based upon the standpoint he had already reached in his *Hauptpuncte*. Because of its historical and systematic importance, we do well to examine its content and arguments.

The *Hauptpuncte* is brief but dense, discussing in very concentrated form some of the central problems of metaphysics. Unfortunately, its exposition is uncompromising, offering few aids to the ordinary reader. The subtitle of the book warns us that it is "composed for prepared listeners" (*vorgeübten Zuhörern zusammengestellt*), who were advanced students of Herbart's own lectures. The preface refuses to make further explanations for the reader and warns us that it contains only what is necessary from a "strict scientific point of view". Such an approach poses serious challenges to the contemporary reader, however, who cannot count himself among Herbart's "prepared listeners". The major challenge is the sheer obscurity of the work, which makes for different, even conflicting, interpretations. We will attempt to compensate for this obscurity by placing Herbart's work in its historical and systematic context.

Prima facie it seems odd for Herbart, who now has Kantian predelictions, to be embarking on metaphysics, the very discipline whose impossibility had been demonstrated by Kant in the first *Kritik*. Yet it is important to understand what Herbart meant by metaphysics. It is decidedly not the science of the absolute, as it was in

---

[75] *Hauptpuncte der Metaphysik* (Göttingen: J.C. Baier, 1806). A second edition, published with Danckwerts, appeared in 1808. All references above are to the first edition as reprinted in SW II, 175–226.
[76] See Herbart to Carl von Steiger, August 23, 1806, SW XVI, 296.

Schelling and Hegel. Though the dense exposition of the *Hauptpuncte* tells no secrets, some of Herbart's lectures on the introduction to philosophy, which were given around the same time, reveal his meaning.[77] There metaphysics is defined in Kantian terms as "the science of the conceivability of experience" (327).[78] The task of metaphysics, Herbart further explains, is to show how the central concepts of experience are possible. It will do so by showing how one concept is possible only through its relations to other concepts. To demonstrate these relations, Herbart will follow "a method of relations". This was the method which he had baptized in the 'Beylage' to his dissertation, and which he had expounded in the introduction to *Pestalozzi's Idee.*[79]

The Kantian conception and approach behind the *Hauptpuncte* emerges in the few elucidatory comments in the preface. These comments are polemical and directed against Herbart's opponents, who are the Schellingians. In his view, they have a dogmatic metaphysics which claims to have knowledge of the absolute. Against them, Herbart reminds us of the progress of metaphysics since Kant. We now know that it is an error to regard cognition as a mirroring of its object, and that we cannot know things-in-themselves (177–178). We also know since Fichte, Herbart adds, that whoever talks about being also thinks about it, and that for just this reason he will have to justify his thinking (178). This comment, which is an allusion to Fichte's dispute with Schelling, shows Herbart taking sides with his former teacher. He was essentially accusing the Schellingians of dogmatism, of trying to escape the question of justification by appealing to an intellectual intuition. Herbart was reminding them that it is impossible to escape the demand for evidence. The question always remained: How do they know that what they intuit is the divine? To drive his point home, Herbart cites some lines from Kant: "Even the holy gospel must be compared with moral perfection before one recognizes it as such?"[80]

The *Hauptpuncte* begins with a discussion of method, specifically with "the method of relations". While he had sketched only a rough idea of that method in his earlier writings, he now gives for the first time a technical and logical account of it.

Herbart introduces his discussion with a classical problem of logic: What is the connection between ground and consequent? There seems no simple and precise way to specify that connection. If we say that the consequent is *identical with* the ground, the inference shows us nothing new and is only a tautology. If, however, the consequent is *distinct from* the ground, there is no necessary connection and no valid inference (179). For Herbart, this problem is the same as Kant's fundamental problem: How is

---

[77] *Entwurf zu Vorlesungen über die Einleitung in die Philosophie*, SW II, 297–327.

[78] See too Herbart's definition in the 'Praenoscenda Generaliora' to his *Theoriae de Attractione Elementorum Principia Metaphysica* where metaphysics is defined as "*ars experientian recte intelligendi*". See SW III, 160, §1.

[79] See Section 5 in this chapter.

[80] Herbart refers to Kant's *Grundlegung zur Metaphysik der Sitten*, *Schriften* IV, 408. His citation is selective but accurate.

synthetic unity possible? How can there be a necessary connection between distinct terms? The same problem recurs because the necessary connection requires identity between the terms, though they should be distinct from one another. As we have seen, Herbart's reflections on this problem go back to the 1790s. Only then Herbart saw this problem as identical with the issue of self-consciousness. In the *Hauptpuncte* that Fichtean perspective disappears entirely, with the "*Ich*" abruptly dismissed as "the most annoying of fantasies" (185–186). The problem of synthetic unity is now discussed on a strictly logical level.

How can we resolve the problem of synthetic unity? We do so, Herbart says, if we postulate a third term, a mediating concept between the distinct terms (180). This mediating concept is a whole having distinct parts or aspects. The whole *connects* its parts or aspects because it is in both of them; but it also *separates* them because it is not in them in the same way at the same time. To show how synthetic unity is possible in any specific case, we must determine how the parts of a whole are both identical to and distinct from one another.

The task of the method of relations is to show us how synthetic unity is possible for the general concepts of experience. It does so by exposing and resolving contradictions involved in the use of these concepts (181). There is a danger of contradiction involved in all these concepts, Herbart points out, because, as synthetic unities, their terms need to be identical to yet distinct from one another (182). To resolve the contradiction, we show the respects in which the terms are the same and the respects in which they are different. But this is not the end of the matter because contradictions can arise on a deeper level. The parts M and N of the whole A are themselves wholes having parts m and n. The problems that we have found *between* M and N now arise *within* M and N themselves. Their parts m and n appear in contradiction because they too are synthetic unities, which are both the same and different; so the same operation of finding the respects in which m and n are different and the same must continue. And so on. Herbart poses no limit to how far we can pursue the analysis involved in the method of relations.

Whatever its exact formal structure, the chief point behind the method of relations is transcendental: to show how a synthetic a priori concept is possible. Such a concept, Herbart thinks, is a necessary condition of experience, basic to how we conceive and perceive our world. The method of relations shows how these concepts are possible by removing the contradictions in their use, which it does by showing how each concept forms a coherent whole, a synthetic unity where some of its elements are the same in some respects and different in other respects. Through the method of relations, metaphysics can then claim to be "the science of the conceivability of experience."

A procedure of exposing and resolving contradiction, and of doing so by showing how concepts form coherent wholes, makes Herbart's method of relations sound very much like Hegel's dialectic, which was developed around the same time.[81] The

---

[81] Hegel's dialectic makes its first formal and official appearance in 1807 in the *Phänomenologie des Geistes*. Arguably, Hegel had the idea much earlier, since its rudiments already appear in his 1801

method of relations seems a dialectic for Hegelians, the dialectic a method of relations for Herbartians. Are, though, these methods really the same? Though there are indeed structural similarities, it is noteworthy that they have utterly opposed uses or goals. The aim of Herbart's method is to show only the possibility and reality of experience, to remove the contradictions discovered by idealist philosophers who are all too ready to declare the world of experience a realm of illusion. The aim of Hegel's method, though, is the exact opposite: to show that the finite world on its own is illusory and that it has reality only as an appearance of the absolute or idea.

After his opening reflections on methodology, Herbart takes us into the depths of metaphysics proper. His "transcendental enquiry", as he calls it, consists in an abstruse discussion of the most abstract concepts of metaphysics, viz., being, essence, force, substance, change. The entire metaphysics is sketched in fourteen sections, whose extreme density poses a challenge to the most patient reader. We cannot provide here an analysis, let alone a summary, of these sections. Our only task is to focus on those passages relevant to Herbart's emerging conception of transcendental idealism.

Herbart begins with that most basic of metaphysical concepts: being (*Seyn*) (§1). Before analyzing it, though, he reminds his reader: "Transcendental enquiry bears in mind that the thinker always remains enclosed in the circle of his representations" (§1; 188). For this reason, he says, we can speak of being only insofar as we attach a thought to it. What is that thought? What is the act of thinking that expresses being?

Herbart equates the thought of being with the simple act of positing, that is, assuming that something exists. "To explain that A is, is to explain that the matter rests with the simple positing of A." (§1; 188). Being is therefore sheer existence, nothing more. Herbart insists that we should not assume from the mere concept of being that there is a plurality of beings. The concept of being is neither one nor many but simply that which is posited.

Like Kant, Herbart insists that existence is not a predicate. It adds no new content to the subject of an assertion; to say that something exists is not to attribute a determinate property to that thing. Since it is not a property, existence has no degrees, so that the whole notion of a most perfect being, an *ens realissimum*, makes no sense (189). And since it is only in virtue of a property that one thing relates to another, being in itself is self-sufficient, having no relations to anything else. It is therefore utterly simple, indeed completely inexplicable, because to explain something means to determine its relations to, or connections with, other things (189).

Differenzschrift. See the section entitled 'Reflexion als Instrument des Philosophierens', in *Werke in zwanzig Bänden*, eds Eva Moldenhauer and Karl Michel (Frankfurt: Suhrkamp, 1970) II, 25–30. However, there is no question of a direct influence of Hegel on Herbart, or conversely, since the two philosophers were never in the same place at the same time, and their chief metaphysical writings appear almost simultaneously. It is noteworthy that in his later years Herbart took note of Hegel's dialectic, and that he was more sympathetic to it than other neo-Kantians, especially Fries. In his *Kurze Enzyklopädie der Philosophie*, which appeared in 1831, he stated that the contradictions of Hegel's logic have their basis in experience itself. "*Der Kern seiner Logik ist die Erfahrung selbst.*" See SW IV, 215.

Having explained the concept of being, Herbart proceeds to that of essence (*Wesen*) (§2). What is thought of as being, something that exists, is *a* being (*ein Wesen*) (§2; 190). Essence is therefore the being of this or that thing. Essence as such, however, is necessarily one, Herbart argues, because being is utterly simple, excluding all relation. It is one not in the sense that it is one indivisible thing among many, but in the sense that it excludes all plurality. Since it has no relations, it has neither plurality, nor quantity, nor degree, nor infinity, which all presuppose relations in some form. It is only a figure of speech, therefore, when Herbart talks about "a being" in the singular, as if it were one among a plurality of beings. Strictly speaking, we cannot assume that there is a plurality of things, at least not insofar as we consider the sheer being of a thing. All things that have being are the same insofar as they have being, that is, insofar as we regard their essence alone (§2; 190). If, then, there is a multiplicity of things, their plurality must come from some other source than their mere existence.

So far, Herbart's analysis of being or essence makes it seem utterly ineffable. We cannot state anything definite about being, because to do so would be to ascribe some property to it when being is utterly propertyless. Since being is utterly simple, excluding all relations, and since to explain something is to relate it to other things, being seems utterly inscrutable. Still, the fact remains that we do talk about being, that we do say what it is. The question then arises: What status should we give to our talk about being? Not fearing the consequences of his radical position, Herbart places all talk of being outside being itself (§2; 190–191). When we talk about being, he says, we use an image (*Bild*), which should not be confused with what it is an image of, that is, with being itself (§2; 190). These images are only how we view being and they are accidental to being itself. Herbart therefore calls them "accidental views" (*zufällige Ansichten*) (§2; 190).

After treating the very general and abstract concepts of being and essence (§§1–2), Herbart then proceeds to consider their application to experience (§§3–9). More specifically, he examines the concept of being as a particular thing in experience (§§3–5). This involves investigating first of all the concepts of substance and its accidents (§3).

It is a basic fact of our experience, Herbart says, that the simple sensations of experience are never found on their own but that they are always in connection with one another; they appear in complexes, which we call things or substances (§3; 191). There is a problem, however, with the concept of a thing. We think of the thing as a unity, as the whole of all its properties. But these properties are utterly different from one another. Each of them refers to a distinct kind of sensation, which is utterly unique and simple; for example, no one can make a single sensation comprising the yellowness and heaviness of gold. The form and the matter of the thing are then in conflict: the form (the complex) posits one single being; the matter (the distinct properties) gives us a multiplicity of beings (§3; 192). Yet this one being and these many beings should be, somehow, one and the same. Here, then, lies one of those contradictions that Herbart claims to be pervasive in the ordinary concepts of experience.

Already at this point in his discussion Herbart reaches a significant conclusion: "that we cannot know things-in-themselves" (§3 Anm.; 192). We have already seen how sections §1–2 make being itself unknowable, but that does not give us the conclusion that *particular things* are unknowable. Why does that additional point follow? Though Herbart does not explain, we can reconstruct his reasoning from his other assumptions. Herbart has made several contrasts between the thing itself and the properties by which it is known: while the thing is one, its properties are many, each distinct from the other; while the thing is unique, its properties classify it and compare it to other things; and while the thing is indivisible, the properties divide it into distinct aspects. The basic problem seems to be that each thing is essentially propertyless, whereas all knowledge of things takes place through their properties. To know a thing is to be able to say what it is; but to say what it is involves the attribution of some property to the thing. So Herbart seems to be reasoning as follows: if the essence of the thing is propertyless, and if all knowledge is through properties, then the essence of the thing is unknowable.

Having determined that things-in-themselves are unknowable, Herbart goes on to draw another significant conclusion to vindicate the critical philosophy: that empiricism and rationalism are both necessary and complementary. This follows from the fact that we need to postulate a single thing beyond the senses (as rationalism demands), and that we must see each of its properties as given in experience (as empiricism insists). Whatever weight we care to give to Herbart's reasoning for these conclusions, they show how his metaphysics intends to confirm fundamental doctrines of Kant's transcendental philosophy.

After discussing the concept of substance and accident, Herbart introduces the concept of change (*Veränderung*) (§4). This concept brings with it, however, further contradictions in our concept of a thing. We sometimes regard a thing as just the conjunction of its properties. Asked what the thing is, we just list its properties; gold, as Locke tells us, is that substance that is yellow, malleable and soluable in *aqua regia*. Because the thing is just the conjunction of its properties, it requires *all* of them, such that if only one were changed, we would have a new thing (§4; 193). But this means that the identity of things will be constantly changing, and that we will never be able to talk about the same thing amid change. To avoid these consequences, we adopt another conflicting conception of a thing, which is no more plausible. According to this conception, we ascribe identity to a thing throughout change, so that even if some of its properties change—even if it has gained some new ones or lost some old ones—we still regard it as one and the same thing. So we identify the thing with, yet distinguish it from, its many properties. "A contradiction therefore lies before our eyes: that one substance ought to be many, and that many ought to be one." (§4; 193)

How do we resolve this contradiction? Content for now to play the role of dialectician, Herbart does not propose a solution. Rather than resolving the tension, he increases it by posing another contradiction. In a passage showing uncanny parallels with Hegel,[82] Herbart introduces the concept of force (*Kraft*) (§5). The concept of force seems to explain the unity of a thing and the diversity of its properties (§5; 194). The force unifies all these properties, which are one and all its manifestations. The concept of force and its manifestation now takes over the role of substance and accident. But we quickly discover that the concept of force is no less problematic than its predecessor. The problem is trying to explain how all these properties form a unity, how they belong to a single thing. On the one hand, each property has its determinate quality in virtue of contrast or negation, in virtue of the fact that it is *not* another property; on the other hand, each is a simple unique positive quality, "a unique, simple what", and as such stands alone and does not negate another (195). Neither view explains the unity of the thing: the former gives us contrasting qualities that exclude one another, whereas the other gives us unique and independent qualities standing indifferently alongside one another.

Somewhat mysteriously, Herbart ascribes to each being "an act of self-preservation" (*Act der Selbsterhaltung*) (§5; 195). Though he introduces this concept with little explanation, its rationale follows from some of his earlier moves. He has used the concept of force to explain the unity of a thing; and he has also stressed a thing's identity over time. Putting these together, one gets the idea of a force to maintain one's identity, that is, self-preservation. If there is such a force, Herbart reasons, there must be also another countervailing force, which he calls a disturbance (*Störung*). These disturbances do not change the inner identity of a thing, however, which is maintained in its being by its inner power of self-preservation. This account of acts of self-preservation and their disturbances play a fundamental role in Herbart's psychology, as we shall soon see.[83]

After treating the concepts of substance, change and force (§§3–5), Herbart examines the no less fundamental concepts of space, time, motion and causality (§§6–9). The most striking feature of his account of space and time is his departure from Kant's Transcendental Aesthetic. Herbart had already showed his misgivings about the Transcendental Aesthetic in the introduction to his book when he argued that the Kantian doctrine that space is an a priori form of intuition cannot explain the origin of specific spatial appearances, that is, that we see here a triangle and there a circle (186). That quarrel with the Transcendental Aesthetic continues when Herbart questions the assumptions of absolute space and time (§§6–7). Herbart constructs the concept of an intelligible space from the places occupied by objects, so that space follows from the relations between these places (§7; 198–199). The notion of an absolute space preceding all these constructions Herbart dismisses as a mere abstraction (201). Absolute time is dismissed on similar grounds. It is simply the form in

---

[82] G.W.F. Hegel, 'Kraft und Verstand', *System der Wissenschaft. Erster Theil, Phänomenologie des Geistes* (Bamburg: Goebhardt, 1807), pp. 59–100.
[83] See Section 10 in this chapter.

which something goes through space, that is, succession, the way in which one body continuously changes its place (§8; 203). Time is nothing more than the quantity of succession, divided by speed (203). Just as Herbart found contradictions in the concept of a thing and its properties, so he finds contradictions in the concepts of absolute space, time and motion. In devising these contradictions he takes his cue from Zeno's paradoxes.

Throughout his analysis of experience, Herbart is preoccupied with finding contradictions in the most basic concepts. This is just what we should expect from his method of relations, whose task is to expose such contradictions. It is striking, however, that Herbart poses no solutions to these contradictions, which is no less a task of his method. On several occasions he invokes the method of relations to analyse the contradictions; but these analyses only clarify the reasons for the contradictions without resolving them. What is going on? It is only in a section titled 'Uebergang zum Idealismus', attached at the close of section §9, that we are given some explanation of the aim of the proceedings. Here Herbart states that the doctrines of the nothingness of space, time and motion, and the unknowability of things-in-themselves, belong to a *realistic* metaphysics (204). All these doctrines, he says, are connected with the positing of something real, which seems to be indicated by experience. This entire realism, he then adds, is "the inevitable booty of idealism". This idealism, though apparently irrefutable from the outside, explodes from its inner contradictions (205).

What does Herbart mean with these cryptic lines? Is he committing himself to idealism or realism? And what does he mean "idealism" and "realism"? It is on the basis of these lines that some scholars regard Herbart as a realist opposed to Kant's transcendental idealism. But a closer look at the context shows that Herbart is not taking issue with Kant but siding with him.

Herbart seems to suggest that the contradictions arising within experience arise from transcendental realism, that is, the assumption that appearances are things-in-themselves. Herbart is then alluding to the Kantian doctrine that the antinomies arise from transcendental realism, and that their solution rests upon transcendental idealism. The idealism that explodes from inner contradictions is not, however, transcendental idealism but the idealism criticized by Kant in the *Prolegomena,* that is, that idealism which holds that space, time and the things of experience are only illusory. That Herbart has in mind this sense of "idealism" is clear from his closing remark that Kant has used the term "idealism" to designate "those early doctrines of the nothingness of space and time, etc." Herbart complains about the confusions created by Kant's usage, not least because he uses the term "idealism" to describe his own "transcendental idealism".

That Herbart regards transcendental idealism as the solution to these contradictions is apparent from section §10, 'Idealismus'. For here we learn that there are two realms, a realm of appearance (*Schein*) and realm of being, which is that of "intelligible nature" (205). Herbart insists that these two worlds are completely separate: that, though the realm of being appears through the form of appearance, it cannot explain anything in that realm, either individually or collectively. But there must be something that carries or bears the realm of appearance, and that is some representing being. The sharp division between noumena and phenomena, being and appearance, suggests that the contradictions involved in the basic concepts of experience are resolvable through something like the Kantian strategy in the dynamical antinomies: making the thesis apply to things-in-themselves, the antithesis to appearances. Though Herbart never states that he is employing such a strategy, it is consistent with his general adoption of transcendental idealism (i.e. the distinction between appearances and things-in-themselves) and his insistence that the antinomies be resolved through the method of relations.

The transcendental idealism that emerges from the *Hauptpuncte der Metaphysik* is Kantian in its broad outlines. It adopts the central Kantian distinction between things-in-themselves and appearances, which Kant uses to define his own transcendental idealism. It also maintains that we have knowledge of appearances alone, that things-in-themselves are forever inaccessible to us. *Prima facie* Herbart comes to these very Kantian conclusions from very non-Kantian premises, from the analysis of the concepts of being, substance, change and power. The Transcendental Aesthetic, which is so central to Kant's transcendental idealism, plays no role in Herbart's. Yet, from another perspective, even Herbart's premises are Kantian, because he comes to his distinction between appearances and things-in-themselves by extending the strategy of the Antinomies to the concepts of experience. The *modus operandi* of Herbart's book is indeed to bring the antinomies of the Transcendental Dialectic right into the realm of experience itself.

Still, Herbart's transcendental idealism is not exactly or entirely Kant's. There is a greater element of realism in Herbart's transcendental idealism insofar as it stresses the givenness and irreducibility of the particular qualities of the manifold of sense. My world is not simply reducible to the realm of my consciousness because that consciousness arises from my interaction with other beings which disturb my pure activity. Hence Herbart writes about his own "strict realism" (*strenge Realismus*), according to which the appearances of representing beings arise from "the most colourful mixture of disturbances" involved in their interaction with one another (§14; 215–216). To this extent, then, those who ascribe realism to Herbart are not entirely wrong; it's just that his realism has to be placed in the context of his transcendental idealism as a whole.

7. The Idea of Philosophy

The Göttingen years were Herbart's most productive. Having overcome the crisis of his Bremen days and eager to make a name for himself, Herbart began to publish one book after another. In 1806 he published not only the *Hauptpuncte der Metaphysik* but also his *Allgemeine Pädagogik*, which put forward his educational ideas in systematic form.[84] Shortly after both these works appeared, he published another shorter one on philosophy, his *Ueber philosophisches Studium*, which appeared in 1807.[85] In style, expression and audience this work is the very opposite of the *Hauptpuncte*: it is clear and straightforward, directed not towards the initiated but the novice. Its aim is pedagogic: to introduce the student to the goals and methods of philosophy.

Apart from its pedagogic value, *Ueber philosophisches Studium* has an important place in Herbart's intellectual development. It was his first systematic attempt to define his conception of philosophy and its methodology. Though it is not so explicit, Herbart's account is partisan, indeed polemical. He sets forward his conception of philosophy in deliberate opposition against the speculative idealism of Fichte and Schelling, and in doing so falls back on the Kantian tradition. Herbart's conception of philosophy in this work is decidedly Kantian in spirit, anticipating ideas common in the neo-Kantian tradition. To see the roots of neo-Kantianism, we should study Herbart's text, not Trendelenburg's *Logische Untersuchungen*.

Herbart begins by rejecting the view, which was characteristic of speculative idealism, that philosophy should provide the first principles of all knowledge, or that it should be the foundation for all the sciences. Rather than starting with first principles, which it grounds on an esoteric intellectual intuition, philosophy should start with the examination of the logic of our ordinary concepts and the principles of the special sciences (234). It is not that Herbart thinks that everything is in order with these concepts and principles as they stand, and that the philosopher should do nothing more than comment upon them. Rather, he insists that philosophy must be a *critical* examination of these concepts and principles. All too often some of them—viz., being, activity, cause, continuity—raise paradoxes and contradictions, and it is the task of the philosopher to resolve them. True to the Kantian tradition, Herbart rejects both empiricism and rationalism as one-sided strategies for solving these problems. Empiricism tries to escape these problems, as if experience were given and unproblematic, while rationalism attempts to solve them on the basis of some higher principles that transcend experience. Neither approach works: empiricism needs to resort to rational analysis to solve problems; and the abstract principles of rationalism are empty if they are not based on experience. Proper philosophical method, Herbart implies, involves the abstract reasoning of rationalism *combined with* the reference to experience of empiricism.

Like many modern philosophers, Herbart sees philosophy as a problem-solving enterprise. It should first and foremost focus on the problems raised by ordinary discourse and the principles of the special sciences. Its task is then to find "the true construction of a problem", that is, to see all the factors that compose it and the requirements for its solution (237). The true method of philosophy should be "pure

---

[84] Johann Friedrich Herbart, *Allgemeine Pädagogik* (Göttingen: Röwer, 1806), SW II, 1–139.
[85] Johann Friedrich Herbart, *Ueber philosophisches Studium* (Göttingen: Dieterich, 1807). All references in parentheses are to SW, II, 227–296.

self-surrender to the nature of the problem" (*reine Hingebung an die Natur des Problems*). Or, as Herbart puts it more simply: "Speculation is the striving toward the resolution of problems" (267). This does not mean, however, that philosophy should be nothing more than piece-meal problem solving. Herbart insists on the value of striving for greater unity of knowledge, on the need to construct a general system in which all partial perspectives are organized into a coherent whole (249). Yet at the same time he also warns about the pitfalls of premature system-building: it forces the data of experience into preconceived moulds, and it prematurely ends enquiry (243–244). The striving for a system should move forward, he advises, only insofar as it can correct itself.

No less than Fries, Herbart recommends an analytic method for philosophy, one that begins with "the bathos of experience", the analysis of ordinary concepts and concrete intuitions. The philosopher needs to immerse himself into his subject matter, sinking into "the black night of eternal death and the furious fires of hell" (239). After his experience he should form a "basic concept" (*Hauptbegriff*) to articulate what he has seen, and which will serve as the starting point of his investigation. He should explore the logic of this concept, all the while testing its implications against the particulars of experience (240–241). In forming his basic concept the philosopher will have to rely on intuition; but this intuition should be simply a provisional starting point for later critical reflection. On no account does it provide a rationale or evidence for a first principle, as an intellectual intuition is supposed to do. Herbart envisages many different starting points for a philosophical investigation, where each starting point depends on the philosopher's individual "standpoint" or "attitude" (*Ansicht*). But the variety of these viewpoints, he stresses, should be taken as an opportunity rather than a problem. The best philosophical system will be one that brings together all basic concepts, all partial standpoints, which together form the truth (245).

The title and timing of Herbart's work indicate that he intended it to compete with Schelling's earlier lectures on philosophical method.[86] Sure enough, much of the work consists in a polemic against the methods of "the two great men", who, though unnamed, are unmistakably Fichte and Schelling. Herbart takes exception chiefly to their a priori methods, their appeal to intellectual intuitions to justify their first principles, their imposition of abstract schemata upon the wealth of particular facts, and their beginning philosophy with abstract principles or concepts, viz., the absolute or the ego, which are not derived from experience (254, 271). While Herbart thinks that philosophy should indeed aspire to systematic unity, he thinks that it is important to realize that this unity is only for us as knowers and that it need not correspond to reality itself; he again insists upon distinguishing between the *ratio cognoscendi* and *ratio essendi*, the order of knowledge and being, just as he once did in his critique of

---

[86] See F.W.J. Schelling, *Vorlesungen über die Methode des akademischen Studiums* (Tübingen: Cotta, 1803). In Schelling, *Sämtliche Werke* V, 211–352. Schelling lectures were originally given in the Summer Semester of 1802 at the University of Jena.

Schelling. What distinguishes philosophy from other disciplines, Herbart insists, is that it is *second-order*, an investigation into our concepts of things rather than things themselves (274).

In the course of his polemic against Fichte and Schelling, Herbart announces his departure from a fundamental doctrine of the idealist tradition: the unity of reason (259–60, 275). Though the aspiration towards systematic unity is indispensable, there is one basic dualism that no system will ever surmount: that between norm and fact, between practice and theory. There is no "principle of unification" for such distinct kinds of discourse, Herbart contends (285–286). He thinks that both Fichte and Schelling have confused this distinction: Fichte by attempting to derive experience from the moral law; and Schelling by introducing a teleological perspective into nature (255–259).

For all his critique of idealist methodology, Herbart still does not break with it entirely. On one important score he is still a follower of Fichte: in his use of a dialectical method. In his *Grundlage der gesamten Wissenschaftslehre* Fichte had applied a combined method of analysis and synthesis to discover and resolve contradictions between concepts. Herbart took this as the inspiration for his "method of relations",[87] which he first expounded in his *Hauptpuncte* and now reaffirms in *Ueber philosophisches Studium*.[88] As Herbart now explains it, the method of relations consists in the progressive analysis of a concept by finding the middle terms between its components (273). A middle term C that connects A and B is determined by analysis to be connected to A and B only by virtue of another term C', which connects C to A and C to B; and so on. Given his ban on a priori methodologies, it is somewhat surprising to see Herbart following Fichte on such an important score. Herbart believes, however, that his use of this method is more "critical" than that of his predecessors, that is, he regards it as strictly a method of exposition rather than one of discovery.

8. Aesthetic Foundation of Ethics

The final work of Herbart's Göttingen years was his *Allgemeine praktische Philosophie*, which was published in 1808.[89] This work laid down the basis for his ethics, just as the *Hauptpuncte* set forth the foundation for his metaphysics. True to his insistence on maintaining a firm distinction between the normative and natural, the practical and theoretical, Herbart makes metaphysics and ethics two distinct domains of philosophy. They are for him not just separate parts but equal co-ordinate ones. Fichte was as wrong to subordinate the theoretical to the ethical as Spinoza was to subordinate

---

[87] Herbart admits its Fichtean provenance in his 'Über philosophisches Wissen und philosophisches Studium', SW I, 94. Just how his method follows and differs from Fichte's is a complicated matter that we cannot explore here.

[88] Cf. *Ueber philosophsiches Studium*, SW II, 273 and *Hauptpuncte der Metaphysik*, SW II, 181–182.

[89] Herbart, SW II, 333–354. It is worthwhile supplementing the introduction with Herbart's handwritten remarks on the text, which appear in SW II, 464–470.

the ethical to the theoretical. Though insisting on their equal status, Herbart devoted most of his time and energy to metaphysics and the theoretical branches of philosophy. The *Allgemeine praktische Philosophie* was his only systematic work on ethics.

There is something of a mystery to Herbart's ethics. For he had insisted that, of all parts of his philosophy, it showed his greatest debts to Kant.[90] Yet in ethics Herbart departs from Kant in the most fundamental ways: he denies that there is a single principle of morality; he insists that reason is not the source of moral obligation; he maintains that obligation has to be determined on the basis of particular situations; and he bases morals on aesthetics. Where, then, lies the debt to Kant? We can only imagine Kant reciting that old Italian saying he had once applied to Fichte: "May God protect us from our friends; against our enemies we can take care of ourselves."[91] The solution to the mystery, as we shall soon see, is that Herbart constructed his ethics from building blocks taken from Kant's aesthetics.

Herbart's best account of his foundation for morality appears in the introduction to the *Allgemeine praktische Philosophie*. He begins with the classic problem of ethics: whether something should be good because we desire it, or whether we should desire it because it is good (334). Herbart's solution sides with the latter alternative. Although he recognizes that values by their very nature involve human desires, he denies that values are determined by desire alone (335). Indeed, he insists that the good takes precedence over desire. For it is only on that basis that it is possible to judge and value desires themselves. It is the "basic presupposition" of practical philosophy, he maintains, that there be such a thing as "will-less valuation" (*Willenlose Schätzung*) (335).

Though fundamental, this presupposition is undermined by every prevalent form of ethics, in Herbart's view. There are three current theories about the foundation of ethics: a theory of the good (*Güterlehre*), which bases ethics on the good; a theory of virtue (*Tugendlehre*), which founds it on virtue; and a theory of duty (*Pflichtenlehre*), which gives primacy to duty. Herbart rejects all three, because they share one common faulty assumption. That assumption is that the will is primary, the basic rule and source of value (337). Thus the theory of the good assumes that the good is the goal of the will; the theory of virtue makes the will the supreme power behind virtue; and the theory of duty assumes that the will is the source of duty, the supreme commander (338). The fundamental problem with this assumption, Herbart argues, is that it becomes impossible to judge the will (338). These theories do not go far enough in their search for the source of morality, because they do not enquire into the basis of the value of the will itself (337–338).

Herbart's position will make more sense if we see it as a critique of Kant's concept of autonomy. Kant had made the third formulation of the moral law his principle of autonomy, according to which a human being is "subject only to laws which are made

---

[90]   See Herbart's 'Rede, gehalten an Kants Geburtstage, den 22 April', in SW III, 69.
[91]   See Kant's 'Erklärung gegen Fichtes *Wissenschaftslehre*', *Schriften* XII, 370–371.

by himself", so that the subject "is bound only to act in conformity with a will which is his own".[92] Herbart finds this conception problematic because a will that makes the laws also can break them; it stands above all responsibility and accountability since it can by sheer fiat invalidate any law that would dare to pronounce a sentence against it; as the sovereign source of law itself, such a will can "loosen" just as easily as it can "bind". Of course, Kant insists that the moral will is rational, that its laws should be universalizable, binding everyone's desires and inclinations on all occasions. But, rejecting the categorical imperative as a sufficient criterion of morality, Herbart doubts that the Kantian will can have a rational content; there are all kinds of universalizable imperatives, depending on the will from which one begins.[93] Given the emptiness of the Kantian criterion, the sheer formality of the universalizability requirement, the Kantian will becomes a serious danger, having the power to make virtually anything into a universal law. Since the will cannot regulate itself, there needs to be some higher source of moral authority. Herbart's practical philosophy was his attempt to determine that source.

Given that practical philosophy has to be based on will-less valuation, on judgement that has authority over the will, what kind of valuation or judgement should that be? Without providing any argument, Herbart simply declares that this kind of valuation or judgement should be aesthetic.[94] Morality should take from aesthetics, he advises, a model of judgement that is independent of the will, and which has authority over it (390). *Prima facie* aesthetic judgement satisfies this requirement, because it determines something to be beautiful or sublime even if it is not an object of desire or the will. Though Herbart does not refer to Kant here, his reliance on Kant's theory of aesthetic judgement is obvious, indeed so much so that he probably felt no need to point it out. In the third *Kritik* Kant had famously argued that judgements of taste are independent of interest, and that their pleasure comes strictly from the act of contemplation (intuition or reflection) alone.[95] Since aesthetic judgements are disinterested, and since interest involves desire or will, aesthetic judgements are also independent of desire and the will.[96] This doctrine of disinterested aesthetic contemplation was one of the crucial building blocks of Herbart's own ethics.

We can explain Herbart's appeal to aesthetic judgement as a solution to the problem of moral obligation if we consider it as a response to Kant's confessed failure to

---

[92] *Grundlegung zur Metaphysik der Sitten, Schriften* IV, 432.

[93] Herbart does not explicitly reject the categorical imperative as a criterion of morality in the introduction to the *Allgemeine praktische Philosophie*; however, in the handwritten remarks he states that Kant's attempt to make the mere form of the law into the criterion of morality naively assumes that an immoral will will attempt to make an exception for itself. See SW II, 477.

[94] As we have seen in Section 4 of this chapter, Herbart does provide something of an argument in his earlier essay 'Ueber die ästhetische Darstellung der Welt'. There he argues that the source of obligation cannot be practical or theoretical and therefore has to be aesthetic as the only remaining alternative. See SW I, 264. Herbart does not repeat or refer to this argument in the *Allgemeine praktische Philosophie*.

[95] Kant, *Kritik der Urteilskraft*, §2, V, 204.

[96] Kant, *Kritik der Urteilskraft*, §4, V, 207; §5, V, 210.

resolve that problem. In the third section of the *Grundlegung* Kant admitted that he could provide no explanation for why we should take an interest in the idea of moral-ity, or for why we should subject ourselves to the moral law. Granted, it is rational to act on the categorical imperative; but that still begs the question why I should be rational. As Kant explained:

Why should I subject myself to this principle [the moral law], and indeed as a rational being in general? I readily concede that no interest *drives* me, for that would not give a categori-cal imperative; but I must still *take* an interest and see how that happens; for this obligation (*Sollen*) is properly a willing (*Wollen*), which holds for every rational being under the condi-tion that reason is practical in him without any hindrance … If someone asks why the univer-sality of our maxim as a law should be the limiting condition of our action, and upon what we base the worth that we attribute to it, we cannot give him any answer.[97]

Citing this very passage,[98] Herbart takes it as evidence that Kant has not taken his enquiries far enough. He accepts Kant's point that the interest in the moral law can-not derive from sensibility, from any inclination, need or desire, because that would destroy the integrity of the moral law, which demands that duty should be the *sole* motive for our action. He also recognizes that the interest cannot derive from rea-son, given that the question is what interest we should take in being rational. What, then, should provide an interest in acting according to reason? It is precisely here that Herbart thinks that aesthetics comes to the aid of moral philosophy. It is aesthetics alone that can explain why we should take an interest in morality. An aesthetic inter-est is neither sensible nor rational but something in between: it gives us a disinterested pleasure in witnessing morally good actions, and indeed in inspiring us to do them. It is the beautiful and the sublime that motivates and inspires us to act morally. Here again Herbart can be seen to be developing an idea already implicit in Kant, who had himself stressed the moral dimension of the idea of the sublime.[99] Kant came close to an aesthetic point of view in morality, Herbart maintains, when he set forth the idea of humanity as an end in itself.[100] That idea presupposes the idea of dignity, which also invokes that of the sublime, the idea of a value transcending all the forces of nature.

Though basing much of his theory on Kant, Herbart goes on to provide his own account of aesthetic judgement. He declares that he is especially concerned to sepa-rate aesthetic from moral judgement, so that it never collapses back into the moral, and so that it never loses its authority over the will (341). He finds two basic differ-ences between aesthetic and moral judgement. First, the representation of the beauti-ful or sublime in aesthetic judgement should be singular and complete, whereas the

---

[97] Kant, *Grundlegung zur Metaphysik der Sitten, Schriften* IV, 449–450. The translation above is taken from Herbart's inaccurate citation of Kant.

[98] In the handwritten remarks to *Allgemeine praktische Philosophie*, SW II, 479–480.

[99] In sections §27 (V, 257–259) and §28 (V, 261) of the *Kritik der Urteilskraft* Kant explains that the pleasure we take in the sublime arises from our awareness of our moral powers transcending the world of sense. In section §59 (V, 362) he famously states that beauty is a symbol of the morally good.

[100] Herbart, SW II, 478.

representation of the good in moral judgement is general and incomplete (343–344). Second, the representation of the object in an aesthetic judgement must be separate from our attitude towards it, whether we approve or disapprove it, whereas the representation of the good in moral judgement involves our approval of it (344). Herbart qualifies this last point regarding aesthetic judgement: it is only the *content* that we perceive with indifference; the *relations* between its content are immediately perceived with approval or disapproval (345). He gives this example from music: though we are indifferent to any particular sound, we perceive the combination of sounds with either pleasure or displeasure. For Herbart, as indeed for Kant, the special object of aesthetic appraisal is form. He envisages a science of aesthetics that determines the most basic forms and which kinds of pleasures are connected with them (345).

Pursuing his aesthetic analogy, Herbart maintains that moral judgement is based on what he calls "moral taste".[101] Taste in general he defines as a power of perceiving and judging particular forms or unique relations between things (350). Just as a form of taste, moral judgement is not different from other kinds of taste, namely, poetic, musical and plastic (347). Like aesthetic taste, it perceives and judges particular relations or unique forms. Excellence in moral taste, just like that of aesthetic taste, requires sensitivity to the particular features of objects—what Hume called "delicacy" and Herbart calls "tenderness of feeling" (*Zartheit des Gefühls*) (353). Moral taste does have, however, some distinctive features of its own apart from aesthetic taste. What is distinctive about it is that it judges desire itself and not simply (as other forms of taste) the object of desire (348). It concerns especially our own inner states and not simply objects outside us (347–348). Its special concern is the human will, and specifically how these wills relate to one another in particular circumstances.

The most obvious problem for an aesthetic theory of morality is that it seems to forfeit the universality required of moral judgement. Judgements of taste are notoriously personal and contradictory, so that there seems no hope of deriving the universality of moral judgements. Herbart considers the objection in some detail in a special section of his introduction.[102] His response to it is surprising and dramatic: that we should just drop the universality requirement in moral judgement. The ideal of a fundamental moral principle that provides a standard of judgement for all circumstances is illusory, he argues. He comes to this conclusion *not* from a critique of the Kantian categorical imperative—though that does lie at the back of his mind—but from an appreciation of the fact that moral judgements always concern very complex and unique circumstances. "Human life is much too colourful for us to know a priori all the simple relations of the will and how they will encounter one another." (351) Herbart does allow for a minimal kind of universalizability, and does not permit the possibility of conflicting judgements about the same case; he insists

---

[101] The phrase is redolent of the moral sense school. In a reply to a review of his book, however, Herbart distanced himself from that school. See SW II, 514.

[102] Herbart, 'Wiefern kann der praktische Philosophie Allgemeinheit zukommen?', SW II, 349–354.

upon consistency, that people should judge alike in the exact same circumstances. The problem is that when we specify the circumstances, all the factors making for the judgement, the law ceases to be very general at all; it is universalizable only in the sense that it is consistent but not in the sense that it is general (350). Hence the lack of generality is more a strength than a weakness of an aesthetic theory of morality. For the aesthetic theory rightly emphasizes the particularity and uniqueness of the object of moral judgement. Just as aesthetic judgement concerns a particular work of art, so moral judgement concerns a particular action under particular circumstances.

Although Herbart stresses the unique situations of moral life, he does not throw overboard all general rules and guidelines in ethics. While there is no general principle of morality that will be sufficient in all cases, there are still many general guidelines that we might or might not want to apply in a particular situation, depending on the exact circumstances of the case. We can form general moral concepts when we focus on the similarities between different cases and abstract from the peculiarities of the particular circumstances. These general concepts Herbart calls "practical ideas", which we acquire not through induction but by an act of intellectual rather than sensible intuition (352).[103] The rest of Herbart's ethics is then devoted to outlining the specific ideas governing our practical life, though an account of them goes well beyond our purposes here.

9. Professor in Königsberg

Though Herbart was happy in Göttingen, and so much so that he even declined an offer from Heidelberg, his happiness was not to last. Political events soon cast a cloud over his future there. After Napoleon's victory over Prussia in the battles of Jena and Auerstadt in October 1806, Prussia lost control of all its territories west of the Elbe, first and foremost among them Hannover, which now became a puppet kingdom of Napoleon's brother Jérome. Göttingen was within the principality of Hannover, and so now came under French rule. Though the new French government professed to protect the university and to guarantee academic freedom, the university was forced, on short notice, to raise enormous sums of money to lend to the government. This "Zwangsanleihe", or compulsory loan, brought the University to the verge of financial ruin. To add insult to injury, the new government also abolished the old tax exemptions for professors, who were now forced to pay "back taxes". Herbart himself had to pay the new government, within twenty days, 1,500 francs, an enormous sum for him, which he could raise only by borrowing from his old friend Smidt.[104] As a result of these events, and the glum prospect of renewed French exploitation,

---

[103] The introduction of intellectual intuition here is still consistent with Herbart's disputation thesis "*Intellectualis intuitio nulla est*" (SW I, 278). The intellectual intuition he forbids is the Schellingian kind whose object is the "*An-sich*", that is, the universal substance or absolute. The intellectual intuition he permits is the intuition of practical ideas.

[104] See Herbart to Smidt, January 17, 1808, SW XVII, 3.

the general mood in Göttingen was very bleak.[105] It seemed that Göttingen had no future—especially so for Herbart. Not only was there the oppression of living under French rule, but there was also the realization that all his plans for the reform of the university would come to nothing. All his pedagogical hopes and ideals were now dashed. To escape it all, Herbart longed to leave Göttingen. As he told Smidt, February 15, 1808: "Everything is now so bleak–I often seriously think of getting *completely* away from this place."[106]

Thus it came almost as deliverance, when, entirely unexpectedly on October 1808, Herbart received news of an impending offer from the University of Königsberg.[107] The first successor to Kant's chair, Wilhelm Traugott Krug, had accepted an offer from Leipzig, thus leaving Kant's throne vacant. Because of his writings, success with students and expertise in pedagogy, Herbart seemed to the Prussian authorities the best man for the job. His knowledge of pedagogy, they noted, was especially valuable for the reform of education in Prussia. After some quick and easy negotiations, Herbart accepted the offer, 1,100 thalers, which was enough to remove all his financial worries and debts. For the next twenty-four years (1809–1833), Herbart would remain in Königsberg, which would be the apex of his academic career.

For Herbart, the call from Königsberg was the fulfilment of a boyhood dream. Now he really would be the successor of the philosopher whom he had venerated since childhood! Such was the gist of the happy news he conveyed to Smidt in December 1808:

I am once again going to be a Prussian subject. Doubtless you will recall that we Göttingers were that once; then against our will. But now Krug in Königsberg has had the honor of being called to Leipzig . . . and so for me I now have the unexpected luck of getting that place that I so often dreamed of as a youth when I studied the works of the Königsberg sage! To be sure, in those days things stood differently with the Kantian philosophy and the Prussian monarchy; but in both there is still something that greatly attracts me . . . I will happily see it as a duty of the position to preserve the memory of Kant.[108]

After resigning from Göttingen, Herbart undertook the long journey to Königsberg in mid-March 1809. Along the way he stopped in Berlin to see Fichte, who, despite their disagreements, received his old student warmly, introducing him to the Prussian authorities as "a man of intelligence and many talents."[109] Herbart arrived in Königsberg by the middle of April, in plenty of time to celebrate Kant's

---

[105] See Herbart to von Halen, July 1808, SW XVII, 10; and Herbart to Carl von Steiger, April 1808, SW XVII, 6.

[106] See Herbart to Smidt, February 15, 1808, SW XVII, 6.

[107] All the documents surrounding Herbart's appointment are in SW XIV, 1–20.

[108] Herbart, SW XVII, 28.

[109] See Fichte to Karl Freiherr von Altenstein, April 2, 1809, in J.G. Fichte, *Briefwechsel*, ed. Hans Schulz (Leipzig: Haessel, 1930) II, 530–531; and Fichte to Friedrich Stägemann, April 2, 1809, Fichte, *Briefwechsel*, II, 531–532.

birthday, which was honoured every April 22 by Kant's old *"Tischgenossen"*. Among the guests, Herbart, as Kant's successor, now took a place of honour.

Just what the Kantian legacy meant to Herbart in these days is apparent from a speech he gave several years later on the occasion of Kant's birthday.[110] To assess Kant's remarkable achievements, Herbart notes, we first have to place him in the context of his time. Philosophy in the period before Kant was devoted to the cause of enlightenment, to making philosophy popular for the general public, and it had ignored or neglected fundamental problems. Rather than thinking through problems, which challenge our ordinary intuitions and feelings, it would simply appeal to common sense and have done with the matter. Hume's scepticism aroused more dumb astonishment than serious thinking. It was Kant's great contribution, Herbart maintains, to have returned philosophy to its fundamental problems, to have made it take seriously once again scepticism and its challenges to our ordinary view of the world. Rather than fearing the direction and results of radical thinking, Kant would fearlessly investigate an issue regardless of the consequences. We must never underestimate, and we should forever cherish, Herbart thinks, the critical dimension of his philosophy, which insists that we constantly ask the questions: "How much do I know?" and "What is it that I know?" (64). But Kant's critique went beyond a mere examination of previous philosophy, of this or that special system or school of thought; for it was first and foremost a critique of reason itself. This critique of reason is most apparent, Herbart maintains, in the antinomies, where Kant discovers the necessary contradictions in reason itself (65, 67). Herbart stresses that the antinomies are no mere sceptical trope, that they are not some easily resolvable puzzle or paradox. Rather, they are endemic to the very enterprise of metaphysics, which inevitably gets caught in contradictions whenever it thinks about the basic concepts of experience (67). Still, despite standing far above his own age, we must never forget, Herbart advises us, that Kant too was a child of his own time. As much as he did to overthrow the prejudices and dogmatism of his own day, he was still to some extent captive to them. For Herbart, this is especially apparent in Kant's psychology, which still clung to the old faculty psychology. About that psychology, Herbart openly declares: "here I must confess frankly my regret that such a great mind had to be bound in such shackles!" (68)

Herbart's early years in Königsberg are marked by two developments: his growing identification with Kant and his increasing alienation from the general direction of German philosophy.[111] The two trends were tightly interwoven: Herbart saw Kant's legacy as the bulwark and remedy against the excesses of contemporary German philosophy. That philosophy, as Herbart saw it, was dominated by his old

---

[110] 'Rede, gehalten an Kants Geburtstage, den 22 April, 1810', SW III, 59–71. The speech was first published in the *Königsberger Archiv*, 1812.

[111] He expressed this alienation shortly before going to Königsberg. See his November 1808 letter to C.L. Reinhold, SW XVII, 23.

nemesis, his erstwhile rival for Fichte's attention and recognition: Schelling. There were, in his view, two corrupting forces behind Schelling's influence. First, his formalism and a priori methodology, especially his tendency to explain everything by imposing some a priori conceptual scheme upon it. Rather than examining things for their own sake, Schelling began with general principles and described all facts in their terms. Second, his mysticism, a tendency deriving from appeals to intellectual intuition. Herbart expressed his misgivings about Schelling in a polemical essay, *Ueber die Unangreifbarkeit der Schellingschen Lehre*, which he published in 1813.[112] Here Herbart declared that there was not much point in refuting Schelling's philosophy, which was a task already performed by Fries and Köppen.[113] The problem was not in refuting Schelling but in explaining why, despite such thorough refutations, Schelling's philosophy still managed to persist as a corrupting force. Herbart's chief explanation for the persistence of Schelling's philosophy was its appeals to intellectual intuition. These were not only popular, because they avoided the need for hard thinking, but they were also irrefutable. Who could question an intellectual intuition if it was esoteric, the privilege of a talented elite? Herbart charges the Schellingians with dogmatism because they fail to ask basic questions about how they know their intuitions to be true. If the Schellingians only took to heart Kant's call for criticism, they would never have dared to presume to be in possession of infallible intuitions. Herbart does not dispute that intuition is often a sound starting point in philosophy; but he insists that it cannot be the end point, because intuitions have to be refined and elaborated into concepts, judgements and inferences, which are indeed subject to criticism. Much of Herbart's polemic in this piece is reminiscent of Kant's famous essay *Von einem neuerdings erhobenen vornehmen Tone in der Philosophie*, where Kant once railed against the esotericism and dogmatism of Platonic intellectual intuitions.[114] Fighting the pretensions of mysticism was another score on which Herbart could identify with the Kantian legacy.

All Herbart's alienation from contemporary German philosophy came to a head in a pamphlet he wrote in 1814, *Ueber meinen Streit mit der Modephilosophie dieser Zeit*.[115] The pamphlet was an act of self-defence against two reviews of two of his recent books, his *Allgemeine Pädagogik* and his *Lehrbuch zur Einleitung in die Philosophie*. *Modephilosophie*, it is not surprising, turns out be the philosophy of Schelling, whose corrupting influence Herbart detects in his anonymous reviewer. Laying aside all Herbart's rhetoric and bluster against intellectual fashion, one fundamental

---

[112] Herbart, *Ueber die Unangreifbarkeit der Schellingschen Lehre* (Königsberg: Degen, 1813). In SW III, 241–258.
[113] This piece stands in marked contrast to Herbart's early essays on Schelling when he praised Schelling's writings as expositions of idealism. Disingenuously, Herbart tells his audience that he never bothered to write against Schelling (III, 252).
[114] Kant, *Schriften* VIII, 387–406.
[115] Herbart, *Ueber meinen Streit mit der Modephilosophie dieser Zeit* (Königsberg: Unzer, 1814). SW III, 311–352.

philosophical issue emerges from his pamphlet. Namely, how are we to define philosophy? In his *Lehrbuch* Herbart defined philosophy as "the cultivation of concepts" (*die Bearbeitung der Begriffe*).[116] The reviewer took exception to this because he felt that philosophy should deal straightaway with reality itself, not simply with our concepts of reality. Like a good Schellingian, he wanted the philosopher to grasp reality immediately through an intuition. Herbart's response to this criticism reveals how much he prefers Kant's legacy to the fashionable philosophy of his day:

> It is a well known fact that, if there is to be knowledge for us, we know *only through representations,* and that in all philosophizing we deal immediately only with our representations. Whoever forgets this, and wants to jump right away into reality, lands in that old morass from which Kant with great effort rescued his contemporaries. (325)

Before this passage, Herbart provides a short statement of his own philosophical *credo,* where he makes it entirely plain that he accepts the basic principles of Kant's transcendental idealism: that all our inner and outer intuitions are representations within us, and that they do not provide us with knowledge of things in themselves (320). If we put this statement in its context, namely Herbart's opposition to Schelling, it becomes clear how much he opposed his own transcendental idealism to Schelling's absolute idealism. While transcendental idealism is critical, not assuming that our representations of things directly reveal things themselves, absolute idealism is dogmatic, assuming that we have an immediate and direct grasp of reality in itself through intellectual intuition. This statement should be noted well by those scholars who classify Herbart as a realist and who assume he is opposed to transcendental idealism.

10. Psychology

Now that we have placed Herbart in Kant's chair in Königsberg, it seems that our story about his path to Kant might well come to a close. We have already taken stock of the deep Kantian dimension of his philosophy: his transcendental idealism, his critical conception of philosophy, his reformation of ethics through Kantian aesthetics. What more could we possibly add to make Herbart more Kantian? We might as well crown his head with Kant's peruke! Yet there is one more factor to ponder in examining Herbart's relationship to Kant, and we would be remiss not to consider it. This is Herbart's psychology. It is here that Herbart's relationship to Kant becomes especially fraught and critical. Herbart not only thinks Kant failed as a psychologist, but that the foundation of his philosophy has to be based on a new psychology. So, to have a completely balanced picture of that relationship, we need to know something about Herbart's psychology.

---

[116] Herbart, *Lehrbuch zur Einleitung in die Philosophie,* §4, SW IV, 38–39.

Though Herbart's later reputation rested mainly on his psychology, it was only in his Königsberg period that he fully devoted himself to the subject. Reflections on psychology were always an integral part of his early epistemological and pedagogical writings, so psychology was never far from his central concerns. Still, before Königsberg, Herbart wrote little specifically devoted to the subject. There is a short section on psychology in the *Hauptpuncte der Metaphysik*,[117] though little more.

Herbart's first systematic work on psychology is his *Lehrbuch zur Psychologie*, which first appeared in 1816.[118] Although intended as only a compendium for his lectures, the *Lehrbuch* is still a historically significant text. It is here that Herbart first launched his attack on faculty psychology, which made him famous; and it is here that he first sketched the doctrines that he would put forward in his 1824 *Psychologie als Wissenschaft*, which is his major work on psychology. In some respects the *Lehrbuch* is the more revealing text, because it explains premises presupposed in the later work.

The preface and introduction to the *Lehrbuch* are very revealing about Herbart's views on the method of psychology and its place in the sciences. We learn right away that psychology is not an independent empirical science but only one part of philosophy. Herbart indeed conceives of his textbook as part of a larger course preparing the student for philosophy. According to his classification of the sciences,[119] psychology is a form of applied metaphysics, and only one of three such forms, along with physics and physiology. Still, psychology is the most important of these forms, and it is of special importance to philosophy in general. Why? This, Herbart explains, is for two reasons. First, because it is necessary to raise the psychological question of the possibility of knowledge; and second, because psychology has been used as a weapon in philosophy against all kinds of prejudices, though it is laden with prejudices itself. Both these points mean, Herbart concludes, that improving psychology is "a basic condition of correcting the errors in all parts of philosophy" (297).

Herbart thinks that the method of psychology should be, as far as possible, like that of the other empirical sciences. Namely, it should be what he calls "rational empirics", that is, the method of deriving laws from observations, and then from these laws making predictions and further observations (§4; 304). Herbart's psychology is intentionally naturalistic, attempting to explain the mind according to natural laws, so that it is part of the general fabric of nature. Hence he states that the goal of psychology should be to provide "a natural history of the mind" (303; §3 Anm. 2). On no account, however, does Herbart intend his psychology to be materialistic: subsumption under

---

[117] See Herbart, *Hauptpuncte der Metaphysik*, §13, 'Elemente einer künftige Psychologie', SW II, 210–215.

[118] Johann Friedrich Herbart, *Lehrbuch zur Psychologie* (Königsberg: August Wilhelm Unzer, 1816). SW IV, 295–436. All references in parentheses are to the edition in SW. The first number is to the page, the second to the paragraph, indicated by the '§' sign. 'Anm.' designates 'Anmerkung', a remark appended to a paragraph.

[119] For this classification, see the 'Encyklopädische Uebersicht der Psychologie und Naturphilosophie', in the *Lehrbuch zur Einleitung in die Philosophie*, SW IV, 233, §134 and IV, 264, §140.

laws of nature does not mean for him subsumption under laws of matter. In any case, matter, true to his transcendental idealism, turns out to be nothing more than appearance (365; §114).

Despite prescribing a strict methodology, Herbart is not very sanguine about the prospects of following it. He warns us that we cannot expect "pure empirics" in psychology, that is, the possibility of describing experience just as given without the intrusion of prior thinking (302; §3).[120] There is no such thing as pure data in psychology, pure facts independent of how we observe them; the mind is not like a lump of clay that exists independent of the sculptor who would form it.[121] Self-observation often distorts the phenomena of consciousness, tears them out of context, and then surrenders them to general concepts (302–303; §3). Herbart flatly denies the classic Cartesian doctrine that inner experience enjoys any epistemic advantages or superiority over outer experience (305; §5). It is just as difficult to know ourselves through introspection as it is to know objects through the external senses. In his scruples about the methods of self-observation Herbart surpasses Fries and Beneke, who were much more naive and self-confident. Such are his doubts, however, that one wonders why he thinks psychology can be a science at all.

To some extent, Herbart addresses this problem. Despite the problems of self-observation, he still maintains that there are some prospects for success in psychology—*provided that* we make certain guiding assumptions. We must assume that mental life consists in particular events, that these events are in constant change, and that they are a manifold within one consciousness. We must also adopt as a working hypothesis that representations are forces whose activities are capable of measurement (306; §6). It is this hypothesis, Herbart thinks, that allows psychology to approach scientific status, because it alone permits a mathematical treatment of psychological phenomena. The ultimate justification of these guiding assumptions, he maintains, lies in metaphysics, whose task is to examine the presuppositions that make empirical psychology possible. So, though Herbart has modest hopes for psychology as an empirical science, he insists that it must have a metaphysical foundation. For these reasons he puts forward his psychology as little more than an "acceptable hypothesis" (306).

The antithesis of empirical psychology, the great obstacle to its realization, Herbart finds in the old faculty psychology, which he regards as a relic of scholasticism. Accordingly, the first part of the *Lehrbuch* is devoted to a thorough critique of the concept of a psychological faculty. The greatest damage to psychology occurs, he complains, when we pass from "what happens in us" to "powers that we have" (303; §3). The attribution of a faculty to similar mental phenomena he likens to a form of mythological thinking; it is as if there were a special animate force behind each kind

---

[120] See 'Herbart's handschriftlich Bemerkungen in seinem Handexemplar des Lehrbuchs zur Psychologie', Anhang 2, SW IV, 614.

[121] See 'Herbart's handschriftlich Bemerkungen', Anhang 2, SW IV, 617.

of natural event, so that just as there is one god for thunder and lightening, another for rain and the harvest, so there is a distinct faculty for each kind of mental phenomena. On no account should we assume that the concept of a faculty is like that of a natural law, as if the faculty works always in specific ways under specific conditions; for the concept is always much too vague for that, applying under all kinds of different conditions.[122] The very idea of a faculty is for Herbart a hypostasis, the reification of an abstract concept. We assume that there is some kind of thing lying behind the concept we use to refer to similar phenomena. Behind Herbart's critique of mental faculties there lies a deep nominalism: "There are no general facts; the true psychological facts lie in the momentary states of the individual; and these are immeasurably far from the height of the general concept: man in general." (310; §11). For this reason, Herbart will begin his own psychology with particular events alone, avoiding all commitment to general concepts not derived from facts.

One faculty theory in particular is the subject of Herbart's wrath in the *Lehrbuch*: the tripartite theory that divides the soul into representing, desiring and feeling. This classification finds its *locus classicus* in Kant, and under his influence it had become very widespread in Herbart's day. Herbart throws a battery of objections against it: that it is based on an incomplete induction; that its distinctions are not firm and clear, so that one phenomena falls under several headings; that it is impossible to regard these powers as separable, as if they could function apart from one another (310–312; §§13–15). The main problem with the theory, though, is that it tears apart the indivisible unity of the mind (311; §15).

Such was Herbart's faith in the importance of psychology that he implicitly subordinates epistemology to psychology, as if there could no question of epistemology being a separate discipline on its own. One reason psychology is such a crucial discipline, he writes, is because of "the *psychological* question of the possibility of knowledge." (297; my italics). The dependence of epistemology upon psychology becomes a prominent theme in the *Lehrbuch*, for here Herbart argues that epistemology will come closer to proper scientific status only through the work of empirical psychology. This point is driven home especially with regard to Kant, who becomes the foil for most of Herbart's objections. We are told in no uncertain terms: "The foundations of Kantian philosophy, if they are to be tenable, must also be a rational empirics" (304). Kant has made all kinds of mistakes in epistemology due to his faulty psychology, namely, it is just false that people represent space as an infinite quantity, that substance and cause are universal principles for understanding experience in all stages of life and culture, that all people have implicit in their moral consciousness a categorical imperative, and so on (304–305; §4 Anm.). Herbart even says that, since Kant, psychology has gone backwards rather than forwards (307; §9 Anm.). Leibniz and Locke put psychology on a better foundation because they at least based it upon

---

[122] See 'Herbart's handschriftlich Bemerkungen', Anhang 2, SW IV, 615–616.

experience, whereas Wolff and Kant spoiled that promising beginning by making psychology into a scholastic discipline. Rather than relying on empirical observation, they followed an a priori method and simply presupposed, and constantly applied, the concept of a faculty. Kant was not only led astray by Wolff: he made things worse by attacking Wolff where he was most plausible, namely, in the idea of the mind as a substance. Instead of tearing apart Wolff's intricate web of faculties, Kant drew it ever more tightly and finely. Herbart's verdict on Kant's psychology could not be more damning:

And so it came to pass that the Kantian doctrine was weakest where it should have been strongest. The critical weapons were sharpened with great finesse; but they were fashioned from a brittle metal which shattered with use, and which must be completely reforged. (308; §9 Anm.).

After his critique of faculty psychology in Part I of the *Lehrbuch*, Herbart turns to the exposition of his positive doctrine in Part II. The guiding assumption behind his psychology, as he now explains it, is that the mind consists in acts of self-preservation which express themselves as representations (364; §112). Herbart refuses to begin his psychology with the soul (*Seele*), which *ex hypothesi* does not exist anywhere or at any particular time, and which is therefore ultimately unknowable (363–364; §§109–111). His psychology will begin, true to his nominalist leanings, with nothing more than particular acts of self-preservation. It will not assume any subject in which these acts inhere, still less will it speculate about their source or origin (370; §125). That said, Herbart does think that he has a metaphysical justification for his guiding assumption: namely, his doctrine, expounded in the *Hauptpuncte,* that essence consists in power (*Kraft*), which consists in acts of self-preservation.[123] We are reminded here, though Herbart does not explicitly mention it, of Leibniz's theory of *nisus,* the striving of each monad towards representation.

We begin, then, with only representations, with acts of striving or self-preservation. These representations do not exist on their own, of course, but stand in relation to one another, which gives rise to a system of striving and counterstriving, action and reaction. Explicitly invoking a physical analogy, Herbart states that representations stand in relations of pressure and counterpressure to one another, just like forces in the physical world (364; §112). Representations are indeed forces themselves, standing in a system of mutual attraction and repulsion like physical forces. Herbart insists, however, that representations become powers (*Kräfte*) only through their relations to one another, and more specifically only when they resist one another (369; §124). None has a power in itself—for that would be only another hypostasis—but only in resisting other representations (370; §124). Each representation must both resist and yield to the pressure of other representations, without which tension it would cease to be a striving, and so even a representation (370; §125).

---

[123] See Part I, Chapter 2, Section 6.

Assuming that each representation is a force, Herbart argues, permits us to ascribe to each a certain degree or quantity, which appears as its clarity or obscurity (370; §126). It is in virtue of this degree or quantity that we can *measure* the force of the representation, and so treat it mathematically. Herbart agrees with Kant that a discipline is a science only to the degree that it permits of mathematics; he disagrees with him, however, that psychology cannot permit mathematics. Once we understand representations as forces, we open the path to their measurement and so their scientific treatment.

Each representation consists in infinitely many smaller ones, or what Herbart calls "elementary apprehensions" (*elementarischen Auffassungen*), the analogue of Leibniz's *petit perceptions* (384; §160). For them to make one representation they must fuse together and form one "*Totalkraft*". Like Leibniz, Herbart thinks that most representations are subconscious, and that they come to consciousness only when the striving of a representation surmounts the resistance against it (372; §130). When a representation reaches a certain degree of strength, it reaches what Herbart calls "the threshold of consciousness" (*Schwelle des Bewußtseins*). There is, however, a limit to the strength of consciousness, Herbart thinks, since no representation is infinite in its strength (384; §159). Hence he proposes his law of decreasing receptivity: that the stronger a representation is, the less its strength increases (384; §159). When we add together all representations of sufficient strength to reach this threshold, we have consciousness itself, which just designates "the totality of all simultaneous actual representations" (372; §130 Anm.).

Having achieved such a reduction of the realm of consciousness to individual representations, Herbart then seems to re-introduce the soul through the backdoor, for we are told in no uncertain terms that "the unity of the soul" is the ground for the opposition of representations, for their forming a system within consciousness (374; §136). The same point is made later when Herbart insists that "the unity of the soul" is the source of the unity of our experience (401; §196 Anm.). The lingering presence of the soul in the background seems a relic of Herbart's Kantian-Fichtean heritage, which scarcely coheres with his teaching elsewhere that representations by themselves form the unity of experience through their laws of interaction (399–400; §194).

Herbart ponders the objection that his psychology is too reductivist because it considers only the quantitative aspects of the mind, leaving aside its qualitative dimension (380–382; §§146–151). Since the qualitative aspect would involve feeling and desire, Herbart attempts to respond to the objection by proposing his own theory of feeling and desire. The soul is called the mind (*Geist*) insofar as it represents something; and it is called the spirit (*Gemüth*) insofar as it feels and desires (380; §146). Herbart then insists: "spirit has its place in the mind". In other words, feeling and desire are functions of representation, and so they too are ultimately capable of quantitative treatment. Herbart explains that feeling and desire are really only specific kinds of representation (382; §151). Desire arises when a representation is driven forth yet held back, events that give rise to an unpleasant feeling, which is the source of desire (381; §149). Feeling occurs when a representation comes forth from its own power and is assisted by other forces so that it is strengthened (381–382; §150). It is ironic here how close Herbart comes to Wolff's own theory of the mind as a *vis representativae,* the power of representation, of which desire and feeling are only aspects or functions. The Kantian tripartite theory, which has been the target of so much of Herbart's criticism, grew out of the critique of this Wolffian theory, whose simple scheme, Kant argued, could not accommodate the specific functions of desire and feeling. It must be said that Herbart's schematic treatment of this complicated topic is too simplistic, failing to address these Kantian objections.

Such are the basics of Herbart's psychology as he first presented it in the *Lehrbuch.* The question remains, however, of its value and limits. Just how much did Herbart think he could explain of the mind according to his mathematical method? Though Herbart does not treat this question in the *Lehrbuch* itself, he turned to it more directly in a later essay, 'Ueber die Möglichkeit und Notwendigkeit Mathematik auf Psychologie anzuwenden'.[124] Here Herbart admits that mathematics is of no use in metaphysics (101), and that its use is limited to the realm of quantity. He denies, however, that the realm of the mind is qualitative alone. There is a broad quantitative dimension of psychic life, and it is just this which is amenable to mathematical treatment. This dimension includes the following: 1) the strength of each representation, namely, its degree of clarity or obscurity; 2) the degree of resistance between representations; 3) the degree of connection between representations and the number that are connected (102); 4) the length and duration of a series of representations; and 5) the speed or slowness in changes of representation (107). It is especially significant, Herbart notes, that representations fall into series of different kinds, for each of which we can provide precise equations (103). Yet Herbart admits that there is one fundamental aspect of mental life that his psychology cannot explain: namely, the content of the representations themselves (107). "What is represented," he flatly concedes, "does not come into further consideration except insofar as their resistance or connection depends on it." (107)[125] This is, of course, a remarkable concession. For it means that Herbart's psychology really cannot have the epistemological value and implications he promises; for epistemological issues concern first and foremost the content of representations, what they mean and whether they have a truth and reference.

So, though Herbart promised to put epistemology on a firm psychological basis, there is not much left of epistemology at all in his psychology. Least of all is there anything left of Kant's epistemology. Throughout the *Lehrbuch* Herbart rejects one

[124] Herbart, SW V, 91–122.
[125] Herbart made the same concession in his *Psychologie als Wissenschaft*, SW VI, 125; §123. See also Herbart's *Ueber meinen Streit mit der Modephilosophie*, SW III, 326–327, where he clearly separates logic and psychology, insisting that logic has nothing to do with psychology and that its results concern the content of thought quite independently of how we happen to think.

basic Kantian doctrine after another, all on the grounds that they are poor psychology. Rather than putting Kant's epistemology on a new psychological foundation, as he promised, Herbart uses psychology to destroy it, piece by piece. He denies, for example, that the unity of our experience is the product of an act of synthesis, insisting instead that representations cohere with one another through their own inner force (318; §21). Unity is not a creation of the mind but it is a given of our experience, into which we later introduce distinctions (399, 400–401; §§194, 196). The whole idea of inner sense is dismissed summarily as an invention of psychologists, and as a rather poor invention at that because we know nothing about the specific representations it supplies or the law by which it operates (323; §32). The main assumption behind the metaphysical deduction—that all thinking is judging—is also questioned on the grounds that thinking does not necessarily involve speaking or the use of language (328; §40). Most striking of all, Herbart rejects the assumption that we have a faculty of understanding that consists in concepts (326; §37). Since there is no such thing as concepts, which are only abstractions, all that we can say in the end is that concepts are ideals to which our thinking should approximate (393–394; §§179–181). The whole idea of a priori powers and activities of the mind, which is so central to Kant's problematic, collapses in the face of Herbart's critique of psychological faculties. The mind does not consist in innate powers and faculties but only in the interconnections of representations, which are formed by their own activity.

Given Herbart's trenchant critique of Kant's psychology, and given that his psychology became by far the most influential aspect of his philosophy, it is hardly surprising that Herbart's Kantianism has been overlooked. It is so hard to square Herbart's mechanist and naturalist psychology with Kant's transcendental philosophy that we have to forgive those who have stressed his opposition to Kant. And yet, as we have seen, apart from his psychology, Herbart was a deeply Kantian thinker, just as he said he was. His transcendental idealism, his critical conception of philosophy, his re-working of ethics according to Kantian aesthetics, his loyalty to the basic Kantian dualisms, all make him very Kantian. So it was with neither hyperbole nor irony that Herbart declared that October day in 1833 "*Kantianum ipse me professus sum*". That was a public confession, coming from the heart, of his deepest philosophical convictions. They were the hard won result of his philosophical development from Jena to Königsberg, yet they were also there from the beginning in the little boy.

3

Friedrich Eduard Beneke, Neo-Kantian Martyr

1. The Last Anthropologist

The youngest thinker in the empiricist-psychological tradition of neo-Kantianism was Friedrich Eduard Beneke (1798–1854). Born twenty-five years after Fries and twenty-two years after Herbart, Beneke belonged to a completely new generation from his predecessors. When he came of age in the early 1820s, the *Wunderjahre* in Jena, which both Fries and Herbart had experienced first-hand, were becoming a rapidly fading memory. While Fries and Herbart were ordinary professors at the height of their careers, Beneke was still a student in Berlin. Yet, despite these differences in age, these philosophers shared one common experience, one which became a bonding force among them. Namely, they all suffered under the shadow of Romanticism and speculative idealism, which had become the dominant forces in German philosophy in the 1820s. All reacted against these forces, and as such regarded themselves as outsiders, as rebels against the philosophical culture of their day. Against Romantic enthusiasm and idealist speculation, they allied their philosophy with the new empirical and mathematical sciences, and they identified themselves with that philosopher who seemed to represent best the spirit of those sciences: Immanuel Kant.

Though much younger than Fries and Herbart, Beneke still belongs to the same philosophical tradition. He shares with them the same fundamental positions: the central role of empirical psychology for epistemology; the fundamental truth of transcendental idealism; the reaction against the neo-rationalism of speculative idealism; the need for an empirical and analytical method in philosophy; and allegiance to the Kantian tradition, which he too believed was betrayed by speculative idealism. With Herbart, Beneke preached a situation ethics and the need for an aesthetic foundation for morality.

Beneke's affinities with Fries and Herbart are not simply the product of historical hindsight. For Beneke himself was fully aware of them. He had read Fries when he was still young, and listed him among those authors who had most influenced his early thinking.[1] He greatly admired Herbart, whose metaphysical writings he

---

[1] See F.E. Beneke, *Die neue Psychologie* (Berlin: Mittler, 1845), p. 81.

deemed "indisputably the most acute and profound that our century has shown."[2] Although Herbart was a lesser influence upon him, chiefly because he discovered his writings only after most of philosophy was already formed,[3] Beneke still felt that they had so much in common that it warranted collaboration; he duly proposed joining forces with him,[4] though nothing came of that proposal.

It is not hard to see why. While Herbart had encouraged Beneke and written favourable reviews of his early writings,[5] he treated him more as a student than an equal. More importantly, Herbart knew that there were unbridgeable philosophical differences between them. He found Beneke's radical empiricism wildly implausible, a relapse into the bad old days of pre-Kantian empiricism.[6] Furthermore, he had stressed the need for a metaphysical foundation of psychology, which had become a sticking point with Beneke, who insisted that psychology be entirely empirical and cast aside all metaphysics.[7]

Of the three thinkers in the empiricist-psychological tradition, Beneke had the most radical programme, which pushed the claims of empiricism and psychologism to their ultimate limit. His empiricism was so extreme that, at least in his early years, he denied the existence of the a priori entirely, insisting that experience alone is the foundation for knowledge. And his psychologism was so excessive that he regarded all intellectual disciplines as so many parts of psychology, which was for him "the basic science" (*Grundwissenschaft*). In both respects Beneke went further than Fries or Herbart, who not only retained aspects of the Kantian a priori but who also believed that psychology is one science among others.

Beneke's place in the history of neo-Kantianism is not very secure. For the most part,[8] the standard histories of the movement have ignored him. To some extent, this

---

[2] See F.E. Beneke, *Beiträge zu einer reinseelenwissenschaftlichen Bearbeitung der Seelenkrankheitskunde* (Leipzig: Reclam, 1824), p. xix.

[3] This is on Beneke's own testimony. See his *Die neue Psychologie*, p. 84. Beneke was responding to the charge that he had plagiarized Herbart's psychology. These charges were made by Herbart's disciple M.W. Drobisch, *Empirische Psychologie nach naturwissenschaftlicher Methode* (Leipzig: Voß, 1842), pp. 325–327. Beneke's reply is his 'Ueber das Verhältnis meiner Psychologie zur Herbart'schen', *Die neue Psychologie*, pp. 76–121.

[4] Beneke proposed an alliance with Herbart first in March 1823 in a public essay, and then in May 1824 in a private letter. See Beneke's essay 'Soll die Psychologie metaphysisch oder physisch begründet werden? Ein Schreiben an den Herrn Professor Dr. Herbart zu Königsberg', in *Beiträge zu einer reinseelenwissenschaftlichen Bearbeitung der Seelenkrankheitskunde* v–l; and Beneke's May 22, 1824, letter to Herbart, in *Ungedruckte Briefen*, eds Renato Pettoello and Nikola Barelmann (Aalen: Scientia Verlag, 1994), pp. 127–130. Herbart never responded to these proposals.

[5] See J.F. Herbart, review of *Erfahrungsseelenlehre*, *Jenaer Allgemeine Literatur-Zeitung* 1822, Nr. 47, reprinted in SW XII, 153–157; review of *Grundlegung zur Physik der Sitten*, *Jenaer Allgemeine Literatur-Zeitung* 1822, Nr. 211–213, reprinted in SW XII, 171–189; and review of *Schutzschrift für meine Grundlegung zur Physik der Sitten*, *Jenaer Allgemeine Literatur-Zeitung* 1823, Nr. 178, reprinted in SW XII, 215–222.

[6] See Herbart's review of Beneke's *Erfahrungsseelenlehre*, SW XII, 155.

[7] Beneke raised this issue with Herbart in his essay 'Soll die Psychologie metaphysisch oder physisch begründet werden? Ein Schreiben an den Herrn Professor Dr. Herbart zu Königsberg', published in the beginning of his *Beiträge*, v–l.

[8] Lehmann, Ollig, Beck and Willey do not even mention Beneke.

neglect is perfectly understandable. As a radical empiricist, Beneke seems to belong more to the tradition of British empiricism than anything having to do with Kant. Following that tradition, he rejects every rationalist strand in Kant's philosophy— viz., Kant's theory of a priori intuitions and concepts, his theory of the synthetic a priori, his philosophical method, his categorical imperative. After rejecting all these doctrines, it seems difficult, indeed impossible, to be a Kantian. Beneke also sought publicity as a critic of Kant. His early work on ethics, his 1822 *Grundlegung zur Physik der Sitten*, was a blistering polemic against Kant's moral doctrine. Finally, no less than Herbart's psychology, Beneke's was empiricist, naturalist and mechanist, making for a great contrast with Kant's own transcendental psychology.

Nevertheless, despite all these factors, Beneke still deserves a significant place in the history of neo-Kantianism. For the fact remains that he greatly identified with Kant, and even regarded himself as the Königsberger's only legitimate son. His 1832 tract *Kant und die philosophische Aufgabe unserer Zeit* is indeed one of the very first neo-Kantian manifestos. Beneke identified with Kant for two chief reasons. First, he regarded Kant's transcendental idealism as a powerful statement of the fundamental anthropological truth that all knowledge revolves around man.[9] Second, he saw Kant's philosophy as the most potent antidote against the ills of speculative idealism. For Beneke, the heart of Kant's philosophy was its critical spirit, and that ultimately rested on its empiricism. It was with his empiricist principles—primarily, his insistence that all knowledge be limited to experience—that Kant did battle against the rationalism of Descartes, Leibniz and Wolff. Beneke wanted to continue that battle in his day against the neo-rationalism of Fichte, Schelling and Hegel.

Beneke was the last major thinker in the German anthropological tradition. It was his great contribution to have kept that tradition alive in the 1820s when it was rapidly becoming forgotten with the rise of Romanticism and Hegelianism. Beneke was schooled in all the great authors of this tradition—Platner, Locke, Hume, Garve, Tetens and Fries—and he remained true to its central teachings all his life. He very much took to heart the central doctrine of this tradition: that all knowledge originates in man, and therefore should revolve around him. That alone was sufficient for him to make psychology into the master science. When Herbart later demanded that Beneke justify his radical psychological programme, he would take refuge in this old doctrine, citing it again and again like a mantra.

Even in his own lifetime, Beneke's psychology was quickly becoming obsolescent. True to the anthropological tradition, Beneke continued to maintain the value and necessity of the concept of the soul and the method of self-observation. Unlike Herbart, he was very ambivalent about the use of mathematics, ultimately doubting its utility in explaining the qualitative aspects of mental life.[10] In all these respects

---

[9] See F.E. Beneke, *Das Verhältnis von Seele und Leib* (Göttingen: Vandenhoeck & Ruprecht, 1826), p. vii.
[10] See Beneke's *Beiträge*, p. xliii.

Beneke was clinging to the past. Already in the 1830s, in Beneke's own lifetime, psychology had little use for introspection or the soul, and it was becoming much more experimental, physiological and mathematical. It was in Leipzig in the 1830s that Gustav Fechner, Alfred Volkmann, Ernst and Eduard Weber began to conduct their pioneering experiments in visual perception, which, in their rigorous experimental techniques, went far beyond anything Beneke had practised or even dreamed. The neo-Kantianism of the 1860s would ally itself more with the new experimental and physiological psychology of Helmholtz and the Leipzig school than the old anthropological tradition.[11]

For better or worse, Beneke's influence on his age was slight. Unlike Fries and Herbart, he never got the recognition that he so deeply craved and so truly deserved. No school formed around him to spread his teaching and to keep his memory alive, as happened with Fries and Herbart. He had a few disciples,[12] though they were largely concerned with applying his psychology to pedagogy. Later in the 19th century, Beneke finally received some recognition, finding a modest place in several histories of philosophy.[13] Since, then, however, he has been largely forgotten. Only very recently, in the work of Klaus Christian Köhnke,[14] has Beneke received some of the attention he deserves.

2. A Tragic Life

Friedrich Eduard Beneke was born in Berlin on February 17, 1798.[15] His family was upper-middle class. His father was a high-ranking Prussian bureaucrat, a commissioner of justice and finance; and his mother, née Wilmsen, came from a well-known literary family. About Beneke's early education little is known. We do know that he went to the best primary schools in Berlin, and that he progressed so rapidly that, by age 12, he was in the top third of the *Friedrichs-Werderschen Gymnasium*. From an early age, Beneke showed talent for classical languages and mathematics as well as a

---

[11] As we shall see in Chapter 8, Jürgen Bona Meyer is an exception to this generalization.
[12] On Beneke's disciples and their writings, see Francis Brandt, *Friedrich Eduard Beneke: The Man and his Philosophy* (New York: Macmillan, 1895), pp. 161–163, 166–167; and Otto Siebert, *Geschichte der neueren deutschen Philosophie seit Hegel* (Göttingen: Vandenhoeck & Ruprecht, 1898), pp. 207–215.
[13] See Julius Bergmann, *Die deutsche Philosophie von Kant bis Beneke*, Volume II of his *Geschichte der Philosophie* (Berlin: Mittler, 1893), II, 544–583; Albert Stöckl, *Geschichte der neueren Philosophie von Baco und Cartesius bis zur Gegenwart* (Mainz: Kirchheim, 1883), II, 258–282; and Friedrich Ueberweg, *Die deutsche Philosophie des XIX. Jahr hunderts und der Gegenwart*, Volume IV of *Grundriss der Geschichte der Philosophie*, tenth edition (Berlin: Mittler, 1906), IV, 134–145.
[14] See Klaus Christian Köhnke, *Entstehung und Aufstieg des Neukantianismus* (Frankfurt: Suhrkamp, 1986), pp. 69–88.
[15] The main source on Beneke's life is in Friedrich Adolf Diesterweg's *Pädagogisches Jahrbuch für Lehrer und Schulfreunde-1856* (Berlin: Diesterweg, 1856), pp. 1–105, which contains an account of Beneke's life by his student J.G. Dressler and his friend 'Dr. Schmidt'. Also see Brandt, *Beneke*, pp. 15–37; and Otto Gramzow, *Friedrich Eduard Benekes Leben und Philosophie* (Bern: Steiger, 1899).

fondness for poetry. At the *Gymnasium* he graduated at the very top of his class at the age of seventeen.

In 1815 Beneke enlisted as a volunteer in the campaign against Napoleon. We know little about what he did during that campaign or his wartime experiences. Returning from his military service at Easter 1816, he matriculated at the University of Halle to study theology. There he read the Bible, learned Hebrew and Arabic, and wrote two prize-winning essays on religious themes.[16] It was also in Halle that he developed an interest in philosophy, which was sparked off by two prominent Kantians there, Ludwig Heinrich Jakob (1759–1827) and Johann Christian Hoffbauer (1766–1827). After only a year in Halle, Beneke returned at Easter 1817 to Berlin, where he went to lectures on theology and philosophy at the new university. He attended Schleiermacher's lectures, which were to have a significant effect on him.

It was during his Berlin student days that Beneke discovered his calling in life. To pursue his pastoral training in theology, he made a habit of going to sermons; and while listening to Schleiermacher one fine Sunday, he had an epiphany. It was nothing Schleiermacher said that inspired him; he was so lost in thought that he could have been anywhere. It was what was said on the way to church that moved him. While walking there he had been talking with his brother about the dire state of contemporary philosophy and about the urgent need to make it change course. It was this line of thought that engrossed him and made him pay scant attention to Schleiermacher's sermon. Upon leaving the church, he resolved, henceforth, to devote the rest of his life to philosophy. And so, at the tender age of nineteen, Beneke found his mission in life: the reform of philosophy.[17]

Unfortunately, Beneke tells us very little about the precise content of his epiphany, about what was wrong exactly with contemporary philosophy and how it should be reformed. Fortunately, though, his historical context and later writings make it easy to reconstruct some of his thinking. The contemporary philosophy in question was the grand metaphysical systems of Fichte, Schelling and Hegel, which held sway over the philosophical scene in Berlin. Though Fichte had died in January 1814, his spirit still haunted the halls of the university; and in October 1818 Hegel began his famous lectures in Berlin, which would soon become the talk of the town. It was not that Hegel reigned unopposed. The source of resistance to his philosophy came from Schleiermacher, who strongly disapproved of its overweening rationalism and a priori methodology. Battle lines began to form between "the philosophical school" under Hegel and "the historical school" under Schleiermacher.[18] Modelling

---

[16] Gramzow, *Benekes Leben*, p. 14, states that these were not published. Neither Brandt's nor Dressler's bibliographies list them.

[17] This story was told by Beneke to Dressler, who wrote about it in the biographical essay in Diesterweg's *Pädagogisches Jahrbuch*. It is cited by Gramzow, *Benekes Leben*, p. 16.

[18] The most extensive account of the dispute between the historical and philosophical schools is still that of Ernst Simon, *Ranke und Hegel, Beiheft der Historische Zeitschrift* 15 (1928), pp. 16–119. For a shorter illuminating account, see John Toews, *Hegelianism* (Cambridge: Cambridge University Press, 1980), pp. 49–67.

its methodology on the new empirical sciences, the historical school believed in the value of careful empirical and historical research. To the historians, Hegel's dialectical method, with its a priori reasoning and rigid schematic form, seemed to be a relapse into "scholasticism", the very antithesis of the scientific revolution inaugurated by Bacon and defended by Kant.

Taking into account all these facts, we can reconstruct the content of Beneke's epiphany along these lines: the dire state of philosophy came from its scholasticism or excessive rationalism; the remedy for it should be advocating and following a more empirical method in philosophy. Ultimately, Beneke's epiphany was probably very much inspired by the historical party in Berlin. So it was perhaps no accident after all that it occurred during a sermon by Schleiermacher.

The day after his epiphany Beneke marched straight to the dean of the university and declared his intention to qualify as an instructor in philosophy. Only two months later, on August 9, 1820, he submitted his inaugural dissertation, *De veris philosophae initiis*,[19] a short statement of his new programme for a reform of philosophy and a sharp critique of the prevailing methodology. Immediately thereafter, in the Winter Semester of 1820, Beneke began his first lectures as a *Privatdozent*.

Lecturing at Berlin in the early 1820s was a bold and risky undertaking. Beneke had to compete with Hegel, who enjoyed not only great popularity but also the patronage of the Prussian government. Schopenhauer's experience was a signal lesson about these hazards. He attempted to give lectures in Berlin in the spring semester of 1821, even daring to schedule them at the same time as Hegel's; but with catastrophic results: only five students appeared. But where Schopenhauer failed miserably, Beneke had conspicuous success. In the winter semester of 1821–22, he had thirty students in each of his lectures, one on logic and metaphysics and the other on mental illnesses.[20] Such success could only have troubled Hegel, who would have seen Beneke as a Schleiermacher ally, and who was intent on consolidating his power over the philosophical faculty in Berlin. At the very least, it was not in his interest for Beneke to continue lecturing.

Sure enough, Beneke heard from the Philosophical Faculty in February 1822 that his lectures for the forthcoming semester were to be cancelled, his *venia legendi* withdrawn.[21] No reasons were given. After begging for an explanation from Baron von Altenstein, the Minister of Education,[22] Beneke was told that the reason had something to do with his latest book, *Grundlegung zur Physik der Sitten*. Altenstein could not tell him, however, what precisely about that book that had proven so offensive;

[19] Beneke, *De veris philosophiae initiis* (Berlin: Mittler, 1820).
[20] See Beneke to Altenstein, December 4, 1821, in Beneke, *Ungedruckte Briefe*, p. 95.
[21] The full story is told by Brandt, *Beneke*, pp. 18–25, Gramzow, *Benekes Leben*, pp. 23–29, and useful supporting documents are in Rudolf Murtfeld, 'Vergeblicher Kampf gegen den Idealismus. Friedrich Eduard Benekes Schicksal und seine Wissenschaftstheorien', *Zeitschrift für Geschichte der Erziehung und des Unterrichts* 26 (1936), 1–48, esp. 44–48.
[22] Beneke to Altenstein, March 1, 1822, *Ungedruckte Briefe*, pp. 97–98.

on that matter, he had to refer Beneke to his secretary, Johannes Schulze, who might know more about it. On February 7, 1822, Schulze had written a memorandum about the reasons for a rescript against Beneke's lectures, citing passages from the Appendix to Beneke's *Physik der Sitten*. Schulze found it especially problematic that Beneke had maintained that reason is only a refined form of sensibility, and that thinking is a purely natural process.[23] Apparently, though, Schulze did not inform Beneke about the contents of the memorandum or the reasons for the decision. Deliberately, Beneke was left in the dark, the victim of an inscrutable bureaucratic decree. He again wrote Altenstein on March, begging for an explanation and complaining that he knew only from hearsay that it had something to do with his *Physik der Sitten*.[24] After months of waiting, Beneke's uncle, a civil servant who had intervened on his behalf, received a letter from Schulze, dated July 15, 1822, stating that he still believed it necessary to uphold the rescript against "Dr. Beneke".[25] But little explanation was given, and Beneke himself was still not informed.

Undaunted, Beneke wrote in October 1822 to Karl August Hardenberg, Minister of State, begging for the right to defend himself and declaring his incomprehension at the rescript, which was contrary to the University's policy of academic freedom.[26] Receiving no answer by December, Beneke went to the very pinnacle of government, appealing to Prince Friedrich Wilhelm himself.[27] Eventually, he was granted an interview with Altenstein, who told Beneke in no uncertain terms that "a philosophy that could not explain everything in relation to the absolute was no philosophy at all."[28] Altenstein's explanation suggests that Beneke was the victim of Hegelianism. That, at least, is the explanation of Beneke's supporters.[29]

It is still unclear, however, whether Hegel himself had intervened with the Ministry against Beneke.[30] It is possible that Altenstein was only voicing his personal opinion to Beneke. There is another simpler explanation for the rescript: that Schulze, as minister responsible for executing the Karlsbad decrees, was only doing his job.[31] Books

---

[23] Murtfeld, 'Benekes Schicksal', p. 47.
[24] Beneke to Altenstein, March 1, 1822, *Ungedruckte Briefe*, p. 97.
[25] Diesterweg, *Pädagogisches Jahrbuch*, p. 11.
[26] Beneke to Hardenberg, October 18, 1822, *Ungedruckte Briefe*, pp. 105–108.
[27] Beneke to Friedrich Wilhelm, December 9, 1822, *Ungedruckte Briefe*, pp. 110–112.
[28] Beneke an Twesten, May 11, 1823, *Ungedruckte Briefe*, p. 121.   [29] Brandt, *Beneke*, pp. 19–21
[30] But was Hegel himself really behind the rescript? It is widely accepted in Beneke scholarship that he was indeed the culprit. For its part, as far as I know, Hegelian scholarship has not discussed the Beneke affair. There is evidence for and against Hegel's role. The evidence for it, which is only circumstantial, is Hegel's willingness to use his influence on the government to oppress opponents and critics. For example, he attempted to get the government to censure the *Hallesche Allgemeine Literatur-Zeitung* for its critique of his treatment of Fries in the preface to his *Philosophie des Rechts*. On this episode, see Karl Rosenkranz, *G.W.F. Hegels Leben* (Berlin: Duncker & Humblot, 1844), pp. 336–37. The evidence against it is that Hegel himself, at least in 1831, had nothing against Beneke's receiving a professorship in the Faculty of Philosophy. See Beneke to Altenstein, November 28, 1831, *Ungedruckte Briefe*, p. 189. It could well have been, however, that Hegel had relented from his earlier stance.
[31] The decrees were very explicit and emphatic about the need for press censorship and for controlling university faculty. See *Karlsbader Beschlüsse*, 'Universitätsgesetz' §§1–2 and 'Preßgesetz' §§1, 6, in Manfred Görtemaker, *Deutschland im 19. Jahrhundert* (Opladen: Leske, 1983), p. 75.

like Beneke's were dangerous, expressing views likely to undermine public morality and religion.

Whatever the reason for the rescript, Beneke found himself unemployed. Now that his career had abruptly ended, he was forced to explore opportunities elsewhere. After having banished Fries, the University of Jena was eager to get Beneke as his replacement, and it was even willing to grant him an ordinary professorship. The condition of his coming to Jena, however, was that Altenstein declare that he had nothing against Beneke's employment in Saxony. Beneke duly beseeched Altenstein for a letter to this effect.[32] But Altenstein was not obliging. He declared that, though he found nothing personally wrong with Beneke's character, his teachings were evidence of his intellectual immaturity and his unsuitability to teach at a university. That was a sentence of damnation. However, Altenstein, like Schulze, was only following official policy. According to the Karlsbad decrees, a rescript against an instructor at one university automatically barred him from employment at any other land of the German confederation.[33]

For two years Beneke struggled to reinstate himself in Berlin. All to no avail. In mid-January 1824 he went to Göttingen in the hope of becoming a *Privatdozent* there. He habilitated at the end of January, and in the next weeks began his lectures, which initially proved very successful.[34] It soon became clear, however, that he could not make his living as a *Privatdozent* in Göttingen, whose students had little interest in philosophy.[35] For two and a half years Beneke struggled in Göttingen, eking out a precarious existence. For family reasons he returned to Berlin in April 1827. Again and again he supplicated Altenstein for reinstatement of his right to lecture in Berlin. Finally, in the summer of 1827, Altenstein relented and Beneke could resume his career as a *Privatdozent*.

But then came the even longer struggle for promotion. Beneke found it humiliating to be only a *Privatdozent* at his age and with his publications. He constantly appealed to Alteinstein to be made a professor, and he could produce strong arguments in favour of his promotion: his lectures were popular, his books were getting widespread recognition, and he had no personal resources. It was only in April 1832, after Hegel's death and the strong recommendations of the Philosophy Faculty, that Beneke was named an extraordinary professor. But he still received no money; and since all faculty members were obliged to contribute 30 thalers to their "widow's pension", Beneke, a bachelor, liked to say that he actually received "a negative salary" from the university. Even after Hegel's death, the Ministry of Education was intent on preserving his legacy, so they appointed as many Hegelians as possible. Beneke

---

[32] Beneke to Altenstein, April 5, 1823, *Ungedruckte Briefe*, pp. 112–113.
[33] *Karlsbader Beschlüsse*, 'Universitätsgesetz', §2, in Görtemaker, *Deutschland im 19. Jahrhundert*, p. 75.
[34] See Beneke to Twesten, February 21, 1824, *Ungedruckte Briefe*, pp. 123–124.
[35] See Beneke to Twesten, November 24, 1824, *Ungedruckte Briefe*, p. 113; and December 22, 1825, *Ungedruckte Briefe*, p. 115.

struggled on, living in dire poverty despite the increasing success of his lectures and writings. He complained that his destiny in life was to be the "*Schutzmauer gegen die Hegelei*".[36] To fight his isolation in Berlin, Beneke established contacts with English intellectuals, with John Herschel and William Whewell, whose views were more congenial to his own thinking.[37] After Altenstein's death, Beneke finally received a small salary from the University, yet he was never promoted to an ordinary professorship. He stayed in Berlin until the very bitter end.

Beneke died under mysterious circumstances. On the way to a lecture March 1, 1854, he disappeared. A search was made by the police, friends, family and students, but all to no avail. Some two years later his badly decomposed body was found in the Spree near Charlottenberg. It is unclear whether he committed suicide or was murdered.[38] Two workers were indicted for his murder when they were found to be in possession of his coat and gloves; but they claimed to have found them along the Spree and were eventually acquitted for lack of evidence. The fact that money was still found on the corpse counts against the robbery hypothesis. Though he was seen to be in a good humour on the day of his disappearance, Beneke was known to be in poor health and to be very depressed by his isolation and the lack of advancement in his career;[39] the fact that the faculty of philosophy had recently decided to pass him by for promotion must have been another heavy blow. The evidence suggests suicide as the most likely cause of death, a sad but understandable end for a very tragic life.

3. Epistemological Foundations

Shortly after his epiphany Beneke set to work to realize his grand ambition. It was probably in the spring of 1819, when just twenty-one years old, that he wrote his first philosophical work. This was his *Erkenntnißlehre*, which he finished in May 1819 and then published in 1820.[40] This work laid down the basis of his epistemology, and thus the foundation for much of his philosophical programme. Though he would later refine and revise it, he would follow its central theses for the rest of his life.

The preface to Beneke's book is very revealing about his intentions and programme. Right away we see how much the young Beneke was inspired by Kant. His grand plan is to complete Kant's philosophical revolution. We are told, however, that the promise

---

[36] See Beneke to Twesten, May 19, 1834, *Ungedruckte Briefe*, p. 207.

[37] On Beneke's contacts and correspondence with these figures, see Gramzow, *Benekes Leben*, pp. 232–241.

[38] The difficulties with both hypotheses are discussed thoroughly by Gramzow, *Benekes Leben*, pp. 270–276.

[39] See, for example, Beneke to Herschel, July 17, 1845, *Ungedruckte Briefe*, pp. 237–238.

[40] Friedrich Eduard Beneke, *Erkenntnißlehre nach dem Bewußtsein der reinen Vernunft in ihren Grundzügen* (Jena: Frommann, 1820). All references in parentheses are to this edition. The first number refers to a page, the second to a paragraph. The preface to the work is dated May 1, 1819, which places it before Beneke's doctoral dissertation, which was defended August 9, 1820. In the preface to his *Erfahrungsseelenlehre* Beneke states that the dissertation was written after the *Erkenntnißlehre*.

of Kant's philosophy has been scarcely fulfilled (vi–ix). Rather than creating eternal peace among philosophers, the critique of pure reason has only incited more conflict among them. There is now a *bellum omnium contra omnes* in the philosophical world, where each system claims to be the universal standard of pure reason. It is striking that Beneke puts the blame for this situation on Kant himself (x). Though he was right to call for a "lawbook of pure reason", a tribunal to settle the disputes between philosophers, Kant had still not laid down its proper foundation (x). The task of Beneke's *Erkenntnißlehre* is to do just that. Its business is to determine "the basic guidelines", if not all the precepts, of this lawbook of pure reason (xii).

To rethink the foundations for the critique of pure reason, Beneke insists that we go back to the basis of all epistemology: the theory of judgement. We need to ask the question: What is judgement? What makes a judgement true or false? (9; §2). Although Kant rightly began his critique with a classification of the forms of judgement, his classification is deeply flawed, and as a result the critique has been put on a faulty foundation.

All judgement for Beneke involves the comparison between two activities of the mind: one represented by the subject term and the other by the predicate. The judgement is true if the two activities are partially or completely identical with one another (20, 28; §4). In other words, it is true if the intuition represented by the predicate is contained in, or part of, that intuition represented by the subject (12; §2). The judgement "This lily is white", for example, states that my intuition of white is part of, or contained within, my intuition of this lily (11–12; §2). In saying that the predicate is contained in the subject by virtue of a partial or complete identity, Beneke implied that all true judgements are essentially, in Kantian terms, "analytic". Sure enough, he insisted on banishing Kant's distinction between analytic and synthetic judgements (16–17; §3). Kant wrongly believed that there are synthetic judgements because he had the wrong idea of the subject of a judgement. He equated that subject with our *concept* of it, in which case some judgements are indeed synthetic because the concept of the subject does not contain the predicate. But the proper subject of a judgement is not just any concept of it but our whole *intuition* or *perception* of it, in which case the subject term does indeed contain or involve the predicate (13, 16–17; §3). Beneke admits, however, that there can be synthetic judgements in cases where we have an *incomplete* intuition or perception of the subject. It turns out that complete identity between subject and predicate is only an ideal of knowledge, which we attain only in the sciences when we have an adequate knowledge of the subject (25; §4). Ultimately, whether a judgement is analytic or synthetic, Beneke argues, depends on how we define the subject; and how we define the subject is essentially a pragmatic affair, depending on our purposes (28–29; §4). In ordinary life many of our judgements are synthetic because we have a rather inadequate concept of the subject; but in science, where we have a more adequate knowledge, they are analytic. But a judgement that is analytic in one science also can be synthetic for another, because the terms have different definitions depending on the different ends of enquiry (27–28; §4).

Beneke does not hesitate to generalize his theory of judgement, applying it to all kinds of judgement, even those in mathematics (31; §5). He therefore questions Kant's theory that the judgements of mathematics are synthetic a priori. *Prima facie* they do appear to be synthetic because it is hard to see how the predicate is contained in the subject in judgements like "The three angles of a triangle are equal to two right angles". Beneke assures us, however, that they can be made analytic through further analysis of the subject term (33–34; §5). He does not dispute that we often begin proofs in mathematics with intuitions; but he insists that we can analyse and refine these intuitions, and then on that basis define the subject term so that it is equivalent to the predicate (90–91; §14). Having rejected the synthetic a priori status of mathematics, Beneke then went on to question Kant's thesis that mathematics requires the a priori status of space and time (132; §18). Since mathematical propositions are, after proper analysis, analytic, their truth would not be jeopardized if space and time were entirely empirical.

Although Beneke, like Leibniz before him, proposed that all true judgements be reducible to identities, he knew all too well that such identity alone does not amount to knowledge. The reason was all too simple: a formula or identity by itself has no necessary application to reality (47; §7). The judgement "All dryads live in the forest", for example, is just as much a judgement of identity as "All bodies have weight" (48; §7). What is necessary for a formula to be knowledge, Beneke insists, is that it applies to reality or being itself (46; §7); and we can determine whether that is so only by consulting experience (60; §8). What distinguishes knowledge from mere fiction is therefore perception (*Wahrnehmung*) (52; §7).

Beneke's insistence that judgements, to count as knowledge, be confirmed in experience is simple and straightforward enough. It was the fundamental principle of his empiricism, which he saw as the bedrock of his agreement with Kant (212–213; §25). But in developing his theory Beneke encountered two difficulties. First, he stressed that no amount of experience can ever confirm a universal judgement (36; §5). For such a judgement to be true, it must hold for *all* instances; but it is impossible to confirm whether this is true because we cannot make a complete induction. This means that many judgements of empirical science, which are universal, cannot be true in a strict sense. We can make them true only by convention, that is, by so defining the subject term that the predicate follows from it; but that still leaves us with the problem whether the conventions give us knowledge of reality; we have no guarantee that they are not judgements like "All dryads live in the forest". Second, Beneke found it difficult to explain objective knowledge of things in space beyond our own subjective states. Since he insists that the immediate objects of knowledge consist in our own representations (70–71; §10), we need some criterion to distinguish those representations that refer to objective things in space from those that are only illusory. Only if we know such things do we have *objective* knowledge (79; §11). But what is this criterion? Since Beneke does not specify it, his foundation of knowledge is left hanging in the air. It seems possible that the knowing subject is caught inside the circle of his own consciousness. We will consider in later sections how Beneke attempted to solve these problems.

Whatever its difficulties, Beneke believed that his theory of knowledge had provided the necessary foundation for a critique of pure reason. The critique of pure reason now had a clear and simple criterion of truth: the identity, complete or partial, of a subject with its predicate. Beneke realized, of course, that most judgements fall far short of such an ideal, especially in ordinary life but even in the sciences, for they too seldom have an adequate idea of the subject. Still, the point was to have a clear conception of the *ideal* of knowledge, the *goal* to which investigation must aspire. Kant's conception of the synthetic a priori left the tribunal of critique bereft of a workable criterion, because it seemed impossible to assess when such judgements are true. Kant resorted to his transcendental deductions of such judgements; but these arguments are problematic, resting on subtleties and scholastic reasoning.

Seen as a whole, Beneke's *Erkenntnißlehre* seems a curious mixture of rationalism and empiricism. Its standard of true judgement goes back to Leibniz's predicate-in-notion principle,[41] while its talk about comparing ideas to determine their agreement or identity sounds like no one more than Locke.[42] Although Beneke insists that true judgements be confirmed in experience, he still entertains the rationalist ideal of a deductive system of the sciences, "a mathematical philosophy" like Newton's that will demonstrate all its basic truths (117–118; §16). This seems to affirm the very scholastic methodology that Beneke repudiates in Kant. The two strands of his epistemology can be made consistent, however, provided that Beneke insists that mathematical philosophy comes at the end rather than the beginning of enquiry. While a mathematical system is fine to organize and systematize empirical discoveries, it should never be used to replace or anticipate them.

4. The Psychological Programme

Shortly after the *Erkenntnißlehre* Beneke published his *Erfahrungsseelenlehre*,[43] which also appeared in 1820. The two works are complementary. The *Erfahrungsseelenlehre* states and defends the psychological programme and premises behind the earlier epistemological work. Epistemology, Beneke firmly believed, should be completely merged with psychology. The study of the powers and limits of human knowledge is therefore for him only one chapter within psychology, which is the study of the human mind as a whole. This conviction had been fundamental to, yet implicit in, the *Erkenntnißlehre*; it was now time to explain and justify it.

---

[41] See Leibniz, *Discours de Métaphysique* §8.
[42] See Locke, *An Essay Concerning Human Understanding*, Book IV, Chapter 1, §2.
[43] Friedrich Eduard Beneke, *Erfahrungsseelenlehre als Grundlage alles Wissens, in ihren Hauptzügen dargestellt* (Berlin: Mittler, 1820). All references in parentheses are to this edition; the first number refers to a page, the second to a section.

The *Erfahrungsseelenlehre* was the first full statement of Beneke's youthful dream, his plan to reform all of philosophy. The work attempts to provide a psychological foundation not only for epistemology but for *all* philosophy, for ethics and aesthetics as well. Its psychology serves strictly philosophical ends. Its intent is not to establish a complete system of psychology—a larger task for a later occasion—but to lay down just enough psychology to serve as a foundation for the central parts of philosophy. The ultimate intent of Beneke's programme, which emerges only later, is to make all parts of philosophy into parts of psychology. "If my view wins out (as I am fully convinced it will)," he wrote in 1822, "all philosophy will become the natural science of the human soul."[44]

Why psychology? Why did Beneke think it held the solution to all the problems of philosophy? There was a tangled web of motives behind Beneke's faith in psychology. First of all, he believed that psychology alone could make epistemology into a science. Psychology was, or at least in principle could be, an empirical science. It could follow the same methods of observation, experiment and induction that are used in physics, chemistry, biology and physiology. "True science," Beneke writes in his introduction, "cannot be founded on anything else but perception and the experience arising from comparing and correlating it." (7) An epistemology could be scientific, therefore, if it were founded on psychology, whose methods of observation and induction were the same as those of the empirical sciences.

Another rationale for Beneke's faith in psychology was his conviction that understanding the mind is the key to understanding knowledge itself. What we know is determined by how we know, by the activities of the mind that shape and form the object of knowledge. Hence self-knowledge of these activities is the basis for all knowledge, the key to understanding everything knowable. This rationale for psychology appears clearly in Beneke's introduction when he tells us that psychology is the most basic science of them all, indeed "the science of science". Why? Because the soul is the very medium or instrument that creates science (7). All knowledge is fundamentally a knowledge by man, for man and of man, because it depends so much upon his powers of perceiving the world (5).

Still another rationale for Beneke's confidence in psychology lies in his theory of meaning. We have already noted this theory at work in the *Erkenntnißlehre* where Beneke analyses judgement into "psychological activities". Only at the close of the *Erfahrungsseelenlehre* do we find the basis for this theory (166–167; §12). There Beneke reasons that we can identify and name the object of knowledge only through basic mental activities, namely, through the use of speech and hearing. Since the words that designate what we know are products of such basic mental activities, their meaning ultimately derives from them. Alternatively, whatever we know is the product of activities within ourselves, so the words we use to designate what we know are

---

[44] This statement appears in the preface to Beneke, *Grundlegung zur Physik der Sitten* (Berlin: Mittler, 1822), p. x.

grounded in these activities. Outside these activities, Beneke tells us, there is noth-ing *in* man, and therefore nothing *for* man. And so Beneke concludes: "The com-plete expression of all simple and complex activities exhausts the secret of all human knowledge." (167)

For better or worse, then, Beneke here seems intent on breaking down any dis-tinction between psychological activities and their objects. The realm of intentional objects dissolves into mental activities because these activities create these objects, which have no existence apart from them. Since the objects of mental acts are con-structed by these acts, they ultimately acquire their sense and reference from them. The idea that there is some realm of intentional objects distinct from the activities that create them Beneke would regard as an artificial abstraction; to believe literally in its existence he would regard as hypostasis.[45]

From a Kantian perspective, Beneke's psychology seems a relapse into the bad old ways of the past, a regress to the old empiricist tradition of epistemology whose shortcomings had been exposed by Kant in the first *Kritik*. In Beneke's defence, how-ever, it must be said that going back to the old empiricist project was the only way of going forwards, and precisely because of the defects of Kant's epistemology. It was one of Kant's greatest failures, Beneke believed, that he had not reflected on "the meta-critical question", the question of the basis of his own methodology.[46] There was indeed a remarkable discrepancy between Kant's methodology and his own stand-ards of knowledge. His methodology in the first *Kritik* is a priori reasoning; but his standard of knowledge is possible experience. How could Kant square such a scholas-tic methodology with his own standard of knowledge? The only way to comply with Kant's own standard of knowledge, it seemed, would be for epistemology to adopt the same empirical methods as the other sciences. So, in Beneke's view, it was not he but Kant who had relapsed into the bad old ways of the past, for his method of a priori reasoning was precisely that used by Wolffian rational psychology. In thus charging Kant with following a scholastic methodology in his psychology, a methodology at odds with his own empirical standards of knowledge, Beneke was following in the footsteps of Fries and Herbart. On this point the empiricist-psychological tradition formed a united front against Kantian orthodoxy.

The method of Beneke's psychology is supposed to be observation and induction. He writes in his introduction that psychology should proceed by the same meth-ods as the other empirical sciences. It has to collect and compare phenomena; find what they have in common; and then trace them back to their causes (1). Beneke later describes his method as "genetic", meaning that it analyses psychic phenomenon into

---

[45] These important assumptions are implicit in the *Erfahrungsseelenlehre*. Beneke began to explore them more explicitly only much later in his *System der Logik als Kunstlehre des Denkens* (Berlin: Dümmler, 1842), I, 35–42.

[46] Beneke made this point explicit later on in his *Kant und die philosophische Aufgabe unserer Zeit* (Berlin: Mittler, 1832), pp. 32–33. It is fair, I think, to make it part of the rationale for his earlier work.

their more basic elements, and then shows how they arose, how they came into being through the process of their genesis, through the combination of these elements (85; §8). Though keen to follow the methods of the other sciences, Beneke says nothing about experiment. He is still far from envisaging the kind of experimental psychology developed by Volkmann, Fechner and the Webers in the 1830s. And what he means by observation seems to be little more than introspection. On any point of doubt about his results, he simply requests the reader to look into himself. This was the standard practice of *Erfahrungsseelenkunde*.[47]

Beneke's programme in his *Erfahrungsseelenlehre* is very reductivist, attempting to explain all mental activities as appearances or functions of what he calls "basic activities" (*Grundthätigkeiten*). These basic activities consist in all those necessary to sustain animal life (e.g. digestion and reproduction), the senses and muscle movements involved in action (10; §1). This seems to be a materialist programme, though that is definitely not Beneke's intention. He stresses that it is impossible to separate mind and body within these basic activities, which are not only physical but also mental (10; §1). He also maintains that the mind is not only passive in receiving stimuli but also active in responding to them (11; §1). Though his programme is very reductivist, there is also a holism behind Beneke's general position. He insists that a human being is indivisibly one, so that to act in any particular way he or she has to act as a whole. Hence he writes: "the whole human being has to be active if any activity at all is to arise in him." (11; §1). The point of his explanatory programme is to show that all activities are part of a single vital human being, so that we must not divide it into independent faculties.

No less than Herbart's programme, then, Beneke's is directed against the old faculty psychology that divided the soul into independent faculties. It is interesting to note, however, that Beneke, unlike Herbart, does not intend to banish the concept of a faculty entirely. He prefers the term "activity" over "faculty" because it is in line with his fundamental belief in the vitality of the human being. But he sees nothing wrong in principle with the concept of a faculty, which, he says, designates nothing more than "the arousal of activity in a thing with the appropriate stimulus" (12; §1). Beneke adds that a faculty should designate "a kind of activity", and warns against postulating a new faculty for each activity. Because we must first determine the kinds of activities before we attribute faculties to the soul, we need to begin by examining and classifying its various activities, and only after that can we determine the basic faculties (13; §1). Hence, for Beneke, the concept of an activity still proves more basic than that of a faculty.

True to his reductivist programme, Beneke argues that all the higher activities of the soul—conceiving, judging, language, understanding—arise from the action of the environment on the basic activities, and then from their combination or

---

[47] See Introduction to Part I, Section 4.

interaction with one another (54–76; §6). The basic mechanisms for the derivation of these higher activities are association and the repetition of a stimulus, or what Beneke calls "re-awakening" or "re-arousal" (*Wiedererweckung*). We form concepts from the repeated stimulation of similar activities and the weakening stimulation of different activities (15; §2). We create language when we associate a sound with a concept (26; §2). And we make judgements when we state through words that one mental activity is the same as, or part of, another (27; §3). On no account, Beneke claims, should we postulate a special independent faculty for conceptualization, language or judgement, because these are only functions of our basic activities. For similar reasons, Beneke thinks that there is no reason to postulate a special faculty of inner sense to explain self-awareness, which arises only after our basic activities recreate impressions they have had in the past (58–61; §6).

Although Beneke believes in the fundamental unity of the mind, he maintains that there are two basic series of activity involved in human knowledge (42–44; §5). One series has its source in acts of perceiving, with the stimulation of the senses; the other comes from relating or connecting these acts of perceiving, which chiefly happens according to cause and effect, where cause–effect relations arise from the constant conjunction of successive representations (38; §4). We seem to return here to Locke's old distinction between ideas of sensation and reflection.[48] The point of Beneke's distinction is indeed empiricist. For he is concerned that we not confuse his distinction with another one: that between the a posteriori and the a priori (45; §6). What Kant and others call a priori knowledge, he argues, really ultimately arises from experience. Kant's a priori concepts are only the most general concepts that we abstract from experience. We consider some knowledge to be a priori or innate only because we have not done a sufficient account of its genesis (47–48; §6). It is noteworthy, however, that Beneke would eventually qualify such radical empiricism, admitting that the mind has inherent activities that make all knowledge possible.[49]

On the basis of his psychological analysis Beneke attempts to draw further epistemological conclusions. We are told that the whole question whether our knowledge is subjective or objective is rather vague and suspicious (13–14; §1). Some of our senses, namely, seeing and hearing, are more "objective" than others, because different people see and hear the same thing, or because the same person sees and hears the same thing at different times. But all the senses are to an extent both subjective and objective because they depend on our inner activity as much as an external stimulus (14, 23; §§1, 2). It is very difficult to draw a fine line, he argues, between the subjective and objective component of our representations, between what we receive from outside

---

[48] John Locke, *An Essay Concerning Human Understanding* I, ii, §2; I, I, §24.
[49] In the preface to his *Die Philosophie in ihrem Verhältnisse zur Erfahrung* (Berlin: Mittler, 1853), Beneke states that he agrees with the speculative systems that there are a priori forms or powers of the mind, and that there is philosophical knowledge independent of experience (vi). This marks a shift in position from his earlier work. It is possible that Herbart's harsh judgement made him retreat from his extreme empiricism.

and what we supply from within, because our receptivity and spontaneity are so intermingled (22; §2). Beneke does think, however, that psychology gives some basis for belief in things-in-themselves. Though he does not explicitly defend Kant's notorious concept here, he maintains that the stimulus behind our perception of an object and the object itself are beyond cognition by our perceptual activity (44; §5). We can think about and perceive the world only insofar as it reveals itself to us.

The fundamental question for Beneke's empiricism, however, is whether and how it can justify some of the basic propositions of natural science. Some of the most important of these propositions are laws, which claim that there is a universal and necessary connection between kinds of events. Kant had rejected empiricism precisely because he believed that it cannot justify such propositions; experience, as Hume taught, shows us only constant conjunctions and never warrants the inference to a universal and necessary connection. Fully aware of this problem, Beneke address it in section §3, though he still does not develop a completely unequivocal position regarding it. He again insists, as he did in the *Erkenntnißlehre*, that all universal judgements are valid only if they hold for all cases falling under them (29; §3), and that we can be certain that they are valid only through a complete induction (32–33; §3). He also admits, however, that that certainty is only in proportion to the degree of the induction (32; §3), and that no induction can ever be complete (29; §3). In that case, it seems we should admit that all natural science is uncertain, however rigorously we have proceeded in our observation and experiment. To an extent, Beneke seems willing to accept this result, and he even endorses Hume's account of the concept of causality as amounting to nothing more than constant conjunction (38; §4). But he also seems to hesitate, stopping short of this sceptical conclusion. Rather than flatly admit the uncertainty of all universal propositions, he appeals to the phenomenon of mathematical construction, which shows how we can base a universal proposition from considering a single case (29–30; §3). From the construction of a single triangle we can see, for example, that all its sides must be equal to 180 degrees or two right angles. All universal judgements arise in this way, Beneke then suggests (30–31; §3), though he provides no further explanation. To escape scepticism, then, Beneke entertains the possibility that all universal judgements can be verified through a process akin to mathematical construction. But why this is so, and how it is so, is left unexplained. The *Erfahrungsseelenlehre,* no less than the *Erkenntnißlehre,* leaves the question of the foundations of knowledge hanging in the air.

The *Erfahrungsseelenlehre* attempts to provide a new foundation for aesthetics and ethics as well as epistemology. Accordingly, more than half of the work is devoted to these disciplines. First comes the new foundation for aesthetics, which is for Beneke a theory of feeling. Feeling is explained on the basis of the same activities as the faculty of knowledge. It consists in those states arising from the ratio between the mind's receptivity and spontaneity, between what Beneke calls "stimulus" (*Reiz*) and "power" or "energy" (*Kraft*) (86–87; §8). There are three kinds of feelings: pleasure (*das Angenehme*), when stimulus preponderates over power; sublimity (*das*

Erhabene), when power preponderates over stimulus; and beauty (*das Schöne*), when stimulus and power are in equilibirum.

This very sketchy and schematic account of feeling then provides the foundation for Beneke's ethics. For Beneke, no less than Herbart, ethics is ultimately based on aesthetics. This is because ethics is based upon human feelings, the study of which is aesthetics, the doctrine of feeling (130; §10). Why is this so? We judge the morality of actions, Beneke explains, according to whether they arouse feelings of sublimity or beauty within us (132; §10). A virtuous action gives us feelings of sublimity or beauty, and a vicious one gives the opposite of those feelings (the common or ugly). Such a reduction of ethics to aesthetics comes as a surprise, especially for someone who otherwise avows to follow the spirit of Kant's philosophy. But in the field of ethics Beneke is more the antagonist than protagonist of Kant. He thinks that the whole concept of practical reason is an occult quality, which he wants to reduce to its more basic elements, which are to be found in feeling (133; §11). More radically, he wants to abolish the entire doctrine of duties from ethics and to replace it with a doctrine of virtue alone (163; §11). Judging human actions according to general rules is for Beneke an abomination: it abstracts from the particular factors necessary for each moral judgement, and it measures all human beings according to a single standard of mediocrity (144; §11). Like a good student of Schleiermacher,[50] Beneke is critical of Kant's belief in absolute duties because it ignores the realm of individuality, that is, the particular motives of a person's action, the particular circumstances in which a person must act, the particular constraints and limits of action. Moral judgement has to be aesthetic because it is first and foremost a matter of feeling, of learning how to sympathize with people, of acquiring the power to re-enact another person's state of mind (127–128; §11). The great advantage of feeling over general rules is that it is more perceptive of the individual features of each case of action, and so more likely to result in fair and accurate moral judgement (144–145; §11). *Erfahrungsseelenlehre* has for Beneke, as it had for its early protagonists, a liberal social and political agenda. Its aim is to make the judge or magistrate see the world from the standpoint of the defendant, so that they are more tolerant and provide more humane judgements.

Such, in crude outline, was Beneke's early philosophical programme. It was all very sketchy and schematic, stated in dense and awkward prose. But in 170 small pages Beneke believed that he had provided the basis for a complete reform of philosophy, the foundation for the *philosophia perennis*, forever sought and never caught. However, he was confident, as only a very young man can be, in his discovery and its success. In the concluding section he went so far as to claim that his philosophy was not just "this or that philosophy" but "philosophy in itself" (166; §12). Soon, though,

---

[50] On Schleiermacher's ethics and critique of Kant, see my 'Schleiermacher's ethics', in *The Cambridge Companion to Schleiermacher*, ed. Jacqueline Marina (Cambridge: Cambridge University Press, 1995), pp. 53–71.

Beneke would learn the fate of all great reformers of learning: that they have to give a foundation to their new foundation.

5. A Trying Encounter

Sometime in 1820, just around the time he wrote his *Erkenntnißlehre* and *Erfahrungsseelenlehre,* Beneke had a trying encounter with another young and ambitious philosopher in Berlin, one who later would become as famous as Hegel: Arthur Schopenhauer. Schopenhauer and Beneke both habilitated in Berlin in 1820, though Schopenhauer began to lecture one semester before Beneke. Curious about his future colleague, Beneke attended Schopenhauer's lectures twice in the spring of 1820. He was later given the opportunity to examine Schopenhauer's work when the editor of the *Jenaische Allgemeine Literatur-Zeitung* invited him to review *Die Welt als Wille und Vorstellung,* which had appeared in January 1819. Though hesitant, Beneke agreed to write the review, which duly appeared in December 1820.[51]

A review of Schopenhauer was a very delicate task for Beneke. The two new *Privatdozenten* were rivals for student audiences in Berlin, and any review was likely to arouse suspicions about the reviewer's motives. Well aware of this danger, Beneke strived to write a fair, balanced and objective review. He would be free and frank in his philosophical judgements; but philosophical differences should never be a cause for personal animosity. Beneke pointed out that Schopenhauer had been highly critical of Kant, even though he had the greatest respect for him; he wanted Schopenhauer to take his criticisms in a similar spirit. And then in one sentence he summarizes all his admiration and reservations about the author:

The book before us shows such great philosophical insight, such a richness of thought, such a rare gift for clear and vivid exposition; it contains in its refutation of other views, and in its account of its own, so many illuminating remarks about all parts of philosophy, that (the reviewer must now bring this panegyric to an end) we cannot complain enough about its many errors bordering on insanity, to which its author has been led through consistent deduction from a few false principles. (378)

Beneke's review, which is nearly thirty pages long, contains many insightful criticisms of many aspects of Schopenhauer's work, to which we cannot begin to do justice here. On the whole Beneke strives to evaluate Schopenhauer by his own standards, and contents himself with finding inconsistencies. Among these inconsistencies: Schopenhauer insists that knowledge is limited to experience but then claims to have knowledge of reality in itself; Schopenhauer limits the principle of sufficient reason to appearances but assumes that the will in itself is the cause of

---

[51] *Jenaische Allgemeine Literatur-Zeitung,* December 1820, No. 226–229, pp. 378–403. Along with Schopenhauer's book, Beneke also reviewed a polemic against it by J.G. Rätze, *Was der Wille des Menschen in moralischen und göttlichen Dingen aus eigener Kraft vermag, and was er nicht vermag. Mit Rücksicht auf die Schopenauerische Schrift: Die Welt als Wille und Vorstellung.* (Leipzig: Hartmann, 1820).

appearances. The gross errors Beneke finds in Schopenhauer's book—those "bordering on insanity"—concern the vast metaphysical conclusions that he draws from scanty empirical premises. Beneke questions whether the immediate knowledge we have of our own mental activities gives us sufficient evidence to infer the existence of a single cosmic will that appears in all of nature and in every human being (388). By the end of the review, the main differences between Beneke and Schopenhauer are plain: Beneke's more cautious empirical approach clashes with Schopenhauer's metaphysical ambitions. Beneke accepts wholeheartedly Schopenhauer's many statements to the effect that science gives us knowledge only of the appearances of things; but he cannot endorse Schopenhauer's statements that philosophy gives us knowledge of reality in itself. If philosophy is a science, it should be subject to all the limits of science. Whence then this bold ambition to know the inner nature of things? (382–383)

Beneke knew that in writing the review of a rival he was skating on thin ice. But there was another reason that he was fearful about the reaction to his review: Schopenhauer's arrogance and sensitivity, his open contempt for other philosophers, was well known. His book was sprinkled with caustic and vituperative remarks about Fichte, Schelling and Hegel. Would not Beneke, by writing his review, soon became a similar target for Schopenhauer's wrath? Beneke was hopeful that he could make the whole discussion more civilized. At the end of his review he chastens Schopenhauer for his venomous remarks, which he finds "unworthy of a philosopher". He agrees with the philosophical failings of these authors; but philosophical failings should not be treated as if they were moral vices. In thus chastening Schopenhauer, Beneke was hoping that he would discourage him from treating him as he had done to so many others. His plea was for "*Sachlichkeit*", sheer objectivity, sticking to the issues and leaving one's ego behind.

It was a grievous miscalculation. Schopenhauer could not have been more incensed by Beneke's review, which he saw as the work of a rival intent on undermining him.[52] He immediately wrote an indignant letter to the editor of journal, Heinrich Karl Eichstädt, demanding that he publish immediately, without any delay and the slightest editorial changes, his response to the review, which he enclosed.[53] If Eichstädt did not do so, he would find six other journals that would publish it, in which he would add his own explanation for the whole affair.

Why was Schopenhauer so angry? In his response he explained that it was not the reviewer's opinion about his book; he expected criticism and disagreement, and even welcomed it. What he took exception to, however, was all the "lies" and "slander". Beneke's review was indeed "a forgery" and "fraud" because, on at least ten occasions, he had used quotation marks for sentences that never appeared in Schopenhauer's

---

[52] Schopenhauer said as much many years later. See Schopenhauer to Julius Frauenstädt, March 26, 1854, in *Arthur Schopenhauer, Gesammelte Briefe*, ed. Arthur Hübscher (Bonn: Bouvier, 1978), p. 336.
[53] See Schopenhauer to Heinrich Karl Abraham Eichstädt, January 6, 1821, in *Gesammelte Briefe*, pp. 63–66.

book. Allegedly, Beneke omitted phrases, pushed together disparate sentences, added words with wild abandon, and then used quotations marks as if this farrago were the author's exact words. It was one thing to criticize the content of the book; but it was quite another to distort it. This incoherent pastiche, this clumsy prose, this monstrous dog's dinner, was presented to the whole world as if they were the *ipsissima verba* of the author! What could that be but lies and slander?

Eventually, Eichstädt acceded to Schopenhauer's demands, though he did so only by giving Beneke the space to reply to Schopenhauer's accusations. Schopenhauer's riposte, with Beneke's reply immediately following it, duly appeared in the *Intelligenzblatt der Jenaischen Allgemeinen Literatur-Zeitung* for February 1821.[54] Beneke found it easy to reply to Schopenhauer's accusations. Some of the changes were due to printer's errors; but most of them were due to abridgements, which Beneke felt obliged to make for his readers and reasons of space. In no case were the abridgements such that they destroyed the meaning of Schopenhauer's sentences. Such abridgements are the common practice of all reviews nowadays, Beneke said, so that Schopenhauer need not feel that he was the special target of a conspiracy. If Schopenhauer felt that these abridgements damaged the beauty of his prose, Beneke was sorry for that; but then he had some bad news for him: the latest review of Schopenhauer's work in the *Leipziger Literatur-Zeitung* had made the same kind of abridgements.[55] As for the tone of Schopenhauer's riposte, Beneke felt no need to censure it; it spoke for itself.

Towards the close of his review, Beneke made reference to one extraordinary fact about his encounter with Schopenhauer. He said that, to prevent all the trouble and embarrassment of a public dispute, he had tried to discuss matters with Schopenhauer personally. Indeed, on two occasions, Beneke paid a visit to Schopenhauer's lodgings in Berlin and asked to speak with him. On both occasions, however, the maid sent him away; and on the second she even told him that Schopenhauer was at home. "The poor young man turned completely pale", the maid told Schopenhauer after the second visit.[56] Schopenhauer revelled in Beneke's humiliation, which he felt to be due revenge for the review.

However brief, Beneke's clash with Schopenhauer was portentous. It was symbolic of the future rivalry between Schopenhauer and the later neo-Kantians, who, like Beneke, disapproved of Schopenhauer's grandiose metaphysics. Refusing to acknowledge Schopenhauer's claim to be Kant's only legitimate heir, the neo-Kantians would subject his metaphysics to sharp criticism throughout the 1860s. Though

[54] Beneke's review, Schopenhauer's response, and Beneke's counter-response, along with all other early reviews of Schopenhauer's *Die Welt als Wille und Vorstellung*, are reprinted in 'Die Zeitgenössischen Rezensionen der Werke Arthur Schopenhauers', ed. Reinhard Piper, *Jahrbuch der Schopenhauer-Gesellschaft* VI (1917), pp. 47–178, esp. 149–158.

[55] Beneke was referring to the review of Traugott Krug, which appeared in *Leipziger Literatur-Zeitung*, No. 21 (January 24, 1821), pp. 158–175 (Schopenhauer Gesellschaft edition).

[56] See Schopenhauer to Frauenstädt, March 26, 1854, *Gesammelte Briefe*, p. 336.

Schopenhauer did not live to see the Kant revival of the 1860s, we can be certain that he would have vented a hefty dose of spleen over it. After all, the neo-Kantians were "university philosophers" and he had also expressed his contempt for Herbart and Fries just as he had done for Beneke. We will have occasion to examine the neo-Kantian clash with Schopenhauer in later chapters.[57]

6. The Physics of Morals

The early 1820s was a period of extraordinary creativity for the young Beneke, whose high ambitions were matched only by his inexhaustible energies. In 1822, only two years after his *Erfahrungsseelenlehre* and *Erkenntnißlehre,* he published his first work on ethics, *Grundlegung zur Physik der Sitten.*[58] His major work on ethics was his three-volume *Grundlinien des natürlichen Systems der praktischen Philosophie,* which appeared from 1837 to 1840.[59] There are important differences in emphasis and meaning between the earlier and later works, though these do not concern us here. Our interest will be limited strictly to Beneke's earlier work, which was more controversial and which laid down the basis for his later work.

Beneke's *Grundlegung zur Physik der Sitten* is a much more full exposition of the ethical doctrines already sketched in his *Erfahrungsseelenlehre.* There is the same naturalistic programme, the same emphasis on the central role of feeling, and the same opposition to an absolutist morality. On one very important point, though, the texts differ: the aesthetic foundation of morality, so pronounced in the earlier work, falls into the background in the later one. Beneke retains the distinction between beauty and sublimity, though these aesthetic concepts no longer play a foundational role but only distinguish between two kinds of virtue.[60]

For Beneke's ethics, no less than his epistemology, Kant proves to be the decisive figure. But it is almost entirely in a negative sense. The antagonism towards Kant already apparent in the *Erfahrungsseelenlehre* now becomes more explicit and emphatic. On point after point Beneke takes issue with Kant, defining his position in opposition to him. The *physics* of morals is meant to refute and replace Kant's *metaphysics* of morals. The very subtitle of Beneke's work reveals his intentions: "*ein Gegenstück zu Kants Grundlegung zur Metaphysik der Sitten.*" The work was conceived in epistolary form, where Beneke's imaginary correspondent, "Karl", is a Kantian. After twenty long letters, Karl finally comes to see the light: the untenability of virtually every

---

[57] See Introduction, Section 4.

[58] Friedrich Eduard Beneke, *Grundlegung zur Physik der Sitten, ein Gegenstück zur Metaphysik der Sitten, mit einem Anhange über das Wesen und die Erkenntnißgränzen der Vernunft* (Berlin: Mittler, 1822). All references in parentheses are to page numbers in this edition.

[59] Friedrich Eduard Beneke, *Grundlinien des natürlichen Systems der praktischen Philosophie* (Berlin: Mittler, 1837–1840). Band I: *Allgemeine Sittenlehre* (1837). Band II: *Specielle Sittenlehre* (1840). Band III: *Grundlinien des Naturrechts, der Politik und des philosophischen Kriminalrechts* (1838).

[60] See Beneke, *Grundlegung zur Physik der Sitten,* pp. 226–234.

tenet of Kant's moral philosophy. Because it takes such a diametrically opposed view
to Kant on so many issues, Beneke's *Grundlegung zur Physik der Sitten* is one of the
most interesting and important works on ethics to appear in the early 19th century.
Beneke's criticisms still resonate, anticipating positions later advanced in the 20th
century.[61]

Just what does Beneke mean by a "physics of morals"? Though it is left undefined in
the work itself, he went to some pains to explain himself in a later appendix and apology.[62] The term gave rise to suspicions of materialism, which Beneke was eager to dis-
pel.[63] The physics of morals is meant to be an application of the naturalist-empiricist
programme Beneke had already outlined in his *Erfahrungsseelenlehre*. This project
would trace the fundamental principles of morality back to their origins in human
sensibility and feeling, which are held to be the sources of all mental activity.[64] The
method of the physics of morals would be "genetic", that is, it would show how moral
principles and concepts that seem to be eternal, innate and a priori are really the
products of education and environment.[65] To address concerns about materialism, Beneke insists that a physics of morals is not a materialist or "sensualist" programme.[66] "The physics of the soul" means only "the nature of the soul", according
to the old Greek sense of *phýsis,* and Beneke insists that its nature is distinct from
matter itself.

Though no materialist, Beneke is a naturalist. He is perfectly clear that his project
intends to explain all the characteristic phenomena of the soul according to natural laws.[67] And he even endorses Lessing's naturalism, according to which there is
nothing supernatural and everything happens of necessity (66). Such naturalism was
alone sufficient to get him into trouble in the repressive environment of the 1820s.
When Schulze complained about Beneke's book, he never mentioned materialism,
but he did express his disapproval of a doctrine which held that thinking is "a purely
natural process".

Beneke's *Grundlegung zur Physik der Sitten* was first and foremost an attempt to
rehabilitate the sentimentalist ethics of Hutcheson, Hume and Smith, which had
been once endorsed but then repudiated by Kant. Though his ultimate debts are to
his British forbears,[68] Beneke's more immediate ones are to Jacobi, who, via Rousseau,

---

[61] In his emphasis on the role of virtue, Beneke's views are close to those of Alasdair MacIntyre; and
in his emphasis on the importance of particular situations, his views are like those of Sartre and the
existentialists.

[62] The appendix, entitled *Anhang über das Wesen und die Erkenntnißgränzen der Vernunft,* consists of
a set of five distinct letters on the meaning and limits of reason. The apology was Beneke's *Schutzschrift
für meine Grundlegung zur Physik der Sitten* (Leipzig: Karl Heinrich Reclam, 1823).

[63] The suspicion of materialism shadowed Beneke all his life, and even after it. In 1862 Johann Gottlieb
Dressler, Beneke's student, attempted to refute it. See his *Ist Beneke Materialist?* (Berlin: Mittler, 1862).

[64] Beneke, *Anhang über das Wesen und die Erkenntnißgränzen der Vernunft,* pp. 313–316.

[65] Beneke, *Anhang,* pp. 308–309, 332–333.

[66] Beneke, *Schutzschrift,* pp. 15–16; Beneke, *Anhang,* p. 344.   [67] Beneke, *Schutzschrift,* p. 16.

[68] These debts are most apparent from Beneke's favourable opinion of Hume, *Physik der Sitten,*
pp. 21–22. Jacobi's own philosophy was very indebted to Hume's.

had imported sentimentalism into Germany. Never one to conceal his debts, Beneke explicitly declared that Jacobi's views were closest to his own, and he acknowledged that it was Jacobi who first gave him the idea for a genetic account of morality.[69] Beneke's central thesis is indeed straight out of Jacobi and the sentimentalist tradition: that moral principles are derived from, and indeed must be based upon, sentiments or feelings. We know what is right or wrong first through feelings, which we later formulate into concepts and principles (10, 80). So it is not principles that determine our moral feelings; it is our moral feelings that determine our principles. To be sure, concepts and principles are necessary to clarify and explain these feelings; but they cannot ever replace them and ultimately have to be based upon them (279). If, for example, we were purely rational beings who never had a feeling of sympathy, we would never have motive or reason to be kind to others. We approve benevolent actions, and disapprove selfish ones, only because we have that feeling of sympathy. Generalizing from this point, Beneke assumes that there is a *sui generis* class of moral feelings, which it is the business of ethics to discover, define and clarify (86–87). The decisive role of feeling in morality has been so ignored, he argues, because so many philosophers have a false conception of sensibility. They see it as a purely passive and physical capacity opposed to reason, though it is in reality active and spiritual. Following Hume and Jacobi, Beneke regards sensibility as the source of all our vital energies, indeed as the dominating power of the soul, of which reason is only one function.[70]

The flipside of Beneke's enthusiasm for sentimentalism is his vehement reproof of Kant's rationalism. Not the least reason to be an empiricist and sentimentalist in ethics, he believes, is that rationalism is so bankrupt. All the problems of the rationalism of Kant's epistemology resurface in his ethics. Kant's categorical imperative makes the same mistake as all rationalist speculation: it attempts to squeeze blood from a turnip, that is, to derive concrete or particular results from a general or universal principle. The categorical imperative, as a purely formal principle, proves to be "empty" because all kinds of maxims, whether moral and immoral, are universalizable (37–38). The only reason Kant's principle seems to provide results, Beneke argues, is that the arguments for it tacitly presuppose feelings, which are necessary to tell us whether we accept a maxim as a universal law (39–40). On the whole, Beneke finds Kant's criterion useless because it is too vague. Kant does not specify exactly how to formulate a maxim, so we get inconsistent results depending on the formulation (37–39, 257). He also fails to give a precise account of the moral will that is to be the ultimate determinate of the value of a maxim (42–43).

---

[69] On Beneke's debts to Jacobi, see Beneke, *Grundlegung*, p. 2; Beneke, *Schutzschrift*, p. 10; and Beneke, *Anhang*, p. 309. See also his June 6, 1849 letter to Josephine Stadlin, *Ungedruckte Briefe*, pp. 265–266. For all his debts to Jacobi, Beneke was very critical of his distinction between understanding and sensibility, see *Anhang*, pp. 320–322.
[70] Beneke, *Anhang*, pp. 315–316.

Contrary to Kant, and very much like Herbart, Beneke sees no special moral value attaching to universality. Since immoral principles can be universalized no less than moral ones, the distinction between universal and particular commands is purely logical (247). Focusing upon the universality of a maxim to determine the morality of an action is in any case a distraction, because it does not consider the very special circumstances of each case and the complicated motives of an agent (130). Each case is unique and each agent is different, so that it becomes almost impossible to generalize what we should do (199–200). It is indeed precisely here, Beneke argues, that we can see the great value of moral feeling over universalizability as a test of morality (278). Feeling is perceptive of, and responsive to, different circumstances and motives, and so is more likely to provide a more tolerant and accurate moral judgement.

For Beneke, the most objectionable aspect of Kant's moral theory lies in its doctrine of absolute or unconditional moral values. No value is so absolute, Beneke argues, that there cannot be some higher one (94). None is so unconditional that it should not be surrendered under specific circumstances (31–33, 269–272). Consider, for example, the prescription against murder. There seems to be no higher precept, no more absolute prohibition; but sometimes we even excuse it, namely, in times of famine the Greenlanders murder their children rather than see them starve to death (100–101). While Kant makes it a fundamental principle that we always treat humanity as an end in itself, it is still the case that we often make exceptions to this principle, viz., we execute criminals, we command soldiers to sacrifice their lives in time of war (95). Beneke sees no problem at all in admitting a kind of relativism, one which accepts opposing moral assessments of the same kind of actions, so that whether we approve or disapprove of polygamy or suicide should depend on the circumstances, time and age of the agents (269–272). Following the spirit of his historical age, Beneke insists that a *Rechtslehre* that pretends to be independent of time and place is *"eine leere Dichtung"*, and stresses that all legitimate *Rechtslehre* has to be "in part an historical science" (186, 192).

Given his critique of absolute values and universality, it is not surprising that Beneke's position in *Physik der Sitten* comes close to a complete virtue ethics. Like all virtue theorists, he insists that we cannot formulate general rules that hold for all cases, and that we can determine what we ought to do only by considering particular circumstances. A general principle by itself has no moral force because it cannot tell us under particular circumstances how, and indeed whether, we should follow it. A proper moral imperative does not take simply the general form "Be kind!", but the more particular form "Be kind in this case!" (246). Beneke's virtue ethics is most explicit when he states that the moral law should be derived from our model of the virtuous man (228, 230). Accordingly, he cites a maxim he attributes to Aristotle: "The good is what the excellent man does".[71] Beneke even defines morality in terms of

---

[71] The source of this maxim is obscure. The cited dictum goes in German *"gut sei, was der vortreffliche Mann thue."* (228) Beneke is directly citing Jacobi, who, he claims, is citing Aristotle. Beneke is

virtue because it consists for him in having power over one's sensible desires and in following one's system of values, whatever they might be (214, 217, 209–210). Since morality is independent of precepts, he even leaves it open-ended what these values should be. People can be virtuous, that is, moral, whatever the desires they control and whatever the values they have.

Whatever his leanings towards a virtue ethics, it is striking that Beneke does not completely disavow general moral principles. He even goes so far to say that, at least in particular cases, we can determine right or wrong with mathematical accuracy (179, 278). It turns out, though, that we determine right or wrong not by consulting the categorical imperative but by reckoning according to the utilitarian calculus, that is, by weighing gains and losses and choosing that option that maximizes pleasure or minimizes pain (172, 179). The strong utilitarian streak in his ethics emerges most clearly when Beneke states that a sound moral system should be grounded on the value of "pleasure as pleasure" (213).[72] He even goes so far in his utilitarianism as to claim that no crime is committed if a thief, who is in dire need, steals from someone who does not derive any benefit from his property (174). Beneke disavows consequentialism, however, because he thinks that it is a mistake to take into account the success of an action to determine its morality, which is ultimately determined by the will (21, 187).[73] The apparent tension is resolvable if we follow through with Beneke's distinction between *Sittlichkeit* and *Recht*, between the morality and legality of an action (196–198). While the legality of an action considers its consequences, its morality concerns its motives (196).

No aspect of Kant's ethics more aroused Beneke's ire than its theory of metaphysical freedom, which ran counter to his own deep-seated naturalism (66). The Kantian concept of a noumenal self he saw as a lapse into obscurantanism (66–67).[74] It seemed absurd to place moral motivation and character into a mysterious realm beyond time and space. Since it is plain that moral volition and action occur in time, it should follow, at least by Kant's own reckoning, that they must be part of nature, which encompasses the entire temporal realm (67). Kant's aim, of course, was to protect moral freedom, to save moral responsibility from the determinism of nature; but Beneke insists that there is no need to assume that freedom excludes determinism in the first place. All that freedom presupposes in a moral sense is that we have the power to control our impulses, and that our actions are free from constraint; but neither presupposition means that an action has no cause.[75] All acts are indeed the product of

probably referring to Jacobi's *Woldemar*, in Jacobi, *Werke* (Leipzig: Fleischer, 1820), V, 79. Here Jacobi cites Aristotle, though he too does not give a source.

[72] It was indeed no accident that Beneke was an admirer of Bentham and became the editor of a German edition of *Principles of Morals and Legislation*. See Beneke, *Grundsätze der Civil- und Kriminalgesetzgebung* (Berlin: Amelang, 1830). Beneke translated Bentham from the second French edition of Etienne Dumont.

[73] See *Physik der Sitten*, p. 21, where Beneke criticizes Hume for confusing morality with utility. Cf. *Schutzschrift*, pp. 18, 25–26.

[74] Cf. Beneke, *Schutzschrift*, pp. 41–46.   [75] Beneke, *Schutzschrift*, p. 47.

previous causes; but that does not make the will superfluous, because it too is a necessary cause of our actions (72). Beneke goes on to argue, like all compatibilists, that
morality is not only compatible with causal necessity but even presupposes it (67–68).
Moral judgements presuppose that people's actions will follow causal laws, namely,
"Do X if you want Y" assumes that X is in appropriate circumstances a cause of Y
(67–68).[76]

All told, the *Physik der Sitten* was a remarkably bold and original work, at least if we
place it in its historical context, which was still dominated by Kant's ethics and speculative idealism. Its empiricism, naturalism and relativism proved very challenging for
his contemporaries. It was not surprising, then, that the *Physik der Sitten* led to the
rescript against Beneke's lectures in Berlin. Sadly, Beneke would never live down the
fate that the *Physik der Sitten* imposed on him. It was no work for the age of reaction.

7. Cracks in the Foundation

Shortly after the *Erfahrungsseelenlehre* appeared in February 1820 Beneke realized
that his programme faced grave obstacles. His grand vision was to make philosophy into a science by transforming it into empirical psychology. All his confidence
in that revolutionary project came from his belief that psychology too could be an
empirical science, a science on par with physics, physiology and chemistry. Soon
enough, however, he learned that belief stood in urgent need of defence. For there
had been some powerful critics of empirical psychology, even dangerous sceptics,
who doubted the very possibility of psychology as a science. Responding to these
critics and sceptics became one of Beneke's priorities in the early 1820s. This was a
central task of three early works, *Neue Grundlegung zur Metaphysik, Das Verhältniß
von Seele und Leib* and *Beiträge zu einer reinseelenwissenschaftlichen Bearbeitung der
Seelenkrankheitskunde.*[77]

One of the chief critics of empirical psychology was no less than Kant himself. In
the first *Kritik* he had treated psychology like a stern stepfather.[78] While he seemed to
allow the possibility that it could be an empirical science, he insisted that it was only
part of *applied* philosophy, and that it should be "banished entirely" from metaphysics or pure philosophy. Psychology had still not proven itself, and it was scarcely a
discipline in its own right. Hence one had to treat it as "a stranger whom one suffers

---

[76] In rejecting Kant's concept of transcendental freedom and in advancing compatibilism, Beneke
found himself in company with Herbart, a point noted with some satisfaction by Herbart himself. In a
review of the *Physik der Sitten* he declared the chapter on transcendental freedom the best in the entire
book. See Herbart, SW XII, 181.

[77] *Neue Grundlegung zur Metaphysik* (Berlin: Mittler, 1822); *Das Verhältniß von Seele und Leib*; and
Beiträge zu einer reinseelenwissenschaftlichen Bearbeitung der Seelenkrankheitskunde. Though the second work appeared in its final form in 1826, Beneke had written an earlier version by 1821, which appeared
in *Nasses Zeitschrift für psychische Aertze*, Heft 1 (1821), 1–55.

[78] Kant, KrV, B 876–877.

for a while, and grants residence for a time, until he can move into his own lodging in a comprehensive anthropology (the pendant to empirical natural science)." In the preface to his *Metaphysiche Anfangsgründe* Kant went on to doubt whether empirical psychology could be a science at all.[79] A discipline was a science only to the degree that one could apply mathematics to it; and it is impossible to apply mathematics to the phenomena of inner sense, which are too fleeting to be properly measured.

As if these pronouncements on the scientific status of psychology were not challenging enough, Beneke was disturbed even more by another central Kantian doctrine. This was the Kantian theory of inner sense, according to which we know ourselves only as appearances. Kant had maintained in the first *Kritik* that while we can know *that we exist* as spontaneous subjects, we cannot know *how* we exist as such a subject, whose essence or intrinsic nature is an unknowable noumenon or thing-in-itself.[80] The reasoning behind this apparently paradoxical doctrine seemed perfectly straightforward: that all knowledge, including self-knowledge, is limited by the form of inner sense, which is time; and that form provides us with knowledge only of appearances.[81] This thesis had far-reaching consequences: it meant downgrading self-knowledge from its once privileged position in modern philosophy. While Descartes, Locke and Hume saw self-knowledge as certain and immediate, they held knowledge of the external world to be uncertain and mediate because it has to be inferred as the cause of my ideas or representations. With his doctrine of inner sense, however, Kant puts self-knowledge and knowledge of the external world on the same footing. Both are certain and immediate; but both gave us knowledge only of appearances. The thing-in-itself, whether as an external cause of sensation or the subject behind all representations, is unknowable.

It was one of the central aims of Beneke's psychology to restore the primacy and immediacy of self-consciousness, to reinstate its privileged place in epistemology after its demotion in the Kantian *Kritik*. In his *Neue Grundlegung zur Metaphysik* Beneke attempted to provide a knock-down refutation of Kant's doctrine of inner sense. Here he tries to prove *more geometrico* that we can know ourselves as we really are, and that our self-knowledge is privileged over knowledge of the external world, which has to be inferred from our knowledge of our own inner states. *Prima facie* it is odd to find Beneke resorting to the method of mathematical demonstration so loved by rationalists and so scorned by empiricists; but Beneke had to resort to "metaphysics" here, because it is obvious that the question at stake is not empirical. When questions are not empirical but metaphysical, Beneke thinks that the only exact methods to decide them are mathematical. In general, he questions Kant's distinction between the mathematical and philosophical methods, and believed that philosophy could have all the certainty and exactitude of the mathematical method—provided, of course, it rigorously follows that method.[82]

---

[79] Kant, *Metaphysische Anfangsgründe der Naturwissenschaften*, IV, 471.
[80] Kant, KrV, B 158.   [81] Kant, KrV, B 152.
[82] See Beneke, *Erkenntnißlehre*, 88–98, §§13–14. Here Beneke argues in detail against Kant's distinction.

Beneke thinks that his very first proof is sufficient to refute the Kantian doctrine (8). He sets himself the following task: to find one representation that corresponds with being (6). We find that representation in the very act of becoming aware of a representation, he argues, because that representation, simply as a representation, has a being of its own (7). It does not matter whether this representation conforms to something else beyond itself (in this case another representation); it still exists as something in its own right, and it therefore has being. The simple facts that we can be aware of this representation, and that this representation has a being of its own, demonstrates that we can have knowledge of being, at least in our own case through the awareness of our own representations.

It is evident, however, that Beneke laid too much on such a simple and slender proof. The argument is clearly insufficient to prove his thesis. For the question remains whether the representation we know belongs to ourselves in ourselves or as an appearance. The representation indeed amounts to "being" (*Sein*), but only in a very general sense, which leaves open the question whether it is being in itself or mere appearance. Furthermore, Beneke seems blind to the deeper problem of self-knowledge: How can we know the act of representing ourselves except on pain of an infinite regress? This was the kind of problem that tormented the young Herbart, who did not fail to remind Beneke of their importance.[83]

Beneke turned to the question from another angle in his *Das Verhältniß von Seele und Leib.* After explaining his earlier proof in less technical language, he adds the following argument: that there is a fundamental difference between knowing ourselves and knowing the external world, because to know the external world we have to go outside ourselves to see if our representations correspond to something external to us; but in the case of ourselves we do not have to go outside ourselves at all; rather, what we know lies before us in immediate self-observation (43–44; §3). This basic difference between the two forms of knowledge is denied on the Kantian doctrine, Beneke implies, because it makes it seem as if self-knowledge is just as difficult and problematic as knowledge of the external world.

Here again, though, Beneke's argument is too thin. It begs the question because if *all* cognitive activity conditions and determines how things appear to us, as Kant argues and Beneke admits (33–34; §2), we are still left with the question how we know ourselves in ourselves. Even our self-knowing activity should condition and determine what it knows. This means that even in our own case the self-knowing subject has to go outside itself to know itself as an object in itself. The distinction between knowledge of ourselves and the external world collapses; but this is the price we have to pay for the Kantian principle that all cognitive activity shapes what it knows.

Another potent critic of empirical psychology was Hume. Although his science of human nature was an ancestor of Beneke's own project, Hume's legacy was a very

[83] See Herbart's review of Beneke's *Psychologische Skizzen*, SW XIII, 124.

ambivalent one, having the power to destroy as well as inspire. For resting uneasily beside David Hume the naturalist there was David Hume the sceptic. And the two Humes are not happy bedfellows: Hume's critique of the principle of causality seems to undermine the science of human nature he is so intent to establish. That science claims to consist in universal and necessary laws, much like Newton's laws of motion; but the thrust of Hume's doubts about causation is that there is no evidence for the idea of necessary connection involved in a natural law. Beneke was a great admirer of Hume, whom he read carefully and in the original English. Such, indeed, was his admiration that in his *Erfahrungsseelenlehre* he had even endorsed Hume's analysis of causality into constant conjunction (38–42; §4). Later in the 1820s, however, Beneke saw the troubling consequences of such scepticism. Hume's doubts about causality work against not only the laws of nature but also the laws of mind.

Beneke addresses the source of his new doubts in section §5 of *Das Verhältniß von Seele und Leib*. There he tackles head-on Hume's scepticism. He declares that he is in full agreement with Hume's fundamental principle: that we can demonstrate the reality of an idea only if we can find an impression corresponding to it (59, 41–42n). But by this very standard, he argues, we can vindicate the reality of the idea of causal connection. We have an immediate feeling of causal power in the case of our own will, Beneke argues (63, 64; §5). When we resolve to close the door, for example, we have a feeling of our effort to close it, the force by which we push the door against the resisting air and onto its frame. That feeling, Beneke believes, is nothing less than a simple impression of force or power, which is sufficient to ground the idea of necessary connection behind our idea of cause and effect. This impression of force and power is given and simple, and it is not an idea resolvable into more simple impressions; hence it is not created by the imagination, which has the power to join together and take apart impressions but never to create them (40; §3).

It is remarkable to find Beneke falling back on this tired old argument, which had a long and inglorious history. As Beneke well knew, its weaknesses had already been exposed by Hume in the *Enquiry*.[84] Indeed, on these grounds he had rejected it himself in his *Erfahrungsseelenslehre* (38, 40; §4). But now, out of sheer desperation, Beneke attempts to rehabilitate it and to vindicate it against Hume's objections. Too much was at stake: the very possibility of providing a sound foundation for universal laws in psychology. And so Beneke sifts through Hume's objections and tries to wiggle out of them. But it is all to no avail. His efforts are no more successful than those before him. For while we might indeed have a simple impression or feeling of effort or force, there is no reason to think that this impression or feeling involves the experience of a necessary connection. We have two distinct impressions—the feeling of effort and the closing of the door—but no evidence of a necessary connection between them, and so no reason to call one the cause and the other the effect. The fallacy of Beneke's

---

[84] Hume, *Enquiry Concerning Human Understanding*, in *Essays and Treatises on Several Subjects* (London: Cadell, 1777), pp. 48–57.

argument becomes very clear from his description of the experience involved in feeling how one mental state follows another. Beneke says that we feel not only the effort but also how the succeeding state is "conditioned" (*bedingt*) by the preceding one (69; §5). But where is the impression of something "conditioning" or "determining" something else? It is plain that Beneke had simply read into the experience the very causal principle needing justification.

8. Settling Accounts with Kant

Though a sharp critic of Kant in his *Erfahrungsseelenlehre* and *Physik der Sitten*, Beneke never ceased to define and orient his philosophy around him. Never did he renounce the claim to be the legitimate heir of Kant's legacy, the true spokesman for the spirit of the critical philosophy. It was important, however, that he justify such a bold claim, which was very controversial in the 1820s. Just because the Kantian spirit was such a potent imprimatur, philosophers of many stripes would claim to be its true disciples. Not the least among them were the great idealist system builders themselves, Fichte, Schelling and Hegel, whose work Beneke regarded as a betrayal of Kant. Somehow, then, Beneke would have to defend his claim against other contenders for the Kantian mantle.

He turned to just that task in his 1832 tract *Kant und die philosophische Aufgabe unserer Zeit*.[85] The tract is subtitled *Eine Jubeldenkschrift* (literally, 'a celebratory memorial') because it was written to celebrate the semi-centennial of the publication of the *Kritik der reinen Vernunft*. Coincidentally, it appeared in November 1831, the very month of Hegel's death. That aroused Hegelian suspicions.[86] Was Beneke, a known enemy of Hegel, covertly celebrating the death of their beloved master? If so, it was an insult to "*der Verewigten*"! To counter such mistrust, Beneke felt obliged to add a prefatory note attesting that the date was sheer coincidence and that his work had been in fact finished earlier in August; however, its printing had been prevented by the spread of cholera in Berlin (the very pestilence that had claimed Hegel's life).

Beneke's tract has been seen as the beginning of the neo-Kantian movement, as the first explicit call for a return to Kant.[87] But, as we have seen, it was preceded in that role as early as 1803 by Fries' *Reinhold, Fichte und Schelling*. Still, it was an early manifesto, to say the least. It appeared at least thirty years before Otto Liebmann's *Kant und die Epigonen*, which is often seen as the beginning of neo-Kantianism.

The *Jubelschrift* (as it is known) begins with a broad assessment of Kant's achievement and place in history. Beneke saw Kant's work as the great watershed of modern

---

[85] Friedrich Eduard Beneke, *Kant und die philosophische Aufgabe unserer Zeit. Eine Jubelschrift auf die Kritik der reinen Vernunft.* (Berlin: Ernst Siegried Mittler, 1832).

[86] Karl Rosenkranz, for one, seemed very sceptical of Beneke's motives. See his *Geschichte der kant'schen Philosophie* (Leipzig: Voß, 1840), pp. 436–437.

[87] Brandt, *Beneke*, p. 29.

German philosophy. The critical philosophy was revolutionary, he believed, primarily because it broke with the predominant rationalism of its day and led philosophy back to the foundations of true knowledge, which lay in the "bathos of experience". Beneke regarded Kant's philosophy as the culmination of the *empiricist* tradition, as the last great representative of the lineage beginning with Bacon and continuing with Locke, Berkeley and Hume. If modern German philosophy would only follow that precedent, he believed, it would finally march down the road towards science.

Yet, Beneke lamented, the great promise of Kant's revolution came to nothing. Rather than following in the footsteps of the empirical tradition, philosophy after Kant had turned into a new form of rationalist speculation. It was the grand metaphysical systems of Fichte, Schelling and Hegel that had dominated German philosophy after Kant, and they represented a remarkable rehabilitation of rationalism. They were based on abstract reasoning and a priori deductions following methodologies fundamentally akin to the rationalism of Leibniz and Wolff. Worst of all, though, this resurgence of rationalism was in the name of Kant. Fichte, Schelling and Hegel all claimed to fulfill "the spirit of Kant's philosophy". How could this be? What went so wrong with Kant's revolution that it inspired the very rationalism it condemned?

That was the chief question Beneke wanted to answer in his *Jubelschrift*. The ultimate reason for the failure of Kant's revolution, he argues, was that Kant himself was still too much a child of his own age. Though a penetrating critic of rationalism, his own philosophical method was still too indebted to it. Kant had defined philosophy as "rational knowledge by means of concepts"; and, sure enough, the method of the first *Kritik* is still very much the old a priori reasoning of Leibnizian-Wolffian rationalism (29–30). Thus Kant derived the forms of understanding from the forms of judgement through conceptual analysis; and he defended the categories as necessary conditions of experience through "transcendental deductions", that is, abstract reasoning from first principles. Thus the very rationalist methodology Kant had banished in metaphysics he had endorsed in epistemology. As Beneke puts it:

Kant drove speculation from mere concepts out of the front door only to re-introduce them through the back door; in place of the objective fictions (fictions with respect to the world and God), against which he had rightly pronounced a sentence of death, he put subjective fantasies. (33)

It was Kant's use of an a priori method, Beneke contended, that set such a bad example for his successors. His rationalist methodology was the model for Fichte, Schelling and Hegel, who believed that they could know the first principles of experience by sheer a priori reasoning. No wonder, then, that they claimed to represent the spirit of Kant!

Beneke insisted, however, that Kant's rationalist methodology represents only one side of his teaching, and indeed the more antiquated and least original side. The more novel and innovative side is its empiricism, its demand that all claims to knowledge be justified by experience. There is a striking tension between these two sides of

Kant's philosophy, Beneke maintained. While his methodology is a relic of rational-ism, his standard of knowledge is entirely empiricist. That raises the question about how Kant can justify his own epistemology. For what warrant in experience could there be for the transcendental deduction of the concepts of the understanding? Or, for that matter, the metaphysical deduction of the table of the categories? For Beneke, there is only one way to resolve the tension: abandoning the rationalist method and following a strict empirical one in epistemology itself (92–93, 98). It was an argument, as we have seen, strongly reminiscent of Fries in the 1790s.[88]

It becomes clear from the *Jubelschrift* that Beneke saw Kant's chief contribution to philosophy as essentially negative. The great value of Kant's philosophy, in his view, lay in its critique of rationalism, and that critique went hand-in-glove with its empiri-cism, which was the stick with which Kant beat rationalism. The fundamental intent of the critical philosophy is indeed, true to name, critical. In responding to critics who charged him with ignoring the positive side of Kant's teaching, Beneke remained unrepentent.[89] The positive aspect of Kant's teaching is problematic, he maintained, because it comes from his rationalism. Like Fries and Herbart, Beneke downplayed the role of the *Kritik der Urteilskraft* in Kant's philosophy, which, he insisted, intro-duced no major systematic changes (xii). The third *Kritik* was no less critical than the first, and the speculative excesses it inspired came from ignoring its critical messages about the limits of teleological judgement.

Although the *Jubelschrift* stresses the negative side of Kant's achievement, it would be wrong to infer that this was Beneke's final or complete assessment of Kant. For it is a striking feature of the *Jubelschrift* that it leaves out of account Beneke's more posi-tive assessment of Kant's achievement. When we consider other writings of Beneke, it becomes clear that Kant's philosophy was important to him not only because of its critique of rationalism, but also because it had laid down the very foundation of philosophy. It was Kant who had established for Beneke that first philosophy must be ultimately anthropology or psychology. Kant's greatest achievement, Beneke maintains, is that he showed once and for all that philosophy must begin with, and revolve around, the knowing subject. Kant had shown that we cannot understand our world until we first have knowledge of ourselves, because all knowledge of the world is ultimately conditioned by human beings. In the preface to an earlier work, *Das Verhältniß von Seele und Leib,* Beneke declared that this orientation of philoso-phy around the subject was "the proper living spirit of the Kantian philosophy" (vii). Beneke, in other words, strongly endorsed Kant's Copernican Revolution.

This more positive assessment of Kant becomes clear from another work Beneke wrote in the early 1830s, his *Die Philosophie in ihrem Verhältnisse zur Erfahrung, zur*

---

[88] See Chapter 1, Section 3.
[89] See Friedrich Eduard Beneke, *Die Philosophie in ihrem Verhältnisse zur Erfahrung, zur Spekulation und zum Leben* (Berlin: Mittler, 1833), pp. xii–xiii.

Speculation and zum Leben.[90] Beneke called the work a polemic (*ein Plänker*),[91] and so indeed it is, for here he spells out in more detail than ever before the problems of idealist speculation. But this work also reveals more clearly Beneke's allegiance to Kant's positive doctrines.

Beneke's account of philosophy in this work shows, despite his empiricism, how much he is still indebted to Kant's method and conception of philosophy. Although Beneke thinks that the method of philosophy should be empirical, he still accepts the basic Kantian point that its aims should be epistemological, and indeed critical. For Beneke, no less than Kant, philosophy should be first and foremost an examination of the powers and limits of knowledge, an account of "the universal laws of the foundation of knowledge" (4). Beneke even endorses the standard rationale of epistemology as *philosophia prima*. He thinks that Locke and Kant were right to insist that before we make claims to knowledge we should first investigate the faculty of knowledge itself (12–13). The standard Hegelian objection to that strategy—that investigating knowledge involves claims to knowledge—does not much impress Beneke, who thinks that second-order knowledge claims are still much less hazardous than first-order ones, especially metaphysical ones (13). Though empirical psychology is a *first-order* investigation into the nature of inner experience, Beneke still understood epistemology as a *second-order* enterprise, one whose primary task is to determine *how we know* the world rather than anything about the world itself. Thus he defines philosophy as "a science of science" whose task is to determine the methods of the sciences. It is the specific mission of philosophy, he wrote, to engage in "an exact analysis and examination of scientific procedure", all for the sake of defining and preserving the method of empirical investigation first championed by Bacon (6). One of its tasks is therefore to determine "the universal distribution and limitations of the matter of knowledge", that is, to settle the border disputes between the sciences, so that one knows the extent to which the methods used in the examination of inanimate nature also apply to animate (6).

Beneke praises Kant for making the subject "the middle point of philosophy", the centre from which philosophy explains everything (11–12). The starting point of philosophy should be, as Descartes and Kant taught, self-awareness, the awareness of our own existence and mental activity. Descartes was right to begin his philosophy with the "*cogito*" and Kant with the "*Ich denke*". Philosophy should start with what is certain, with immediate knowledge, and that certainty and immediacy comes only with knowledge of ourselves and inner states (1–12). However much we can doubt whether our representations are true of the world, we at least cannot doubt that we have those representations. Self-awareness should therefore be the foundation and medium of all knowledge (12, 14). Beneke does not intend this endorsement of self-awareness to

[90] See Friedrich Eduard Beneke, *Die Philosophie in ihrem Verhältnisse zur Erfahrung, zur Spekulation und zum Leben* (Berlin: Mittler, 1833).
[91] Beneke to Twesten, May 19, 1834, *Ungedruckte Briefe*, p. 207.

be, however, a rationale for a kind of rationalist foundationalism. Unlike Reinhold and Fichte, he does not think that we can begin with some self-evident first principle, grounded in self-awareness, and then from it derive the rest of our knowledge; his only point is that we should acknowledge that awareness of ourselves, and of our own representations, is the ultimate evidence for all knowledge. Knowledge of the external world and other worlds is mediate knowledge, based upon or inferred from the immediate knowledge of our own selves and representations.

It is ironic, however, that Beneke was riding roughshod over Kant precisely when he believed he was embracing his very spirit. For the doctrine that we have an immediate knowledge of ourselves, and only mediate knowledge of the external world, had been the central target of Kant's criticism, in both the 'Critique of the Fourth Paralogism' in the first edition of the *Kritik* and in the 'Refutation of Idealism' in the second edition. Beneke had conflated Kant's position with this old Cartesian doctrine despite Kant's persistent efforts to refute it. We have seen, however, that Beneke was perfectly well aware of Kant's attempt to place self-knowledge and knowledge of the external world on a par, and that he went to great (though futile) pains to refute Kant's limitation of self-knowledge to appearances. In expounding Kant in these terms, then, Beneke was going against his own better knowledge of Kantian doctrine. In short, he was making Kant the philosopher he wanted him to be rather than the philosopher he was. This at least shows the extraordinary importance Kant had for Beneke: he was willing to distort Kant to enlist him in his cause.

Just how far Beneke was willing to go in embracing Kant is apparent from his endorsement of one of his most controversial doctrines: the thing-in-itself. What Fichte, Schelling and Hegel regarded as Kant's biggest mistake, Beneke saw as common sense. Since we know directly only our own inner states, we must infer the existence of the world outside us, which we know only to the extent that it is like us or conforms to our own inner nature (22). We know external objects only insofar as they affect us but not as they are in themselves (23, 41, 82).

Beneke's abiding attachment to Kant is in inverse proportion to his aversion to the great post-Kantian system builders. In his view, they have cast aside what is solid in Kant—his limitation of knowledge to experience—and they have affirmed what is most suspect—his a priori method in philosophy. Beneke credits the post-Kantians with being more consistent than Kant in developing and applying that a priori method. But in following it, they also commit their gravest error, he is convinced. That methodology does nothing more than create "castles in the air". "A philosophy a priori", he insisted, is only "an empty phantom".

What exactly is wrong with the great speculative systems? Beneke gives his clearest diagnosis of the problem in *Die Philosophie*. Here we are told that there are two defining characteristics of speculation, both of which make it illegitimate (65–67). First, speculation derives from mere concepts the existence of what is thought in them (65). This was a constant if implicit theme of classical rationalism, which appears in Descartes, Spinoza, Leibniz and Wolff. Beneke sees the source of this rationalism in Descartes' dictum that the perception of the clarity and distinctness of our ideas is sufficient evidence for their truth (66 n.1). Fichte, Schelling and Hegel continued this tradition, because they used pure reasoning about mere concepts, namely, the absolute, the ego, the indifference point, to determine the nature of things. Second, speculation attempts to derive concrete or determinate conclusions from abstract or indeterminate premises (67). This enterprise is most apparent in Fichte, who attempted to deduce all of reality from his abstract and empty first principle "I am I".

Each characteristic suffers from fatal difficulties, Beneke argues. The problem with the first is that it attempts to derive existence from essence; and the problem with the second is that it attempts to derive determinate from indeterminate content, or, as Beneke loves to put it, "the concrete from the abstract, the full from the empty, something from nothing". Both problems, Beneke insists, were already fully exposed by Kant in his critique of rationalism (112). The first problem appears in his critique of the ontological argument; and the second problem is the main lesson of the Amphibolies and Paralogisms. Beneke notes that Kant himself was fully aware of his differences with his successors, and that it is absurd of them to claim to represent the spirit of his philosophy. To this end, he cites in full Kant's famous declaration against Fichte's *Wissenschaftslehre* (103–104).

From a broad historical perspective, we can see that Beneke's critique of neo-rationalism reaffirms the earlier critiques of Fries and Herbart. However much Beneke would disagree with Fries and Herbart about positive doctrine, he was entirely at one with them in their opposition to neo-rationalism. If we accept the maxim "the enemy of my enemy is my friend", we can see on this ground alone that Fries, Herbart and Beneke formed a single tradition or alliance.

With Beneke's tragic death, the lost tradition too will come to its sad and sorry close. Its existence, however, was not in vain. It will live on in a new transfigured form. We call its transfiguration "neo-Kantianism". But before we examine that movement proper, we must see what happened in between its rise and the lost tradition's fall.

4

The Interim Years, 1840–1860

1. Years of Transition

The lost tradition came to an anticlimactic close in the 1840s. Its heroes wandered off and withered away, largely unsung and forgotten. Herbart had died in 1841, and Fries in 1843; and though Beneke would stagger on until 1854, he was a marginal figure in Berlin. His isolation, loneliness and suicide there stands as a stark symbol of the fate of his tradition.

That said, the legacy of the lost tradition was of inestimable value for neo-Kantianism. It had kept alive central Kantian doctrines that had been cast aside by the speculative idealists. While Fichte, Schelling and Hegel wanted to bury these doctrines, Fries, Herbart and Beneke did their best to nurture and sustain them. Among these doctrines were Kant's transcendental idealism, his limitation of knowledge to experience, his regulative strictures on teleology, and the crucial dualisms between form and matter, understanding and sensibility, essence and existence. Without the preservation and protection of these doctrines, the Kant revival of the 1860s would have been unthinkable. For that revival was first and foremost a rehabilitation of these doctrines. When the later neo-Kantians reaffirmed them, they were upholding a torch passed down to them by the lost generation.

Yet the lost tradition alone could never have given birth to neo-Kantianism. Only a few of its progeny became neo-Kantians.[1] Its influence was simply too thin and weak to produce a neo-Kantian movement. The Friesian school had dissipated by the late 1840s, its journal having ceased publication in 1849, after only two issues. Though Herbart's school lasted for decades in Germany and Austria, it had almost entirely revolved around his psychology rather than his epistemology and metaphysics. And Beneke, for his part, had only a few disciples, none of whom followed him very closely.[2]

---

[1] Carl Fortlage was a student of Beneke, and Ernst Mirbt was a student of Fries; Jürgen Bona Meyer was also influenced heavily by Fries. Helmholtz attended some of Beneke's lectures in Berlin in the 1830s, though they had no discernible influence upon him.

[2] On Beneke's influence, see Otto Siebert, *Geschichte der neueren deutschen Philosophie seit Hegel* (Göttingen: Vandenhoeck & Ruprecht, 1898), pp. 207–215. As Siebert points out, Fortlage was not, in the strict sense of the word, a disciple of Beneke.

The lost tradition also could not claim to have budged the chief obstacle to the emergence of neo-Kantianism: the speculative idealist regime that had dominated German cultural life from the 1790s to 1840s. Despite all the attacks of Fries, Herbart and Beneke, that regime never swithered, swerved or swayed. The lost ones, though they had conducted a heroic underground resistance against speculative idealism for more than thirty years, never enjoyed their day of liberation. They lived long enough to enjoy a flash of *Schadenfreude* at Hegel's death; yet they went to their graves under the shadow of his disciples.

The great cultural and political event of the interim period was, of course, the Revolution of 1848.[3] The effect of the Revolution on German philosophy might be thought negligble, and indeed many scholars have written about the decade after the Revolution as the end of the classical period of German philosophy.[4] For just this reason, the interim period has been regarded as a stagnant one for German thought. Because the political world was in such turmoil—so the explanation goes—people had to devote their time and energy on politics, so that there was little left for philosophical reflection. Yet we must not confuse a lack of philosophical production with a lack of philosophical significance. While it is indeed the case that people were not as philosophically productive in the interim period, there can still be no doubt that the Revolution had a profound effect on German philosophy. In its own way the Revolution helped prepare the ground for neo-Kantianism. Some of the fundamental ideals of Kant's moral and political philosophy were enshrined in the *Verfassung des Deutschen Reiches*, which the Frankfurt Parliament had proclaimed in March, 1849. Section VI on the *Grundrechte des deutschen Volkes* reads like extracts from Kant's *Metaphysik der Sitten*. Article II, §137, makes everyone equal before the law; Article III, §138, states that personal freedom is inviolable; Article IV, §143, grants everyone freedom of opinion and liberty of press; Article V, §144, ensures that everyone has freedom of belief; Article VI, §158, gives everyone the freedom to choose their own occupation; and Article IX, §164, states that the right of property is inviolable.[5] These were just the kind of personal rights and freedoms that Kant had defended so passionately in his moral and political philosophy. Now, it seemed, they were on the verge of becoming a political reality.

That did not happen, of course, and the *Verfassung des deutschen Reiches* remained only a dream. Yet, as it happened, the failure of the Revolution played more into the hands of neo-Kantianism than its success ever would have. For the collapse of the Revolution made it necessary to defend by intellectual or philosophical means

---

[3] For an account of the Revolution from a contemporary philosopher, see Julius Duboc, *Hundert Jahre Zeitgeist in Deutschland* (Leipzig: Wigand, 1893), II, 46–99.

[4] This was the opinion of contemporaries themselves. See, for example, Rudolf Haym, *Hegel und seine Zeit* (Berlin: Gaertner, 1857), pp. 5–6; and Friedrich Albert Lange, *Geschichte des Materialismus*, Zweite Ausgabe (Iserlohn: Baedeker, 1875) II, 64–65.

[5] See David Hanseman, ed., *Die deutsche Verfassung vom 28 März, 1849. Mit Anmerkungen* (Berlin: Unger, 1849), Abschnitt VI: Die Grundrechte des deutschen Volkes, pp. 44–55.

what could not be achieved by political means on the barricades or through the ballot box. It was necessary to ascend to a higher plateau of abstraction and analysis than is possible on the streets or on the debating floor. A defense of the ideals of the Revolution would mean first and foremost, however, a defense of that philosopher who best represented those ideals; and that philosopher was, of course, Immanuel Kant.

Why, one might well ask, did it not mean a defense of Hegel? After all, he too stood for some of the same basic rights as Kant, and his philosophy was of more recent memory than that of the old sage of Königsberg. Yet the Hegelians were the great losers in the Revolution of 1848. They saw the imminent realization of its ideals—national unity and self-determination—as the final proof of Hegel's thesis that there is reason in history. For the Hegelian, the ultimate rationale for these ideals lies in historical necessity, in the *telos* of history, which is the self-awareness of freedom. It is useless to provide a purely normative justification of these ideals—to prescribe what ought to be—and it is necessary instead to give them an historical justification, which means showing how they are immanent in the past. So the Hegelians rested all their cards on history—and they lost. When Kaiser Friedrich Wilhelm IV refused the crown the Frankfurt Parliament offered to him, he not only crashed all hopes for a constitutional monarchy, which had been the main ideal of the Hegelian centre, but he also demonstrated how little reason there really is in history. The collapse of the Revolution of 1848 was the ultimate defeat of Hegelianism.[6]

The defeat of Hegelianism left the path open for a return to Kant. Already in the 1840s, there were calls for a return to Kant. Consider the following instances of nascent neo-Kantianism from the 1840s and 1850s.

- In 1841 Ernst Sigismund Mirbt (1799–1847) published the first volume of his *Kant und seine Nachfolger*,[7] whose aim was to trace the origins and reception of the critical philosophy. After the decline of speculative idealism, Mirbt felt it necessary for the public to have a better historical understanding of the starting point of German philosophy. While Hegel had reduced Kant down to a preliminary stage of his own system, it was important to understand Kant in his own right, Mirbt insisted. He then went on to provide a sympathetic, if somewhat simplistic, account of Kant's philosophy. Though not the first history of Kant's philosophy in the 1840s,[8] it was still the first written from a neo-Kantian perspective.

---

[6] On the Hegelian reaction to the 1848 Revolution, see Hermann Lübbe, *Politische Philosophie in Deutschland* (Munich: Deutscher Tascnenbuch Verlag, 1974), pp. 77–82.

[7] Ernst Sigismund Mirbt, *Kant und seine Nachfolger oder Geschichte des Ursprungs und der Fortbildung der neueren deutschen Philosophie* (Jena: Hochhausen, 1841). Mirbt planned another volume—the first bears the title 'Erster Band'—though it never appeared. Mirbt appears to have been a Friesian. See the preface to his *Was heisst Philosophieren und was ist Philosophie? Sieben einleitende Vorlesungen* (Jena: Karl Hochhausen, 1839), p. x.

[8] That honour goes to Rosenkranz's *Geschichte der kant'schen Philosophie* (Leipzig: Voß, 1840); Rosenkranz's history was written from a Hegelian point of view.

- In 1847 Christian Hermann Weiße (1801–1866) gave his inaugural lecture in Leipzig on the theme *In welchem Sinn die deutsche Philosophie jetzt wieder an Kant sich zu orientiren hat.*[9] Though an eclectic and isolated thinker,[10] Weiße was still a force to reckon with: he was ordinary professor in Leipzig, a prestigious appointment, and he was the teacher of Lotze and Fischer. In his lecture Weiße argued that Kant's philosophy should be the "orientation point" for all future philosophy in Germany, because it wisely avoided the mistakes of the warring parties of the present. The Hegelians had failed to appreciate the importance of experience, assuming that they could reach substantive conclusions from the realm of thought alone; and the Herbartians had exaggerrated the importance of experience because they refused to recognize the fundamental role of a priori concepts in constituting our experience. It was Kant's great achievement to have recognized the merits and deficiencies of both rationalism and empiricism.
- In 1852 Carl Fortlage (1806–1881), a student of Beneke's, published his *Genetische Geschichte der Philosophie seit Kant*,[11] whose express purpose was to make philosophers self-conscious that their work was ultimately inspired by Kant (vi). All modern philosophers were "collectively and individually nothing more than variously shaped Kantians" (7). Kant was the greatest philosopher of the modern world, and it was around his model that all philosophers should be educated (4). One of Fortlage's aims in writing his *Geschichte* was irenic, to quell the constant battles between the sects and schools, and he believed that there was no better way of doing this than showing how all recent philosophy, whether Hegelian or Herbartian, had its ultimate roots in Kant. Lamenting the oppressive atmosphere of the 1850s after the failure of the Revolution, Fortlage believed that philosophers had to learn to assert themselves, to have pride in stating their own opinions; but they could apply this remedy only if they went back to Kant, whose revolution in philosophy was more a way of thinking than a set of dogmas, a way of thinking that stressed the importance of autonomy and thinking for oneself (5). Against the bleak atmosphere of the early 1850s, Fortlage could only advise: "as long as we do not forget Kant and Fichte we are not lost." (vii)[12]

---

[9] Christian Hermann Weiße, *In welchem Sinne die deutsche Philosophie jetzt wieder an Kant sich zu orientiren hat* (Leipzig: Dycke, 1847).

[10] On Weiße, see the excellent account by Olaf Briese, 'Im Geflect der Schulen. Christian Hermann Weißes akademisches Karriere', in *Konkurrenzen: Philosophischen Kultur in Deutschland 1830–1850* (Würzburg: Königshausen & Neumann, 1998), pp. 65–77.

[11] Carl Fortlage, *Genetische Geschichte der Philosophie seit Kant* (Leipzig: Brockhaus, 1852).

[12] Fortlage had already made the case for a Kant revival as early as 1838 in his 'Die Stellung Kants zur Philosophie vor ihm und nach ihm', *Deutsche Vierteljahrs Schrift*, Heft IV (1838), 91–123. Here Fortlage stresses, as he later did in his *Genetische Geschichte*, that the roots of all modern philosophy lie in Kant's system, and that it is necessary to return to it (93, 94, 119, 120–121). Fortlage likens Kant to the Socrates of the modern age (114–119).

– In two hectic weeks in 1854 Otto Friedrich Gruppe (1804–1876) wrote his *Gegenwart und Zukunft der Philosophie in Deutschland*,[13] his final attempt to set the course for future philosophy in Germany. Writing on the occasion of Schelling's death, Gruppe noted that Schelling's recent "positive philosophy" had taken philosophy back to its starting point in Kant. The positive philosophy was based on the distinction between essence and existence, which was essentially a vindication of Kant against Hegel. Gruppe saw Schelling's philosophy as the end of an era—the end of the great systems—and the dawn for a new age of philosophy, one where philosophers collaborated and worked in piecemeal fashion rather than producing grand systems as monuments to their own vanity. While Gruppe himself did not advocate a return to Kant, he saw the course of recent philosophical history as a vindication of Kant's teachings about the limits of knowledge in experience.

But all these instances of neo-Kantianism were mere glimmerings, mere foreshadowings. Two long and eventful decades, the 1840s and 1850s, separate the end of speculative idealism from the rise of neo-Kantianism in the 1860s. Why such a long interregnum? The simple and classical explanation points to the politics of these decades. With the 1840s came the great March Revolution (1848), and with the 1850s came the Restoration. Such dramatic and epoch-making events, whether one is a spectator or participant, do not give the time, leisure or composure to think about abstract philosophical issues. For these reasons it has been received wisdom that these decades mark a nadir for German philosophy. Philosophers were simply too involved in politics in the 1840s, and too repressed by government in the 1850s, to do much philosophy.

While there is an important element of truth to this view, we must not push it too far. For the 1840s and 1850s also witness the most profound philosophical developments, without which neo-Kantianism would never have taken place. Among these developments were the materialism controversy, the rise of materialism, the identity crisis of philosophy, and the coming of age of three great thinkers, Hermann Lotze, Adolf Trendelenburg and Hermann Helmholtz, all of whom would have a great influence on the young neo-Kantians. Our task in the rest of this chapter will be to consider each of these developments in their broad outlines.

2. The Materialism Controversy

The most important intellectual dispute of the 19th century—one can declare with complete confidence—was the materialism controversy, which began in the 1850s, and whose shockwaves reverberated until the end of the century. No philosopher of

---

[13] Otto Friedrich Gruppe, *Gegenwart und Zukunft der Philosophie in Deutschland* (Berlin: Reimer, 1855).

that epoch could ignore it, and every philosopher had to stake his position with reference to it. The controversy raised the troubling question whether modern science,
whose authority and prestige were now beyond question, necessarily leads to materialism. The dispute posed a disturbing dilemma: either a scientific materialism or a
leap of faith in theism, immortality and free will. The controversy was reminiscent
of the famous "pantheism controversy" between Moses Mendelssohn and Friedrich
Heinrich Jacobi in the late 18th century. Just as that controversy determined the contours of intellectual life in the late 18th century, so the materialism controversy did
the same in the 19th century.

We can assign a definite time and place for the official beginning of the materialism controversy. It was September 18, 1854, in Göttingen. It was then and there
that Rudolph Wagner, the head of the Physiological Institute in Göttingen, gave his
opening address to the thirty-first *Versammlung deutscher Naturforscher und Ärtze*.
Wagner's address, entitled *Menschenschöpfung und Seelensubstanz*,[14] was an ad hoc
piece that he had hurriedly and reluctantly thrown together just days before the conference at the request of some of its leading participants. It was only appropriate,
they believed, for the host to hold the opening address. They soon got more than they
bargained for.

To have maximum effect, Wagner chose a topic from anthropology that he believed
would interest everyone: the origin of man and his fate after death. The main question
he wanted to pose for the participants at the conference was whether natural science
had been able to shed any light on these grand old questions. It was his own personal
view, he openly confessed, that the latest research had not been able to demonstrate
or refute the Biblical doctrine that all human beings came from an original single
pair (17). There were some natural scientists who held that, given the variety of human
races, there must have been different original pairs, an Adam and Eve for each race;
but they lacked concrete empirical evidence for their views. All the data from the
most recent empirical investigations did not contradict the Biblical doctrine at all,
which therefore should remain "inviolate" (17). Regarding the grand question about
the fate of man after death, Wagner asked what recent research had to say about the
human soul. He noted how psychology was becoming more and more the object of
natural science, and less and less the preserve of theology and philosophy. And here
he believed that he had to issue a warning about the direction of the latest physiology.
It was a sad but indisputable truth that some physiologists were inclined towards materialism, and they were not only doubting but denying the existence of the soul and free
will (18). The problem with this new materialism, Wagner intoned, is that it was undermining a belief crucial to the moral and political order: the belief in the immortality

---

[14] Rudolph Wagner, *Menschenschöpfung und Seelensubstanz. Ein anthropologischer Vortrag, gehalten
in der ersten öffentlichen Sitzung der 31 Versammlung deutscher Naturforscher und Ärtze zu Göttingen am
18 Sept. 1854.* (Göttingen: Wigand, 1854). All references in parentheses above are to this edition.

of the soul. The Christian doctrine of a moral world order—a divine providence that rewarded the virtuous and punished the vicious—rested on this belief. Whoever wanted to preserve morality and religion among "the de-christianized masses" should strive to uphold that belief at all costs (26–27). Wagner then closed his address with the plea: natural scientists should consider where their research is heading; they should refrain from spreading doctrines damaging to morals, religion and state.

Judging from its brisk sales,[15] Wagner's address had an impact well beyond the confines of the conference. Many participants were shocked by Wagner's boldness in obtruding moral and political considerations into what was supposed to be a purely academic conference. Yet he had raised questions on the minds of many, ones difficult to ignore. Namely, is natural science heading towards materialism? And if so, what are the consequences for moral and religious belief? Similar questions had been posed by Jacobi some seventy years earlier. It seemed to Jacobi in the 1780s that the new natural sciences were leading inevitably towards the atheism and fatalism of Spinozism, which he regarded as the most consistent and rigorous form of naturalism. Jacobi confronted his contemporaries with a powerful dilemma: either naturalistic atheism and fatalism or a *salto mortale,* a leap of faith in a personal creator and freedom. With no less urgency and bluster, Wagner was *in effect* posing the same dilemma for his generation with regard to the beliefs in divine creation and the immorality of the soul.[16]

Wagner's opening address was only his first salvo in what had now become his holy war against materialism. Only a few weeks after the conference, and in response to the controversy aroused by his address, he published his *Ueber Wissen und Glauben,*[17] which stated his general position regarding the classic issue of reason versus faith. In this piece Wagner reaffirmed his view that the latest results of the natural sciences provide no evidence against belief in the existence of immortality. While there is no proof for this belief, there is also no disproof of it either, so that the believer is free to keep his faith with no fear that science stands against him (8–9). Wagner then put forward his main rationale for this point: the classic double-truth doctrine of Protestantism.[18] According to that doctrine, faith and reason operate in separate spheres; neither contradicts the other as long as each stays within its boundaries. Faith should not pronounce on matters of science, which we can know through sense experience and reason; but science should not presume on matters of faith, which we know through the Bible, the record of divine revelation. Faith was not for Wagner

---

[15] Wagner stated in the preface to his *Ueber Wissen und Glauben* that it had sold 3,000 copies in a few weeks.

[16] I stress "in effect" because Wagner believed that he could avoid such a dilemma; but it is arguable if he really could.

[17] Wagner, *Ueber Wissen und Glauben, Fortsetzung der Betrachtungen über Menschenschöpfung und Seelensubstanz.* (Göttingen: Wigand, 1854).

[18] The *locus classicus* for this doctrine is Luther's disputation *De sententia: Verbum caro factus est,* in Luther, *Kritische Gesamtausgabe Weimarer Ausgabe* (Weimar: Hermann Böhlaus Nachfolger, 1883), XXXIX/2, 3–33. On Luther's doctrine, see my *The Sovereignty of Reason* (Princeton, NJ: Princeton University Press, 1996), pp. 24–30.

simply a matter of belief, but, as Luther and Calvin had taught, a kind of immediate experience (14–16). Faith gives us knowledge of supernatural things just as reason does for natural things; and just as a blind man should not presume to judge what he cannot see, so the non-believing natural scientist should not dare to doubt what the Christian sees through the eyes of faith. Despite insisting that faith and science should respect their boundaries, Wagner had to admit that there were "points of contact" *(Berührungspunkte)* between them, and in these cases conflict was difficult to avoid. These cases concerned issues about the origins of things or matters of historical revelation (18). The Bible, for example, stated that the earth was only thousands of years old, whereas geological and historical evidence showed that it had to be much older than that. Who was one to believe in such cases? Science or faith? One must practise "double bookkeeping" was Wagner's answer (20). That meant that one should still strive as far as possible to resolve the conflict by assigning the apparently contradictory views to their separate spheres. One should limit one's conclusions as a natural scientist strictly to the empirical evidence; and one should not reject matters of faith out of hand but wait for their eventual reconciliation with that evidence. It was plain, however, that this solution was nothing more than a stop-gap, another kind of *salto mortale*, a leap of faith in the eventual reconciliation of faith and reason.

Raising a major intellectual issue is necessary for a good public controversy, but it is rarely sufficient. To attract public attention, something more is necessary, namely, bile, pathos and scandal. These the materialism controversy offered in spades. The history behind Wagner's opening address lay in his bitter quarrel with one very angry young man: Karl Vogt.[19] It is no exaggeration to say that Vogt was one of the most fascinating figures of 19th century German intellectual history. A corpulent man with a savage wit and boundless energy, he was an intellectual raging bull, a formidable opponent in any dispute.[20] Having studied chemistry with Liebig at Gießen in the 1830s, Vogt had received a doctorate in medicine and then gradually became a journalist. He had acquired a reputation for himself in the 1840s by publishing a number of popular books on geology and physiology. These works had revealed a growing sympathy for materialist views, especially a denial of creation *ex nihilo* and a belief in a complete naturalism.[21] A man of decidedly left-wing political views, Vogt had hung out with Bakunin and Proudhon in Paris in the early 1840s and he had engaged in revolutionary activity in Berne in 1846.[22] In 1848 he was elected as a member to the Frankfurt Parliament, where he stood on the extreme left of the Assembly. Predictably, Vogt's radical views got him into trouble, and after the collapse of the

[19] On Vogt, see Frederick Gregory, *Scientific Materialism in Nineteenth Century Germany* (Dordrecht: Reidel, 1977), pp. 51–79; and Annette Wittkau-Hogby, *Materialismus: Entstehung und Wirkung in den Wissenschaften des 19. Jahrhunderts* (Göttingen: Vandenhoeck & Ruprecht, 1998), pp. 77–95.

[20] See the pencil sketch in Gregory, *Scientific Materialism*, p. 63.

[21] Vogt states his *credo* fully and openly for the first time in his *Ocean und Mittelmeer: Reisebriefe* (Frankfurt: Literarische Anstalt, 1848), pp. 9–26.

[22] See Vogt's own vivid account of these activities in *Ocean und Mittelmeer* I, 165–200.

Revolution he found himself dismissed from his post in Gießen. From his exile in Italy he would rile against the German establishment, especially its universities. No one represented more the worst side of that establishment, in Vogt's bilious view, than one professor in Göttingen: Rudolph Wagner. In his *Bilder aus dem Thierleben* Vogt singled out Wagner as the worst German science had to offer, a superstitious theist whose beliefs set limits to his research.[23] Vogt's attack was not entirely unprovoked, for in a series of articles in the *Allgemeine Zeitung* Wagner had already warned the public about the dangerous materialist tendencies of Vogt's writings. In his opening address he cited long passages from Vogt's *Physiologische Briefe* to the effect that there is no free will, that the mind is nothing more than the activity of the brain, and that there is no such thing as the immortality of the soul.[24]

After hearing about Wagner's address in Göttingen, Vogt became enraged. Wagner had the nerve to use a public podium to attack him when he was not there to defend himself! When Wagner promised in a later session to discuss the question of the materiality of the soul, he abruptly cancelled it, claiming that he was suffering from "a sudden cold". That seemed to Vogt the excuse of a coward; Wagner was withdrawing from the very fight he had started. Vogt was determined that he not escape so easily. Now that Wagner had thrown down the gauntlet, Vogt would pick it up and pursue his opponent relentlessly. And so, in a few heated and inspired weeks in the autumn of 1854, Vogt wrote a blistering and brilliant polemic against Wagner, his *Köhlerglaube und Wissenschaft*, which first appeared in 1855.[25] The first part is a vicious personal attack on Wagner's moral and intellectual integrity. It indicts Wagner for his sloppiness as a scientist, for allowing his personal beliefs to interfere with his research, and for his temerity in taking credit for publications for which he had done little or nothing. The second part addresses the major intellectual issues raised by Wagner. Vogt found Wagner's distinction between the realms of science and faith utterly artificial and arbitrary. He insisted that there is overwhelming empirical evidence *against* the two beliefs that Wagner was so eager to protect: that human origins came from a single original couple, and that there is an immaterial soul. Regarding the first belief, all the evidence from geography and anatomy reveals such differences between the various human races that each must have had its own original pair; it is also evident from geology that the age of the earth is much older than anything said in the Bible, and that human beings originated much earlier than four thousand years ago. So, rather than standing inviolate above empirical falsification, the Biblical doctrines are flatly contrary to the facts, in which case it is clear that one has to side with science against

---

[23] Carl Vogt, *Bilder aus dem Thierleben* (Frankfurt: Literarische Anstalt, 1852), p. 367.

[24] Wagner, *Menschenschöpfung und Seelensubstanz*, pp. 20–21. Without mentioning Vogt or his work by name, Wagner cites passages from the second edition of Vogt's *Physiologische Briefe* (Gießen: Ricker, 1854), pp. 322–323, 626–637.

[25] Karl Vogt, *Köhlerglaube und Wissenschaft: Eine Streitschrift gegen Hofrath Wagner in Göttingen* (Gießen: Ricker, 1856). All references in parentheses above are to this edition.

them (81–83). Regarding the belief in an immaterial soul, the latest physiological research gives no evidence whatsoever for the existence of a soul separate from the brain; on the contrary, it shows how closely mental activity is tied to brain functions. If the brain were injured, mental activity would cease; and it is even possible to identify specific parts of the brain that are used for specific mental functions (107–114). While Vogt admitted that it is difficult to explain how brain processes give rise to consciousness and mental events, he insisted that all the evidence indicates the utter dependence of consciousness upon brain processes (109). Given such a fact, it is not likely that human beings possess an immortal soul that somehow survives the death of the body (121–122). Against all Wagner's warnings, Vogt then declared that he had no fear in drawing the appropriate conclusions from all these facts: that the religious beliefs are nothing but superstitions. To uphold such beliefs when they are contrary to all the plain evidence of science is to take a desperate leap into the irrational.

Lying just underneath the surface of Vogt's dispute with Wagner were their clashing politics. While Vogt was a radical who had fought for democracy in Bern and Frankfurt, Wagner was a reactionary whose fondest hope was a return to the monarchic rule of the *ancien régime*. It was indeed telling that, at the close of his speech, Wagner cited, and vowed to uphold, the political testament of a leading conservative statesman and publicist, Joseph Maria von Radowitz.[26] The politics of Vogt and Wagner were decisive for their philosophical positions. Wagner wanted *to uphold* the beliefs in providence and immortality to legitimate the monarchy and to control "the dechristianized masses"; Vogt intended *to undermine* these beliefs for just that reason: they were an ideological weapon to control the people, a veil of deception to prevent them from taking control over their own lives in a new democratic order. Thus the dispute between Vogt and Wagner was not only philosophical but also political. It was indeed a battle between two complete worldviews, a life and death struggle of the materialism of the left against the theism of the right.

Given its acrimonious and scandalous beginning, it should not be surprising that the controversy spread rapidly. Vogt's dispute with Wagner was only the beginning of a much longer and more complex controversy, which would eventually pull every major thinker into its vortex. As it happened, Wagner's warnings backfired. Rather than frightening the materialists, they provoked them. Out of their closets they came, now marching headstrong, banners waving, in a thick phalanx to challenge the establishment. 1855, the very year Vogt published *Köhlerglaube und Wissenschaft*, also witnessed the appearance of two mighty materialist tomes: Heinrich Czolbe's *Neue Darstellung des Sensualismus* and Ludwig Büchner's *Kraft und Stoff*.[27] What

---

[26] Wagner, *Menschenschöpfung und Seelensubstanz*, pp. 26–27. Wagner does not name the author. I assume that it is Radowitz from the comments of Reclam and Vogt in *Köhlerglaube und Wissenschaft*, pp. 33, 40. Vogt makes clear his political antipathy to Radowitz's views, p. 33.

[27] Louis Büchner, *Kraft und Stoff* (Frankfurt: Meidinger, 1855); and Heinrich Czolbe, *Neue Darstellung des Sensualismus* (Leipzig: Costenoble, 1855).

Vogt had announced in a polemical context—that the natural sciences are heading inevitably towards materialism—that Czolbe and Büchner would now defend in a more general and systematic manner. These works laid out the basic principles for a materialist worldview, arguing that it is based on nothing less than the empirical findings of the new natural sciences. Thus Wagner's worst nightmare had become reality. The satyrs of Lucretius had been resurrected, and they were now dancing on the streets of Germany.

3. The Identity Crisis

Of no less significance than the materialism controversy for the intellectual map of Germany in the 19th century was the so-called "identity crisis of philosophy".[28] Beginning in the 1830s, philosophers began to ask some very hard and basic questions about themselves, about who they were, what they were doing and where they were going. What is philosophy? What kind of questions should it attempt to answer? And what should be its place within the division of the sciences? Neo-Kantianism, like many other philosophical movements in the second half of the 19th century, arose first and foremost from an attempt to answer these questions.

Before the decline of speculative idealism, philosophers felt no need to raise such questions. They all seemed to have received convincing answers within that tradition. Speculative idealism from Reinhold to Hegel had a clear conception of the aims and methods of philosophy *vis-à-vis* the natural sciences. According to that conception, philosophy should provide a foundation for all the sciences, one that is immune from sceptical doubt, and it should construct a system of all the sciences, assigning each a special place in the general body of human knowledge. Such was the conception of philosophy proposed by Reinhold in his *Fundament des philosophischen Wissens*, developed by Fichte in his *Über den Begriff der Wissenschaftslehre,* tweaked by Schelling in his *Vorlesungen über die Methode des akademischen Studiums,* and then finally realized by Hegel in his vast and imposing three volume *Enzyklopädie der philosophischen Wissenschaften.*

There were two main reasons why, after the 1830s, these answers no longer satisfied philosophers. The first came with the many criticisms of this foundationalist programme. These criticisms came from many quarters: from Fries, Herbart and Beneke; from the early Romantics, especially from Friedrich Schlegel and Novalis; and from the many opponents of the methodology of *Naturphilosophie* (viz. Mathias Schleiden, Emil du Bois-Reymond, Justus Liebig, Hermann Helmholtz). By the 1840s their cumulative result seemed to be that this programme cannot get off the ground. We cannot from abstract and general first principles, no matter how certain, derive all the content of concrete experience. Appeals to intellectual intuition, the strategy

---

[28] This is the phrase of Herbert Schnädelbach, *Philosophy in Germany 1831–1933* (Cambridge: Cambridge University Press, 1984), p. 5.

of Fichte and Schelling, also seemed to ring hollow, to be even desperate ploys, for they could never convince sceptics. After all, who could refute those with opposing intuitions? Intuitions having significant content need justifications of their own, which cannot just come from another intuition. Hegel's dialectical method, which was meant to replace intellectual intuition, seemed problematic too, because its pure thinking seemed to grind out substantive results only by sleight-of-hand. By attempting to get content from pure ratiocination, the dialectic seemed to be a specious art for squeezing blood from a turnip, or, as Kant once put it, for milking a billy goat with a strainer. Such, very crudely, was the conclusion of Feuerbach in his 1839 *Zur Kritik der Hegelsche Philosophie,* of Trendelenburg in his 1840 *Logische Untersuchungen,* and of Lotze in his 1841 *Metaphysik.*

The second reason for the identity crisis came with the rapid rise and specialization of the empirical sciences. The new sciences of chemistry and biology, the old sciences of physics and astronomy, and the ancient once reviled but now revived discipline of history, had achieved great success for themselves by following their own methods and standards. They no longer needed philosophy to provide them with a foundation and to secure them a place within a general system of the sciences. Now that the empirical sciences had become autonomous, they spurned the guidance of philosophy. While philosophy had once been the mother of all the sciences, her children had now come of age and wanted to leave their maternal nest. This new attitude of the sciences to philosophy was well put later in the century by the neo-Kantian Jürgen Bona Meyer: "The daughters now demand independence from their common mother, and they do not suffer it gladly when they are supervised or corrected; they would prefer that their old and morose mother lay herself to rest in her grave."[29]

It was the combination of these two developments in the 1840s—the collapse of the foundationalist programme of speculative idealism, and the demand for autonomy of the particular sciences—that plunged philosophers into an identity crisis and forced them to redefine themselves. If philosophy cannot provide a foundation for the sciences, what should it be? And if all the particular sciences have already carved up the entire *globus intellectualis* among themselves, what room is left for philosophy? The mother of the sciences, it seemed, was utterly superfluous, a tired old matron of no relevance to the modern world.

From the 1840s to 1860s, philosophers responded very differently to their identity crisis. There were in these decades at least four responses.

- The most drastic and dramatic answer came from the materialists, who simply declared the death of philosophy. They reasoned: since philosophy has no method of its own, and since the empirical sciences achieve reliable results by their own methods, there just is no need for philosophy anymore. The proper method to acquire *all* knowledge, they assumed, is that of natural science,

---

[29] Jürgen Bona Meyer, *Zeitfragen* (Bonn: Adolph Marcus, 1870), p. 1.

namely, patient and painstaking empirical research, observation and experiment; and so, if philosophy is to provide any knowledge of the world at all, it should just become one with the empirical sciences. Hence Ludwig Feuerbach wrote in 1843: "Philosophy must unite with natural science, and natural science with philosophy."[30] The real intent behind this programme—the eradication of philosophy—Feuerbach spelled out a few years later: "The true philosophy is the negation of philosophy; it is no philosophy at all."[31]

– A novel response to the identity crisis came from an original, profound but much neglected thinker, someone already alluded to above: Otto Friedrich Gruppe.[32] Reflecting on the state of philosophy after Schelling's death,[33] Gruppe argued that Schelling's final system demonstrated that German philosophy had made no progress whatsoever during the age of speculative idealism. In affirming a dualism between essence and existence, Schelling had taken German philosophy full circle: back to its starting point in Kant. Why had speculative philosophy failed? For Gruppe, its chief problem is that ever since the ancient Greeks it suffered from the illusion that there could be a speculative method, that is, a means of grasping reality through pure thought alone. All thought on its own is entirely formal and empty, however, deriving its content from experience alone. Gruppe then went on to suggest a diagnosis for the illusions and failures of speculative metaphysics. They all came from a faulty logic, from not having a clear understanding of the workings of ordinary language. Philosophers, Gruppe argued, tend to reify words, to think that they have a definite and given meaning of their own, and that as such they designate a particular aspect of reality. But words derive their meaning from use, and their use depends on a particular context. We cannot set down any a priori constraints on what their use or context should be, and so we have to resign ourselves to the "relativity of all concepts", the recognition that meaning depends on use and context. The traditional logic is mistaken in taking concepts as the primary unit; their meaning depends on their use in judgements in a particular context. The meaning of concepts changes constantly, depending on the judgements that we make with them; every new true judgement changes the meaning of its concepts from its previous uses. On

---

[30] Ludwig Feuerbach, 'Vorläufige Thesen zur Reformation der Philosophie', in *Werke in sechs Bänden*, ed. Erich Thies (Frankfurt: Suhrkamp, 1975), III, 243. The 'Thesen' were first published in 1843. In a similar vein and following Feuerbach, see Jakob Moleschott, *Der Kreislauf des Lebens* (Gießen: Emil Roth, 1852): "Experience must dissolve into philosophy and philosophy into experience."

[31] Ludwig Feuerbach, 'Vorwort' [zu Ludwig Feuerbach's *Sämmtliche Werke* (Leipzig: Wigand, 1846)], *Werke* IV, 158.

[32] On Gruppe, see Hans Sluga, *Gottlob Frege* (London: Routledge, 1980), pp. 19–26. Sluga rightly stresses the proto-Wittgensteinian dimensions of Gruppe's philosophy, p. 26.

[33] See Otto Friedrich Gruppe, *Gegenwart und Zukunft der Philosophie in Deutschland* (Berlin: Reimer, 1855). Gruppe had sketched his views much earlier, first in his *Antäus, Ein Briefwechsel über speculative Philosophie in ihrem Conflict mit Wissenschaft und Sprache* (Berlin: Nancke, 1831), and then in his *Wendepunkt der Philosophie im Neunzehnten Jahrhundert* (Berlin: Reimer, 1834).

THE INTERIM YEARS, 1840–1860 191

the basis of this diagnosis of the problems of speculative idealism, Gruppe made his recommendations for the philosophy of the future: it should be first and foremost logic, but a new and reformed logic that is based on the philosophy of language. The fears about philosophy's obsolescence are misguided, he argued, because there will always be a need for logic, which is the distinctive enterprise of philosophy.

– Still another solution to the identity crisis—and one of great importance for neo-Kantianism—appeared in Adolf Trendelenburg's *Logische Untersuchungen,* which was first published in 1840.[34] Accepting the autonomy of the new empirical sciences as his starting point, Trendelenburg held that there was no necd for a *philosophia prima* in the sense of speculative idealism. Philosophy could not, in any case, provide a foundation for the empirical sciences, because pure thinking on its own is barren and empty, acquiring its content only from experience. However, dropping foundationalist aspirations does not mean, Trendelenburg insisted, that there is no end or point to philosophy at all. On the contrary, philosophy should now become "a theory of science" (*Wissenschaftstheorie*), whose task is to examine the logic of the sciences. There is still a serious need for philosophy, Trendelenburg noted, because the particular sciences do not reflect on their most basic concepts and presuppositions; they are more concerned to apply their methods and standards than to explain them. So Trendelenburg reversed the speculative idealist view of the relationship between philosophy and science. Rather than basing the empirical sciences upon philosophy, philosophy should be based on the empirical sciences. Instead of prescribing the methods and principles of the natural sciences, philosophy should investigate the methods and principles developed by the natural sciences themselves. In this new scientific age, Trendelenburg taught, philosophy must recognize "the fact of science", that is, the fact that the sciences are forces in their own right, that they have proven their own success, and there is no point in worrying ourselves with scepticism about them.[35]

– A final response to the identity crisis came from left-wing Hegelianism, which identified philosophy with criticism. Many of the left-wing Hegelians—Karl Marx, David Friedrich Strauss, Kuno Fischer, Eduard Zeller and Bruno Bauer— had accepted Feuerbach's criticisms of Hegelian metaphysics, which they saw as the end of traditional philosophy. However, they still believed that philosophy has a valuable role to perform as critique, as the critical second-order examination of all beliefs, especially political and religious ones but also those of traditional philosophy. In identifying philosophy with criticism, the left-wing

---

[34] Friedrich Adolf Trendelenburg, *Logische Untersuchungen*, second edition (Leipzig: Hirzel, 1862). See especially the preface, introduction and first chapter. The first edition, which does not differ substantially from the second, appeared in 1840 with Bethge Verlag in Berlin.

[35] Trendelenburg, *Logische Untersuchungen*, I, 130–131.

Hegelians both affirmed and denied the materialist call for the abolition of philosophy: they affirmed it in holding traditional philosophy to be bankrupt; but they denied it in turning philosophy into the criticism of philosophy. Ironically, philosophy could resurrect itself as the criticism of philosophy, thus escaping those critics of philosophy who foretold the death of philosophy itself.

4. Late Idealism and Neo-Kantianism

Besides the materialism controversy and identity crisis, there was another philosophical development of the interim decades of great importance for neo-Kantianism. This was the emergence of two neo-idealist thinkers, Adolph Trendelenburg (1802–1872) and Hermann Lotze (1816–1881), who became the most influential thinkers in Germany in the middle of the 19th century. Both held prestigious positions, which they occupied for nearly half a century. Trendelenburg was professor in Berlin from 1833 to 1872, and Lotze professor in Göttingen from 1844 to 1881. Both were teachers of prominent neo-Kantians: Lotze of Windelband, Trendelenburg of Cohen and Bona Meyer. But their influence extends far beyond their teaching; their writings reached an entire generation. Trendelenburg's *Logische Untersuchungen* and Lotze's *Mikrokosmus* were two of the most influential philosophical works of the 19th century.

The importance of Trendelenburg and Lotze for neo-Kantianism has not gone unappreciated. In his *Entstehung und Aufstieg des Neukantianismus* Klaus Christian Köhnke devotes an entire chapter to Trendelenburg, whom he regards as the decisive figure in the transition from speculative idealism to neo-Kantianism.[36] Köhnke deserves much of the credit for lifting Trendelenburg out of obscurity and noting his pivotal role in the history of philosophy in the 19th century.[37] He rightly stresses the importance of Trendelenburg's re-orientation of philosophy around the empirical sciences, which he sees as "the beginning of the history of modern epistemology and philosophy of science, which finds its summit in neo-Kantianism".[38] Though Köhnke is silent about him, Lotze is the subject of a complete chapter of Thomas Willey's *Back to Kant*. According to Willey, Lotze was "the most important fore-runner of the neo-Kantian movement."[39] Willey explores Lotze's chief contributions to neo-Kantianism: "constructive scepticism, a distrust of purely conceptual thought, a

[36] Klaus Christian Köhnke, *Entstehung und Aufstieg des Neukantianismus* (Frankfurt: Suhrkamp, 1986), pp. 23–57.

[37] See *Friedrich Adolf Trendelenburgs Wirkung*, eds Gerald Hartung und Klaus Christian Köhnke (Eutin: Eutiner Landesbibliothek, 2006). This collection contains a complete and accurate bibliography, compiled by Köhnke, of Trendelenburg's writings.

[38] Köhnke, *Entstehung und Aufstieg*, p. 23.

[39] Thomas E. Willey, *Back to Kant: The Revival of Kantianism in German Social and Historical Thought, 1860–1914* (Detroit, MI: Wayne State University Press, 1978), pp. 40–57.

deep interest in the problem of values and an admirable effort to bring philosophical idealism into harmony with nineteenth-century science."[40]

There is little point here in replicating Köhnke's and Willey's efforts in explaining Trendelenburg's and Lotze's positive influence on neo-Kantianism. It is perhaps worthwhile, however, to see their relationship from the opposite angle, one which notes the important differences between these neo-idealists and the neo-Kantians. Only then will we be able to see their relationship from a broader and more balanced perspective.

For all their importance for neo-Kantianism, Trendelenburg and Lotze belong to an earlier generation. They were essentially neo-Romantics, striving to uphold the heritage of absolute or objective idealism. We tend to think of the idealist tradition dying off with neo-Hegelianism in the 1840s; but Trendelenburg and Lotze, the two most influential thinkers of the mid-19th century, were very much in the idealist tradition, and they lived on until 1872 (Trendelenburg) and 1881 (Lotze). What came to an end in the late 1840s was *speculative* idealism, the attempt to justify metaphysics through a priori methods, but not idealism as such. Lotze and Trendelenburg rejected the *methods* of absolute idealism, though they attempted to preserve its content, which they tried to justify by more empirical means. Neo-Kantianism, however, rejected not only the method but also the content of absolute idealism; and to this extent there is a gulf between the late idealists and the neo-Kantians.

Lotze and Trendelenburg were absolute idealists in the sense that they, like the Romantics, Schelling and Hegel before them, held that all reality conforms to the idea, which is the form or purpose of the good. Both were committed, therefore, to the validity of teleology, which they defended against materialism or a mechanistic naturalism. They were indeed explicit in describing their metaphysics in such terms. In the preface to the second edition of his *Logische Untersuchungen* Trendelenburg calls his philosophy "the organic worldview",[41] according to which the entire universe forms a single organic being. This was the very worldview that we find in the Romantics, Schelling and Hegel. Trendelenburg's main aim in the *Logische Untersuchungen* was to defend it against materialism, to show how it conforms to the findings of the latest scientific research, and to free it from the old conceptions of providence and theism. Lotze had a very similar intention in his massive *Mikrokosmus,* which appeared from 1856 to 1864.[42] Already by 1852 Lotze began to describe his worldview as "spiritualism", which he distinguished from "idealism", a term he had used for his philosophy in his 1841 *Metaphysik*.[43] Spiritualism for Lotze

[40] Willey, *Back to Kant*, p. 57.

[41] Adolf Trendelenburg, *Logische Untersuchungen*, 3rd edition (Leipzig: Hirzel 1870), I, ix.

[42] Hermann Lotze, *Mikrokosmus. Ideen zur Naturgeschichte und Geschichte der Menschheit. Versuch einer Anthropologie* (Leipzig: Hirzel, 1856–1864). All references here are to the fourth edition, which appeared from 1884 to 1888.

[43] Lotze first used the term "spiritualism" to describe his position in his *Medicinische Psychologie* (Leipzig: Weidmann, 1852).

is the thesis "that spirit alone is primary existence, and that matter is to be seen as secondary".[44] This doctrine was essentially panpsychism, according to which the substance, or the inner nature or essence of anything, consists in spirit or soul. In advancing his spiritualism Lotze was not discarding absolute idealism but attempting to revise it. Absolute idealism, in his view, had failed to stress the agency behind the realization of the idea and the personal dimension of the absolute. A central purpose of *Mikrokosmus* was to defend this spiritualism and to show how it is an improvement on absolute idealism. All the while, however, Lotze continued to uphold the basic idealist thesis that all reality conforms to the idea.[45]

It should be plain from this very brief statement of Lotze's and Trendelenburg's worldviews that they are fundamentally metaphysical, and in a profoundly *anti*-Kantian sense. Contrary to Kant's critical idealism, both are attempts—in a limited, hypothetical, partial and provisional fashion—to know reality in itself, the unconditioned, or the absolute. Lotze and Trendelenburg never hid their attempts to move beyond the Kantian limits on knowledge. This is especially apparent from their efforts to defend teleology against Kant's regulative constraints. In the *Logische Untersuchungen* Trendelenburg would deliberately take aim at Kant's regulative doctrines and argue that it is necessary to give constitutive status to the idea of a purpose.[46] And in his *Mikrokosmus* Lotze would engage in a more subtle defence of teleology,[47] though one no less anti-Kantian in its intentions and implications. Lotze maintains that we must distinguish between the realms of existence and validity: though we must not posit the *existence* of purposes, we still have to assume their *validity*. While what is valid need not exist, its validity makes it true independent of human consciousness or whatever anyone thinks about it.

Lotze's and Trendelenburg's attempts to move beyond Kantian constraints also emerge from their reaction against transcendental idealism. Both feared that the critical limits of transcendental idealism would result in a kind of solipsism or scepticism, according to which the individual subject could know nothing beyond its own representations. Trendelenburg believed in the importance of a realistic worldview, according to which we know reality in itself and not simply how the world appears to us.[48] It was for this reason that he refused to accept the alleged idealistic implications of Kant's arguments in the Transcendental Aesthetic. While Trendelenburg accepted the arguments themselves, he maintained that they did not rule out a much stronger realism, that is, that even if space and time are forms of a priori intuition, it is still possible that they are also true of things-in-themselves. While Lotze had no commitments to transcendental realism, one purpose behind his own distinction between

[44] Lotze, *Medicinische Psychologie*, p. 61, Section 48.
[45] See *Mikrokosmus* Book V, Chapter 1, II, 157–169, where Lotze argues that the essence of things consists in their ideas.
[46] Trendelenburg, *Logische Untersuchungen*, II, 46–54.
[47] See Lotze, *Mikrokosmus*, Book IV, Chapters 1 and 2, II, 3–17, 43–44
[48] See Trendelenburg, *Logische Untersuchungen*, I, 160, 163.

the realms of existence and validity was to escape the solipsistic snares of scepticism or subjective idealism.[49] The truths of the Lotzean realm of validity are objective not in the sense that they exist independent of the mind, but in the sense they are true even if no one ever thinks of them. Though Lotze's doctrine of validity will later become the source of the theory of value of the Southwestern school, it is worthwhile to note that its original intention was to avoid the unpalatable consequences of scepticism and Kant's subjective idealism.

The distance between the neo-idealists and the neo-Kantians is perhaps most visible when we consider their contrasting attitudes towards epistemology. The neo-Kantianism of the 1860s saw the solution to the crisis of philosophy in going back to epistemology, in making philosophy once again a critique of knowledge as Kant had once envisaged it. It was a reaction against the grand old metaphysics of Schelling and Hegel, and an attempt to take philosophy back to its limits within experience. There is an extent to which Trendelenburg encouraged this move by re-orienting philosophy around the empirical sciences and by abandoning Schelling's and Hegel's speculative methods. But to another extent Trendelenburg discouraged it, because he never intended his re-orientation of philosophy around the sciences to mean limiting philosophy to epistemology. Far from it. As the first chapter of the *Logische Untersuchungen* makes clear,[50] Trendelenburg still saw philosophy as metaphysics, as knowledge of the universe as a whole. In a striking Platonic formulation, he states that philosophy is "the science of the idea", where the idea determines the whole in its parts, the universal in the particular.[51] Even though, unlike Schelling and Hegel, he regards such knowledge as an ideal that we can approach but never attain, he still stressed the priority of metaphysics in resolving the problems of philosophy. Epistemology could never be first philosophy for Trendelenburg because its problem of knowledge could be resolved only through the metaphysics of absolute idealism, which alone could mediate the opposition between thought and being.[52] A very similar attitude appears in Lotze, who, in his 1841 *Metaphysik*, argued that "the critique of reason is not a question preceding metaphysics but one immanent within it".[53] Epistemology, as the attempt to examine knowledge before making claims to knowledge, is naive, Lotze thought, because even the attempt to know these conditions involves a claim to knowledge, and moreover a metaphysics in its conception of the object of knowledge.[54] Though Lotze was intent on providing metaphysics with a critical foundation, he never ceased to stress the importance of metaphysical enquiry

---

[49] See Hermann Lotze, *System der Philosophie: Erster Theil: Drei Bücher der Logik* (Leipzig: Hirzel, 1874), I, 493–511.

[50] Trendelenburg, *Logische Untersuchungen*, I, 4–14.

[51] Trendelenburg, *Logische Untersuchungen*, I, 5.

[52] This is the crux of Trendelenburg's argument in Chapters IV and V of the *Logische Untersuchungen*, I, 130–155.

[53] Hermann Lotze, *Metaphysik* (Leipzig: Weidmann, 1841), p. 280; §58.

[54] Lotze, *Metaphysik*, p. 279; §58

in answering the fundamental questions of philosophy. The philosopher had to be self-critical, but he should never let the demands for self-criticism prevent him from pursuing metaphysical questions. As he put it in an oft-cited metaphor: "The constant whetting of the knife proves boring when we have nothing to cut."[55]

The neo-Kantians and neo-idealists were not always aware of their differences, though now and then they would emerge into broad daylight. In the second edition of his *Kants Theorie der Erfahrung* Cohen would often take issue with Lotze's metaphysical talk about the "plan and meaning of life".[56] The most dramatic encounter between these traditions was the clash between Trendelenburg and Fischer regarding Kant's theory of space and time, which was very much a struggle between Kant's transcendental idealism and Trendelenburg's absolute idealism. But to witness the conflicts between neo-Kantianism and neo-idealism we do not have to look *after* the interim period; we can also look *before* it, because Trendelenburg's and Lotze's absolute idealism was in no small measure a reaction against the transcendental idealism and mechanism of Fries and Herbart.[57] In fighting against Fries and Herbart, it was as if the neo-idealists saw neo-Kantianism forthcoming and did their best to nip it in the bud.

All these points about the differences between the neo-idealists and neo-Kantians do not undermine in any way Köhnke's and Willey's accounts about the importance of Lotze and Trendelenburg for neo-Kantianism. They do show, however, that the relationship between these movements is much more complicated than an account of their positive influence alone can provide.

5. Helmholtz's Programme: Introduced and Adopted

Besides Trendelenburg and Lotze, there was another thinker of crucial importance for neo-Kantianism during the interim years: Hermann von Helmholtz (1821–1894). While it is a mistake to see Helmholtz as the founder of the neo-Kantian movement,[58] he definitely played a powerful role in the development of neo-Kantianism. Not the least reason for this was his scientific reputation. Helmholtz was one of the most celebrated natural scientists of 19th-century Germany. He became famous for his

---

[55] Lotze, *System der Philosophie*, II, 15.

[56] Hermann Cohen, *Kants Theorie der Erfahrung*, Zweite neue bearbeitete Auflage (Berlin: Dümmler, 1885), pp. 289, 581–582, 602, 603.

[57] See especially Trendelenburg's *Über Herbarts Metaphysik und neue Auffassungen derselben. Erster und Zweiter Artikel* (Berlin: Bethge, 1854 and 1856). Trendelenburg would also take issue with Herbart throughout his *Logische Untersuchungen*. On Lotze's views on Herbart, see especially his *Streitschriften* (Leipzig: Hirtel, 1857), pp. 1–16. Lotze's 1841 *Metaphysik* constantly takes issue with Herbart.

[58] This was the opinion of Alois Riehl, *Hermann von Helmholtz in seinem Verhältnis zu Kant* (Berlin: Reuther & Reichard, 1904), p. 1.

discovery of the law of conservation of force, his invention of the opthalmoscope, and his research on physiological optics.

Although Helmholtz was primarily a natural scientist, and saw himself as such, he also had a deep interest in philosophy, which he acquired during his youth. He remembered hearing his father, a Gymnasium teacher, discuss epistemological questions with his friends, who were devotees of Kant, Fichte and Hegel.[59] At an early age he read Kant, who made a deep impression upon him.[60] He later said of his youth that he had been "a faithful Kantian"; and, though he would later diverge from his master on some points, he never lost his basic Kantian convictions.[61] Even as an old professor in the late 1890s, Helmholtz would preach Kant's enduring relevance.

Although Helmholtz wanted to be a physicist, there was no career in that field in the 1830s, and so he studied medicine instead. As a student at the Medical Institute in Berlin he attended the lectures of Beneke in logic, of H.G. Magnus (1802–1870) in physics, and of Johannes Müller (1801–1858) in physiology. It was Müller, the foremost physiologist of his day, who guided Helmholtz into the new scientific approach to the study of human physiology.[62] As we shall soon see, Müller's account of the nerves and senses will have a decisive effect on his later approach to epistemology. Because of his promise and early achievements, Helmholtz had a meteoric academic career.[63] In 1849 he became chair of physiology at Königsberg; in 1855 professor in Bonn; and from 1858 to 1871 he was professor of physiology at Heidelberg. He crowned his career in 1871 by taking over Magnus' chair in physics at Berlin, and by becoming the first director of the new Physico-Technical Institute. During his illustrious career Helmholtz developed some personal connections with neo-Kantians: he was a friend of Zeller, a teacher of Lange, and an acquaintance of Liebmann.

Helmholtz's importance for neo-Kantianism mainly rests on his programme to wed philosophy with natural science, and more specifically on his attempt to rehabilitate Kant's epistemology through modern physiology. This programme made it seem as if Kant's philosophy was not an obsolete faculty psychology from the 18th century, as Herbart used to say, but that it was at the cutting age of science in the mid-19th century. Given the growing authority of natural science, and given Helmholtz's stature as a scientist, what more compelling endorsement could there be for Kant's philosophy? It was a seductive message, especially now that the materialists were becoming such a potent force; and it was a winning strategy, which many saw as the best way to promulgate Kant in the new scientific age.

---

[59] See Helmholtz's 'Erinnerungen', in *Vorträge und Reden*, 4th edition (Braunschweig: Vieweg, 1896), I, 17.

[60] See Helmholtz's letter to his parents, written sometime in early 1839, in Leo Königsberger, *Hermann von Helmholtz* (Braunschweig: Vieweg & Sohn, 1902–1903), I, 29–30

[61] See 'Vorrede zum ersten Bande' to the third edition of Helmholtz, *Vorträge und Reden*, p. viii (as reproduced in the fourth edition cited n. 59).

[62] On Helmholtz's study with Müller, see Laura Otis, *Müller's Lab* (Oxford: Oxford University Press, 2007), pp. 111–131.

[63] On Helmholtz's life and career, the standard account is Leo Königsberger, *Hermann von Helmholtz*.

Helmholtz's attempt to rehabilitate Kant began with his famous lecture *Über das Sehen des Menschen*, which was delivered on February 27, 1855 on the occasion of the unveiling of a statue of Kant in Königsberg.[64] It is difficult to exaggerate the importance of this lecture for later neo-Kantianism. The programme it puts forward—what later became known as "physiological neo-Kantianism"—would become the inspiration for the 1860s generation. Zeller, Liebmann and Lange became its advocates.

Helmholtz's lecture is best read as his response not to the materialism controversy but to the identity crisis of philosophy.[65] While Helmholtz is concerned with materialism, specifically its claim about the death of philosophy, this is not his explicit or main worry. His chief adversary in his lecture is not materialism, about which he says nothing, but the speculative idealism of Schelling and Hegel, about which he says a lot. He feared that the collapse of speculative idealism had discredited not only philosophy in general but even Kant's philosophy in particular, which had inspired speculative idealism, and which was closely associated by many with it. Helmholtz's strategy for resolving the crisis was twofold: first, dissassociate Kant's philosophy from speculative idealism; and, second, show that the latest physiological and psychological research confirms the guiding principles of Kant's epistemology. That second move quashed in one solid blow the materialist's claims about the death of philosophy. Natural science was not making philosophy obsolete but reviving it, and indeed pushing it in an anti-materialist direction.

Prima facie Helmholtz's programme does not seem so original. For did not Fries and Beneke try to base Kantian philosophy on psychology since the early 1800s? Yet there was something new and important in Helmholtz's programme, something that went far beyond anything forseen by his predecessors. For Helmholtz insisted upon strict observation and experiment from the standpoint of an objective observer, upon placing the epistemological subject in the laboratory. The old methods of self-observation or introspection, which had been recommended by Fries and Beneke, were declared obsolete. The problem with these old methods, Helmholtz pointed out, is that some of the most important workings of our physiology and psychology are subconscious and have to be inferred (34, 36). Too much escapes the first-person observer, who notices only what happens on the surface of consciousness. So Helmholtz's programme elevated psychology onto a new plateau, onto the field of observation and experiment; what counts is what one does in a laboratory, not what one records by introspection.

---

[64] Hermann Helmholtz, *Über das Sehen des Menschen. Ein Populär wissenschaftlicher Vortrag gehalten zu Königsberg in Preussen. Zum Besten von Kant's Denkmal. Am 27. Februar, 1855.* (Leipzig: Voß, 1855). Also published in Helmholtz, *Vorträge und Reden*, I, 85–118. All references in parentheses are to the original edition.

[65] Here I take issue with Köhnke, who thinks that the context of Helmholtz's argument is provided by the materialism controversy. See Köhnke, *Entstehung und Aufstieg*, pp. 152–153. While Helmholtz is indeed concerned with materialism, his immediate and explicit concern in this lecture is with the obsolescence of philosophy.

It was a bold undertaking on Helmholtz's part to try to bring philosophy and science together in the 1850s, given that they seemed to be drifting further apart. Taking the bull by the horns, Helmholtz addresses this very issue in the beginning of his lecture. He notes that the division between science and philosophy is a peculiar fact of the present. It did not exist in the 18th century and least of all for Kant, whose early philosophy was based on Newtonian physics (4). Kant's philosophy is still very much in accord with the spirit of modern science, Helmholtz insists, because it teaches that knowledge is founded on experience. The source of the breach between philosophy and science in the 19th century Helmholtz finds in the speculative idealism of Schelling and Hegel. Rather than resting content with knowledge from experience, Schelling and Hegel tried to answer the ultimate metaphysical questions from "pure thinking alone" (6). Anticipating a common neo-Kantian trope, Helmholtz claims that these efforts ended in abject failure because they failed to heed Kant's lessons about the limits of knowledge. But the collapse of speculative idealism should not lead to disillusionment about philosophy in general, Helmholtz advises (6), because one should not confuse these systems of philosophy with philosophy itself. There is a way of regenerating philosophy if we attempt to bring it in closer accord with the natural sciences, just as it was in Kant's day.

There is one important point where philosophy and science do coincide, Helmholtz notes, and that is the field of sense perception (6–7). This field is as much a concern for the epistemologist, who studies the origins of knowledge, as it is for the physiologist, who investigates the physical structure of sense perception. To show how epistemology and physiology come together in the latest scientific research, Helmholtz explains to his audience the basic conclusions of Johannes Müller's theory of specific nerve energies, which he praises as "the greatest progress that the physiology of sense organs has made in recent times" (18). According to Müller's theory, the content of our perception, or "the quality of our sensations", is determined by our sense organs and their nervous apparatus.[66] One and the same stimulus in the physical world—the oscillation of aether—is perceived as light or heat according to whether we see or touch it. What we perceive thus depends on the specific sense organ with which we perceive it. As Helmholtz puts it somewhat paradoxically: "Light becomes light when it hits the seeing eye; without that it is only an oscillation of the aether." (18) Helmholtz does not hesitate to stress the analogy between Müller's theory and Kant's epistemology. "Exactly what the physiology of the senses had shown through experience", he contends, "Kant tried to show earlier for the representations of the human mind, since he made clear the extent to which the innate laws of the mind, as it were its organization, determine our representations." (19; cf. 41–42).

---

[66] See Johannes Müller, *Zur vergleichende Physiologie des Gesichtsinnes des Menschen und der Thiere* (Leipzig: Knobloch, 1826), pp. 6, 44–45. Also see his *Handbuch der Physiologie des Menschen* (Coblenz: Hölscher, 1838–1840), II, 251–254.

Helmholtz does not leave the connection between Kant's epistemology and science simply on the level of *physiology*, however. He takes it a step further by also considering the *psychology* of perception, that is, the psychic acts that are necessary for
perception. Helmholtz is far from thinking that we perceive the world just by having sensations; he goes on to consider some of the many psychic acts of inference
and judgement—most of them automatic and subconscious—necessary to convert
sensations into perception. The very content of perception, he argues, is formed by
inference and judgement. What we see is very much the product of the intellectual
processes by which we see it. We see three-dimensional objects in space, for example,
though that perception is not just given to us but is the product of the mind constructing one image from the many it receives from its two eyes, and from walking around
the object and seeing it from many perspectives (25–27). We are "jugglers with the
eyes", as it were, because we engage in the most complicated acts in seeing things. We
are not aware of this art, though, because we have learned it so long ago and repeated
it so many times (39). While Helmholtz thinks that we learn this art by habit and
experience, he is far from ruling out innate or a priori mechanisms in the formation
of perception. One of the fundamental assumptions behind all perception, he notes,
is that there is a cause for all events, and that assumption we do not learn from experience because all experience presupposes it. Kant was right, therefore, to regard the
principle of causality as an a priori or innate mechanism behind all perception (41).

It is striking that Helmholtz does not contrast his Kantian theory of perception
with materialism, whose theories of perception had just begun to appear in the
mid-1850s as he was delivering his lecture. That contrast will later be developed by
Lange, who will make Helmholtz's theory a counter against materialism. Helmholtz's
own contrast is with the theories of perception of Schelling and Hegel. They attempt
to prove, he says, "the identity of our sensations with the actual properties of the perceived bodies" (19).[67] Their theory assumes that the idea reveals and manifests itself
in sense qualities, so that we can know the world in itself through immediate experience. They completely failed to take into account, therefore, the extent to which
that experience is a construction of the creative cognitive subject. While Helmholtz
has some sympathy for Schelling's and Hegel's theory of subject–object identity—it
embodies an aesthetic attitude towards the world—he thinks that it does no justice to
the epistemology of natural science, which demands that the scientist gets behind the
veil of sense perception to grasp the laws lying underneath experience.

Helmholtz concludes his lecture by expressing his conviction that there is no necessary conflict between philosophy and science, that there is instead a common bond
between them (42). This is indeed the crux, though it was just here that Helmholtz's
lecture became vague and left many questions. For what, exactly, is the relationship
between Kant's epistemology and the sciences? Is that epistemology only a form of

---

[67] Helmholtz refers us here to an earlier paper, 'Ueber Goethe's naturwissenschaftlichen Arbeiten',
which first appeared in 1853. See Helmholtz, *Vorträge und Reden* I, 23–45, esp. 36–42.

proto-physiology and psychology, so that it can be eventually replaced by them? Or is there a kind of parallelism between them, so that what epistemology determines on the transcendental level, physiology and psychology determine on the empirical level? As important as these questions were, Helmholtz had no answers to them. They were questions he would leave later neo-Kantians to explore.

6. Helmholtz's Programme: Reaffirmed and Abandoned

Some thirty years after his Königsberg lecture, Helmholtz returned to his neo-Kantian programme with his Rectoral Address at Berlin University, 'Die Thatsachen der Erfahrung', which he delivered on August 3, 1878.[68] This lecture is remarkable for revealing Helmholtz's enduring loyalty to Kant amid his willingness to criticize and re-interpret him. Without the slightest hesitation, he reaffirms his old Kantian standpoint: "In what appears to me the progress of Kant's philosophy, we still stand on the ground of his system." (42). But he immediately adds that this does not mean he swears allegiance to "all the subordinate points *in verba magistri*". Indeed, for reasons we shall soon see, Helmholtz takes to task what he mockingly calls "*die Kantianer stricter Observanz*" (22). The crucial question is what Helmholtz means by "the progress of Kant's philosophy". To understand that, we have to take a close look at the lecture itself.

Helmholtz began his lecture by revisiting the old conflict between philosophy and science, which he had already thematized in *Über das Sehen des Menschen*. He reaffirmed his old strategy for resolving it: namely, showing how Müller's theory of specific nerve energies supports Kant's epistemology. Now, however, Helmholtz takes Müller's theory in an interesting direction, elaborating it into a theory of his own about the relationship between representation and object.[69] Müller's theory states that one and the same external stimulus (viz. aether oscillations) can produce two very different kinds of sensation (sounds, colours), and that two very different stimuli (an oscillation and pressure on an optical nerve) can produce the same sensation (a flash of light) (9–10). These facts show that what we perceive, the quality of sensation, depends on the sensory nerves of a specific sense organ. Now if we keep this point in mind, Helmholtz argues, then we cannot claim that a sensation is an "image" (*Bild*) of its object; all that we can say is that it is a "sign" (*Zeichen*) for it (12). While an image resembles its object by virtue of some natural similarity, a sign designates its object

[68] *Die Thatsachen in der Wahrnehmung. Rede gehalten zur Stiftungsfeier der Friedrich Wilhelms Universität zu Berlin am 3. August 1878* (Berlin: August Hirschwald, 1879). Also in Helmholtz, *Vorträge und Rede* II, 213–248. All citations here are to the original edition.

[69] Helmholtz had developed his sign theory much earlier. Its first statement appears in his 'Ueber Goethe's naturwissenschaftlichen Arbeiten', which appeared in 1853. See Helmholtz, *Vorträge und Reden*, I, 41.

only in virtue of some convention or interpretation. Though Helmholtz is not so explicit, his sign theory should be regarded as a reformulation of a Kantian doctrine. For Kant had departed from the traditional theory of ideas precisely on the grounds that ideas do not resemble their objects; what makes them represent an object is the concepts behind them, which are not images but ways of organizing sensations into laws (i.e. a rule of synthesis).[70]

Helmholtz's sign theory immediately raises the question to what extent we do have knowledge of an external world, of a reality independent of our perception. If sensations are signs having no resemblance to their objects, are we not caught in a web of signs of our own making? It is a question that much troubles Helmholtz, and which he addresses in different ways in his lecture. There is an element of realism in his position because he holds that sensations arise from external causes (12), and that what particular sensations we have, and the order and context in which we have them, depends on "external influences" (*äusserern Einwirkungen*) and not just our physiological organization (23). Still, he admits that there cannot be any scientific justification for such realism. This is because there cannot be any theoretical refutation of an extreme subjective idealism, which holds that all reality consists in representations and that life is only a dream (34). The only justification of realism is that it is the simplest hypothesis and agrees with common sense (35). He advises us to treat idealism and realism as "scientific hypotheses", that is, to avoid making them into dogmas or claiming that they are necessary truths (35–36).

So Helmholtz is a realist to the extent that he thinks that there is an independent reality, that is, that something continues to exist when we do not perceive it. But that still leaves the question: What knowledge do we have of this reality? To what extent can we know it? Helmholtz is *not* a realist to the degree that he holds our sensations give us direct knowledge of this external reality. The whole point of the theory of signs is to exclude transcendental realism, which assumes that our representations in experience give us knowledge of reality in itself. But if transcendental realism is false, and if there is some independent reality, are we not forced to assume the existence of Kant's unknowable thing-in-itself? Helmholtz is rather skittish about this whole issue. He knows that he is stepping on contested ground and stands aback with the following remark: "That it is a *contradictio in adjecto* to want to represent the real or Kant's 'thing-in-itself' with positive properties, without putting it in the form of our representations, is something I do not need to explain to you. That has often been discussed." (39). But this was more avoiding the issue than answering it.

When push came to shove, Helmholtz took his stand in affirming a limited kind of scientific realism according to which we can know the laws of nature (40). Immediately after introducing his sign theory, he qualifies it by saying that there is some degree of resemblance between representations and reality after all, because

[70] See Kant, KrV, B, 235–236, 242.

we can use signs so that they designate lawful relationships between objects (12–13). Since the same signs designate the same objects, and different signs different objects, we can place them in relationships to signify causal relationships perceived to hold between objects. So, though signs themselves are not images, the relations between them, which we can express precisely mathematically, can be (12–13). In thus making relations do the work of representation, Helmholtz anticipates one of the later doctrines of the Marburg school.[71]

Now, though, another hoary question arises, a classical one for just such a scientific realism: What justification can there be for the principle of causality? Helmholtz was troubled by this question too, though he fails to give a completely unambivalent answer to it. Sometimes he declares dogmatically that it is "a fact without hypothetical supposition" that appearances are lawful (37), and he even says that these lawful connections are "directly perceived" (37). Yet Helmholtz eventually retreats to the more modest position that we have no guarantee of the applicability of the causal principle other than its success (41). He even reaffirms the Kantian position that the principle of causality is "a transcendental law", and one that cannot be demonstrated from experience because experience is possible only by assuming it (41). Here Helmholtz saw, if through a glass darkly, the limits of his whole programme, his attempt to build philosophy on the basis of science. If science has presuppositions, which it is the purpose of transcendental philosophy to investigate, then how can it be the basis of transcendental philosophy? Should it not be the other way around, so that transcendental philosophy is the basis of science? The old idea of a *philosophia prima* was not so easily buried after all.

Helmholtz's theory of signs was only one of the innovations of his 1878 lecture. Another no less important one is his reformulation of the Kantian theory of the a priori status of space. Helmholtz notes that Kant went much further than the sign theory of perception in affirming the subjectivity of experience, for he held that not only sensations but also space and time themselves are only forms of intuition. Even here, Helmholtz maintains, modern physiology can follow Kant, though, he hastens to add, only "up to a certain limit" (14). He then proceeds to sketch his own theory of spatial perception (14–15). In the great battle between "nativists" and "empiricists" about the origins of spatial perception, Helmholtz comes down firmly on the empiricist side (30).[72] While the nativists hold that space is an innate intuition, which is simple, given and unanalysable, the empiricists hold that it is constructed from experience, association and habit. Helmholtz's theory attempts to explain how we construct our representation of space from these sources. According to his theory, we construct it through locating things, by associating the movement of our eyes and

[71] See especially Ernst Cassirer, *Substanzbegriff und Funktionsbegriff* (Berlin: Cassirer, 1910).
[72] For a detailed treatment of Helmholtz's position in this controversy, see Gary Hatfield, *The Natural and the Normative: Theories of Spatial Perception from Kant to Helmholtz* (Cambridge, MA: MIT Press, 1990), pp. 165–234.

bodies with certain sensations from certain locations. We locate bodies by moving our eyes towards them, by walking around them and seeing them from different perspectives. The object is for us the totality of perspectives that we have of it by walking around it, from seeing it from this or that angle. So space for Helmholz is, as it were, the field we construct by moving our eyes and body about things.

What, we might ask, is the Kantian aspect of this theory? As an empiricist theory, it seems to be at odds with Kant's "nativism" because it denies the a priori status of space. Helmholtz, though, still thinks that we can give some content to the Kantian theory. Space is "a subjective form of intuition" insofar as it is a construction we create to perceive things (16). Insofar as the power of movement, the feelings that we have from that movement, and the connections we make with these feelings, are all part of our physiological and psychological organization, they can be regarded as a priori conditions of space. "Space is a given form of intuition, prior to all experience, insofar as its perception is connected with the possibility of motor impulses, the mental and physical capacities of which are given by our organization before we have any intuition of space." (16).

It seems Helmholtz is bending over backwards to give some sense to Kant's a priori theory of space. It is not a realist theory, to be sure, since it holds that space is created rather than a given reality. But since it is an empiricist theory, it is not strictly Kantian either. Of course, Helmholtz knows this perfectly well, and it is in just this respect that he wants to take issue with "*die Kantianer stricter Observanz*". He differs from them in two important respects. First, he does not think that space is given a priori as a complete whole intuition; rather, it is constructed by us, the result of our encounter with sensual stimuli as we move around objects (28). The representation of space is indeed not simple and unanalysable, as the Kantians assume, but the result of complex psychic acts, or what Helmholtz calls "subconscious inferences" (27). A subconscious inference is like a quasi syllogism: its major premise is some generalization that we have learned from past experience; its minor premise states some particular observation; and the conclusion subsumes the particular observation under the generalization. In attributing such inferences to spatial perception, Helmholtz was effectively saying that they are not really the immediate given intuitions that strict Kantians made them out to be. Second, Helmholtz maintains that the basic axioms of Euclidean geometry are not a priori truths about the structure of space, but that they are contingent properties that we learn about our own space (23). Here much of his argument is based on an earlier essay, 'Ueber den Ursprung und die Bedeutung der geometrischen Axiome',[73] where Helmholtz had argued that it is only a contingent feature of our spatial world that the Euclidean axioms apply to it. Basing his case on the new non-Euclidean geometries of Riemann and Lobatschewsky, Helmholtz pointed out that the Euclidean axioms hold only for a space with no curvature, and

---

[73] Helmholtz, *Vorträge und Reden*, II, 1–32. This lecture was first given in Heidelberg in 1870.

that there are other possible spaces (viz. those with a constant negative or those with a constant positive curvature) for which non-Euclidean axioms hold. He explicitly contested the Kantian thesis that the Euclidean axioms are necessary consequences of an a priori transcendental form of intuition.[74] It is still possible that we human beings, equipped with our peculiar sensibility, perceive a different space for which non-Euclidean axioms hold. Helmholtz insisted on separating two claims: that space is a priori, the product of our human sensibility; and that Euclidean axioms are necessary to that sensibility (22–3).[75] What Helmholtz regards as the a priori structure of space—our power to locate objects through the movement of our bodies—he also holds to be logically compatible with non-Euclidean axioms.[76] In other words, if we human beings, with our peculiar a priori sensibility, were in a different spatial world, namely, a curved spherical one, we would formulate non-Euclidean axioms that we could find as intuitive as Euclidean ones in our non-curved flat spatial world.

Towards the close of his lecture, Helmholtz distances himself from not only the strict Kantians but Kant himself. Here he notes how "the metaphysicians"—and here he means Schelling and Hegel—have taken their inspiration from Kant's metaphysics, and specifically from his metaphysical foundations of natural science. He decisively rejects that metaphysics, however, on the grounds that it is based on Kant's mistaken view that the axioms of geometry and the principles of mechanics are "transcendental, a priori given propositions" (43). Rather than seeing Kant's metaphysics as an integral part of his philosophy, Helmholtz insists that it "contradicts his whole system". So, for Helmholtz, there were two sides to Kant: the scholastic or metaphysical side, and then the empirical or scientific side. The former, Helmholtz assures us, is the product of outdated science (23, 43). Fortunately, the latter, which can be confirmed by modern science, represents the real Kant.

On the whole, Helmholtz's 1878 lecture, for all its interest and importance, has to be judged a failure. Its shortcomings derived less from any particular doctrine or argument than from its entire programme, from its attempt to base Kant's philosophy upon science. That had not only led to a distorted and contorted interpretation of Kant's theory of space, but it had also misunderstood the aims of Kant's transcendental philosophy, which cannot be grounded on natural science if its purpose is to investigate its very possibility. As Helmholtz spoke in Berlin on that August day in 1878 his programme had already grown old. The younger generation of neo-Kantians—Otto Liebmann, Hermann Cohen and Wilhelm Windelband—had already challenged his interpretation of Kant and the entire programme behind it. We shall eventually see how, at their hands, the Helmholtzian programme came to grief.

[74] Helmholtz, *Vorträge und Reden*, II, pp. 23, 30.
[75] See also the appendix to 'Die Thatsachen in der Wahrnehmung', 'Der Raum kann transcendental sein, ohne dass es die Axiome sind', pp. 51–54; and in Helmholtz, *Vorträge und Reden* II, 391–93.
[76] Helmholtz, 'Ueber den Ursprung und die Bedeutung der geometrischen Axiome', in *Vorträge und Reden*, II, 22, 28.

PART II

Introduction

The Coming of Age

1. The Resurrection of Immanuel Kant

The 1860s seemed to mark the dawn of a new age in Germany.[1] The liberal hopes for greater democracy, for constitutional government and national unity, which had been defeated in 1848, began to stir again. After the oppressive atmosphere of the 1850s, when the forces of reaction bore down heavily on German lands, the air began to clear. Several developments of the late 1850s created this change of atmosphere. Some German states (viz. Baden and Bavaria) were forced to make concessions to liberal parliaments; more liberals were elected to local parliaments; more enlightened reform-minded ministers came to power (viz. Radowitz in Prussia and Schmerling in Austria); and the new Prussian monarch, Wilhelm I, seemed more amenable to reform and liberal ideas than his predecessor, Friedrich Wilhelm IV, a figurehead of the reaction. As the repressive policies of reactionary forces began to weaken, so political activity among liberals began to strengthen. With renewed hopes, the old leaders of 1848 again began to agitate for their cause. They would now proceed more slowly and prudently than in the past, however, calculating that gradual reform could succeed where revolution had failed.

The 1860s was also the breakthrough decade for neo-Kantianism. The calls for a return to Kant now became more vocal and frequent. The few disparate voices of the interim years grew in number and seemed to speak in unison. Some of the most dynamic young philosophers in Germany wrote articles, manifestos, essays, and even whole books, championing the cause of Kant's philosophy. No longer seen as obsolete or dated, Kant's philosophy was now deemed not only worthy of study in its own right but the best solution to the crises and controversies of the day.

It was no accident, of course, that the 1860s witness both the Kant revival and a new political atmosphere. While Kant never advocated, let alone foresaw, German

---

[1] See James Sheehan, *German History 1770–1866* (Oxford: Oxford University Press, 1989), pp. 863, 869, 876.

national unity, he was famous for his advocacy of liberal ideals, such as constitutional and representative government. He was no less well-known for his critical project, according to which all political institutions, "whether the state in its majesty or the church in its holiness", had to submit to the tribunal of critique. No one had done more to secure Kant's reputation as a fearsome critic of the political and religious establishment than Heinrich Heine, who, in his *Zur Religion und Philosophie in Deutschland*, had portrayed Kant as "this great destroyer in the realm of thought who surpassed the terrorism of Maximilian Robbespierre".[2] To some liberals, the "old destroyer" (*der alles Zermalmende*) would be just the man to invoke against those reactionaries who wanted to return to the old alliance of throne and altar.

This connection between the new political atmosphere of the 1860s and the rise of neo-Kantianism is very plain in a very timely and symbolic book published in the beginning of the decade, Ludwig Noack's *Immanuel Kant's Auferstehung aus dem Grabe*.[3] Writing in 1860, Noack made a plea for Kant's resurrection, for a return to the original more radical Kant, whose critical spirit had been buried by the forces of reaction. "The romantic foxes", who populated the theological faculties at the universities, Noack charged, had tried to render Kant harmless by building a foggy metaphysics on his philosophy; but the young Hegelians led by Feuerbach, and "the buddhist saint and pessimist Schopenhauer", had now smoked them out of their refuge. "It is time to get away from the Kantian foxpelt, which is how the philosophical romantics bring him to market, and to return to the true spiritual form and heroic armor of the old man from Königsberg".[4] We should have our Kant neat and straight, Noack advised, and that means pushing his critical project to its limits, whatever the consequences for state and church. What the critical philosophy stands for above all, in the realms of science as well as religion and politics, is free enquiry, the right, indeed duty, to free our minds of all prejudices and superstitions. Doubtless, Noack's pleas expressed the standpoint of many liberals in the early 1860s. The prophecy expressed in the title of Noack's book was becoming true: slowly but surely, Kant's spirit was rising from his grave.

Of course, there were more than political reasons for the Kantian revival of the 1860s. Political reasons alone cannot explain why Kant became the head of a *philosophical* movement. The philosophical reasons for Kant's resurrection lay, as we have already seen,[5] in his power to solve the crises and controversies of the interim decades. The neo-Kantian writers of the 1860s advocated the critical philosophy because, in their view, it alone could solve the materialism controversy and the identity crisis.

There were five major figures who helped to re-establish Kant in the 1860s: Kuno Fischer (1824–1907), Eduard Zeller (1814–1908), Otto Liebmann (1840–1912), Jürgen Bona Meyer (1829–1897) and Friedrich Albert Lange (1828–1875). All of them published

---

[2] Heinrich Heine, *Zur Religion und Philosophie in Deutschland*, in *Sämtliche Schriften*, ed. Klaus Briegleb (Munich: Hanser, 1976), V, 595. This work was first published in 1834.

[3] Ludwig Noack, *Immanuel Kant's Auferstehung aus dem Grabe* (Leipzig: Wigand, 1861).

[4] Noack, *Immanuel Kant*, pp. 27–28.   [5] See the General Introduction, Section 2.

their chief writings on Kant some time during the 1860s, and so, despite their different ages, they still belong to the same period from the standpoint of neo-Kantian history. Several themes unite these authors. All saw Kant as a bulwark against materialism; all made criticism the central vocation of philosophy; all advanced a psychological interpretation of Kant; and all, with one complicated exception, repudiated the neo-rationalism of speculative idealism.

Our task in the following five chapters will be to provide an introduction to each of these thinkers, determining their contribution to neo-Kantianism, and retracing their intellectual development up to their conversion to Kant. Before we turn to that larger task, though, we will provide a brief overview of some of the main themes of the 1860s.

2. Common Themes

The neo-Kantian thinkers of the 1860s were by-and-large the heirs of the psychologism of Helmholtz and the lost tradition. Meyer and Lange were wholehearted advocates of this tradition; and while Fischer, Zeller and Liebmann had some doubts about it, they still affirmed its fundamental tenets. All these thinkers saw Kant's epistemology essentially as psychology, as an investigation into the basic mental activities behind human cognition. Although they were perfectly aware of Kant's distinction between the *quid juris?* and *quid facti?*, they still saw his epistemology primarily as a first-order account of the *causes* of human cognition rather than a second-order evaluation of the *reasons* for it. They reaffirmed Herbart's and Beneke's view that Kant's psychology was simplistic and archaic, in desperate need of modernization to meet the standards of the new empirical sciences. They stressed therefore the value of empirical method in epistemology, whether it is a form of introspection, in the manner of Fries and Beneke, or a form of experiment and observation, in the manner of Helmholtz. Although they upheld Kant's thesis of the a priori dimension of the mind against empiricism, most still believed that the proper way of knowing this a priori dimension is through empirical means.[6]

By the standards of contemporary Kant scholarship, the psychological tradition itself seems archaic and obsolete. We are today the heirs of the Marburg and Southwestern schools, which saw Kant's epistemology in logical rather than psychological terms, and which regarded it as a second-order evaluation of the evidence for beliefs instead of a first-order causal enquiry into their origins. We should not assume, however, that the neo-Kantians of the 1860s were guilty of simple confusions between logic and psychology. They were well aware of the distinction between the normative and natural, the logical and psychological; but they still chose to read Kant in psychological and natural rather than normative and logical terms. The reason for

---

[6] Fischer was an exception to this generalization, holding that the a priori had to be known through a priori means. See Part II, Chapter 8, Section 4.

this lies chiefly in the extraordinary pressure to bring epistemology in line with the empirical sciences, which had set the intellectual standards of the 19th century after the decline of speculative idealism. It was hard for the mid-century neo-Kantian to detach a purely logical and normative epistemology from the scholastic enterprise of Wolffian psychology, or even worse the speculations of the idealist tradition.

During the 1860s, however, cracks began to form in the wall of the psychological tradition. Serious doubts arose whether Kant's epistemology could or should really be simply a form of psychology. Fischer and Liebmann, for example, asked whether Kant's epistemology could be a form of psychology if its task were to examine the necessary conditions of all empirical knowledge. Since psychology is supposed to be a form of empirical knowledge, it should be more the object rather than mode of investigation. It should be the business of transcendental philosophy to investigate the possibility of empirical psychology, to examine its conditions and methods, so that it cannot be reducible to empirical psychology. Fischer and Liebmann raised these doubts, even though they, on the whole, continued to uphold the psychological ways of thinking about epistemology. But their doubts were not forgotten: they became the rationale for a complete break with the psychological tradition later in the 1870s.

There were more than just cracks in the foundation of psychologism. There was also a deeper crisis looming in the background, one that became evident only by the end of the 1860s. The source of the crisis lay in two clashing ambitions of the neo-Kantians: on the one hand, they wanted to psychologize philosophy, so that its methods were more in accord with the empirical sciences; on the other hand, however, they wanted philosophy to have autonomy vis-à-vis the natural sciences, for it to have its own distinctive methods and standards. Clearly, though, the neo-Kantians could not have it both ways. But this impossibility seemed possible in the murky context of the 1860s because the status of psychology was still very much unsettled and undefined. It was not clear then whether psychology was a unique kind of science having its own methods, or whether it was just another empirical science with methods like those of physiology and biology. The more psychology progressed in the later half of the century, however, the more it seemed to be just another empirical science, reaching its results through observation and experiment, and having as its goal the formulation of general causal laws. If this were so, then the identification of philosophy with empirical psychology meant surrendering philosophy's claim to autonomy. Rather than avoiding the danger of obsolescence, philosophy fell prey to it; it became redundant, becoming just another empirical science, empirical psychology.

Another fraught theme of the 1860s was the status of the Kantian thing-in-itself. This had been the major stumbling block to the critical philosophy ever since Jacobi's famous criticism in his *David Hume*, which made affirming the existence of the thing-in-itself the chief reason for both entering and exiting the Kantian system. The 1860s generation continued to wrestle with this dilemma, though it remained unresolved. This generation did not explicitly affirm the existence of the thing-in-itself, as the lost generation once had; but nor did it attempt to eliminate it entirely, turning it into a regulative ideal, as the Marburg and Southwestern schools will later do. Initially, Fischer, Zeller, Liebmann and Lange attempted to remove the thing-in-itself; but, ultimately, they reluctantly admitted its ineliminability. Since, as good Kantians, they stressed the role of the subject in creating the form of its experience, and since, as good students of Helmholtz, they also emphasized the active role of sensibility in conditioning the content of experience, they had to admit that we could not know the object in itself, as it exists apart from and prior to the workings of our cognitive faculties. None of the neo-Kantians were willing to accept a complete Fichtean idealism, which derives all the content of experience from the knowing subject; they insisted that, to some extent, the matter of experience, the content of sensation, is given. They were loyal Kantians in accepting the dualisms between form and content, the posited and given, even if they did not always formulate it in the Kantian manner. If, however, we accept a given content to experience, and if we insist that all objects of knowledge are conditioned or determined by the activities by which we know them, it becomes impossible to avoid the unknowable thing-in-itself. This was the bitter lesson learned by the neo-Kantians of the 1860s.

Still another major theme of the 1860s was the tenability of the epistemological conception of philosophy. Though entrenched, salient and prevalent, this definition came under increasing stress during the decade and thereafter. Granted that this definition is very strategic in helping philosophy overcome its crisis of obsolescence, nagging doubts remained whether it is too narrow. If philosophy is simply epistemology in the strict intended sense, that is, the second-order examination of the logic of the sciences, then it has to forfeit its traditional role as a worldview, as an attempt to answer basic questions about the meaning and purpose of life. These questions had been placed at the centre of philosophy since antiquity. How, then, could they be ignored? Is it not the purpose of philosophy to answer them, to try to resolve "the riddle of existence"?

There was no unanimity about how to answer these questions in the 1860s. There was a positivist strand to neo-Kantianism that wanted to get rid of old fashioned worldviews, which smacked too much of metaphysics; this attitude appears most strongly in the work of the early Liebmann and Lange. There was also, however, an anti-positivist strand to neo-Kantianism in the 1860s, which grew stronger as the century grew older. This anti-positivist strand reaffirmed the value of a worldview and stressed the need to answer the traditional questions about the meaning of life. In other words, philosophy should be not just epistemology but also metaphysics. We find this view best represented in the older Liebmann; but it also appears in Meyer, Zeller and Fischer, who all insist upon the importance of metaphysics. But revitalizing metaphysics was always a testy matter for any neo-Kantian who had taken on board the hard lessons of the first *Kritik*. How could philosophy be a worldview without violating Kant's strictures against metaphysics?

3. The Fischer–Trendelenburg Dispute

One of the most important and striking intellectual events of the 1860s—one crucial for the development of neo-Kantianism—was the famous dispute between Adolf Trendelenburg and Kuno Fischer regarding Kant's Transcendental Aesthetic.[7] This bitter controversy began in the early 1860s and continued until the end of the decade. After Trendelenburg and Fischer, battered and bruised, withdrew from the fray in 1870, a younger generation took over, which debated the issues well into the 1880s. When the dust finally settled at the end of the century, Hans Vaihinger counted some fifty books, brochures and articles devoted to the dispute.[8]

The immediate issue behind the Fischer–Trendelenburg dispute was a question of Kant scholarship. Namely, do Kant's arguments in the Transcendental Aesthetic of the first *Kritik permit* or *prohibit* the possibility that the a priori forms of space and time apply to things-in-themselves? It was Kant's central thesis in the Transcendental Aesthetic that space and time are a priori forms of sensibility, that is, they are the universal and necessary manner in which the human mind perceives the matter given to it by sensation. In other words, the human mind, by the necessary laws of its operation, must perceive things in some space and at some time. These forms, Kant argued, cannot be abstracted from experience because they are necessary conditions of experience; before we abstract anything from experience, they must already be in operation. Since these forms are therefore subjective, arising from our own mental activity, Kant concluded that they are valid only for how we perceive things, that is, only for appearances and not things-in-themselves. But the question arose whether Kant's arguments really give this conclusion. Are the forms of space and time, simply because they arise from the mind, valid *only* of appearances? Or is it still possible that they are *also* valid of things-in-themselves? Even though these forms arise directly from the mind, it should still be possible, so it seemed, for them to apply to things-in-themselves.

In Chapter VI of his *Logische Untersuchungen*, Trendelenburg raised just these questions and claimed to have found a gap in Kant's reasoning.[9] All Kant's proofs for the subjectivity of space and time in the Transcendental Aesthetic, he insisted, do not exclude the possibility that they are also true of things-in-themselves. Trendelenburg did not dispute Kant's intentions. He realized that Kant *intended* to argue that space and time are *only* subjective, and that he had expressly *stated* that they are valid only of appearances. But the crucial question was not about Kant's intentions or

---

[7] For a detailed analysis of the dispute, see my *Late German Idealism: Adolf Trendelenburg and Hermann Lotze* (Oxford: Oxford University Press, 2013), pp. 107–120. For a survey of the course of the dispute as a whole, see Christopher Adair-Toteff, 'The Neo-Kantian Raum Controversy', *The British Journal for the History of Philosophy* II (1994), 131–148.

[8] Hans Vaihinger, *Kommentar zu Kants Kritik der reinen Vernunft* (Stuttgart: Deutsche Verlags Anstalt, 1922), II, 545–548.

[9] Friedrich Adolf Trendelenburg, *Logische Untersuchungen* (Leipzig: Hirzel, 1862), I, 155–232.

statements but the logic of his arguments, that is, does admitting the a priori status of space and time logically entail that they are true of appearances alone? Trendelenburg insisted that there is no such implication at all: although the forms of space and time are a priori and not derived from experience, it is still possible for them to apply to things-in-themselves.

In a later article Trendelenburg laid out the issue as follows.[10] There are three possibilities regarding the ontological status of space and time: 1) they are *only subjective*, that is, forms of intuition valid for only how we perceive the world or for appearances alone; 2) they are *only objective*, that is, the structure of things that exist whether or not we perceive them; and 3) they are *both subjective and objective*, that is, though they are forms arising from our mental activity, they are also true of the objective structure of things-in-themselves. It was this third possibility that Trendelenburg embraced and that he believed Kant's reasoning had failed to exclude.

It was just this third possibility that Fischer adamantly rejected. He could see no gap in Kant's argument whatsoever. In the second edition of his *Logik und Metaphysik,* which appeared in 1865, Fischer mounted two arguments against Trendelenburg's third possibility.[11] First, he makes the exegetical point that Kant's arguments, when read in context, do demonstrate that space and time cannot be properties of things-in-themselves. Fischer points out and underlines one of Kant's crucial background assumptions: that if space and time were objective qualities of things, they would have to be derived from experience; but in that case they would be empirical concepts, so that mathematical propositions would have to forfeit their universality and necessity. Second, he makes the philosophical point that Trendelenburg's position does not avoid scepticism but reinvokes it, for it raises the inevitable problem of how we know that our representations of things in space correspond to things in objective space (175). The sceptic will answer that we have no means of ever establishing a correspondence between our representations and things-in-themselves, so that all the difficulties return about the possibility of a mathematical knowledge of nature (176–177).

Though much of the dispute got bogged down in details of textual exegesis, it is important to see that much more was at stake than issues of Kant scholarship. Underneath the dispute lay fundamental philosophical issues. The chief issue was formulable in terms of that classic Kantian question: How is mathematical knowledge of nature possible? Trendelenburg and Fischer had conflicting views about the necessary conditions of such knowledge. Both accepted Kant's arguments for the a priori status of our representations of space and time; both rejected an empiricist account of the origins of these representations because they feared it would

---

[10] Trendelenburg, 'Ueber eine Lücke in Kants Beweis von der ausschliessende Subjektivität des Raums und der Zeit', in *Historische Beiträge zur Philosophie* (Berlin: Bethge, 1867), III, 215–276.
[11] Kuno Fischer, *System der Logik und Metaphysik oder Wissenschaftslehre*, Zweite umgearbeitete Auflage (Heidelberg: Bassermann, 1865), §66, pp. 175–178.

undermine the universal and necessary validity of mathematics. But they were at odds concerning the question: Under what conditions do these a priori forms give knowledge of nature? Trendelenburg adamantly affirmed a transcendental realism, according to which these forms give knowledge of nature only if they are true of things-in-themselves, that is, for reality independent of how we perceive it. If these forms apply only to appearances, he argued, then we are caught inside the circle of our own representations, given that these appearances are, as Kant says, "only representations in us". An empirical realism, which would hold only within the realm of appearance, was not an option for Trendelenburg, because, in his view, appearance (*Erscheinung*) is not far removed from illusion (*Schein*).[12] "It is the vital nerve in all knowing", he wrote, "that we want to reach things as they are; we want the thing, not only us."[13] Fischer, however, passionately defended transcendental idealism, insisting that transcendental realism is unnecessary for an objective knowledge of nature. All that is necessary, and indeed possible, for objective knowledge of nature, Fischer contended, is a Kantian *empirical realism*, according to which objectivity is possible *within* the realm of appearances. According to empirical realism, objectivity means not the correspondence of representations with things-in-themselves—an impossible standard to meet, as Kant had argued—but simply the conformity of representations with universal and necessary norms of consciousness.

The dispute between Fischer and Trendelenburg also raised the broader issue of the comparative merits of transcendental versus absolute idealism. The question at issue concerned which worldview bests explains the possibility of mathematical knowledge of nature: transcendental or absolute idealism? Fischer's transcendental idealism states that the subject is the first condition of all knowledge, that all knowledge is limited to appearances, and that empirical realism is sufficient to account for the possibility of mathematical knowledge of nature. Trendelenburg's absolute idealism, on the other hand, claims that there is a single ideal structure equally instantiated in the subjective and objective realm, that empirical realism is insufficient to account for the mathematical knowledge of nature, and that it is instead necessary to assume something like transcendental realism, that is, the doctrine that our knowledge is about nature in itself. Like all absolute idealists, Trendelenburg assumed that there is a single activity of reason that manifests itself in both the subjective and objective realms, and that this activity manifests itself as space and time both in consciousness and nature. In making such as assumption, Trendelenburg had returned to an older position once championed by Schelling and Hegel. Fischer, like Fichte before him, rejected that absolute idealism because, in postulating knowledge of nature in itself, it transcends the limits of knowledge, and so lapses into "dogmatism". The dispute between Fischer and Trendelenburg was therefore more than a bit *déjà vu*. It was a

[12] Trendelenburg, *Logische Untersuchungen*, I, 160.
[13] Trendelenburg, *Logische Untersuchungen*, I, 163.

repeat of the old battle between Fichte's "subjective idealism" and Schelling's "objective or absolute idealism" which took place in the early 1800s.[14]

That the key issue involved a choice between absolute and transcendental idealism was often obscured in the thicket of Kantian exegesis. Nevertheless, it was stated clearly by Trendelenburg later in the dispute. In his 1869 *Kuno Fischer und sein Kant* he wrote that the question of the third possibility is not only of historical but also of philosophical importance.[15] If Kant's arguments prove exclusive subjectivity, then transcendental idealism is true; but if they do not, the possibility is open "to show the ideal in the real". "To show the ideal in the real"—that was the absolute idealist's catch phrase for demonstrating how nature, which exists independent of consciousness, manifests the intelligible or intellectual form of things. In other words, Trendelenburg saw the third possibility as opening the door for his own version of absolute idealism, according to which the subjective and objective manifest one and the same intelligible activity. Schelling, in his battle with Fichte in the early 1800s, had made a similar argument on behalf of his own absolute idealism.

Though it raised substantive philosophical issues, the dispute between Fischer and Trendelenburg eventually degenerated into a personal brawl. By the late 1860s the quarrel had become a notorious spectacle. Here were two of the most eminent philosophers in Germany, professors at two of its most prestigious universities—one in Berlin, the other in Heidelberg—locked in a bitter personal feud over a question of Kant interpretation. The dispute attracted such attention chiefly because of the animosity it aroused between its contestants. They began by discussing Kant interpretation; but they ended by abusing one another. Each cast doubt on the ability of their adversary to discuss exegetical or philosophical questions in an honest and impartial manner. Both quit the field bristling with indignation and nursing wounded vanity. Not surprisingly, the dispute was widely reported in the press and heavily discussed in lectures, reviews, articles and books. Battle lines were drawn, and parties rallied around one contestant or the other.

If the Trendelenburg–Fischer dispute showed anything, it was how important Kant had become to German philosophy. It was not only that Kant interpretation could be seen to arouse intense passions and heated controversy; it was also that so much seemed to depend upon it philosophically. Whether personally or philosophically, Kant mattered; he was now at the centre of attention.

4. The Great Pretender

Our list of the leading neo-Kantians of the 1860s in Section 1 seems to commit a major oversight. For it does not mention a man who claimed to be Kant's sole legitimate heir, and who did probably more than anyone else for his revival in the 1860s. I mean,

[14] On that dispute see my *German Idealism: The Struggle against Subjectivism, 1781–1801* (Cambridge, MA: Harvard University Press, 2002), pp. 491–505.
[15] Trendelenburg, *Kuno Fischer und sein Kant: Eine Entgegnung* (Leipzig: Hirzel, 1869), pp. 2–3.

of course, Arthur Schopenhauer. Although his major work, *Die Welt als Wille und Vorstellung*, was published in 1819 and neglected for decades, it was rediscovered in the 1850s, and had even become popular by the 1860s. Its rediscovery and popularity was of the greatest importance for the revival of Kant. For Schopenhauer, long before the 1860s, had stressed the revolutionary importance of Kant's philosophy, and he had made it very clear that it was the foundation for his own. In the preface to the first edition of his book he made a special request to the reader: that he study "the most important publication that has appeared in philosophy in the past two thousand years", namely, "the main writings of Kant".[16] The effect of reading Kant's writings Schopenhauer compared to the results of a cataract operation: where once there was blindness, now there was sight.

There are features of Schopenhauer's philosophy that make his exclusion from the neo-Kantian canon seem puzzling. For, no less than the neo-Kantians, Schopenhauer was an opponent of the neo-rationalism of the speculative tradition, and he too insisted on returning to Kant's critical teachings. All knowledge, he stressed, had to begin with, and to be verified through, experience; the attempt to gain knowledge through a priori reasoning alone is futile. Schopenhauer was also an opponent of the foundationalism of the speculative tradition, which he too regarded as an attempt to squeeze blood from a stone.[17] Like Herbart, Fries and Beneke, Schopenhauer championed an empirical method for philosophy, a procedure that would begin with experience and determine through analysis its content and necessary conditions. It was chiefly on these grounds that he claimed the right to ascend Kant's throne. While the speculative idealists flaunted Kant's limits on knowledge and indulged in a priori reasoning, he alone remained loyal to Kant's critical doctrines.

For these reasons historians of philosophy before the 1860s were often inclined to include Schopenhauer within the neo-Kantian movement. Thus Karl Rosenkranz added a section on Schopenhauer in his 1840 *Geschichte der kant'schen Philosophie*, and Carl Fortlage had a chapter on him, right along with Herbart, Fries and Beneke, in his 1852 *Genetische Geschichte der Philosophie*.[18] Yet later historians ceased to place Schopenhauer in the neo-Kantian tradition. The one-time pretender to the throne had been completely cast out of the Kantian palace. It is as if all Schopenhauer's claims to the Kantian title were spurious, as if all his suffering in the wilderness during the reign of speculative idealism counted as nothing. How could this be?

---

[16] See Schopenhauer, 'Vorrede zur ersten Auflage', *Die Welt als Wille und Vorstellung*, in *Sämtliche Werke*, ed. Wolfgang Freiherr von Löhneysen (Stuttgart: Insel, 1968), I, 10. All references in parentheses are to this edition. A Roman numeral indicates a volume number, an Arabic numeral a page number; and '§' a paragraph number, which is standard in all editions.

[17] See Schopenhauer, 'Über das metaphysische Bedürfnis', §17 of *Die Welt als Wille und Vorstellung*, *Werke* II, 229.

[18] See Karl Rosenkranz, *Geschichte der kant'schen Philosophie* (Leipzig: Voß, 1840), pp. 475–481; and Carl Fortlage, *Genetische Geschichte der Philosophie seit Kant* (Leipzig: Brockhaus, 1852), pp. 407–423.

The more we consider Schopenhauer's relations with the neo-Kantians, the more we find solid grounds for his exclusion from the club. Understandably, the leading neo-Kantians of the 1860s saw Schopenhauer not as an ally but as an enemy. They did so for two reasons: one is political, which we will consider below;[19] and the other is philosophical, which we need to look at now.

The philosophical issue is simple: the neo-Kantians cast Schopenhauer into the very speculative tradition that he had so vocally opposed. To be sure, Schopenhauer had opposed the rationalism and foundationalism of the speculative tradition no less than the most orthodox neo-Kantian. But the problem was that his conception of philosophy ran completely counter to that of the neo-Kantians. Philosophy, for Schopenhauer, is not simply an analysis and investigation into the logic of the sciences; it is first and foremost a metaphysics, and metaphysics in the grand old traditional sense: knowledge of reality in itself and as a whole. Despite his claim to observe Kantian limits, Schopenhauer insisted that philosophy should provide us with an immediate knowledge of ultimate reality, reality in itself as opposed to mere appearances.[20] The thing-in-itself that the neo-Kantians wanted to eliminate or make into a limiting concept Schopenhauer wanted not only to keep but to know. Philosophy was for him "unconditional knowledge of the essence of the world", knowledge of "the in-itself" (das An-sich), just as it had been for Schelling and Hegel.[21] Though Schopenhauer pretended to know this reality through more cautious empirical methods, that hardly detracted from his metaphysical ambitions.

Schopenhauer's affinities with the speculative tradition, and his differences with later neo-Kantianism, are especially apparent from his *Naturphilosophie*. Although Schopenhauer strived to distance himself from the methods and worst excesses of the *Naturphilosophen*, his arguments for a metaphysics of nature, and for the limits of empirical science, seem to come straight out of the pages of a Schelling, Oken or Steffans. Schopenhauer argues repeatedly and emphatically that empirical science can know nature only as appearance, and that it presupposes a metaphysics, which alone grasps the ideas and inner nature of things. This was the very doctrine that physicists, chemists and physiologists had rebelled against and rejected by the 1830s. In this struggle the neo-Kantians sided with the empirical scientists against the *Naturphilosophen*. They accepted the autonomy of the sciences, and they disputed the need for a metaphysical foundation for them. Schopenhauer, however, was claiming the kind of priority and privilege for philosophy that had become discredited and unfashionable by the 1830s. This was not the least reason why *Die Welt als Wille und Vorstellung* was neglected for so long in the first half of the 19th century. To

---

[19] See Chapter 10, Sections 1, 3–4.
[20] See Schopenhauer, *Die Welt als Wille und Vorstellung, Werke* I, 160, §18; 170, §21; and 'Anhang. Kritik der kantischen Philosophie', I, 675.
[21] Schopenhauer, *Die Welt als Wille und Vorstellung*, I, 190, §24; I, 135, §15.

the empirical scientists, and the neo-Kantian philosophers sympathetic with them, Schopenhauer seemed to be calling for the revival of a dead cause.

Nowhere are Schopenhauer's metaphysical intentions, and his differences from the neo-Kantians, clearer than in his theory of ideas in Book III of *Die Welt als Wille und Vorstellung*. Here Schopenhauer makes it perfectly clear that his philosophy is essentially a version of Platonic idealism. The thing-in-itself, Schopenhauer informs us, is nothing more nor less than the Platonic idea (I, 247; §31). He stresses the great affinity between Kant and Plato: that both distinguish between appearance and reality in itself, that both think that the realm of appearances is subject to space and time. Where Kant needs to go a step further, Schopenhauer avers, is in making his things-in-themselves into ideas. With that extra step, the philosophy of Plato and Kant, the two greatest philosophical systems, are joined in holy matrimony. Schopenhauer admits that there is an obvious difference between Kant and Plato: Kant's thing-in-itself, unlike Plato's form, is in principle unknowable (I, 252; §32). Still, he thinks that this difference is only the result of Kant's unnecessary restriction of all forms of experience to sense perception. What Schopenhauer does not mention, or refuses to recognize, is Kant's own sharp distinction in the *Prolegomena* between his own critical idealism and Plato's idealism: that critical idealism limits knowledge to appearances while Plato's idealism strives to transcend it. And what he also conveniently ignores is Kant's withering criticism of the possibility of immediate and intuitive forms of knowledge. It was not least for these all-too Kantian reasons that the neo-Kantians were never ready to accept Schopenhauer's conflation of Platonic with transcendental idealism; that to them grossly flaunted Kant's restrictions on metaphysics. Following Kant, the neo-Kantians reject the possibility of an intuitive or immediate knowledge of reality in itself, and they insist upon a regulative reading of the Platonic ideas following the guidelines of the Transcendental Dialectic.

Thus the neo-Kantians' interpretation of Schopenhauer, which they will develop gradually throughout the 1860s and 1870s, strategically place him in the tradition of speculative idealism, which, by the 1850s, almost everyone saw as surpassed and antiquated. All Schopenhauer's bluster and tirades against this tradition only disguised his real affinity with it. The Schopenhauer revival of the 1860s therefore seemed to the neo-Kantians a step backwards, both philosophically and politically, a call for a return to the bygone Romantic age.

Yet in an important sense it was Schopenhauer who had the last laugh, and who ultimately trumped the neo-Kantians. For the old grouch showed them, and made them admit, that he was ultimately more timely and relevant than any of them. One reason for Schopenhauer's enduring popularity throughout the last half of the century is that he placed one fundamental question at the front and centre of his philosophy: "the question of existence". By this he meant not only why the universe exists at all, but also whether life is worth living. The big question, to which his entire philosophy is an answer, is whether we should affirm or deny the will to live (I, 423; §56). Schopenhauer insisted that these questions had always been at the heart of philosophy, and that no philosophy worth the name could ignore them. Man was a "*homo metaphysicus*" and he would pose the question of the purpose and value of his existence as long as he was an intelligent being at all. "To be or not to be", that was the crucial question for Schopenhauer, as it is indeed for all of us.

It was no accident that later in the century the neo-Kantians would be accused of neglecting this all-important question, of coming too close to an arid positivism in their insistence that philosophy should be primarily epistemology and the investigation into the logic of the sciences. This criticism, and the continuing popularity of Schopenhauer, put great pressure on the neo-Kantians to revise and broaden their own conception of philosophy. Neo-Kantianism could survive in the intellectual marketplace only by showing that it too could provide a plausible answer to this basic question. Thus, by the 1880s, such neo-Kantians as Wilhelm Windelband, Friedrich Paulsen, Otto Liebmann and Alois Riehl moved away from their original positivism, towards a more practical philosophy that reflected on the value and purpose of life. The thinker pushing them in this direction—let us give credit where it is due—was that old pessimist, Arthur Schopenhauer. He was an educator not only for the young Nietzsche but for the entire neo-Kantian generation!

5

Kuno Fischer, Hegelian Neo-Kantian

1. A Mysterious Figure

Of all the major figures behind the Kant revival of the 1860s the strangest is Kuno Fischer.[1] Few thinkers threw themselves so fully and forcibly behind Kant's rehabilitation. No one stressed more the abiding relevance of Kant's philosophy, and no one was more successful in explaining Kant's arcane doctrines to a wide audience. And yet Fischer was not, at least in any strict sense of the word, a Kantian. He was raised a Hegelian, and that he remained his entire life.

It is very misleading to refer to Fischer as a Hegelian manqué, as if he were a failed, second-rate, mock or would-be Hegelian.[2] For Fischer was in the very centre of the neo-Hegelian movement, having as his close associates no less than Arnold Ruge and David Friedrich Strauß. His first articles in philosophy were devoted to the neo-Hegelian cause; and he wrote some very compelling defences of the Hegelian position against two of its most formidable radical critics, Ludwig Feuerbach and Max Stirner. Such, indeed, was Fischer's allegiance to neo-Hegelianism that, like Ruge and Strauß, he became one of its martyrs, forced out of academia for proclaiming pantheism from the podium.

Yet how could it be that this staunch neo-Hegelian became such a powerful spokesman for neo-Kantianism? That, in short, is the mystery of Kuno Fischer. There was indeed a Kantian side to his thinking; but that Kantian side did not coalesce with his Hegelian one, and the two remained locked in conflict all his life. Not that Fischer was unaware of their conflict. The major project of his philosophy was *to synthesize* Hegel and Kant, *to unite* both thinkers in a single system. Such was the task of two of

---

[1] On Fischer's biography, the standard source has been the article by Hugo Falckenheim, 'Kuno Fischer', in *Biographisches Jahrbuch und Deutscher Nekrolog* 12 (1907), 257–272. Another valuable source is Reinhold Hülsewiesche, *System und Geschichte: Leben und Werke Kuno Fischers* (Bern: Peter Lang, 1989), pp. 17–46. Hülsewiesche has used Fischer's unpublished autobiographical manuscripts, 'Lebenlauf zum Abitur verfaßt' and 'Mein Lebenslauf'.

[2] This is the epithet of Thomas Willey, *Back to Kant: The Revival of Kantianism in German Social and Historical Thought, 1860–1914* (Detroit, MI: Wayne State University Press, 1978), p. 58. Willey does not investigate Fischer's early neo-Hegelian writings.

his major philosophical works, his 1852 *Logik und Metaphyik* and his 1865 *System der Logik und Metaphysik*.

All throughout his philosophical development Fischer would struggle with these contradictions. His thinking was dynamic and protean, so that sometimes Hegel would get the upper hand over Kant, and sometimes Kant would get the upper hand over Hegel. From one angle his system appears a Kantianized Hegel, from another a Hegelized Kant. Yet, struggle though he did, it cannot be said that Fischer was successful in his syncretic ambitions. The contradictions between the Kantian and Hegelian sides of his system are so deep and fundamental that it proved impossible to resolve them. So obvious and basic are the contradictions that it is indeed hard to understand how Fischer attempted to put them together in the first place.

Part of the explanation for the mystery lies in Fischer's historical empathy. It was Fischer's great gift as an historian of philosophy to be able to enter into the spirit of each great philosopher and to recapture the essential core of his thought, the point from which everything followed. He could see the world from the point of view of the philosopher he attempted to revive and reconstruct. Like Hegel, he saw each philosophy as a work of art, an integral, autonomous whole. If we practise this methodology, it is easy to adopt and sympathize with incompatible philosophical views without seeing how to reconcile them. In his funeral speech for Fischer, Wilhelm Windelband said that Fischer once told him he did not regard himself as called upon to create a new system of philosophy, and that he did not think that the times were ready for one.[3] That statement explains Fischer's failure to develop a coherent system, and reveals that he saw his vocation more as an historian than philosopher.

Fischer's Hegelianism seems to give the lie to our thesis that neo-Kantianism arose from a reaction against the neo-rationalism of the German idealist tradition. We have confirmed that generalization in all the early neo-Kantians we have considered so far. Fries, Herbart, Beneke and Helmholtz all called for a return to Kant to serve as a counter against speculative neo-rationalism. Yet, upon closer examination, Fischer is the proverbial exception that proves the rule. The Kantian strands in his thinking were in clear conflict with the Hegelian ones, and Fischer never succeeded in finding a stable synthesis of both. He demonstrated through this conflict that a neo-Kantian really cannot be a Hegelian after all. To be a Hegelian, Fischer had to transcend the Kantian critical limits upon knowledge; and to be a Kantian, he had to abjure the central theses of his Hegelian metaphysics. Fischer struggled for decades, from the 1840s to the 1880s, to reconcile this conflict, though, for reasons we shall soon see, he never succeeded.

Given Fischer's pivotal role in the development of neo-Kantianism, and given our interest in the origins of neo-Kantianism, we have no choice but to examine Fischer's philosophical development. Such an examination will show us the stresses

---

[3] Wilhelm Windelband, *Kuno Fischer. Gedächtnisrede bei der Trauerfeier der Universität in der Stadhalle zu Heidelberg am 23. Juli 1907* (Heidelberg: Winter, 1907), pp. 27–28.

and strains on Fischer's thinking that made him at once both neo-Hegelian Kantian and neo-Kantian Hegelian. It will also offer us a glimpse into the evolution of neo-Kantianism in one of its central figures at one of its most critical periods.

2. The Young Hegelian

Kuno Fischer was born July 23, 1824, in the Schlesian village of Sandewalde. His father, Karl Theodor Fischer, was a pastor in the local church. His mother died when he was very young, a loss Fischer felt his entire life. Fischer received his first education from his father, and then from a private tutor after his father moved in 1832 to serve as the *pastor primarius* in the neighbouring village of Winzig. He attended the Gymnasium in Posen, where he excelled in classical languages and German literature.

Fischer began his university education in 1844 at Leipzig, where he stayed only one semester. He then moved to Halle, where he studied for the next three years. It was little wonder that the young Fischer became a Hegelian. In both Leipzig and Halle he was exposed to strong Hegelian influences. During his semester at Leipzig, he heard the lectures of Hermann Christian Weiße (1801–1866), whose philosophy was permeated with Hegelian themes. Though a sharp critic of Hegel, Weiße still adopted some of the fundamentals of his philosophy, primarily his dialectic and logic.[4] After moving to Halle, Fischer again came under strong Hegelian influence. There he was a student of two prominent Hegelians, J.E. Erdmann (1805–1892) and Julius Schaller (1810–1868), both of whom made an impact upon him. Schaller and Erdmann were Hegelian hardliners, apologists for Hegel's philosophy when it was becoming less fashionable. Schaller wrote a tract defending Hegel against his critics, who, he argued, had criticized Hegel from a standpoint he had already overcome.[5] Erdmann, one of the great historians of philosophy of the 19th century, formulated a programme for a scientific history of philosophy, a programme inspired by Hegel and the model for Fischer's own work.[6]

While still a student at Halle, Fischer entered the ranks of the neo-Hegelian movement. In 1846 he began to write reviews and articles for Oswald Marbach's

---

[4] Weiße wrote one of the first critiques of Hegel's philosophy, *Ueber den gegenwärtigen Standpunct der philosophischen Wissenschaften* (Leipzig: Barth, 1829). Though Weiße criticizes Hegel's speculative logic for failing to account for the concrete facts of the empirical world, he still maintained that his logic is unsurpassable, and that the dialectic is the basis for the form or structure, if not the content, of all natural science (pp. 11, 163, 174). On Weiße, see Chapter 4, Section 1.

[5] See Julius Schaller, *Die Philosophie unserer Zeit: Zur Apologie und Erläuterung des hegelschen Systems* (Leipzig: Hinrichs, 1837). On Schaller, see Otto Siebert, *Geschichte der neueren deutschen Philosophie seit Hegel* (Göttingen: Vandenhoeck & Ruprect, 1898), pp. 16–17.

[6] Johann Eduard Erdmann, *Versuch einer wissenschaftlichen Darstellung der Geschichte der neuern Philosophie* (Riga and Dorpat: E. Frantzen, 1834–1853), 7 vols. On Erdmann, see Hermann Glockner, 'Einführung in Johann Eduard Erdmanns Leben und Werke' in Volume I of the new edition of his *Versuch* (Stuttgart: Frommann, 1932), pp. 1–200. See especially Chapter 13, pp. 155–185, which discusses Erdmann's relationship to Fischer.

Literatur- und Kunstbericht,[7] all of which defend a strict Hegelian position. The 1840s was not the most promising time to be a young Hegelian. This decade marks the beginning of the end of the neo-Hegelian movement. Ever since the accession of Friedrich Wilhelm IV in 1840, the movement had ceased to enjoy the patronage of the Prussian government, and it had come under increasing censorship and prosecution. The government had shut down Arnold Ruge's *Hallische Jahrbücher,* the main journal of the movement in 1840, and it did the same to its successor, *Die Deutsche Jahrbücher,* in 1843. Still undaunted, Ruge and others made renewed attempts to revive a neo-Hegelian journal, a common organ for the movement. One enthusiastic supporter of this cause was the young Kuno Fischer himself. In an article for the *Literatur- und Kunstbericht* he claimed that the most pressing task of the age was to revive a common Hegelian journal.[8] Fischer went on to praise the *Hallische Jahrbücher,* which "had dominated five years of German cultural history", and whose editor was the "the Daniel O'Connell of the Hegelian philosophy." After reading these lines, Ruge befriended Fischer, recruiting him for more neo-Hegelian journalism.[9] And so, for the next two years, Fischer wrote articles on Hegelian philosophy for neo-Hegelian journals and newspapers, first for the *Leipziger Revue,* then for Otto Wigand's *Die Epigonen* and Arnold Ruge's *Die Akademie.*[10]

In the complicated neo-Hegelian spectrum of the 1840s, Fischer occupies a middle position, steering between the extremes of right and left, conservative and radical.[11] Following Schaller and Erdmann, he defended Hegel's metaphysics because he saw it as a bulwark against the radical materialism of the left and the supernaturalistic theism of the right. Such a stand put Fischer at odds with the left-wing neo-Hegelians, with radicals like Max Stirner and Ludwig Feuerbach, who saw Hegel's metaphysics as little more than a relic of Christian theology, the final form of alienation and hypostasis. On the other hand, Fischer did not endorse the position of those right Hegelians, such as Phillip Marheineke and Karl Daub, who wanted to rescue Christian theology through Hegel's philosophy.[12] While Fischer held that some core Christian beliefs,

---

[7] All the articles appeared in *Literatur- und Kunstbericht,* ed. Oswald Marbach (Leipzig: Wigand, 1846). Fischer wrote the following signed articles: 'Die Autorität', Nr. 43, 169–170, and Nr. 44, 174–176; 'George Sand und Ida Gräfin Hahn-Hahn', Nr. 27, 109–112, and Nr. 29, 113–115; 'Philosophie der Geschichte in der Geschichte der Philosophie', Nr. 20, 78–79; Nr. 21, 81–84; Nr. 22, 85–87 and Nr. 23, 90–92; 'Philosophische Literatur', Nr. 58, 229–232; Nr. 59, 233–235; and Nr. 60, 237–239; and 'Theologische Fragen', Nr. 73, 289–292; Nr. 74, 293–295; Nr. 75, 298–299.

[8] Fischer, 'Philosophische Literatur', Nr. 58, p. 229.

[9] See Ruge's letters to Fischer in Arnold Ruge, *Briefwechsel und Tagebuchblätter* (Berlin: Weidmann, 1896), I, 425–426, 427, 429–430, 433–435, 437–439.

[10] See the signed articles entitled 'Moderne Sophisten' in the *Leipziger Revue* (1847), Nr. 3, 9–11; Nr. 4, 13–14; Nr. 5, 17–20; Nr. 6, 21–23; Nr. 8, 30–32; Nr. 12, 45–48; Nr. 13, 50–52. See also 'Ein Apologet der Sophistik und ein „philosophischer Reactionär"' in *Die Epigonen* 4 (1847), pp. 152–165; and 'Das Wesen der Religion von Carl Schwarz', *Die Epigonen* V (1848), 177–208. See too 'Ludwig Feuerbach und die Philosophie unserer Zeit', in *Die Akademie. Philosophische Taschenbuch* I (1848), 128–190. See also 'Arnold Ruge und der Humanismus' in *Die Epigonen* 4 (1847) 95–140.

[11] Here I summarize only Fischer's theological views; his political views are much less explicit and do not appear in his early articles.

[12] On these and other figures on the Hegelian right, see John Toews, *Hegelianism: The path toward dialectical humanism, 1805–1841* (Cambridge: Cambridge University Press, 1980), pp. 141–155.

namely, the trinity or incarnation, could be rationalized according to Hegel's dialectic, he saw that rationalization as a transformation, stripping the beliefs of their mythical and anthropocentric meaning; on no account could the beliefs be saved in their original meaning and form.[13] Fischer stressed against the orthodox that Hegel's dialectic had completely destroyed traditional Christian theism.[14] Theism had presupposed a dualism between man and God, where man sees God as an alien, transcendent being; but the dialectic negated such alienation, placing man within God and making him a living appearance of the divine. It is important to see, however, that while Fischer regarded traditional Christian *theology* as outmoded, he still believed, unlike left Hegelians, that *religion* itself is perfectly legitimate as a form of life, as feeling, devotion and ritual.

Fischer's critical stance towards conservative Christianity appears in full force in his endorsement of David Friedrich Strauß' biblical criticism, which he regarded as revolutionary, the complete destruction of traditional theology.[15] According to Fischer, Strauß had shown that religious belief is essentially a form of myth, and that it cannot be rescued as dogma. "A formal restoration of previous dogmatics can be no more", he declared in one of his review articles.[16] Just as Fischer's endorsement of Ruge led to friendship, the same happened with Strauß. Fischer and Strauß met in 1854 in Heidelberg and they soon became close friends. Fischer's friendships with Ruge and Strauß, two leading figures of neo-Hegelianism, show his deep involvement in the very heart of that movement.

The most important of Fischer's early neo-Hegelian articles was his critique of Stirner and Feuerbach. The critique of Stirner is in an article entitled 'Moderne Sophisten', which appeared in several installments in the 1847 *Leipziger Revue*.[17] The critique of Feuerbach came in the article 'Ludwig Feuerbach und die Philosophie unserer Zeit', which appeared in 1848 in *Die Akademie*.[18] Though published separately, both articles defend Hegel, and criticize Stirner and Feuerbach, for similar reasons. Stirner and Feuerbach were rebels against Hegel's metaphysics because they saw his absolute, the single infinite substance, as an alien, abstract being standing over and above the individual and oppressing him. Hegel's philosophy did not free the individual from the alienation of religion and theology, they argued, but only reinstated that alienation in a more abstract intellectual form. Hegel's critique

---

[13] See Fischer, 'Theologische Fragen', in *Literatur- und Kunstbericht*, Nr. 73, p. 289.

[14] See Fischer, 'Ludwig Feuerbach und die Philosophie unserer Zeit', *Die Akademie*, p. 149.

[15] See 'Theologische Fragen', p. 290. See also Fischer's essay 'Strauß' "Leben Jesu"', in *Über David Friedrich Strauß* (Heidelberg: Winter, 1908), pp. 103–126.

[16] Fischer, 'Theologische Fragen', p. 289.

[17] Fischer, 'Moderne Sophisten' in the *Leipziger Revue* (1847), Nr. 3, 9–11; Nr. 4, 13–14; Nr. 5, 17–20; Nr. 6, 21–23; Nr. 8, 30–32; Nr. 12, 45–48; Nr. 13, 50–52. Under the pseudonym 'G. Edward' Stirner replied to Fischer's article in 'Die philosophischen Reaktionäre', in *Die Epigonen* 4 (1847), 141–151. Fischer responded in the same issue, 'Ein Apologet der Sophistik und ein „philosophsiche Reactionär"', *Die Epigonen* 4 (1847), 152–165.

[18] Fischer, 'Ludwig Feuerbach und die Philosophie unserer Zeit', *Die Akademie, Philosophische Taschenbuch* I (1848), 128–190.

of hypostasis, when taken to its ultimate conclusion, explodes his own philosophy as well, because his absolute turns out to be only another subtle and sophisticated form of hypostasis. Against this line of argument, Fischer first admits that Stirner and Feuerbach both have a point, insofar as right-wing Hegelians often give an alienated and hypostasized interpretation of Hegel's philosophy. But he then goes on to argue that their critique rests upon a one-sided interpretation of Hegel's thought. They stress the objective, universal and abstract side of that philosophy, failing to realize that it was Hegel's aim *to unite* the objective and subjective, the universal and particular, the abstract and concrete. Hegel would have agreed with everything they said against a one-sided objectivist conception of the absolute; but his aim was to go further and to integrate the subjective with the objective, to restore "the rights of subjectivity". Thus Stirner and Feuerbach only said against Hegel what Hegel himself had already said against Christianity. They rail against the Hegelian absolute from the perspective of the finite, individual self; but they lose sight of Hegel's important argument that the self is more than finite and individual, that it realizes itself only by becoming part of the infinite and universal, the community of ethical life. The self realizes itself not through its personal or individual needs, as Feuerbach and Stirner assume, but only in and through the mutual self-consciousness of spirit. First and last Hegel's philosophy is a philosophy of freedom, which teaches that freedom is realized only in the community, only in accepting the rational authority of law. Seeing freedom as little more than the right to satisfy my arbitrary individual wishes, Stirner and Feuerbach do not appreciate this dimension of Hegel's philosophy. Hence they are little more than "modern sophists".

Fischer's advocacy of the neo-Hegelian cause eventually went beyond the confines of political journalism. It became the motive for something even grander, namely his first book, *Diotima. Die Idee des Schönen*,[19] which appeared in 1849, in the wake of the Revolution of the previous year. The ostensible aim of this book was to provide a popular introduction to aesthetics, especially for women; but Fischer insists that aesthetics has to be set in the context of a general worldview.[20] Aesthetics, he argues, is not just one branch of learning but "a world principle". *Diotima* was meant to be a popular introduction to Hegelian metaphysics, using aesthetics as a lure for broader educational and political goals. What, though, did aesthetics have to do with neo-Hegelianism? What, indeed, did it have to do with the Revolution that was now convulsing the political world? "Why do I write about beauty when the world now strives bloodily for freedom?", Fischer asks, much like Schiller had some fifty years

---

[19] Kuno Fischer, *Diotima. Die Idee des Schönen. Philosophische Briefe* (Pforzheim: Flammer und Hoffmann, 1849). All references in parentheses are to this edition. *Diotima* became a very successful book. It went through two more editions in Fischer's lifetime: (Leipzig: Reclam, 1849) and (Suttgart: Scheitlin, 1852). It lived on into the 20th century. The last edition appeared as late as 1928 with Reclam in Leipzig.

[20] See Fischer's 'Vorrede', *Diotima. Die Idee des Schönen*, pp. viii–xii.

earlier.[21] And he responds, much like Schiller, that "freedom achieved is beauty, and it is no treason against that striving if one recalls its happy goal". (xii)

Diotima is an important and interesting document in Fischer's philosophical development because it gives a simple and straightforward exposition of his early neo-Hegelian metaphysics. The main principle behind that metaphysics is what Fischer calls "the principle of subject-object identity", that is, the thesis that mind and nature, subject and object, are ultimately the same. This principle is common to Schelling and Hegel, Fischer explains. While Schelling invented it, Hegel gave it its proper logical foundation. The central question about this principle is which side of the equation should predominate, the subjective or objective, mind or nature (45). Do we resolve the subjective into the objective, the mind into nature, or the objective into the subjective, nature into the mind? "Is it spirit that creates and does everything, or is it nature that is everything in everything?" Schelling tried to give equal weight to both sides, but Hegel was right, Fischer thinks, to give primacy to mind over nature, to the subjective over the objective. "The unity of spirit and nature cannot be natural but must be spiritual . . . The nature of spirit is the logic of actuality." (49) Why is this so? The point follows, Fischer argues, from the chief principles of Schelling's *Naturphilosophie* (46–50). According to *Naturphilosophie*, all of nature consists in a hierarchy of stages of development, in increasingly greater degrees of organic development and organization, the highest level of which consists in nothing less than human self-consciousness. Hence nature finally realizes its own energies and powers in subjectivity, which is the inner truth of nature herself. The single activity that appears as necessity in nature becomes freedom in man. The realm of freedom is history, which consists in the self-consciousness of freedom (50).

Though its metaphysics is fundamentally Hegelian, it would be a mistake to describe *Diotima* as a purely Hegelian work. Some of Fischer's attitudes prove to be more Romantic than Hegelian. The entire atmosphere of the work is Romantic, taking us back to the early Romantic circles in Jena and Berlin. True to its namesake, *Diotima* is a paean to the powers of art and beauty, reaffirming the apotheosis of art of the early Romantic circle. The essentials of Fischer's aesthetic theory are straightforwardly Romantic. He puts forward what he calls "an aesthetic worldview", which is "the aesthetic pantheism" of *Frühromantik*. According to this worldview, God is one with the entire universe, which is a work of art. The divine appears in nature as beauty, and the goal of the artist is to reproduce that beauty (86). Elements of this aesthetic pantheism also reappear in Hegel, of course, but Hegel had always distanced himself from the Romantic circle, and in two basic ways. First, he placed philosophy above religion, and religion above art, as a means of knowing the truth. Second, he maintained that art was obsolete in the modern world, because the rational comprehension

---

[21] Friedrich Schiller, 'Zweyter Brief', *Ueber die ästhetische Erziehung des Menschen*, in *Schiller, Nationalausgabe*, ed. Benno von Wiese (Weimar: Hermann Böhlaus Nachfolger, 1962) XX, 310–312.

of philosophy stood above the intuition and feeling of art. It is a strong indication of Fischer's independence from Hegelianism that he does not accept either of these Hegelian theses. While he does not explicitly take issue with Hegel, he maintains their very opposite. Rather than placing religion above art, Fischer places art above religion, because it is only in art that the feelings of religion are articulated and become visible. And rather than maintaining the obsolescence of art, Fischer thinks that the arts will be reborn in a new social and political order (108, 112). It is only in Fischer's attitude towards Romantic irony that his persistent Hegelianism reasserts itself. Like Hegel before him, Fischer finds Romantic irony the most extreme form of egoism and alienation from the social and political world (156–175).

Such, in sum and substance, was Fischer's early neo-Hegelianism. It is hard to read Fischer's *Diotima* and early articles without admiring his grasp of Hegel's philosophy and without admitting that he had a strong defence against Hegel's critics. This was no superficial convert to the Hegelian cause. The young Fischer had his reasons, and good ones, for being a Hegelian. All this leaves us, then, with the question: Why did such a convinced Hegelian ever become a Kantian? That is the mystery we have to unravel in the following sections.

3. Banishment

In September 1850 Fischer took his habilitation exam in Heidelberg, which he passed with flying colours. Now having the necessary qualification to teach at the university, Fischer began to lecture on logic, metaphysics and the history of philosophy in the autumn semester. His lectures proved to be extremely popular, so much so that a larger lecture hall was necessary to accommodate his growing audience. The students were drawn to Fischer's lectures partly because of his rhetorical skills, and partly because they liked what they heard. Fischer was teaching them the latest doctrines, the modern, progressive and liberal ideas behind the Revolution of 1848. Not least because of the success of his lectures, these early years in Heidelberg were some of the happiest in Fischer's life. It seemed he had found his calling in teaching.

That happiness vanished suddenly in September 1853. Fischer's popularity had brought him enemies, especially in the theology faculty, who not only envied his success but who also suspected his neo-Hegelian ideology. Daniel Schenkel, professor of theology and head of the theology faculty, was alarmed by the popularity of Fischer's lectures, whose content undermined the Christian dogmas taught by the theology faculty. Fearing for the reputation of the theology faculty, Schenkel duly informed the High Consistory in Karlsruhe of Fischer's dangerous lectures, which were corrupting the youth. Although Schenkel insisted that he had advised only employing another lecturer in philosophy to combat Fischer's influence,[22] the Consistory pushed for something more harsh and drastic: the revocation

---

[22] Schenkel insisted that he had never pushed for the interdict against Fischer's lectures, and that he even protested against it. See his *Abfertigung für Herrn Kuno Fischer in Heidelberg* (Heidelberg: Akademie

of Fischer's lectureship. Even though the university senate and philosophy faculty rejected this measure, matters were taken out of their hands by a change in government in June 1853. The early 1850s were dangerous times for young liberals and radicals, especially for those who espoused their views from the lecterns. For these were years of reaction and retrenchment after the Revolution of 1848, and the new authorities were determined to keep tight controls over press and education. The new education minister Friedrich von Wechmar, a staunch reactionary, peremptorily deprived Fischer, without appeal or hearing, of his *venia legendi*, his right to lecture. And so for the next three years Fischer would live in the wilderness, with no prospect of employment or a steady income. An outcast, he now joined the company of Feuerbach and Strauß. Fischer had become the latest neo-Hegelian martyr.

What, exactly, did Fischer teach that proved so provocative to Schenkel and the theology faculty? We know well what Fischer said on the podium from 1850 to 1852 because he published the first part of his lectures in 1852, which eventually became the first volume of his *Geschichte der neuern Philosophie*.[23] It would be these lectures that Schenkel would later cite as evidence against Fischer. The especially offensive parts are the 14th and 29th lectures, which are blunt statements of rationalism and pantheism. There Fischer puts forward the bold argument that all philosophy, if it is only consistent and complete, ends in pantheism. He defines pantheism as the thesis that God is the world-order, the universe as a whole. All philosophy is pantheistic, Fischer argues, because philosophy is the attempt to know things through reason, and to know anything through reason requires knowledge of the universe as a whole. Since everything in the universe is connected with every other thing, to know one thing requires knowing all things. The attempt to know anything through reason therefore demands that we know the universe as a whole, which is God itself. Hence all philosophy is pantheism. As Fischer summarized his argument: "For philosophy, rationalism [and] pantheism are the same; philosophy says we should know; rationalism says that we should know through concepts; and pantheism says that the conceived or known God is the eternal order." (553–554)

Fischer's thesis was not a little *déjà vu*. In 1786, in his *Briefe über Spinoza*, Jacobi sparked off "the explosion" of the famous "pantheism controversy" by advancing the thesis that all philosophy, if it is only consistent, ends in pantheism. That thesis had lost none of its power to provoke in the 1850s. Fully aware of this precedent, Fischer saw in Jacobi a kindred spirit.[24] He agreed with Jacobi that rationalism ends in pantheism,

---

Anstalt für Literatur und Kunst, 1854), pp. 9, 11. Fischer, however, was convinced that Schenkel was the main agent and force behind the proceedings against him. On the proceedings against Fischer, see Hülsewiesche, *System und Geschichte*, pp. 29–36. The documents assembled by Hülsewiesche show that Schenkel had indeed voted against a rescript and instead proposed only warning Fischer (p. 34); yet this seems to have been a retreat from a harder position, because he had first endorsed the motion for his expulsion (pp. 30–31).

[23] Kuno Fischer *Vorlesungen über Geschichte der neueren Philosophie. Abtheilung I: Einleitung in das Studium der Philosophie* (Stuttgart: Scheitlin, 1852). The entire volume was later published under the title *Geschichte der neuern Philosophie: Erster Band, Das classische Zeitalter der dogmatischen Philosophie* (Mannheim: Bassermann & Mathy, 1854). All references will be to this later more accessible edition.

[24] See the 18th lecture of the *Geschichte* (1854), pp. 299–313.

that faith consists in feeling and action rather than dogma and doctrine, and that Leibniz's philosophy is only a halfway house on the road to Spinozism. There were, however, two important differences between Fischer and Jacobi. First, Fischer did not equate pantheism with Spinoza's naturalism. According to Fischer, Spinoza's naturalism is indeed atheism, just as Jacobi always taught; but not all pantheism is naturalism. There is a *generic* concept of pantheism, which simply identifies God with the world-order; and there are more *specific* concepts depending on just how one defines that world-order. There is *naturalistic* pantheism, which identifies the world-order with nature; and there is *spiritualistic* pantheism, which identifies the world-order with spirit. Second, Fischer refuses Jacobi's *salto mortale*, his leap of faith in a personal God and freedom. It is not necessary to resort to such desperate measures to save religion, Fischer argues, because the standpoint of philosophy stands above religion and explains its essential truths in rational terms. Rationalism does not destroy religion but preserves its essential content in conceptual and systematic form.

It was Fischer's equation of pantheism with rationalism that proved so offensive to Schenkel and the theological faculty. Schenkel explained the rationale for the withdrawal of the *venia legendi* in an article in the *Darmstadtischen Kirchen Zeitung*, 'Das Christenthum und modernes Philosophenthum'.[25] The High Consistory in Karlsruhe, he said, based its charges against Fischer on those passages from his *Geschichte der neuern Philosophie* where he had affirmed that pantheism is the only rational worldview. That seemed to imply that Christian theism is irrational, given that it is completely opposed to pantheism. Schenkel states simply and firmly some of the classical reasons why theism and pantheism are incompatible. Theism demands a dualism between God and the world; but pantheism identifies the one with the other. Theism requires a personal God; but the absolute of pantheism is impersonal. Theism holds that God creates the world from nothingness and by free will; but pantheism maintains that the world is eternal and exists of necessity. For all these reasons, Schenkel concluded that Fischer's pantheism was utterly at odds with Christian doctrine. Rather than the personal living God of Christianity, Fischer had simply divinized the world itself, which was tantamount to paganism and atheism. Schenkel's defence of the faith was very much the standard orthodox position. Refusing to take a *salto mortale*, he affirmed that the characteristic doctrines of Christianity are based on revelation, on the divine word as stated in Scripture. Schenkel ended his piece by citing a rather implausible ally: Heinrich Heine. It was Heine who admitted all when he said that pantheism is really only "a bashful atheism".

Although Fischer could make no appeal against his dismissal, he defended himself against Schenkel's charges in two tracts, *Das Interdict meiner Vorlesungen* and *Apologie meiner Lehre*, which both appeared in 1854.[26] Neither makes for edifying reading. Both

---

[25] *Darmstadter Allgemeine Kirchenzeitung*, Nr. 12 (1854). Reprinted by Kuno Fischer in *Das Interdict meiner Vorlesungen* (Mannheim: Bassermann & Mathy, 1854), pp. 65–78.

[26] *Das Interdict meiner Vorlesungen* (Mannheim: Bassermann & Mathy, 1854); and *Apologie meiner Lehre* (Mannheim: Bassermann & Mathy, 1854). The *Interdict* is a reply to Schenkel's 'Das Christenthum und modernes Philosophenthum'; the *Apologie* is a response to Schenkel's *Abfertigung*.

are filled with petty polemics and righteous indignation. For the most part, they add little to clarify Fischer's own philosophy. Indeed, they even obscure and distort it. Rather than clearly stating his views, taking his stand and accepting the consequences, Fischer is evasive, denying the obvious implications of his views and twisting their meaning to make them appear less heterodox. He insists that he never wrote that non-pantheistic philosophy is irrational,[27] though that is the clear implication of his thesis that *all* rationalism ends in pantheism. Rather than disputing with conservative Christian theists, Fischer protests that his real target was the radicals, "certain materialists, certain sophists, certain legal philosophers of today".[28] Nothing from the original context, however, indicates that he ever had these figures in mind. Fischer had indeed done battle against the radicals in some of his early journal articles, but these are not explicit in the *Geschichte*. On the whole, though he squirms and squawks, Fischer is guilty as charged. While we can accept his protestations that he has nothing against religion, his pantheism is fundamentally heterodox, flatly contrary to Christian dogma, and for just the reasons Schenkel cited. While Fischer distances himself from Spinozian naturalism, the monism and rationalism of his pantheism still undermine Christian theism. Its monism leaves no place for the distinction between God and world; and its rationalism gives no room for revelation or divine mysteries. Rather than admitting these points, Fischer simply chooses to ignore them. Because he was so evasive, and even twisted his original meaning, Schenkel could come to only this damning conclusion about the motives of his opponent: "*Carrière um jeden Preis*".[29]

Not that these tracts are complete write-offs, non-entities from a philosophical point of view. Towards the close of the *Apologie meiner Lehre* Fischer gives us what we have been long waiting for: a clear and simple statement of his general worldview.[30] Fischer had already made it very clear in *Diotima* and his *Geschichte* that he, as a philosopher, is a pantheist; he did not explain, however, what form his pantheism took. Although he made it clear that he rejected Spinoza's naturalistic pantheism, he said very little about the idealistic or spiritualistic pantheism that he opposed to it. Now in the *Apologie* we get a clearer account of this idealistic or spiritualistic version of pantheism. According to this version, the order of things consists in spirit and everything is its creation, a mode of this single infinite living and self-conscious substance. This spirit is not something supernatural and mysterious because it appears as the world-order itself, the intelligible unity of all things. Fischer conceives this spiritualistic or idealistic pantheism as the middle path between two extremes: naturalistic and supernaturalistic pantheism. A naturalistic pantheism is materialism, and a supernaturalistic pantheism is irrationalism. The problem with naturalistic pantheism is that it cannot explain the phenomena of mental life—religion, art, science and morality—and so ends in a dualism between these phenomena and nature. The

---

[27] Fischer, *Interdict*, pp. 40, 45; Fischer, *Apologie*, pp. 57–58, 69.
[28] Fischer, *Interdict*, p. 40; Fischer, *Apologie*, p. 66.   [29] Schenkel, *Abfertigung*, p. 23.
[30] Fischer, *Apologie*, pp. 93–95.

difficulty with supernaturalistic pantheism is that it makes the essence or whole of things mysterious. The great advantage of idealistic pantheism is that it maintains the unity of the world while making it perfectly comprehensible. Fischer insists that this idealistic pantheism is not only compatible with Christianity but that it even provides it with its necessary foundation. Christianity conceives of the divine as spirit, which is the incarnation, the idea of the divine becoming human, the infinite becoming finite. It is precisely this idea that is affirmed in idealist pantheism, which sees the infinite in the finite. Having expounded such a doctrine, Fischer now felt that he could rest with an easy conscience, fully able to claim that he is a true Christian.

Whatever we make of Fischer's crudely sketched world-view, it shows his distance from left and right Hegelians alike: the left would never accept his sympathy with religion and his attempt to rationalize the incarnation; the right would not like his pantheistic rendition of the incarnation that left no place for the uniqueness of Christ or miracles. It was with his idealistic pantheism that Fischer hoped to save the Hegelian legacy, which represented for him the rational *via media* between materialism and supernaturalism.

4. A Hegelian Kantian or a Kantian Hegelian?

In our account of Fischer's philosophical development so far we have found a very convinced and able young Hegelian, one surprisingly mature for his age, and one who had the will and power to defend Hegel's system against its most potent critics. After his dismissal from Heidelberg, Fischer had even become a martyr for the Hegelian system. This would have made him all the more a convinced and passionate Hegelian, given that martyrs, almost by definition, do not recant the cause for which they suffer. But all this leaves us with some difficult questions: When, how and why did Fischer become a Kantian?

All these questions are posed for us by a book that Fischer published in 1852 during the halcyon Heidelberg years: *Logik und Metaphysik oder Wissenschaftslehre*.[31] This work is very much what we would expect from Fischer's philosophical development hitherto. That is to say: it is very much a Hegelian work. It has all the trappings of a textbook of Hegelian logic and metaphysics. In his exposition Fischer follows the general structure and method of Hegel's logic, adopting the same general categories and sub-categories, and using the same dialectic to reveal their inner contradictions and connections. But not only the structure and method of the work is Hegelian. In his introduction Fischer provides an historical account of the development of philosophy

---

[31] Kuno Fischer, *Logik und Metaphysik oder Wissenschaftslehre. Lehrbuch für akademische Vorlesungen* (Stuttgart: C.P. Scheitlin, 1852). All references in parentheses in this section are to this edition. "§" indicates a paragraph number, "Z" a *Zusatz* or Addition; Arabic numerals refer to page numbers. The second edition completely revised the first and appeared under the new title *System der Logik und Metaphysik oder Wissenschaftslehre* (Heidelberg: Friedrich Bassermann, 1865). We will consider the changes of that edition in Section 6.

from Kant to Hegel that is pure Hegel. According to this account, the contradictions and inadequacies in the philosophies of Kant, Fichte and Schelling are overcome in Hegel's system. It is a story straight out of Hegel's *Geschichte der Philosophie*.[32]

Yet there is another aspect of Fischer's early text that is very puzzling, indeed downright mysterious. Despite its many Hegelian features, there is also a deep Kantian dimension to Fischer's early logic and metaphysics, one that seems to come out of nowhere. Now, for the first time, it seems as if Fischer has become, if only in part, a Kantian. Just what this new Kantian dimension amounts to Fischer explains in his preface. Here he states that "the problem of logic" is one and the same as "the problem of knowledge", and that the problem of knowledge has to be seen from the transcendental standpoint formulated by Kant (xii). We can solve the problem of knowledge, Fischer maintains, only if we assume that there is one and the same being that acts in nature and that thinks in the mind, that is, only if we suppose that nature and spirit are identical (xiv). This is the so-called "principle of subject-object identity", that Fischer already espoused in *Diotima*. That principle is central to, and characteristic of, Schelling's and Hegel's absolute idealism. Fischer stresses, however, that he adopts this principle *"only within transcendental philosophy"* (xiv; his italics). If he follows Hegel, he explains, that is only because Hegel "grasped and systematically developed the concept of identity in a transcendental spirit." (xv) It is for this reason, and only for this reason, Fischer insists, that he makes common cause with Hegel. This means that the Hegelian system, as he puts it, *"must be placed under the control of Kant"* (xv; his italics). Because of the Kantian qualifications he places on the Hegelian system, Fischer calls his standpoint *"critical philosophy of identity"* (xvi).

A *critical* philosophy of identity! The Hegelian system *"under the control of Kant"*! That, in a phrase, is the new Kantian dimension of Fischer's philosophy. But nothing in his earlier philosophical development prepares us for this. Whence this Kantian dimension? The mystery only deepens when we consider Fischer's views on Kant just before or around the same time he wrote *Logik und Metaphysik*. In his *Geschichte* Fischer had espoused the most extreme rationalism, according to which everything in the universe must be knowable (at least in principle).[33] From this perspective, the Kantian notion of a limit upon knowledge is utterly absurd. In his *Apologie* Fischer even stated that Kant's philosophy is irrationalist because it places limits upon reason with its thing-in-itself.[34]

One apparent solution to the mystery is just to say that Fischer is still not that much of a Kantian after all. This is because the critical dimension of his philosophy is enveloped by the Hegelian, limited to just one moment of his Hegelian system. After all, the Hegelian dialectic comprises a negative or critical moment, which is intended to

[32] See Hegel, *Vorlesungen über die Geschichte der Philosophie*, in *Werke* XX, 329–462.
[33] See Fischer, *Geschichte der neuern Philosophie* (1854), 'Neun und zwanzigste Vorlesung', pp. 543, 546, 547.
[34] Fischer, *Apologie*, pp. 70–71.

address the demands of Kantian criticism. Surely, this is what Fischer had in mind, it seems, when he wrote that Hegel grasped the concept of identity in a transcendental spirit. On this reading, then, Fischer's Kantianism is a very domesticated kind, one under the control of Hegel.

Is this an *accurate* reading of the *Logik und Metaphysik?* The crucial question is how we are to understand the crucial qualifying adjective *"critical"* in Fischer's philosophy of identity? Is the critical standpoint external or internal to Hegel's system? Is it added onto the system as a watchguard to control or prevent its inherent dogmatic tendencies? Or is it already integral to Hegel's system as one moment of the dialectic? So the question now before us is: Was Fischer a Kantian Hegelian, who made Kant the controlling force over Hegel? Or was he a Hegelian Kantian, who made Kant a mere moment of the Hegelian system?

At first Fischer seems to leave no doubt about his answer to this question. In his introductory historical exposition he makes it clear that the critical aspect is *internal to* Hegel's system and central to its guiding spirit. Hegel's philosophy is "the critical philosophy of identity" because it removes the dogmatic tendencies in Schelling's "philosophy of identity". Schelling understood the philosophy of identity in a purely dogmatic manner because he appealed to intellectual intuition, thus failing to provide a proper demonstration of the absolute standpoint (§17; 32). Hegel's logic is a critical version of Schelling's philosophy of identity because it attempts to demonstrate what Schelling simply presupposed (§16; 33). In attempting to show the necessity of the absolute standpoint in the *Phänomenologie,* Hegel synthesized the critical dimension of Fichte's philosophy with the metaphysical aspect of Schelling's philosophy (§18; 33–34).[35] So the answer to our question seems clear: the critical aspect of Fischer's system is absorbed into the Hegelian; in other words, Fischer is indeed a Hegelian Kantian.

Yet the whole business turns out to be more complicated. It would be a mistake to read Fischer's early *Logik und Metaphysik* as a strictly Hegelian work, either by intention or implication. For the more we read into the details of the work, the more we find that Fischer is not simply expounding Hegel but also revising him, and indeed according to Kantian guidelines. In his account of some of the transitions of Hegel's logic Fischer insists on giving them a new formulation, one that intends to improve on Hegel's own texts. When discussing the transition from being to nothingness, for example, Fischer insists that the normal account of that transition misses the crucial factor empowering the move from being to nothingness: namely, the activity of thinking itself (§29Z; 56). The normal account states that being goes over into nothingness because being is completely indeterminate and therefore the same as nothingness. But this removes all reason for further development of the dialectic, Fischer

---

[35] Fischer had developed this formulation of Hegel's philosophy as early as 1848. It appears clearly in his article 'Das Wesen der Religion von Carl Schwarz', *Die Epigonen* V (1848), 192.

complains, because the result of equating being with nothingness in this manner is a tautology, a mere zero, so that any further movement is stalled or a creation *ex nihilo* (§29Z; 56). The reason that being becomes nothingness is because the pure activity of thinking is not a thinking of anything, and so it is a thinking of nothingness. We must not think of the content of the concepts of being and nothingness, apart from the thinking of them, because that would be purely dogmatic. We must rather stress *the thinking* of these contents, the activity of the subject which makes them possible. In emphasizing the role of thinking, instead of the content of the thoughts themselves, Fischer was pointing to the subjective, transcendental dimension of these concepts.

We will leave aside here the question whether Fischer's revision really improves upon this transition in Hegel's logic. The point to see now is much simpler: that Fischer is *re-writing* the transition, introducing factors that are not present in Hegel's own version. When Fischer takes issue with the normal account of the transition it is clear that he does so against Hegel himself, who stressed that being is nothingness because of being's complete abstractness and indeterminacy.[36] Hegel had insisted that his transitions are generated entirely by the content of the concepts themselves, so that we do not have to introduce or presuppose any activity behind them.[37] But for Fischer everything rests upon introducing this activity of thinking, because for him it represents the transcendental standpoint, the ineliminable aspect of subjectivity that is necessary to all thought. He had insisted in his preface that one fundamental lesson of Kant's philosophy is that "There cannot be any categories without a self-consciousness which produces them." (xv) This was Fischer's way of reaffirming the Kantian principle that the "I think" must be able to accompany all representations, that is, a concept has no meaning at all unless it could be the content for some self-consciousness. Schelling had insisted that we abstract from this "I", the subject of knowledge, to get to the standpoint of subject–object identity;[38] but Fischer regards such an effort as self-defeating: to abstract from myself I still presuppose myself. What makes Hegel's philosophy of identity critical, in contrast to Schelling's dogmatism, is partly its retention of the dimension of subjectivity, of self-awareness within the absolute standpoint.

Just how much Fischer was revising and transforming Hegel becomes apparent when we consider the tensions between his transcendental standpoint and Hegel's philosophy. The transcendental standpoint means that we recognize limits upon our knowledge, that we do not pretend to know anything about reality in itself, that is, reality as it exists apart from and prior to consciousness itself. As transcendental philosophers the limits of our world are the limits of possible

[36] G.W.F. Hegel, *Wissenschaft der Logik*, ed. Georg Lasson (Hamburg: Meiner, 1971), I, 66–67. In the 1869 edition Fischer is explicit that this version of the transition is a mistake of Hegel's (§77; 219).

[37] Hegel, *Wissenschaft der Logik*, I, 31, 36, 47.

[38] See F.W.J. Schelling, *Darstellung meines Systems der Philosophie*, §1, *Werke* I/4, 10–11.

experience. Fischer himself duly takes note of these restrictions, endorsing them when he writes that the categories are applicable only to appearances, and that there can be only a metaphysics of appearances and not supersensible objects (§11, Z2b; 21).[39] Such restrictions can hardly be described as Hegelian because they clash with fundamental claims of Hegel's logic. Hegel had insisted that the movement of the dialectic is that of things themselves, and that his categories express the very essence of things. He famously described the realm of logic as "the exposition of God as he exists in his eternal being before the creation of nature and any finite mind."[40]

So, given Fischer's emphasis on subjectivity, on the activity as well as content of thinking, and given his limitation of knowledge to appearances, it seems more accurate to describe him as a Kantian rather than Hegelian. The Kantian dimension of his thinking is not absorbed into the Hegelian, as if it were only a moment of the dialectic; rather, it stands as a watchguard over the Hegelian, preventing it from transcending the limits of experience and from dispensing with the role of the subject in constituting the world. In the final analysis, then, Fischer seems to be really a Kantian Hegelian rather than a Hegelian Kantian.

This would seem finally to resolve the matter. Yet there are more complications still, because Fischer, having stressed the role of Kantian limitations of knowledge, never surrendered his earlier rationalism. Thus he tells us that the *ordo idearum* is one and the same as the *ordo rerum* (§24; 43), that "the objective dialectic is the self-development of objective reason (the essence of things)" (§24; 44), and that the idea studied by logic is "the real world itself", which is the world "not in some state of appearance but in its true essence" (§22; 40). All this raises the question: How do we reconcile these metaphysical claims with Kant's critical restrictions? How does Fischer square his radical rationalism with his critical principles?

We still have not fully answered our original question: When, how and why did Fischer become a neo-Kantian? The mystery has only increased, because Fischer's apparent neo-Kantianism seems to come out of nowhere and to be utterly at odds with his Hegelianism. Rather than one question, we now have two. First, where did Fischer's neo-Kantianism come from? Second, is Fischer's system consistent? Is it possible to reconcile the Kantian and Hegelian sides of his logic and metaphysics? To answer these questions, we have no choice but further to unravel the tangled thread of Fischer's philosophical development.

---

[39] Fischer is not simply expounding Kant here but also reaffirming him. Though he criticizes the concept of the thing-in-itself as a residue of pre-critical dogmatism (§12; 23), he also endorses Kant's restriction of knowledge to experience as part of his critical doctrine (§11, 20; §13; 22). As we shall see, Fischer also accepts Kant's theory of space and time, according to which they are valid for human intuition alone.

[40] Hegel, *Wissenschaft der Logik*, I, 31.

5. Birth of a Neo-Kantian

After the rescript against his lectures, Fischer languished in the wilderness for three years, from September 1853 to November 1856. Though unemployed, he was not idle, for he devoted himself to writing his *Geschichte der neuern Philosophie*, specifically the volumes on Bacon and Leibniz.[41] The University of Berlin had attempted to acquire Fischer in the autumn of 1855, when several luminaries of that storied time and place—Alexander von Humboldt, August Böckh and Adolf Trendelenburg—pushed for the appointment.[42] Yet the cultural minister Karl von Raumer blocked these efforts on the grounds of Fischer's *Lehrverbot* in Heidelberg. Just as all seemed lost for Fischer in Berlin, he received from Moritz Seebeck, the head of the board of trustees at the University of Jena, the offer of an honorary ordinary professorship there. "And so little Jena has once again saved the honor of Germany", Humboldt wrote to a friend upon hearing the news.[43] Naturally, Fischer gladly and graciously accepted the offer. Not since Wolff's restauration in Halle in 1740 had an academic appointment been so celebrated in Germany. For the next sixteen years Fischer would be a professor at Jena, the birthplace of classical German philosophy.

Fischer's appointment to Jena brought with it a renewed interest in Kant. He had begun to lecture on Kant in his early Heidelberg years, but that came to an abrupt end with the rescript. A draft of a book on Kant was pushed to the backburner as Fischer worked on Bacon and Leibniz.[44] But, in Jena, Fischer would have to lecture on Kant again, and the preparation for that made him rethink all his work on Kant. His inaugural lecture, appropriately enough, was on Kant. Entitled portentously *Clavis kantiana,*[45] this lecture was little more than a summary of Kant's doctrines and the stages by which he developed them. But it showed Fischer's intentions and interests on an auspicious occasion. In the next years Fischer would devote himself to giving lectures on Kant at the university.

It is only from these lectures that we begin to see the reasons for Fischer's steadily evolving Kantianism. Already in his 1852 Heidelberg lectures Fischer took a crucial step towards Kant by acknowledging his central role in the history of philosophy. Fischer taught that there are three basic stages in the history of modern philosophy: the *dogmatic*, which simply assumes, without examination, that thinking can know being; the *critical*, which examines this assumption but ends in scepticism; and the *philosophy of identity*, which restores this assumption on a critical level through

---

[41] See Kuno Fischer, *G.W. Leibniz und seine Schule* (Mannheim: Bassermann, 1855); and *Francis Bacon und seine Nachfolger* (Leipzig: Brockhaus, 1856).

[42] On the story behind the attempt to appoint Fischer, see Falckenheim, 'Fischer', pp. 261–262.

[43] As cited in Falckenheim, 'Kuno Fischer', p. 262.

[44] See Fischer's own account of his work on Kant in the preface to his *Immanuel Kant: Entwicklungsgeschichte und System der kritischen Philosophie* (Mannheim: Bassermann, 1860), pp. vii–ix.

[45] See Kuno Fischer, *Clavis kantiana. Qua via Immanuel Kant philosophiae criticae elementa invenerit* (Jena: Schreiber, 1858).

dialectic.[46] The thesis that the second stage is necessary to avoid dogmatism shows Fischer's recognition of the pivotal role of the critical philosophy. Criticism would have to be one component of the Hegelian philosophy. Yet the 1852 lectures still do not go far enough because the final synthesis, the culminating stage of development, is still Hegelian. But in the late 1850s Fischer begins to give Kant an even greater importance, and one that even trumps Hegel. Like many philosophers in the 1850s and 1860s, Fischer felt that philosophy was going through a crisis, and that nothing less was at stake than the future of philosophy itself. The rapid growth of the empirical sciences seemed to doom philosophy to obsolescence; and philosophers like Stirner and Feuerbach saw philosophy as little more than disguised theology. Who could save philosophy from this crisis? Who could rescue it from imminent death? The answer was clear: Immanuel Kant. It was not Hegel, because he was more part of the problem than the solution. Hegel's speculative metaphysics had become increasingly disreputable and unpopular because its methodology seemed utterly at odds with the new empirical and historical sciences. While Stirner and Feuerbach would only scoff at Hegel, they would have to respect Kant, whose critical method had been their ultimate inspiration too.

The impending crisis of philosophy, and Kant's central role in resolving it, was the central theme of three important lectures that Fischer gave in the spring of 1860. These lectures, which were later published under the title *Kant's Leben und die Grundlage seiner Lehre*,[47] have often been regarded as a milestone in the history of neo-Kantianism—and with good reason. Not the least reason for their influence was the occasion and manner of their original delivery. Fischer spoke before a large audience in the palace of Sophie Luise, the grand duchess of Sachsen-Weimar; and the style of the lectures was clear, simple and lively, so that even a layman could follow. In simple and straightforward terms Fischer spelled out the reasons for the relevance of Kant's philosophy to his age. Kant was now declared the saviour of philosophy, the Immanuel to lead philosophy out of the wilderness.

The aim of his lectures, Fischer tells us in the preface, is to explain "the foundations of the critical philosophy" and "the intellectual greatness of Kant" (v). His lectures will provide the shortest, but also a fully sufficient, answer to two important questions: "Who was Kant?" and "What is meant by critical philosophy?" (viii). The lectures are devoted to three specific topics: the character of Kant, the problem of knowledge, and the doctrine of space and time (vi). Kant's greatest achievements, in Fischer's opinion, were his discovery of the problem of knowledge and his theory of space and time. Two of the lectures are devoted to these achievements; a third discusses Kant's life and personality.

---

[46] See Fischer, *Geschichte der neuern Philosophie* (1854), pp. 89–100. This is a later edition of lectures originally given in 1852.

[47] Kuno Fischer, *Kant's Leben und die Grundlagen seiner Lehre* (Mannheim: Friedrich Bassermann, 1860). All references in parentheses are to this edition.

Indisputably, the most important and influential of Fischer's three lectures for the later reception of Kant was the second, that devoted to the problem of knowledge.[48] This text is a *locus classicus* for the neo-Kantian conception of philosophy.[49] If its ideas are familiar to us today, that is not least because Fischer put them forward so long ago. It is in this lecture that Fischer makes his case for why Kant's conception of philosophy is still relevant to, and indeed crucial for, contemporary philosophy. He argues that only Kant's conception rescues philosophy from its impending obsolescence. His lecture considers what he somewhat dramatically calls "*die Lebensfrage der Philosophie*", that is, the question of its life or death, whether philosophy has a right to exist at all. Fischer's argument is that philosophy deserves to exist if, and only if, it follows the Kantian conception.

Fischer begins his lecture with the basic question "What is philosophy?" It is necessary to raise this question anew, he explains, because philosophy is no longer the mother of all the sciences as it had been in the past. Philosophy gave birth to all the special sciences, though they have now grown independent of her. We need to re-examine, then, how philosophy differs from the other sciences, what are its distinguishing characteristics, and what special role it plays in the general economy and classification of the sciences. It is especially important to do this, Fischer stresses, because nowadays some deny that philosophy has any place at all in the general scheme of the sciences. For them it seems that philosophy is destined for obsolescence because it satisfies none of the basic criteria of a science. Each science should have its special subject matter, its specific part of reality to investigate; but the problem is precisely that every part of reality has already been taken by one of the empirical sciences (94–95). It appears, then, that philosophy has no role to play at all and might as well disappear. Fischer is especially worried by those advocates of empirical science—he does not give them a name—who insist that everything has to be explained on the basis of natural laws (96). They regard physics as the only science, and they insist that we should explain only what we observe. By their criteria of science—observation, experiment, explanation by general natural laws—philosophy should not be a science at all. Though Fischer does not name them, it is clear from the context that he has in mind the materialists.

Fischer's response to the materialists is to ask them to reflect on their own methods and presuppositions (96). To explain facts or events in nature, they have to use and apply concepts like cause and effect, force and manifestation, substance and property. These concepts are the *instruments* of their enquiries; they are not, however,

[48] Fischer, 'Das Problem der menschlichen Erkenntniß als die erste Frage der Philosophie', pp. 89–115.

[49] It is a commonplace to see Zeller's 1862 lecture 'Ueber Bedeutung und Aufgabe der Erkenntnistheorie' as the beginning of this neo-Kantian conception of philosophy. See, for example, Richard Rorty, *Philosophy and the Mirror of Nature* (Oxford: Blackwell, 1980), pp. 133–135. Rorty cites Fritz Mauthner and Hans Vaihinger to bolster Zeller's claim to priority (135, nn. 5–6). Though Fischer does not use the term "Erkenntnistheorie", it is noteworthy that his conception of the epistemological task of philosophy precedes that of Zeller.

their *objects*. It is just here that a space opens for the role of the philosopher. He makes into an object of enquiry what the empirical scientist uses, applies and presupposes but does not reflect upon. What the physicist cannot explain is the possibility of physics itself. All the empirical sciences explain *specific objects* in experience; but they cannot explain the possibility of experience in general. They explain things, but not *knowledge* of things (97).

The special task of the philosopher, then, is to explain what all scientists presuppose but can never explain themselves: the possibility of empirical science. All the empirical sciences aspire towards knowledge; but they have no explanation of knowledge itself, of how and whether it is possible and in what it consists. Philosophy therefore has to ascend to a higher order of reflection than all the empirical sciences. While they study objects themselves, philosophy makes their study its object. It therefore stands above the empirical sciences, and so transcends them. Hence Kant calls this second-order reflection "transcendental" (99).

The specific problem and concern of philosophy, as Fischer now conceives it, is "the problem of knowledge". He outlines three possible positions regarding the possibility of knowledge: 1) we can accept that possibility on good faith; 2) we can deny that possibility and attempt to refute it; and 3) we can investigate that possibility and show not only that but how it is possible. The first option is dogmatism; the second is scepticism; and the third is criticism (100). By putting forward the options in these terms, Fischer made it clear that only the third is possible. As Kant had put it in the final paragraph of the *Kritik*: "The *critical* path alone is still open." (B 883) The implications of this new schema should be clear: Hegel had now been silently dethroned in Fischer's thinking. For now the schema of dogmatism–scepticism–criticism had put criticism in the culminating position once occupied by the philosophy of identity.

Fischer goes no further in his lecture than explaining the problem of knowledge according to Kant. He does not attempt to sketch Kant's solution to the problem. "My lecture therefore ends," he concludes, "on just that point where the solution of the problem begins" (115). Yet in explaining the problem so clearly, and in stressing the crucial role of Kant in resolving it, Fischer had done much. He had secured a place for philosophy in the realm of the sciences, and he had shown how and why Kant's critical philosophy alone deserves to occupy that space. The *Lebensfrage* had been decisively answered, and not thanks to Hegel.

6. Interpretation of Kant

The three lectures of Fischer's *Kant's Leben und die Grundlagen seiner Lehre* were only the prelude for something much larger and grand. Shortly after the lectures appeared, Fischer published a two-volume work on Kant which eventually became Volumes III and IV of his general *Geschichte der neuern Philosophie*. Volume III treated Kant's development and the *Kritik der reinen Vernunft*; Volume IV examined the entire structure of the critical philosophy, all Kant's major works after the first *Kritik*.[50] The publication of this work was an important event in the history of neo-Kantianism. It was by no means the first scholarly study of Kant, having been preceded by the works of Rosenkranz, Fortlage and Erdmann,[51] to name a few. Nevertheless, it was more exacting, painstaking and complete than its predecessors. And, more importantly, despite its size, it was no dry or dull tome. Written in a lively and engaging style, it made Kant comprehensible for a wider public. With Fischer's book, Kant ceased to be another dead philosopher from the past and became a living thinker of vital concern to the present.

Kant scholars from the late 19th century give clear testimony about the importance of Fischer's work. Emil Arnoldt wrote that, thanks to Fischer's book, a great shift took place in the public's attitude towards Kant in the 1860s.[52] Rather than seeing Kant as a historical figure superseded by the great system builders, people now began to take Kant on his own terms. And, speaking at Fischer's funeral in 1907, Wilhelm Windelband stressed its importance for neo-Kantianism:

This work, which still deserves the most eminent place in the now immeasurably swollen Kant-literature, had doubtless the greatest influence in arousing the movement of neo-Kantianism, which, in the last decades of the 19th century, has decisively influenced philosophy in Germany and beyond its borders.[53]

Given the great importance of Fischer's work, it is worthwhile to examine its aims, methods, genesis and content. Since it is impossible to summarize all its contents, whose two volumes comprise more than a thousand pages, we will consider only two aspects of Fischer's work that are of special historical and philosophical importance: namely, his interpretation of transcendental idealism, and his account of the method of transcendental philosophy.

In the preface to the first edition of his work Fischer tells us a little about its genesis. The work took at least nine years to complete. The first draft of what became the first volume was already finished in 1851. After his dismissal from Heidelberg in 1853, however, Fischer's work on Kant was interrupted, and he devoted himself instead to the study of Bacon, Spinoza and Leibniz. With his appointment to Jena in 1856, he again began to lecture on Kant, and these lectures were a major revision of the original

---

[50] The whole work bore the title *Immanuel Kant, Entwicklungsgeschichte und System der kritischen Philosophie* (Mannheim: Friedrich Bassermann, 1860). The first volume has the subtitle *Entstehung und Begründung der kritischen Philosophie. Die Kritik der reinen Vernunft;* the second volume has the subtitle *Das Lehrgebäude der kritischen Philosophie. Das System der reinen Vernunft.* The first volume was Volume III of his *Geschichte der neuern Philosophie;* the second volume became Volume IV. In the ten-volume *Jubiläumsausgabe* the Kant volumes became Volumes IV and V.

[51] See Karl Rosenkranz, *Geschichte der kant'schen Philosophie* (Leipzig: Voß, 1840); J.E. Erdmann, *Versuch einer wissenschaftlichen Darstellung der Geschichte der neuern Philosophie* (Leipzig: Vogel, 1848), III/1; and Carl Fortlage, *Genetische Geschichte der Philosophie seit Kant* (Leipzig: Brockhaus, 1852).

[52] Emil Arnoldt, *Kant nach Kuno Fischers neuer Darstellung* (Königsberg: Beyer, 1882). Reprinted in *Gesammelte Schriften*, ed. Otto Schöndörffer (Berlin: Cassirer, 1908), III, 213–214.

[53] Wilhelm Windelband, *Kuno Fischer*, pp. 24–25.

draft. As he lectured on Kant, Fischer's views kept changing, so that hardly a sentence from the original draft remained (vii). He found it necessary to correct and simplify essential points; but he was least satisfied with the exposition. The need to lecture on Kant—to make his philosophy clear and accessible to a general audience—forced Fischer to improve the exposition from its original version. The work had now so grown in size that it had become a two-volume work (ix).

As it happened, Fischer's Kant book became a never-ending work-in-progress, a virtual sounding board for its author's constantly evolving views. Five editions of the book were published in Fischer's lifetime,[54] and these editions differ considerably from one another in organization and content. Fischer kept adding and taking away material, and he was constantly revising the exposition. As a result, the structure and outline of the chapters constantly change. Some editions contain polemics that are responding to current issues; but these are simply dropped in later editions in favour of new polemics. In short: the book is an editor's nightmare. Students and scholars are advised to cite carefully the edition they use. Here, for historical reasons, we will consider chiefly the first edition of 1860.

Fischer's aim in writing his book, as he explains in the preface, was to provide "an exposition and reconstruction of the Kantian philosophy in its genuine and still little understood spirit" (xiii). The throng of systems following Kant claimed to have superseded him. Rather than examining Kant on his terms, they had used him for their own purposes, either as material for their systems or as a target for criticism. Fischer wanted to put an end to that practice: "My exposition will reproduce the Kantian philosophy in its *original* spirit" (xiv). That sounds presumptuous and naive, but it is understandable enough when one considers its context: the general state of Kant interpretation before Fischer, which was much as he had described it. To provide a sound historical interpretation of Kant, Fischer stressed the great value of knowing his philosophical development and his historical context (xv).

Fischer's understanding of Kant's transcendental idealism rests chiefly on his interpretation of the Transcendental Aesthetic. Like Schopenhauer, who greatly influenced his reading of Kant, Fischer saw Kant's theories of space and time as his great achievement. "The transcendental aesthetic is Kant's most spectacular deed. In both its result, and in the path to this result, this investigation is a model of scientific precision and method." (293) This part of the *Kritik* was also the basis for Kant's central and characteristic doctrine, his transcendental idealism. As Fischer wrote in the preface: "The correct and sound understanding of the critical philosophy depends on one major point: correct insight into the new doctrine of space and time, the transcendental aesthetic, as Kant called this doctrine." (xiv–xv) Sure enough, Fischer later defines Kant's transcendental idealism in his chapter on Kant's theory of space and

[54]   The first three editions were published by Bassermann in 1860, 1867 (Mannheim) and 1882 (Munich); the fourth and fifth by Winter in Heidelberg in 1889 and 1898–1899. Starting with the third edition, the general title for both volumes was *Immanuel Kant und seine Lehre*.

time.[55] Kant's doctrine is called transcendental idealism, we are told, because it maintains "the transcendental ideality of space and time" (317). This doctrine means that space and time are forms of our representation only, that they are nothing more than a priori intuitions, and so not true of things-in-themselves. Space and time, as Fischer bluntly puts it, are "mere representations", and they are "nothing as such" (309).

There are two crucial points behind the transcendental ideality of space and time, Fischer explains (317–318). First, it means that space and time are conditions of appearances only. As conditions under which we perceive the world, they cannot give us knowledge of how the world is in itself, apart from and prior to our perception of it. Second, they are *necessary* conditions of appearances (317–318). This means that space and time, though only forms of intuition, are still indispensable in that everyone must perceive the world according to them. It is on the basis of their universality and necessity, Fischer holds, that Kant can justifiably talk about their *empirical* reality. Space and time are not arbitrary and accidental representations of things in experience, but they are conditions under which we have any experience at all. Although they are not true of things-in-themselves, they are still necessarily and universally true of objects in our experience (314). Hence we can talk about the transcendental ideality and the empirical reality of space and time. While space and time are transcendentally ideal with respect to things-in-themselves, they are empirically real with respect to objects of possible experience (316–317).

What, then, about the thing-in-itself? What is Fischer's stance towards this enduring conundrum? Like Adickes long after him,[56] Fischer thinks that Kant is committed to the reality of the thing-in-itself, that is, its existence as an entity, as something that exists beyond our experience. What exists apart from and prior to the application of the a priori forms of intuition cannot be represented by us, and that is the thing-in-itself (313). Fischer had no sympathy for the demand of Otto Liebmann, his later student, to banish the thing-in-itself from the critical philosophy; and he would later disapprove of the interpretation of the Marburg school, which would attempt to make the thing-in-itself only a limiting concept, an ideal for enquiry.[57] Such interpretations had simply too many texts against them, Fischer maintained. Without the thing-in-itself Kant's transcendental idealism made no sense, because it is essentially the doctrine that appearances are not things-in-themselves. Nevertheless, though Fischer insists on a realist interpretation of the thing-in-itself, he cautions against interpreting it as the cause of our sensations. When Kant writes that the qualitative dimension of sensation is "given from the outside" (*von Außen gegeben*), he does not mean that it is the product of something independent of our consciousness. "To say that something is given from without in the proper meaning of the Kantian philosophy can only mean: the origin is not pure reason, that is, it is not given a priori, it is no product of

---

[55] Buch II, Zweites Capitel: 'Transcendentale Aesthetik', pp. 291–318.
[56] Erich Adickes, *Kant und das Ding an sich* (Berlin: Pan Verlag, 1924).
[57] Kuno Fischer, *Kritik der kantischen Philosophie* (Munich: Bassermann, 1883), p. 90.

reason." (312) We must not assume, then, that there is something out there, "as if we were the receiver, and some other being outside us, I know not what, were the giver." (313)

Fischer adopts a two worlds reading of Kant's transcendental idealism, according to which noumena and phenomena designate distinct kinds of entity. He rejects firmly the opposing thesis that noumena and phenomena are simply different ways of representating one and the same thing, as if phenomena were the thing as perceived by the senses and noumena the thing as understood by the understanding (404). This, he says, is the old dogmatic conception of the relationship between things-in-themselves and appearances, which Kant explicitly denies. The appearance and thing-in-itself differ not in degree, as if there were one and the same thing seen clearly by the understanding and confusedly by the senses. Rather, because understanding and sensibility are so heterogeneous, they differ in kind; and because they differ in kind, they should be regarded simply as different objects (405). For this reason it is also a mistake to interpret appearances as if they were simply aspects or properties of things-in-themselves (405). Appearances are for Fischer merely representations within us, and as such they do not have to be attached to things-in-themselves (396). He does not dispute that Kant sometimes writes about appearances as if they were aspects of things-in-themselves; but he claims that these passages are limited to the second edition of the *Kritik* where Kant was eager to distinguish his idealism from Berkeley's (404). This was a falling off from his original doctrine in the first edition, where Kant had identified appearances with representations alone.

Does Fischer assume, then, that Kant's idealism is the same as Berkeley's? Raising just this question in Book II, Chapter 4, Fischer replies that the equation of Kant with Berkeley is a grave mistake (397). The two philosophers agree that the objects of knowledge consist in representations, that what we perceive exists only for some subject. But Fischer stresses that Kant's idealism has something Berkeley's does not: a *transcendental* dimension, the universal and necessary forms of understanding and sensibility, which allows him to distinguish between illusion and reality. These forms are necessary conditions of experience, so that they are not objects in experience (and so representations) but that which makes any such object possible. Because Berkeley did not recognize this dimension of experience, his idealism fell prey to Hume's scepticism, which pointed out the weakness of the distinction between illusion and reality on Berkeley's premises. It is solely this transcendental dimension of his doctrine that Kant needed to distinguish his idealism from Berkeley's, Fischer insists. Kant went astray, however, when he added the 'Refutation of Idealism' to the second edition of the *Kritik*. By distinguishing between objects and our representations of them, Kant violated the spirit of his own transcendental idealism (397). In thus stressing the differences between the first and second editions of the *Kritik*, an authentic first edition and apocryphal second one, Fischer had given his imprimatur to one of Schopenhauer's more controversial readings.[58]

---

[58] See Arthur Schopenhauer, 'Kritik der kantischen Philosophie', Anhang to *Die Welt als Wille und Vorstellung*, in *Sämtliche Werke*, ed. Wolfgang Freiherr von Löhneysen (Stuttgart: Insel, 1968), I, 586–587.

Regarding Kant's method, Fischer stresses the great importance of first having a solid understanding of Kant's problem. We will understand the purpose and logic of that method only if we first examine the questions Kant intends to answer with it. The main question the critical philosophy poses is "How is knowledge possible?" (263) But Kant cannot answer this question, Fischer insists, until he raises two more. He cannot simply presuppose that there is knowledge because this will be questioned by the sceptic. He therefore has to ask the more basic question: "Is there knowledge?", or "Is there really a fact of knowledge to investigate?" (263). And since he cannot answer this question until he knows what knowledge is, he has to ask the even more basic question: "What is knowledge?" (264). The critical philosopher therefore has to answer three basic questions: "What is knowledge?", "Is there knowledge?", and "How is such knowledge possible?".

It is striking that Fischer first writes about Kant's method in epistemological rather than psychological terms. It seems that the problem is not to show the causes or processes by which we arrive at knowledge but to examine the evidence for claims to knowledge. In a telling metaphor Fischer likens the procedure of the critical philosopher to that of a lawyer (264). Just as the lawyer intends to examine the "basis in right" (*Rechtsgründen*) of a question, so the critical philosopher has to examine the "question of right in knowledge" (*Rechtsfrage der Erkenntniß*). As Fischer puts it:

Kant has to deal with the question of right regarding knowledge. To speak legally, he wants to put knowledge on trial. The first thing is to introduce the proceedings, the second is to come to a judgement. We introduce the proceedings when we show in what the case consists, and that the case lies before us. We decide the case when we show its possibility, i.e., when we show in virtue of what right knowledge takes place, or when we deduce it in a legal sense. (263–264)

Fischer goes on to explain Kant's distinction between the *Quaestio facti* and the *Quaestio juris* (265). The *Quaestio facti* concerns the questions what is knowledge and whether there is knowledge. The *Quaestio juris* concerns the question how knowledge is possible. It is remarkable, however, that Fischer, despite his insistence on a close reading of the texts, does not explain these questions in Kant's own terms. For Kant, the *quid facti?* concerns the origins of knowledge, the attempt to explain its causes or basis in fact. It is the *quid juris?* that examines the right of knowledge and investigates the basis for synthetic a priori knowledge.[59] Kant is firm and explicit that answering the *Quaestio facti* does not solve the problem of knowledge, because showing how concepts arise from experience does not substantiate their claims to universality and necessity.[60] It is really the *Quaestio juris* that takes up the question of justification, which Fischer places under the *Quaestio facto*. Fischer's readings of Kant's questions arise not from carelessness but, as we shall soon see, from his own peculiar and tendentious interpretation of the method of the *Kritik*.

[59] Kant, KrV, B 116–117.   [60] Kant, KrV, B 119.

Fischer's initial explanation of Kant's method seems entirely epistemological rather than psychological. It seems that the critique of pure reason is more like a legal tribunal, which assesses claims to knowledge, and that it is not really a psychological enquiry into the origins and causes of knowledge. This is entirely in keeping with Fischer's reservations about Fries' interpretation of Kant: that in conflating Kant's enquiry with empirical psychology, Fries misunderstood the transcendental dimension of the critical philosophy, which was to investigate the very possibility of an empirical science like psychology.[61] Nevertheless, contrary to all these appearances, it is remarkable that Fischer never fully broke with the naturalistic paradigm of doing epistemology, that he never carefully and consistently distinguished the methods of empirical science from those of the critical philosophy. Hence, in his original explanation of the task and place of the critical philosophy in the sciences, he wrote as if Kant simply applied the method of the natural sciences to the fact of knowledge itself:

The fact of exact science is indisputable. The natural scientific and empirical method of investigation is indisputable. And the new investigation that Kant carried out with such success in the field of philosophy consists in applying this method to that fact. If a natural scientist wants to explain some physical fact, he seeks the conditions under which the phenomenon follows, the forces from whose combination it proceeds. Kant followed just the same investigation, now directed at the fact of science itself. (14)

So, despite explaining the critique as a legal enquiry, and despite his criticism of Fries, Fischer still understood Kant's method as similar in kind to the natural sciences. Transcendental philosophy was an investigation not into the logic of cognition but into its origins. The critical philosopher would treat science as a fact just as the natural scientist would regard his data as facts.

Why did Fischer still cling to this naturalistic interpretation of Kant's method? Doubtless, part of the explanation was the prevalent authority and prestige of the natural sciences, whose methodology had proven so successful, and which had cast a shadow over the more a priori methods of philosophy (viz. Hegelian dialectic, Schellingian construction). Yet this is only part of the explanation.

The other part becomes clear as soon as we consider Fischer's peculiar conception of Kant's empirical method. It was not the method of empirical psychology, as Fries assumed, but that of natural history. It was indeed nothing less than the natural historical method that Kant had first developed in his early pre-critical work *Allgemeine Naturgeschichte und Theorie des Himmels*. Remarkably, Fischer argued that this method was also that of the critical philosophy itself![62] According to that method,

---

[61]   Fischer, *System der Logik und Metaphysik*, §55; 112.

[62]   Fischer became fully explicit and clear about this in his *Kritik der kantischen Philosophie*, pp. 39–57. In developing this interpretation Fischer refers us to the third newly-revised edition of Volumes III and IV of his *Geschichte der neuern Philosophie* (Munich: Bassermann, 1882), III, 514–518 and IV, 401–407. These passages do not appear in the first and second edition. Still, this conception of Kant's methodology seems to have been implicit in the two earlier editions of the *Geschichte* (1860, 1867).

everything in nature has its history, and to understand it consists in tracing its origins and path of development. What at first appears to be static and eternal in nature will turn out to be, when properly understood, the product of a long and gradual history; for example, the circular orbits of the planets around the sun seem like an eternal fact but they are the result of the action of the forces of attraction and repulsion upon a primal mass of dust. Fischer believed that Kant had followed this method throughout his career, and that it was by no means a relic of his pre-critical years. Indeed, it was because of this method that Kant had come to a "developmental-historical world-view", according to which everything in nature has a history, and everything in history has a purpose. Fischer argued that Kant intended to apply this same method to epistemology; his aim was to explain the fact of knowledge from a genetic perspective, so that it too could be seen as the result of history. Transcendental philosophy was therefore meant to be "*die Entstehungs- und Entwicklungslehre der menschlichen Erkenntniß*".[63]

This was an extraordinary interpretation, one especially remarkable because it flew in the face of Kant's texts. For Kant went to great pains to distinguish his transcendental enquiry from Locke's "plain, historical method" whose task was to explain the origins of our knowledge from experience. But, as we have just seen, Fischer had his own tendentious reading of the *Quaestio juris*, which he made into the question *how* knowledge is possible, thus removing the normative and logical dimension and making it seem more like a genetic or historical enquiry. The motive for Fischer's peculiar interpretation should now be clear: he was assimilating Kant to Hegel in the interests of his own "critical philosophy of identity". For it was Hegel rather than Kant who had followed a genetic and historical method in his epistemology to expose the ahistorical illusions of philosophy. Hegel himself would have been astounded by Fischer's interpretation of Kant, given that he had used his historical method to expose what he regarded as Kant's ahistorical illusions. But Fischer was striving and struggling to fit Kant into a Hegelian mould. That Fischer was still Hegelian, despite his growing Kantianism, shall soon become perfectly clear.

7. The Loyal Hegelian

Given Fischer's work on Kant in the early 1860s, it would appear as if his Hegelian days were finally over. How, indeed, could Fischer be anything but a full-blown Kantian? In his lectures and book he had stressed how Kant's philosophy alone could solve the crisis of philosophy, and how all modern philosophy is either a preparation for or development of the critical philosophy. Furthermore, Fischer had now endorsed Kant's theories of space and time in the Transcendental Aesthetic, which he saw as

---

[63] Fischer, *Kritik der kantischen Philosophie*, p. 43.

the basis of Kant's transcendental idealism. Where, then, could Fischer go but down the critical path he had so clearly marked out for himself?

Prima facie this is just what happens. In 1865 Fischer published a new edition of his *Logik und Metaphysik,* now renamed *System der Logik und Metaphysik.*[64] This was not, however, just a reissue of its 1852 Hegelian predecessor. What the reader now has before him, Fischer assures us in the preface, is "a completely new work" (iv). He not only rewrote many sections, but he also added new ones, so that the new introduction alone was now as long as the whole old edition. Fischer explained that the old edition was riddled with obscurities and difficulties, and that it no longer reflected his new way of thinking, which was the product of all his lectures on logic and metaphysics in the past twelve years (iii–iv). It seems that this new way of thinking is going to be much more Kantian because Fischer writes that the new edition takes into account "two things that one may not neglect in philosophy: Aristotelian logic, and the critical, I mean Kantian philosophy" (vi). He also suggests that many of the errors of the previous edition came from a "scholastic adherence to a traditional and prescribed doctrine"—an obvious reference to his own Hegelianism (iv). One expects, therefore, a much more Kantian, a much less Hegelian, work in this new reformed and improved *System der Logik und Metaphysik.*

Yet, as reasonable as they are, the reader's expectations are utterly dashed. Rather than abandoning or modifying his Hegelian doctrines, Fischer reaffirms them, embarking upon a new defence of the philosophy of identity against its latest critics. One of the major changes of the second edition is its new much longer historical introduction, which examines the latest developments in philosophy since Hegel's death, and specifically the attempts by Herbart, Schopenhauer and Trendelenburg to surpass Hegel. Special sections are devoted to the exposition and critique of each of these philosophers. Fischer regards their attempts to go beyond Hegel as total failures, either because they relapse into realism (Herbart), or because they grasp subject–object identity in a one-sided manner, not recognizing that its subjective dimension is as important as its objective one (Schopenhauer and Trendelenburg). These were points Fischer made against Hegel's critics back in the 1840s, in the days of the *Leipziger Revue* and *Epigonen* articles. Fischer also had not budged on his basic metaphysical principles. The solution to the problem of knowledge still remains for him the principle of subject–object identity, which he regards as the fundamental pillar of Schelling's and Hegel's absolute idealism. Upholding that principle, he argues, demands giving equal weight to its subjective and objective factors, to thought as well as being (§67; 183). Fischer's account of the method of logic is also still fundamentally

---

[64] Kuno Fischer, *System der Logik und Metaphysik oder Wissenschaftslehre.* Zweite völlig umgearbeitete Auflage (Heidelberg: Friedrich Bassermann, 1865). The new title also drops the subtitle of the first edition, *Lehrbuch für akademische Vorlesungen,* because of its increased size. All references in parentheses in this section are to the second edition, where "§" indicates a paragraph number and Arabic numerals indicate page numbers.

Hegelian. Logic consists in the development of pure thinking (§68; 188), and to study this development philosophy needs to follow a method that is both genetic and critical: genetic, in that it traces thinking from its origin through its stages of development (§72; 197), and critical, in that it evaluates thinking according to its own aims or goals (§72; 199). That genetic and critical method was, of course, nothing less than the Hegelian dialectic. In his second edition of the *Logik und Metaphysik* Fischer provides a completely new account of the dialectic of being and nothingness, one more explicitly critical of Hegel (§77; 219); but he still retains the broad outlines of Hegel's logic, dividing it into a doctrine of being, essence and concept (§75, 212).

Fischer's 1865 *Logik und Metaphysik* very much remained, then, "the critical philosophy of identity" of its 1852 predecessor. The tenacity of its author is remarkable in view of the tensions that infected his earlier formulation of that doctrine. We have seen how Fischer both recognized Kant's critical limits upon knowledge yet advanced Hegel's grander metaphysical claims about knowledge of the absolute. Rather than resolving this tension in the 1865 version, Fischer only let it grow. His new endorsement of Kant's Transcendental Aesthetic, which appears in the 1860 edition of his *Geschichte*, means that he is more committed than ever to Kant's critical limits upon knowledge, for Kant's teaching there insists that space and time are a priori intuitions valid only of appearances and not things-in-themselves. Fischer does not shirk from these implications but even insists upon them. For he defends Kant's critical teaching that space and time are valid only for appearances against Trendelenburg's "third alternative", according to which space and time could be a priori intuitions and still true of things-in-themselves (§66; 175). The clash with Hegelian metaphysics is made perfectly explicit when Fischer himself insists that the Transcendental Aesthetic is incompatible with Hegel's own teaching, according to which space and time have an objective rather than subjective status (§§65, 66; 157, 175). All this raises anew the question how Fischer plans to reconcile this critical doctrine with his own Hegelian metaphysics. It is in vain, however, that the reader searches for an answer to this question.

There are other tensions between Kantian and Hegelian doctrines in the second edition of the *Logik und Metaphysik*. The ultimate source of Fischer's attraction to Kant's theory of space and time is that it could serve as a bulwark against naturalism, which assumes the objective existence of space and time. If the existence of matter in space and time is only the result of our forms of perception, there is no longer the danger that the self will be the product of natural forces alone, still less that it will be one cog in the vast machine of nature. It makes all the difference in our worldview, as Fischer put it, whether the self is in space and time or whether space and time are in the self. Yet in the new *Logik und Metaphysik* Fischer does not develop these anti-naturalistic inclinations and intuitions; instead, he continues to affirm the philosophy of identity, which affirms a strong naturalism of its own, according to which everything in the universe unfolds according to the necessity of the concept (§70; 193). The great virtue of this philosophy, we are told, is that it maintains a unified vision of the world and overcomes the Kantian dualism between freedom and nature, idea and reality (§71; 195).

Another remarkable tension arises from Fischer's vascillation about the method of philosophy. He had stated clearly in the new *Logik und Metaphysik* the problems with Fries' anthropological and psychological interpretation of the critical philosophy. The categories and forms of intuition of the critical philosophy cannot be objects of experience for psychological or anthropological investigation, he insists, because that makes them empirical, depriving them of their universality and necessity (§55; 112). The method of the critical philosophy cannot be psychological or anthropological, he further argues, because its purpose is to investigate the very possibility of psychology or anthropology (§58; 112). Yet Fischer also continued to uphold the value of a genetic method in epistemology, according to which everything is understood as a stage in the historical development of reason (§72; 197–199). It was precisely this method, though, that Fries saw as constitutive of his own psychological and anthropological viewpoint. It was hard to see how the genetic method does not involve the very psychological and anthropological tools that it is the purpose of the critical philosophy to investigate.

Thus Fischer's logic and metaphysics of 1865 remained the same unstable, combustible mixture of the "critical philosophy of identity" of 1852. Clearly, this compound could not last; eventually, it would have to explode. Fischer would have to be either a Kantian or a Hegelian, but he could not be both.

What finally *seems* to push Fischer in a firmer and clearer Kantian direction is his new views about human freedom, which first appear in a lecture he gave in 1875, 'Ueber die menschliche Freiheit'.[65] In re-examining the classical question of human freedom, Fischer praised the Kantian solution to the problem, claiming that in it "the question of human freedom is seen for the first time in its true meaning" (45). Fischer had adopted something like the Kantian distinction between the intelligible and phenomenal character. He distinguished between our *natural* character, which is completely subject to natural necessity, and our *moral* character, which has the power to change our natural character according to the will. While our actions are necessary as expressions of our natural character, they are free in the determinations of our moral will, which gives us the power to do otherwise (38, 42). Again like Kant, Fischer maintains that we know we have this power to transform ourselves from the fact of conscience, which tells us that we could have done otherwise even though our natural character and all its actions are necessary (39, 40). This affirmation of the Kantian doctrine of freedom marks a silent and implicit repudiation of the metaphysical doctrines of his 1865 *Logik und Metaphysik*. For there Fischer had stressed, in true Hegelian fashion, that freedom develops of necessity (§70; 193), and he praised the

---

[65] Kuno Fischer, *Ueber die menschliche Freiheit* (Heidelberg: Winter, 1875). Reprinted in *Kleine Schriften* (Heidelberg: Winter 1896), I, 1–47. All references here are to the later edition.

philosophy of identity for grasping this point and overcoming the Kantian dualism between freedom and necessity (§71; 195).

Fischer had now embraced two central and characteristic Kantian doctrines: the theory of space and time of the Transcendental Aesthetic, according to which everything in space and time is only an appearance; and the Kantian theory of freedom, according to which there is a dualism between our noumenal moral character and our phenomenal natural character. It is hard to imagine two doctrines more opposed to the philosophy of identity of Schelling and Hegel. And yet, as we shall soon see, Fischer still could not bring himself to abandon his Hegelian metaphysics. Rather than interpreting Hegel in Kantian terms, he interpreted Kant in Hegelian ones.

8. A Hegelian Kantian

Fischer's final settling of accounts with Kant came in 1883 with his *Kritik der kantischen Philosophie*.[66] This tract is as much a critique of the rapidly evolving neo-Kantian movement as it is of Kant himself. Fischer makes criticisms of prominent neo-Kantians, of older ones like Fries and Herbart, but also of more recent ones like Hermann Cohen and Emil Arnoldt. The very idea of a critique of Kant's philosophy signals that Fischer, unlike the neo-Kantians, does not take Kant as the final word in philosophy. Fischer seems to be asserting the enduring values and relevance of his old Hegelianism.

Kritik der kantischen Philosophie is less a critique of Kant than a complete reinterpretation of him according to Fischer's Hegelian metaphysics. Fischer conceives Kant's philosophy as a metaphysics of freedom, according to which the noumenal substratum of appearances is the moral will, and the phenomenal world is the appearance of freedom. The Hegelian flavour of such a doctrine is unmistakable. Whether intentionally or not, Fischer had made Kant into the spokesman for a famous Hegelian doctrine: that the purpose behind nature and history is the self-consciousness of freedom. He had already affirmed that Hegelian doctrine in his *Diotima* in 1849; and he now reaffirmed it in 1883.

Fischer's reinterpretation of Kant is a "metaphysics" in a non-critical sense of the word because he maintains that it has not a regulative but a constitutive validity. In other words, he claims that we can know that the world *is* the appearance of freedom, and not only that we are obliged on moral grounds to think *as if* it were so. Even more remarkably, Fischer thinks that we are justified in assuming such knowledge on Kantian premises. If Kant were only consistent, he argues, he would have to accept the legitimacy of a Hegelian metaphysics.

How was Fischer led to such a radical reinterpretation of Kant? Part of the inspiration for his reinterpretation came from a philosopher who had much preoccupied

---

[66] Kuno Fischer, *Kritik der kantischen Philosophie*.

him in the 1860s and 1870s: Arthur Schopenhauer. The very title of Fischer's tract is reminiscent of Schopenhauer's famous appendix in *Die Welt als Wille und Vorstellung*.[67] Not surprisingly, Fischer devotes an entire section to discuss his agreement and disagreement with Schopenhauer's interpretation and critique of Kant (75–79). Fischer agrees with two fundamental theses of Schopenhauer's interpretation of Kant: 1) that transcendental idealism is the doctrine of the ideality of all appearances, that is, that appearances consist in representations; and 2) that Kant affirms the reality of the thing-in-itself, which is completely distinct from all appearances (78). More significantly, he also accepts Schopenhauer's fundamental thesis that the thing-in-itself appears to us as the will. Schopenhauer held that Kant had vaguely felt the truth of this doctrine, though he insisted that it was his achievement to have expressly formulated it and made it into a general metaphysical principle. Fischer, however, wants to deprive Schopenhauer of his claim to originality on this score. Kant, he insists, was not only aware of this doctrine but expressly teaches it (79). It is indeed the fundamental principle behind his own metaphysics. Kant knew exactly what he was doing, Fischer contends, when he identified things-in-themselves with ideas, ideas with purposes, purposes with decisions of the will, and the will with freedom (80). According to Kant's own teaching, the world is the appearance of purposiveness; and since purposiveness makes sense only through the concept of a will, the whole world should be seen as "the progressive revelation of freedom" (81).

The most crucial—and controversial—premise behind Fischer's reinterpretation is his identification of the thing-in-itself with the will. The premise is fully explicit: "The intelligible world is the world as will" (25; cf. 79, 92). The thesis is somewhat surprising, however, because there seems to be no reason to interpret the *entire* noumenal world in these terms. *Prima facie* the will is *one* thing-in-itself or noumenon; but that does not mean that it is *the* thing-in-itself, that it exhausts the entire world of noumena. Fischer argues, however, that this equation is central to Kant's attempt to unify the critical philosophy, to find a single basis for the worlds of nature and morality (49, 50, 79). It is well-known that in the third *Kritik* Kant had attempted to unify these worlds according to the idea of purposiveness (*Zweckmäßigkeit*), which demands that we treat the entire natural world as if it were created according to purposes. Fischer points out an important premise behind that attempt at synthesis: that we conceive of purposes according to human intentions (50, 81). We understand the self-organizing activity of living things in nature only according to human ends or purposes, which make sense to us only insofar as they are matters of choice or freedom. We simply have no other way of grasping their activity, Kant believes, except on the analogy of our own human intentionality and voluntary activity. If, therefore, we unite the realms of morality and nature according to purposiveness, and if we understand purposiveness according to human intentionality or the will, and if, finally, the will is the

---

[67] Arthur Schopenhauer, 'Kritik der kantischen Philosophie', 'Anhang' to *Die Welt als Wille und Vorstellung*, in *Sämtliche Werke*, I, 559–715.

domain of freedom, then the conclusion is inevitable: freedom becomes the key to understanding the entire world itself. We should understand all of nature and history as the self-realization of freedom.

There are, of course, many Kantian texts to provide support for such an interpretation. There is the concept of the final purpose of nature in §84 of the *Kritik der Urteilskraft*, which saw the realization of human morality as the highest end of nature. There is also the concept of world history in the 'Idee zur einer allgemeine Weltgeschichte', according to which the realization of human freedom is the very end of history itself. Finally, there is Kant's doctrine about the primacy of practical reason, which makes the noumenal will independent of phenomena but phenomena subordinate to the will (25–26). Fischer's interpretation of Kant came from texts like these, which he does not hesitate to cite. But the most important source for his reinterpretation of Kant is his long-standing view that Kant's philosophy was fundamentally a *"Entwicklungslehre"*, that is, a doctrine that everything in the world is subject to historical change and development. According to Fischer, Kant first conceived of this doctrine in his *Allgemeine Weltgeschichte und Theorie des Himmels*, and the doctrine persists throughout his philosophical development, appearing in his critical writings no less than his pre-critical ones (42). The idea of development makes no sense, however, without the concept of a purpose or end (48). Fischer argues that Kant has to extend this idea not only to living but also non-living beings, since it is only by this means that we can avoid dualism and have a single unified conception of the world (49).

Yet, however much these texts support Fischer, they still do not go far enough for him. For Kant would insist that we should give the idea of purposiveness a strictly regulative validity, which means that we should only treat nature and history *as if* they were governed according to ends. Kant always held himself back from the metaphysical doctrine that nature and history actually *are* only the appearances of freedom. Fischer believes, however, that Kant is not entirely consistent on this score, and that he progressively abandoned his regulative constraints with the development of his system (92–93). Though he insisted in the first *Kritik* that we cannot have knowledge of things-in-themselves, that restriction applied specifically to our *theoretical* knowledge. In the second *Kritik* Kant allowed for *practical* knowledge of things-in-themselves when he made consciousness of the moral law into the *ratio cognoscendi* of freedom (92). In the third *Kritik* Kant had developed a concept of appearance that makes no sense at all without granting knowledge of noumena, for there an appearance is not simply what appears to our senses, as in the first *Kritik*, but what manifests or develops a purpose (81–82). If we cannot know noumena, then we cannot know purposes, and so we cannot know that anything is in this sense an appearance. It is crucial for Kant to drop his regulative constraints, Fischer argues, for the simple reason that his own transcendental philosophy does not comply with them (82). If it were the case that we can know only appearances, then we cannot have knowledge of the conditions of knowledge, because these too do not fall within experience.

With his final essay on Kant, Fischer had reversed the position he had initially adopted in his 1852 *Logik und Metaphysik*. There Fischer had developed a Hegelian system "under the control of Kant", a "critical philosophy of identity". He had expounded the main principles of absolute idealism—the unity of self and nature, the organic structure of the world—though he had tried, in vain, to keep these doctrines within Kantian limits. Now, however, he had done just the opposite: he had created a Kantian system under the control of Hegel. For Fischer had now adopted the essentials of Kant's transcendental idealism—the ideality of space and time and the distinction between thing-in-itself and appearance—but insisted that such transcendental idealism reveals a much deeper metaphysical truth: that all reality is the appearance of freedom. Hence the Kantian Hegelian had become a Hegelian Kantian. In making Kant's philosophy utter this Hegelian truth, Fischer had revealed, once and for all, his deep and abiding Hegelian convictions.

6

Eduard Zeller, Neo-Kantian Classicist

1. Zeller and Fischer

Eduard Zeller is best known today for his *Outlines of the History of Greek Philosophy*,[1] a compendium which is still widely used as a quick introduction to classical philosophy. If it were not for the stiffness and awkwardness of the English prose, which belie a translation from German, one might assume the author was a penurious classics scholar eager to make a few bob from the sale of a potboiler. But Zeller was no ordinary scholar. He was not only an eminent 19th century philosophical historian but also a central figure in the revival of neo-Kantianism. No study of neo-Kantianism can afford to ignore him.

Zeller and Fischer were in many respects perfect counterparts. They were two of the greatest philosophical historians of their age. What Fischer was to modern philosophy, Zeller was to ancient. Just as, for generations, the standard work on the history of modern philosophy was Fischer's *Geschichte der modernen Philosophie*, so, even today, the standard work on the history of classical philosophy is Zeller's *Philosophie der Griechen*.[2] It could not have hindered the rise of Kant's stature in Germany that, from complementary historical perspectives, the two most eminent philosophical historians declared their allegiance to Kant. Whether seen from a classical or modern viewpoint, Kant seemed to be the saviour of German philosophy.

Though near contemporaries of equal stature, Zeller and Fischer met only late in their careers, and then only occasionally.[3] When Zeller went to Berlin in 1872, Fischer

---

[1] Eduard Zeller, *Outlines of the History of Greek Philosophy*, translated by S.F. Alleyne and Evelyn Abbott (London: Longmans, Green & Co., 1886). This was the first English translation of Zeller's *Grundriss der Geschichte der griechischen Philosophie* (Leipzig: Reisland, 1883). The translation has been reprinted at least fifteen times.

[2] For a contemporary assessment of Zeller's importance as a historian of classical philosophy, see *Eduard Zeller: Philosophie und Wissenschaftsgeschichte im 19. Jahrhundert*, ed. Gerald Hartung (Berlin: de Gruyter, 2010).

[3] When Zeller first met Fischer is unknown. There is no mention of their first meeting in their published correspondence or autobiographies. In his November 6, 1854 letter to Zeller, Strauß mentions his meetings with Fischer in Heidelberg, making it clear that Zeller has not yet met Fischer. See Strauß, *Ausgewählte Briefe von David Friedrich Strauß*, ed. Eduard Zeller (Bonn: Verlag von Emil Strauß, 1895), p. 334. Zeller mentions visiting Fischer in his August 8, 1905 letter to Hermann Diels, implying that the

became his successor in Heidelberg. For a while the two men were rivals for the post in Heidelberg, which Zeller eventually received only because Fischer turned it down.[4] Laden with honours and memories of glorious careers, the two men lived in retirement in Stuttgart, where Zeller would sometimes visit Fischer. Zeller, who lived to be a sprightly ninety-four, went to see Fischer in August 1905, only to be turned away from the door.[5] He was crushed to learn that Fischer, who was ten years younger, was so unwell and senescent that he could not receive guests.

For the revival of Kant in the 1860s, Zeller was of no less importance than Fischer. In the early 1860s both gave influential lectures calling for a return to Kant. Though there is no evidence of collaboration, their neo-Kantian programmes show remarkable parallels. Both contend that only Kant can solve the identity crisis of philosophy and save it from imminent obsolescence. Both argue that philosophy should be re-conceived as epistemology if it is to have its own place in the modern division of the sciences. And both see Kant's philosophy as the middle path between the rosy fantasies of speculative idealism and the grim realities of materialism. Their neo-Kantian paths would diverge only over one central issue: Zeller supported Trendelenburg in his famous dispute with Fischer.[6]

Not the least respect in which Zeller and Fischer are counterparts concerns their early backgrounds. Both were Hegelians in their early careers. Both wrote for Arnold Ruge's *Jahrbücher*; both were close friends of David Friedrich Strauß, who had a decisive influence in shaping their early theological views; and both shared a common fate in suffering persecution for their left-Hegelian pantheism. The stories behind their conversions to Kant are, however, very different. While Fischer, as we have seen, never became a complete convert and never fully renounced his Hegelianism, Zeller became a total disciple and abandoned his Hegelianism entirely.

The story of Zeller's conversion to Kant is of great interest to us as students of the history of neo-Kantianism. Why, exactly, did Zeller abandon Hegel? And why did he convert to Kant? Given Zeller's importance for neo-Kantianism, the answers to these questions should shed some light on the origins of the movement. Yet it is precisely here that the historical record proves to be very obscure. Nowhere in his published correspondence or in his writings does Zeller himself offer an explanation. We have to reconstruct the history from the few clues available to us. A large part of our task in this chapter will be to retrace Zeller's intellectual development and to show how he was led away from Hegel and towards Kant. We will then examine Zeller's major writings on Kant.

---

two have already met. See *Hermann Diels, Hermann Usener, Eduard Zeller, Briefwechsel*, ed. Dietrich Ehlers (Berlin: Akademie Verlag, 1992), II, 94.

[4] On their rivalry for the post in Heidelberg, see Heinrich von Sybel to Zeller, June 21, 1860, in *Heinrich von Sybel and Eduard Zeller, Briefwechsel (1849–1895)* ed. Margret Lemberg (Marburg: N.G. Elwert Verlag, 2004), p. 296.

[5] See Zeller to Diels, August 8, 1905, in *Diels, Usener, Zeller Briefwechsel*, II, 362.

[6] On Zeller's position in this dispute, see Section 6, in this chapter.

2. Early Tübingen Years

Eduard Zeller, the eighth of nine children, was born January 22, 1814, in the village of Kleinbottwar in Swabia.[7] Though descending from a long line of Protestant clergy, his father, Johann Heinrich Zeller, was a minor civil servant in Kleinbottwar. At a very early age Zeller learned classical languages, and already at eight showed a proficiency in ancient Greek, a talent which would serve him well for his later work on classical philosophy. When still very young Zeller decided, in accord with family tradition, to study theology for a career in the church. And so, in October 1827, after finishing primary school, he went straight to the evangelical seminary at Maulbronn. It was during his Maulbronn years that he first met a figure who would later play a fateful role in his life: David Friedrich Strauß (1808–1874).[8] A temporary teacher at the seminary, Strauß recognized Zeller's precocious talents, little knowing then how fate would later intertwine him with his student.

In autumn 1831 Zeller went to the *Tübinger Stift*, the fabled Protestant seminary, where, nearly half a century earlier, Schelling, Hegel and Hölderlin had been students. There Zeller was the student of Ferdinand Baur (1792–1860), who had joined the *Stift* in 1826.[9] Baur was the father of the Tübingen critical school of theology, whose aim was to apply the new historical methods to the study of early Christianity and the Bible. An imposing yet beloved teacher, Baur soon became the decisive figure in Zeller's intellectual development. According to Dilthey, "the ideal of Zeller's life" was "to appropriate, support and continue [Baur's] researches."[10] The closeness of Zeller to Baur was such that, in 1847, he married Baur's daughter.

For his four years of study at the *Stift*, Zeller had to study philosophy for the first three semesters. In his first semester he read Plato's *Republic* and Kant's *Kritik der reinen Vernunft*, chosing as his first essay topic Kant's distinction between phenomena and noumena.[11] Already in these semesters Zeller had acquired a thorough grounding in classical German philosophy, reading the major writings of Kant, Fichte, Schelling, Jacobi and Hegel.[12] Another early essay, written in the Summer

---

[7] On Zeller's biography, see first and foremost his autobiography, *Erinnerungen eines Neunzigjährigen* (Stuttgart: Uhland, 1908). See also Hermann Diels, *Gedächtnisrede auf Eduard Zeller* (Berlin: Akademie der Wissenschaften, 1908); and Wilhelm Dilthey, 'Aus Eduard Zellers Jugendjahren', in *Gesammelte Schriften* (Leipzig: Teubner, 1921) IV, 432–450.

[8] For two excellent introductions to Strauß, see John Edward Toews, *Hegelianism* (Cambridge: Cambridge University Press, 1980), pp. 255–287; and William Brazill, *The Young Hegelians* (New Haven, CT: Yale University Press, 1970), pp. 95–132.

[9] On Baur, see Zeller's own account, 'Ferdinand Christian Baur', in *Vorträge und Abhandlungen*, II, 354–355, 434; and Dilthey, 'Ferdinand Christian Baur', in *Gesammelte Schriften* IV, 403–432.

[10] Dilthey, 'Aus Zellers Jugendjahre', p. 438.

[11] Zeller, *Erinnerungen*, p. 73. The title of the essay was 'Darstellung und Beurteilung der Lehre von den Phänomenen und Noumenen in Kants Kritik der reinen Vernunft'. This essay was in Zeller's literary remains when they were classified by Otto Leuze in his 'Chronologisches Verzeichnis der literarischen Arbeiten Eduard Zellers', in Volume III of his edition of *Eduard Zellers Kleine Schriften* (Berlin: Reimer, 1910–1911), III, 522.

[12] See the items listed in Leuze, 'Verzeichnis', III, 522–523.

Semester of 1832, was on the development of transcendental idealism after Kant, which, according to his tutor, "left nothing to be desired" for its historical accuracy and philosophical insight.[13] Zeller says that in those early days he had not heard the name Schopenhauer, and that he knew about but had little interest in Herbart.[14]

Zeller's main philosophy teacher at the *Stift* was the very man who once briefly taught him at the Maulbronn seminary: David Friedrich Strauß. In May 1832, Strauß, a graduate at the *Stift*, had become an instructor there. He had just spent the winter of 1831–32 in Berlin, where he had attended Hegel's last lectures. Strauß introduced Zeller not only to Plato and Schleiermacher but also to Hegel, who was then hardly known at his *alma mater*. A self-confessed Hegelian, Strauß took extra pains to explain the intricacies of Hegel's system in plain and simple language to his young students. A close friendship developed between Strauß and Zeller, a bond strong enough to last for the rest of their lives. Though Zeller was intellectually and personally closer to Baur,[15] he would support Strauß throughout all the dramas and struggles of his later career. He eventually became Strauß's biographer and the editor of his correspondence.[16]

After the completion of his studies in 1836, Zeller, following a *Stift* tradition, received a stipend for a *Wanderjahr*. Following in Strauß's footsteps, he decided to make a pilgrimage to Berlin, then the centre of theological and philosophical studies in Germany. Though Hegel and Schleiermacher were now dead, Zeller thought that he could at least learn from Hegel's disciples. So, well supplied with introductions from Strauß, he duly met the leaders of the Hegelian school: Karl Michelet (1801–1893), Phillip Marheineke (1780–1846), Eduard Gans (1797–1839) and Leopold Henning (1791–1806). He also met an old friend of Strauß, Wilhelm Vatke (1806–82), who managed to arrange for him a tea with Hegel's widow.

In the summer of 1837 Zeller returned to his Swabian homeland, where he began his clerical career by preaching in rural districts. But the lure of academic life proved too great for him. By 1839 he had returned to his *alma mater*, first as a *Repetent* (i.e. a tutor) and then in 1840 as a *Privatdozent*. The early years as a *Dozent* in Tübingen were Zeller's halcyon days. It was during these years that he formed a close intellectual circle with other Baur students—Christian Märklin (1807–1849), Friedrich Vischer (1807–1887), Albert Schwegler (1819–1857), Gottlieb Planck (1819–1880), and Ernst Rapp (1806–1879)—to discuss philosophy, theology and politics. This circle shared common philosophical, theological and political views, which could be loosely described as moderate to left of centre Hegelianism.[17] Together, they created

---

[13] Diels, *Gedächtnisrede*, p. 7. 'Über die historische Entwicklung des transcendentalen Idealismus'. See Leuze, 'Verzeichnis', p. 522.

[14] Zeller, *Erinnerungen*, p. 73.

[15] Dilthey, 'Aus Zellers Jugendjahre', p. 439, remarks that Zeller's own work followed Baur more than Strauß.

[16] See Eduard Zeller, *David Friedrich Strauss* (Bonn: Verlag von Emil Strauss, 1874); and Strauss, *Ausgewählte Briefe von David Friedrich Strauss* (Bonn: Verlag von Emil Strauss, 1895).

[17] See Dilthey's description of their general views in 'Aus Zellers Jugendjahren', p. 440.

two journals to serve as mouthpieces for their views, the *Jahrbücher der Gegenwart*,[18] which was edited by Schwegler, and the *Theologische Jahrbücher*,[19] which was edited by Zeller himself.

That the young Zeller was something of a Hegelian there cannot be any doubt.[20] He was a frequent contributor to Arnold Ruge's *Hallische Jahrbücher*, a Young Hegelian journal begun in 1837 but supressed in 1841, and to Schwegler's *Jahrbücher der Gegenwart*, a more moderate replacement for Ruge's journal.[21] Zeller's allegiance to Hegel is made plain from a letter Strauss wrote to him in February 1844, praising Zeller for his respectful attitude towards "our old master" and for not treating him, like so many upstart youths, "like a dead dog".[22] "Our old master" meant, of course, Hegel. Strauss was referring to Zeller's recent treatment of Hegel in his *Philosophie der Griechen*, where he defended Hegel's history of philosophy against Fries' objections.[23]

Yet the question remains: *How much* of a Hegelian was the young Zeller? Unlike Fischer, he was never a died-in-the-wool disciple, and already by the mid-1840s he had developed a critical distance towards Hegel. In his *Philosophie der Griechen*, the very text Strauß praises for having a respectful attitude towards their "old master", Zeller is careful to expound a method that is *not* strictly Hegelian, and that is indeed partially *anti*-Hegelian. He recommends a method that *combines* the speculative with the historical, and he is very wary of the dangers of an entirely speculative method: the invention of arbitrary constructions, the imposition of a priori schemata on the subject matter. While Zeller approves the Hegelian practice of tracing "the organic development of thought", "the connection of the systems", he does not think that this should come from above but only from below, from dwelling in the particularities of the facts of history (v, 7–8). In suggesting these criticisms of Hegel, Zeller was endorsing the common complaints made against his methodology by the historical school. It is also noteworthy that though Zeller advises the philosophical historian to determine "the organic development of thought", he does not identify this concern with Hegel alone. While Hegel was its most conspicuous protagonist, Zeller finds the same concern in the work of Schleiermacher, Ritter and Hermann (2).

---

[18] Albert Schwegler, ed., *Jährbücher der Gegenwart* (Tübingen: Fues, 1843–1847). 6 vols.

[19] Eduard Zeller, ed., *Theologische Jahrbücher* (Tübingen: Fues, 1842–1857). 16 vols.

[20] In his autobiography, *Erinnerungen* p. 76, Zeller writes of Strauß and his early Hegelianism: "Our young twenty-four year old teacher was not Hegel's critic but his apostle; but exactly for that reason he was very welcome for us. We needed a philosophy we could enthuse about, a world of thought in which we could live; the question whether we could stay within it, whether and how we could improve upon it, naturally could only be raised later. The time for the independent examination of the Hegelian system still had not come for us or Strauß."

[21] See Albert Schwegler's 'Das preußische Cultusministerium und die Hegel'sche Schule', *Jahrbücher der Gegenwart* (Tübingen: Fues, 1845), 1–13. See also Zeller's account of the origin of this journal in *Erinnerungen*, p. 136.

[22] See Strauß to Zeller, February 8, 1844, *Ausgewählte Briefe*, p. 156.

[23] Eduard Zeller, *Die Philosophie der Griechen. Eine Untersuchung über Charakter, Gang und Hauptmomente ihre Entwicklung* (Tübingen: Fues, 1844), pp. 6–8.

The programme behind Zeller's *Theologische Jahrbücher* was also far from a strictly Hegelian enterprise. In his early 1846 article 'Die Theologie der Gegenwart',[24] his account of all the theological schools of his day, Zeller does take a stand on behalf of what he calls "speculative theology", which was the usual term for the Hegelian version of the discipline. But it soon becomes clear that he does not mean anything particularly Hegelian by this phrase. He defines "speculative theology" as the attempt to explain religion from the universal essence of mind, which could hardly be described as a unique or characteristic Hegelian enterprise (19). Although Zeller praises Hegel's philosophy for providing the most up-to-date form of such theology, and even for having taken it a step further than Schleiermacher, he does not identify speculative theology with Hegel alone. He says that the same enterprise was carried on by Schleiermacher;[25] and he even imagines a progression beyond Hegel that might realize more fully the ideal of a speculative theology (20). What form that progression might take he does not explain.

That Zeller was already taking decisive steps away from Hegel in the mid-1840s is fully apparent from some other articles in his *Theologische Jahrbücher*. In an article on the nature of religion,[26] Zeller shows himself to be highly critical of Hegel's philosophy of religion, which he finds much too intellectualistic. By identifying religion with a stage of consciousness, the representation of the infinite, Hegel came close to reducing it down to a mental attitude, neglecting its practical side in ritual and moral conduct (55–64). And in an article on freedom of will,[27] Zeller, in self-conscious opposition to Hegel's and Schleiermacher's determinism, defends the concept of freedom as the power to choose, the ability to decide and act otherwise. Such freedom requires the possibility of contingency, a possibility that Hegel denies (394, 444). For Hegel, contingency is possible only from the standpoint of reflection, which cannot know entirely all the causes behind an event (393). Significantly, in defending freedom in this sense, Zeller had already broke decidedly with the monism and determinism of Hegel's pantheistic worldview.

Yet, despite his growing distance from Hegel, the young Zeller was no closer to Kant. He was just as critical of Kant's philosophy of religion, which committed the opposite error of Hegel's: in reducing religion down to morals, Kant saw its practical but not its intellectual side.[28] Although Zeller's position on freedom would seem to bring him closer to Kant, who had famously defended freedom of choice, Zeller explicitly rejects Kant's theory of freedom (433, 437–438).[29] Zeller does not think that

---

[24] Eduard Zeller, 'Die Theologie der Gegenwart und die theologische Jahrbücher', *Theologische Jahrbücher* V (1846), 1–28.

[25] In an earlier essay he had even called Schleiermacher "the founder of speculative theology". See Zeller, 'Erinnerung an Schleiermachers Lehre von der Persönlichkeit Gottes', *Theologische Jahrbücher* I (1842), 284.

[26] Eduard Zeller, 'Ueber das Wesen der Religion', *Theologische Jahrbücher* IV (1845), 26–75, 393–430.

[27] Eduard Zeller, 'Ueber die Freiheit des menschlichen Willens, das Böse und die moralische Weltordnung', *Theologische Jahrbücher* V (1846), 384–447.

[28] Zeller, 'Ueber das Wesen der Religion', pp. 40, 42.

[29] Here I take issue with Dilthey, who, in his 'Aus Zellers Jugendjahren' p. 447, suggests that Zeller's move away from Hegel towards Kant came with his early articles on freedom of the will. These articles

we can harmonize moral choice with natural necessity, as Kant had, and he attempts to make them compatible by arguing that the general laws of nature are valid only *en masse* but not in all particular cases (398, 439). So, for Zeller, unlike Fischer, affirming freedom of choice was no reason to return to Kant.

Zeller's distance from Kant in the 1840s leaves us with the question of why he became a Kantian at all. Obviously, we still have a lot of explaining to do. The answer lies with another crucial aspect of Zeller's early intellectual career, one which we must now examine in detail: his project of historical criticism. It was only through the thorny thickets of historical criticism that the young Zeller would discover the path towards Königsberg.

3. Historical Criticism

The core of Zeller's intellectual life during his later Tübingen years (1844–1847) revolved around Baur's project of historical criticism. The circle that formed around Baur later became known as the "Tübingen historical school", or more simply as "the Tübingen school" or "the critical school". Zeller played a pivotal role in its organization and development as the founder and chief editor of its common journal, the *Theologische Jahrbücher*.[30] Since this project was so crucial to Zeller's intellectual development, we need to examine it in a little detail.

Fortunately, the best account of the Tübingen school, at least for our purposes, is that provided by Zeller himself, who wrote a long retrospective article about it in 1859 for the *Historische Zeitschrift*.[31] What was fundamental to, and characteristic of, the Tübingen school, Zeller informs us, was its methodology, its manner of treating sacred texts strictly as historical documents, that is, as writings produced by human beings under particular social, historical and cultural circumstances (268). This meant laying aside the traditional orthodox assumption that the Bible was the product of supernatural inspiration, as if everything it said had divine authority. The method of the Tübingen school, as Zeller describes it, was that of historical criticism, pure and simple. Such criticism consists in the rigorous examination of the evidence behind historical texts to determine their authorship and accuracy, so that we accept or reject what a text states about the past strictly according to the degree of evidence for or against it. The origins of this methodology lay with the new critical history

---

indeed take him away from Hegel but not towards Kant. Dilthey ignores the crucial fact that in these articles Zeller explicitly repudiates Kant's theory of freedom.

[30] Zeller alone edited the *Theologische Jahrbücher* for its first six years; thereafter it was co-edited with Baur.

[31] Eduard Zeller, 'Die Tübinger historische Schule', *Historische Zeitschrift* IV (1860), 90–173. The article was reproduced in *Vorträge und Abhandlungen* (Leipzig: Fues Verlag, 1865), I, 267–353, which is the edition cited in parentheses above. In the 'Vorwort' Zeller states that this article was written in 1859. Zeller also gave an earlier account of historical criticism, 'Ueber historische Kritik und ihre Anwendung auf die christlichen Religionsurkunden', *Theologische Jahrbücher* V (1846), 288–321.

formed in the early 1800s by Barthold Niebuhr (1776–1831) and Leopold Ranke (1795–1886). Niebuhr had applied the method to Roman history in his *Römische Geschichte* (1811–1812), and Ranke had done the same to early modern history in his *Geschichte der germanischen und romanischen Völker* (1824). The programme of the Tübingen school was simply to extend that method to sacred history. This was indeed just how Zeller himself viewed the origins of the historical school when he wrote in the final sentence of his article: "Its ruling principles are only the same as those that have governed all German historical writing outside theology since Niebuhr and Ranke" (353).

Zeller stresses two additional features of historical criticism. First, it is meant to be entirely "free" or "radical", that is, it lays aside all theological presuppositions or ecclesiastical guidelines, and it takes its method to its ultimate conclusions, whatever the consequences for church and dogma. Hence, in the forward to the *Theologische Jahrbücher*, Zeller vows to devote his journal to the ideals of "free enquiry", "the freedom and consistency of thought" independent of all confessional loyalties.[32] This means, as he later put it, that dogma should follow critique, not critique dogma (268). Second, historical critique is intended to be "scientific". This means that it adopts the general scientific view of the world, that is, it accepts the universal validity of the laws of nature discovered by the empirical sciences. It assumes that natural laws hold without exception, that the laws true for the universe now were also so in the past, so that testimony about the extraordinary and abnormal has little or no probability. Such a method, when applied rigorously to the Bible, immediately renders suspect its entire supernatural dimension, all its prophecies and miracles. Perfectly aware of this consequence, Zeller himself insisted on this naturalism, which he saw as integral to the scientific status of criticism; he indeed admitted that there could be no compromise between it and the supernaturalism of the Bible: "Belief in miracles and critique are two things that exclude one another" (299).[33]

Zeller was eager to distinguish historical criticism from two older forms of Biblical interpretation. Following his account, the Tübingen programme differs from not only Protestant orthodoxy, which saw the Bible as a divinely inspired document, but also from the old rationalism of the Enlightenment, which read the Bible as if its content were entirely rational and written by philosophers. The theologians of the Enlightenment had attempted to tone down the supernatural dimension of the Bible by interpreting its language about inspiration, miracles and prophecies in terms of symbols for moral and metaphysical truths, viz., the snake speaking to Eve, or the devil appearing to Jesus, were parables about inner spiritual conflicts. The chief problem with this rationalism, Zeller maintains, is that it was not sufficiently historical or critical. Although it had questioned whether the events narrated in the Bible are supernatural, it never doubted that these events occurred (273). Rather than

---

[32] See 'Vorwort' to the first volume, *Theologische Jahrbücher* I (1842), v.
[33] Zeller was forced to defend his view of miracles espoused here. See Zeller, 'Die historische Kritik und das Wunder', *Historische Zeitschrift* VI (1861), 356–373.

interpreting texts in their historical context and trying to understand them in the authors' terms, the rationalists imposed their own constructions on the text, giving them a metaphysical or moral meaning never intended by their authors. It had assumed that the authors of the Bible were like modern *Aufklärer* or free-thinkers who were writing parables for the people in poetic and ornate language; once placed in their historical context, however, it becomes clear that these authors actually believed their prophecies and miracles.

Zeller also distinguishes the Tübingen school from two trends of contemporary theology: a tepid rationalism, which dares not take its criticism far enough, and a mellow orthodoxy, which softens its belief in the supernatural by making piecemeal concessions to rationalism (274).[34] Thus a theology of "timid compromise" has become the order of the day, Zeller complains. He insists that neither Schleiermacher nor Hegel have done much to change this sad state of affairs. Neither were sufficiently critical or historical because they never really challenged the sacred texts. Thus Schleiermacher's dogmatics began with the assumption of "the basic mystery of Christ", while the Hegelians simply accepted the claims to revelation in the Bible because their only interest was casting them in terms of the speculative concept (274–275).[35] In foisting all kinds of dialectical constructions on the text, the Hegelians proved themselves no better than their rationalist forbears.

For Zeller, the culmination of the historical criticism of the Tübingen school came with David Friedrich Strauß's *Das Leben Jesu*.[36] Taking the programme of radical criticism to its ultimate limits, Strauß came to the conclusion that all the narratives in the Bible are false if they are taken as straightforward accounts of supernatural events. Strauß found inconsistencies in the testimony of the four gospels; and he was rigorous in applying the standards of ordinary induction to the texts, coming to the unsurprising conclusion that it was improbable that any miracles ever occurred. Strauß denied, however, that these stories were the product of self-conscious deception on the part of a conspiracy of priests—the old account of the free-thinkers—and instead explained them as myths. Myth was the central theme of Strauß's book, the concept he invoked to replace the reason of the rationalists and the inspiration of the orthodox. According to Zeller, Strauß made three central claims about myth: 1) it is poetry, not history; 2) it is the work not of an individual alone but of an entire community; and 3) it is not a legend created by the imagination but a story serving practical and dogmatic interests (278). In short, myths are "Christian folktales" (*Volkssage*), though folktales created for religious interests (278). The interests of the early Christians were

[34] See also Zeller's account in 'Die Theologie der Gegenwart und die theologischen Jahrbücher', in *Theologische Jahrbücher* V (1846), 1–28, esp. p. 9.
[35] In an earlier article, Zeller had accused the Hegelians of designing their dialectic so that it would prove Christian dogmatics. See his 'Ueber das Verhältniß der Theologie zur Wissenschaft und zur Kirche', *Theologische Jahrbücher* IX (1850), 93–110, esp. 99.
[36] David Friedrich Strauß, *Das Leben Jesu, kritisch bearbeitet* (Tübingen: C.F. Osiander, 1835).

twofold: to glorify Christ; and to demonstrate that the Judaic prophecies about the messiah had been fulfilled.

Although he saw Strauß's book as the epitome of the Tübingen school, Zeller himself was far from endorsing it entirely. Like Baur, he felt that the book was much too negative and much too polemical. After demolishing all the narratives of the Bible, Strauß had made no effort to construct a more truthful history (279–282). Zeller was also critical of the Hegelian assumptions behind Strauß's concept of religion, which understood religion in a much too theoretical manner.[37] Strauß wrote as if the ancient prophets and apostles were want-to-be Hegelian philosophers! Still, despite these reservations, Zeller stood by the negative teachings of Strauß's book, which he regarded as indisputable and epochal. Although one could quarrel with Strauß on particular points, one could not contest his general scepticism about the old Protestant dogma of the literal truth of the Bible (277–278). Thanks largely to Strauß, Zeller came to the conclusion that the entire worldview of the Christian church—its concept of revelation, its principle that salvation came with faith alone—could no longer be accepted in the modern age.[38] Although Zeller was worried about "the nihilism" of a completely negative critique, and although he demanded nothing less than "a complete reconstruction" of theology, he made few positive suggestions about how to avoid this nihilism or what this new theology should be. One thing alone was entirely clear to him: that after Strauß there could be no going back to the past.

Seen from a broader historical perspective, the historical criticism of the Tübingen school was the result of three powerful historical influences. One was the historical criticism of Niebuhr and Ranke, as we have already seen. Another influence was Spinoza, whose naturalist biblical criticism was the precedent for Strauß. Last but not least, there was Kant. While Zeller never mentions Spinoza, probably because he still remained so controversial, he does not hesitate to acknowledge, on two different occasions, his debts to the sage of Königsberg. At the close of 'Die Theologie der Gegenwart' Zeller states expressly that the standpoint of criticism of the historical school grew out of the Kantian Copernican Revolution (27); and in the beginning of his article 'Ueber das Wesen der Religion' he claims that only since Kant based philosophy on human self-consciousness has it been possible to explain the place of religion in the general economy of mental life (28). In stressing the importance of Kant for the Tübingen school, Zeller was *inter alia* alluding to Kant's Transcendental Dialectic. The disposition to hypostasize concepts, which Kant saw as the fundamental fallacy behind rationalism, the Tübingen school found in myth. Just as the doctrines of the rationalist metaphysician (viz. the simplicity of the soul) are hypostasizations, so the objects of myth are the products of the religious consciousness, which subconsciously objectifies its own creations into powers ruling over it.

---

[37] See Zeller, 'Ueber das Wesen der Religion', *Theologische Jahrbücher*, IV (1845), 26–75, esp. 66.
[38] Zeller, 'Die Theologie der Gegenwart', p. 20.

Whatever the reasons behind it, Zeller's tendency to identify the project of historical criticism with Kant was significant for his emerging neo-Kantianism. It meant that Zeller already understood himself to be engaging in a Kantian project in the mid-1840s, a period in his career which is usually understood to be Hegelian. So the neo-Kantianism Zeller will later announce in the early 1860s did not spring fully born out of the head of Medusa. It had been gestating ever since his Tübingen days.

4. From Hegel to Kant

In discussing Zeller's early critical project it seems we have gone a long way around the barn. For how does this bring us closer to understanding his neo-Kantianism? Although Zeller understood this project in Kantian terms, this was still not enough to make a Kantian out of him. After all, in the mid-1840s, Zeller was as critical of Kant as Hegel. What then happened to push Zeller closer to Kant and further from Hegel? We can answer this question only by going further *through* and not *around* Zeller's early Tübingen years. For it was only by following what happened with his project of radical criticism during these years that we can begin to understand why Zeller finally became disillusioned with Hegel and embraced Kant.

Zeller's first official public declaration of his neo-Kantianism appears in his 1862 Heidelberg Inaugural lecture, 'Ueber Bedeutung und Aufgabe der Erkenntnistheorie', which we will examine closely in Section 6. Suffice it to say for now that Zeller begins his lecture with a denunciation of Hegel's logic for its confusion of the form and content of knowledge, for its illusion that we can generate content from thinking alone. The great strength of Kant over Hegel, Zeller contends, is that he avoided such confusion and illusion with his distinctions between form and content, understanding and sensibility. What was decisive for Zeller's move away from Hegel and towards Kant, then, was his endorsement of these Kantian dualisms. So the crucial question is: What led Zeller to affirm these dualisms?

The answer ultimately lies with Strauß's and Zeller's experience with historical criticism, with their motives for adopting it and the conclusions they drew from it. Back in the early 1830s, when Strauß first attended the lectures of Hegel's disciples in Berlin, he was struck by their naive assumptions in translating the representations of religion into the conceptual terms of Hegel's system.[39] Rather than subjecting the claims to revelation in the Bible to criticism, the young Hegelians—Marheineke, Gabler and Göschel—simply accepted them at their face value; and so, in translating them into philosophical terms, they were attributing a conceptual necessity and eternal validity to what might prove to be, in the light of historial criticism, a simple falsehood. Determined to avoid such an embarrassing fallacy, Strauß insisted that one must first subject the Biblical record to historical criticism; only *after* determining the

---

[39] For a fuller account of Strauß's early days in Berlin, see Toews, *Hegelianism*, pp. 255–287, esp. 256–259.

authenticity and reliability of a claim to revelation could one begin to reconstruct it in philosophical terms. But Strauβ's subsequent investigations into the Biblical record had come to such an overwhelmingly negative verdict—that all the claims to revelation in the Bible were myths, having no historical foundation at all—that there was no justification for a translation of revelation into conceptual terms. The net result of Strauβ's historical criticism left him staring at what he called "a great chasm, a deep ditch filled with the dragons and monsters of doubt and despair".[40] This was his way of referring to Lessing's famous "broad and ugly ditch" between the facts of history and the truths of reason. The only way to get across that chasm, it now seemed, was through "a leap of faith", Jacobi's famous *salto mortale*.

These results of historical criticism were very bad news for a Hegelian. They meant that the Hegelian dialectic could not bridge the gulf between history and reason after all. The dialectic is an engine designed to cross Lessing's ditch: it would, if all went to plan, show how the contradictions in the realm of finitude, which is the sphere of the particular and contingent, are resolved in the realm of the infinite, which is the sphere of the universal and necessity. Applied to religious experience, the dialectic is supposed to transform the particular and contingent representations of religious experience into the universal and necessary concepts of the system of philosophy. While some aspects of religious representations are to be cancelled, others are to be preserved, in that wondrous transformative process known as *Aufhebung*. While the dialectic has its moment of "negativity", that is, the contradictions inherent in the realm of finite experience, it is also supposed to have a "positive result", that is, the transformation of the particular and contingent representations of religion into universal and necessary thoughts. But the dialectical engine stalls, shutting down right in front of the ditch it is supposed to cross. For the result of Strauβ's historical criticism is that there is really no solid spot to jump from; the alleged facts of Biblical revelation are not really facts at all. Hence the dialectic ends, to put it in Hegelian terms, in "abstract negativity" alone, because the content of religious belief is completely cancelled. It leaves us still standing before Lessing's ditch, that yawning gap between the particular and contingent realm of finite experience and the universal and necessary realm of thought.

That the young Zeller realized the impact of these results for the Hegelian dialectic there cannot be any doubt. We have already seen how he endorsed the negative results of Strauβ's historical criticism, and how he criticized the Hegelians for naively accepting the Biblical record. But Zeller had gone much further than this: he explicitly criticized the whole procedure of the Hegelian dialectic. In an important article in the *Theologische Jahrbücher*, 'Ueber das Wesen der Religion',[41] he argued that the dialectic is much too reductivist (412–413). We could indeed translate religious experience into the realm of thought, just as we could distil the main thought behind

---

[40]   Strauss to Käferle, January 17, 1836, *Ausgewählte Briefe*, p. 18.
[41]   Zeller, 'Ueber das Wesen der Religion', *Theologische Jahrbücher* IV (1845), 26–75, 393–430.

a poem into prose. But who would claim that the experience of the poem is noth-ing but the thought? Like Kierkegaard, who came to similar conclusions around the same time, Zeller stressed how religion is essentially about an individual's unique and personal experience with God, a dimension left behind by the Hegelian dialectic (399, 404, 409). Most important of all, though, Zeller claimed that the translation of religious representation into philosophical concept is impossible in principle because it requires bridging a gulf between two completely distinct realms (65). The religious representation is in the realm of the unique and temporal; the philosophical concept is in the realm of the universal and eternal. Since they are completely opposed to one another, how could one be transformed into the other? How could the unique and temporal become the universal and eternal? It could be only through a total negation or self-contradiction. What the collapse of the dialectic means, as Zeller puts it, is "the opposition between transcendence and immanence" (65).

We can now see why, already by 1845, Zeller was ready to break with Hegel and side with Kant on the all-important question of the relationship between form and con-tent, thought and sensibility. The Hegelian dialectic could not bridge these dualisms. The most severe examination of the particular, contingent and temporal domain of experience had failed to identify the alleged common content between religion and philosophy, which had been the main presupposition of the Hegelian dialectic. There just was no such content.[42] Kant, it seemed, had good reasons for his dualisms after all. Rather than trying to leap beyond Lessing's ditch, the old fox of Königsberg wisely chose to recognize its existence. It was this Kantian lesson that Zeller had learned in the mid-1840s, I suggest, that became the decisive factor in pushing him down the road towards his later neo-Kantianism.

5. Running the Gauntlet, Tübingen to Heidelberg

Zeller's career began under an unlucky star. The so-called *Vormärz* period, the years between the Revolutions of 1830 and 1848, which roughly coincided with those between Zeller's entry into the *Stift* and his first professorship, were notable as a period of political reaction and conservatism. Eager to prevent revolution in their German homeland, conservative forces—the princes, nobility and clergy—did eve-rything in their power to guard their prerogative and privileges, especially by con-trolling the press and universities. In 1835 these forces were suddenly mobilized by the appearance of Strauß's *Das Leben Jesu*, which hit the public, to use Zeller's phrase, "like a bombshell".[43] Strauß's book seemed to confirm all the conservative's worst fears about radical criticism and left-wing Hegelianism. In attacking the historical

---

[42] In his 1850 article 'Ueber das Verhältnis der Theologie zur Wissenschaft und zur Kirche', pp. 101–103, Zeller questions the whole Hegelian doctrine of identity of content throughout change of form in reli-gious representation. What is represented in religion is claimed to be inseparable from its form.

[43] Zeller, *Erinnerungen*, p. 100.

testimony behind the Bible, Strauß was undermining the very basis of the Protestant faith, and with it the alliance of throne and altar. Somehow, sooner rather than later, this Schwabian "Anti-Christ" would have to be crucified.

The hysterical reaction against Strauß spread rapidly throughout Germany, quickly reaching even sleepy Tübingen. The first victim was Strauß himself, who was peremptorily dismissed from his post in the *Stift*. Now everyone in Strauß's circle also stood under suspicion, and they would have to be careful about all they said, wrote or taught. Zeller himself began to feel the heat in 1840 when he gave some lectures on dogmatics to replace another theology professor. For simply stating his sympathy with Strauß, he was censured by conservatives in the theology faculty.[44] The censure was a rude shock to Zeller, who now feared that that no Hegelian or Straußian would ever be promoted in Schwabia. Subsequent events were only to confirm this bleak forecast. When, in 1842, the theological faculty applied to the Ministry of Education for Zeller's promotion as an extraordinary professor, the request was flatly denied. And when, in 1844, they applied for his promotion in philosophy instead of theology, that too was bluntly refused. Zeller was not alone in such misfortunes. None of Baur's students were promoted, and some were simply dismissed.[45]

The new winds of 1848 brought the prospects of redemption. Not, however, from anywhere on German soil, but from Switzerland, where a friend of Zeller's, Friedrich Ries, had secured an offer for him as extraordinary professor of theology at Bern.[46] Having no other options, Zeller accepted the offer from Bern without hesitation, January 16, 1847. But at first it seemed Zeller would get the same reception in Bern that Strauß once received in Zurich. When Strauß was offered a position in Zurich in 1839, the outcry was so great among the clergy and general public that the city council was forced to back down and to retire their just-appointed professor at half-salary. The Strauß affair threatened to repeat itself with Zeller, because the conservative clergy in Bern raised a clamour and organized a campaign against the *"Zeller Religionsgefahr"*.[47] The conservative motion to have Zeller's appointment revoked was defeated, however, by the deft political manoeuvres of the new radical government in Bern.[48] Still, such was the animosity stirred by Zeller's appointment that there were fears for his safety, so that the government found it necessary to provide him with police protection.

---

[44] On this incident, see Diels, *Gedächtnisrede,* p. 16.
[45] Hartung, 'Leben und Werk' in *Zeller,* p. 3; Dilthey, 'Aus Zellers Jugendjahre', p. 449.
[46] On Zeller's appointment in Berne, see Diels, *Gedächtnisrede,* pp. 24–25.
[47] The case against Zeller's appointment was argued by C. Baggesen, the Archdeacon of Münster at Bern, in his *Bedenken gegen die Berufung des Herrn Dr. Eduard Zeller an eine theologische Professur* (Bern: Stämpflichsche Verlagsbuchhandlung, 1847). Baggesen's tract was not a screed against Zeller but a careful examination of his writings to demonstrate how they fell short of Christian orthodoxy. Baggesen objected to Zeller's Hegelian pantheism (32, 34), his critique of the historical foundations of the faith (48–49), and his claim that the unity of the infinite and finite was not realized solely in the person of Christ (64).
[48] On these events, see Zeller, *Erinnerungen,* pp. 152–153.

Eventually, 1848 brought change to Germany too. The University of Marburg, once a provincial backwater, had a new liberal administration eager for reform and new faculty. The administration turned a sympathetic ear to the efforts of Johannes Gildemeister, a professor in the theology faculty, to recruit Zeller.[49] Not happy with his precarious position in Bern, Zeller told Gildemeister that he was willing to come to Marburg, even though he had been warned about another "storm". Sure enough, when the conservative clergy found out about Zeller's appointment, they were furious and organized protests against it. The theology faculty did everything in its power to block the appointment, and prince Friedrich Wilhelm refused to sign the final documents. Only after a massive protest by the liberal assembly did Zeller finally get an appointment, though it was in philosophy rather than theology. Zeller was hired under the condition that he not teach theological topics.

After the initial fire storm, Zeller did manage to settle down in Marburg, where he would stay for the next thirteen years (1849–1862). He was not an especially popular lecturer in Marburg, apparently because his thick Schwabian accent was not so comprehensible there.[50] Zeller was part of a circle of close friends—the theologian Wilhelm Gildemeister, the philosopher Franz Theodor Weitz, and the historian Heinrich von Sybel—which became known as the "Tuesday club". The main preoccupation of Zeller's Marburg years was with the second edition of his *Philosophie der Griechen*, which had expanded from one volume into three very large tomes.[51]

It was most probably during his Marburg years that Zeller completed his conversion from Hegel to Kant. For it was immediately after these years, in 1862, that Zeller would proclaim his Kantianism from the podium in his inaugural lecture at Heidelberg. Unfortunately, it is impossible to determine how and when the conversion took place. None of Zeller's published letters or writings from the Marburg years explicitly concern Kant's or Hegel's philosophy; and there are no notes on Zeller's lectures on logic and metaphysics from this period.[52] Since, however, Zeller was most probably a Kantian already in Marburg, we have to revise or qualify the common claim that Lange, who would come to Marburg ten years later, was the father of Marburg neo-Kantianism.[53]

---

[49] On Zeller's appointment in Marburg, see Sieg, *Aufstieg und Niedergang des Marburger Neukantianismus* Würzburg: Königshausen & Neumann, 1994), pp. 49–53.

[50] Sieg, *Aufstieg und Niedergang*, p. 51. That the accent was the source of the problem seems to be confirmed by his popularity as a lecturer in Tübingen.

[51] Eduard Zeller, *Die Philosophie der Griechen in ihrer geschichtlichen Entwicklung dargestellt* (Tübingen: Fues, 1856–1868), 3 vols.

[52] See Sieg, *Aufstieg und Niedergang des Marburger Neukantianismus*, p. 53, n.135. Sieg notes that there are no extant notes on Zeller's lectures on logic and epistemology for the winter semester 1860/61 and 1861/62.

[53] Sieg, *Aufstieg und Niedergang des Marburger Neukantianismus*, p. 86, accepts this claim. Yet he assumes, p. 49, that Zeller was still a neo-Hegelian in Marburg. As we have seen, however, Zeller had already moved away from Hegelian fundamentals by the 1840s.

Zeller's Marburg period came to a close in 1862 when he received an offer from Heidelberg for an ordinary professorship in philosophy. Unlike the Bern and Marburg appointments, there was no political controversy surrounding the offer from Heidelberg. Not only were the 1860s more settled times, but Zeller's appointment was in philosophy rather than theology, thus avoiding all controversy. As in Marburg, Zeller soon found himself as part of an illustrious circle of friends, including Robert Bunsen, Georg Gervinus and Hermann Helmholtz. With Helmholtz, Zeller would often discuss his new interest in psychology.

It was in Heidelberg that Zeller finally became an integral part of the new up-and-coming movement to revive Kant. Just what his contributions were to this movement we must now examine.

6. Return to Kant

One of the milestones of the Kant revival of the 1860s was Zeller's inaugural lecture at Heidelberg, 'Ueber Bedeutung und Aufgabe der Erkenntnisstheorie', which was delivered October 22, 1862.[54] It is in many respects the counterpart of Fischer's 1860 Jena lectures. Like Fischer, Zeller too thinks that German philosophy is in a state of crisis, and that the only way to resolve it is by going back to Kant. Both Zeller and Fischer see the vocation of philosophy as epistemology, "the theory of knowledge" (*Erkenntnistheorie*), rather than metaphysics.[55] That message, proclaimed from two prestigious podiums, could not fail to have a wide impact on the philosophical scene in Germany.

The affinity between Fischer's and Zeller's lectures raises the question of their relation to one another. Was Fischer an influence on Zeller? Or did they even co-operate with one another? The two men certainly knew of one another, and Fischer's lecture had been published in 1860, which makes it plausible that Zeller knew of its contents. There is no evidence, however, from Zeller's published writings or correspondence that he had read Fischer's lectures. In any case, Fischer and Zeller seem to have come to their conclusions independently, because, for all the similarities in their lectures, there were also interesting differences between them.

These differences become apparent as soon as we raise the question: What, exactly, is the crisis of philosophy for Zeller? Fischer had stressed the danger of obsolescence from the rise of the new empirical sciences, which had left no place for philosophy. While Zeller agrees with that diagnosis, he emphasizes a factor ignored by Fischer: the

---

[54] Zeller, *Vorträge und Abhandlungen*, II, 479–496. All references in parentheses are to this edition.

[55] Ernst Cassirer suggested that Zeller's lecture is the first use of the modern term *Erkenntnistheorie*. See his *Das Erkenntnisproblem in der Philosophie und Wissenschaft der neueren Zeit* (Stuttgart: Kohlhammer, 1957), IV, 12. However, the term had been used widely before then, and its origins date back to the beginning of the 19th century. For a full discussion, see Köhnke, *Entstehung und Aufstieg des Neukantianismus* (Frankfurt: Suhrkamp, 1986), pp. 59–69.

vacuum left behind by the collapse of the great idealist systems. While Fischer had still not abandoned hope of rehabilitating that tradition, Zeller saw its decline as irreversible and final. Philosophy in Germany is now at a turning point, he declares, because it has proven to be impossible to repair the Hegelian system, which has broken down irremediably (489). If philosophy is to go forward at all, it must completely transform itself and start from a new foundation. The best way to determine what that foundation should be, Zeller advises, is to go back to one's starting point, the place from which philosophy began before the rise of speculative idealism (490). That starting point was, of course, Kant's critique of pure reason (490). Kant marked a new beginning for philosophy insofar as he made it into a theory of knowledge. Zeller realizes that some of Kant's predecessors, namely, Locke and Leibniz, were also engaged in the theory of knowledge; but Kant's great contribution was to make that theory more thorough, comprehensive and systematic; he made the theory of knowledge into the chief vocation of philosophy itself (485). Reviving epistemology is precisely the remedy for philosophy in its present impasse, Zeller contends, because only such an examination will diagnose why the great systems have failed.

Zeller also has a different account of the sources of obsolescence. While Fischer thinks that this danger arises from the special sciences usurping the role of philosophy, Zeller maintains that it derives from them divorcing themselves from philosophy. The relationship between philosophy and the special sciences has veered from its natural course, Zeller says, because the sciences pretend that they do not need philosophy at all, and they even fear that it will interfere with their operations (490). Rather than a divorce, there should be a symbiosis between philosophy and the empirical sciences, where each supports and learns from the other. Just why and how there should be such a symbiosis Zeller does not explain.

The most striking contrast between Zeller's and Fischer's lectures concerns their attitudes towards Hegel and the idealist tradition. When Fischer gave his lecture he was still working within the tradition of Hegelian metaphysics; Zeller, however, renounces that tradition as bankrupt from the very beginning. He starts his lecture by declaring it a mistake to assume with Hegel that logic has some kind of content, that it determines the chief structures of the world itself. Logic, for Zeller, has to be completely separated from metaphysics; it is a purely formal discipline, and we have no reason to identify the forms of thought with those of being itself. These forms are the means by which we *know* being, and we cannot simply equate them with being itself (482). Contrary to the speculative principle of subject–object identity, Zeller lays down the principle that knowing and being are distinct: "The operations of thinking by means of which we know the essence of things are distinct from that which we know through them." (482) Zeller accepts that formal logic stands in need of some kind of foundation, but he insists that foundation lies with epistemology rather than metaphysics (482). The foundation cannot lie in metaphysics because it, like all the special sciences, presupposes the validity of certain methods that it is the very purpose of epistemology to investigate. Not metaphysics but epistemology is the *philosophia prima,* because we need to investigate the origins and limits of knowledge before we engage in metaphysics (483).

As much as Zeller stresses the need for philosophy to return to Kant, he also maintains that Kant made one fundamental mistake, an error of such prodigious proportion that it was the source of all the errors of speculative idealism. That mistake was his assumption of the unknowability of things-in-themselves (492). Kant made this mistake because he reasoned that if the forms of our faculty of knowledge determine or condition what we know, then we cannot know how things exist apart from and prior to the application of those forms. But there is a *non sequitur* lurking in Kant's reasoning, Zeller maintains, because even though these forms originate from ourselves, it is still possible that they conform to things-in-themselves (492). In holding out for this possibility, Zeller was following Trendelenburg's argument for such a stronger realism in his *Logische Untersuchungen.* According to that argument, even though the forms of space and time are a priori, arising from the mind, it is still possible for them to apply to things-in-themselves.[56]

Here, then, lay another major difference between Zeller and Fischer. For, though it is not made explicit, Zeller was siding with Trendelenburg in his famous dispute with Fischer, which was just beginning in 1862. No less than Trendelenburg, and contrary to Fischer, Zeller insisted that truth in the empirical sciences requires knowledge of more than just appearances; it is not enough that we know just our representations of things; we also demand that we have knowledge of things themselves. There is a hard element of realism in Zeller's thinking, which consists in more than a Kantian empirical realism (the conformity of representations with the a priori forms of consciousness), and which demands a stronger kind of transcendental realism (the identification of the objects of experience with a reality that exists independent of them). This stronger realism comes to the fore when Zeller maintains, against Kant, that it is false that sensation gives us only disorganized matter and that all form comes from ourselves (491–492). That Kantian dualism is implausible, Zeller argues, because the particular relations between things in space and time (viz. the clock standing two feet from the window, the ball taking sixty seconds to drop from 6,000 meters) cannot be derived from the general forms of intuition and understanding; these relations are therefore simply given to us, having a reality independent of our consciousness.

Zeller was so confident in his realism that he was not phased at all by the objection that we cannot get outside our representations to see if they correspond with reality itself. We have within our experience a means of knowing whether our representations are only illusions or appearances of things themselves, he reassures us. We do not have to determine the reality of a representation simply from its own content; rather, we determine its reality by comparing it with other representations. We compare different representations of the same sense, representations of different senses,

---

[56] Adolf Trendelenburg, *Logische Untersuchungen* (Berlin: Bethge, 1840), I, 124–133.

and many different perspectives of all the senses; it is only when they all agree with one another that we claim they are of reality itself (493). Besides comparing representations among one another, we have another test for the reality of a representation in the laws of the empirical sciences (494). We ascribe reality to a representation only if it conforms to these laws, and we regard it as illusory if it fails to comply with them.

It is ironic, however, that Kant used just these kinds of arguments to demonstrate the sufficiency of empirical realism. Kant would have agreed with Zeller that we do not have to get outside our representations to determine their reality, and that we have sufficient criteria to do so within consciousness itself; he would have disagreed with Zeller's conclusion, however, that satisfying these criteria guarantees knowledge of reality itself. For Kant, that extra inference on Zeller's part would be pure *non sequitur*. Belief in the correspondence of representations with reality itself was a leap of faith, which no sceptic would be prepared to make or approve.

Some fifteen years later, when Fischer's dispute with Trendelenburg was a rapidly fading memory, Zeller returned to the topic of knowledge of the external world in some reflections he added to his original lecture.[57] Zeller here retreats from his earlier position, though he does not recant or attempt to smooth over the inconsistency. Stressing now the role of our senses and physiology as conditions of experience, he maintains that the Kantian conception of the a priori can be extended, so that it applies not only to the forms of intuition and understanding but even to sensation itself (501). We can talk about a priori factors of sensation because it is just a fact—and here Zeller has in mind the experiments of Müller so stressed by Helmholtz—that the quality of sensation depends on the specific qualities of our nerves and brain. We cannot reduce the quality or content of a sensation down to the character of the stimulus, because the nerves and brain so transform the stimulus that their product, the representation, is nothing like them (500). Having emphasized the creative role of the senses in producing experience, Zeller now finds it difficult to retain the realism he had so optimistically affirmed in his original lecture. Although he again insists that the particular content of sensation, and the relations between particular facts in experience, cannot be produced by us and that it has to be given by stimuli outside us (522), and although he again stresses that the definite content of perception simply cannot be explained in terms of the general forms of sensation, intuition or understanding (499, 522), he now explicitly concedes that our representations do not directly reflect things-in-themselves (523). This is because the senses transform what we know, or because the nerves and brain affect the very content of sensation. All that we know directly is simply how these things affect us and how we react to them; and it is impossible for us to get outside ourselves to know the thing as it exists in itself (523). Indeed, the form and content of representations, the role of our own activity and the role of the stimulus in producing it, are impossible for us to separate (523). Although

---

[57] Zeller, 'Zusätze', *Vorträge und Abhandlungen* II, 496–526. These additions were written in 1877, apparently for the republication of the original lecture.

Zeller again insists that we can determine the reality of a representation by its coherence with others, it is now obvious that this test shows only facts about appearances—about how the world affects us—and nothing about things-in-themselves. In these reflections Zeller had discovered a point that Lange and Liebmann were also forced to admit: that the thing-in-itself is, however horrible and nonsensical, ineliminable.

Whatever the merits or flaws of his arguments for the unknowability of things-in-themselves, Zeller's original lecture preaches the doctrine that the assumption of their unknowability was the source of all the errors of the idealist tradition after Kant. Rightly seeing the problems behind this assumption, Fichte, Schelling and Hegel attempted to eliminate things-in-themselves and to explain the origin of experience without having to postulate some mysterious cause behind it. Fichte tried to explain experience on the basis of idealism, by assuming that the opposition between subject and object within experience arises from the absolute ego; but this explanation did not work, because, as Schelling reasoned later, the absolute ego is not really a subject at all, given that the meaning of a subject comes only from its contrast with an object (487). Hence Schelling and Hegel attempted to explain the origin of experience, the division between subject and object, from the standpoint of absolute identity, which is neither subject nor object but the complete identity between them. But, Zeller insists, in ascending to such a high level of abstraction, Schelling and Hegel went beyond the limits of experience itself and indulged in a kind of transcendent metaphysics (488). It is impossible to begin from above, from some abstract absolute standpoint, and then to derive the basic facts of experience from it. In doing so Schelling and Hegel illegitimately attempted to derive the particular and determinate from the universal and indeterminate; they were trying to squeeze blood from a turnip, milk from a billygoat, in the usual rationalist manner. The deductions demanded by the Hegelian dialectic are impossible in principle, because they attempt to derive content from form, the concrete from the abstract (488–489). Here in Zeller's diagnosis of the problems of Hegelian speculation we can see his reason for thinking that the idealist tradition had collapsed and stood beyond redemption.

It was a central theme of Zeller's lecture that philosophy had to be first and foremost epistemology because that alone would ensure it against dogmatism and the spectacular errors committed by speculative idealism. Zeller insisted in classical manner, much like Locke and Kant before him, that it is necessary first to examine the conditions and limits of knowledge before attempting to acquire knowledge itself (483). Since the methods we employ determine the results we get, we first need to investigate the value of these methods themselves (481); we need to determine the standards of knowledge, which we derive from the conditions under which the mind acquires knowledge (483). Zeller makes these old points as if they contain profound lessons for future philosophy, as if the speculative idealists had forgotten them entirely, and as if it were for this reason alone they had committed the classical mistakes of rationalist dogmatism. But was Zeller preaching a timely lesson for the fallen or just an old homily for the converted? His argument on behalf of epistemology sounds naive in the face of some of the objections made against it. Hegel had lampooned the attempt to learn how to swim before jumping in the water; Lotze had complained about those who forever sharpen their knife but never try to cut anything with it; and Dilthey had contended that we cannot determine the limits of knowing except by undertaking attempts to know and seeing whether they are successful or not. It was a weakness of Zeller's position that he never replied to these common objections.

For all its naivety, Zeller's lecture had its merits: within the short span of fifteen pages, it had sketched a new approach to philosophy, a new way forward from the morass of speculative idealism. If Zeller's arguments were sketchy, hasty and inconclusive, we cannot expect more from a single lecture. The value of the lecture lay more in its proposals and suggestions than its arguments or answers. Last but not least, Zeller's diagnosis of the failures of the idealist tradition—his claim that the entire tradition came to grief over the thing-in-itself—will prove fruitful. As we shall soon see, it will be made into the central theme of one of the most influential neo-Kantian manifestos of the 1860s, Otto Liebmann's *Kant und die Epigonen*.[58]

7. Unfinished Business

For all its richness in content, Zeller's 1862 lecture had not fully answered the most pressing question of them all, the very question he intended to answer in the first place: How can philosophy avoid imminent obsolescence? Although Zeller had explicitly posed that question, and although he had even suggested an answer, he had not explained or justified it. He had recommended that philosophy should go back to Kant, that it should revive the project of epistemology to avoid the problems of metaphysics. But Zeller had not gone into any detail about *how* epistemology solves the crisis of philosophy, about *how* it saves philosophy from redundancy by the special sciences. Zeller finally turned to that task in a later lecture, 'Ueber die Aufgabe der Philosophie und ihre Stellung zu den übrigen Wissenschaften',[59] which he delivered in Heidelberg on November 23, 1868, on the occasion of the birthday of the Prince Karl Friedrich von Baden.

Now, in much more detail than in his first lecture, Zeller sketches the scenario that threatens philosophy. The account he now provides is very similar to Fischer's. After having freed itself from theology in the modern world, philosophy returned to its old vocation of providing a general worldview, a theory of the universe as a whole. But this conception of its calling was threatened by the growth of the special sciences (447). Each of them had its own special domain, its own unique methodology, which made them independent of philosophy. Since all of reality was carved up among the special sciences, it seemed as if there was nothing left for philosophy to do (450). Philosophy was like that poet who, after finding that the sciences had carved

---

[58] See Chapter 7, Section 2.   [59] Zeller, *Vorträge und Abhandlungen* II, 445–466.

up reality for themselves, had nothing more for himself than "the dream world of abstractions".

Given this predicament, what should be the relationship of philosophy to the special sciences? "What remains left for philosophy?", Zeller asks (450). The answer to this question will depend on our general epistemological position, he answers. If we assume that there is a source of a priori knowledge within the mind independent of experience, then we can make philosophy the science of such a priori knowledge, so that it is distinct from the special sciences, which all pursue empirical or a posteriori knowledge (448). This, Zeller thinks, was just the position of the idealist tradition, which saw philosophy as an a priori science that could construct all reality by deductive reasoning. But this position has now shown itself to be bankrupt, he claims. That we cannot have a priori knowledge of reality, that we will never succeed in providing an "a priori construction of the universe", Zeller says, is plain from the failures of Hegel's dialectical method (449). This method either produces results in conflict with experience or it smuggles in premises from experience to get its results (449).

So, granted that there is no a priori knowledge, granted that all knowledge of the world in some way depends on experience, how do we distinguish philosophy from the special sciences? Zeller assumes that philosophy too will have to adopt an empirical methodology, and that there cannot be any fundamental difference in method between it and the empirical sciences. The problem of defining the difference between philosophy and the sciences has now become all the more acute, however, given that both share the same method and that both depend for knowledge upon experience. We can now see clearly why Zeller thinks that the collapse of idealism left philosophy with an identity crisis: once one rejects the old a priori methods of dialectic or construction, the old border line between the empirical sciences and philosophy disappears. But now that philosophy too has to dwell in the realm of experience, it seems utterly redundant, given that the special sciences have carved up that entire realm among themselves. And so the urgency of Zeller's question: "What remains left over for philosophy?" (450).

Zeller has three answers to that question, three solutions to the problem of obsolescence, though he never precisely distinguishes them. His first solution reaffirms the main proposal of his 1862 lecture: that the special vocation of philosophy consists in logic and epistemology (459). Now, though, the argument for this proposal is more explicit and better developed. Zeller explains that the activity of thought is the same in all the sciences, and that it is the special task of philosophy to determine the laws of this activity (459). Philosophy determines, in other words, "the general conditions and forms of all scientific thinking" (460). Insofar as it does this, philosophy is logic, but logic understood in a broad sense as the theory of knowledge, a theory whose special concern is "universal scientific methodology" (460). Logic or theory of knowledge does not have to fear redundancy at the hands of the special sciences, then, because it determines the foundation of all the special sciences, and so transcends their particular concerns (461).

The second solution to the obsolescence problem is more novel, having no precedent in the earlier lecture. Zeller explains that each of the special sciences has its own fundamental presuppositions and concepts; it uses and applies these presuppositions and concepts to investigate its particular sector of reality; but it does not investigate them itself (462). Such an investigation is the task of philosophy. Zeller explains that physics, for example, uses the concepts of matter, motion and space, but it does not investigate what they mean exactly, whether they have ultimate reality or are only modes of our awareness (462). The same is the case for psychology, which uses the concept of a mind but which does not explain its precise meaning (463). For each of the special sciences, then, there will be a philosophy of that science which has the special task of investigating its fundamental concepts and presuppositions. So, in addition to a general logic which investigates what all sciences have in common, philosophy will also divide into separate parts for each discipline.

Having laid out these solutions to the redundancy crisis, Zeller now goes a step further and suggests even a third vocation for philosophy, yet another task to distinguish it from the special sciences. There must be a science, he reasons, that examines the interconnections between the special sciences, one that transcends their limited boundaries and connects them together into a single theory. The special task of this science will be "the connection of all sciences" (465). It will be a science of all the sciences, a *Gesamtwissenschaft* so to speak, that summarizes and synthesizes the results of all the special sciences. Zeller calls the subject matter of this science "the infinite ground of all being" (464). What he has in mind, though he does not use that dirty word, is metaphysics. For all his criticism of the metaphysics of speculative idealism, Zeller was not ready to banish metaphysics as such. It's just that he wanted metaphysics to be based on the methods and results of the particular sciences rather than any a priori methodology.

So, *summa summarum,* Zeller gave philosophy plenty to do in his scientific age. Philosophy could be logic and epistemology, a study of the conditions and limits of knowledge and science in general; it could be a study of the concepts and presuppositions of any particular science; and it could be a general metaphysics that pulled together all the results of the sciences. What is so striking about Zeller's general position is that it is still so traditional. Zeller was not willing to abandon the old conception of philosophy as a worldview, a general theory of reality as a whole, the very conception that seemed to have been rendered obsolete. Some of his neo-Kantian colleagues, namely, Lange and Windelband, had already written off this conception as archaic. The precise status of metaphysics remains a troublesome question within neo-Kantianism, with some insisting on its rehabilitation with new methods and others preaching the need for its complete abandonment.

Another remarkable feature of Zeller's conception of philosophy is that he sees no difference in method or discourse between philosophy and the empirical sciences.[60] The

---

[60] In his *Philosophy and the Mirror of Nature* (Oxford: Blackwell, 1980), pp. 133–136, Richard Rorty

distinction between philosophy and the sciences rests on two factors: its broader scope or generality and its higher level, that is, it is second order, dealing with knowledge of things rather than things themselves. As far as epistemology is concerned, however, Zeller makes no distinction between the *Quid juris?* and the *Quid facti?*, the normative and natural. Under the influence of Helmholtz, and in the tradition of Fries, Herbart and Beneke, Zeller continued to see epistemology as a kind of empirical psychology. He shared Helmholtz's view that if philosophy were to become a science, epistemology would have to engage in the experiments and observations of psychology and physiology. It is ironic, however, that this belief seems to push philosophy even closer to obsolescence, because it makes epistemology, properly pursued, just another form of psychology. As we shall soon see, Windelband will soon press just this point against Zeller.[61]

8. A Neo-Classical Ethics

On January 24, 1872, after nearly 40 years in the role, Adolf Trendelenburg, professor of classical philosophy at the University of Berlin, died. The University was eager to find someone of similar stature to replace him. They could think of only one person fit for the position: Zeller. The university duly made him the offer of full professorship in July 1872.[62] To be called to Berlin was the crowning glory for any German academic in the 19th century. The city was the cultural centre of the new Reich, and its university had the most illustrious faculty in Germany. Despite the honour, Zeller hesitated, not least because of fears about his age. He was now 58 and unsure if he had the energy for such a new and demanding role. It was only after Helmholtz, "in the personal service of the government", travelled to Heidelberg to persuade him that Zeller relented. He began his lectures in the Winter Semester of 1872.

It was a sign of changed times that the outcast in the 1840s had become the celebrity of the 1870s. But Zeller himself had changed too. Although he had never renounced his basic liberal principles, his advocacy of the rights of radical criticism, and least of all his support for David Friedrich Strauß, Zeller's political convictions were now more in accord with the new *Zeitgeist*. Though a Schwabian, Zeller now celebrated Prussia's rise to power. He was a passionate defender of German unification, and specifically of the Prussian or *Kleindeutsch* version of it; and he was a staunch supporter

fails to see this point. Rorty says that Zeller makes philosophy a "non-empirical discipline" distinct from empirical psychology (p. 134). But Zeller never says that epistemology is a non-empirical discipline; just the opposite: he insists that philosophy has to adopt empirical standards and methods of knowledge like the empirical sciences. Rorty's reading of Zeller is anachronistic, seeing him from the prism of later neo-Kantianism (Windelband and Cohen).

[61] See Wilhelm Windelband, *Die Philosophie im deutschen Geistesleben des XIX. Jahrhunderts* (Tübingen: Mohr, 1909), pp. 82–85.

[62] On the history behind Zeller's appointment in Berlin, see Volker Gerhardt, Reinhard Mehring and Jana Rindert, *Berliner Geist: Eine Geschichte der Berliner Universitätsphilosophie bis 1946* (Berlin: Akademie Verlag, 1999), pp. 95–100.

of Prussia in its war against France. In 1872, in a series of lectures,[63] Zeller, like a true liberal, defended the separation of church and state; but this was also a statement on behalf of Prussian Protestantism in its emerging *Kulturkampf* with Roman Catholicism. Zeller's cosiness with the Prussian establishment reached its height in 1886 when, on the centenary of Frederick the Great's death, he published a book celebrating the great ruler as a philosopher.[64]

For his inaugural lecture in Berlin in October 1872,[65] Zeller returned to the topic of his inugural lecture in Heidelberg ten years earlier: the identity crisis of philosophy. Now, however, Zeller is much more confident that this crisis is finally resolved. There is no danger of obsolescence for philosophy, he assures, because "the German spirit" will never turn its back on philosophy. It will always want to reflect on the fundamental questions of life, and to examine the chief presuppositions of the empirical sciences (469). But the way philosophy should pursue these questions in the future, Zeller declares, will have to be very different from the methods of the past. Rather than attempting to provide a priori deductions from first principles, in the idealist tradition, it will have to investigate the conditions and limits of knowledge according to empirical methods, following the observation and experiment of the new psychology. Never was Zeller so explicit and adamant in his affirmation of empiricism: "Our philosophy should, as far as the nature of its objects permit, take as its model the exact methods of the natural sciences." (474). And never was he so clear and firm about the realism of his epistemological outlook: "We should comprehend things as they are, and we should not impose on them our thoughts and fantasies; our philosophy should be realism, an image of reality." (474). This empiricism and realism are fully in accord with the new temper of the times, Zeller reassures us, with the advance of the natural sciences and the growth of technology and industry. In making such a virtue out of following the *Zeitgeist,* Zeller seemed to have forgotten the programme of radical criticism of his youth.

Zeller's most important writings on Kant during his Berlin years were two substantial essays on moral philosophy. The first of these essays, 'Ueber das kantische Moralprinzip', was read before the Prussian Academy of Sciences in December 1879; the second, 'Ueber Begriff und Begründung der sittlicher Gesetze', was read before the Academy of Sciences in December 1882.[66] The essays complement one another and present a single point of view. In them Zeller sketches his own moral philosophy, one formed chiefly on the basis of his critique of Kant.

---

[63] Eduard Zeller, *Staat und Kirche. Vorlesungen an die Universität zu Berlin.* (Leipzig: Fues, 1893).
[64] Eduard Zeller, *Friedrich der Grosse als Philosoph* (Berlin: Weidmann, 1886).
[65] Eduard Zeller, 'Ueber die gegenwärtige Stellung und Aufgabe der deutschen Philosophie', *Vorträge und Abhandlungen* III, 467–478.
[66] Eduard Zeller, 'Ueber das kantische Moralprinzip und den Gegensatz formaler und materialer Moralprinzipien', in *Vorträge und Abhandlungen* III, 156–187; and 'Ueber Begriff und Begründung der sittlichen Gesetze', *Vorträge und Abhandlungen* III, 189–224. All references in parentheses are to this edition.

Zeller's aim in both articles is to find a middle path between Kant's formalism and hedonism. Kant had cast his moral philosophy as the only alternative to hedonism. It was either acknowledging duty for its own sake or lapsing into the relativism and egoism of hedonism.[67] Zeller thinks that there is a middle path between such dire options: the humanist ethic of self-realization or excellence presented by Plato and Aristotle. The great advantages of this ethic are that, by basing ethical precepts on the general laws of human nature, it avoids the emptiness of Kantian formalism as well as the relativism of hedonism. It provides a content for ethics—the needs of human nature—yet it also does not have to surrender to relativism because it bases these needs on *universal* laws of human nature. In putting forward this classical ethic against Kant, Zeller was following the precedent of his illustrious predecessor in classical philosophy in Berlin: Trendelenburg.[68] Both Zeller and Trendelenburg therefore represent the standpoint of neo-classicism in modern moral philosophy.

The chief problem with Kant's ethics Zeller finds in its formalism. Kant had rightly seen that the moral value of maxims cannot be based on their consequences; but on these grounds he wrongly concluded that they should not be based on experience at all. Having rejected experience as an arbiter of moral value, Kant sought its criterion in formal features alone, namely, whether a maxim could be made into a universal law. But this put him in an untenable position, Zeller argues, because the purely formal criterion is empty, capable of sanctioning virtually any content (166–167). This is precisely what we should expect, because once we abstract from all content, as Kant demands, it is no longer possible to distinguish between right and wrong content (164). The mere demand that a maxim be universalizable cannot determine its moral rightness or wrongness alone, given that an egoist is willing to universalize his maxim; it is perfectly consistent for him to will to live in a state of nature where he is ready to compete with others (166–167). If we are to give content to morality, Zeller contends, then we have to consider the *purpose* to be achieved by it (206). Contrary to his own principles, Kant himself does exactly this, often using teleological reasoning and language. When, for example, he universalizes a maxim, he asks us to consider what would happen—that is, what would be the consequences—if everyone were to do the same (165). And he formulates his principle in teleological terms when he states that every rational being should so act that through his maxims he becomes a member of the kingdom of ends (206).

While Kant's ethics suffer from emptiness, Zeller holds that hedonism provides no viable alternative to it because it leads to relativism. He agrees entirely with Kant that hedonism, understood as the doctrine that pleasure alone is the highest good, cannot provide a justification for the universality and necessity of moral principles. It is just

[67] See Kant, *Kritik der praktischen Vernunft*, AA V, 21–23.

[68] See Adolf Trendelenburg, 'Der Widerstreit zwischen Kant und Aristoteles in der Ethik', in *Historische Beiträge zur Philosophie* (Berlin: Bethge, 1867), III, 171–214. Zeller cites this article, which he calls a *"werthvollen Abhandlung"*. See Zeller, 'Ueber das kantische Moralprinzip', III, p. 188, n.10.

a fact, pointed out by Plato long ago, that people take pleasure in different things, so that we cannot have a universal prescription to strive for pleasure except in a very general and abstract sense (175–176, 210–211).

In both essays Zeller's repudiation of hedonism is unequivocal, so that it is incorrect to state with Willey: "Zeller stated the eudaemonistic principle unequivocally: Pleasure is good, pain is bad."[69] Such a statement comes from reading some sentences of Zeller's 1882 essay out of context, and from equivocating about the meaning of "eudemonism".[70] Zeller distinguishes carefully between a hedonistic eudemonism, which takes pleasure alone to be happiness, and a perfectionist eudemonism, which regards human perfection as the chief source of happiness. More significantly, he distinguishes between a subjective and objective justification of moral actions: where a subjective justification values actions because they are a means to attain pleasure, an objective justification values them for their own sake (209–210). With the subjective justification we regard pleasure as the good, whereas with the objective justification we take pleasure in an action because it is good.

If hedonism ends in relativism, and if Kantian formalism is empty, how do we sustain the universality of moral principles? For Zeller, the answer to this question lies only in the sphere of psychology and anthropology, whose task is to determine "the essential needs and the common laws of human nature" (173). What matters in determining the moral value of maxims should be "the proper nature of human beings, by virtue of their inner, a priori laws" (174). In putting forward this position, Zeller was reaffirming Aristotle's position in the *Nicomachean Ethics* that the task of ethics is to determine what is good for man as man. This is an enquiry into happiness, of course, though not happiness in the sense of pleasure but in the sense of self-realization or perfection, that is, what makes a human being excellent or do well at its characteristic activities. Engaging in these characteristic activities brings pleasure, but the pleasure that results from them is not the reason for doing them.

There is a certain plausibility to Zeller's position, and it is indeed the natural and inevitable one for the classicist to take. But it faced severe problems that Zeller did not squarely face. It is by no means evident that an appeal to human nature or excellence will give the universality that Zeller desires. Does not human nature vary with culture and epoch, and are there not accordingly different, indeed incommensurable, conceptions of human excellence? Herder had already preached that in the 1770s; and Nietzsche was publishing his relativist conclusions from his "historical philosophy"

---

[69] Willey, *Back to Kant*, pp. 75–76.

[70] Zeller writes: "*der Werth jeder Handlung wird nach dem Lust beurtheilt*" (p. 210). But this is an exposition, not an endorsement, of the hedonist version of the eudemonistic position. Zeller does accept the position that states happiness is the final end of human action: "*Um so mehr scheint eben diese, also mit Einem Wort: die Glückseligkeit, das natürliche Ziel des Strebens, und alles menschlichen Thun nur ein Mittel für dieses Zweck zu sein.*" (p. 208). But he does not equate happiness with pleasure. There are for him two forms of eudemonism: a hedonistic form that sees happiness as pleasure; and a perfectionist form that identifies happiness with human excellence. Zeller argues on behalf of the second form.

just when Zeller gave his first speech before the Academy.[71] Wisely, Kant avoided appeals to human nature because he realized they cannot escape relativism.

Besides relativism, there was another problem with Zeller's appeal to human nature. Zeller had defended Kant's distinction between the normative and factual against Schleiermacher's objections (199–201). But if we accept that distinction, how do we derive the norms of ethics from facts about human nature? Seeing the force of this point, Zeller noted that we could not simply list some common human needs and then rest content with having provided a foundation for ethics (208). We need to know not simply what people want but what they *ought* to want, a criterion of *valid* needs; but that leaves the question on what that criterion is based. Zeller had no answer to this crucial question.

Throughout the 1870s, and for decades thereafter, these questions about the foundation of ethics will continue to preoccupy the neo-Kantian tradition. The crucial problem for a Kantian ethics is how it could provide a foundation for morality in the face of two challenges: the apparent formalism or emptiness of the categorical imperative, and the rise of historicism, which seemed to make relativism inevitable. We shall consider some attempts to meet these challenges.

---

[71] See Herder, *Auch eine Philosophie der Geschichte der Menschheit*, in *Werke*, eds M. Bollacher *et al.* (Frankfurt: Deutsche Klassiker Verlag, 1985–2000), IV, 38–39; and Nietzsche, *Menschliches, Allzumenschliches*, in *Sämtliche Werke*, eds G. Colli and M. Montinari (Berlin: de Gruyter, 1967–77), II, 23–25, §§1–2.

7

Rehabilitating Otto Liebmann

1. Rise and Fall of a Reputation

One of the most controversial figures in the history of neo-Kantianism is Otto Liebmann (1840–1912). If we are to believe popular or textbook accounts,[1] Liebmann is the very founder of neo-Kantianism. His book *Kant und die Epigonen*, which first appeared in 1865, is its opening manifesto. Its celebrated refrain *"Back to Kant!"* became the slogan for the whole movement. Such has been Liebmann's reputation for at least the past half century.

Recently, however, Klaus Christian Köhnke, in his brilliant *Entstehung und Aufstieg des Neukantianismus*, has pleaded for a drastic reassessment of Liebmann's reputation and historical significance. Liebmann's work is hardly groundbreaking, Köhnke argues, because it comes at the end, rather than the beginning, of the first period of neo-Kantian programmatics (1849–1865).[2] Furthermore, there is little of scholarly or philosophical value in his book, whose interpretation of Kant is crude and simplistic, and whose critique of idealism is tendentious and rhetorical. Köhnke's reassessment is driven chiefly by his contempt for Liebmann's politics. Liebmann is for him the epitome of the conservative German nationalist, a chauvinist zealot who preaches loyalty and obedience to the fatherland. Here is Köhnke's vivid portrait of the man:

He was born in 1840 ... and thus was a child of the Bismarck era: a spirited fraternity member, with moustache and short, exactly-parted hair; he looked, if the comparison could be permitted, more like a Prussian lieutenant or a German engineer on the Turkish railways than any philosopher before or after him. Mathematically and scientifically educated, Liebmann was an admirer of Treitschke and a firm hater of the French and British, though in that respect he hardly differed from the German national average. His whole style had nothing to do with an "angry young man" (Willey), but rather more to do with the ruthlessness and brutality of the central figure of *Der Untertan*.[3]

---

[1] See, for example, L.W. Beck, 'Neo-Kantianism', in *The Encyclopedia of Philosophy*, ed. Paul Edwards (New York: Macmillan, 1967), V, 468; and Hans-Ludwig Ollig, *Der Neukantianismus* (Stuttgart: Metzler, 1979), pp. 9–15.

[2] Klaus Christian Köhnke, *Entstehung und Aufstieg des Neukantianismus: Die deutsche Universitätsphilosophie zwischen Idealismus und Positivismus* (Frankfurt: Suhrkamp, 1986), p. 214.

[3] Köhnke, *Entstehung und Aufstieg*, pp. 215–216. The reference is to *Der Untertan*, a satirical novel by Heinrich Mann, which was published in extracts in *Simplicissimus* from 1911 to 1914. Its anti-hero,

After this damning caricature, Köhnke attempts to expose the shady politics behind Liebmann's neo-Kantianism. He maintains that Liebmann's philosophy was motivated by a political agenda: the attempt to make Kant's philosophy into propaganda for the new Bismarckian *Reich*. After all, Liebmann expressly says that the spirit of the categorical imperative appears in Prussian military discipline, in the strict obedience and complete submission of the individual to the state. Because of that agenda, the case against Liebmann, as far as Köhnke is concerned, is closed. There is little more worthwhile to say about him. Apart from a scanty summary of two of his early works, Köhnke ignores the rest of Liebmann's *corpus*.

Yet Köhnke's reappraisal of Liebmann needs reappraisal itself. To take it as the final word would not only result in a grave injustice to Liebmann but also in a drastic distortion of the history of neo-Kantianism. There can be no question that Köhnke is right to assail Liebmann's popular reputation: he is not the founder of neo-Kantianism, and his call for a return to Kant was preceded by the manifestos of Beneke, Helmholtz, Zeller, Weiße and Fortlage. Furthermore, his critique of German idealism was nothing new, but simply carried on the tradition begun by Fries, Herbart and Beneke. The rest of Köhnke's reappraisal is, however, groundless. The attempt to discredit Liebmann's philosophy on the basis of his politics is misconceived: it throws the baby of philosophy out with the bathwater of politics. Politics should not be the basis for an evaluation of his philosophy, whose epistemology and metaphysics should be judged by different criteria. In any case, as we shall soon see,[4] Köhnke's account of Liebmann's politics is not only wildly anachronistic but grossly inaccurate.

Any accurate and complete picture of neo-Kantianism demands that we give a fuller and fairer treatment to Liebmann. Even if he was not the founder of the movement, he remains a central figure in its history. He was one of the first neo-Kantians to see the problems with the psychological interpretation of Kant; he was also one of the first to provide a neo-Kantian critique of positivism; and he was one of the very few who had the qualifications to discuss the relationship between Kant's philosophy and the new developments in mathematics and natural science. An inspiring and beloved teacher, Liebmann was an important influence upon some later neo-Kantians, among them Wilhelm Windelband, Bruno Bauch and Erich Adickes.[5] Liebmann's first book not only created a stir, but some of his later writings were widely read, often discussed and favourably reviewed. Last but not least, it is necessary to add that Liebmann was the best writer of the neo-Kantian tradition. In a tradition not distinguished for

---

Diedrich Heßling, defers to those above him and brutalizes those below him. After 1945 Heßling has been invariably read as a Nazi prototype.

    [4] See Section 5, in this chapter.
    [5] See especially *Kant-Studien* 15 (1910), which contains many articles devoted to Liebmann. Among the contributors were Windelband, Bauch and Adickes. Volume 17 (1912) of *Kant-Studien* contains funereal speeches by Bruno Bauch and Rudolf Eucken.

stylistic grace, Liebmann's writings stand out for their elegance, urbanity and wit. Though his style is popular, it sacrifices nothing in philosophical rigour and subtlety.

Seen from a broad historical perspective, Liebmann reveals himself to be a transitional figure in the history of neo-Kantianism. His work appears between the psychological-physiological phase of Kant interpretation, which prevails from the 1790s through the 1860s, and the epistemological phase, which was dominant from the 1870s to 1890s. Caught between these phases, Liebmann's work shows traces of both. He believed that the new physiology could confirm the fundamentals of Kant's epistemology; but he also stressed the *sui generis* epistemological dimension of transcendental philosophy. There is a tension in Liebmann's work between a physiological and epistemological interpretation of transcendental philosophy, a disparity which he struggled to resolve. In his later years Liebmann stressed the epistemological side of Kant's philosophy, which he saw as its chief intention, and he sharply distinguished between the normative and natural, questions of value and fact. In these latter respects his work anticipates that of Windelband and Cohen.

From 1859 to 1864 Liebmann studied philosophy, mathematics and natural science at Jena, Leipzig and Halle. In Jena Liebmann was a student of Karl Fortlage and Kuno Fischer, who were decisive in shaping his own neo-Kantian programme.[6] At Leipzig he attended the lectures of Fechner and Drobisch, who taught him the basis of the new psycho-physics and the mathematical approach to psychology. In 1864 Liebmann became a *Privatdozent* in Tübingen, where he habilitated the following year. After a short stint in the military in 1870, Liebmann became extraordinary professor in Straßburg in 1872, then ordinary professor in 1878. In 1882 he returned to his *alma mater*, Jena, serving as professor there until his death in 1912.

It is questionable whether Liebmann had a consistent systematic philosophy. He regarded a complete system as an ideal he could approach but never attain. His style of philosophizing was to approach problems analytically and piecemeal, and he constantly stressed how his results were provisional, depending on the results of future enquiry. The lack of consistency and system is most apparent from Liebmann's philosophical development, which largely consisted in the rediscovery and reaffirmation of something he had initially repudiated: metaphysics. Liebmann began his career with an almost positivist contempt for metaphysics, with a brusque dismissal of the relevance of the transcendent; but he ended it with a convinced defence of metaphysics and an almost pious acknowledgement of the value of the transcendent. The fear of materialism, and the aversion to positivism, pushed him away from his former "tough-minded" neo-Kantianism, which paid little heed to moral values, and towards a more "tender-minded" neo-Kantianism, which gave a central place to moral value in the universe.

---

[6] In his inaugural address at Jena, *Ueber Philosophische Tradition* (Straßburg: Trübner, 1883), pp. 5–6, Liebmann paid tribute to his two teachers at Jena.

Our task in this chapter will be to provide a reassessment of Liebmann's place in the history of neo-Kantianism. We will consider the main phases in his philosophical development from a close study of his major writings from 1865 to 1900, from his early *Kant und die Epigonen* until his *Gedanken und Thatsachen*, his last major work. Our chief focus will be Liebmann's epistemology and metaphysics, which is where his main contribution lies. On no account does our study pretend to be complete or exhaustive, to do justice to all the nuance, subtlety and detail of Liebmann's thinking. We attempt to provide only an introduction for some of its chief themes.

2. *Kant und die Epigonen*

Liebmann shot to fame in 1865 with the publication of his first book, *Kant und die Epigonen*.[7] The book was a sensation, partly because of its lively and engaging style, partly because of its passionate stand on behalf of Kant. The young author, then only twenty-five years old, preached that Kant was the be-all-and-end-all of philosophy—"the most important thinker of Christian humanity"—and that every attempt to go beyond him had ended in disaster. Fichte, Schelling, Hegel, Schopenhauer, Fries and Herbart—all these epigoni had failed to surpass Kant. The proper direction for philosophy was not forwards beyond Kant but backwards towards him. No work of scholarship, still less a contribution to Kant philology, *Kant und die Epigonen* is more a manifesto, a feisty polemic on behalf of Kant. What Liebmann lacked in scholarly depth he made up for in rhetorical flair. His style is emphatic, witty and humorous. And just to make sure no one mistook him for a literary naif: the tract is sprinkled with quotations in English, French, Italian, Greek and Latin. Each chapter ends with the refrain *"Es muß auf Kant zurückgegangen werden."* Its shorter version—'*Zurück zu Kant!*'—, though more famous, was never used by Liebmann.

The title of Liebmann's tract—*Kant und die Epigonen*—seems to belittle Kant's successors. It is as if the author intends to diminish their reputations so that they do not presume to stand above his hero. The word *Epigone* suggests as much, because it means in modern German "an imitator without creativity" (*Nachahmer ohne Schöpfungskraft*).[8] There is good reason to assume, however, that Liebmann did not intend the word in that derogatory sense. Bruno Bauch, the editor of the later *Kantgesellschaft* edition of Liebmann's book, tells us that he meant it in the original Greek sense, according to which it signifies only "those born afterward".[9] Nothing more upset the older and wiser Liebmann, Bauch informs us, than the

---

[7] Otto Liebmann, *Kant und die Epigonen: Eine kritische Abhandlung* (Stuttgart: Carl Schober, 1865). There is also a Kant Gesellschaft Neudruck: Berlin: Reuther & Reichard, 1912, ed. Bruno Bauch. All references in parentheses will be to the original edition, which is cited on the margin of the Kantgesellschaft edition.

[8] *Duden. Rechtschreibung der deutschen Sprache und der Fremdwörter.* 19th edition (Mannheim: Dudenverlag, 1986), I, 244.

[9] Bauch, 'Vorwort des Herausgebers', p. X.

widespread view that he had treated Fichte, Schelling and Hegel as disrespectfully as Schopenhauer once had.[10] The content of the book bears out Bauch's interpretation. Liebmann is careful to say in his introduction that his epigoni—Fichte, Schelling, Hegel, Fries, Herbart and Schopenhauer—were all "independent thinkers" and "great architects" of their own original systems (8). And he often distanced himself from Schopenhauer's diatribes about Fichte and Hegel, which he found "inexcusable" (76, 157–158, 214). Liebmann chose "epigoni" more to stress the dependence of these philosophers on Kant, and his careful examination of their systems shows that he does indeed respect them.

An essential part of Köhnke's reassessment of Liebmann is his appraisal of his first book. As we have seen, Köhnke questions its historical significance, because it came not at the beginning but the end of the early period of neo-Kantian programmatics. But he also deprecates the intellectual content of the book. Liebmann's interpretation of Kant, and his polemics against the post-Kantians, are, in his opinion, crude, rude and tendentious. Liebmann had no real interest in questions of Kant scholarship, he says, because his true agenda was political: the attempt to popularize Kant on behalf of the authoritarian Wilhelmine state.[11] The only significant feature of Liebmann's book, in Köhnke's view, is that scholars had made so much out of something so insignificant.[12]

Here again Köhnke's political convictions trump his historical sense. He goes too far in belittling the impact of Liebmann's book. Though it was not the first manifesto of neo-Kantianism, it is still of some historical significance, partly because it was widely read and attracted much attention in its day, and partly because it was prized by later neo-Kantians, most notably Wilhelm Windelband and Bruno Bauch.[13] Köhnke's attribution of a political agenda to the work is also a misreading, because, as we shall soon see, Liebmann developed his political views only later in response to the military situation of 1870. It is for this reason that there is no mention of politics at all in the book—a very puzzling feature on Köhnke's reading. Though Köhnke is correct in pointing out the brashness of Liebmann's polemics and the weaknesses in his interpretation of Kant, he is also unfair in dismissing the work's intellectual qualities. For all their passion and conviction, Liebmann's polemics sometimes do strike their target; and his interpretation of Kant is in an important respect groundbreaking. For Liebmann saw more clearly than most of his contemporaries that there are serious shortcomings to the psychological interpretation of Kant, which was the predominant interpretation of the 1860s; he recognized before Cohen and Windelband, if

[10] Bauch, 'Vorwort des Herausgebers', p. viii. Köhnke, *Entstehung und Aufstieg*, p. 216, repeats this old view.
[11] Köhnke, *Entstehung und Aufstieg*, pp. 221–222, 228.
[12] Köhnke, *Entstehung und Aufstieg*, p. 218.
[13] See Wilhelm Windelband, 'Otto Liebmanns Philosophie', *Kant-Studien* 15 (1910), iii–x; and Bruno Bauch, 'Nachruf auf im Sarge im Namen der Kant-Gesellschaft gesprochenen Worten', *Kant-Studien* 17 (1912), 5–8.

only through a glass darkly, that transcendental philosophy is more epistemology than psychology.

Liebmann wrote his book in response to the philosophical situation of the 1860s. The context and content of his book suggests that it was written in response to the Trendelenburg–Fischer dispute, which had been set on its fateful course in the early 1860s.[14] As a student of Fischer, to whom he felt greatly indebted, Liebmann would have wanted to defend the position of his teacher against Trendelenburg. The motive for Liebmann's critique of the thing-in-itself would be to undermine the very possibility of Trendelenburg's third alternative, which stipulated that a priori forms of sensibility correspond with things-in-themselves. If there are no things-in-themselves, then the a priori forms of space and time would have to be true of appearances or experience alone. In that case Fischer would win out over Trendelenburg almost by default.[15]

The explicit explanation that Liebmann provides for his book is that it is a response to the current crisis of philosophy. Like Fischer and Zeller, Liebmann is greatly worried by the decline in prestige of philosophy, which seems increasingly dispensable to the public. In his introduction he complains about the recent general mistrust towards philosophy. The public are either indifferent about it or, even worse, they are tempted by materialism (5). The main reason for this loss of confidence Liebmann finds less in the danger of obsolescence than in the interminable strife between the new systems. People listened in awe to Schelling's oracles–only for Herbart to condemn them as nonsense. They were astounded by the boldness of Hegel's dialectic–only for Schopenhauer to dismiss it as hocus-pocus. They read Fries' polemics against Fichte, Schelling and Hegel; but then they heard about Herbart's critique of Fries, and finally Schopenhauer's diatribes against them all. And so the general picture is one of confusion and chaos:

Sadly, the Babylonian tower of German philosophy in our century is distinguished from the biblical one not only in that its builders believed they really reached heaven, but also in creating a confusion of thought as well as a confusion of tongues. (6)

What is the path out of this predicament? Liebmann has the same advice as Fischer and Zeller: go back to fundamentals, return to the common starting point of these systems. Those fundamentals, that starting point, lie with Kant's philosophy. All forms of recent philosophy are only so many interpretations of Kant, so that to see what is right or wrong with them it is only necessary to go back to him. If we know

[14] Trendelenburg had made his criticisms of Fischer in the 1862 edition of the *Logische Untersuchungen* (Leipzig: Hirzel, 1862), I, 121–127; and Fischer had responded to them in *System der Logik und Metaphysik oder Wissenschaftslehre* (Heidelberg: Bestermann, 1865), §§65–66, 77 Zusatz.

[15] There is no direct evidence that Liebmann wanted to take part in the brewing controversy. He makes no explicit mention of it. But this might have been because Fischer did not want him to broaden the dispute, which was still limited in 1865.

what is valid or invalid in Kant's philosophy, we will have a criterion to measure the value, or lack thereof, in all forms of recent philosophy (13).

What, then, is right, and what is wrong, with Kant's philosophy? Liebmann is entirely confident that Kant's philosophy is sound and solid in its basic principles. That the a priori forms of sensibility and understanding are necessary conditions of experience; that the object and subject of knowledge are interdependent; that there cannot be knowledge beyond possible experience; that human forms of representation are limited to time and space; that the transcendental subject is the ineliminable condition for all experience—all these principles are incontestable, the starting point for any sound philosophy (20–26). Showing their truth constitutes Kant's "epoch making" achievement. Kant has done for the philosophical world what Copernicus and Columbus did for the physical world.

Still, Kant's philosophy is not without its flaws, it too is not above critique. For one thing, it is marred by its technical terminology, artificial symmetries and rigid systematics. Behind all that rococo ornamentation, Liebmann writes, "we can almost physically detect the powered and bewigged Magister" (12). More importantly, however, there is another major flaw, one that lies deep in the Kantian system "like the worm in the fruit" (26). This is the postulate of the thing-in-itself. This postulate is the thesis that reality in itself, apart from and prior to cognition, is utterly unknowable, and unknowable in principle. This thesis is problematic, Liebmann argues, because it is utterly inconsistent with Kant's fundamental principles, especially the limitation of knowledge to possible experience. If all that we know to exist is within experience, how do we know of the existence of the thing-in-itself, which *ex hypothesi* exists beyond experience? Hence Liebmann demands that the thing-in-itself be expurgated from the body of Kant's philosophy. The only reason that Kant postulated it in the first place was to serve as "a transcendental scarecrow" to frighten the rationalists from speculating beyond the limits of possible experience (205). But the concept backfired, because the epigoni took the scarecrow for "a signpost pointing to the irrational beyond".

Armed with this account of Kant's insights and illusions, Liebmann had his criterion to determine the merits and shortcomings of all forms of recent philosophy. All are illusory, Liebmann argues, because they amount to so many attempts to know the thing-in-itself. There are four directions to modern philosophy, each of which has its own formulation for the thing-in-itself. There is the *idealist* direction of Fichte, Schelling and Hegel, which interprets the thing-in-itself as the absolute; there is the *realist* direction of Herbart, which turns things-in-themselves into simple real substances; there is the *empiricist* direction of Fries, which re-invokes the thing-in-itself as the object of faith; and finally there is the *transcendent* direction of Schopenhauer, which construes the thing-in-itself as the will. Once we have seen how each of these systems ends in conceptual disaster, Liebmann argues, we will see that there is no point in trying to go beyond Kant, and no alternative but to go back to him. Accordingly, each chapter of *Kant und die Epigonen* is devoted to a critique of one direction of recent philosophy.

It is in Liebmann's critique of post-Kantian philosophy that we find the most daring and provocative aspect of his book. For the most part, Liebmann shared, and was indeed indebted to, Fischer's interpretation of Kant. Like Fischer, he saw Kant's theories of space and time as the very heart of Kant's transcendental idealism; and he stressed the ineliminability of the knowing subject and the limitation of knowledge to experience. It was indeed Fischer who had argued that the very concept of the thing-in-itself is unintelligible and has to be eliminated because it is incompatible with Kant's critical principles.[16] Yet, despite these deep Kantian strains in his thinking, Fischer continued to be a Hegelian in his metaphysical views. The 1865 edition of his *Logik und Metaphysik* persisted in its Hegelianism despite its endorsement of central Kantian doctrines.[17] It was in just this respect that Liebmann was taking issue with his former teacher. The hidden but pointed message behind his critique of Hegel was that Fischer needed to abandon his Hegelianism. If Hegel's metaphysics is a gigantic attempt to know the thing-in-itself, then it is a misconceived enterprise which needs to be aborted. Liebmann was in effect telling Fischer: "if you accept Kant's critical limits, you also cannot be a Hegelian metaphysician." In calling for a return to Kant, Liebmann was making a plea to his old teacher, begging him to take his critical principles to their ultimate conclusion.

Whoever its intended audience, the chief contention of Liebmann's book seems deeply paradoxical. If Kant is the source of the postulate of the thing-in-itself, and if all forms of recent philosophy go astray because they rehabilitate this postulate, why go back to Kant? It would seem better to go forward with a new philosophy rather than returning to the old one, which has been the source of so much trouble. The solution to the paradox is Liebmann's tacit assumption that Kant's postulate is dispensable. We can have the core of Kant's epistemology without the thing-in-itself, Liebmann assumes. Indeed, since the postulate is inconsistent with Kant's basic principles, we not only can but must get rid of it.

But that answer only poses another question: If the thing-in-itself so blatantly violates Kant's principles, why did he postulate it in the first place? Liebmann owes us an explanation. To his credit, he attempts to provide one, indeed two. He thinks that there is both a historical and psychological explanation for Kant's unseemly postulate. The *historical* explanation is that Kant could not completely renounce the language of the Leibnizian-Wolffian system if he were to be intelligible to his age (35–36). The thing-in-itself was an old tattered hand-me-down: the *ens per se* of Wolffian ontology. Kant kept using it so that he could warn the Wolffians that what they were trying to know is really unknowable. The *psychological* explanation lies in our deep-seated

---

[16]   See Kuno Fischer, *Logik und Metaphysik oder Wissenschaftslehre* (Stuttgart: Scheitlin, 1852), §12, p. 23.

[17]   As we have seen in Chapter 5, Section 7. Though *Kant und die Epigonen* appeared in March 1865, half a year before Fischer's 1865 *Logik und Metaphysik*, Liebmann would have had many opportunities before then to know of Fischer's persistent Hegelianism.

human tendency to ask the question 'Why?', even when we know we cannot answer it (51–66). The final goal of all knowledge is to know the unconditioned, that which completes the series of conditions. The thing-in-itself is just another concept for the unconditioned. We are led by a very natural chain of reasoning to assume its exist-ence. The reasoning goes: everything conditioned depends on something outside it as its cause; the empirical world in space and time is conditioned; therefore it depends on something outside it as its cause (38).

Whatever Kant's reason for postulating its existence, Liebmann was confident that the thing-in-itself could be easily removed from the corpus of the critical philoso-phy. But here his confidence bordered on the rash and reckless. It is remarkable that, throughout *Kant und die Epigonen,* Liebmann does not consider Kant's major motive for postulating the thing-in-itself: the need to make room for faith. It is as if Kant's entire concern with morality and religion were misconceived. Liebmann's justification for this apparent neglect seems to be that if the thing-in-itself is inconceivable, then it cannot be an intelligible object of moral or religions belief. On just these grounds, he mocks Fries for having made the thing-in-itself the object of religious faith (156). In gen-eral, Liebmann had little sympathy for Kant's attempt to rescue morality and religion with the thing-in-itself, which he dismissed as "the feeble side of this great thinker".[18]

It is even more remarkable that Liebmann does not attempt to reconstruct, and then deconstruct, the line of reasoning that led Kant to postulate the thing-in-itself in the first place. However problematic, the thing-in-itself is hard to avoid on Kantian premises. If 1) the forms of intuition and understanding condition how the world appears to us, and if 2) they do not create the manifold of intuition, which has to be given to us, then it only seems natural to assume that 3) there is something that exists apart from and prior to the application of these forms. This something will be unknowable to us because the a priori forms of intuition and understanding condi-tion and therefore alter what they know. Strangely, Liebmann accepts both premises yet denies the conclusion.

The question still remains: Why does Liebmann think the thing-in-itself is incon-sistent with Kant's principles? This claim too is controversial and stands in need of justification. Liebmann is largely content to reaffirm G.E. Schulze's arguments in *Aenesidemus* (49–51). Schulze had maintained that Kant has no right to assume the existence of the thing-in-itself, or to hold that it is the cause of our experience, because this amounts to a transcendent application of the categories of existence and cau-sality beyond experience.[19] Although Liebmann endorses these now standard argu-ments, he thinks that Schulze is far too tentative. While Schulze holds that it is still possible for the thing-in-itself to exist, limiting himself to saying that Kant cannot

---

[18] See Liebmann's later essay 'Die Metamorphosen des Apriori', in *Zur Analysis der Wirklichkeit. Eine Erörterung der Grundprobleme der Philosophie* (Straßburg: Trübner, 1876), p. 218.

[19] Anonymous [G.E. Schulze], *Aenesidemus oder über die Fundamente der von dem Herrn Prof. Reinhold in Jena gelieferten Elementar-Philosophie* (sine loco: 1792), pp. 296–299.

provide a justification for its existence, Liebmann corrects him by adding that it is completely absurd to think that the thing-in-itself could exist at all (51). The thing-in-itself is sheer nonsense, a *"contradictio en adjecto"*, "wooden iron" (27).

Whence this stronger claim? Liebmann sometimes writes as if it were self-evident because to postulate the unthinkable is already to think it, which is contrary to its unthinkable nature (27). This was an old criticism of the thing-in-itself, one already made by Fichte and Hegel, and one reaffirmed by Fischer. But, however venerable the tradition behind it, the criticism rests on a simple confusion: it confounds the concept of the thing-in-itself (its sense or connotation) with the thing it intends to designate (its reference or denotation). While *ex hypothesi* we cannot think of the object designated by the unthinkable, we can think of the *concept* of the unthinkable; otherwise, even the claim of its unthinkability would make no sense.

Fortunately, however, Liebmann does not leave it at this, and goes on to provide two more substantial arguments for his stronger claim. 1) According to the Transcendental Aesthetic, all representations conform to the a priori forms of inner sense, space and time. We therefore cannot represent something existing beyond space and time; so it is impossible for us even to represent the thing-in-itself, which is *ex hypothesi* beyond space and time (26–27). 2) We assume that the entire realm of experience is conditioned and that there must be something unconditioned as its source, which would be the thing-in-itself. But the concept of the conditioned has meaning only within experience, that is, with regard to particular events, so that it cannot be applied to experience as a whole (39). In other words, experience is conditioned only in its "immanent constitution", by what lies *within* itself and not by what lies *beyond* itself. It makes no sense to seek for a cause of experience as a whole because the category of causality has meaning or significance only *within* experience.

There are serious weaknesses to both arguments. First, Liebmann simply ignores Kant's reply to these criticisms in the preface to the second edition of the *Kritik*: that it is necessary to distinguish *thinking* about the thing-in-itself from *knowing* it (B xxvi). Kant explained that all his restrictions against knowledge of the thing-in-itself did not forbid the possibility of thinking about it according to the categories of the understanding. Second, Liebmann's argument from the Transcendental Aesthetic equivocates with the concept of representation, which might mean the possibility of *imagining* something or the possibility of even *conceiving* it without contradiction. The Aesthetic indeed shows that we cannot imagine something that is not within space and time; but these limits of the imagination do not hold for the pure concepts of the understanding, which can be meaningfully extended beyond experience, even though they are then without any reference and so cannot provide knowledge.

Fortunately, the most important and interesting contribution of Liebmann's book does not rest on his arguments against the thing-in-itself. Rather, they lie elsewhere: in his critique of psychological interpretations of Kant. Liebmann criticizes Schulze, Schopenhauer and Fries for interpretating Kant's philosophy as if it were a kind of empirical psychology, little more than an investigation into the faculties of the mind. He makes two basic points against this interpretation. First, it is a mistake to equate, as Schulze and Schopenhauer do, the a priori with the cause of experience, or with an innate mental capacity (45, 183–185). Rather, the a priori signifies the logically necessary conditions for knowledge of experience. Kant's central concern is not with the origins or causes of experience but the truth conditions for empirical judgements. Second, it is also an error to assume, as Fries does, that we can determine the general principles of epistemology from empirical enquiry, from inner observation and inductive generalizations. These methods give results that are only particular and contingent; but the general principles of experience are synthetic a priori, claiming a universal and necessary validity (147–149).

The ultimate lesson of Liebmann's critique of Schulze, Schopenhauer and Fries is that Kant's transcendental philosophy is more than psychology for the simple reason that it is supposed to investigate the very possibility of psychology. An empirical psychology cannot replace transcendental philosophy because it presupposes the very methods and principles that transcendental philosophy should investigate. In making this point Liebmann anticipated the later interpretations of Kant of the Marburg and Southwestern schools. Unfortunately, in *Kant und die Epigonen* Liebmann did not develop a more positive account of transcendental enquiry and how it differs from empirical psychology. We are left with a negative message with little more than vague suggestions about the distinctive status of transcendental enquiry itself. This was a shortcoming that Liebmann would address in later writings.

Seen from a later perspective, *Kant und die Epigonen* was a rash and reckless work, altogether the product of a tempestuous young man. Its arguments against the thing-in-itself are weak; it had failed to develop the implications of its critique of psychologism; and it had brushed aside Kant's moral and religious concerns. The older and wiser Liebmann admitted his youthful folly and dismissed the work as a *"Jugendarbeit"*.[20] He quickly learned the errors of his ways. Soon he would see the need for the concept of the thing-in-itself, which he had too quickly dismissed; and soon he would grow to appreciate Kant's concern for morality and religion, which he had too readily rejected. We can well say of Liebmann what Hegel once said of Schelling: he made his philosophical education before the public. This is the classical problem of publishing too young. We shall soon see how Liebmann learned this bitter lesson.

3. Perils of the Transcendent

In the concluding chapter of *Kant und die Epigonen* Liebmann begins to reveal some of the moral motivation behind his diatribe against the thing-in-itself. The Kantian Copernican Revolution in philosophy had shown that man is the centre of his

---

[20] See Liebmann, 'Vorwort des Herausgebers' to the *Kantgesellschaft* edition, p. v.

universe, and that he cannot go beyond the limits of his experience. For Liebmann, this fundamental epistemological lesson should also be an ethical one: that we *should* make man the centre of our universe. All of our problems, as Liebmann puts it, are ultimately "*immanent*", that is, they are problems only for we human beings who exist in space and time, and which we should strive to solve in the here and now (208, 212). We should not trouble ourselves, then, with metaphysical or theological speculation about a transcendent realm beyond our human world. In advocating this ethical doctrine, Liebmann was reaffirming, if only implicitly, the old tradition of German anthropology, the tradition of Herder, Schiller, Platner, Fries and Beneke. That tradition was always profoundly humanist, preaching that philosophy should be not only *about* man but also *for* him.

But Liebmann had even deeper moral motivations for his campaign against the thing-in-itself. The problem was not simply that speculation about the transcendent drew attention away from the immanent human realm. More gravely, it could also undermine the moral convictions that we need to act within this realm, more specifically, the beliefs in human freedom and responsibility. Kant had postulated his noumenal realm precisely to rescue these beliefs from the determinism of the natural world. But Liebmann was convinced, for reasons we shall soon see, that Kant's strategy had backfired. His doctrine of transcendental freedom did not support but undercut our beliefs in moral freedom and responsibility. So, unless we eliminate the noumenal realm, which is the basis for that doctrine, we jeopardize some of our most important moral beliefs.

To save the concepts of freedom and responsibility for the immanent realm, to rescue them from the perils of the transcendent, Liebmann wrote another book, his *Ueber den individuellen Beweis für die Freiheit des Willens*,[21] which appeared in spring 1866, only one year after *Kant und die Epigonen*. This tract is a caustic critique of the concept of transcendental freedom and a dogged defence of a compatibilist conception of human freedom. Liebmann's intent is to save freedom and responsibility within the immanent domain, which is also for him the realm of nature where all events are determined according to causal laws. The ultimate message of the book is that there is no need to postulate a transcendent will to save freedom; indeed, that the concept of noumenal freedom undermines the facts of moral consciousness and the real relative freedom that we do possess.

The dangers of the doctrine of transcendental freedom were apparent to Liebmann less from Kant himself than his cranky would-be heir, Arthur Schopenhauer. It was Schopenhauer who seemed to take the Kantian doctrine of transcendental freedom to a radical and absurd extreme, violating our normal moral intuitions and undermining our beliefs in freedom and responsibility. Schopenhauer's popularity in the 1860s had also made him an inviting and

---

[21] Otto Liebmann, *Ueber den individuellen Beweis für die Freiheit des Willens. Ein kritischer Beitrag zur Selbsterkenntniß* (Stuttgart: Carl Schober, 1866). All references in parentheses are to this edition.

important target. Liebmann had already subjected Schopenhauer's metaphysics to sustained criticism in the longest chapter of *Kant und die Epigonen*.[22] In his new book he turned against Schopenhauer's moral philosophy, which seemed to him the best example of how excessive metaphysical speculation is a danger to morals.[23] Liebmann specifically targets Schopenhauer's 1839 *Preisschrift über die Freiheit des Willens*,[24] which had discredited the testimony of self-awareness as an arbiter of the question of free will. Schopenhauer argued that my self-awareness does not give me evidence for the power of choice, the ability on any specific occasion to choose between X or not-X.[25] Liebmann wishes to restore the worthiness of that testimony, so that each person has within his own consciousness "an individual proof of the freedom of the will".

As Liebmann portrays it,[26] Schopenhauer's theory of the will is a heavy and harsh determinism. It maintains that a person's actions are the necessary result of his character and motives. A person's character is given at birth and normally unalterable, the result of the transcendent will expressing itself through him.[27] Given his character, a person will choose to act only on certain motives rather than others; and given his character *along with* these motives, his action follows of necessity, such that it could not be otherwise. One and the same person, with the same motives and under the same circumstances, must always act in the same manner.[28] When we feel that we could have done otherwise, we are simply ignorant of our own character and the causes compelling it to act in just one manner. Belief in the *liberum arbitrium indifferentiae*—the power to act and choose equally between two alternatives—is an illusion, arising from confusing the correct proposition "I could have done otherwise on this occasion *if my character were different*" with the incorrect proposition "I could have done otherwise on this occasion *with my present character*" (62). I am responsible, Schopenhauer thinks, not because of what I do but because of the kind of person

[22] Liebmann, *Kant und die Epigonen*, pp. 157–203.
[23] Liebmann examines two works of Schopenhauer, *Die beiden Grundprobleme der Ethik* and Band I, Buch IV of *Die Welt als Wille und Vorstellung*. Here these works will be cited according to *Sämtliche Werke*, ed. Wolfgang Freiherr von Löhneysen (Stuttgart: Insel, 1968).
[24] Schopenhauer, *Preisschrift über die Freiheit des Willens*, first published in German as the first part of *Die beiden Grundprobleme der Ethik* (Frankfurt: Hermann, 1841). See *Sämtliche Werke* III, 481–627.
[25] Schopenhauer, *Preisschrift*, III, 535, 537, 541–542.
[26] Since my aim here is to understand Liebmann, I follow his exposition of Schopenhauer rather than Schopenhauer's own exposition. Whether Schopenhauer is entirely the total determinist Liebmann sees in him is a matter of some debate, not least because Schopenhauer's position is complex. At §55 of *Die Welt als Wille und Vorstellung* Schopenhauer contends that our noumenal will is free to create or not create our phenomenal character, and that it can even create a different phenomenal character (I, 396); but he also maintains that the noumenal character, given certain motives, acts of necessity in specific circumstances, and that the appearance it could do otherwise arises only from ignorance (I, 400–401). In general, Schopenhauer defends predestination of all human actions from the original act of will (I, 404), and maintains that only the certainty of the necessity of human actions gives us some solace about them (I, 421).
[27] See Schopenhauer, *Die Welt als Wille und Vorstellung*, §55, I, 404.
[28] See Schopenhauer, *Die Welt als Wille und Vorstellung*, §55, I, 398–399, 402; and *Preisschrift*, III, 567, 570.

I am (68). It is the character, rather than the deed, that is the ultimate subject of moral praise and blame.[29]

So far this seems to be straightforward and unqualified determinism, one that stresses the role of character in the necessity of human actions. Yet, as Liebmann notes, Schopenhauer qualifies his determinism in one important respect (94–97), namely, he allows a person, in rare moments of great insight, to see through to the source of all suffering and to deny the will to live, which otherwise determines his phenomenal character. When a person finally realizes the futility of life, the nothing-ness of individual existence in space and time, or when their own will has been bro-ken by suffering, they can elevate themselves to a moment of "transcendent change", which involves "the complete annulment of individual character".[30] In these cases a person does have the power to transform his character and to change his life. And so there was something like moral redemption in Schopenhauer's universe after all, though it came from a conversion as mysterious and magical as that of divine grace.

Liebmann is sceptical of such mystical transformative experiences, which he finds hard to square with Schopenhauer's general determinism (94–95, 97). But in some important respects he agrees with Schopenhauer's theory of the will. He too finds the *liberum arbitrium indifferentiae* unacceptable, and he too affirms a universal cosmic necessity. Any tenable theory of freedom, Liebmann believes, has to be compatible with the general determinism of nature, which ultimately derives from the principle of suf-ficient reason itself. Yet, beyond these points, Liebmann's agreement does not go. He maintains that Schopenhauer had pushed the case for determinism too far, to the point that it violates the testimony of our normal experience. The task of a moral theory is to explain this experience, not to dismiss it as an irrelevance if it contradicts the dictates of our theory. Schopenhauer's theory contradicts, blatantly, our normal moral conscious-ness, Liebmann contends, because it makes nonsense of our common practice of prais-ing right actions and blaming wrong ones (71–72, 75). What is the point of such praise and blame if, as Schopenhauer holds, our characters are completely unalterable? Surely, the purpose of our moral practice of praise and blame, approval and disapproval, is to change our characters, to make us act differently the next time. But, barring some bizarre mystical insight, Schopenhauer does not allow this kind of change to occur.

Is it truly the case that our normal characters are as unalterable as Schopenhauer portrays them? Liebmann doubts that this is the case. He maintains that we do con-stantly change our character in the course of our normal moral development, that character alters with the growth of knowledge, experience, education (96). This makes Schopenhauer's determinism incorrect in one important respect: the same person need not always act in the same way under the same circumstances.[31] Since

---

[29] See Schopenhauer, *Preisschrift*, III, 618.

[30] Schopenhauer, *Die Welt als Wille und Vorstellung* §68, I, 514–515; §70, 546–547.

[31] Here Liebmann's criticism is unfair. Schopenhauer does *not* maintain that we always act in the same way in the same circumstances; he allows for the possibility that, if we acquire new knowledge about our

the person can change his character, he or she can act differently the next time in the same circumstances (99). This goes some way to explaining, Liebmann believes, our common moral conviction that we could do otherwise. Though we cannot do otherwise on the same occasion, at one and the same moment of time, and with the same character, we can still do otherwise in the future once we change our character.

The least acceptable side of Schopenhauer's moral theory Liebmann finds in its metaphysics, specifically its doctrine of a transcendent will. The reason I am the kind of person I am, Schopenhauer holds, rests on my intelligible or noumenal character, which, through "a supertemporal act of will", ultimately drives my phenomenal character (68).[32] This act of will is, however, unknowable to me, because it is the basis of all consciousness and as such transcends it (69). Such a doctrine, Liebmann protests, undermines all our normal intuitions and feelings about moral responsibility. It means that I, as a rational self-conscious person, should be responsible for an action even though I do not know its ultimate source, a supertemporal act of will. It is absurd, however, to be held responsible for something I could not know myself to do. The fundamental condition of all responsibility, Liebmann contends, is self-consciousness, the awareness of my doing something and consciously choosing it as my course of action (10). But this condition is violated by Schopenhauer's supertemporal act of will, which directs and controls my life even without my knowledge.

The ultimate source of Schopenhauer's determinism, Liebmann stresses, lies in his metaphysics, and especially in his theory of the will. This theory postulates the existence of a single universal impersonal will in all human beings and throughout all of nature, which is the ultimate source of each person's individual character. This theory poses a grave danger to our beliefs in personal freedom and responsibility, because this will creates our character and makes us act in ways of which we cannot be self-conscious and so cannot control. Whether rightly or wrongly, Liebmann is clear in blaming this metaphysics for Schopenhauer's harsh determinism: "From the wind-egg of so-called transcendental freedom the supposed absolute unfreedom of will and action is demonstrated [on Schopenhauer's theory]" (81). Here we see explicitly articulated the motive for Liebmann's campaign against the thing-in-itself: transcendent freedom, the most important form of the thing-in-itself, does not save but undermines human freedom.

Attempting to defend a completely immanent theory of freedom—one that dispenses with its illusory transcendent dimension—Liebmann advances a form of compatibilism according to which our actions are still free even though they

---

desires and the means to attain our ends, we will act differently. See Schopenhauer, *Die Welt als Wille und Vorstellung*, §55, I, 405–406; *Preisschrift*, III, 572. This point is important because it allows Schopenhauer's subject, despite having a fixed character, to reform its conduct. Schopenhauer holds that, in addition to our noumenal and phenomenal characters, we have "an acquired character", which arises in the course of experience from greater knowledge of our own individuality, of what we want and how we can get it. See Schopenhauer, *Die Welt als Wille und Vorstellung*, §55, I, 416–419.

[32] See Schopenhauer, *Die Welt als Wille und Vorstellung*, §55, I, 414–415.

are determined of necessity according to the laws of nature. It is possible to over-come the dilemma between determinism or indeterminism (i.e. belief in uncaused causes), Liebmann argues, by questioning the common premise of both these dire alternatives: that the necessity of an action amounts to a form of constraint or com-pulsion (122–123). The incompatibilist insists on uncaused causes as a condition of freedom, and the determinist attempts to eradicate freedom entirely, because both wrongly equate necessity with constraint. Deny that common premise and the middle path is clear. It is only necessary to recognize, Liebmann contends, that for an action to be determined does not mean that it is coerced or constrained. Coercion or constraint makes sense only when I cannot do that which I will to do; but it is still possible for my decision and action to be necessary, the product of strict natural laws, and for it to be what I want to do. I am constrained or coerced only by a necessity that I have not willed, one that rules against my will (122). But if there is sometimes a necessity that rules within me—through my will—then there is no constraint or coercion at all. It takes the fear away from determinism, Liebmann thinks, once we realize that our wills too are necessary moments in the causal chain of nature. Our wills are indeed determined, a product of everything that has happened before them; yet it is still the case that they too are causes of action, that without them the action would not follow; they are still a necessary, though not a sufficient, condition of action (118, 128).

Much could be said on behalf of Liebmann's second book. His critique of Schopenhauer is compelling, at least in places, and his compatibilist theory of the will is plausible; and, as usual, the argument is put forward with great clarity and vigour. Yet at the close of his *Beweis* Liebmann undermines the very freedom he was so intent on defending. Throughout his book he aspired to explain the facts of moral consciousness, to uphold the common belief that we are the causes of our actions and that we have the power to do otherwise. While he rejects the *liberum arbitrium indif-ferentiae*, he does want to make sense of the power we have as moral agents to change our lives and to act otherwise on future occasions. Yet Liebmann undermines his own project by arguing at the end of his book that for an agent to be free he or she has to act morally, that is, to follow maxims that impose the moral law upon his or her will (128–131). If we are to be free, he stresses, we should have the power to resist incli-nation and to act according to reason alone (128). This was the old Kantian thesis, put forward in the *Kritik der praktischen Vernunft*, that freedom of will consists in moral autonomy, the power to act on the categorical imperative. As a Kantian, Liebmann finds that an admirable thesis, and duly makes it part of his own theory of freedom. Yet this thesis has a disturbing consequence: it undermines freedom because it means that a person is free only insofar as he or she is moral, that someone is not free if he or she is immoral; in other words, there is really no freedom of choice at all. If we are to be free, however, we must be free in choosing either of two alternatives, whether right or wrong. Kant himself had seen through this problematic consequence of his origi-nal theory of freedom and accordingly revised it in his *Religion*. Liebmann, though, fell into the old error, undercutting the freedom of choice that had been his original intention to uphold.

One could say of Liebmann's *Beweis* what he had said of his first book: it too was a "*Jugendarbeit*", the work of a youth. For Liebmann did not remain true to his own critique of transcendent freedom. In a much later essay we find him defending as the source of human freedom "that mysterious something that thinks the 'I am' and 'I think' without knowing in what it ultimately consists and what it really is".[33] For reasons we shall soon see, Liebmann found it necessary to transcend the limits of his own philosophy of immanence.

4. Rediscovering the Transcendent

In the late 1860s Liebmann failed to develop his promising critique of empirical psychology suggested at the close of *Kant und die Epigonen*. That critique invited the prospect of a new epistemological account of transcendental philosophy, one that broke finally with the psychologistic mould established by Fries in the 1790s. Yet this was the 1860s and the hold of the empirical sciences over philosophy was still far too great to move in such a new direction. Rather than shunning empirical psychology, Liebmann remained in her embrace. For his next work on transcendental philosophy was a foray into a psychological domain, the theory of vision. In the tradition of Descartes' *Dioptrice*, Berkeley's *New Theory of Vision* and Schopenhauer's *Über das Sehen und die Farben*, Liebmann's *Ueber den objectiven Anblick* explores the epistemological implications of visual psychology.[34] Its chief aim, as Liebmann explains in its 'Vorwort', is to show that exacting empirical research into human physiology provides decisive evidence against realism and for "an idealistic worldview" (iv–v). In embarking upon such a project Liebmann seems to have been inspired by the latest work on visual psychology, by the research of Lotze, Müller and Helmholtz, whose work he often cites.

Another motive for Liebmann's new work, though never made fully explicit, was to fill an enormous gap in the argument of his *Kant und die Epigonen*. Though Liebmann wanted to convince all philosophers of the need to return to Kant, he had not really provided any positive argument for doing so. *Incredible sed verum*: Liebmann had still not vindicated Kant's basic principles! *Kant und die Epigonen* was a polemic against speculative positions, and it suggested the truth of the critical one only by default. Worst of all, the battle against materialism was not joined in the least, for there was nothing to stop a materialist from happily endorsing Liebmann's critique of the epigoni while snubbing his nose at Kant himself. Hence *Ueber den objectiven*

[33] Liebmann, 'Geist der Transcendentalphilosophie', in *Gedanken und Thatsachen: Philosophische Abhandlungen, Aphorismen und Studien* (Straßburg: Trübner, 1904), II, 89.
[34] Otto Liebmann, *Ueber den objectiven Anblick. Eine kritische Abhandlung* (Stuttgart: Carl Schober, 1869). All references in parentheses are to this work.

Anblick would go the extra step further to provide a positive argument for Kant's basic principles. Now the materialists will be fought with their own weapons: the results of scientific research.[35]

The first chapter of *Ueber den objectiven Anblick* is devoted to the *physiological* conditions of sense perception. Liebmann lays down all his cards at the very beginning by stating two fundamental principles. The first principle is perfectly straightforward: that sense perceptions are representations in us. The second principle, however, is more controversial: that the *content* of sense perception consists in nothing more than inner states; in other words, what we see, sense qualities such as colours, sounds and smells, are "affections of the psychic subject" (3). While the first principle is compatible with idealism or realism, the second is incompatible with direct realism, the thesis that what we sense is nothing less than qualities of objects themselves.

Though it is more controversial, Liebmann assures us that his second principle is the immediate consequence of recent physiological research, and specifically of Müller's theory of specific nerve energies. This theory, for which there is allegedly abundant experimental proof, holds that each nerve conducts its specific kind of sensation. The same stimulus striking different nerves has different effects; and different stimuli striking the same nerve have the same effect. This shows, Liebmann concludes, that the content of sensations depends not on the quality of the stimulus but on the nerves by which we perceive it (32). The stimulus for visual perception is like the striking of a piano key, whose action is only the occasion for the content of the perception (the sound), which is completely unlike the stimulus. There is a great disparity between the nature of the stimulus (the oscillation of light or sound waves) and the sensible qualities in the mind (sounds, colours) (57).

After treating the *physiological* conditions of visual perception in his first chapter, Liebmann proceeds to examine its *intellectual* conditions in his second chapter. The main problem in understanding visual perception, we are told, is to explain how sensations inside us are perceived as objects outside us. If the content of sensation is only something inside us, a psychic event having no width, length or breadth, why do we perceive it as if it were outside us, a three-dimensional object? "The great mystery of perception," we are told, "is not how sensations come inside us but how we perceive them as outside us" (66). Liebmann does not claim to have a definitive theory to solve this mystery, though he does attempt to identify the basic mechanism by which it takes place. This mechanism consists in the hypostasization of our sensations, their projection outside our body in the direction of the stimulus of the sensation (70–71). Since this mechanism works subconsciously, we are not aware that the sense qualities are really only our projections, hypostasizations of our own sensations (71). The mind is thus like a *laterna magica* which projects images inside it as if they were outside it.

---

[35] Liebmann's concern with materialism is apparent from the 'Vorwort', pp. viii–ix; and the close of Chapter 3, pp. 142–145. His statement that materialism is *"unter Kritik"* is an attempt to mask how much it really troubles him.

Just as those images are nothing real but only appear to be so, the same holds for our sensations.

The central thesis of Liebmann's second chapter is that the motor behind this *laterna magica* lies primarily in our intellect. The ultimate source of the objective view of the world resides in the concepts of substance and causality, which are universal and necessary principles that govern all sensations. Since these principles are synthetic priori, operating of necessity for everyone alike, they ensure that the content of experience conforms to intersubjective norms. We see the world as something external to us, as something objective, because sensations have to comply with these norms, whose dictates are independent of our will and imagination. What appears independent of our private will and imagination is hypostasized, as if it came from outside us, though it really comes from the necessity of perceiving the world according to these intersubjective norms.

So far, so good. In the third and final chapter of *Ueber den objektiven Anblick*, however, Liebmann's argument collapses. This chapter attempts to determine the "transcendent" conditions of psychological perception, just as the first did the sensible and the second the intellectual. But in his effort to spell out these transcendent conditions Liebmann stresses a paradoxical but indisputable conclusion, one that follows of necessity from his basic principles, and one that seems to undermine any psychological interpretation of Kant. The conclusion is this: that the mechanisms by which we perceive the world are themselves only appearances! The brain, the eyes, the nerves. What are they but representations in the psyche of the physiologist? He studies the mechanisms of visual perception, which consist in muscles, nerves and tissues, and treats them as if they were also events in the physical world because they too belong to the human body. But this means that all these mechanisms, like everything else in the spatial phenomenal world, are only so many representations, so many perceptual states, in the mind of the physiologist. Hence these mechanisms cannot really be the ultimate explanans of experience but only part of the explanandum. The explanation of experience now has to ascend to higher transcendent principles, conditions that explain the possibility of all psychological phenomena.

What are these transcendent principles? What are the ultimate conditions of experience?

They are a subject who perceives and an object that causes its perception. The subject alone cannot be the sole condition of its experience, because it does not create its objects, which must be given to it. But as transcendent conditions of experience this subject and object do not fall within experience itself; and so, since all knowledge is limited within experience, they are unknowable. The transcendent conditions of experience turn out to be an unknowable X (the object) and an unknowable Y (the perceiving subject), which somehow interact with one another to make us perceive an objective world (153).

The objection is as obvious as it is inevitable: How can these unknowable transcendent conditions be anything other than things-in-themselves? Willy-nilly, it seems, Liebmann has found himself postulating the very entities he had once denounced. Since the inconsistency is glaring, Liebmann squirms, attempting to deny it to save face. At the close of the third chapter of *Ueber den objectiven Anblick* he adds a long remark to the effect that his transcendent conditions are not things-in-themselves (155–156). The thing-in-itself is something absurd, a *contradictio en adjecto*, which, he assures us, his transcendent conditions are not. But this only leaves us with the question why Kant's things-in-themselves are absurd when, properly understood, they play the same roles as Liebmann's transcendent conditions of experience? When Liebmann goes on to provide a long description of the attributes of the thing-in-itself—this supposedly unknowable entity—the inconsistency only becomes more embarrassing, because all the attributes he lists are equally attributable to his own transcendent conditions. And so, at the close of *Ueber den objectiven Anblick,* Liebmann had finally discovered, though he refused to admit it, that the thing-in-itself is not so dispensable after all.

To add one self-inflicted injury upon another, there is another disturbing problem with the argument of Chapter 3 of Liebmann's treatise. If all the facts of physiology are empirical, presupposing the transcendental conditions of experience, then how are they relevant to transcendental philosophy at all? Liebmann's treatise was based on the premise that visual psychology is relevant to transcendental philosophy; but his argument in Chapter 3 means that it is utterly irrelevant because these conditions are in principle unknowable. Any attempt to know these conditions through empirical means presupposes them, and so proves to be circular. All the facts of empirical psychology really concern the world as appearance alone, nothing about the conditions that make this appearance possible. This was precisely the kind of argument that Liebmann had invoked against empirical psychology in *Kant und die Epigonen*. But it was as if he had forgotten it in the first two chapters of *Ueber den objectiven Anblick*. Although he remembered it in Chapter 3, it was too late to prevent a devastating conclusion: the irrelevance of his entire project, the futile attempt to prove transcendental idealism through physiology.

Yet, as we shall soon see, this was not the end but only the beginning of Liebmann's travails, his many attempts to unravel the complicated relationship between natural science and transcendental philosophy.

5. War and Peace

In July 1870 Liebmann's academic career was abruptly interrupted by a dramatic political event: the advent of the Franco-Prussian war. On July 19 Kaiser Wilhelm I had called upon all the German provinces to unite and to defend the fatherland against "the aggressions" of their traditional foe, France. A wave of patriotic enthusiasm swept through the land in response to the Kaiser's appeal. Among those who responded was the young Liebmann himself, who later admitted to having been infected with the "*furor teutonicus*". He duly enlisted as a volunteer in the Prussian

Gardefüsilierregiment. For four months, from September 1870 to January 1871, Liebmann participated in the siege of Paris, sheltering in little villages outside Paris which were under constant French bombardment. After his return to civilian life, he published his memoirs and diaries from these months, which appeared in September 1871 as *Vier Monate vor Paris.*[36]

Prima facie it would seem that there is little of philosophical value in Liebmann's reminiscences. This is indeed the case for most of the book, which is chiefly of historical interest. Still, these four months mark one of the most formative periods of Liebmann's life, not only morally but also intellectually. There is nothing like the experience of war to collect the mind and to make it think about the meaning of life. Several sections of Liebmann's tract are filled with general reflections, sometimes in verse, about death, war, peace, history and human nature in general. We cannot ignore these sections, not least because they are the basis of Köhnke's damning portrait of Liebmann as Heinrich Mann's *Untertan.*

There is a remarkable passage from Liebmann's diary, dated September 24, 1870, where he praises the discipline and *esprit du corps* of the Prussian Army. Though such discipline might seem ridiculous to an outsider, someone like Heinrich Heine, that would be only a superficial view of its meaning and purpose, Liebmann declares. What reveals itself in such discipline is the spirit of self-sacrifice, devotion to law and the state (30). Egoism is held in check as the individual becomes a working member of the social and political whole. This spirit of obedience and public purpose does not oblige the subject alone, Liebmann is careful to add, but also the Prussian monarch himself, who is only "the first servant of the state" (31). Viewing the Prussian army through a Kantian prism, Liebmann then declares that this ethic of discipline and self-sacrifice is nothing less than "the spirit of the categorical imperative". Here are the crucial lines:

In this army everything down to the smallest detail and in the greatest extreme is made "exact", "proper", [it is] pedantically and painfully prescribed and executed. For an outside observer this might appear as servitude (*Kamaschendienst*) ... But in it is revealed the spirit of discipline and subordination, the postulate of selfless, strict fulfillment of duty, the consciousness of duty to the point of complete self-sacrifice toward law and state. Resistant egoism has to keep silent, and the individual feels himself constantly an obedient member of the whole. Such is the spirit of the categorical imperative. (30)

It was largely on the basis of this passage that Köhnke formed his interpretation of Liebmann. From these lines there seems to speak the true "Prussian lieutenant", one whose idea of ethics is obedience and subordination to authority. According to Köhnke, Liebmann takes the Prussian military as his model for social order in general, and therefore preaches the complete subordination of the individual to the

---

[36] Otto Liebmann, *Vier Monate vor Paris: 1870–1871. Belagerungstagebuch eines Kriegsfreiwilligen im Gardesfüsilierregiment* (Stuttgart: Schober, 1871). A second commemorative edition was published in 1896 by Beck Verlag, Munich. All references here are to the second edition.

Prussian state.[37] Liebmann's reference to the categorical imperative in this passage is his idea of "the spirit of the Kantian philosophy".[38] Because he forces Kant's ethics into this Prussian mould, Köhnke reasons, Liebmann uses Kant's philosophy to legitimate the authoritarian Prussian state.

Is it fair to interpret Liebmann in this light? Does this passage really represent his general social and political viewpoint? Hardly. One only needs to read further in Liebmann's text to see the full context and meaning of these lines. There is another remarkable passage where Liebmann records a dialogue between himself and his comrades during *Sylvesternacht* 1870–71 (238–247). There it becomes clear that Liebmann thinks that the ethic of subordination and obedience is only appropriate in times of war, and then only when the fatherland is in danger. He makes it very clear that it is only as a Prussian soldier that one should live for the state. This life as a soldier is, however, "only for now, only *ad hoc*", and it will cease with the peace (244). Like a true liberal, Liebmann then goes on to insist—flatly contrary to Köhnke's account— that the state is made for the individual, not the individual for the state (245). He looks forward to the end of the war and the return to peace where everyone can follow their own career and go their separate ways.

A closer look at the text also shows that Liebmann does not equate "the spirit of the Kantian philosophy" with the Prussian military ethic. To be sure, Liebmann says that ethic is "the spirit of the categorical imperative". But there is nothing in *Vier Monate vor Paris* to suggest that Liebmann read Kant's philosophy as a whole in such terms. The more modest interpretation, and all that the textual evidence supports, is that Liebmann saw military discipline as one application of the categorical imperative, an application specifically appropriate to times of war. It is noteworthy that when Liebmann later came to write explicitly about "the spirit of the Kantian philosophy" he understood its ethics entirely in terms of moral autonomy, which he explains as taking responsibility for one's own actions.[39] That is hardly the submission to authority that Köhnke sees as the heart of Liebmann's ethics.

As part of his general portrait of Liebmann, Köhnke stresses his nationalism and chauvinism, especially his contempt for the French and British.[40] Here Köhnke is closer to the mark. There can be no doubt about Liebmann's nationalism, specifically his fervent wish to see Germany united under Prussia. The book has a loving portrait of Kaiser Wilhelm, whom Liebmann sees as the saviour of Germany. The book ends with the enthusiastic declamations: "*Lang lebe Kaiser Wilhelm! Deutschland für immer!*" There can also be no question about Liebmann's contempt for the French, whom he would often describe as a rabble, a nation of dishonest, decadent egoists. Yet how extraordinary is such nationalism and chauvinism? It was the common ethos

---

[37] Köhnke, *Entstehung und Aufstieg*, p. 223.
[38] Köhnke, *Entstehung und Aufstieg*, pp. 228–229.
[39] Otto Liebmann, 'Geist der Transcendentalphilosophie', in *Gedanken und Thatsachen*, II, 73–74, 79.
[40] Köhnke, *Entstehung und Aufstieg*, pp. 216, 224.

of the age, and we cannot claim that Liebmann's attitudes are especially extreme or notable. This is duly noted by Köhnke. What he completely fails to mention, however, is Liebmann's later recantation of his earlier chauvinism in the preface to the second edition of *Vier Monate vor Paris*. For here Liebmann distances himself from his "blunt and harsh judgments" about the French, which, he confesses, "go beyond the bounds of fairness". He decided to retain them in the second edition not because they were his persistent convictions but only because of their historical interest, because they revealed something about the common view of the time (iii–iv).

The more serious shortcoming in Köhnke's portrait, however, is that he completely ignores the other side of Liebmann's early political philosophy: namely, his pacifism and cosmopolitanism. There are several prominent passages in *Vier Monate vor Paris* where Liebmann expresses such convictions (184, 240, 246–247, 285). Liebmann was confident that the conclusion of the war would mark a new epoch in history, one more cosmopolitan and peaceful than all the preceding. The age of nationalism was a step forward beyond the dynastic age, just as the dynastic age was a step forward beyond feudalism; but now there will be a new cosmopolitan age that is a step forward beyond the age of nationalism. This new epoch will be "the period of humanity and peace" (240), one that acknowledges "the equal validity of all cultural nations" (247). In this new world order Germany and France will cease to compete with one another and will begin to learn from one another; their virtues will even complement one another to serve as a model of culture in general. What Liebmann admires in Germany is not its peculiar national virtues but its "cosmopolitan sense and its humanist cultural ideals" (285). He believes that it is Germany's special mission to serve as the motor for this new cosmopolitan and irenic age because its self-interest ultimately lies with peace rather than war. The French cannot perform this role, because they see war as a cause of *Gloire et Prestige,* and so fail to see how the self-interest of all nations lies in peace (246).

The source of Liebmann's pacificism and cosmopolitanism are all too Kantian: Kant's *Zum ewigen Frieden*, a text which Liebmann cited and knew well (xii, 166). His arguments on behalf of peace come straight out of that Kantian text: that war is becoming too expensive; that war disrupts international commerce; and that the instruments of war are becoming so potent that no one can engage in it without terrible causalities (184).[41]

How did this cosmopolitanism cohere with Liebmann's nationalism? Liebmann himself was not so sure. In the preface to the second edition he poses the question, and admits that his own thinking suffers from this common tension (viii). Nationalism is natural and instinctive for human beings, he notes, because it springs from their attachment to their roots and belongs to their very identity. The cosmopolitan man, who is bereft of all national characteristics, is a mere abstraction. If we were to abolish the ties of family, ethnicity, language and nation in favour of some cosmopolitan ideal

---

[41] It is therefore difficult to understand Köhnke's claim, p. 228, that Liebmann makes no use at all of Kant's philosophy of history.

we would most likely end with the war of all against all (x). Still, Liebmann thinks that nationalism has to co-exist *with* cosmopolitanism, because it is only in recognizing the equal rights of all nations that we achieve the peace to which all nations aspire.

Seen in context and from a broader historical perspective, Liebmann's political convictions in *Vier Monate vor Paris* are those of a conservative liberal rather than a reactionary monarchist. Like many conservative liberals of his day, Liebmann held dear basic liberal ideals—cosmopolitanism, individualism, belief in personal autonomy—but he was also wary of socialism and communism because he was fearful of their levelling tendencies (110–111). If he was sceptical of French republicanism, it was not because he repudiated its democratic ideals, but because he believed, following Montesquieu, that the French people were still not ready for the virtue that a republic required (169). Liebmann shared the general conviction of Weimar culture that Germany's humanist and cosmopolitan ideals should be a model for all nations. Germany was for him, as it was for Schiller, Goethe and the Romantics, *der Kulturstaat, der Land der Dichter und Denker*. In the light of later history we can object to these ideals as quixotic and naive; but they are hardly the attitude of a Nazi party functionary. To read Liebmann in that light is a forced and blind anachronism.

6. Natural Science and Transcendental Philosophy

A year after his return to civilian life, in 1872, Liebmann became extraordinary professor of philosophy at the University of Straßburg, which was now a German institution after the accession of Alsace-Lorraine to the newly-founded second Reich. Liebmann would remain in Straßburg for the next ten years, starting the tradition that would make the Southwest a centre of neo-Kantianism. Eventually, Windelband, Rickert and Lask would also migrate to Straßburg.

In the 1870s Liebmann continued to investigate the fraught relationship between natural science and transcendental philosophy. Although his first foray into that field, *Ueber den objektiven Anblick*, had ended in disaster, with him having demonstrated what he intended to refute (the thing-in-itself) and having refuted what he intended to demonstrate (the relevance of physiology for transcendental philosophy), Liebmann pushed on regardless. Well that he did so, for the relationship between natural science and transcendental philosophy is much too complicated, much too amorphous, much too slippery, to be answered with a simple positive or negative verdict about its relevance or irrelevance. The crucial question is *how* and *in what respects* it is relevant or irrelevant. The task now was to spell out these respects through more detailed and precise investigations. The product of these efforts was one hefty tome, *Zur Analysis der Wirklichkeit*, which first appeared in 1876.[42]

---

[42] Otto Liebmann, *Zur Analysis der Wirklichkeit. Philosophische Untersuchungen* (Straßburg: Trübner, 1876). There were three more editions of this work, in 1880, 1900 and 1911. The 1880 and 1900 editions were enlarged. All citations here are to the third edition of 1900.

REHABILITATING OTTO LIEBMANN 307

Liebmann's thinking greatly matured in the early 1870s. The manifest weaknesses of his earlier work taught him the need for caution. Rather than rushing to conclusions and flaunting generalities, Liebmann now realized that it was necessary to proceed piecemeal, investigating topics in detail and in a more neutral and tentative manner, bracketing any preconceived views. His method, as he put it in the 'Prolegomenon' to *Zur Analysis der Wirklichkeit*, would be "analytic", proceeding from the particular to the general rather than conversely (15–16). Such an analytic method made a general system of philosophy a distant goal, a regulative ideal, which we should strive to approach but which we could never attain.

There can be no question that *Zur Analysis der Wirklichkeit* is Liebmann's best work. The book went through four editions, and it was highly regarded since its publication.[43] Liebmann considers every major problem of philosophy, penetrates to the core of the issue, and he does so in clear, simple and elegant prose. It is a book from which every philosopher can learn something, even if he or she does not agree with the author's viewpoint. In its style and method, the careful investigation of concepts and arguments, Liebmann's book anticipates modern analytic philosophy, though its scope is much broader, indeed so broad that a single worldview emerges from its individual chapters. Wilhelm Windelband wrote of the work: "It is one of the most unique works in which a philosopher ever put forward his worldview. There is, it seems, no trace of a complete picture; each chapter treats its separate problem. . . But whoever looks more closely will find that all these special treatments are parts of an organic whole, that they require and condition one another and present a unified living whole."[44]

It is one of the merits of Liebmann's *Zur Analysis der Wirklichkeit* that it discusses Kant's philosophy in relation to the latest results of the natural and mathematical sciences. Not all philosophers could do so. But, originally trained in mathematics and physics, Liebmann was well-equipped to deal with technical questions. Although his discussions are lucid and informed, we must bear in mind that they are also dated, limited by the state of the sciences in the 1870s. Liebmann was writing *after* the development of neo-Euclidean geometry, the rise of Darwinian theory, and the new psychology of Fechner, Weber and Helmholtz, but also *before* Einstein's theory of relativity, which would revolutionize physics in the early 20th century. Still, his essays remain of great historical interest because they show how neo-Kantianism attempted to adapt to and evolve with the empirical sciences.

Three essays in *Zur Analysis der Wirklichkeit*—'Phenomenalität des Raumes', 'Raumcharakteristik und Raumdeduktion' and 'Zur Theorie des Sehens'—are a re-examination of visual psychology, a topic that Liebmann had already treated in his

---

[43] See, for example, the notice of the first edition in *Westermann's Jahrbuch der Illustrierte Deutsche Monatshefte* 43 (October 1877–March 1878), p. 448; and the review of the third edition by Friedrich Steudel in the *Protestantische Monatshefte* 6 (1902), 413–425.
[44] Wilhelm Windelband, 'Otto Liebmanns Philosophie', p. v.

Ueber den objectiven Anblick. Now, though, Liebmann approaches the matter with greater clarity and caution. The question at stake is whether Kant's thesis of the phenomenality of space has been verified by the empirical sciences. The phenomenality of space means, Liebmann explains, that it has only a "relative" or "conditioned" reality, that is, one that depends on our consciousness and sensibility, such that if they disappear so does space (37). Now does empirical science confirm this thesis? Liebmann is still convinced that it does, rehearsing arguments that he had already advanced in his earlier work. He continues to hold that the theory of specific nerve energies has established that "the quality of sensation is not the quality of the sensed object but a modification of the sensing sensibility" (41). He also still maintains, with Helmholtz, that the general form of space is an intellectual construction, arising from the organization and co-ordination of visual and tactile sensations according to regular laws. "What we see is always optical phenomena, having empirical and not transcendental reality; not only that which we see in space but also visual space itself is projected by our intellect." (49–50). What is new in these essays is Liebmann's treatment of the question of how we see the content of our sensations outside us in three-dimensional space (172–186). He now explains in more detail the mechanism by which we project sensations outside ourselves. This projection is an act that locates our sensations in definite places. The process begins when we take ourselves as the centre of our visual world, the axis, as it were, of a co-ordinate system in which we locate all our visual and tactual sensations. We make ourselves, in the simplest case, the vertex of the angle a-C-b, where 'a' and 'b' designate any two distinct sensations and 'C' the centre of our visual world. We locate sensations to the left and right of C, so that we can construct a line consisting of the segments a-C and C-b. The addition of these segments into the single line a-C-b gives us the dimension of length. We can do the same for other sensations, say d and f, which are above and below C; we then have the vertical line d-C-f, which gives us the dimension of height. We then do the same for two more sensations g and h, which are before and behind C, so that we get the line g-C-f perpendicular to the other two, which gives us the dimension of depth. By thus locating our sensations in this primitive co-ordinate system we construct a three-dimensional space. A larger space spreads out in wider concentric circles around the original space whose centre is C. Thus space is an intellectual construction, the result of co-ordinating sensations by placing them in particular locations in the direction of their stimulus. This leads Liebmann to the general conclusion: "The space that we see, from our visible body to the stars in heaven, and everything that rests and moves, is nothing absolutely real *extra mentem* but a phenomenon within our sensible consciousness." (51)

Two essays in *Zur Analysis der Wirklichkeit*—'Subjektive, objektive und absolute Zeit' and 'Relative und absolute Bewegung'—consider the classic question of whether space, time and motion are absolute or relative, and end with a qualified defence of Kant's theory that space and time are absolute. Liebmann maintains a thesis that physicists would now regard as dated: that modern physics presupposes the ideas of absolute space and time. Time cannot be relative, he argues in the first essay, because there are axioms about time—namely, "Time is a continuum", "Two parts of time are not simultaneous but succeed one another"—that are valid only for an absolute time like Newton's (105). Space cannot be relative, he explains in the second essay, because, as Newton held, the rotation of a single body in empty space has a motion that takes place in absolute space alone (141). Furthermore, Galileo's law of inertia presupposes absolute space, because it assumes that a body will move in a straight line, and with a uniform velocity, even when no other body acts upon it (139). It is indeed the case, Liebmann concedes, that any space, time or motion in the empirical world is relative, and that in an empirical regress we will never find any absolute space, time or motion. Still, physics requires the ideas of an absolute space and time for motions that take place independent of other motions (viz. the rotating body, perfect inertia).

The most interesting and original of Liebmann's essays—'Raumcharakteristik und Raumdeduktion'—discusses the Kantian theory of space with reference to "meta-geometry", that is, the new non-Euclidean geometries recently developed by Gauß, Riemann and Lobachevski. Liebmann thinks that non-Euclidean geometry supports rather than refutes Kant's theory of space (45). According to his interpretation, the new meta-geometry constructs the possibility of spaces of any number of dimensions by seeing them as the product of a co-ordinate system having any number of co-ordinates (58). Just as in analytic geometry we locate a point in Euclidean space with three co-ordinates, so in meta-geometry we can locate a multidimensional space with any number of co-ordinates. Meta-geometry makes Euclidean space simply a special instance of space in general; it holds for a space having three co-ordinates, even surfaces and no curvature. *Prima facie* this would seem to undermine Kant's theory of space in the Transcendental Aesthetic, because it shows that Kant's theory holds not for space as such but only one kind of space, namely, Euclidean space of three dimensions. Liebmann insists, however, that Kant's analysis is not damaged in the slightest. Kant never said that Euclidean space is the only possible; indeed, he insisted that his analysis of space and time held only for creatures having our *human* sensibility, and that it is perfectly possible for creatures having different sensibilities to perceive the world according to different spaces.[45] In his early 1746 *Gedanken von der wahren Schätzung der lebendigen Kräften* Kant even imagined that there could be alternative geometries for creatures not limited by our kind of sensibility.[46]

To clarify the implications of non-Euclidean geometry for Kant's theory, Liebmann distinguishes between two kinds of necessity: *logical* necessity, where the opposite of a proposition is contradictory; and *intuitive* necessity, where the opposite of a proposition is not contradictory but cannot be imagined by us (77). No particular space is logically necessary, such that it alone is the only possible and all other forms of space involve a contradiction. Indeed, meta-geometry shows us that there are as many

---

[45] See KrV A26/B43 and A 42/B 59.
[46] Kant, *Gedanken von der wahren Schätzung der lebendigen Kräfte*, §10, *Schriften* I, 24.

logically possible forms of space as there are co-ordinates in our system of analytic geometry. Of course, most of these spaces do not exist; yet it is still possible that some of them do, so that there might exist other kinds of spaces beside that of Euclidean geometry. Just because we cannot imagine these spaces does not mean that they do not exist for us. Liebmann warns against the inference *non posse videri ad non posse existere* (63). He even says that he has discussed the whole matter personally with Helmholtz, who also believed that it is possible for spaces of many dimensions to exist (64). Still, though Euclidean space is only one possible space, the fact remains that it has an *intuitive* necessity for us. Our intuitions about space are entirely Euclidean, because we cannot imagine any spaces beyond three dimensions. We cannot construct a space where parallel lines intersect, or where two straight lines intersect in more than one point. To this extent, then, Kant is entirely right: our sensibilities work according to Euclidean space, whose axioms and theorems are universal and necessary truths only for beings with sensibilities like ours.

Liebmann summarizes the relationship between Kant's theory of space and the new meta-geometry along the following lines. The Transcendental Aesthetic consists in three central propositions: 1) that the axioms of Euclidean geometry are not logically necessary; 2) that they are necessary only for a being with a sensibility like our own, that is, they are intuitive necessities or a priori intuitions; and 3) that they are subjective because they are determined by my sensibility alone (77–78). The mathematicians (viz. Gauß and Riemann) accept 1), which is indeed a condition of their postulating the possibility of other geometries. Regarding 2) and 3), however, they have no clear position, because they write as if Euclidean space is only a logical possibility; they leave out of account its intuitive necessity. It is precisely in this later respect, though, that Kant's theory comes into play. Its central claim is that Euclidean space has an intuitive necessity, a thesis that ultimately rests upon an investigation into human psychology. Liebmann again raises the question why we human beings are so constituted that we perceive a three-dimensional space, though he now admits that his own theory of projection does not completely resolve the mystery and that more research remains to be done (86, 186).

It was altogether fitting that Liebmann, trained in mathematics and physics, should be an apostle for mathematical natural science and a critic of the *Naturphilosophie* of Goethe, Schelling and Hegel. In the tradition of Fries and Herbart, he deplores the neglect of mathematics in *Naturphilosophie* and endorses the Kantian dictum that there is only as much science in a discipline as there is mathematics in it. One of the more revealing essays in *Zur Analysis der Wirklichkeit*—'Philosophischer Werth der mathematischen Naturwissenschaft'— is a frank and blunt apology for the method of mathematical natural science against that of *Naturphilosophie*.[47] The method of *Naturphilosophie* is bankrupt,

---

[47] Liebmann, *Zur Analysis der Wirklichkeit*, pp. 275–308.

Liebmann argues, not only because concrete conclusions cannot be derived from abstract principles, but also because its *qualitative* concepts cannot derive or express the exact *quantitative* ratios of natural laws (280). Precisely because *Naturphilosophie* neglects mathematics, a vast dimension of nature will be forever inaccessible to it: namely, its quantitative aspect. Nature is a fundamentally quantitative realm, Liebmann insists, where everything has its precise measure and quantity. Although Schelling and Hegel regard this realm as merely accidental or sheer appearance, it is really essential, because what something is, its very individuality, is determined by its precise measure and quantity (279). *"Magnitude, to be quantitatively determined, is absolutely everything; and without its quantitative determination everything=zero, i.e., nothingness."* (280; Liebmann's emphasis). The ideal of natural science is therefore to have "a mathematical theory for all kinds of events in space and time" (281). Liebmann recommends that this ideal replace the metaphysics of *Naturphilosophie*. Reason in the universe does not consist in spirit, the absolute or the will, but in nothing less than the system of all natural laws (283).

Nevertheless, Liebmann's mathematical conception of nature and his critique of *Naturphilosophie* should not lead us to the conclusion that he rejected *Naturphilosophie* as a whole. The more Liebmann distanced himself from positivism and materialism, the closer he came to the conception of nature characteristic of Goethe's, Schelling's and Hegel's *Naturphilosophie*. For reasons we shall soon see, the conception of nature as purposive, as forming an organic unity and realizing a rational plan, which is so charateristic of *Naturphilosophie*, proved to be essential in Liebmann's battle against materialism. It is now time to take a close look at that battle.

7. Against Materialism

Like so many neo-Kantians, Liebmann formulated his philosophy against the backdrop of the materialism controversy of the 1850s. Materialism was for him the great nemesis, that force for intellectual and moral evil that had motivated him to develop and defend his own Kantian convictions. His concern with materialism, only implicit in *Kant und die Epigonen*, is evident from the forward to *Ueber den objektiven Anblick,* where Liebmann complains that there is still no viable strategy against it (ix). Yet it is remarkable that, when it came to providing actual criticisms of materialism, Liebmann held back, saying little or nothing. He was so contemptuous of *"Herren Vogt und Consorten"* that he declared their ideas "beneath criticism" (144n). Their theories were *"Quark"*, having been already refuted by the *Kritik der reinen Vernunft*. Yet it is obvious that Liebmann's contempt only betrayed his deeper anxiety. The growing power and popularity of materialism had thrown him on the defensive. If he were not to succumb to the very dogmatism he forswore, he would have to do battle against materialism, sooner or later.

Sure enough, Liebmann turned to this task in several essays in *Zur Analysis der Wirklichkeit*. One of the most substantial of these, 'Platonismus und Darwinismus',[48] outlines his position on Darwinism, which we will consider in a later chapter.[49] Another essay, 'Gehirn und Geist',[50] treats the materialist thesis that the mind is identical with, or at least inseparable from, the brain. This thesis had been put forward by Carl Vogt, materialist *extraordinaire*, who held that the organ for thought is the brain, and who notoriously likened the brain's production of thought to the kidney's secretion of urine.[51] After having dismissed such a thesis as beneath criticism in the 1860s, it is interesting to find that Liebmann now makes deep and drastic concessions to it in the 1870s. As if to correct himself, he now explicitly declares that the materialist is not to be reproached for holding that consciousness is only an efflorescence of the brain (535). There is so much evidence on behalf of the materialist thesis that the brain is the organ of thought, he now admits, that it is safe to conclude that intelligent activity is a function of brain activity (531). Only someone very partisan and blind (viz. Liebmann in the 1860s) would deny that the brain is "the physical place of individual self-consciousness and all higher mental activities" (532). We should even adopt a kind of "empirical materialism" as our research programme, Liebmann proposes, where we attempt to make exact correlations between sequences of brain events and sequences of thought (536). The motto behind this proposal is a dictum of Lichtenberg: "Materialism is the asymptote of psychology" (536).[52]

Having made all these concessions to materialism, Liebmann goes no further. He insists that all the facts apparently confirming mind–brain interdependence are ultimately not decisive for our worldview (538). Lichtenberg was wise to say that materialism is the asymptote of psychology, because that means the lines will never reach the curve. For no matter how far we go in correlating brain events with mental ones, there is still the problem of the disparity in kind between them. "What does protein, calcium and phosphorus in the substance of the brain, and the integrity of the two brain hemispheres, have to do with logic?" (540). They have as much to do with one another, Liebmann answers, as the chemical analysis of the water of the ocean with the plans of the sailors who travel across it. He then asks us to imagine the following scenario: our brain research has advanced so far that we can correlate precisely sequences of physical events in the brain with sequences of thoughts in the mind, so that the sequences of brain events "a-b-c-d-e-f" determines exactly

[48] Liebmann, *Zur Analysis der Wirklichkeit*, pp. 317–360. We shall also examine this essay in Chapter 11, from a different perspective.

[49] See Chapter 11.   [50] Liebmann, *Zur Analysis der Wirklichkeit*, pp. 518–565.

[51] Carl Vogt, *Physiologische Briefe für Gebildete aller Stände*, Zweiter Auflage (Gießen: Ricker, 1854), p. 323. Vogt's statement goes back to the French materialist Pierre Cabanis, whom Vogt studied with in Paris. See P.J.G. Cabanis, *Rapports du Physique et du Moral de l'Homme*, in *Œuvres complètes de Cabanis* (Paris: Bossange, 1823), III, 159.

[52] See Georg Christoph Lichtenberg, 'Einfälle und Bemerkungen', Heft F 1776–1779, No. 485, in *Lichtenbergs Werke in einem Band*, ed. Hans Frederici (Berlin: Aufbau, 1982), p. 102.

the sequence of thoughts "A-B-C-D-E-F" in the mind. Assume that the thought sequence "A-B-C-D-E-F" corresponds with the sentence "I went to the market to buy some wood". This means that if the brain sequence were in the slightest different, so that it becomes, say, "a-c-b-d-e-f", it would have to produce a non-sensical thought sequence "A-C-B-D-E-F", so that the sentence would now become "I went to the wood to buy the market". But what is the connection between the brain event sequence and logical sequence? Why is it that one sequence makes sense and not the other? There is nothing in the brain sequences themselves that show why one order is logical and not the other. Though Liebmann thinks that finding correlations between brain and thought sequences is entirely possible, and is indeed the goal of all brain research, he insists that such correlations ultimately show the very opposite of what the materialist assumes: that nature has it within its power to produce "an *automaton materiale logicum*" (561). It is possible to understand this power, and its resulting correlation between brain and thought sequences, Liebmann contends, only if we assume that the brain has been created and organized according to a rational plan in the first place. Thus brain events will produce logical thoughts only because the brain has been created and organized according to logic. Nature cannot produce these thoughts as a blind mechanism but only if it is constructed according to some underlying rational plan (561, 564). As Liebmann summarizes his argument: "If reason is a product of nature, then nature must have reason" (564). Ironically, in drawing this conclusion, Liebmann had come close to the position of Schelling's *Naturphilosophie*, whose metaphysics he had just spurned.

It seems that Liebmann, in stressing the rationality underlying nature, had affirmed a teleological conception of nature, according to which nature is created and organized by purposes or ends. This suspicion is duly confirmed by other articles in *Zur Analysis der Wirklichkeit*. While the teleological conception is only implicit in 'Gehirn und Geist', it is more explicit in 'Aphorismen zur Kosmogonie',[53] where Liebmann argues that there is no conflict between a mechanical and teleological conception of nature. The whole dispute over teleology versus mechanism is obsolete, he argues, because there is no contradiction between them (393). Recently Haeckel has thrown teleology into the dustbin because he assumes it contradicts the mechanical explanation of nature;[54] but this only goes to show that he does not know the history of philosophy. One only needs to read Leibniz, Kant and Newton, Liebmann contends, to see that it is possible to combine both paradigms of explanation. There would be indeed a contradiction between teleology and mechanism if one assumes with the old theism that God creates miracles, disrupting the course of nature to realize his ends. But there is no need to accept this antiquated doctrine. We can easily reconcile teleology and mechanism

[53] Liebmann, *Zur Analysis der Wirklichkeit*, pp. 370–414.
[54] Liebmann refers to 'E. Haeckel's' "*Allgemeine Morphologie*"' but gives no precise citation. He is probably referring to the forward to the first volume of Haeckel's *Generelle Morphologie der Organismen* (Berlin: Reimer, 1866) pp. xiii–xv.

if we understand mechanism as the necessary means for the realization of a cosmic plan (394). The cosmic mechanism must work with necessity, in lawful regular ways, to realize divine ends, just as a machine must do so if it is to realize our ends. Although Liebmann, following Bacon and Descartes, had banished teleology from physics, that is, from the explanation of particular events in nature, he still insisted that it played a crucial role in metaphysics, in the explanation of nature as a whole (396n).

Liebmann's revival of teleology raises the uncomfortable question of whether he was violating Kantian strictures against metaphysics. In the third *Kritik* Kant had laid down strict regulative guidelines for teleology, which mandated treating nature only *as if* it conforms to ends; there is no empirical evidence whatsoever, Kant held, for the assumption that nature really does act purposefully. Liebmann duly notes Kant's critical doctrine, but only to brush it aside, saying that he will focus instead on the pre-critical Kant, Leibniz and Newton (393). The rationale for this apparently dogmatic move appears only later in another essay, 'Die Einheit der Natur',[55] where Liebmann addresses head-on the question whether he is transcending the Kantian limits of knowledge in assuming purposes in nature. In this essay Liebmann attempts to provide a rationale for a *constitutive* use of teleology through a probabilistic argument. He maintains that the probability that the regularities and uniformities in nature arose from mere chance alone is infinitely low, whereas the probability that they came from some common real cause is infinitely high (572). The root of his argument is an analogy: just as Laplace had argued that there is an enormously high probability, namely, four billion to one, that the homogeneity of planetary movements has a common cause, so Liebmann now contends that it is equally probable that the homogeneity of natural laws as a whole must have a common cause. It is left open what this cause must be, but it is clear that Liebmann thinks that it must be purposive, some form of rational design, because the Epicurean hypothesis that it is due only to the chance movement of atoms in the void is highly improbable (573). So, in the end, Liebmann does advocate the constitutive status of teleology, the assumption that the universe *is* truly guided by ends and that we need not merely treat it (regulatively) as if it were so. In this respect he differs from the lost generation and most neo-Kantians.

Liebmann's analogical argument seems to violate another Kantian stricture against metaphysics: he is making inferences about the universe as a whole from events within the universe. That kind of inference Kant regards as illicit, and Liebmann himself had affirmed just that teaching in his *Kant und die Epigonen*.[56] Liebmann's argument seems void, then, by his very own standards.

What defence did Liebmann have for such flagrant hypocrisy? His excuse is surprising, indicating an important shift in his thinking in the late 1870s (574–575).

---

[55] Liebmann, *Zur Analysis der Wirklichkeit*, pp. 566–578. This essay first appears in the second edition of the book, which was published in 1880. Since the preface to the first edition is dated October 1875, it must have been written between then and September 1879, the date on the preface to the second edition.

[56] Liebmann, *Kant und die Epigonen*, p. 39.

Liebmann fully admits that Kant was completely opposed to such inferences. There is no way that his texts can be twisted to condone them. One half of the first *Kritik* and one half of the *Prolegomena* are directed against them. Nevertheless, Liebmann points out that Kant himself has not obeyed his own strictures. In assuming the existence of the thing-in-itself and in making it the cause of experience, he has taken the principle of causality beyond particular events in experience and applied it to experience as a whole. Thus, even though Kant insists that all knowledge is limited to experience, he assumes that the thing-in-itself is the cause of experience. Now comes the bizarre twist in Liebmann's argument. Since Kant himself has violated his own standards, he asks, why should we comply with them? (575) Why indeed! But with that move, Liebmann had effectively buried his own philosophy of immanence and had given the green light for a new transcendent metaphysics.

8. Critique of Positivism

Liebmann has sometimes been taken for a "positivist neo-Kantian"[57]—with some justification. There are indeed positivist strands in his thought. *Kant und die Epigonen* has its positivist moments, namely, its attack on metaphysics, and its relegation of talk about the transcendent to poetry. Liebmann's mathematical conception of science, and his critique of *Naturphilosophie*, also represent a standard positivist position. Last but not least, Liebmann reaffirmed the old positivist dogma that there are only two forms of knowledge: that verifiable by matter of fact, and that demonstrable according to the law of contradiction.

It would be a serious mistake, however, to regard Liebmann as a positivist *simpliciter*; there are strong reasons for placing him at the very forefront of the neo-Kantian *reaction against* positivism, which began in the 1880s. With age, Liebmann's distance from positivism grew. His critique of materialism, as we have seen, had made him more sympathetic towards classical metaphysics. In *Zur Analysis der Wirklichkeit* he had argued against a completely mechanistic view of mental life, and he had defended substantial forms and the purposiveness of nature.[58] While Liebmann stopped short of regarding metaphysics as a science, he still believed that it involved a legitimate aspiration: trying to understand the world and existence as a whole.[59] Liebmann had also developed a more critical attitude towards the sciences. Although he stressed the importance of bringing philosophy into alignment with the sciences, he also warned against uncritically accepting their results. The preface to the third edition of *Zur Analysis der Wirklichkeit*, which was written in March 1900, reveals fully the anti-positivist views that he had nurtured for years. Here we are told that it is a

---

[57] See, for example, Michael Ermath, *Wilhelm Dilthey: The Critique of Historical Reason* (Chicago: University of Chicago Press, 1978), p. 72.

[58] As we shall see in Chapter 11, Section 4.

[59] The new attitude towards metaphysics is especially evident in the essay 'Das ethische Ideal' in *Zur Analysis der Wirklichkeit*, pp. 716–722.

"fundamental mistake" to think that science alone can solve the problems of philosophy. Science is a useful, and indispensable aid to philosophy, but it cannot be its basis.
The naturalistic explanation of the world cannot be the complete story, Liebmann
assures us, for the simple reason that human beings are not only the product of nature
but also its basis.

Liebmann's evolving anti-positivism is especially apparent from a curious book
he published in 1884, his *Die Klimax der Theorieen*.[60] On the face of it this tract is a
straightforward epistemological exercise whose business is to distinguish between
different kinds of theories about the natural world. There are no explicit polemics
in the book, and Liebmann is content to give his main opponent a generic name,
namely, "the empiricist". But as the book unfolds it becomes evident that it is
intended as a critique of positivism. Liebmann's target is most likely to have been the
up-and-coming *Dozent* Richard Avenarius, whose 1876 tract *Philosophie als Denken
der Welt* was something of a positivist manifesto.[61] Avenarius wanted to penetrate
to the very heart of experience—to experience denuded of all metaphysical presuppositions, which is the basis of all true science. To this end, he announced a programme for "the purification of experience", which would remove from the given all
theoretical accretions and metaphysical baggage.[62] Avenarius saw this programme
as a completion and correction of Kant: Kant's critique had determined the a priori
components of experience; but it had failed to strip them away and to get down to its
raw basic elements.[63]

Liebmann's central contention against Avenarius is simple: that if we pursue his
purification programme to its end, we get nothing. The idea of a pure experience is
a chimera, because experience stripped of the fundamental principles by which we
come to interpret and understand it is nothing more than mute and meaningless sensations. Avenarius' ideal of pure experience forgets one of the fundamental lessons of
the Transcendental Deduction of Kant's first *Kritik*: that even the given intuitions of
sensibility are possible only because of the a priori functions of the understanding.
Avenarius underestimates the constitutive role of the concepts of the understanding; it is as if the material of sense were given and as if the concepts of the understanding were only added to them; but a close reading of the *Kritik* shows that even for that
matter to be given, the work of the imagination and understanding must already have
come into play. Though it is the inspiration for his argument, Liebmann does not cite
this Kantian text against Avenarius. Instead, he lays out his own account of the basic

---

[60] Otto Liebmann, *Die Klimax der Theorieen. Eine Untersuchung aus dem Bereich der allgemeinen
Wissenschaftslehre* (Straßburg: Trübner, 1884). All references in parentheses are to this edition.

[61] Richard Avenarius, *Philosophie als Denken der Welt gemäss dem Princip des kleinsten Kraftmasses.
Prolegomena zu einer Kritik der Erfahrung* (Leipzig: Fues, 1876). This work, as the subtitle indicates, was
purely programmatic. Avenarius carried out his programme for a critique of experience in his *Kritik der
reinen Erfahrung* (Leipzig: Fues, 1888–1890), which appeared after Liebmann's work. The earlier work,
though, would have been more than sufficient to make Avenarius' intentions clear.

[62] Avenarius, *Philosophie als Denken*, §§71–73, pp. 39–40.

[63] Avenarius, *Philosophie als Denken*, p. iv.

a priori principles of all science, namely, the principles of identity, continuity and causality (78–92). These concepts are not given in experience, or verifiable by it, but they are a necessary condition to make experience intelligible at all. Without them, experience becomes nothing more than a blur of sensations, having neither meaning nor connection.

What is so remarkable about Liebmann's tract, however, is more its exposition than its argument, which is standard Kantian fare. For most of the book, for six out of seven chapters, Liebmann outlines the different forms of theory, and his account seems to follow along predictable positivist lines. There are three levels of theory, according to Liebmann's analysis. The first order never leaves experience; its basic principles and concepts are taken from experience, and they derive dependent and secondary facts from basic and primary ones, for example, the theory of wind, which derives air currents from an imbalance in temperature and moisture (18–22). The second order goes beyond the level of experience and explains the phenomena through hypothetical constructs, for example, the atomic theory, or the imponderables of physics (aether, electric fluids) (23–34). The third order is metaphysical. Metaphysics is for Liebmann the attempt to grasp the unconditioned or absolute and to explain everything conditioned and relative on its basis (35–49). As if he were a good positivist, Liebmann states that the ideal for science should be theories of the first order. Such theories should be the basis for all higher attempts at explanation, because only they can be conclusively verified or falsified (22, 54–56).

The positivist reader of the first six chapters of Liebmann's tract is likely to think that he has found a friend. But the final seventh chapter comes as a rude shock, a surprise punch, a kick in the stomach, for now Liebmann declares that his classification is incorrect, resting on a crude and popular error. We now learn that there really is no such thing as a theory of the first order (107). All theories are ultimately of the second and third orders because they are based on transcendental principles which, as preconditions of experience, cannot be derived from it. The positivist doctrine that scientific theories can be based upon and verified by experience proves illusory, the result of the naive realist assumption that the world is simply given to us.

Besides its critique of the idea of pure experience, Liebmann's tract contains another important anti-positivist theme: that metaphysics is a perfectly legitimate, indeed necessary, enterprise. The defence of metaphysics in *Die Klimax der Theorieen* goes beyond that already stated in *Zur Analysis der Wirklichkeit*. For now Liebmann maintains that metaphysics is a necessity for the programme of the unity of science so loved by positivists. There is a dogmatic metaphysics, which speculates about the unconditioned; but there is also a critical metaphysics, which determines how the various sciences fit together to form a coherent systematic whole (112). Positivism thinks that science stands above metaphysics, which is a lower level in the development of human thinking. But the truth of the matter is that positivism is "an inferior kind of dogmatic metaphysics" because it is uncritical, failing to recognize the presuppositions of its own ideal of pure experience (113).

9. The Spirit of Transcendental Philosophy

Liebmann's understanding of transcendental philosophy gradually evolved in the course of his philosophical development. In the 1860s he had an inconsistent conception of its purpose and logic. On the one hand, he realized that transcendental philosophy is not empirical psychology because its concern lies in determining the conditions of all natural science, including empirical psychology; on the other hand, he continued to see empirical psychology as the basis for transcendental philosophy. In the 1870s, however, Liebmann began to resolve this inconsistency, slowly unravelling the complicated issues concerning the relationship between empirical science and transcendental philosophy. The result was an essentially epistemological conception of transcendental philosophy, one that anticipated the work of Windelband and Rickert.

One of the most important essays for Liebmann's new understanding of Kant's transcendental philosophy is his 'Die Metamorphosen des Apriori', which appeared in 1876 in the first edition of *Zur Analysis der Wirklichkeit*.[64] Liebmann now explains in more depth the meaning of the a priori in Kant. In *Kant und die Epigonen* he had chastened G.E. Schulze for having construed the a priori in psychological terms, for having interpreted it as the cause of our representations; but he did not go on to explain how the a priori should be more properly understood. That shortcoming is now addressed. Liebmann first notes how Kant transformed the Leibnizian meaning of the a priori, which made it an innate idea in the soul. Rather than understanding the a priori in such psychological terms, Kant conceived it in essentially epistemological ones, Liebmann contends. The a priori means for Kant the "basic forms and norms of the cognizing subject" (222). These forms and norms are not innate ideas, psychological faculties or dispositions, Liebmann explains, because they have a "metacosmic" dimension, that is, they hold for everything in the cosmos, so that both the subject and object of knowledge fall under them. They govern not only everything we know about nature but also everything we know about ourselves. They are neither subjective nor objective but that which makes the subjective and objective possible. This was a real "revolution in the manner of thinking", Liebmann says alluding to a famous phrase,[65] because Kant turned Leibniz upside down: while Leibniz makes the soul the basis of the a priori, Kant makes the a priori the basis of the subject itself. "Previously it [the a priori] was a psychological apparatus in the head of the earthdweller; now it is extra terrestial, an Atlas that carries on its broad shoulders our entire *globus intellectualis*" (224). This doctrine that norms and forms have a metacosmic dimension, governing the subject as well as the object of knowledge, Liebmann now regards as the very heart and soul of the critical philosophy (238).

---

[64] Liebmann, *Zur Analysis der Wirklichkeit*, third edition, pp. 208–258. The essay appears in its entirety in the first edition, pp. 191–240. All citations in parentheses are to the third edition.

[65] See Kant, KrV, B xviii, where Kant refers to his Copernican view as "*die veränderte Methode der Denkungsart*".

Liebmann is also much clearer in this essay about the distinction between the transcendental and the psychological. The a priori has two meanings in Kant, he tells us (241). There is the metacosmic and the psychological sense. In its metacosmic sense the a priori concerns the basic forms and norms that govern the entire empirical world. In its psychological sense the a priori deals with "the intellectual process in the head of the individual person". Liebmann thinks that both senses are present in Kant's philosophy, and that we should acknowledge one as much as the other. The psychological sense is perfectly legitimate, so that it should be possible to talk about the a priori in Leibniz's terms of "*connaisances virtuelles*" and "*idées innées*" (241n). Indeed, Liebmann assures us that he has nothing against even a physiological or "fleshly" interpretation of the a priori, that is, one that talks about it in terms of "dispositions of the brain" along the lines of the theory of evolution (241–242n). Though both forms of the a priori are present in Kant's philosophy, Liebmann insists they should not be confused. The metacosmic and psychological a priori each follow distinct kinds of laws, which are generically distinct from one another (252). While the metacosmic a priori consists in epistemic, intellectual or "dianological" laws, the psychological a priori consists in natural laws. The epistemic laws are "norms and categorical prescriptions" about how to obtain truth, whereas the psychological laws are natural laws that govern all thought processes, whether true or false (253). In the psychological sense, the distinction between the a priori and the a posteriori is a distinction between the different origins of our ideas, namely, innate versus acquired. In the epistemic sense, it is between different kinds of evidence, namely, universal and necessary versus contingent and particular (240).

Liebmann's talk about the "metacosmic" significance of Kant's norms and forms seems to bring him close to objective idealism, according to which such norms and forms subsist by themselves as impersonal laws detached from the knowing subject. He seems on the verge of abandoning his subjectivist principles, given that he now maintains "the basic norms and forms of the intellectual world" are neither subjective nor objective but govern the subjective and objective alike. It then seems to follow that the subject is no longer the source of these norms and forms but only one more appearance or phenomenon governed by them. Yet, in the end, Liebmann resists taking the plunge into objective idealism. He reaffirms his subjectivist principles by insisting that these norms and forms have their source in our "representing and cognizing consciousness" (251). Apparently, though Liebmann is not so explicit, the empirical subject that falls under the norms and forms is very different from the transcendental subject that imposes them.

Liebmann's final attempt to explain the discourse of transcendental philosophy is his *Geist der Transcendentalphilosophie*, a short tract which he first published in 1901 but then added to the second volume of his *Gedanken und Thatsachen*.[66] This tract was

---

[66] Otto Liebmann, *Geist der Transcendentalphilosophie*. Straßburg: Trübner, 1901. Reproduced in *Gedanken und Thatsachen*, II, 1–90. All references in parentheses are to the later edition.

Liebmann's final reckoning with the psychological interpretation of Kant, his closing statement of the enduring truths of Kant's transcendental philosophy. It is not an
interpretation of Kant's texts so much as an argument on behalf of his basic principles.
Liebmann is now more explicit and emphatic than ever before that the chief purpose
of transcendental philosophy is epistemological rather than psychological. Kant's
central concern, we are told, is to determine "the universal, typical preconditions
of knowledge of the world in general" (3), "the ultimate preconditions of all human
knowledge in general" (8). While the epistemological and psychological sides stood
on an equal footing in 'Die Metamorphosen des Apriori', the epistemological is now
given priority. It was a mistake of Kant to write about psychology at all, Liebmann now
argues, because this deflected from the real meaning and purpose of his philosophy
(3, 8–9). What ultimately concerns Kant is not the *quaestio facti* but the *quaestio juris*.
Psychology deals with the *quaestio facti* because its concern is to know how as a matter of fact knowledge arises; it wants to know the causes of knowledge. Epistemology,
however, deals with the *quaestio juris*, because it wants to know the evidence or reason
for the fundamental principles of our knowledge. It was primarily the *quaestio juris*
that Kant attempted to answer in his transcendental deduction in the first *Kritik*. These
questions are still confused by empiricists, however, because they, like Locke, think
we can justify transcendental principles simply by tracing their origins in experience.
They fail to see that such principles have a universality and necessity that transcends
all possible empirical justification. Even if we were to show that these transcendental
principles are not innate at all, it still would not matter for the purpose of their justification. They would still play a fundamental role in knowledge as the preconditions for
the possibility of empirical knowledge. Following his previous analysis in his *Klimax
der Theorieen,* Liebmann now understands the a priori simply in terms of the logical
status of the most basic principles for knowledge of experience. These basic principles
are identity, causality, and continuity of existence and occurrence. Liebmann drops
the Kantian term "categories", probably because of its psychological associations, and
calls these principles instead "theoretical interpolation maxims of empirical science".
They are "interpolative" principles in the sense that they add to, or insert something
in, experience that is not originally given within it.

Since we cannot justify such principles by the law of contradiction or experience,
the problem of their justification still remains. How, then, does Liebmann attempt
to justify them? Remarkably, though he clearly poses the question, he does not provide a clear answer to it. Following Windelband, he suggests that the answer to it is
ultimately pragmatic.[67] The problems of transcendental philosophy are brought into
a sharp focus, he proposes, if we formulate them in "teleological" terms, that is, if
we ask what are the means for the end to knowledge? (36). The a priori conditions
of knowledge are justifiable in these terms, if they prove to be necessary means for

---

[67] See Chapter 13, Section 5.

the end of attaining knowledge of nature. If, without them, we cannot acquire such knowledge, they have all the justification we need to give them.

In *Geist der Transcendentalphilosophie* Liebmann reaffirms his conception of the "metacosmic" dimension of transcendental principles, insisting again that they are "indispensable preconditions of the existence of the world" (36). He again resists, however, any move towards objective idealism. These transcendental principles are preconditions for the existence of the world *for the subject*, whatever it is, and they do not claim to be true of things-in-themselves. Liebmann is now much clearer, however, about the status of the transcendental subject that is the source of these conditions. The "I" of the unity of apperception must be sharply distinguished from our personal and empirical self-consciousness, he insists, because it is the condition for it (29, 34). The "I" can therefore be regarded as "superpersonal" (*überpersonlich*). This universal and impersonal "I" exists equally in each and every particular and personal "I", so that when the latter knows its world, it does so through the former which lies deep within it. Adopting a Platonic metaphor, Liebmann describes how each personal and individual self "participates" in the knowledge of the impersonal and universal self just as an ectype participates in its archetype (36). The language again seems to flirt with objective idealism, though Liebmann still resists it, making it clear that it is one *subject* participating in another.

Liebmann is very firm in these later writings that the ultimate subject of knowledge is unknowable in principle. In 'Metamorphosen des Apriori' he states that the subject behind the metacosmic norms and forms is intrinsically unknowable (251). Though we can grasp this subject in its knowing function, it is an unknowable X (252). In *Geist der Transcendentalphilosophie* he maintains that the "I" that is the knowing subject is never an object, and he forbids the transcendental philosopher to reflect upon it because that would be the worst kind of transcendent metaphysics (35). Though Liebmann does not admit it, this transcendental self is nothing less than that old bugbear he was once so intent on eradicating: the thing-in-itself. It is evident from these passages, however, that Liebmann's concept of the thing-in-itself had been transformed: it has ceased to be a fiction and has become a reality, though an unknowable one; it now has virtually the same function Kant had assigned it in the first *Kritik*. Ironically, it was Liebmann who returned to the concept around the very time Cohen and Windelband were so intent on eliminating it.

10. A Critical Metaphysics

Liebmann's defence of metaphysics in his *Klimax der Theorieen* was the prelude to a metaphysics of his own, his *Grundriß der kritischen Metaphysik*, which he first published in 1901 as part of his collection *Gedanken und Thatsachen*.[68] It was largely on

---

[68] Otto Liebmann, *Grundriß der kritischen Metaphysik*, in *Gedanken und Thatsachen* (Straßburg: Trübner, 1904), II, 91–234. This work should be read in tandem with other essays in *Gedanken und*

the basis of this work that Überweg deemed "a tendency toward metaphysics" to be the distinguishing feature of Liebmann's work within the neo-Kantian movement.[69] Yet Liebmann's turn towards metaphysics was a later development of his thought, appearing only after an inner struggle against the positivist tendencies in his early work. Liebmann's thinking was moving in a metaphysical direction ever since the first edition of *Zur Analysis der Wirklichkeit*; he announced a programme for a critical metaphysics in his *Ueber Philosophische Tradition*, his 1882 inaugural lecture at Jena; but the self-conscious attempt actually to construct a metaphysics appears only in the *Grundriß*.

Liebmann's metaphysics was not meant to be, of course, a rehabilitation of post-Kantian idealism, still less of pre-Kantian rationalism. It was to be first and foremost a *critical* or *immanent* metaphysics, one that would acknowledge the Kantian limits on knowledge and refrain from speculation about the unconditioned or absolute. To some extent, Liebmann keeps to these self-imposed limits. Throughout the *Grundriß* he approaches the classical metaphysical questions—the relation of mind and body, of the one and many, of subject and object, of mechanism and teleology—and shows the limits to which they are answerable. Furthermore, he warns against speculation about the ultimate origin of life, consciousness, and the union of mind and body; he insists that the unconditioned is unknowable and refuses to adopt a specific view about its nature; and he constantly advises against drawing hasty metaphysical conclusions from limited scientific evidence. Nevertheless, despite such admirable self-restraint, Liebmann does not always heed his own self-imposed critical guidelines. Towards the classical questions he does not rest content with a simple agnosticism, as if no answer could be given. Rather, he takes a definite stand of his own, defending some of the classical answers. Indeed, in explaining the common source of the lawfulness of nature, Liebmann explicitly endorses speculation that transcends the limits of experience. It has to be said, then, that Liebmann's speculative practice hardly squares with his critical ideals. Metaphysics, a forbidden fruit, was for him too much of a temptation.

The more one reads through Liebmann's *Grundriß*, the more one sees the outlines of a Platonic metaphysics. In classical terms, the *Grundriß* is a defence of a Platonic worldview against an Epicurean one, that is, it supports a teleological conception of nature against one that would explain everything according to mechanical causes. Liebmann's "Platonism" (using that term in a broad sense) is really a version of Aristotelianism, one which affirms that forms exist in individual things.[70] It is

---

Thatsachen, especially 'Die mechanische Naturerklärung', I, 46–88, 'Idee und Entelechie', I, 89–121, and 'Gedanken über Natur und Naturerkenntniß', I, 123–300.

[69] Friedrich Überweg, *Die deutsche Philosophie des XIX. Jahrhunderts und der Gegenwart*, Volume IV of *Grundriss der Geschichte der Philosophie* (Basel: Schwabe & Co., 1951), IV, 417, 424.

[70] Liebmann sometimes uses the term "Platonism" in a generic sense for any theory of the reality of universals. For his account of the difference between Plato and Aristotle, see his 'Idee und Entelechie', in *Gedanken und Thatsachen*, I, 100–104.

striking, however, that it is not a Kantian Platonism, that is, one which gives the forms only a regulative status; and still less is it a Lotzian Platonism, that is, one which gives the forms validity but not existence. Rather, it gives a constitutive status to the forms, attributing reality or existence to them as the inherent structures and purposes of living things.

Appropriately enough, the *Grundriß* begins with a spirited defence of metaphysics, which has fallen on such hard times since the rise of positivism. Metaphysics derives from the natural need of human reason to always ask the question 'Why?', the urge to push enquiry to its ultimate limits, Liebmann says. That need is perfectly legitimate, and the refusal to permit that question beyond any definite point is the hallmark of dogmatism (92). Like Herbart, Liebmann insists that antinomies inevitably arise in our ordinary ways of thinking about the world—whether the world is finite or infinite?, whether matter is indivisible or infinitely divisible?—and the only means of resolving them is through metaphysics. The positivists pretend that metaphysics is a primitive form of thinking, now made obsolete by the empirical sciences. But the theories of Plato and Aristotle, of Heraclitus and Parmenides, have not been superseded by the sciences; rather, they represent typical or classical answers to fundamental problems (118). The positivists' attitude towards metaphysics is untenable, Liebmann argues, not least because they have no answers to the antinomies that are inescapable for all human thinking; they either refuse to answer them, or they adopt an answer without having a rationale for it. The positivists have their own naive metaphysics, which they disguise rather than examine. Because of their naivety and dogmatism, they stand not above but below metaphysics in the hierarchy of intellectual development.

Liebmann first considers the classical metaphysical question of the reality of change or becoming.[71] This question arises as soon as we reflect upon the classical paradoxes of the infinite, which make change or motion seem unreal because time and space are infinitely divisible. Liebmann insists that we take Zeno's paradoxes seriously, and he rejects many of the standard solutions to them. Some of the greatest metaphysicians regarded them as unsolvable, and as a result they saw change or becoming as contradictory. Admitting the contradictory status of motion, Parmenides and Herbart denied all reality to the world of becoming, whereas Hegel and Heraclitus accepted its reality but attributed contradiction to it. Liebmann rejects both positions because they rest on a false common premise: that the principle of contradiction is a principle of being rather than thought (121). Things do not contradict one another, only propositions, he insists. Adopting a famous Kantian distinction, Liebmann contends that these positions conflate *logical* with *real* opposition, where logical opposition is the contradiction between two propositions and real opposition is the conflict between forces. Accepting that change is a reality, there are two ways of explaining

---

[71] Liebmann, *Grundriß der Metaphysik*, pp. 114–139.

it while still allowing for permanence in nature: the atomistic or mechanical view that there are a plurality of unchanging substances standing in changing interactions with one another; or the Platonic view that everything in the empirical world undergoes change while only their forms or patterns are ideal (123). Liebmann adopts the Platonic view over the mechanistic one on the grounds that everything in nature, even a simple substance, is subject to change. If there is to be permanence at all, then it cannot be within the realm of nature. All that does remain the same in nature are the laws according to which things change (134). The Platonism Liebmann defends here is a modern and revised Aristotelianism. On his reading, the Platonic forms become scientific laws. Although he states that these laws are the expression or manifestation of powers or forces that constantly work within nature, he insists, true to his critical guidelines, that these powers or forces are unknowable for us. We know only the "*causa formalis et mathematica*" of things, as Newton said, but not their "*causa vera*".

It is in treating another classical question of metaphysics—the relationship between mechanism and teleology—that Liebmann's Platonic metaphysics comes most clearly into focus.[72] In the explanation of life, Liebmann argues, we will never be able to dispense with the idea of form. Like everything in nature, organic beings are in ceaseless flux, constantly changing their material constituents, which are always perishing. What remains the same throughout this flux is their form or structure. It is in virtue of this form or structure that we identify living things and regard them as one and the same (143). We attribute, then, a kind of *substantial* reality to their form or structure, which is what holds together their various elements. This is a kind of Platonism, Liebmann says, which is for him basically "a realism about forms" (144). Although modern evolutionary theory appears to undermine the assumption of substantial forms or unchanging prototypes in nature, we can still reformulate the Platonic theory to show its abiding validity, Liebmann contends. According to this reformulation, the Platonic idea behind a natural kind is the natural law according to which, under the same natural conditions, the same kind of creature will necessarily evolve (145). Hence the theory of evolution does not refute the existence of Platonic ideas but really presupposes them.

Liebmann's reading of Platonic ideas as natural laws does not reflect entirely the full meaning he gives to them. For he also insists that the Platonic idea should be understood in teleological terms, as the Aristotelian formal-final cause. The idea is not simply the law by which the same organisms evolve under the same conditions— a much too mechanical conception by his own standards—because it is more specifically the inherent purpose or end of the organism. Liebmann argues that, at least for the present state of our knowledge, teleological explanation remains a necessary part of the scientific explanation of life. We still do not know the causal mechanism that led to the birth of life from the primal state of the earth. In addition to all the physical

---

[72] Liebmann, *Grundriß der Metaphysik*, pp. 140–172.

and chemical elements that make up the composition of life, we have to assume something like a "*Bildungstrieb*", "*Nisus formativus*", or "*Lebenskraft*" which controls and directs these elements towards ends (161). Liebmann holds, therefore, that teleological explanation is *sui generis* and irreducible to mechanical explanation. He stresses that the technique of nature to produce its ends is much greater than the technique of man to produce his ends, so that the more intricate organization of nature must proceed from a greater intelligence than man (156).

Liebmann defends teleology against all the traditional objections of Lucretius, Bacon, Descartes and Spinoza.[73] He points out, quite correctly, that teleology need not involve committment to physiotheology; he notes that teleology need not be anthropocentric because the concept of inner purposiveness means that an organism is an end in itself and not a means for human ends; and he adds that teleology need not be a refuge of ignorance because its task is not to replace explanation by mechanical causes. All these points are well-taken, though they are hardly sufficient to legitimate teleology on its own terms. Liebmann's critique of mechanism is at its most topical and controversial when it comes to the Darwinian theory of evolution (163–165). He insists that the basic concepts of Darwin's theory are still teleological, and belong more to the realm of Aristotle's metaphysics. Concepts like development, reproduction and the struggle for existence all presuppose that organic beings are purposive (164–165).[74]

Despite his defence of teleology, Liebmann insists that the complete mechanical explanation of life is an ideal of reason, a goal we should strive to approach even if we cannot attain it (171). He still reassures us, however, that even if this ideal were attained, it would not invalidate teleology, given that teleology and mechanism are still perfectly compatible. The mechanism of nature, the strict working of its causally efficient laws, can still be only a necessary means for the realization of the purposes of things. Just as human artifices must have a mechanism to achieve their end, so organisms in nature must have such a mechanism too (167, 172). But it is at just this point that a gap appears in Liebmann's defence of teleology. Granted that teleology is still compatible with mechanism, that means only that it is a *possible* form of explanation. The question remains whether it is a *necessary* form of explanation. Liebmann thinks that we still need teleology to explain "the inexplicable wonder of organic purposiveness" (172). But that begs the question: What wonder would there be to life if it were fully explicable on mechanical grounds? Liebmann has no definite answer to this question because he vascillates on the crucial issue whether life is in principle inexplicable or whether it so only for the present state of the sciences. There is an anti-mechanist side to him that wants the mystery always to be there; but there is another scientific side

---

[73] Liebmann further pursued his critique of mechanism in 'Die mechanische Naturerklärung', *Gedanken und Thatsachen*, I, 46–88; and in 'Gedanken über Natur und Naturerkenntnis', *Gedanken und Thatsachen*, I, 208–230.

[74] See also 'Idee und Entelechie', *Gedanken und Thatsachen* I, 113–115.

that refuses to block the progress of the sciences and recognizes the possibility of an eventual mechanistic explanation of the origins of life.[75]

Liebmann's Platonism and anti-mechanism emerge from his treatment of another basic philosophical problem: the relationship between mind and body.[76] All the empirical evidence about this relationship seems to confirm, he admits, a "psycho-physical parallelism" according to which all changes in mental states correspond with changes in brain events (187). He stresses, however, that this assumption is only a hypothesis, because we are still far from determining exactly how mental states and brain events correlate with one another (189). We still cannot identify the precise brain event that corresponds to just this thought and no other. But even assuming that we could find a precise correlation between them, Liebmann cautions, this still would not prove materialism, because the correlation is still compatible with other metaphysical systems, viz., Leibniz's pre-established harmony or Spinoza's neutral monism, which are no less capable of explaining this correlation than materialism (187, 191). Liebmann's reservations about psycho-physical parallelism are much greater, however, than his merely warning about its hypothetical status. For it turns out that, on his reckoning, some aspects of mental life will forever remain inexplicable according to this hypothesis. There is no physical analogue, substratum or correlatum, for example, for the unity of the self, which is a precondition of experience and not a datum within it (190, 196–197).

In his 'Gehirn und Geist' in *Zur Analysis der Wirklichkeit* Liebmann was willing to entertain the possibility, at least in principle, that there could be a precise correlation between brain events and mental states. He was ready to concede for the sake of argument that psycho-physical parallelism is correct. Having made that concession, he then contended that the parallelism would only go to show that there is an inherent logic or rationality within nature, such that it could produce something as complicated as a "material thinking machine". In the *Grundriß der Metaphysik*, however, Liebmann is not willing to make such concessions. The reason is that he thinks it is impossible for the naturalist or mechanist to ever surmount the dualism between the natural and the normative. While brain events take place according to natural laws, thinking has to conform to normative laws, which differ from one another as much as "is" and "ought". The normative laws of thinking require intellectual freedom, the possibility that the thinker does not comply with them. If these laws are to be valid, it must be possible for the thinker to act contrary to them; no less than the rules of morality, they require the possibility that one could have done otherwise, that we could have been more careful and vigilant in drawing the right inference (201–202). What brain event could possibly correspond to this hypothetical, indeed counterfactual, possibility?

[75] See Liebmann's ambivalent attitude in 'Idee und Entelechie', *Gedanken und Thatsachen* I, 109–111. Liebmann's ambivalence reflects an ambivalence he also finds in Kant. See 'Gedanken über Natur und Naturerkenntniß', in *Gedanken und Thatsachen*, I, 248–249.

[76] Liebmann, *Grundriß der Metaphysik*, 172–204.

The transcendent dimension of Liebmann's metaphysics is most apparent at its close when he treats the classical question of the one and many.[77] He raises the question of why there is so much regularity and uniformity within nature. Why are there laws rather than just chaos? The fact that there are so many laws, and that we can unite these laws under even higher ones, indicates that there is probably only a single cause for everything. Liebmann repeats his Laplacean argument in 'Die Einheit der Natur' that the probability of a single cause of the regularity or uniformity of nature is overwhelming (217).[78] The assumption that there is such a cause seems transcendent because it generalizes from the order within nature to some general cause of nature as a whole (218). Though Liebmann concedes that this is indeed the case, he sees nothing wrong with such a transcendent inference, given that Kant himself made one in assuming that the thing-in-itself is the cause of experience (218). Here Liebmann virtually admits that he will not follow his own guidelines for a completely immanent metaphysics.

Liebmann's case for having a critical metaphysics is further weakened when it comes to the topic of the source or basis of consciousness. We are duly warned that this source is completely unknowable to us. Since all consciousness, even self-consciousness, involves a distinction between subject and object, knower and known, it is impossible for us to be conscious of the unity that lies at the base of all consciousness, the single source of both subject and object (219). After noting these limits to our knowledge, Liebmann then suggests a way of getting around them: mysticism. Liebmann opens the door for mysticism when he points out that there is "a psychological analogue" for the primal source of the subject and object: dreamless sleep (220). In that state consciousness disappears, so that the subject becomes one with the object; it is as if the subject returns to the source of all consciousness (220). Liebmann then pays homage to the Upanishads and the Vedanta, "whose wisdom has no parallel on earth", for cultivating a mysticism that would bring us in touch with the ultimate unity at the source of all things (221).

Whatever the value of mysticism, to suggest it as a path around metaphysical limits was scarcely a Kantian attitude. For Kant, the limits of discursive thinking are the limits of all thinking; and mysticism is only a bogus means of avoiding the difficulties of conceptual thought. Nowhere had Liebmann strayed further from the spirit of Kant's philosophy than in his late flirtation with mysticism. His philosophical development had now run its course, going from one extreme to the other. The man who had once insisted on staying within the bounds of immanence had acquired the urge to transcend them, and through the most desperate means.

---

[77] Liebmann, *Grundriß der Metaphysik*, pp. 204–234.
[78] Liebmann, *Zur Analysis der Wirklichkeit*, 3rd edn, pp. 566–578.

8

Jürgen Bona Meyer, Neo-Kantian Sceptic

1. Life and Career

Of all the neo-Kantian thinkers who came of age in the 1860s the least known has been Jürgen Bona Meyer (1829–1897). Though much neglected in comparison with Fischer, Zeller, Liebmann and Lange, Meyer played a major role in the Kant revival of the 1860s. His early articles on the materialism controversy were some of the most subtle and sophisticated, and his main contribution to it, his 1856 *Zum Streit über Leib und Seele*, appeared years before the pro-Kantian manifestos of Fischer, Zeller and Liebmann. In the 1870s Meyer was a major player in the neo-Kantian discussions of Schopenhauer and Darwin.[1] Two of his books occupy a worthy place in the neo-Kantian tradition. His *Kant's Psychologismus* was one of the last and best statements of the psychologistic interpretation of Kant; and his *Zeitfragen* was one of the first and finest attempts to sketch a neo-Kantian worldview. Last but not least, Meyer was the first neo-Kantian to consider the issues posed by the philosophy of history, issues that will preoccupy the Southwestern school only decades later.

Meyer's importance for the neo-Kantian movement was first fully recognized by Klaus Christian Köhnke.[2] Though Köhnke's discussion is brief, limited to Meyer's early articles on the materialism controversy, it is an important step in the right direction. Here, following in Köhnke's footsteps, we will take the opportunity to take a broader and closer look at this important but neglected figure.

It is a token of Meyer's obscurity that little is known about his life. Fortunately, the main facts are well-established and easily told.[3]

Jürgen Bona Meyer was born October 25, 1829, in Hamburg, the son of a wealthy businessman. As a youth he went to the famous Hamburg Gymnasium *Johanneum* from 1842 to 1849. In the autumn of 1849, he enrolled at the University of Bonn to

---

[1] We will discuss Meyer's contributions to these controversies in Chapter 10, Sections 2 and 4, and Chapter 11, Section 3.

[2] Klaus Christian Köhnke, *Entstehung und Aufstieg des Neukantianismus* (Frankfurt: Suhrkamp, 1986), pp. 157–163.

[3] The main source on Meyer's life is the article by Theodor Lipps in the *Biographischer Jahrbuch und Deutscher Nekrolog* II (1898), 397–400. See also *Allgemeine deutsche Biographie* 55 (1910), 560–563.

study medicine and natural science, a training that later benefited him in discussing Darwinism. Gradually, Meyer gravitated towards philosophy, and in 1851 migrated to Berlin to study it. There he worked with Trendelenburg, writing a dissertation on Aristotle's biology, *De principiis Aristotelis in distributione animalium adhibitis.* On the basis of his dissertation he then wrote a larger book, *Aristoteles Thierkunde,*[4] which appeared in 1855. Meyer also did work on the *Index Aristotelicum* of the Berlin Academy of Science,[5] for which he wrote the entries on Aristotle's natural philosophy. During his early Berlin years, then, Meyer seemed well on the road towards becoming a classical scholar, a career which Trendelenburg encouraged him to follow.[6] But Meyer had different plans for himself, eager to pursue broader and more contemporary interests.

After the completion of his studies in Berlin, Meyer went to Paris in 1855, undertaking studies for a history of recent philosophy in France. Nothing came of the history; but the stay in France had a major impact on his philosophical thinking. There he acquired a command of French and he learned to appreciate classical French thinkers, most notably Voltaire and Rousseau.[7] His knowledge of French philosophy will emerge in many of his later writings, giving them a wider international perspective.

Later in 1855 Meyer returned to Hamburg, and, suffering the fate of Fries, Herbart and Fischer before him, became a private tutor. The image of neo-Kantians as sequestered academics is least accurate in the case of Meyer, who was socially and politically active all his life. Upon his return from France, he threw himself into the civic life of Hamburg, engaging in work to establish an art museum, a Schiller memorial, a *Volksbibliothek,* and a school of higher education for businessmen. He also became a co-editor of the *Hamburgische Volksblatt.* Economic insecurity eventually drove Meyer to find a more settled academic career.[8] In 1862 he habilitated in Berlin, becoming a *Privatdozent* there. He found a position teaching philosophy at the *Kriegsakademie*; and when Trendelenburg resigned his role on the committee to examine teachers for the public school system, Meyer took his place. By the mid-1860s, then, Meyer's career was truly established. By the late 1860s he was considered for professorships in Marburg and Kiel.[9]

---

[4] Meyer, *Aristotles Thierkunde, ein Beitrag zur Geschichte der Zoologie, Physiologie und alten Philosophie* (Berlin: Reimer, 1855).

[5] Jürgen Bona Meyer, Hermann Bonitz and Bernhard Langkauel, *Index Aristotelicus* (Berlin: Reimer, 1870).

[6] See Trendelenburg to Hermann Lotze, December 14, 1856, in *Hermann Lotze, Briefe und Dokumente,* ed. Reinhardt Pester (Würzburg: Königshausen & Neumann, 2003), p. 293. Trendelenburg seemed to disapprove of Meyer's interest in French philosophy, which he saw as a diversion.

[7] This bore fruit with his 1856 Hamburg lectures on Voltaire and Rousseau, published under the title *Voltaire und Rousseau in ihrer socialen Bedeutung* (Berlin: Reimer, 1856).

[8] See Meyer's July 3, 1861, letter to Hermann Lotze, in *Lotze, Briefe und Dokumente,* pp. 379–381.

[9] Ulrich Sieg, *Aufstieg und Niedergang des Marburger Neukantianismus* (Würzburg: Königshausen und Neumann, 1994), p. 71, n.47.

In 1868 Meyer was made ordinary professor in Bonn, taking over the position in classical philosophy once occupied by Christian August Brandis. For his *Einladungsschrift* he submitted a piece on not classical philosophy but Kant's psychology.[10] Meyer would stay in Bonn for the rest of his career. He proved to be a popular teacher, appreciated for his devotion to his students. In 1887 Meyer became a pillar of the establishment, the rector of Bonn University. Just as in Hamburg, he was active in social and political affairs, making it his special calling to promote *Volksbildung* in the Rheinland. He played a major part in founding the *Verband der Bildungsvereins Rheinlands* and a leading role in the *Gesellschaft zur Verbreitung von Volksbildung*. Given these interests, it is not surprising that many of Meyer's publications are devoted to education.[11] Such was his fame as an educator that in 1877–1878 Meyer became one of the teachers of Prince Wilhelm of Prussia.

In his later years Meyer's philosophical views underwent a shift away from Kantian dualism and towards monism. He planned to write a book explaining his new position, but in 1895 he suffered a severe stroke; in the next years he progressively weakened. He died on June 22, 1897 in Bonn.

The chief hallmark of Meyer's neo-Kantianism was his emphasis on the critical, non-metaphysical dimension of Kant's philosophy. Meyer maintained that the critical philosophy is not a metaphysics, that it is not a species of idealism in conflict with materialism; rather, its critical concerns with the limits of knowledge mean that it stands above the dispute between idealism and materialism. He stressed that transcendental idealism is essentially *critical* idealism, that is, it sticks closely to the limits of knowledge and forbears from all metaphysical claims about the nature of reality in itself.

Like all the neo-Kantians of the 1860s, Meyer was an advocate of the psychological approach to Kant founded by Fries and developed by Helmholtz. He has none of the growing doubts about this approach that we find sometimes in Fischer and Liebmann. Though no disciple of Fries, Meyer found the Friesian approach to Kant's transcendental philosophy to be the most plausible and promising.[12] He would advocate a neo-Friesian psychologism as late as 1869 in his *Kant's Psychologie*. Remarkably, Meyer did not adopt Helmholtz's more physiological approach to Kant, and he did not fully appreciate Helmholtz's critique of Fries' introspective methods.

[10] Jürgen Bona Meyer, *Kant's Ansicht über die Psychologie als Wissenschaft. Einladungsschrift zum Amtsantritt der ordentlichen Professur der Philosophie an der Rheinischen Friedrich-Wilhelms-Universität am 9 Januar 1869* (Bonn: Adolph Marcus, 1869).

[11] Among these writings: *Die Fortbildungsschule in unserer Zeit* (Berlin: Luderitz, 1873); *Zum Bildungskampf unserer Zeit* (Bonn: Adolph Marcus, 1875); *Deutsche Universitätsentwicklung: Vorzeit, Gegenwart und Zukunft* (Berlin: Habel, 1874). Meyer also produced an anthology of the pedagogical writings of Frederick II: *Friedrichs der Grossen pädagogischen Schriften und Ausserungen* (Langasalza: Beyer & Söhne, 1875).

[12] The origin of Meyer's Friesianism is obscure. He perhaps learned about Fries from Friedrich von Calker (1790–1870), a disciple of Fries who was a professor in Bonn when Meyer was a student there.

It has been wisely said of Meyer's intellectual ambitions: "His ideal was to revive the cultural aspirations of the age of enlightenment from the higher standpoint of the 19th century, to bring together science and the education of the people."[13] Meyer was indeed a 19th-century *Aufklärer*. This was the spirit behind all his pedagogical work as well as his philosophy. Placing himself in the Enlightenment tradition of Kant and Voltaire, he advocated the classical liberal ideals of toleration, freedom of conscience, separation of church and state; he was intent on Enlightenment in the classical 18th-century sense, which meant breaking down the barriers between theory and practice and making science better known among the public. We shall soon see how these ideals shaped even his neo-Kantian perspective.

2. Criticism and Metaphysics

Like so many neo-Kantians, the crucible for the formation of Meyer's philosophical views was the materialism controversy of the 1850s. As a participant in the fateful 31st meeting of the *Gesellschaft Deutscher Naturforscher und Ärtze* in Göttingen in autumn 1854, Meyer was an eyewitness at the very beginning of the dispute. There he heard Rudolph Wagner's notorious speech about the dangers of materialism, and he listened to the many heated discussions arising from it.[14] While fully appreciating the importance of the issues, Meyer was astonished by the handling of the dispute. It was filled with rancour, dogmatism and intolerance, with one party denouncing the other for immorality. Wagner's self-righteousness disgusted him as much as Vogt's arrogance. Both parties to the dispute claimed to know so much, though it was evident they knew so little. The whole proceedings reminded him of nothing more than the metaphysical disputes among the earthling philosophers in Voltaire's *Micromegas*.[15] Following Voltaire's example, Meyer would cultivate a sceptical detachment about such disputes. Out of disaffection with the intolerance and dogmatism of the materialism controversy came Meyer's sceptical neo-Kantianism.

Meyer's neo-Kantianism had a very different motivation from that of Fischer or Zeller. Although Meyer too was worried about the imminent obsolescence of philosophy, his chief concern was a very different one: the interminable and undecidable disputes of metaphysics. Meyer saw the raging dispute between idealism and materialism about the essence of life, which arose in the wake of the materialism controversy, as beyond solution by rational means. The great merit of the critical philosophy, he believed, is that it could stand above this dispute and show it to be irresolvable. So,

---

[13] Meyer, ADB 55 (1910), 562.
[14] Rudolph Wagner, *Menschenschöpfung und Seelensubstanz. Einen anthropologischer Vortrag gehalten in der ersten öffentlichen Sitzung der 31. Versammlung deutscher Naturforscher und Ärtze zu Göttingen am 18. Sept. 1854* (Göttingen: Wigand, 1854).
[15] Meyer, *Voltaire und Rousseau*, p. 29.

for Meyer, the rehabilitation of Kant's philosophy was very much a matter of restoring its *critical* role and stature, of rehabilitating the old critical task of setting limits to metaphysics. Just as Kant had found the critical philosophy to settle the disputes of metaphysics in the 18th century, so Meyer would re-found it for the same reason in the 19th century.

Meyer stated the essence of his position in a series of lectures he gave in Hamburg in 1856, which were published as *Zum Streit über Leib und Seele*.[16] The book was widely read and reviewed. Meyer responded to his critics, and gave a further explanation and defence of his position, in two series of articles, one appearing from 1856 to 1857 in the *Deutsches Museum*,[17] the other from 1860 to 1861 in the *Zeitschrift für Philosophie und philosophische Kritik*.[18]

In both his lectures and articles Meyer presents Kant's philosophy as a neutral critical standpoint in the disputes between idealism and materialism. The central task of the critical philosophy is to determine the limits of reason and to show how the disputes of metaphysics are undecidable because they transcend these limits. On Meyer's reading, the critical philosophy is intended to be neither a refutation of materialism nor a demonstration of idealism. Both materialism and idealism are metaphysical theories, which are indemonstrable because they speculate about reality in itself, and therefore transcend the limits of possible experience. Although neither theory is demonstrable, neither is refutable, and so both stand as hypotheses about things-in-themselves. On theoretical grounds, then, the critical philosophy makes no decision between idealism and materialism; it simply points out that the dispute between them is undecidable because it goes beyond the limits of reason.

The bulk of Meyer's *Zum Streit über Leib und Seele* is devoted to showing why the demonstrations and refutations of materialism and idealism fall short and leave unresolved the major question about the essence of life and mind. Meyer first considers the materialism put forward by Czolbe, Moleschott, Büchner and Vogt.[19] They attempt to demonstrate that life and consciousness are fully explicable from the basic laws governing matter. Like the classical materialists, Epicurus and Democritus, they assume that life and consciousness arise from the combinations of material particles, though they now have all the tools and data of modern chemistry to help them formulate their hypotheses. The crucial question for materialism, Meyer argues, is

[16] Jürgen Bona Meyer, *Zum Streit über Leib und Seele. Worte der Kritik. Sechs Vorlesungen am Hamburger akademischen Gymnasium gehalten.* (Hamburg: Perthes-Besser & Mauke, 1856). All references in parentheses are to this edition.

[17] Jürgen Bona Meyer, 'Zum neuesten Stand des Streits über Leib und Seele': 'I. Kann Materie denken?', *Deutsches Museum*, Nr. 49 (4. Dez. 1856), 826–834; 'II. Die Lehre von der Willensfreiheit im Materialismus und Idealismus', *Deutsches Museum*, Nr. 51 (18. Dez. 1856), 906–916; 'III. Willensfreiheit und Sittengesetz', *Deutsches Museum*, Nr. 10 (5 März 1857), 345–358; and 'IV: Ueber den Sinn und Werth des Kriticismus', *Deutsches Museum*, Nr. 11 (11 März 1857), 395–402.

[18] Jürgen Bona Meyer, 'Ueber den Kriticismus mit besonderer Rücksicht auf Kant', *Zeitschrift für Philosophie und philosophische Kritik* 37 (1860), 226–263; and 39 (1861), 46–66.

[19] Meyer, *Zum Streit*, 'Zweite Vorlesung', pp. 25–48.

how and why just these combinations of particles arise to produce life. Vogt leaves it to chance, making the origin of life seem like a miracle; but Czolbe and Büchner insist that these particles come together from the necessity of natural laws, which they fail to specify. The problem is that these laws work only under complicated specific initial conditions, and then the question arises why all these conditions come together in the first place (35). The idealist can admit that life and consciousness arise from combinations of atoms; but he will insist that this explanation is still not sufficient because we need some plan, purpose or ideal to explain why just these combinations come together (54–55). While the materialist attempts to explain life and consciousness on the basis of the chemical interactions between particles, the idealist maintains that a complete explanation involves reference to some plan, purpose or ideal. The idealism that Meyer considers in his lectures is what he calls an "objective idealism", whose defining thesis is that all reality conforms to some idea, plan or purpose (55). Within that general thesis, Meyer distinguishes many variations and sub-variations, devoting a lecture to each kind. Here we note only his main objections to two major kinds of such objective idealism. One form is dualistic, holding that mind and body are distinct substances; the other is monistic, holding that mind and body are essentially one and the same thing. Meyer objects to the dualistic version on the classical grounds: it cannot explain the interaction between such distinct substances (75). He disputes the monistic version because it cannot explain how one and the same substance gives rise to such distinct appearances or manifestations (95). Meyer pays special attention to Lotze's spiritualist version of idealism, according to which the essence of all reality consists in spirit (73–74, 87–88). This does not really resolve the problem of mental–physical interaction, he argues, but only throws the problem back another step: Why is it that spirit creates a world that appears in space?

For Meyer, the diagnosis of the failures of materialism and idealism is simple. Both are attempts to explain the inexplicable, to conceive the inconceivable. Both push their explanations beyond possible experience, and so transcend the limits of reason. There is no point in appealing to any particular facts as a final demonstration or refutation of one view or the other, because both views have their own interpretations for all the facts (100, 103). The chief problem for materialism is that it cannot explain why the laws of chemistry come together in just this complicated way to produce life and consciousness; the main difficulty for idealism is how ideas, plans or purposes, which do not exist in themselves, act upon and come to existence in the material world. Before these problems, Meyer advises nothing less than modesty and restraint. We can speculate about these problems all we want, but we must refrain from dogmatic claims that we alone have the solution for them, and that other positions are wrong. Above all, we must have tolerance for the views of others. One of the worst aspects of the dispute between materialism and idealism, Meyer believes, is its intolerance, because each party accuses the other of undermining morals or religion. But such metaphysical views have no moral implications: the materialist can still be virtuous, and the idealist can still value life on this earth.

Although Meyer maintains that there cannot be any decision between idealism and materialism on theoretical grounds, he still states his personal preference for idealism (122). He accepts the common view that mind and body are distinct substances that somehow come together in some incomprehensible way. Whenever we cannot settle an issue by theoretical means, we are allowed such personal preferences, though we have to admit they have no theoretical worth whatsoever. It was one of the great merits of Kant's philosophy, Meyer contends, that it left a space open for personal belief after showing the limits of reason. The model for his own declaration of idealism came from Kant's *Träume eines Geistersehers,* where Kant, after exposing the limits of all metaphysics, states his preference for idealism on the grounds that it gives us the hope of immorality.[20]

3. Critical Idealism?

Now that we have sketched Meyer's general position, we should ask ourselves if it is a faithful interpretation of Kant. His interpretation raises issues of general importance. One of these concerns the critical versus metaphysical dimension of Kant's philosophy: Is Kant's philosophy entirely critical and non-metaphysical? Or does it have metaphysical commitments of its own?

There is some strong textual evidence for Meyer's interpretation. Not the least of its advantages is that it takes seriously Kant's description of his position as "critical idealism".[21] Transcendental idealism is supposedly critical in the sense that it is an idealism about the limits of our knowledge and not a theory about the essence of the world. The defining feature of transcendental idealism is indeed its distinction between appearances and things-in-themselves, where the realm of appearances circumscribes the limits of the knowable and where things-in-themselves are beyond those limits. While Kant does see transcendental idealism as a corrective to materialism, that is arguably only because materialism claims knowledge of things-in-themselves; he does not claim to refute materialism itself because he states, in a passage duly cited by Meyer, that the soul could have, for all we know, a material substrate (A 360). Another strength of Meyer's interpretation is that it takes into account Kant's statement that the critical philosophy is a middle path between "a soulless materialism" and "a groundless spiritualism" (B 421). The natural reading of such a description, which Meyer adopts, is that both materialism and spiritualism are forms of dogmatism because they claim a knowledge of reality in itself. This reading seems to follow from Kant's statement that the critical philosophy criticizes the grounds of proof for propositions rather than the propositions themselves (A 384, 388–389). This agrees

---

[20] Meyer, 'Ueber den Kriticismus', pp. 47–49. Meyer cites extensive passages from Kant's *Träume,* AA II, 327, 368.

[21] See Kant, *Prolegomena,* AA IV, 373, 375.

exactly with Meyer's view that the critical philosophy does not attack the central theses of materialism or idealism but only their demonstrations.

Despite such evidence, Meyer's interpretation is problematic because there is also compelling textual evidence against it. It faces two major difficulties. The first problem is that Kant is not really as neutral in the dispute between spiritualism and materialism as he seems to suggest, because Kant proudly maintains that the critical philosophy establishes the *falsity* of materialism. So it is not simply that materialism fails to *demonstrate* its central thesis. Kant gives two reasons for the falsity of materialism. 1) Transcendental idealism shows that matter consists in nothing more than representations. If we were to take away the thinking subject, Kant argues, the whole corporeal world would disappear (A 383, 387). We assume that matter exists independent of our representations, he maintains, only because we hypostasize these representations, as if they were entities existing independent of us (A 385, 386, 391). 2) Apperception shows that I am simple, and so cannot be in space, where every object is composite (B 420). "If matter were a thing-in-itself," Kant argues, "then as a composite being it would be completely distinguished from the soul as a simple being." (A 359) The second major difficulty of Meyer's interpretation is that Kant does claim to resolve the metaphysical dispute about the interaction between mind and body. In the section 'Observation on the Sum of the Pure Doctrine of the Soul', which concludes the first edition version of the *Paralogisms*, Kant claims that the mind-body problem is resolvable on the premises of his transcendental idealism. Since transcendental idealism makes matter into "nothing more than a mere form, or a certain mode of representation", there can be some interaction between mind and body, which now consists in only different forms of representation, inner and outer (A 385–386). On Kant's reading, mind and body are not heterogeneous substances but only different forms of representation that fall under common general laws of experience. Whatever one makes of Kant's resolution of this problem, it is in striking contrast with Meyer's interpretation, according to which the problem of mental–physical interaction is completely irresolvable on Kantian principles.[22]

Meyer could say in his own defence that, though Kant indeed intends to demonstrate the falsity of materialism, this is not the proper logical consequence of his own position. There is a gap between Kant's intention and his arguments because all that Kant shows in the Transcendental Aesthetic is that space and time are a priori intuitions arising from the spontaneity of our forms of perception; but that still leaves open the possibility that these intuitions correspond to reality in itself, which also happens to be spatial. Meyer, in other words, still had the option of affirming the Trendelenburgian "third possibility", according to which space and time are a priori intuitions but also correspond with reality in itself. It is striking, however, that Meyer himself did not exploit this strategy. Remarkably, in the famous dispute

---

[22] See Meyer, 'Ueber den Sinn und Werth des Kriticismus', p. 399.

between Trendelenburg and Fischer, Meyer took sides against his former teacher! In his 'Ueber den Kriticismus', he stated his express agreement with Fischer and argued that appearances have no objective status beyond representational states.[23] The price of such disloyalty was that Meyer's interpretation of Kant was harder to defend.

Another general issue raised by Meyer's interpretation concerns the realm of faith and what one should allow within it. Although Kant had famously denied knowledge to make room for faith, the kind of faith he wanted to save was still a *rational* faith, that is, one based on the universal and necessary imperatives of morality, which are ultimately based on reason. Kant had no intention of saving purely personal faith, beliefs that stemmed from one's individual choice and personality. For him that would have been to open a floodgate for all kinds of idiosyncrasy and enthusiasm. Meyer, however, had a completely opposing conception of the realm of faith. What Kant wanted to prevent Meyer wanted to permit, indeed encourage. It was the chief advantage of his version of criticism, he proclaimed, that "it would open the floodgates for subjective opining and believing" (v). For Meyer, the great value of the Kantian restrictions on reason is that they create a realm where personal and individual choice can roam and play.

Behind Meyer's liberal conception of the realm of faith were his criticisms of Kant's own doctrine of rational faith, that is, the attempt to provide a *practical proof* for the beliefs in the existence of God and immortality. Since Meyer saw demonstration as co-extensive with the realm of theoretical reason, he could see no possibility of providing a practical demonstration of these beliefs.[24] He agreed with those critics of Kant who suspected that this doctrine re-introduced metaphysics through the back door of practical reason. Meyer's own conception of the space of practical reason allowed no demonstrations at all, and therefore no universal or necessary prescriptions. The space of practical reason was a sphere of freedom, where individual choice alone reigned. Such "subjectivism", Meyer maintained, is "the only possible completion of criticism".[25]

4. In Defence of Psychologism

Meyer's chief work dealing specifically with issues of Kant scholarship was his *Kant's Psychologie*, which appeared in 1870.[26] This book was "the last great hurrah" of the psychological interpretation of Kant, the final work in the tradition beginning with Fries in the late 18th century. That tradition was coming under increasing

---

[23] Meyer, 'Ueber den Kriticismus', pp. 250–251.
[24] See Meyer, 'Ueber den Kriticismus', pp. 262, 54; Meyer, *Zum Streit*, pp. v, 123.
[25] Meyer, *Zum Streit*, p. 123.
[26] Jürgen Bona Meyer, *Kant's Psychologie, Dargestellt und Erörtert* (Berlin: Wilhelm Hertz, 1870). All references in parentheses are to this edition. Also important for Meyer's interpretation is his *Einladungsschrift* in Bonn, *Kant's Ansicht über die Psychologie als Wissenschaft* (Bonn: Adolph Marcus, 1869). This is a separate work, providing a different exposition of the standpoint of the larger work.

criticism in the 1860s, against which Meyer was fighting a rear guard action. Already by the early 1870s the tide would turn against his interpretation with Cohen's and Windelband's new epistemological readings of transcendental philosophy.[27]

Meyer poses three questions concerning Kant's psychology: 1) What is the role of psychology in Kant's transcendental philosophy? 2) How do we know the a priori? and 3) Why did Kant drop psychology from the foundation of transcendental philosophy, and was he justified in doing so? His answers to all these questions attempt to defend the psychological interpretation. Regarding the first, he contends that psychology provides the foundation of the critical philosophy; regarding the second, he argues that we know the a priori through psychological observation; and regarding the third, he maintains that Kant was mistaken in not seeing the central role of psychology in transcendental philosophy.

Aware of the recent threats to the psychological interpretation, Meyer attempts to address them. He explicitly mentions the recent criticisms of Liebmann and Fischer (122–123). They had argued that transcendental philosophy cannot have a psychological foundation because we cannot know the a priori conditions of experience through empirical self-observation. These conditions are universal and necessary; but empirical self-observation provides only particular and contingent data, so no knowledge of these a priori conditions can be based upon it. As Fischer sharply declared: "What is a priori cannot be known a posteriori."[28] But Meyer finds a confusion in this argument: though a priori principles cannot be *based upon* empirical facts, they still can be *known through* them. We must not confuse the mode of *justification* of a priori principles with the mode of their *discovery* (143, 303). That it is possible for a priori principles to be known but not justified by empirical means was a central contention of Fries, whom Meyer explicitly defends on this score (143, 303).

Meyer thinks that there is substantial textual evidence to show that Kant used a psychological method in his transcendental philosophy. It is striking that he focuses on the very same text Fries once had: Kant's *Prize Essay*, where Kant insisted that the methods of philosophy should be the same as those of the natural sciences (124–125).[29] The method of the critical philosophy is the same procedure of self-reflection, analysis and abstraction that Kant had once outlined in the *Prize Essay,* Meyer insists. According to this method, to know the a priori conditions of experience, we must first reflect upon ourselves to see what principles we actually use in perceiving and understanding experience. We identify these principles by abstracting from the

[27] Cohen wrote a surprisingly favourable review of Meyer's book, *Kant's Psychologie*. See Hermann Cohen, *Zeitschrift für Völkerpsychologie und Sprachwissenschaft* VII (1871), 320–330. See Chapter 13, Section 2.

[28] See Kuno Fischer, 'Die beiden kantischen Schulen in Jena', in *Akademische Reden* (Stuttgart: Cotta, 1862), p. 99.

[29] See Chapter 1, Sections 2 and 7. Meyer probably did not know that Fries gave such importance to this text. He maintains, incorrectly, that Fries did not think Kant had an explicit conception of an empirical method (p. 143).

empirical elements in knowledge, and then by testing to see whether what remains has the hallmarks of the a priori, namely, universality and necessity.

While Meyer insists that Kant followed such a psychological method, he admits that Kant refused to acknowledge it, and that he even downplayed the role of psychology in transcendental philosophy. Famously, in the first *Kritik* Kant made a sharp distinction between the *quid juris?* and the *quid facti?*, stressing that the former question was his main concern, while the latter was a psychological matter about the origin of our representations. We do not justify our representations simply by pointing out their psychological origins, "their birthright from experience", in the manner of "the celebrated Locke", Kant declared (B 118–119). Though perfectly aware of this distinction, Meyer still insists that Kant was too quick in pushing aside the role of psychology in transcendental philosophy. Though psychology is not necessary to justify a priori principles, it is so to discover them. In sidelining psychology, Kant had assumed a much too narrow conception of its methods. He equated its methods with those of ordinary induction, with making observations and assembling facts; but he failed to consider that its methods are much wider, that it also includes analysis, abstraction and self-reflection (166, 304). We must carefully distinguish, Meyer argues, these methods from those of ordinary induction, though both are involved in empirical investigation in a broad sense (167, 168).

It was a source of some confusion on Meyer's part, however, that though he made a distinction between discovery and justification, he did not explain how the methods for these tasks differ. While discovery involves self-reflection, analysis and abstraction, justification requires something quite different: assessment of evidence, inference, reasoning rigorously from first principles. Acknowledging the difference in these methods would have been indeed fatal to his argument for the importance of psychology to transcendental philosophy. For if the *quid juris?* is Kant's main concern, and if answering this question does not require a psychological method, then psychology ceases to be so important to Kant after all. There are passages where Meyer seems to recognize the difference in methods (303, 305), but he does not stress it precisely because it undermines the importance he gives to psychology. There are other passages, however, where Meyer insists that the method of the critical philosophy is *only* psychological (168–169). In these he argues that once we broaden the psychological method to include not only induction but also abstraction and reflection, we can see that *both* the discovery and justification of a priori knowledge can be achieved by psychology (168). Regarding both discovery and justification, Meyer insisted: "It is always only a matter of one kind of knowledge of our soul, of one methodology regarding its factual being and the laws of its activity." (169)

But in making this point Meyer was confusing an important distinction, Cohen and Windelband will later maintain. For the proof or deduction of a priori principles is a matter of logic, they contend, a matter of showing how they are necessary conditions of the possibility of experience; and such deduction is a matter of logical rather than psychological necessity; it is as a priori as the principles themselves. In other words, in a transcendental deduction, Cohen and Windelband hold, we want to show first and foremost the *validity* of the principles; we are not making a point about "the factual being and laws of activity" of the soul.[30]

Meyer's tendency to reduce transcendental discourse down to the psychological is most apparent in his treatment of logic. In his *Logik* Kant had made a sharp distinction between logic and psychology: logic is normative, containing rules about how we ought to think; and psychology is factual, dealing with facts about how we happen to think.[31] To base logic upon psychology, Kant argued, is like founding morals on life. But Meyer takes issue with Kant's distinction on the grounds that logic has to be based upon observation and reflection, upon how we as a matter of fact do think (174, 181). Just as we know the rules of English by observing how native speakers talk and write, so we learn the rules of logic by observing the inferences that people happen to make. Kant's distinction is fine, Meyer concedes, insofar as it informs us that logic is about how people must think and not only how they happen to think (174). But in making logic a matter of how we must think Meyer did not distinguish between psychological and logical necessity. He assumes that the necessity involved is essentially psychological, so that what makes the laws of logic valid is human nature, the basic fact that our faculties must operate in that way and no other. This brings his own account of logic close to Fries' anthropology.[32] Sure enough, Meyer praises Fries for having the best account of logic, because he saw that it should and could not be separated from psychology (180–181). Fries' account of logic is superior to Kant's, we learn, because Kant's sharp and drastic separation of the logical from the psychological turned logic into a strictly formal but also sterile discipline. By keeping its connection with psychology, Fries prevented logic from sliding into sterility and bankruptcy.

Convinced of the fundamental role of psychology in Kant's philosophy, Meyer had to address an even more basic question: Is Kant's psychology obsolete? Has Kant provided a plausible psychological foundation for transcendental philosophy? Or is a completely new foundation necessary? This question too was very controversial. Since the 1830s, the growing influence of Herbart's empirical psychology seemed to ring the death knell for Kant's theory of mind. Herbart had criticized not only Kant's reliance on the old faculty psychology but also his scholastic methodology of definition and a priori reasoning. Kant's psychology was for Herbart a relic of that old Leibnizian-Wolffian rationalism that Kant himself had done so much to overthrow. One of the central challenges Meyer faces in *Kant's Psychologie* is addressing Herbart's criticisms of Kant's psychology.

Fortunately, Meyer did not have to stand alone in his battle against Herbart. In the early 1850s the apparently inevitable triumph of the Herbartian juggernaut ground to a halt due to the opposition of two formidable opponents: Lotze and Trendelenburg.

---

[30] On this topic, see also Chapter 1, Section 11.   [31] Kant, *Logik*, 'Einleitung', AA IX, 14.
[32] But as we have seen in Chapter 1, Section 11, this is not really Fries' account of logic. Fries distinguishes transcendental from purely logical principles.

It was in this decade that Lotze and Trendelenburg began to defend Kant's theory against Herbart, especially its tripartite division of the mind into faculties of feeling, desire and representation.[33] Though no great fans of the old faculty theory, Lotze and Trendelenburg argued that Kant's tripartite division of the mind is more accurate in dealing with the facts than Herbart's reduction of the mind down to the single faculty of representation. Meyer joined Lotze and Trendelenburg to defend Kant against the Herbartian assault. Accordingly, the first part of *Kant's Psychologie* is devoted to explaining and justifying Kant's psychology.

It was a singular feature of Meyer's defence of Kant's psychology that, unlike Lotze and Trendelenburg, it attempts to vindicate the concept of a faculty itself. Herbart had attacked that concept on a battery of grounds: that it was a refuge of ignorance, doing little more than renaming the phenomena to be explained; that it multiplied powers beyond necessity, inventing a faculty for any power of a body to act in certain ways; that it divided the soul into distinct compartments, undermining its identity; and so on.[34] But Meyer thinks that none of these objections are compelling. They ignore the definite sense Kant gave to the concept of a faculty: it stands for not *any* power of a body to act in a certain way, but for its power to act in definite *characteristic* ways under the appropriate circumstances (86–87). The concept of a power applies specifically to a substance, and more specifically to the relation of a substance to its accidents insofar as it is the ground of their reality (84–85). While, admittedly, the concept of a power is not as definite as a natural law, it is still not empty because it serves to designate a definite primitive class of phenomena. We can, and indeed should, distinguish between faculties when each denotes an *original* class of phenomena, that is, a class that cannot be reduced down to or subsumed under another class. So if the soul produces different kinds of effects, some of which are qualitatively distinct from others, then it should have different faculties (119). While Herbart worried about the identity of the soul if it is divided into separate faculties, Meyer points out that it is perfectly possible for one and the same soul to have distinctive ways of acting and functioning (87). Kant rightly saw that a division of the soul into distinct functions is perfectly compatible with its numerical identity (119).

Meyer takes his defence of Kant's psychology a step further by going on the offensive against Herbart. Not only is Kant's idea of a faculty defensible, we are told, but his tripartite theory of the mind is preferable to Herbart's own monolithic theory. It was not Kant but Herbart himself who was guilty of lapsing into the old

---

[33] See Lotze, *Medicinische Psychologie* (Leipzig: Weidmann, 1852), §12, 136–138 and §13, 145–148; *Streitschriften* (Leipzig: Hirzel, 1857), pp. 9–15; and *Mikrokosmus* (Leipzig: Hirzel, 1884), 4th edition, (first published 1856) Vol. I, 188–215. See Trendelenburg, 'Ueber die metaphysische Hauptpunkte in Herbart's Psychologie' in *Historische Beiträge zur Philosophie* (Berlin: Bethge, 1867), III, 97–121. Meyer himself refers to all these sources.

[34] See Herbart, *Lehrbuch zur Psychologie* (Königsberg: Unzer, 1816), *Sämtliche Werke* IV, 310–312; §§13–15,

rationalism. For Herbart had gone back to the old Wolffian theory of the mind as a *vis representativae*, a power of representation, reducing desire and feeling down to different functions of representation. But Kant was entirely correct, Meyer contends, to have criticized the Wolffian theory and to have insisted upon three fundamental faculties of the mind, namely, feeling, desire and representation. These are original or primitive faculties because there is no way one is reducible to the other. Although feeling and desire are aroused by representation and always accompanied with it, they have new qualities all their own (91, 94). Feeling is not the same as just having certain sensations because, as Fries and Lotze stressed, it also involves the act of valuing these sensations; and it is not the same as desire because, as Kant argued, we can have a distinterested pleasure in things. Desire is different from the striving for representation, as Herbart explains it, because desire also includes, as Trendelenburg observes, the desire to get or possess something (95). Desire is not just striving itself but the felt need behind it (96). Conversely, representation is distinct from desire and feeling because we are often indifferent to many things that we perceive or know (105–107).

While Herbart had objected to Kant's method in psychology as a relapse into Wolffian scholasticism, because it imposes a priori methods and concepts upon empirical data, Meyer responded that Kant did follow an empirical method of self-reflection by noting the different kinds of mental phenomena and showing how they are distinct from one another. Herbart had objected to such methods of introspection on the grounds that the data we see often depends on the concepts and presuppositions that we read into them. Though Meyer agrees that introspection could often be unreliable in this manner, he pointed out that throwing out introspection entirely was like throwing out the telescope in astronomy on the grounds that it could sometimes give unreliable results (104). The distinction between objective observation and subjective factors was vital to all the sciences, and there was no reason that psychology too, provided it took sufficient care, could not make such distinctions no less than astronomy (292–293).

After rebutting Herbart's objections, Meyer concludes with an emphatic vindication of Kant's psychology. He insists that Kant's transcendental philosophy rests on a psychological foundation, and that this foundation is essentially sound and secure. Kant followed the right method and he reached the right results (121). He correctly determined the different classes of mental phenomena, and he rightly stressed their unity in the mind. Kant's only shortcoming is failing to acknowledge his psychological methods. The greater use of psychology, Meyer contends, would have saved Kant from the formalism of his logic and ethics.

Such was the ultimate message of Meyer's book, which he had put forward with great rigour and vigour. Yet, by the end of the 1870s, it would seem obsolete, a faint echo from years past. Though Meyer could scarcely have foreseen it, *Kant's Psychologie* would prove to be the last statement of the psychological-physiological interpretation of Kant.

5. Questions of the Times

Meyer's major philosophical work was his *Zeitfragen, Populären Aufsätze*, which appeared in 1870.[35] The work had some success in its day, since it received favourable reviews and went into a second edition. Today, however, it is forgotten, neglected even by neo-Kantian scholars. This is a pity because the work is one of the best in the neo-Kantian pantheon. It is extremely wide-ranging, treating the nature of mind, matter, life, freedom, morality and religion; and its discussions are remarkably thorough, well-informed and incisive. The chief problem with the work is that it is too ambitious: it tries to cover so many issues that it leaves crucial questions dangling. Still, Meyer never pretended to provide definitive solutions to anything; he only wanted to keep the discussion going and to explore aspects of an issue. He engaged in the same kind of tentative, exploratory thinking as Liebmann and Windelband, a species of philosophizing that is a hallmark of much neo-Kantian philosophy.

As the title indicates, *Zeitfragen* was meant to be about topical issues. Meyer discusses the current state of philosophy, the latest literature on the mind–body problem, the merits of Darwinism and the condition of religion in Germany. And as the subtitle shows, the book was intended to be popular, though Meyer promised he would not let popularity compromise intellectual content. It is indeed one of the merits of his book that it is both accessible and rigorous. These two features of the book—its topicality and popularity—are tokens of Meyer's allegiance to the old cause of *Aufklärung*.

We cannot begin to do justice here to the richness of *Zeitfragen*. We will focus in this, and in the following section, solely on three major issues addressed in the book: the crisis of philosophy, free-will and the stature of religion in the modern world. These issues are chosen because they are especially revealing regarding Meyer's place in the neo-Kantian movement.

Meyer, like all neo-Kantians, was worried about the danger of obsolescence facing philosophy, and he formulated his own solution to it, which appears in the first and last chapters of *Zeitfragen*.[36] Like Fischer and Zeller, he thinks that the crisis of philosophy arose from the demise of the great idealist systems. These systems collapsed because they were simply too ambitious; and when they failed to achieve their lofty goals, philosophy itself became rudderless and lost. One of the grand aspirations of the idealist systems was to provide a foundation for all the particular sciences. But these sciences had grown independent of philosophy, achieving great success by using their own standards and methods. Now that they had become autonomous, they saw no need for philosophy at all. Another quixotic goal of the idealist systems

---

[35] Jürgen Bona Meyer, *Zeitfragen. Populäre Aufsätze* (Bonn: Adolph Marcus, 1870). The second edition appeared in 1874. All references in parentheses above are to the first edition.

[36] Meyer, *Zeitfragen*: Kap. I. Die Philosophie und unsere Zeit', pp. 1–14; and 'Die Philosophische Systeme und die Zukunft der Philosophie', pp. 407–434.

was to know the absolute, to gain insight into the origin and end of all things, and to do so by means of pure reason. But this ambition too proved unattainable, chiefly because these philosophers failed to heed Kant's old lesson: that the place of philosophy lay in the bathos of experience (7).

Meyer does not think that philosophy will ever again recover its role as a founder and grounder of the particular sciences, nor that it will ever be able to achieve success in its attempt to know the absolute. This is, of course, for not historical but systematic reasons. Like a good Kantian, Meyer thinks that the idealist systems went beyond the limits of reason. But that leaves the question: whither philosophy? If it cannot be the foundation of the sciences, if it cannot give knowledge of the absolute, what good is it?

A large part of Meyer's answer to this question came, predictably enough, from his psychologistic programme. Philosophy can avoid obsolescence, Meyer thinks, only if it becomes psychology. At first blush this sounds like a paradox or joke: philosophy can save itself only if it becomes something else. Yet we must remember that psychology in the 1870s had no fixed identity, and that it did not necessarily mean the experimental science we now associate with the discipline. Meyer explains that philosophy, conceived as psychology, will have its own unique place in the sciences because it will consider the mind as such and in general, unlike all the particular sciences, which treat the mind in its relation to specific objects. Philosophy will be the study of the mind itself, apart from all its special uses, and apart from its relations to particular things (10).

It is a notable feature of Meyer's solution to the crisis that, unlike Fischer and Zeller, he does not envisage a future for philosophy in epistemology. Since, like Beneke, he sees knowledge as a function of the mind, he subsumes epistemology under psychology. Meyer rides roughshod over Kant's distinctions between *quid facti?* and *quid juris?*, between first-order knowledge of the world and second-order knowledge of knowledge. For him, the chief concern of philosophy involves only a special kind of first-order knowledge: knowledge of the mind itself.

The reduction of epistemology to psychology, and the blurring of the distinction between first- and second-order questions, left Meyer vulnerable to the charge that he really had abandoned philosophy after all. This would later become a standard objection against his psychologism, which the Marburgians and Southwesterners saw as a betrayal of philosophy itself.

Whatever the difficulties with psychologism, it was only one half of Meyer's solution to the crisis of obsolescence. Now relenting from his old reservations about metaphysics, Meyer, like Fischer, Zeller and Liebmann, began to see it as an essential part of philosophy. Despite Kant's critique of that discipline, he believed that philosophy should provide a general "worldview" (*Weltanschauung*) (11, 423). This worldview would not be an attempt to know the absolute or the unconditioned, as in the idealist systems of the past, but it would strive to determine the general principles and interconnections between all things, especially the mind and the body. The task of the critical philosopher was not to provide definitive solutions to the problems of metaphysics—that lay beyond the boundaries of knowledge—but to adjudicate the disputes between the metaphysical systems, to correct their dogmatism and to encourage discussion. Meyer saw his own *Zeitfragen* as the sketch for a worldview, though he refused to claim that it had any ultimate validity or that it was the definitive solution to the problems.

Another major concern of Meyer's *Zeitfragen* is to defend freedom of the will.[37] He had already cast himself in this role in some of his earlier articles,[38] though now he returns to the task more systematically. His aim then was to demonstrate only the *possibility* of freedom of will; a proof of its reality, he insisted, went beyond the limits of knowledge. Meyer returns to this modest position here, though now defending it against a wider range of detractors.

Freedom of the will means for Meyer two things: first, the power of decision, the ability to choose between different course of actions; and, second, the power *to do* what we find right, the ability *to act upon* our decisions. He insists that it does not consist in only self-determination, that is, acting according to the necessity of our own nature, because it also involves the power to do otherwise, to act differently from how we have chosen.[39] Understood in this sense freedom should also not be identified with dutiful action, because we are still free should we choose to act contrary to duty. Freedom in the strong sense of having the power to do otherwise, Meyer maintains, is necessary to moral responsibility.[40]

The main evidence for such freedom, Meyer contends, consists in our normal moral consciousness, in our feeling of responsibility or conscience, which tells us that we have the power to do the good or right, and that we could have done otherwise if we fail to do it. He realizes that the determinist, whether materialist or idealist, questions such testimony on the grounds that it rests on ignorance of the deeper causes of our own action. Still, Meyer holds his ground, stressing that the determinist also cannot disprove such testimony. If he cannot convince the determinist by having him look into his own inner consciousness, then the defender of freedom will do nothing more than "quietly take in his sail and anchor in the harbor of immediate self-consciousness".[41] In the end, Meyer realizes that belief in freedom is a matter of faith, though it is a belief we, as moral agents, find it impossible to renounce.

Meyer defends freedom of will against several detractors, but there is one that especially concerns him in *Zeitfragen*: Arthur Schopenhauer. Not least because of Schopenhauer's growing popularity in the 1860s, Meyer felt it necessary to take pains

---

[37] See Meyer, *Zeitfragen*, Kapitel 8: 'Der Wille und seine Freiheit', pp. 205–278.
[38] See Meyer, 'Zum neuesten Stand des Streits über Leib und Seele. II. Die Lehre von der Willensfreiheit im Materialismus und Idealismus' *Deutsches Museum*, Nr. 51. December 18, 1856, 906–916; and 'III. Willensfreiheit und Sittengesetz', *Deutsches Museum*, Nr. 10, March 5, 1857, 345–358.
[39] Meyer, 'Die Lehre von der Willensfreiheit', p. 911.
[40] Meyer, 'Willensfreiheit und Sittengesetz', p. 354.
[41] Meyer, 'Die Lehre von der Willensfreiheit', p. 714.

in responding to him.[42] His defence of freedom of will against Schopenhauer shows remarkable parallels with Liebmann's own efforts only a few years earlier.[43] Like Liebmann, Meyer wants to defend the testimony of our normal moral consciousness against Schopenhauer, who declares it illusory. On Meyer's reading, Schopenhauer denies freedom of will on the grounds that: a) all actions have motives; and: b) all motives are determined by character in its interaction with particular circumstances (224, 234–237). Meyer agrees with Schopenhauer that all actions must have motives or reasons, that there cannot be a completely motiveless or irrational will that chooses a course of action for no reason at all; but he disagrees with Schopenhauer that we have no choice about our motives, that which motive we adopt is completely determined by character. The crucial question with regard to freedom, he maintains, depends on whether or not we have a free choice about our motives (238). And Meyer is eager to defend the possibility of just such a choice. Motives do not determine choice, but choice determines motives, in that which motive we act upon depends on our powers of deliberation, which give greater weight to some motives over others.[44] But free will is also not simply the last motive after deliberation, because we have the power to choose and act contrary to the reasons we find best. It is one of the dangling threads of Meyer's discussion of freedom that he does not explain, though he assumes, the possibility of weakness of will.

What makes freedom of choice possible, Meyer argues, is precisely that, *pace* Schopenhauer, our character is *not* completely fixed and inflexible. It was a crucial premise of Schopenhauer's determinism that our individual and empirical character is completely determined and settled, that the choices we make are an expression of our character, which we do not have the power to alter. Meyer contests this very premise, however, insisting that character is not always fixed and that it is as much an effect as cause of our choices. He admits that there are a few rare individuals who have rigid and strong characters which makes them always choose one course of action without the slightest doubt or hesitation; but, he insists, most people are not like this; in most cases they find themselves having to struggle to make a decision, having to weigh one motive over another (245–247). The reason that they go through an inner struggle is precisely because their character is not fixed; and they have the power through their will to form their character in one direction or the other (246–247). We say that people have a "second nature", and it is this nature that is the product of the steady and firm resolve of our will to do one thing over another.

Of course, Schopenhauer questioned the so-called "facts" attested by our normal moral consciousness, especially the belief that we could have done otherwise on a particular occasion. To cast doubt upon it, he brought forth a wealth of examples to

---

[42] Meyer will deal with Schopenhauer in two other writings, *Arthur Schopenhauer als Mensch und Denker* (Berlin: Carl Habel, 1872), and *Weltelend und Weltschmerz: eine Rede gegen Schopenhauer's und Hartmann's Pessimismus gehalten im wissenschaftlichen Verein zu Berlin* (Bonn: Adolph Marcus, 1872).

[43] See Chapter 7, Section 3.   [44] Meyer, 'Willensfreiheit und Sittengesetz', p. 348.

show that people often recognize that they could not do otherwise than they did. His favourite cases, drawn from newspapers and novels, were of criminals who first professed their guilt, but who then said, in the very act of confession and contrition, that they would still do the same again if given half the chance. Meyer questions, however, whether these examples show what Schopenhauer reads into them: that the person could not do otherwise and acted of necessity. When the contrite criminal admits his guilt it is precisely because he feels that he could have done otherwise; he asks for punishment because he feels he deserves it; and he blames not his maker for his character but his own self (241).

Schopenhauer's determinism is a qualified one, though, because it holds only for our *empirical* and *individual* character. That character itself, Schopenhauer maintained, is determined by a primal act of will, an act that is free because it can choose one character rather than another.[45] Meyer notes this transcendent indeterminism in Schopenhauer's theory, but, like Liebmann, he declares it irrelevant for the problem of moral responsibility (243). What we hold responsible, he insists, is the will of our empirical and individual character; the primal act that creates this character is not relevant, because, on Schopenhauer's own premises, it is unknowable, standing above and beyond the phenomenal world. Schopenhauer had complained that the normal conception of free will is absurd because it presupposes the existence of something indeterminate, something that could be either A or not A, depending on its arbitrary acts of choice. But Meyer replies that this objection applies more readily to Schopenhauer's primal act of will, which is free to decide between different characters. It does not apply to our empirical and individual will, however, because, even though it is changeable, it is determinate in whatever it decides to be (249).

Though Meyer defends Kant's views about the testimony of our normal moral consciousness, he is otherwise highly critical of Kant's theory of freedom. Rather than upholding the possibility of moral responsibility, he argues, Kant's theory undermines it (242). Taking into account Kant's exposition in the second *Kritik*, Meyer finds the difficulty with Kant's theory in its identification of freedom with the rational will. Since the rational will acts according to the moral law, immoral actions cease to be free. On the Kantian theory, whether we act according to the moral law depends not on an act of choice but on the strength or weakness of our sensible or phenomenal nature, which is locked in a struggle with our moral will. If that nature is strong, then it defeats our moral will; and if it is weak, it complies with it. But in either case it is not a matter of our will whether we are free and act according to the moral law. Kant writes as if our sensible and rational natures are completely determined, as if it were impossible for us to determine what that nature should be. He needs to realize that freedom demands that we also create our nature or character.

---

[45] Arthur Schopenhauer, *Die Welt als Wille und Vorstellung*, in *Sämtliche Werke*, ed. Wolfgang Freiherr von Löhneysen (Stuttgart: Insel, 1968) I, 396, §55.

It is easy to see the point behind Meyer's criticisms of Kant and Schopenhauer. But in his refusal to locate the will in the noumenal realm, and in his insistence on making the empirical and individual will the source of moral action, Meyer raised anew the very danger of determinism that he was so eager to avoid. For if the acts of will take place in the phenomenal and natural world, how do they avoid the determinism of that world? How can we uphold freedom of choice in a phenomenal or natural world where all events conform to the principle of sufficient reason? It seems that we are back where we started: we have to accept a complete determinism with Schopenhauer or place freedom in the noumenal world with Kant. It is another of the dangling threads of *Zeitfragen* that Meyer does not consider this fundamental issue.

Meyer's concern with defending human freedom takes a remarkable metaphysical turn when he considers theological objections against freedom of will. Now Meyer enters into the murkiest depths of metaphysics and theology when he treats the classical questions whether human freedom is compatible with divine omniscience and omnipotence. For a philosopher who has already announced his allegiance to the Kantian limitations on knowledge this seems a surprising turn of thought. But Meyer is forced to go down this path given his original goal of defending human freedom. For he cannot beg one crucial question: *If* there were a God, could human beings be free? Many theologians have held that the divine omniscience and omnipotence make human freedom impossible. Not the least of these theologians, Meyer is eager to remind his Protestant readers, was Martin Luther himself.

Before wading into these treacherous waters, Meyer announces a rule of investigation to hold at bay charges of metaphysical self-indulgence (266). Rather than starting with speculations about the divine nature, and then seeing whether and how belief in human freedom conforms to them, he will begin with human experience and then determine which theological views best explain it. This way of proceeding better suits the order of our knowledge, he thinks, because what we know from human experience is more certain than speculations about the divine nature; we should not forfeit the certainty of human experience for the uncertainty of metaphysical speculation. Since it is an integral part of our human experience that we are self-conscious as free agents, that we have the power to choose between different courses of action, we should take this as the desideratum for any adequate theology. This means that should a theology conflict with belief in human freedom, then so much the worse for it.

Taking this rule as his starting point, Meyer immediately rejects pantheistic views of human freedom (267). He especially targets the position of David Friedrich Strauß, who attempts to explain human freedom from a pantheistic perspective.[46] According to Strauß, pantheism is compatible with human freedom because making God omnipresent and part of myself means that I share in the divine freedom;

---

[46] See David Friedrich Strauß, *Die christlichen Glaubenslehre* (Tübingen: C.F. Osiander, 1840), I, 503–504, 507, 588.

I am not compelled into action by anything outside myself because God's free action is part of myself. But Meyer objects that this does not allow the experience of freedom of choice, given that the individual still has to act according to the *necessity* of the divine nature. Having thus rejected pantheism, Meyer concludes that only theism, which distinguishes between God and the world, is compatible with the human self-awareness of freedom (268). But that leaves the question: Which form of theism? How, exactly, must we conceive of the divine attributes, and God's relation to the world, to uphold belief in human freedom?

One major stumbling block in reconciling theism with human freedom is the attribute of divine omnipotence: if everything is created and maintained by God, then how are human beings free to do anything by themselves? Our freedom would seem to be a limit on the divine omnipotence. Meyer attempts to resolve this conundrum by drawing a limit to God's actions in the world: while God's actions are necessary to create and maintain the *essence* or *being* of things, they are not so for the *actions* of these things (268). We must distinguish between the essence of things and their actions, where only their essence requires the creative and preservative powers of the divine. As a free agent himself, God has created other human free agents in his image, allowing everything necessary for the exercise of their freedom (258). It is not a limit but a reflection of divine power, when human beings use the freedom God has chosen to give them (258, 276).

The other chief obstacle to human freedom is the attribute of divine foreknowledge: if God knows everything, then he knows all human actions, past, present and future; but if he knows our future actions, they should be preordained, so that we are not free after all. Meyer attempts to move around this obstacle by suggesting several possibilities about divine foreknowledge: that is limited to necessary truths, excluding the contingency required of human freedom; that it is still perfect even if it does not include possible actions; that it is eternal, excluding the temporal realm of human action (276). Meyer sees the problems with these possibilities, all of which limit divine omniscience in one way or another. Which is the least problematic? Meyer does not say, leaving his reader hanging at cliff's edge.

Whatever the merits of these reflections, they raise the question whether Meyer, by engaging in them, has gone beyond his own self-imposed critical limits. In his defence it has to be said that Meyer does not claim to provide knowledge of God, only what God must be *if* human freedom is to be possible. The whole enquiry therefore has a strictly hypothetical value. In adopting his rule to base his investigation upon the experience of human freedom, Meyer follows something like Kant's doctrine of practical faith, which would base religious belief upon morality, and indeed ultimately the experience of human freedom. It is precisely here, however, that Meyer's speculations raise questions, for, as we have seen, he is harshly critical of that Kantian doctrine. He had seen Kant's demonstrations of the existence of God and immortality as illegitimate extensions of the powers of reason, and he had insisted that the realm of faith should be that of individual belief alone. But Meyer's own reflections on the nature of

God, however hypothetical, were not intended to be fantasies of his individual belief; they were demonstrations of what must be under certain assumptions (viz. the existence of God and immortality), and they took as their starting point the facts of moral consciousness.

6. Renewing Philosophy of Religion

One of Meyer's major aims as a philosopher was to revitalize the philosophy of religion, which had drastically declined since the 1840s, since the heady and happy years of the Tübingen and Hegelian schools. This aim appears in full force in his chapter on the philosophy of religion in *Zeitfragen,* which is one of the longest in the book.[47] That there is a desperate need to revive the discipline is evident, Meyer thinks, from the stifling indifference towards religion in contemporary German life. There is little philosophical discussion of religion among the public, and even less among philosophers. Religion is regarded as a concern for clerics or a private matter of the individual conscience. Regarding the source of this indifference, Meyer is uncertain. Perhaps it is due to the spread of materialism? Perhaps it comes from the general discredit of philosophy? Perhaps too it is the result of the overwhelming practical interests of the age? Whatever the cause, Meyer thinks that the indifference towards religion should not, and indeed really cannot, last. Without going into details, he refers to the present state of German social and political life, insisting that it is now imperative to hold public discussions about religion. Writing in the late 1860s, Meyer was doubtless referring to the new cultural situation of the second *Reich*, which had integrated Catholics and Protestants into a single state. How could Germany be a single nation yet both Catholic and Protestant? What loyalty would Catholics have to the Prussian state, which was officially Protestant? The forces behind the *Kulturkampf,* which would erupt in 1872, were already brewing. To sort out the many religious and theological issues arising from unification, Meyer thinks that it is necessary to revive the philosophy of religion. Only a philosophy of religion can discuss the most general issues that are the source of all the controversy and partisanship, issues like the relationship between reason and faith, God and the world (355–356).

In making his case for the philosophy of religion, Meyer is eager to combat two old but persistent prejudices about religious belief. One is the old view that there should be a divide, a clear wall of separation, between the religious ideas of the intellectuals and the faith of the people, because what the intellectuals think could be dangerous for the faith of the masses, who should be kept in social and political harness. This view, which appears in Reimarus, Lessing and Kant, is no longer appropriate for our more educated and enlightened age, Meyer argues, because now everyone has an opinion and everyone wants to think for himself. As he roundly puts it: "We have

[47]   Meyer, *Zeitfragen,* 'Religion und Philosophie in unserer Zeit', pp. 353–406.

given up dividing participation in the investigation of truth according to classes and professions" (361). The other prejudice is the claim that religion is a private matter, a purely personal issue of no concern to the public at large. Meyer finds this problematic, because religion is not simply a matter of feeling but also of thinking; it involves claims to truth, and the only means of determining their validity is through open discussion with others (363). To Meyer, something like Kierkegaardian inwardness and subjectivity would have seemed like an evasion.

Given that religion is now a concern for the general public, and given that it is not simply a private matter, there is all the more reason to have public discourse about it. Meyer thinks that it is chiefly the role of philosophers to create this discourse and to clarify the basic issues about it. Adapting some famous lines from Plato, he writes that there will be improvement in the religious affairs of the nation only if religious teachers become philosophers or philosophers become religious teachers (365). Seldom has so much confidence been placed in the role of philosophers in the discussion of religious belief.

True to the critical standpoint he developed in the 1850s, Meyer continues to hold that philosophy has no objective criterion to determine the truth or falsity of religious faith (398). Still, philosophy has a valuable role to perform in clarifying the controversies between the religious parties, in assessing the truth or falsity of their arguments on specific issues, and in showing the exact limits of knowledge (356). Apart from this purely critical role, Meyer assigns another task to the philosophy of religion: it must show in a systematic manner how religion arises from human nature (369, 371). Against the materialists, who think that religion is an eradicable superstition, a religious anthropology will demonstrate how religion is a constant element of all human culture, and that it is so because it arises from basic human needs. Since we cannot eradicate these needs, as the materialist wants, we have to learn to understand and accept them. The common element behind all religion, Meyer maintains, is the feeling of dependence on higher powers in the universe and the need to honour them (376).

Meyer's religious anthropology was a frankly apologetic one. Its task was, as he puts it, "to say the right word on behalf of faith" (276). It was by showing how religion is based on essential human needs that we could find some justification for it. Although reason cannot provide an objective demonstration of religious beliefs, viz., the existence of God, providence and immortality, we can still determine from our experience which religion best suits our needs as human beings (398). This would provide a kind of Friesian "transcendental deduction" of religion: it is not by dogmatic proof or syllogistic reasoning but by tracing beliefs back to their origins in human nature that we provide a justification for them.[48] Since we cannot get beyond our own nature, the deeper questions about the objective truth of religion will be unanswerable for us; but

---

[48] See Chapter 1, Section 10.

it is that very human nature that also provides the ultimate test of the worth of any religion.

Not content merely to state a general programme, Meyer proceeds to sketch the desiderata or foundation for a religious anthropology. Like Zeller, he stresses how religion arises from all sides of human nature, from our three fundamental drives: thinking, willing and feeling. Religion involves thinking since it strives to comprehend the universe as a whole, to grasp everything finite as one part of the infinite; it concerns willing since it lays down moral precepts and prescribes actions; and it consists in feeling, the sense for, or intuition of, the infinite present in the finite. Meyer is critical of his great predecessors—Kant, Hegel, Schleiermacher and Fries—because they all have an overly one-sided conception of religion which reduces it down to one of these factors alone. Kant went too far in reducing religion down to moral duty, because that made its concern with the universe as a whole superfluous. Schleiermacher and Fries were right to stress the importance of feeling and aesthetic experience; but they failed to see how feeling is dependent upon thinking, how the feeling for the infinite in the finite arises from the effort of thinking to get beyond the sensible world. Hegel was right to correct Schleiermacher for his one-sided emphasis on feeling, but he went too far in the opposite direction, overstating the role of thinking. A proper religious anthropology will justify religion by showing how it addresses all these sides of our human nature.

It is especially in his chapter on religion in *Zeitfragen* that one witnesses Meyer's project for the restoration of the Enlightenment. Time and again he pleads for the rehabilitation of the ideal of natural religion, which had been a mainstay of Enlightenment deism. Although he had no intention of reviving the old proofs for the existence of God and immorality, the idea behind his religious anthropology is still to show how religion is lodged in human nature. Even if we could not find religion in nature outside us, as the old deists wanted, Meyer was confident that we could find it within us. Religion would still have a universal sanction, standing above the vagaries of culture and custom. Sure enough, Meyer stresses that one of the values of his religious anthropology is that it will get beyond the sectarian strife of the age, locating the basic core beliefs held by Protestant, Catholic and Jew alike. A broad invisible church would also have the advantage of restoring tolerance, which is the first rule for all intellectual discussion and controversy. Such was the old latitudinarian credo of the early Enlightenment, which Meyer now endorses and recommends for his own age.

In rejecting pantheism, in stressing the natural dimension of religion, and in preaching the need for tolerance, Meyer sounds like nothing more than an 18th-century deist. It was no accident that his great model in religious affairs was Voltaire.[49] He admired Voltaire for his deism, for his scepticism about religious controversy and revelation, for his insistence on the role of reason in religion, and above

---

[49] See Meyer's *Voltaire und Rousseau*, pp. 11, 20.

all for his advocacy of toleration in religious affairs. It is this Voltairean spirit that stands behind his attempt to rehabilitate the Enlightenment, which is the ultimate inspiration behind *Zeitfragen*.

7. First Foray into History

It was one of the weaknesses of neo-Kantianism in the 1860s that it had little to say about history. The neo-Kantians had prided themselves on maintaining a close relationship with the empirical sciences, and they were very quick to censure the speculative idealists for ignoring them or treating them in a stepmotherly fashion. They had indeed made it the special business of philosophy to examine the logic of the empirical sciences, to investigate their methods, standards and presuppositions. But, while they were active in discussing physics and physiology, they had virtually ignored history. This was a glaring omission. For history had been rapidly advancing in the early 19th century, and it had made bold claims to be a science in its own right. The new critical history of Ranke and Niebuhr, and the historical school of law of Savigny and Eichhorn, which had fully emerged by the 1830s, had claimed that history could be a science no less than physics and chemistry. While history could not employ the same methods of observation and experiment as physics and physiology, it still had methods and standards of its own, rigorous procedures for discovering sources, weighing testimony, and for drawing conclusions in proportion to the evidence. Surely, here was fertile ground for philosophical investigation. All kinds of questions arose. What, exactly, are the methods and standards of history? How do they differ from those of the natural sciences? What, indeed, do we mean by science, and how, if at all, does history conform to it? It was inevitable that, sooner or later, the neo-Kantians would turn to these questions. They did so only later in the century, beginning with Dilthey's *Einleitung in die Geisteswissenschaften* and Windelband's Straßburg Rectoral Address.[50] By the turn of the century the logic of history will become the chief interest of the Southwestern school.

Given the neo-Kantians turned so late to history, it is interesting to note that Meyer wrote a very substantial article on the philosophy of history already in 1871, his 'Neue Versuche einer Philosophie der Geschichte', which appeared in the *Historische Zeitschrift* in 1871.[51] This was the first major writing by a neo-Kantian on the logic of history. It was essentially a review article, a critique of the latest writings on the philosophy of history. Meyer passes in review recent efforts in the field by Lotze, Comte,

---

[50] Wilhelm Dilthey, *Einleitung in die Geisteswissenschaften. Versuch einer Grundlegung für das Studium der Gesellschaft und der Geschichte* (Leipzig: Duncker & Humblot, 1883); and Wilhelm Windelband, *Geschichte und Naturwissenschaft: Rede zum Antritt des Rektorats des Kaiser-Wilhelm Universität Strassburg, gehalten am 1 Mai 1894* (Strassburg: Heitz, 1894).

[51] Jürgen Bona Meyer, 'Neue Versuche einer Philosophie der Geschichte', *Historische Zeitschrift* 25 (1871), 303–378.

Buckle, Mill and a host of others.[52] But the article is not just a pastiche of critical comments. Meyer formulates his own position on several important issues concerning the philosophy of history. He is concerned especially with two questions: Is a philosophy of history possible? And what is the precise relationship between the philosophy of history and history proper?

Regarding the first question, Meyer responds affirmatively. He maintains that a philosophy of history should be indeed possible, though he admits that none of the recent forays into the field have made concrete steps towards its realization. His chief criticism of the latest works is that they have stated their general programmes for a philosophy of history but then they have done nothing towards developing or executing them. Meyer gives a special meaning to the philosophy of history: it is a history that follows the naturalistic programmes of Mill, Buckle, Comte and Lotze. According to their programme, a philosophy of history determines the general scientific laws of history, where these are laws of human conduct, that is, laws determining cause–effect relationships between human beings and their natural environment; it does not attempt to determine, however, the purpose, end or design of history. While Meyer does not rule out the possibility of such a teleological history, he thinks that it should follow from a more empirical history, one that determines the laws of human conduct itself. It was a mistake of speculative idealism, he argues, that it proceeded in an a priori fashion, laying down what these general purposes should be and then attempting to find evidence for them in experience (345, 362). It is only after we determine the general laws of human conduct, Meyer maintains, that we can determine whether they conform to broader ends or purposes (374–375).

Meyer's confidence in the possibility of a philosophy of history is based chiefly on his belief in the possibility of psychology itself. He maintains that history, as a science of human action, should be based on psychology, which offers the best explanation of human actions. So if psychology can be a science, so should be the history founded on it. For Meyer, the possibility of psychology as a science is unproblematic, because it can be based upon observation and experiment like all other empirical

---

[52] Meyer reviews the following works: 1) Hermann Lotze, *Mikrokosmus*, Band III (Leipzig: Hirzel, 1864); 2) Conrad Hermann, *Prolegomena zur Philosophie der Geschichte* (Leipzig: Breitkopf & Härtel, 1849) and *Zwölf Vorlesungen über Philosophie der Geschichte* (Leipzig: Fleischer, 1870); 3) Heinrich Rückert, *Lehrbuch der Weltgeschichte in organischer Darstellung* (Leipzig: Härtel, 1857); 4) Christian Bunsen, *Gott in der Geschichte* (Leipzig: Brockhaus, 1857–1858); 5) Erst von Lasaulx, *Neue Versuch alten auf die Wahrheit der Thatsachen gegründeten Philosophie der Geschichte* (Munich: Cotta, 1856); 6) Henry Buckle, *History of Civilization in England* (London: J.W. Parker & Son, 1857–1861) in the German translation by Arnold Ruge, *Geschichte der Civilisation in England* (Leipzig: Winter, 1868); 7) F. Laurent, *Philosophie de l'histoire* (Paris: Librarie Internationale, 1870); 8) John Stuart Mill, *System der deductiven und inductiven Logik*, trans. J. Schiel (Braunschweig: Vieweg, 1862–1863); 9) Auguste Comte, *Cours de philosophie positive* (Paris: Bachelier, 1830–1842) and *Systeme de politique positive* (Paris: Mathias, 1851–1854); 10) Moritz Lazarus, 'Einleitende Gedanken über Völkerpsychologie', *Zeitschrift für Völkerpsychologie* 1 (1860) 1–73; 'Verdichtung des Denkens in der Geschichte', *Zeitschrift für Völkerpsychologie* 2 (1862), 54–62; 'Ueber das Verhältniß des Einzelnen zur Gesammtheit', in *Das Leben der Seele* (Berlin: Dümmler, 1883), 321–411, 'Einige synthetische Gedanken zur Völkerpsychologie' in *Zeitschrift für Völkerpsychologie* 3 (1865), 1–94.

sciences. Kant's doubts about psychology as a science were misplaced, because they rested upon his deductive paradigm of science, which is inappropriate for and inapplicable to all empirical sciences.[53] Assuming that we can determine the general laws of human action, we can then apply them to particular cases, finding more specific laws for how people act in more specific circumstances. These more specific laws will be the laws of history itself (382). What Meyer means by history here is close to anthropology, or what Mill calls "ethology" and Lazarus "folk psychology", projects he explicitly endorses (332, 335, 338).

Meyer's model for the philosophy of history is taken less from Mill and Lazarus than a much more predictable source: Kant. He maintains that Kant's essay 'Idee zu einer allgemeinen Geschichte in weltbürgerlicher Absicht' should be the "the starting point" for all new efforts in the philosophy of history (342). Kant clearly affirmed the general idea of a scientific history when he claimed that, despite the chaos of individual choices, there is still a regular law-like development in history. He provided "the guiding thread" for "any future philosophy of history that comes forth as a science" in his maxims that all natural powers of an individual will develop, and that they will develop in the species as a whole. In seeing history as a story about the development of human powers, Kant also rightly grasped that history has its basis in psychology.

Yet, for all his insistence on the importance of psychology, Meyer knew that history is more complicated than his psychological programme made it appear. The more interesting side of his article is when he takes to task the scientific programme of Mill, Buckle and Lazarus, which he otherwise endorses. Thus Meyer argues against Mill that psychological laws alone do not make up all of history (335). Nations and states are historical structures of their own whose changes cannot be explained by psychology alone (335–336). Meyer implies that these nations and states have their own logic and development which transcends psychology, and that there can be a distinctive science about them provided that it sticks close to determining causal interactions in experience (336). More significantly, he recognizes that the individual, which is the starting point of psychology, cannot be understood on its own but has to be placed in its wider social and historical context (337). Psychological analysis alone cannot answer fundamental questions, namely, whether morality, aesthetics and logic are innate or acquired; to answer them, we have to look into history as a whole. But, having recognized the insufficiency of his psychological starting point, Meyer fails to ask the further question how history in the broader non-psychological sense is possible.

Regarding the question about the relationship between the philosophy of history and history proper, Meyer notes the "struggle of life and death" between them. Each alone claims to be science. History questions the credentials of philosophy of history, which bases its generalizations on too few facts and ignores empirical evidence; and the philosophy of history scorns history, which deals only with particularities

---

[53]   See Meyer's *Kant's Ansicht über die Psychologie*, pp. 30–36.

and never ascends to the level of science, which requires universality and necessity (321). Since it is the task of a critical philosopher to settle disputes between disciplines, Meyer steps in to reconcile the parties. Refusing to draw sharp boundaries between them, Meyer attempts to wed them by stressing their interdependence (340–341). Like a good Kantian, he thinks that theory is empty without the particular facts of history (339), and that historical narrative is blind without the guidance of causal analysis and diagnosis (336).

While Meyer defends the possibility of a general philosophy of history, he does not draw the conclusion that it alone enjoys scientific status. He is eager to defend the status of history as a science on its own, and counters the views of Mill, Lazarus and Buckle that history can be a science only insofar as it becomes a general philosophy of history. These thinkers assume that the status of history as a science rests on it having the same kind of general laws as the natural sciences; a discipline is a science, they hold, only to the extent that it can have general laws, because universality and necessity is the condition of all knowledge in the proper sense. Without general laws, history consists in little more than narrative, a description of facts, which does not amount to science. Yet Meyer does not think that the philosophy of history has a monopoly on the title of science. History too is still a science, he argues, even if it investigates *particular* social and political structures in a *particular* time and place (335–336). Though such an investigation has to be consistent with general laws about human nature, it also does not follow from them. The careful investigation of particular facts, and the analysis and explanation of them, is still scientific, Meyer insists, even if it does not consider their ultimate causes or the basic laws of human actions. Indeed, the closer one sticks to particular facts and experience the more certain the results (336). It is misconceived to dismiss the scientific status of historical narrative, which is never completely separable from causal analysis and diagnosis (336–337). Through a glass darkly, Meyer was anticipating a view of historical discourse that will later be thematized by the Southwestern school: that history is "ideographic" rather than "nomothetic", a science of the particular rather than the universal.

Though Meyer's article is crude and raises more questions than it answers, it still had the merit of inaugurating the neo-Kantian investigation of history. Like so much of Meyer's writing, though, it too was forgotten. When the Southwesterners—Windelband, Rickert and Lask—wrote about history in the 1890s, never would they mention their fellow neo-Kantian who had preceded them. And so, undeservedly, Meyer faded away into the mists of the past.

9

Friedrich Albert Lange, Poet and Materialist Manqué

1. Lange's Legacy

Now that we have examined Kuno Fischer, Eduard Zeller, Jürgen Bona Meyer and Otto Liebmann, we come to the last member of the grand quintumvirate that revived neo-Kantianism in the 1860s: Friedrich Albert Lange (1828–1875). If Lange comes last, he does not come least. His reputation overshadows that of his allies. His *Geschichte des Materialismus*, which first appeared in 1866, was a landmark in the history of neo-Kantianism. No other work did more to revive Kant's reputation, to place him at the centre of German philosophy in the middle of the 19th century. Its influence overshadows Fischer's and Zeller's 1860 lectures and Liebmann's 1865 *Kant und die Epigonen*.

Though Lange's importance and influence is clear and uncontroversial, the same cannot be said for his place in the history of neo-Kantianism. Assessing this place is tricky, and it has been a matter of dispute. It is at least plain and uncontentious that Lange belongs to the physiological-psychological tradition of the interpretation of Kant. Like Fries, Beneke and Helmholtz, he saw that interpretation as the only means of ensuring Kant's relevance in the modern scientific age. The physiological-psychological interpretation was for him nothing less than "improved and refined Kantianism". Yet it would be a mistake to stuff Lange completely in this pigeon-hole, as if it exhausted his understanding of Kant. For Lange also transformed the Kantian dualism between the noumenal and phenomenal into a dualism between ideal and reality, norm and fact, value and existence. The distinction between entities became a distinction between logical types. We can already find in Lange the basis for the theory of value of the Southwestern school.[1]

Lange has often been seen as "the father of Marburg Neo-Kantianism".[2] He acquired this reputation partly because of his academic position, and partly because of his

[1] This point has also been made before by Hans-Ludwig Ollig, *Der Neukantianismus* (Stuttgart: Metzler, 1979), p. 19.
[2] This epithet has been taken over by Sieg, *Aufstieg und Niedergang des Marburger Neukantianismus* Würzburg: Königshausen & Neumann, 1994), pp. 86–106.

patronage of Hermann Cohen, the later leader of the Marburg school. Lange was an ordinary professor in Marburg from 1872 to 1875, the predecessor of Hermann Cohen and Paul Natorp. He was a strong supporter of Cohen, who became a *Privatdozent* largely thanks to his efforts. Forever grateful to Lange, Cohen tended to stress his debts to him and the affinities in their thought. But there are good reasons to doubt that Lange sired Marburgian neo-Kantianism in any more than an external academic sense. There is only a superficial similarity between Lange's and Cohen's thought; and the more closely we consider them, the more they show themselves to be deeply at odds, both in their interpretation of Kant and in their conception of the method of philosophy.[3] Lange's nominalism and empiricism, his psychological interpretation of Kant, his reduction of religion down to aesthetic ideas, his critique of Platonism—all these offended Cohen's sensibilities and clashed with his basic beliefs. The philosophy of the young Cohen, as we shall later see, grew out of his reaction against Lange. If Lange is the father of Marburg neo-Kantianism, then that tradition was based on patricide.

Lange has also been cast in another dubious role: founder of neo-Kantian socialism.[4] This common and venerable view has been recently advocated by Thomas Willey: "His most important contribution to neo-Kantianism was in his use of Kant to go beyond the boundaries of liberal social philosophy."[5] Although some of Lange's political views, namely, the value of co-operatives and the critique of historical inevitability, might have had some influence on later neo-Kantians, there is still a problem in crowning him the founder of neo-Kantian socialism. This interpretation joins together, plausibly enough, two basic facts: that Lange was a neo-Kantian and a founder of the social-democratic movement. However, there is a third stubborn fact that keeps these two apart: Lange himself never really connected his neo-Kantianism with his socialism.[6] Never did Lange, in his defence of social-democracy, appeal to Kantian moral principles, and never did he give a Kantian moral foundation to social-democratic ideals. It is indeed striking that in his two major works on politics—*Die Arbeiterfrage* and *Mills Ansichten über die sociale Frage*[7]—Lange not only

[3] This argument has been made before, though on different grounds, by Lehmann, *Geschichte der nachkantischen Philosophie* (Berlin: Junker und Dünnhaupt, 1931), pp. 177–178. Lehmann's claim that idealism is for Lange "Haus aus metaphysische Dichtung" conflates a reference to speculative idealism with Kant's transcendental idealism.

[4] The source of this view is perhaps Eduard Bernstein, who saw Lange as a forerunner of the social-democratic movement. See Eduard Bernstein, 'Zur Würdigung Friedrich Albert Lange', *Die neue Zeit*, Jahrgang X, (1891–1892), II, 68–78, 101–109, 132–141. Bernstein insisted (pp. 101–102) that there is no dualism between Lange's philosophy and his political views, though he did not explain the connection.

[5] Thomas E. Willey, *Back to Kant: The Revival of Kantianism in German Social and Historical Thought, 1860–1914* (Detroit, MI: Wayne State University Press, 1978), p. 84.

[6] The lack of connection here is seen by Harry van den Linden, *Kantian Ethics and Socialism* (Indianapolis, IN: Hackett, 1968), p. 294, who notes that Lange was rather negative about Kant's ethics.

[7] See Friedrich Albert Lange, *J. St. Mill's Ansichten über die sociale Frage und die angebliche Umwälzung der Socialwissenschaft durch Carey* (Duisburg: Falk & Lange, 1866); and *Die Arbeiterfrage in ihrer Bedeutung für Gegenwart und Zukunft* (Duisburg: Falk & Volmer, 1865). Lange greatly expanded and revised this work for the third edition. Here I cite the fourth edition, *Die Arbeiter Fragen. Ihre*

casts his argument in eudemonistic or perfectionalist terms,[8] but he also rejects Kant's moral philosophy as a guide in questions of political economy. In *Die Arbeiterfrage* Lange criticizes Kant severely for attempting to provide an a priori deduction of the institution of private ownership, and for excluding the possibility of communal ownership of the land.[9] Although Kant tries to justify that institution on eternal rational grounds, it is plain to Lange that it arose from all too natural and all too historical facts: conquest, power and exploitation. In this respect, Lange charges Kant with "a vulgar servility toward the powers-that-be and a hypocritical apology for injustice and exploitation". On the whole, Lange is sceptical of Kant's method in ethics on the grounds that it cannot justify specific precepts from very general principles. In *Mills Ansichten* Lange refers approvingly to Kant's categorical imperative, though only to declare that he prefers Smith's principle of sympathy over Kant![10] Given Lange's empiricism and naturalism, his preference for Smith is perfectly understandable; but it has gone unnoticed by Lange commentators, who cling to their faith that there must be some connection between Lange's neo-Kantianism and his socialism.[11]

Given the absence of Kantianism in Lange's socialism, and given the importance of his *Geschichte des Materialismus*, we will focus in this chapter on Lange's book rather than his social and political philosophy. This is contrary to the practice of most neo-Kantian historians, who dwell fondly and at length on Lange's social and political views, even though, properly seen, they fall outside the history of neo-Kantianism. It is in his *Geschichte des Materialismus* that Lange's significance lies for neo-Kantianism. This work presents a challenging legacy: it is long, complex, rich and subtle, and the source of some controversy. Before we examine its

Bedeutung für Gegenwart und Zukunft (Winterthur: Bleuler-Hausheer & Co., 1879), which incorporates all changes Lange made for the third.

[8] See, for example, *Die Arbeiterfrage*, pp. 126–127, where Lange appeals to the "principle of human perfection". Chapter 4, pp. 147–211, considers the question of "the standard of life", which is measured in eudemonistic terms. In Chapter 6, p. 338, Lange refers to "the idea of humanity", a reference to the tradition of Herder and Schiller.

[9] See Lange, *Die Arbeiterfrage*, pp. 268–274.   [10] Lange, *Mills Ansichten*, p. 21.

[11] In his 'Kant und der Sozialismus', *Kant-Studien* 4 (1900), 361–412, esp. 370, Karl Vorländer notes the lack of systematic connection between Lange's socialism and neo-Kantianism. He still believes, however, that Lange connected the two through his "noble personality". Helmut Holzhey grants that the connection is not overt, but he still insists that it is somehow unmistakable, lurking in the background. See his 'Philosophische Kritik. Zum Verhältnis von Erkenntnistheorie und Sozialphilosophie bei F.A. Lange', in *Friedrich Albert Lange, Leben und Werke*, eds J.H. Knoll and J.H. Schoeps (Duisburg: Walter Braun Verlag, 1975), 207–225, esp. 219. Vorländer notes but Holzhey ignores Lange's critique of Kant in *Die Arbeiterfrage* and his preference for Smith in *Mills Ansichten*. Köhnke too, *Entstehung und Aufstieg des Neukantianismus* (Frankfurt: Suhrkamp, 1986), p. 240, seems to believe there is some connection, because he claims that Lange "composed in Kant's spirit" his 'Aufruf an die Menschenfreunde aller Nationen', an appeal for peace he wrote during the Franco-Prussian War. See this document in *Friedrich Albert Lange: Über Politik und Philosophie, Briefe und Leitartikel, 1862–1875*, ed. Georg Eckert (Duisburg: Walter Braun Verlag, 1968), pp. 296–298. But Köhnke reads more into the document than the evidence warrants. Lange never appeals to Kantian ideas but only "the principles of Christianity and humanity". Köhnke polemicizes against the alternatives "Neu-kantianisch-idealistischer Ethiker *oder* linker Politiker" (p. 246), though he does not see the lack of Kantian ethical principles behind his politics.

contents, though, we must place its author in context and trace his early philosophical development.

2. Early Years and Wild Philosophy

Friedrich Albert Lange was born September 28, 1828, in Wald bei Sollingen.[12] Since his grandfather was a drayman, a wagon driver who hauled beer for local breweries, Lange had working class roots, a fact which must have played a role in forming his later political convictions. His father, Johann Peter Lange, worked his way up in the world, first becoming a pastor and eventually a professor of theology. The family residence was in Duisburg, where Friedrich Albert attended the local school until he was 12. In 1841, the family moved to Switzerland after Lange's father received a call to be professor at the university in Zurich. A man of orthodox faith, Johann Peter Lange was the right man to replace his notorious predecessor, David Friedrich Strauß, who was forced to resign because of the scandal aroused by his *Das Leben Jesu.*

Lange attended Gymnasium in Zurich, where he first acquired his taste for philosophy. One day a teacher gave a talk on Hegel's *Phänomenologie des Geistes,* which was his first exposure to philosophy. Lange was later proud to say that he was one of the few among his classmates to have understood that talk. In April 1847 Lange matriculated at the university in Zurich, where he studied theology and philology. There he also attended the lectures of Eduard Bobrik, who was a Herbartian. From these lectures Lange developed an interest in Herbart's psychology, which would preoccupy him for many years. Lange was first a Herbartian, then a Kantian. It was his disillusionment with Herbart that eventually drove him to Kant.[13]

After attending the university at Zurich for one year, Lange moved to Bonn, where he was a student at the university there from 1848 to 1851. He studied philology under Friedrich Ritschl (1806–1876), and art history under Friedrich Welcker (1784–1868), who both imparted to him a historicist methodology. Rather than going to more lectures, Lange spent most of his time on his own, studying mathematics, physics and classical history. He also enjoyed English, and even learned how to speak it from English students at the university.[14] This facility gave him access to English philosophy, history and literature, which were important in shaping his later outlook on moral, social and economic questions. While at Bonn Lange did not study philosophy

---

[12] The following account is based on Eckert, *Über Politik und Philosophie,* and A.O. Ellissen, *Friedrich Albert Lange. Eine Lebensbeschreibung* (Leipzig: Baedeker, 1894).

[13] Ellissen, *Lange* p. 245, speculates that Lange came to Kant via Schopenhauer, though it seems more likely he came to Kant via Herbart. Lange tells us in his September 27, 1858, letter to Kambli that he now valued Herbart only because he was "a bridge to Kant". See Ellissen, *Lange,* p. 106.

[14] The young Lange had travel plans to go to London, though his father tried to dissuade him by noting what happened to Hamann on a similar adventure. Did Lange want to become a mere *Pachthofverwalter* too? See Ellissen, *Lange,* p. 36.

much, because it took away the time and energy he needed to prepare for examinations in philology. Philology was for Lange a *Brotstudium,* a means to help him qualify as a schoolteacher. After his father advised him not to neglect philosophy, he attended two courses on the history of classical philosophy by Christian August Brandis (1790–1867), who had been a student of Schleiermacher and Trendelenburg. In a meeting with Brandis Lange explained that, though he could not attend more lectures on philosophy, he had not been neglecting the subject and that he had his own "wild philosophy", which he wanted to grow a little before applying a strict method to it.[15]

From his correspondence with friends, we know a little about Lange's "wild philosophy" during his student days. The most revealing letter he wrote sometime in 1851 to Conrad Kambli (1829–1914),[16] an old schoolmate and pastor in Switzerland. Responding to Kambli's inquiries about his religious and philosophical views, Lange wrote that his philosophy was still crude and inchoate, a work-in-progress, and that he proceeded slowly and carefully because, before he adopted any philosophical position, he needed to make a thorough study of its history (this the legacy of Ritschl and Welcker). After these caveats, Lange sketched some of his still developing views, which were indeed radical and crude. He comes close to espousing a complete relativism, declaring that "there is no absolute content to conscience", and that there is no objective reality outside the mind for goodness, beauty or the god of theism. All that we know is relative to human beings, the product of their psychology and physiology. The only objective truths are the laws of nature, which show us how the ideas of goodness, beauty and god arise of necessity from human nature. This belief in natural necessity, the inevitable working of natural laws, makes Lange doubt the reality of freedom, a belief which he regards as antiquated by natural science. All actions are necessary, and we call them "free" only where my decision follows my own nature. All of the radical views suggested in this letter—its historicism, relativism and naturalism—will emerge untamed in Lange's later philosophy.

Lange's student days came to a close in March 1851, when he took his qualifying exams, which he passed with the highest possible grade, "*eximine cum laude*". For his doctorate he wrote a dissertation on Latin verse, *Quaestiones metricae.* In June he passed the state examinations to be a schoolteacher, where he was certified to teach classical languages, history, mathematics and psychology. After a brief year in military service, Lange worked at a Gymnasium in Cologne from 1852 to 1855. Frustrated by working for three years only as an assistant, Lange left the Gymnasium and decided to try an academic career. In June 1855 he habilitated at the University of Bonn with a dissertation on Herbart's psychology.[17] From 1855 to 1858 he worked as a *Privatdozent* in Bonn, holding lectures there on psychology, moral statistics, logic and pedagogics.

---

[15] See Lange to his father, winter 1849/50, in Ellissen, *Lange,* p. 244.

[16] Ellissen, *Lange,* pp. 69–71.

[17] The dissertation eventually became a book: *Die Grundlegung der mathematischen Psychologie. Ein Versuch zur Nachweisung des fundamentalen Fehler bei Herbart und Drobisch* (Winterthur: Bleuler-Hausheer & Co., 1865).

It was during his Bonn *Dozentenjahre* that Lange began his first intensive study of philosophy. In June 1855, Lange wrote a letter to the university registrar in Bonn about his desire to habilitate in philosophy. He explained that all his beliefs had been thrown into doubt, and that he needed to get back to fundamentals.[18] His chief concern had been pedagogical theory, but the basis of modern pedagogy, Herbart's psychology, had proven bankrupt. It was necessary to fashion a new psychology, and that would require intensive work in philosophy.

It was also during these years that Lange began his first study of Kant. It was his need to write a new psychology that seems to have moved him towards the critical philosophy. He had plans to write a critique of psychology, in which he would follow Kant's *Kritik der reinen Vernunft*. We get some insight into his reasons for turning to Kant, and his general philosophical views around this time, from his September 27, 1858, letter to Kambli:

> As far as my "direction" or "confession" is concerned, I have to tell you that you judge me quite falsely as a teacher of philosophy when you speak about deepening oneself in "speculation". That is from times past! And hopefully for all Germany. I regard the Hegelian system as a relapse into scholasticism, from which we are already freed. Herbart, whom I followed in the beginning, is only a bridge for me to Kant, to whom so many solid scholars now return, and who do that to complete what Kant did only half way: destroy metaphysics. I regard every metaphysics as a kind of delusion (*Wahnsinn*), which has only an aesthetic or subjective justification. My logic is probability calculus, my ethics is moral statistics, my psychology rests entirely on physiology; in a word, I try to move only in the circles of the exact sciences.[19]

This letter reveals Lange's positivist attitude, which will emerge as a central force in his mature philosophy. This positivist temper is indeed the chief reason for Lange's later sympathy with materialism. It would be a mistake, however, to regard positivism as the complete or whole spirit of Lange's early philosophy. For there was another side to Lange, one that led him away from the exact sciences and that balanced out his positivist views. This was his "poetic" side, his knack for writing verse, which he would indulge constantly and on every occasion. Writing poetry was his most passionate preoccupation, and he would have made a career out of it if poetry earned any money.[20] This poetic trait was the force behind the other side of Lange's philosophy, what he would later call "the standpoint of the ideal". Lange thinks that there are two sides to humanity: the rational mentality apparent in the exact sciences, and "our poetic nature", which expresses itself in creative activity, in giving voice to the deepest aspirations of humanity through religion and art. We shall later see how Lange's mature philosophy attempts to balance and do justice to these two sides of human nature.

Other passages from Lange's long September 27 letter to Kambli reveal more about his early attitude towards Kant.[21] Lange finds Kant's greatness chiefly in his theoretical

---

[18] Ellissen, *Lange*, p. 90.   [19] Ellissen, *Lange*, p. 106.
[20] According to Ellissen, *Lange*, p. 45, it was only after "a hard inner struggle" that Lange gave up poetry for philosophy.
[21] Ellissen, *Lange*, p. 107.

philosophy, in his critique of metaphysics. He took to heart Kant's critical teaching that philosophy should remain within the limits of possible experience, because that seemed to bring philosophy in accord with the methods and standards of the exact sciences. Like all the neo-Kantians before him, Lange saw Kant's critical medicine as the proper antidote to the "scholasticism" of Hegelianism and the *"Begriffsromantik"* of German idealism. The practical side of Kant's system, however, was something entirely different for Lange. He saw its chief achievement as "Kant's proof of the unprovability of the ideas of God, freedom and immortality", but he had little sympathy for Kant's "positive constructions", that is, his particular practical demonstrations of the beliefs in God, providence and immortality. That effort seemed to him a timid bow to religious orthodoxy. Since Lange also disputes Kant's method in ethics, as we have seen, it seems as if he entirely rejects Kant's practical philosophy. Yet it is important to note that he does accept one crucial aspect of Kant's practical philosophy: namely, "its starting point", the attempt to provide a justification for moral and religious ideas through practical reason. Though Lange rejected Kant's demonstrations of the standard Christian beliefs, he still approved of the general strategy of using practical reason to defend morality and religion.[22] This point, already present in the letter to Kambli, will play a crucial role Lange's later philosophy. For it will be practical reason that provides the foundation for "the standpoint of the ideal".

In 1855, in his first semester teaching at Bonn, Lange wrote drafts for lectures on logic,[23] which he later gave at Marburg in 1873/74. These lectures were later revised by Lange himself, and then published posthumously by Hermann Cohen in 1877 as *Logische Studien*.[24] Though little read, this work is very revealing about Lange's views on Kant and the foundations of logic. Lange's chief concern in these lectures was the possibility of a formal logic, that is, whether there could be a formal logic having apodictic certainty like mathematics, and separate from all the intractable questions of epistemology (*Erkenntnistheorie*). The formal logic Lange has in mind here is nothing like the later Fregean discipline, still decades away from conception; it is rather Aristotle's syllogistic logic separated from questions of grammar and metaphysics. Whether there could be such a formal logic was a controversial issue in the 1850s, because the Trendelenburgian school had stressed the connection of Aristotle's logic

---

[22] This point, often ignored in Lange scholarship, is explicit in Lange's June 2, 1870, letter to Überweg: "*Ob ich z.B. in meiner practischen Philosophie auch dem Grundgedanken Kants folge? Ja: sofern ich ebenfalls—und schärfer als Kant—die sittliche Berechtigung der Ideen von ihrer objektiven Begründung trenne; nein: sofern ich wesentlich andere Ideen brauche und dieselben mit Religion und Dichtung in ein gemeinsames Gebiet verweise.*" See Ellissen, *Lange*, p. 263.

[23] See Klaus Plump, 'Der Nachlaß F.A. Langes im Stadtarchiv Duisburg', in Knoll and Schoeps, *Lange Leben und Werk*, pp. 236–267, esp. 246. According to Plump, there are four manuscripts dating from 1855, totalling some 200 pages. Two manuscripts are entitled 'Die reine Logik' and 'Reine Logik', showing that Lange already had his concern with a purely formal logic in 1855.

[24] Friedrich Albert Lange, *Logische Studien: Ein Beitrag zur Neubegründung der formalen Logik und der Erkenntnistheorie* (Iserlohn: Baedeker, 1877).

with his metaphysics and grammar.[25] Against them, Lange affirms the possibility of a purely formal logic. It is possible to have a formal logic independent of all grammar and metaphysics, he argues, because the validity of Aristotle's syllogisms are not affected by his particular views on grammar and metaphysics. No matter how one theorizes about the syllogisms, and whether one accepts Aristotle's views or not, their sheer formal validity still shines through. What gives them that validity, Lange theorizes, is their intuitability, the immediate perception of their truth, which cuts through all grammar and metaphysics.

The more speculative and controversial aspect of Lange's theory concerns this intuitability (*Anschaulichkeit*). The basis for it Lange finds in a priori spatial intuition. The main premise behind this at first blush very odd thesis seems to be this: that when we reason syllogistically, we place terms into classes, and this relation of inclusion or subsumption is perceived in spatial terms, by the placing of parts within wholes.[26] Lange then goes on to give an account of the fundamental role of a priori spatial intuition in our mental economy: it is the basis of part/whole relationships, all quantitative relationships, of even number itself, and it is the source of time, which we conceive as a point moving along a line (139, 141, 147). Much of Lange's theory is inspired by Kant, to whom he refers constantly in these lectures. But he is forced to take issue with Kant in two important respects. First, he cannot accept Kant's thesis that logical truth is based on the principle of contradiction while the truths of mathematics are synthetic a priori (9). He insists that all necessary propositions are synthetic, and that what connects their distinct terms is a priori intuition. There is no difference between logical and mathematical truth in that both require an intuition where some particular sign or figure represents something universal (23). Second, Lange thinks that Kant commits a fundamental error in separating so sharply understanding and sensibility (9). All intuition requires thought, all thought requires intuition. The presence of intuition in thought is especially apparent, Lange contends, not only in geometrical constructions but in logical truth itself where spatial intuition is behind all reasoning.

The other important work of the *Dozentenjahre* was Lange's *Geschichte des Materialismus*, which was already in gestation in these early years. But its genesis and intentions is a much longer story, which we must now tell.

3. Origins and Aims of a Classic

Lange's *Geschichte des Materialismus* was one of the great works of philosophy of the second half of the 19th century, the peer of Lotze's *Mikrokosmus* and Trendelenburg's *Logische Untersuchungen*. The title of the book is somewhat misleading. It is not only a

---

[25] Lange takes aim at the *"die pseudo-aristotelische Erkenntnistheorie der Gegenwart"*, p. 17. On Trendelenburg's conception of Aristotle's syllogistik, see *Logische Untersuchungen* (Leipzig: Hirzel, 1870), II, 388–389, and *Geschichte der Kategorienlehre* (Berlin: Bethge, 1846), pp. 13, 19–20.

[26] See Lange, *Logische Studien*, pp. 23, 128.

history of materialism from classical to modern times, but, like its peers, the statement of an entire worldview. Lange chose the theme of materialism because he saw it as key to the cultural crisis of his age, and because the conflict between materialism and idealism is central to philosophy itself. The work is as much philosophy as history: it engages in philosophy to make sense of history, and history to give concrete shape to philosophy.

Lange's work appeared to great critical acclaim, somewhat to the surprise of its author. Because of its elegance and topical theme, the work was widely read. It was praised for its clarity, for its scholarship, and for the author's wide knowledge of the latest scientific research. The main message of the work—that materialism is a valuable research programme though an untenable metaphysics—appealed to both left and right, scientists and theologians. Such was the success of the book that it appeared in ten editions, the last in 1974.[27] Two editions appeared in Lange's lifetime, the first in 1866, the second from 1873 to 1875.[28]

Geschichte des Materialismus is almost two books rather than one. The second edition was so enlarged and revised that it is virtually a new book. The first edition was a single volume of 557 pages; but the second edition came in two volumes, the first consisting in 428 pages and the second in 569 pages. Thus the book had almost doubled in size! For the second edition Lange took into account not only new developments in the sciences but also the latest contributions to the materialism controversy. But the second edition did not simply enlarge the first; much of the material from the first edition was dropped or rewritten. There are important changes in opinion and outlook in the second edition, especially with regard to Lange's interpretation of Kant.[29] But there is also a significant shift in Lange's whole conception of the work. In the preface to the first edition he said that he wrote for the enlightenment of his contemporaries, and that he did not want to write an academic monograph; he therefore left aside the scholarly apparatus of footnotes. But the second edition eventually became that monograph: it contains extensive notes after each main chapter.

Writing the first edition of the *Geschichte* took some nine years.[30] The original idea for a book on this theme came almost by accident and not from Lange himself.

[27] Friedrich Albert Lange, *Geschichte des Materialismus und Kritik seiner Bedeutung in der Gegenwart*, ed. Alfred Schmidt (Frankfurt: Suhrkamp, 1974). The last English translation is Ernest Chester Thomas, *The History of Materialism and Criticism of its Present Importance* (London: Routledge, Kegan & Paul, 1975), 3rd edition.

[28] Friedrich Albert Lange, *Geschichte des Materialismus und Kritik seiner Bedeutung in der Gegenwart* (Iserlohn: J. Baedeker, 1866). The second edition appeared in two volumes, the first in 1873 and the second in 1875. See *Geschichte des Materialismsus und Kritik seiner Bedeutung in der Gegenwart, Zweite, verbesserte und vermehrte Auflage. Band I: Erstes Buch. Geschichte des Materialismus bis auf Kant.* Band I (Iserlohn: J. Baedeker, 1873). Band II: *Geschichte des Materialismus seit Kant* (Iserlohn: J. Baedeker, 1875). All references in parentheses will be, unless otherwise noted, to the second edition, Roman numerals for volume numbers and Arabic numerals for page numbers.

[29] See Lange's March 14, 1867, letter to Anton Dohrn and his June 2, 1871, letter to Friedrich Ueberweg, in Ellissen, *Lange*, pp. 258–264.

[30] See Lange to Max Hirsch, November 27, 1865, in Eckert, *Über Politik und Philosophie*, p. 106.

In 1857 Lange's students at the University of Bonn sent him a note requesting that he lecture on the history of materialism for the Summer Semester of 1857.[31] Though himself preoccupied with pedagogical projects, Lange complied with their request. His lectures were the rough draft for part of the book. Ellissen, Lange's first biographer, reports that there was a large manuscript of material for these lectures which corresponds with much of the first part of the later published book.[32] Because of his successive jobs as a schoolteacher, a journalist and a customs official, Lange could work on the book only intermittently and sporadically. Finally in January 1864 he could inform his publisher that part of the manuscript was ready for printing.[33] Suffering from stomach cancer and realizing that his health might not last, he concentrated all his energy on finishing the second edition in the autumn of 1874.[34] In the preface to the second volume of the second edition he regretted that his health had not permitted him to consider all the latest publications relevant to his theme. Still, he managed to muster enough energy to see the second edition through the press. Lange died November 21, 1875, only 47 years old, slightly more than one year after the appearance of the second edition.

Why did Lange write his *Geschichte*? What were his aims or motives? In the preface to the first edition he tells us that he began the book in the hope of providing a solution to some issues raised by the materialism controversy (iii). He does not specify which issues, but we know from the content of the book that chief among them is the conflict between science and faith posed by the materialism controversy. It is also clear from this preface that Kant will play the decisive role in Lange's resolution of this conflict. Thus, immediately after declaring his intention to contribute to the controversy, Lange introduces Kant. It is as if it were self-evident that he would have to discuss the venerable sage of Königsberg. We soon see why: "In recent days Kant has achieved great renown, especially among natural scientists, and the enduring elements in his system are increasingly the common property of leading minds, even outside the narrow circles of academic philosophy." (iv) But if Kant is a decisive figure, Lange warns us not to take him uncritically, as if he were an absolute authority. "It is necessary, however, to crush the false absolutism of his system; the false appearance of a rigorous deduction has to be laid aside, so that the simple truth can come forward in an unmistakable manner." (iv)

What is this "simple truth"? Although Lange does not spell it out for us, the context reveals his meaning. "The simple truth" consists in Kant's strategy for resolving the conflict between reason and faith. In his preface Lange at first explains this strategy in very narrow terms: it is the *via media* between the orthodox and positivist Kantians. The orthodox Kantians, who are dogmatic theologians, underrate Kant's

[31] Ellissen, *Lange*, pp. 96–97. According to Plump, 'Nachlaß', p. 245, there is indeed a 361-page manuscript in the Duisburg Nachlass entitled 'Kritische Geschichte des Materialismus', which he dates back to 'Bonner Vorlesung Sommersemesters 1857'.
[32] Plump, 'Nachlaß', p. 250.   [33] Plump, 'Nachlaß', p. 126.
[34] See Lange to Ernst Haeckel, October 12, 1874, in Eckert, *Über Politik und Philosophie*, p. 336.

affinity with materialism and overrate his doctrine of practical faith. The positivist Kantians do just the opposite: they overrate his affinity with materialism and underrate his defence of moral and religious ideas (iv–v). The real Kant, Lange implies, is neither positivist nor orthodox, because he champions in equal measure *both* natural science *and* religious idealism.

But much more was at stake than a quarrel between Kantian schools. Lange also sees Kant's strategy in much broader terms: it is the middle path between the two clashing ideologies of his age, materialism and speculative idealism. If materialism stands for the triumph of a complete mechanism and naturalism, which undermines moral and religious ideals, speculative idealism represents a revival of metaphysical rationalism, which save these ideals but only by going beyond the limits of reason. Kant's philosophy offers a middle path between these extremes, because it saves the autonomy of our moral and religious ideals without metaphysics, and because it upholds the principles of mechanism and naturalism without jeopardizing morality and religion. Explaining just how Kant could accomplish this feat would be one of the central tasks of Lange's book.

Lange's central theme—that Kant could resolve the conflict between science and faith, speculative idealism and materialism—was not the least reason for the remarkable success of his book. His message was embraced by a younger generation. We know from the correspondence and reminiscences of Friedrich Paulsen, Hans Vaihinger, Benno Erdmann, Paul Natorp and Hermann Cohen that Lange's book made a great impact upon them.[35] To them, Lange had shown where the great value and power lay behind Kant's philosophy: in endorsing modern science without having to accept materialism; in preserving moral and religious belief without having to engage in metaphysics or to indulge in mysticism. Essentially, Lange's book did for the 1860s and 1870s what K.L. Reinhold's *Briefe über die kantische Philosophie* did for the 1790s. Just as Reinhold had popularized Kantian teaching by showing how it could resolve the conflict between reason and faith in the pantheism controversy, so Lange did the same by explaining how it could resolve that conflict in the materialism controversy. Lange was thus the Reinhold of the 19th century.

Lange was well aware of, and very pleased by, the effects of his work in promoting the Kant revival. Hence, in the beginning of the second volume of the second edition of his *Geschichte*, he noted with some satisfaction that it was no longer necessary to justify the importance he had given to Kant in the first edition (II, 1–2). Since the publication of that edition some eight years ago, he wrote, there had been a great revival of interest in Kant among a younger generation. In a footnote Lange mentioned the work of Otto Liebmann, Jürgen Bona Meyer, Emil Arnoldt and Hermann Cohen (115, n.1). There was now a new Kant philology, he observed, that could compete with classical philology in its devotion to detail and accuracy in the interpretation of texts.

---

[35] For Lange's influence on these figures, see Köhnke, *Entstehung und Aufstieg*, pp. 323–327.

Responding to the materialism controversy was a central motive for writing the *Geschichte des Materialismus*. This could not be, however, a complete account of its author's intentions. For Lange often describes his aims in more ambitious and broader terms, as if he has not only philosophical but also social and political goals. Thus he writes in the preface to the first edition that his aims are entirely practical, that he wants to contribute to "the great struggles of his age", that he hopes to promote "the spiritual survival of his nation".[36] Picking up on these lines, some scholars see Lange's goals as primarily social and political, though they have conflicting interpretations of them. Helmut Holzhey sees Lange's aim as the promotion of forthcoming social and political revolution,[37] whereas Hans-Martin Sass thinks that Lange's intent was to warn the public about that revolution and to provide an antidote to it with his "standpoint of the ideal".[38] Which of these interpretations are true? Lange cannot be both promoting revolution and warning against it.

Before we sort out this issue, we do well to note that there are problems with both interpretations. First, Lange developed his socialist agenda only by 1863, when large parts of the *Geschichte* were already written.[39] Though Lange continued writing the book after formulating his socialist views, and though they were indeed worked into the second edition of the book, they alone cannot explain why he undertook a study of materialism in the first place. His reasons are just those he sets forth in his preface, and which we can take at face value: taking a stand on the issues raised by the materialism controversy. Second, it is hard to see how writing a book on the history of materialism could have a vital effect on the fundamental social-political problem of his age, which was what Lange called "the social question", that is, the fact that the great mass of people lived in poverty. If it were Lange's aim to contribute to its solution, he had chosen a very indirect and inefficient means of doing so in writing his *Geschichte*. These were reasons for writing his *Die Arbeiterfrage* and *Mills Ansichten über die Socialfrage*, to be sure, but they were not reasons for writing a whole history of materialism. That seemed like a long way around the barn. In any case, neither Holzhey nor Sass provide a clear account of how the philosophical theses of Lange's book are relevant to his politics, still less how his politics shape these theses.

These problems with the social–political interpretation do not mean, however, that Lange's book has no social–political dimension at all. There is indeed an important connection between Lange's philosophy and politics after all. The connection becomes clear when we note the social and political valence of materialism and idealism around the time of the 1848 Revolution. The materialists (viz. Jacob Moleschott,

---

[36] See Lange, *Geschichte des Materialismus* (1866), pp. viii, 241.

[37] See Holzhey, 'Philosophische Kritik', pp. 212–217.

[38] Hans-Martin Sass, 'Der Standpunkt des Ideals als kritische Überwindung materialistischer und idealistischer Metaphysik', in *Friedrich Albert Lange, Leben und Werk*, eds Knoll and Schoeps (Duisburg: Walter Braun Verlag, 1975), pp. 188–206.

[39] This point is made by Köhnke, *Entstehung und Aufstieg*, pp. 247, 490 n.40, against Sass, though it also applies against Holzhey, whom Köhnke supports "almost on all points", p. 492 n.71.

Karl Vogt and Ludwig Büchner) had stood on the left during the great struggles of the March Revolution; they had advocated a broad franchise, greater social and economic equality, the separation of church and state, and limiting royal prerogative. However, the idealists, who were Hegel, Trendelenburg and the Romantics, at least according to Lange's interpretation,[40] stood on the right and had supported the Restoration. For political reasons, Lange could accept neither extreme. Though he endorsed the progressive causes of materialism, he feared that it was leading towards a completely egoistic conception of society where everyone competed with everyone else.[41] While he despised the Restoration, he still believed that the Romantic and idealist traditions had stood for an important side to human beings: their sacrifice and love for the ideal. Despite their metaphysics, and despite their scholastic and bankrupt methodology, the idealists were right to stand for the integrity and autonomy of the ideal. The task of Lange's book was therefore to develop a philosophical position that could preserve the good sides, and cancel the bad ones, in each philosophy. His aim was to defend the progressive causes of the materialists, without the egoism, while still upholding the moral idealism of the romantics and idealists, without the reactionary politics.

And what about the forthcoming revolution? Was it Lange's aim to promote or to forestall it? There can be no question that Lange was a champion of fundamental social, political and economic change sufficient to resolve the social question. It was the task of philosophy "to carry forward the torch of criticism, to collect the rays of knowledge into one, and to promote and palliate the revolutions of history".[42] Though Lange, unlike Marx, was no believer in the inevitability of revolution, he made plain his solidarity with it should one occur: resistance against it deserved all the curses radicals hurled against reactionaries.[43] He was indeed opposed to attempts to tinker with the capitalist system that would only continue its survival without addressing the deeper needs of the masses. Poor laws, charity, increases in wages, emigration were not solutions to injustice and poverty. Lange was a sharp critic of the *Selbsthilfe* or co-operative movement of Hermann Schulze-Delitzsch, as well as the *Staatshilfe* or parliamentarian movement of Ferdinand Lasalle, on the grounds that they would

---

[40] On Lange's critique of Trendelenburg, see *Mills Ansichten*, pp. 98–103. On Lange's interpretation of Hegel, see *Geschichte* II, 553–554. Lange's more considered view on Hegel is in *Die Arbeiterfrage*, pp. 257–262. Lange's views of Hegel, which are nuanced and complicated, cannot be discussed here. On Lange's interpretation of Hegel, see Hermann Lübbe, *Politische Philosophie in Deutschland* (Munich: Deutscher Taschenbuch Verlag, 1974), pp. 90–94.

[41] Lange vascillates somewhat on the connection between materialism and egoism. He first associates them, as if there is a straightforward connection. See *Geschichte* II, 453. He later weakens the connection, saying that theoretical materialism and ethical materialism (i.e. egoism) are bound up with one another, though the former is also compatible with altruism. See *Geschichte* II, 512–513. In the end he affirms a connection between the two because sympathy always means something else for the materialist, namely, refined self-interest (513). "In the long run" (*auf die Dauer*), he says, a materialist worldview leads to ethical materialism (514). It is inaccurate to say with Köhnke, therefore, that Lange holds ethical and theoretical materialism have "*nichts als den Namen gemein.*" (Köhnke, *Entstehung und Aufstieg*, p. 243). This is to miss the social and political valence that Lange gives to materialism.

[42] Lange, *Geschichte des Materialismus* (1866), p. 328.

[43] Lange, *Die Arbeiterfrage*, 4th edn, pp. 26–27.

not really emancipate workers but would simply mollify them.[44] Still, Lange's advocacy of fundamental social, political and economic change was never a call for violent agitation or revolution; he always stood for cautious and gradual reform. He maintained that Marx's belief in the necessity of revolution was "an obsolete standpoint" because of growing organization and education among the workers, and because of new laws and reforms on the part of the government.[45] So it is indeed correct to say that Lange wrote from "fear of revolution", given that he was very much concerned about the consequences of a violent social and political upheaval. It was his firm conviction that the cruelty and chaos of the French Revolution should never be repeated, and that it serves as a lesson about the dangers of all revolutions.[46] There is no guarantee, he argued, that the social question will be resolved on the day after a political revolution, because the ultimate success of any broad programme of social and political change depends on "the spiritual constitution of a generation and the reform of all its views and principles."[47]

Lange's attitude towards revolution was very much that of the humanists of the *Goethezeit*—Schiller, Herder, Humboldt—who insisted that the success of social and political reform depends on the education of the people, on their acquiring "political virtue" so that they learn to put the needs of their nation over their own self-interest. What Lange feared most of all in a revolution was that it would unleash egoistic impulses, the drive to satisfy material needs alone, with no striving for the higher moral and intellectual ideals upon which culture is based. The purpose of Lange's standpoint of the ideal was to represent the fundamental moral, aesthetic and cultural ideals for the education of the people. These ideals were very much those of the German humanists, whose standpoint Lange explicitly endorses.[48]

4. A Secret Materialist

Lange's *Geschichte des Materialismus* presents itself as a critique of materialism. Its very subtitle, *Kritik seiner Bedeutung in der Gegenwart*, announces its critical intentions. The book was celebrated chiefly because of its penetrating criticisms of the materialists, namely, Büchner, Czolbe, Moleschott, Vogt and Feuerbach. Yet Lange's book was also in an important sense a defence of materialism. Lange not only believed that materialism had been misunderstood and underappreciated by its critics, both ancient and modern, but he also nurtured a fondness for some of its main doctrines. He admired the basic ideal of materialism—a complete scientific explanation of the world—and he embraced some of its fundamental tenets: empiricism, nominalism and mechanism. Much of the *Geschichte* is a defence of these doctrines, which Lange saw as essential to natural science.

[44] See his critique of these figures in Lange, *Die Arbeiterfrage*, pp. 353–364.
[45] Lange, *Die Arbeiterfrage*, pp. 158, 349.   [46] Lange, *Die Arbeiterfrage*, pp. 389–390.
[47] Lange, *Die Arbeiterfrage*, p. 388.   [48] Lange, *Die Arbeiterfrage*, p. 338.

Not the least reason for Lange's attraction to materialism was its ethical agenda: emancipation, the liberation of the individual from arbitrary authority and religious superstition. Behind the materialist critique of religion, Lange rightly saw, lay its ideal of human autonomy, the right and power of the individual to lead his life according to his own laws and aspirations.[49] The great danger to this autonomy came with religion, the materialist taught, because it introduced the fear of the gods, who would punish those who did not obey *their* laws. Such fear grew out of superstition, that is, the belief that natural events had spiritual or supernatural causes. The materialist's antidote to such superstition was natural science, which would show that the true causes of things lay in nature rather than supernatural spirits. Lange embraced this critique, not because it would undermine religion as such, but because it could destroy superstition, which was the basis for what he saw as the greatest source of human oppression, namely, dogmatic theology and ecclesiastical authority.[50] "The greatest curse upon modern nations" Lange believed, came from the power of the church over the very soul of a human being, its right "to bind and loosen", that is, to open and shut the door to eternal salvation (I, 489). By destroying superstition, the materialist critique would remove that curse and clear the path for human autonomy.

The model for Lange's *Geschichte,* though never made explicit, was Gottfried Arnold's *Unparteiische Kirchen- und Ketzerhistorie,*[51] a classic of the radical Protestant tradition, a work much admired by Lessing and Herder. Lange also revered Arnold's work, and it is probably not accidental that he praises it in the *Geschichte des Materialismus.*[52] Writing in the early 18th century, Arnold contended that the true Christians were the heretics, those persecuted by the established churches, which persistently oppressed genuine faith through dogmas and rituals. Just as Arnold's history was a plea for liberty of conscience, a defence of heretics against persecution, so Lange's history was an appeal for liberty of press, a defence of materialists against prosecution. Persecution and prosecution, Lange noted, had been the perennial fate of materialism. Ancient materialists had been persecuted by the state, and now the same was happening to their modern counterparts.

The first book of the *Geschichte des Materialismus,* the entire first volume of the second edition, is a history of materialism from Democritus in the 5th century BC to La Mettrie and Holbach in the 18th century. It is a narrative about how natural science originated in materialism, and how its advance was hindered, in late antiquity and the Middle Ages, by the hegemony of the church and the Platonic-Aristotelian

---

[49] See Lange, *Geschichte des Materialismus,* I, 34, 100: "*dies Streben der Befreiung [ist] gerade der Nerv des epikureischen Systemes*".

[50] On Lange's opinion of ecclesiastical authority, see *Geschichte des Materialismus,* II, 487, 489, 507, 557.

[51] Gottfried Arnold, *Unparteiische Kirchen- und Ketzerhistorie* (Frankfurt: Fritsch, 1729).

[52] Lange mentions Arnold's work and praises it for being "*mächtige Stütze der Denkfreiheit*", *Geschichte des Materialismus* (I, 402). He explicitly adopts the Arnoldian thesis that the heretics are the true Christians and champions of humanity. See *Geschichte des Materialismus,* II, 485–486.

philosophy. The birth of the natural sciences in the early modern era, Lange argues, was due in great measure to the rediscovery of materialism, to the reaffirmation of its central doctrines by Bacon, Hobbes, Gassendi and Descartes. Enlightenment and materialism are for Lange almost one and the same: the more enlightened the philosophy, the closer it stands to materialism.

Why write a whole history of materialism if one's goal is a critique of materialism, especially a critique of its contemporary relevance? This too seems like a long way around the barn. For Lange, however, critique is first and foremost *historical* critique,[53] involving an account of the origins and development of the philosophy, religion or art under investigation. Such a critique is especially important in the case of the materialism controversy, he believes, because both materialists and their critics show a complete lack of historical sense.[54] The materialists think that their materialism is the result of modern science alone, completely unaware how their main ideas, goals and problems go back to 5th-century Athens. They need to realize that what they think and teach did not grow out of the head of some contemporary Medusa, but that it is the result of a long history, that they are the descendents of Democritus, Epicurus and Empedocles. Becoming aware of their own history, Lange believed, would have a great moral and political value for the materialists: they would gain strength and motivation in their struggle against the reactionary forces if they see that they are part of a long glorious tradition, the materialists' centuries long battle on behalf of enlightenment and progress (II, 171). But the critics of materialism were also in desperate need of a historical education. For they liked to dismiss materialism as if it were the latest intellectual fad, as if it were not worthy of discussion even as a form of philosophy. But if one could show that materialism had its sources in antiquity, that philosophers of no less stature than Plato and Aristotle took materialism seriously, then one would show that materialism is indeed a form of philosophy after all. Knowing that might have the valuable effect of producing a discussion or dialogue between idealists and materialists.

Lange's historical education begins with the very first sentence of the *Geschichte des Materialismus*, which is laden with significance. "Materialism is as old as philosophy, but not older."[55] The first phrase of the sentence is directed against modern materialists and their critics. The modern materialists had insisted that their doctrine is science, not philosophy; their critics had claimed that materialism is not even philosophy. The first phrase tells us both are wrong: that materialism is indeed philosophy. This means that the critics of materialism should take it seriously because it is philosophy after all, and that modern materialists should stop claiming their doctrines are purely

---

[53] See *Geschichte des Materialismus*, II, 170: "*Hand in Hand mit der philosophischen Bildung geht die historische.*"; and II, 171: "*Geschichte und Kritik sind oft eins und dasselbe.*"

[54] See *Geschichte des Materialismus*, II, 68, 71, 90, 170.

[55] Lange, *Geschichte des Materialismus*, I, 3. The 1866 edition begins with the same sentence (p. 3), showing the importance Lange gave it. The second edition provides a commentary on the first sentence, I, 123–124 n.1.

scientific, as if they did not emerge from philosophy. The second phrase of the sentence is no less significant. To say that materialism is not older than philosophy means that it did not originate in myth, the first form of human awareness about the world. Myths are forms of belief and art, but they are not theories, attempts to explain the world. Materialism arose with philosophy itself, Lange explains, because it was the first attempt to provide a consistent and general theory of nature (8–9). Its goal was to explain all phenomena according to a single principle, and on a naturalistic basis, so that nature is understood through nature, that is, the supernatural is banished and everything in nature is understood according to its own general laws (4, 8). Modern materialism shares the same ideal.

Materialism, Lange informs us, can take many forms. It can be vitalistic, pantheistic or hylozoistic. The purest and most consistent form, however, is atomism, because it assumes that the basic entities of nature are bodies, to which it attributes no spiritual or mystical qualities but only physical ones, that is, those that are observable and in space and time (I, 123 nn. 1, 8). The chief advocate of atomism was Democritus, for whom Lange's admiration could hardly have been higher: "Among the greatest thinkers of antiquity, Democritus may in fact be counted the greatest." (11). Lange tells us how Democritus went to visit Athens but quickly left the city because he could not abide the sophists, still less Plato, "whose entire philosophy was only dialectical wordplay" (11).

In the second edition,[56] Lange gives a concise summary of Democritus' philosophy (I, 12–19). He lists six chief principles:

1) From nothing comes nothing, and what exists cannot be destroyed. All change is unification and separation of parts.
2) Nothing happens by chance but only for a reason, and from necessity.
3) Nothing exists except atoms and the void.
4) The atoms are infinite in number and form.
5) The differences between things comes from differences in the number, size and shape of the atoms.
6) The soul consists of fine, smooth and round atoms, like those of fire.[57]

---

[56] The first edition gives a very different summary, pp. 7–8.
  1) The principles of all things are atoms and empty space; all else is opinion.
  2) There are infinite worlds in number and extension, which are constantly coming into and going out of being.
  3) From nothing nothing comes, and something can never be destroyed.
  4) The atoms are in constant rotary motion, and all coming into and out of being is due to their unification and separation.
  5) The differences in things comes from the differences in number and shape of atoms; and originally there are no qualitative differences between atoms
  6) Everything happens of necessity; final causes are to be rejected.

[57] One of the difficult points in Lange's account of materialism concerns his understanding of the relationship between materialism and what he calls "sensualism". Sensualism is for him an empiricist

There is no specific chapter or section of the first book of the *Geschichte des Materialismus* devoted to a defence of materialism. Lange's sympathy for it is often implicit and disparate, scattered in various places in the text. It first appears from his comments on the materialists' chief principles. Regarding the second principle, Lange remarks that it was intended as a maxim of mechanical explanation, according to which every event is explained by prior events acting upon it (I, 13). This principle is meant to exclude teleology, the explanation of events by final causes or purposes. Lange makes it perfectly clear that he endorses such mechanism; for him final causes are a refuge of ignorance, "a partial negation of science, an arbitrary cordon around a field that has still not been investigated" (14–15). All teleological explanation is for Lange anthropomorphic, because it explains events by analogy with human intentions. Such explanations violate the chief principle of naturalism, according to which everything in nature should be explained in natural terms (47–48, 63).

Lange's sympathy with materialism is no less apparent from his attitude towards Democritus' chief critics, who were Socrates and Plato. The reaction against Democritus began with Socrates and came to a climax in Plato, Lange tells us (I, 44). Socrates attempted to revive the older teleological way of seeing things, which was explicitly and intentionally anthropomorphic. He conceived the architect of the world as a person, and the reason by which it creates the world as akin to human reason (47, 48). Rather than explaining man from his place in nature, Socrates wanted to explain nature according to man (47). Because he aimed to revive teleology, Lange regards Socrates' reaction against materialism as "a great step backwards" (29).

Attempting to revive teleology, it turns out, was not Socrates' only retrograde step. There was another of no less significance: the belief in the existence of universals. The Socrates-Platonic tradition gave a mystical significance to words, whose meanings were placed in a special intelligible realm. Lange traces this doctrine back to two sources: Socrates' theory of definition, according to which there is a natural relationship between words and their designata (I, 39, 51); and his method of dialectic, which supports an hypothesis by ascending to a higher level of abstraction and universality (39). These Socratic doctrines eventually reached their climax in Plato's theory of ideas, according to which ideas alone have reality (58). Lange thinks that the belief in the existence of ideas is entirely illusory, because it arises from the hypostasis of

---

doctrine that states the immediate object and content of consciousness consists in sensation alone (27). In one passage Lange states that sensualism is "a natural development of materialism" (27). Sensualism derives from materialism because the sensualist holds that the objects and contents of consciousness ultimately reflect and derive from matter, which is the source of all being. Yet in another passage Lange states that sensualism is "a transitional stage toward idealism" (131, n.30), which is the antithesis of materialism because it undermines the materialist's belief in the objective reality of matter. Sensualism leads to idealism because it holds that the immediate objects of consciousness are not material objects but sensations in us, so that it is impossible to know matter directly or in itself (26–27). So just how sensualism relates to materialism is left unclear. It seems to derive from materialism but also to be opposed to it. Lange tries to resolve this tension when he explains that Protagoras, the chief exponent of sensualism, held that matter is indeterminate, realizing itself in all kinds of ways in the different sensations of different minds (29).

meanings, which exist only in the mind (41, 162). He even recommends that the theory of ideas be banished from the sciences, because it turns away from the particular things of nature and towards the hypostases of mere words (60). Nominalism, we shall soon see, is one of Lange's fundamental doctrines, the critique of hypostasis one of the main underlying themes of the *Geschichte des Materialismus*.

It was one of the great misfortunes of the history of philosophy, Lange laments, that Plato's doctrine of ideas and final causes was continued by Aristotle. Although Aristotle attempted to correct Plato's theory that universals exist in some special realm of being, he still assumed that universals exist in things and that they are not simply creatures of the mind. His logic and theory of categories is a deficient organon of science, Lange argues, because it confuses kinds of assertion with kinds of being. The hypostasis of forms of speech, as if properties of language were somehow forms of being, is indeed "the essential characteristic of Aristotelian thinking" (I, 159). Unfortunately, Aristotle's philosophy dominated the Middle Ages. It was entirely due to its hegemony, Lange maintains, that the Middle Ages proved to be so barren for the development of natural science. Thanks to Aristotle, the Middle Ages was an era "dominated by words, by hypostasis, by complete unclarity about the meaning of phenomena given to the senses" (162).

Lange ascribes the rebirth of natural science in the early modern era mainly to two thinkers: Bacon and Descartes. Their thought marks a return to the materialism of the ancient world, insofar as they advocate atomism, nominalism and mechanism. Although Bacon and Descartes explicitly disavowed materialism, they were still able to revive natural science in virtue of the materialist tendencies of their thought. Bacon, Lange believes, should be even called the father of modern materialism (195).

Although Lange's narrative about the history of materialism seems to make it alone responsible for the birth and advance of the sciences, he realizes that such a story is much too simplistic. He admits that the Platonic tradition has been the motivation for some of the most important scientific discoveries in the ancient world (I, 92; II, 174, 178–179). The love of order and harmony, so characteristic of this tradition, was a spur to scientific discovery, enabling it to go much further and faster towards its goal than the grind of ordinary induction. The chief value of materialism towards the advance of science, Lange explains, was its development of a sober and solid methodological way of thinking that demanded considering the phenomena of nature for their own sake, independent of their utility and religious meaning (I, 95).

As much as Lange champions ancient materialism, he still does not hesitate to criticize it. Throughout the first book of his *Geschichte des Materialismus* he emphasizes that there has been one perennial unsolved problem of materialism: the explanation of consciousness and thinking according to the laws of nature (I, 15–16, 18, 110–111, 232, 390). Lange understands this problem in more specific terms: how to explain the qualitative dimension of sensation? The difficulty for the materialist was to account for how sense qualities arise from the motions of material particles (390). There seems to be the greatest heterogeneity between sounds or colours and their causes in the material world, namely, light rays and sound waves, which are measurable and quantifiable. It was a fundamental principle of materialism to explain all differences in things from the differences in number, size, motion and the shape of the atoms (18). But this principle ran into difficulty with the difference in kind between sense qualities and the physical characteristics supposed to give rise to them (15–16, 18). This problem thwarted materialism from achieving its grand goal of explaining all of nature according to a single principle. Lange thinks that this objection is convincing, doubting that there will ever be a bridge to close the gap between consciousness and matter.

While Lange stresses the explanation of sensation as the fundamental problem of materialism, he also suggests another criticism of no less importance. Towards the end of the first book Lange remarks that materialism has been much too dismissive in its attitude towards morality, religion and metaphysics. While the ideas of purposiveness and intelligence in nature are indeed anthropomorphic, lacking all objective validity, they still have an "aesthetic justification" all their own (I, 374). What Lange means by this aesthetic justification is not entirely clear, and it seems to amount to nothing more than giving them "poetic value". Whatever that means, it soon emerges that these ideas are "poetic" in the sense that they are created by us, and that they should be appraised according to their own *sui generis* standards (376). Lange suggests that we evaluate moral and aesthetic ideas according to very different standards from those of objective truth or cognitive worth, and that the materialist has missed their point in dismissing them for not matching such theoretical standards. When we say that a painting is ugly, that a person is evil, that a fallacy has been committed, we are not saying that they are false but that they do not conform to ideals or norms. We shall soon see how this criticism of materialism, only suggested in the first book, eventually becomes a major theme of Lange's general philosophy.

5. A Kantian Critique of Materialism

In the history of materialism Lange gave great importance to Kant. The second book of the *Geschichte des Materialimus*—the second volume of the second edition— begins with his section on Kant, the longest and densest in the entire book.[58] Lange saw Kant's philosophy as a caesura in the history of materialism, as a crisis in the long tradition that had begun in the 5th century BC. Having exposed its major weaknesses, Kant's philosophy was "the beginning of the end, the catastrophe of the tragedy".[59] Though new forms of materialism would arise after Kant, they proved weak and unstable, just because they could not overcome the problems that Kant had posed for them. The only reason materialism returned after Kant, Lange claimed, is that

---

[58] This chapter was heavily revised and expanded in the second edition. All references in parentheses above, unless otherwise noted, are to the second volume of the second edition.
[59] As Lange put it in the first edition, p. 241.

speculative idealism had swept away the constraints of the critical philosophy (II, 67–68). It was Lange's chief goal, therefore, to re-impose those constraints, to teach the materialists some basic critical lessons.

What problems had Kant exposed in materialism? It is striking that Lange does not think it consists in showing the inexplicability of sensation, the classical diffi-culty that had been the chief stumbling block of ancient materialism. It is also notable that Lange, contrary to the orthodox Kantians, gives no weight to Kant's doctrine of practical faith. In the second edition he bluntly declared Kant's practical philoso-phy—and here he meant specifically his doctrine of practical faith—to be the weakest side of his system (II, 2). The real significance of Kant's philosophy, he declared, lay entirely with his critique of *theoretical* reason.[60]

According to Lange, Kant's philosophy posed two fundamental challenges to materialism. First, it exposed the naive realism of materialism, that is, its belief that material things are the immediate objects of perception. The materialist assumed that sense perception gives us the objective truth about the world, that what we see through our senses continues to exist just as we perceive it. Though he would concede that some perceived qualities depend on our perception of them, namely, the so-called "secondary qualities", such as colours, smells and sounds, he insisted that others really do inhere in the object itself, existing in it independent of our per-ception, namely, the so-called "primary qualities", such as size, shape and weight. It was just this realism, Lange argues, that was destroyed by Kant's Copernican Revolution (II, 2, 5, 38). Kant had shown that *all* sense qualities depend upon our perceptive and cognitive organization, so that our entire world would appear dif-ferently had we a different perceptive and cognitive constitution (5). This is true not only for the secondary qualities but also for the primary ones, because Kant had demonstrated that even the perception of space itself depends on a priori forms of sense perception.

Though classical materialism had always been vulnerable to the scepticism of Protagoras, who had taught that man is the measure of all things, Kant marked a more potent threat to materialism, Lange argued, because he had provided a more systematic and scientific justification for Protagoras' teaching (II, 4–5). While the materialists had dismissed Berkeley's arguments against realism as so many sophisti-cal paradoxes, they could not do the same to Kant, because his case was supported by "a new sphere of scientific research", namely, "the physiology of sense organs" (4–5). Here Lange, a student of Helmholtz, was alluding to the experiments of Johannes Müller, which seemed to establish the active role of our physiology in forming the qualities of experience.[61] These experiments seemed to show that what we perceive, the content of our experience, depends on our nervous constitution. If this were so,

---

[60] Lange's statement here, however, has to be compared with his statements elsewhere to see exactly what he accepts and rejects in Kant's doctrine of practical faith. See Section 3, 5 and 9.

[61] On Müller's experiments, see Chapter 4, Section 5.

then the materialists would be beaten at their own game. They had insisted that science is on their side, and that only superstition opposed them. But now Lange was pointing out that science really undermines a fundamental dogma of the materialists, their belief in the existence of an objective world.

The second basic challenge Kant posed for materialism involves its belief in causal necessity. It was a fundamental principle of materialism that everything happens of necessity, that all events conform to regular laws. But this assumption too proved to be naive, especially in the face of Hume's scepticism. Hume had shown that there is no rationale for the belief in causal necessity, that there are no grounds to assume, from either logic or experience, that there is a necessary connection between cause and effect. There is no reason in logic, because there is no contradiction if we affirm a cause and deny an effect; and there is no reason from experience, because our senses give no evidence for a necessary connection. Kant had appropriated this Humean theme, which he used to demonstrate that universal and necessary order derives not from things-in-themselves but from our cognitive constitution (II, 7, 12). All the order we find in the world is order that we create, and it is not given to us with things-in-themselves.

Both these problems of classical materialism are instances of what Kant called "dogmatism". That term means at least two things: first, accepting beliefs without subjecting them to critical scrutiny, holding them without considering whether they are based on solid reasons; and, second, being unaware or unreflective about the subjective sources of one's beliefs, hypostasizing or reifying them, as if they refer to things in the world when they really arise subconsciously from our mental activities. Hypostasis, Kant teaches, is the characteristic fallacy of dogmatism, the common source of its many fallacies, namely, the paralogisms, amphibolies and antinomies. In assuming that our representations refer to actual things in the world, and that the connections we posit between events are really in the events themselves, the materialist shows himself to be guilty of dogmatism in both senses. Criticism stands on a higher level of reflection than dogmatism, Lange implies, precisely because it makes us aware of the subjective sources of our ways of thinking about the world. Thus both dogmatic strands of materialism mean that it is epistemologically naive. This is an especially embarrassing lesson for materialism, which attempts to expose the naivety of religion by revealing its hypostases and anthropomorphic sources. Now Lange had turned those criticisms against materialism itself: the same charges of anthropomorphism and hypostasis applied to the materialist's belief in material objects and causal necessity. Now that materialism had shown itself to be as dogmatic as religion, there seemed no turning back to the naive pre-critical era. Hence Lange's belief that Kant's philosophy represented an irreversible turning point in the history of materialism. The catastrophe was total, putting it beyond redemption or resurrection.

Besides his belief in the existence of matter and causal relations, Lange thinks that the materialist is guilty of yet another hypostasis: belief in the existence of atoms.[62] Büchner thought that it was one of the great merits of modern chemistry that, whereas the ancient materialists had to resort to speculation, it had actually proved the existence of atoms.[63] Lange, however, believed that in saying this Büchner had only revealed, once again, the naivety and dogmatism of modern materialism. He could see no justification whatsoever for the existence of atoms, which were for him only a construction to explain the data. While Lange praised the modern atomists, namely, Dalton and Guy-Lussac, for developing a concept of the ultimate constitution of matter that is very intuitive and intuitable (II, 187, 211)—viz., atoms are like little balls swirling around in a space having a precise size, shape and place—he warned that the intuitability of a theory does not prove its actuality (190). In any case, recent research in physics and chemistry had made the atom something far less intuitable, into something even supersensible, because it has turned the atom into a centre of forces, an unextended point that is the locus of attraction and repulsion (192, 204, 212). More generally, the progress of science consists, Lange declared, in replacing the concept of a thing with that of relations (207), so that the concept of force now replaces the atom (204). After its analysis into forces, the concept of matter amounts to little more than that of a substrate, the subject in which the forces somehow inhere (205). It thus serves the same role as the old concept of substance, and it is no less a hypostasis, the reification of a grammatical subject. But Lange took his critique of hypostasis a step further, applying it to the concept of force itself. Force, he argued, is really only a personification of the mathematical formulae that physicists use to describe and predict phenomena (205). We do not develop the formulae to describe the force, which somehow actually exists in nature, but we develop the idea of force to describe the formulae (205, 206). Force is a personification of what formulae describe, the projection of feelings of pushes, pulls and pressures onto things (204).

In his chapter on Kant in the *Geschichte des Materialismus* Lange had focused chiefly on the conflict between the critical philosophy and materialism, portraying them as antithetical worldviews. Indeed, he sagely remarked at one point: "One can regard Kant's entire system as a splendid attempt to destroy materialism once and for all without falling into scepticism." (II, 65) Yet it is noteworthy this is only one side of the story that Lange told about the relationship between Kant and materialism. There is another side, because Lange also stresses the great affinity between them. Thus he remarks that Kant was not implacably opposed to materialism, that he was much closer to materialism than its other opponents, and that he praised Epicurus for wisely keeping his philosophy within the bounds of experience (5).

---

[62] See Lange, *Geschichte des Materialismus* (1875), II, 181–220. This chapter anticipates the later philosophy of science of the Marburg school.

[63] Ludwig Büchner, *Natur und Geist, Gespräche zweier Freunde über den Materialismus und über real-philosophischen Fragen der Gegenwart* (Frankfurt: Meidinger Sohn & Comp. 1857), p. 102. Büchner is not quite as naive as Lange makes him appear, because a few pages later (pp. 104–105) he notes that the modern atomic theory is still crude and speculative.

Lange even claims that Kant saw materialism, along with scepticism, as the two pre-liminary stages of the critical philosophy (9). The nemesis of the critical philosophy, Lange suggested, is not materialism but Platonic idealism, which transcends the limits of experience and claims insight into things-in-themselves (9–10). It was just this Platonic idealism, we have seen, that had been the great enemy of materialism. So given that the enemy of my enemy is my friend, it seemed that the critical philoso-phy could now embrace materialism as a comrade in the struggle against Platonic idealism.

Prima facie Lange champions Kant because he defeats materialism. But this too is only one side of the story. Lange embraces Kant not only because he destroys mate-rialism (in some respects) but also because he saves it (in other respects), even incor-porating it into his own philosophy. Lange knew all too well that the affinity between Kant and materialism goes much further than the empiricism he mentions in his chapter on Kant. He was fully aware that Kant also supports, even if more implicitly, the nominalist and mechanistic strands of materialism.[64] Furthermore, both phi-losophies are champions of the new natural sciences and the mathematical theory of nature. As Lange saw it, then, the critical philosophy has all the strengths and none of the weaknesses of materialism: all the strengths, because it too is empiricist, mecha-nist and nominalist; and none of the weaknesses because it, unlike materialism, is not dogmatic. In a later chapter of his *Geschichte des Materialismus* Lange is perfectly explicit about the deep and broad affinity between Kant and materialism: "the whole worldview of materialism is, as it were, incorporated into the Kantian system with-out altering its basic idealistic character." (147) For Lange, then, Kant's theoretical philosophy is to be recommended not as the antithesis of materialism but simply as a *critical* or *phenomenalistic* materialism.

6. Lange and the Thing-in-Itself

Stressing such a close affinity between Kant's philosophy and materialism breaks down, however, at one vulnerable point: the thing-in-itself. The whole point of that concept is to set limits to naturalistic explanation, the very kind of explanation cham-pioned by materialism. This raises the important question: What was Lange's stance towards the thing-in-itself?

---

[64] Kant's mechanism is most apparent from his doctrine about the regulative status of teleology, and in his insistence on a mathematical paradigm of explanation. His nominalism appears in at least two major forms: his thesis that the form of experience, the relations between things, originates in the mind; and his doctrine of synthesis, according to which all connection results from the spontaneity of understanding. The theme of hypostasis, which is central to the Transcendental Dialectic, was also a standard nominalist trope. Still, nominalism is only one side of Kant. It has been well-argued that there is also a Platonic side. See, for example, Patrick Riley, *Kant's Political Philosophy* (Totowa, NJ: Rowan and Littlefield, 1983), and T.K. Seung, *Kant's Platonic Revolution in Moral and Political Philosophy* (Baltimore, MD: Johns Hopkins University Press, 1994).

As it had for his contemporaries, this concept created many difficulties for Lange, who never really resolved them. He vascillates about the status of this concept and fails to develop a fully consistent position. In the first edition of the *Geschichte des Materialismus* Lange had tried to defend the existence of things-in-themselves.[65] After taking note of Überweg's objection that the idea of the thing-in-itself as the cause of experience involves a transcendent application of the category of causality, Lange replies that if we can apply that category to everything within experience, it should also determine its limits, at least in the sense that we know there are limits and that there is something beyond them. "The fish in the pond can only swim in the water and not on the earth; or he can still bump his head against the ground and walls. In the same manner we can use the concept of causality to measure the whole realm of experience and find that beyond it there is something other than it, an inaccessible domain for our organs." (267) However, he immediately poses a problem for such reasoning: that if the categories have meaning only with reference to appearances, then the thing-in-itself, which is postulated by the category of causality, should also be only an appearance; in other words, the entire distinction between appearance and thing-in-itself should fall within the realm of appearances (267–268). Undaunted, Lange persists in maintaining the reality of the thing-in-itself. A consideration of our faculty of knowledge shows us, he argues, that what appears is relative to it, that what we know is determined by our specific physiological constitution. This means that the world will appear differently to creatures having different faculties. There must be something that appears so differently to all these creatures, "a common unknown source", and that something will be the thing-in-itself (268).

In the second edition of his *Geschichte des Materialismus,* however, Lange attempts to eliminate the very thing-in-itself whose existence he defended in the first edition. He now argues expressly that the limitations Kant had placed on knowledge do not allow him to assume the existence of the thing-in-itself. If all knowledge is limited to possible experience, as Kant had preached in the first *Kritik*, then he cannot claim that the thing-in-itself exists, given that the thing-in-itself transcends all possible experience. And so Lange writes: "That there are things-in-themselves that have a spaceless and timeless existence Kant could not prove from his own principles, for that would be a transcendent, even if negative, knowledge of the properties of things-in-themselves, and such knowledge is completely impossible according to Kant's own theory." (36) While in the first edition of his *Geschichte des Materialismus* Lange had expressly defended the existence of the thing-in-itself, in the second edition he came to the conclusion that Kant himself had seen the inconsistency in such an assumption and intended to remove the thing-in-itself (48–49).[66] The thing-in-itself, Lange is now

[65] See also Lange's March 14, 1867, letter to Dohrn, in Ellissen, *Lange,* pp. 258–259, which affirms a realistic conception of things-in-themselves. Here Lange writes: "*Ich glaube weder, daß Kant selbst jemals gedacht hat, das „Ding an sich" habe keine Realität außer uns, noch huldige ich selbst einer solchen Ansicht. . . Ich halte dasselbe nur für gänzlich unerkennbar, ebenso aber auch das Wesen unserer Organization für unerkennbar.*"
[66] Lange writes in an endnote (II, 130, Anm. 35) that he was changing his view about the status of the thing-in-itself before he read Cohen's *Kants Theorie der Erfahrung,* which appeared in 1871, between the

convinced, is only "a limiting concept", a "problematic concept" (49). Its main purpose is to show us that we cannot know anything beyond the world we create and experience; but it does not imply that there is some existing realm outside of us.

Yet Lange never entirely succeeded in eliminating the thing-in-itself, not even in the second edition of his *Geschichte des Materialismus*. There are other passages of this edition where, in so many words, Lange commits himself to its existence. In the final chapter of the book, for example, we learn that our cognitive powers of synthesis are limited, and that our representations of things arise from something that does not derive from our own activity, something Lange variously calls an "object", "non-ego", or "power" that cannot be resolved into the forms of knowledge (II, 542). If this were not enough, in Chapter 2 of Book II Lange re-invokes the thing-in-itself as an unknowable entity to curb the dogmatic pretensions of idealism and materialism. Thus he argues that it is utter dogmatism to assume that how we perceive the world according to our cognitive faculties is the only way and form in which it exists or appears. The whole point of the Kantian doctrine of the thing-in-itself is to point out the limiting factors of our own cognitive faculties, and to remind us that our faculties are only one of the possible ways to perceive things-in-themselves (99). When a worm, a beetle, a human and an angel perceive a tree, there are four different representations of one tree; each creature knows the tree only from its perspective and physiology; but none knows the tree in itself (102–103). We should never generalize about reality-in-itself from our own cognitive faculties, Lange cautions, because the difference between the thing-in-itself and the thing for me is as great as the difference between a single factor and infinitely many factors (i.e. all the workings of physiology and the environment) behind a product (consciousness) (103). These arguments occur in the background of a more general theory according to which knowledge arises from the interaction of the subject and object, where the subject fashions the object according to its faculties, and where the object is given as the source of an "objective influence" on our sensibility (98).

Thus Lange, like Liebmann, discovered that the thing-in-itself, the great stumbling block of the critical philosophy, is not so easily eliminable after all: that we are bound to postulate its existence as soon as we consider that our knowing faculties are finite, and that these faculties are only one way in which an independent reality is perceived.

7. Interpretation of Kant

Lange's naturalistic interpretation of Kant's philosophy extended to its methodology. His conception of Kant's transcendental enquiry was greatly influenced by the physiological-psychological tradition of Fries, Beneke and Helmholtz.

---

first and second editions of his *Geschichte des Materialismus*. Now that he had read Cohen, however, he had been encouraged to make a total revision of his views. He says that he agrees with Cohen on most points but that he does not think that Kant is as consistent as Cohen assumes.

"The physiology of the sense organs" was in his view nothing less than "developed or corrected Kantianism" (II, 409). It was "corrected Kantianism" because there were still respects in which Kant clung to the old dogmatic method of Wolff, which demands strict demonstrations and a priori reasoning; but, Lange assures us, this was a vestige of Kant's rationalist heritage, which does not represent the true tendency or spirit of his teaching. That tendency or spirit consists in its "psychological-physiological research programme". We can regard Kant's entire system, Lange says, as "a programme for new discoveries in this field [the physiology of the sense organs]." (409) Like Fries, Beneke and Helmholtz, then, Lange sees Kant's epistemology as fundamentally an empirical investigation into the physiology and psychology of human perception; it deals primarily with first-order questions about the *causes* of experience rather than second-order questions about the *reasons* for beliefs. This interpretation suited Lange's general interpretation of modern philosophy, which stressed its affinity with the natural sciences. With the exception of the "*Begriffsromantik*" of speculative idealism, a perverse aberration, modern philosophy is characterized by its "natural-scientific manner of thought" (145).

Following his naturalistic conception of transcendental philosophy, Lange interpreted the a priori in terms of what he calls our "physical-psychological organization" (II, 30). The a priori consists in those constant, or universal and necessary, factors in our physiological and psychological constitution that condition us to perceive the world in certain ways. This organization is a priori in the sense that it precedes our experience and lays down the necessary conditions under which we perceive it (28). In saying this Lange was still mindful of Mill's critique of innatism, according to which an apparently innate part of our psychology often turns out to be nothing more than an engrained habit. While he accepted Mill's point, he did not think that it demonstrated that *all* the basic ways of perceiving and conceiving the world had to derive from experience. There are still parts of our physiological and psychological constitution that are inherent in our human nature and that determine the nature of our experience. It is the special task of the transcendental philosopher to distinguish between those factors that are a constant part of our human nature and those that arise only from habit and experience (31).

Though intended to give some scientific backing for Kant's theory, Lange's naturalistic conception of the a priori licensed some basic departures from Kantian doctrine. The conception of the a priori should be broadened, Lange argued, so that it extends beyond the Kantian forms of intuition (space and time) and understanding (the twelve categories). Any kind of human functioning that is inherent in, or natural to, our physiological-psychological constitution should count as part of the a priori conditions of experience. There are, for example, a priori conditions of even colour perception, which consist in how our visual nerves respond to light waves (II, 28, 33). Lange also objected to the Kantian assumption that only the form of experience is a priori while its content is a posteriori; he maintained that even its content could have its own a priori dimension. For example, the law that the intensity of the conscious-ness of a sensation is directly proportional to the intensity of its stimulus deals only with sensations, the content of experience, though it too could be regarded among the a priori laws or factors of sense perception (33–34). It is also a mistake, Lange held, to assume that sensation is an entirely passive factor in experience, for sensa-tion is also a conditioning factor in determining how the forms of spatial percep-tion are applied (34). Though Lange advocated broadening the concept of the a priori, and though he stressed the a priori factors in sensation itself, he still maintained that Kant had been broadly correct to argue for the a priori nature of space and time (34). Like Fischer and Liebmann, Lange saw the Transcendental Aesthetic as one of Kant's greatest accomplishments.

Although influenced by Fries, Beneke and Helmholtz, Lange did not take over their physiological-psychological interpretation of Kant unreflectively. He had his own reasons for adopting it, and he went to some pains to justify it. In a long endnote attached to the second edition of the *Geschichte des Materialismus* Lange explained why he introduced the term "physical-psychological organization" for the subject matter of Kant's epistemology (II, 125–127, n. 25). Kant's own vocabu-lary of the "transcendental" smacked of the thing-in-itself, which is very prob-lematic, given that Kant had forbidden all speculation about it. The reason Kant introduced the term "transcendental" was to avoid the danger of materialism; but then he fell prey to the opposite error of sanctioning speculation about things-in-themselves. The whole point about the term "physical-psychological organization", Lange wrote, is to bring the apparently transcendental into the realm of experi-ence itself, so that the a priori is made the subject of proper empirical investigation (126). Lange insisted on defining "physical-psychological organization" in empiri-cal terms, avoiding all reference to metaphysical assumptions. This organization was nothing more than "what appears to our external senses as part of our physical organization, and which stands in an immediate causal connection with our psy-chic functions" (127). Whether this organization was supported by a soul or mat-ter was simply bracketed off as having no relevance for a strictly epistemological investigation.

One of the most obscure and difficult questions about Kant's philosophy, Lange believed, concerns Kant's method, and more specifically how he discovers the a priori or necessary conditions of experience (II, 28). Kant himself gave few explanations about his own methodology, leaving his progeny to piece together his few hints and suggestions dropped here and there. Lange described an apparent dilemma facing any attempt to reconstruct Kant's methodology: Kant cannot discover these condi-tions following either an a priori or an empirical method (II, 29). While an a priori method seems too rationalistic and dogmatic, an empirical method appears inap-propriate to determine a priori conditions, which are universal and necessary and so underivable from empirical data. Yet Lange argues that this is a false dilemma. Like Fries and Meyer, he believes that it is possible to determine a priori conditions through empirical means.[67] It is one thing *to discover* these conditions, quite another *to demonstrate* them (30). While demonstration indeed requires an a priori method, discovery involves nothing more than an empirical one. Kant's method, Lange then assures us, consists in nothing more than reflection on the facts of consciousness and normal ordinary induction (29).

Lange was well aware that Kant would often make claims for his transcendental philosophy that went beyond what any empirical method could provide. He claimed, for example, that his method ensured both "completeness" and "apodictic certainty", though an empirical method could give at best merely piecemeal and hypothetical results. Yet Lange explained those strong claims from the residual rationalism clinging to Kant's philosophy. While Kant had been a powerful critic of rationalist metaphysics, he still had not completely liberated himself from use of its "dogmatic method", namely, rigour in the use of syllogistic reasoning, thoroughness in the analysis of concepts. Indeed, Kant had explicitly endorsed this method in the second preface to the *Kritik* (B xxxv). But, for Lange, this was Kant's great mistake, violating the spirit of the "natural-scientific mode of thought" that was the guiding spirit of modern philosophy. If one of Kant's greatest feats was his critique of rationalist speculation, his attempt to restrict knowledge within experience, one of his greatest failures was his persistent use of the rationalist methodology (32).

Because he rejects Kant's dogmatic method and recommends an empirical one, and because he explains the subject matter of Kant's critique as our "physiological-psychological constitution", there seems no question that Lange embraces a psychologistic interpretation of Kant. There are some places, however, where Lange seems to waver in this interpretation. There is a passage in the second edition of the *Geschichte des Materialismus* where Lange states unequivocally that Kant's concern is not psychological at all. "The psychological side of the question [What must I presuppose to explain the fact of experience?] is not only not his [Kant's] chief interest, but he even attempts to avoid it, since he poses his question in such a general manner that the answer is compatible with the most diverse psychological theories." (29) What does Lange mean here? Did he recognize the limits and problems of the psychological interpretation after all? Not really. The explanation for this confusing statement appears in a footnote attached to the end of the chapter (124, n.23). Here Lange states "the greatest part of the obscurity of the *Critique of Pure Reason* derives from the single fact that Kant conducts what is in its general nature a psychological investigation though he does not have any special psychological theory." Thus Lange acknowledges and reaffirms the general psychological nature of Kant's investigation; he means only that it is not psychological in any more specific sense; in other words, Kant does not intend to develop a specific metaphysical theory about the nature of the soul, namely, whether it is entirely spiritual or physical or some combination of both.

---

[67] See Chapter 1, Section 3; and Chapter 8, Section 4.

Some passages in Lange's *Logische Studien,* however, seem to abandon the psychological interpretation more unequivocally. Here Lange often notes a basic point about Kant's transcendental discourse that seems to belie the psychological interpretation: that the transcendental conditions of experience cannot be in experience itself; the very attempt to know them through experience presupposes them. This point is taken to some remarkable conclusions at the very close of the book. Here Lange remarks that the basic laws of logic and mathematics are the foundation of our intellectual organization, and that they derive not from "the region of our empirical consciousness" but from "the subconscious foundation of our self, together with all appearances in which this world consists" (148). We then learn that the transcendental self, which is the source of these laws, is distinct from the empirical self: the former is the condition for the experience of the latter; but because all knowledge is limited to experience, the transcendental self becomes "the completely in determinate and indeterminable X, of whose existence we cannot make any positive judgment" (149). Thus, remarkably, Lange had made the same discovery as Liebmann: that the thing-in-itself is ineliminable as the condition of knowledge itself. He was also making the very points that had been the source of so much speculation in the German idealist tradition. He sees this all too well, remarking that he had stumbled across "a playground for a febrile speculation" (149). This transcendental self, he writes, is like the old Averroist *Nous* that dwelled as one and the same being in all consciousness. This opens the door to a whole new world, Lange says. But then, having seen that new world, Lange immediately declares that he will not enter into it. Having preached that knowledge is limited to experience, he realized that consistency demands restraint.

It was one of the ironies of Lange's interpretation of Kant that, though he affirmed the first-order psychological nature of transcendental enquiry, he also laid great importance on Kant's reply to scepticism. Unlike Cohen,[68] Lange had fully recognized the challenge Hume posed for Kant, how it affected his intellectual development, and how it determined the shape of the critical philosophy as a whole. Thus he quoted at length Kant's statement in the *Prolegomena* about how Hume had awakened him from his dogmatic slumber, and about how Hume's sceptical doubts about the principle of causality had alerted him to the general problem of transcendental philosophy (II, 39–42). Yet there is an irony here because Kant could not reply to Hume without the use of the very "dogmatic" or rationalist method that Lange saw as Kant's great mistake. After all, Hume would not have been impressed with any attempt to defend the principle of causality through an empirical method. We could use that method to discover that principle; but the sceptical problem concerns not its discovery but its demonstration, that is, not the *quid facti?* about its genesis but the *quid juris?* about its justification. Lange explained that it was a great mistake

---

[68] See Chapter 13, Section 7.

on Kant's part to attempt to provide a demonstration of the principle of causality, to attempt to deduce it from some even higher principles (51). All that Kant needed to demonstrate is that the principle of causality lay deep within our physiology, that it is an essential part of our organization (44, 45). In effect, he was agreeing with Fries that the ultimate response to the sceptic consists in pointing out a deep and ineradicable feature of our physiology. But that too was a premise that Hume would never have questioned. It is noteworthy that Kant had rejected justifying causality on these grounds just because it could not reply to the sceptic. Even if the principle of causality were an integral part of the working of our physiology and psychology, the sceptic would ask, does that alone give it objective validity?[69]

8. The Limits of Monism

As much as Lange admired the materialist's ideal of a unified worldview, of a universe completely explicable according to natural laws, he still believed it to be unattainable. We have already seen how in the first book of *Geschichte des Materialismus* he had maintained that materialism faces an insurmountable obstacle: the explanation of sensation and consciousness. Lange returns to this theme in the second section of book two, especially in its second edition.[70] Now, however, his reflections on this theme are the occasion for a general discussion of metaphysics. Nowhere else in Lange's big book did he engage in such sustained metaphysical reasoning. His conclusions are important for his general worldview.

In this section Lange attempts to vindicate his original objection against materialism by taking into account the latest scientific research. Recent work in physiology and physics has shown, he argues, that the problem of explaining consciousness is as irresolvable now as it had been in antiquity. To prove his point, Lange considers a recent lecture by the physiologist Emil Du Bois-Reymond, 'Ueber die Grenzen des Naturerkennens', which was given in August 1872 at the *Versammlung deutscher Naturforscher und Ärtze* in Leipzig.[71] As a physiologist of some renown, Du Bois-Reymond's lecture carried some weight in the scientific community, and it duly attracted much discussion and aroused much controversy, the famous *Ignorabimusstreit*.[72] Du Bois-Reymond maintains, much as Lange had held in his first edition, that the realm of consciousness remains inaccessible to scientific explanation. Even though everything in the physical world, at least in principle, can be

---

[69] See Kant, KrV, B 167–168.
[70] See Lange, *Geschichte des Materialismus* (1875), Buch I, Zweiter Abschnitt', 'Der Materialismus und die exacte Forschung', II, 139–181.
[71] Emil Du Bois-Reymond, *Ueber die Grenzen des Naturerkennens. Ein Vortrag in der zweiten öffentlichen Sitzung der 45. Versammlung deutscher Naturforscher und Ärtze zu Leipzig 14 August 1872* (Leipzig: Veit & Co., 1872).
[72] On that dispute, see my *After Hegel: German Philosophy 1840–1900* (Princeton, NJ: Princeton University Press, 2014), Chapter 3.

predicted with complete accuracy, and even though we can correlate precisely events in consciousness with brain states, the problem remains that we cannot conceive how consciousness is caused by the brain states; cause (e.g. light rays and sound waves) and effect (colours and sounds) are completely heterogeneous, so that we cannot explain how one arose from the other.

Lange's defence of Du Bois-Reymond's thesis mainly consists in refuting Du Bois-Reymond's critics, whom Lange, borrowing some Kantian lines, likens to the Scottish critics of Hume: they assumed what he had doubted; and they had demonstrated with zeal what he had never thought of bringing into question (II, 153). But it is not Lange's defence of Du Bois-Reymond's thesis that interests us here so much as the broader conclusions he draws from it. Lange sees his thesis as evidence for a more general theory about the existence of "two worlds": a natural world and a mental one (156). These very different worlds are occupied by the same human beings, the same actions, all having the same movements and gestures. Yet in the natural world, human actions take place with no thought or feeling, as if human beings were automatons; and in the mental world, the same actions take place with thought or feeling, as if human beings were free agents.

Perhaps not accidently, Lange's dualism between "two worlds" here is reminiscent of Leibniz's pre-established harmony, according to which two completely different realms are perfectly co-ordinated by one set of laws that governs both. A little later, however, Lange reformulates his theory, so that it is less about "two worlds" than different perspectives or aspects of the same world. To illustrate his point, he now mentions another very different historical precedent: Spinoza. Thus he suggests that Du Bois-Reymond's thesis that brain and mental events coincide, without exerting causal influence on one another, is reminiscent of Spinoza's doctrine that the mental and the physical are distinct attributes of one and the same thing (163).

Having introduced Spinoza, Lange then asks whether the conflict between idealism and materialism is ultimately only a matter of perspective. Du Bois-Reymond had speculated whether the present limits of scientific research could be overcome if one only had a complete understanding of matter.[73] Perhaps then one could say that it belongs to the very nature of matter for it to develop thinking and feeling (II, 158)? But Lange quickly turns this around and suggests the opposite possibility: that if we only knew enough about the mind, then perhaps we could see why the natural world appears to it in the form of matter and force (158)? In this case idealism and materialism would be only two different forms of explanation of one and the same thing. We could then have our unified worldview after all. Though Lange does not admit it, such speculation came close to Schelling's system of absolute identity, according to which all of nature is explicable either from an idealist or realist standpoint.

But no sooner does Lange propose this Schellingian metaphysics than he abandons it. It is as if it were all sheer fantasy and wild speculation. He is not willing or able to

---

[73] See du Bois-Reymond, *Ueber die Grenzen des Naturerkennens*, p. 33.

envisage a complete idealistic explanation of the world anymore than a materialist one. There is still the thing-in-itself lurking in the background, which poses severe limits on any such explanation. Monism, whether in a materialist or idealist form, proved to be an impossible ideal for Lange.

Although Lange thinks that a complete naturalistic explanation of consciousness is impossible, it is noteworthy that he still finds the naturalist's paradigm of explanation—nomological explanation or mechanism—the only possible one. "The limits of natural knowledge are *the limits of knowledge in general.*" (161) Lange rejects any other possible form of explanation. Although he insists that the realm of consciousness is accessible through introspection, he is quick to add that self-consciousness alone is not a sufficient basis for scientific knowledge (160). It is useful as a source of knowledge only if it is confirmed by, complemented with and integrated into a general system of natural laws. While Lange denies that these laws can explain consciousness as such, he still maintains they are sufficient to explain human actions in the external world. It is interesting to note that, in this context, he refers to the debate about the *"Geisteswissenschaften"*—an allusion not to any controversy surrounding Droysen or Dilthey, whose work was still not widely known, but to the recent appearance of a translation of Mill's *Logic*, which had rendered "moral sciences" as *"Geisteswissenschaften".*[74] Remarkably, Lange accepts Mill's thesis that explanation in the moral sciences is in principle the same as that in the natural sciences, though he thinks that Mill has placed too much reliance on introspection (288, n. 4). We are left wondering what Lange's position would have been had he knew about the later course of this debate, which would expand greatly later in the 1880s.[75] Droysen and Dilthey had stressed the insufficiency of naturalistic explanation, and they had argued for the necessity of some form of internal or hermeneutical understanding. Lange, however, was not aware of the hermeneutical forms of explanation later advanced by Dilthey and Droysen.

Lange's metaphysics, as he presents it in section two of Book II of the *Geschichte des Materialismus*, is dualistic in its division of reality into the mental and physical. He presents this dualism sometimes as a difference of entity, sometimes as a difference of attribute of a single entity. We will leave aside these differences of formulation here, however, because they are of small moment compared to an even larger dualism that dominates Lange's philosophy. This is a dualism not *within* the realm of existence or reality but a much broader dualism between the realm of values or ideals and the entire realm of existence or reality. For Lange, the fundamental division in the world

[74] J.S. Mill, *System der induktiven und deduktiven Logik, aus dem Englischen von J. Schiel* (Braunschweig: Vieweg, 1862–1863). Though there were earlier uses of the term *"Geisteswissenschaften"*, Mill's use of it seems especially important for Lange, given that he refers to Mill often and in just this context (II, 288, n.4).

[75] Dilthey published his *Einleitung in die Geisteswissenschaften* first in 1883; and though Droysen's *Grundriß der Historik* first appeared in 1868, it was not widely understood. On the fate of Droysen's historics, see my *The German Historicist Tradition* (Oxford: Oxford University Press, 2011), pp. 289–291.

is not between different forms of existence or being, namely, the mental and physical, but between ideal and reality, values and existence. It was in pointing out this realm of values or ideals that Lange believed that he found the ultimate limit of materialism. Even if the materialist could explain the entire realm of consciousness, he still would face this even greater chasm, the gulf between ideal and reality, value and existence. Thus Lange argues that idealism captures the important truth that we are not only intellectual beings who know about the real world, but that we are also creative beings who have the power to produce an ideal world (II, 176).[76] We go astray if we evaluate these ideas according to the criteria of knowledge. For the point of these ideas is not to give us knowledge about the world that exists, but to create norms for a world that ought to exist (177). They belong to a completely different intellectual order from that of truth: namely, the order of value (*Werth*). Of course, we can explain the origin of these ideas from some psychological viewpoint, but this still fails to understand their purpose and meaning. "An idea distinguishes itself from an illusion through its value and not through its origin." (177) Ideals and norms set or pose values, and we have to evaluate them as such: "We compare the Cologne cathedral with other works of art; and stones with other stones." (178) It was in pointing out this *sui generis* realm of ideals and values that Lange anticipates the later theory of values of Windelband and the Southwestern school.

9. The New Religion

As much as Lange loathed clericalism and ecclesiastical authority, and as much as he admired the materialist critique of superstition and enthusiasm, he was still reluctant to abolish religion entirely. He shared none of the materialists' hostility towards religion as such, and he feared that their critique of superstition and enthusiasm might destroy all religion. As far as he was concerned, the materialist critique was in danger of throwing the baby of religion out with the bathwater of superstition. The more one reads of *Geschichte des Materialismus* the more one is indeed struck by Lange's deep sympathy for religion. Several chapters of the final fourth section of Book II of Volume II are devoted to a defence of religion against its materialist detractors.

These sections assign a great importance to religion in the cultural struggles of the modern era. One of the most potent forces behind the recent revolutions in Europe, Lange writes in Chapter 2, came from the ideas of Christianity, which has inspired the masses to transform the state for their benefit (II, 484). We then learn in Chapter 3 that the main weapon against the stultifying and stupefying forces of materialism, which would transform the world into a marketplace and a competitive scramble of self-interest, has to come from renewed forms of religion (537–538). It was only religion that could inspire the masses to change their world so that it would conform to

---

[76] Cf. Lange, *Geschichte des Materialismus*, I, 374–376.

their justified moral aspirations (557).[77] The importance that Lange gives to religion in social and political change is proto-Weberian and stands in sharp contrast to Marx.

But what form should religion take in the post-revolutionary era? That, for Lange and most of his contemporaries, was the vital and pressing question. The context for his reflections about religion was set by the "free community" movement in Germany—the attempt to break with traditional religious authority, whether Protestant or Catholic, and to create new churches according to more rational and humanitarian ideals. After the 1848 Revolution, there was much discussion about the appropriate forms of ritual, belief and church organization, and many different communities arose reflecting a wide variety of views. In the final chapter of his *Geschichte des Materialismus* Lange discussed some of these issues. His own attitude is deeply ambivalent. Though filled with mistrust about any form of organized religion,[78] he also does not want religion to disappear or to collapse into the state. Comte's "cult of humanity", which would prescribe rituals and dogmas no less than the Roman Catholic Church, was utterly repellent to him (II, 506–7, 510).

Religion, Lange explained, now faces a terrible crisis. The spread of enlightenment and the growth of the natural sciences have had a devastating effect on traditional religious belief, so that it is no longer possible to uphold the old dogmas (II, 547). Not only the beliefs of revealed religion (viz. the trinity and atonement), but also those of natural religion (viz. God, providence and immortality), have shown themselves to be vulnerable to criticism. What, though, is to replace such beliefs? Religion now stood at a crossroad (546). One had to choose between two paths: the complete abolition of religion, where its traditional functions in regulating moral conduct are handed over to the state; or the total reformation of religion, so that it is no longer seen as dogma or metaphysics, and so that it is recognized instead simply as "poetry", a product of the activity of human beings. To go down the first path ultimately would backfire, Lange warns, because the people will resent the state dictating their religion, and they are likely to clamour for some of their old superstitions (547). Furthermore, this path simply represses the feelings and creative forces behind religion, and fails to give them a legitimate outlet. The second path is the more hopeful. What this involves is the gradual transformation and reformulation of religion by artists and poets so that it expresses the highest ideals and values of the people. The artist or poet will now take over the traditional function of the priest. For Lange, the model for such a transformation of religion is the philosophical poetry of Schiller. His poem 'Reich der Schatten', for example, expresses everything that one felt in the suffering

---

[77] For an insightful treatment of this theme, see Adam Weyer, 'Religion und Sozialismus bei F.A. Lange', in eds Schoeps and Knoll, *Lange, Leben und Werk* (Duisburg: Walter Braun Verlag, 1975), pp. 226–235.

[78] Lange seems very sympathetic to the free community movement, but also very wary of its ultimate direction. He writes that "every form of ecclesiastical organization of a community of faith is a state within the state and may in any moment easily trespass into the civil arena." Lange, *Geschichte des Materialismus*, II, 558.

and resurrection of Christ (547–548).[79] The thrust of Lange's programme was thus to transform religion from a form of belief into an aesthetic experience. Everything that we feel in religion, Lange wagers, is ultimately formulable in poetry without loss of meaning, and without involving all the problematic beliefs of dogma, metaphysics or myth. Poetry has the power to express religious feeling in the form of symbols and images, which could have the same function as belief in elevating us above the world of the senses and in allowing us to feel the value or worth of the ideal.

Lange's project for an aesthetic reformation of religion has its roots in the Romantic movement of the late 18th and early 19th centuries. Hölderlin, Schleiermacher, Schlegel and Novalis all stressed the affinity between religion and art, and they too wanted the artist to take over the traditional function of the priest. The artist has the power to evoke in us the feeling of the sublime and beautiful, which give witness to the infinite in the finite, the divine within nature. We have already seen how Fries and Herbart clung to these aspects of romantic religion. Lange follows in their footsteps. There is an important difference, however, between Lange's reformed religion and that of the Romantics: Lange refuses to regard aesthetic experience as a form of cognition; an awareness of the sublime is not an intuition of the infinite. For Lange, as a good Kantian, aesthetic experience is strictly non-cognitive; knowledge is the exclusive prerogative of the exact sciences.

The philosophical basis for Lange's aesthetic reformation of religion is his distinction between the realms of ideal and reality, value and existence. The real core and essence of religion, Lange insists, lies not in trying to know the realm of reality or existence but in creating an ideal world that expresses our ultimate values (II, 547). Traditional religion had been blind to the *sui generis* nature of this ideal world, chiefly because of its deep-rooted tendency to hypostasize ideals, to make them into objects of belief rather than ideals for action. But, for Lange, recognizing the precise logical status of this ideal world, and placing religion firmly within it, is utterly crucial to saving religion in the modern world. If religion is understood as dogma or metaphysics, as an attempt to acquire knowledge about existence or reality, it cannot compete with science, and so it is doomed to eventual destruction. If, however, religion is seen as an attempt to create values and ideals through art, then it stands outside the whole sphere of knowledge, and thus beyond the ken of criticism. After all, who would attempt to refute a Mass by Palestrina or a Madonna by Raphael? (561).

The inspiration for Lange's attempt to rescue religion ultimately came from Kant. *Prima facie* this is surprising because of Lange's statement, in the very beginning of his Kant chapter, that the real significance of Kant's philosophy lay in its theoretical part, and that the practical part was "the changeable and perishable part of the Kantian system" (II, 2). That makes it seem as if Lange *completely* repudiated Kant's doctrine of practical faith. While he indeed rejected Kant's attempt to rescue the old beliefs of natural religion, namely, the beliefs in God, providence and immortality,

---

[79] See Friedrich Schiller, 'Das Reich der Schatten', in *Schillers Werke, Nationalausgabe*, eds Julius Petersen und Friedrich Beißner (Weimar: Hermann Böhlaus Nachfolger, 1943), pp. 245–253.

he still endorsed his attempt to provide a practical or moral justification of religion. Following Kant, Lange would divide science and religion into separate spheres, and he would justify religion by practical rather than theoretical means. His loyalty to the Kantian doctrine is fully apparent from his June 2, 1870 letter to Überweg, where he attempts to answer Überweg's question of whether he follows Kant's practical philosophy in his justification of religion. The answer is 'no', he says, insofar as he does not attempt to justify the same beliefs as Kant; but it is 'yes', insofar as he too attempts to provide a practical justification for moral and religious ideas.[80]

Though Lange followed some basic Kantian guidelines, he still departed from them in important ways. His distinction between value and existence was meant to replace Kant's distinction between noumena and phenomena. In providing a secure space for religion, his distinction would do the same work as Kant's, but it would not require Kant's postulate of a mysterious noumenal realm of existence. Kant, Lange argued, had failed to see that these ideals, values and norms are created by us, and that they do not exist in some special realm of being independent of us (II, 61). There is no need to postulate, therefore, an extra ontological realm to account for the integrity of our ideals and values, to show their difference from the natural world. In postulating a special realm of reality or existence to place religious belief, Kant had lapsed into the very error he had exposed in rationalist metaphysics: hypostasis.

Lange also refused to accept Kant's account of the content of practical faith. For Kant, that content consists in some of the basic beliefs of natural religion, namely, the beliefs in God, freedom and immortality. But Lange refuses to recognize these beliefs as rational, whether by theoretical or practical guidelines. It is no longer the case, he argues, that morality requires the beliefs in God and immortality, because history and common experience has shown that we can be perfectly moral agents without holding these beliefs (II, 488–489). Lange also pointed out that some free communities had already dispensed even with these beliefs, and that they were fully content with a humanistic faith (496). It was Kant's attempt to prove these beliefs on the basis of practical reason that Lange regarded as "the changeable and perishable" side of his doctrine of practical faith. This showed Kant to be a child of the 18th century, just another disciple of Enlightenment deism and natural religion.

Granted that religion falls into the realm of values and ideals, and granted that the old beliefs are obsolete, what standards determine the new values and ideals? What criteria adjudicate between conflicting views about these values and ideals? The new community movement had made this question all the more urgent and important. It was, however, a question for which Lange still had no definite answer in his *Geschichte des Materialismus*.[81] It is clear that we cannot appeal to

---

[80] See Ellissen, *Lange*, p. 263.
[81] In the first chapter of Section II Lange suggests that the standards are those for "inner truth" in art and religion, which determine whether an idea leads to "the harmonic satisfaction of the human mind" (II, 177). What this phrase meant, however, Lange did not begin to explain.

normal *theoretical* criteria, which determine only matters of fact in the natural world. Following Kant's precedent, we now have to resort to *practical* criteria, such as the moral law. But nowhere does Lange explain how the moral law provides such a criterion. We learn only that tolerance towards others is one measure for the possession of spirit (II, 553), but little more. Morality seems to give at best a *negative* criterion to exclude ideas and values that are immoral; but it does not appear strong enough to provide a *positive* criterion to choose between ideas and values that are moral. Between *moral* ideals and values Lange offers nothing but aesthetic criteria. He makes the following puzzling statement: "To put it rather bluntly, this is *a matter of taste*; but, of course, the essential deciding factor is not the subjective taste of the individual, but the general cultural condition of nations, the dominant patterns of the association of ideas and, conditioned by an infinitude of factors, a certain basic attitude of mind." (497)

The shift away from moral to aesthetic criteria is perfectly understandable given how Lange conceives of the creative activity behind religion. That activity he describes as "poetic", though "poetic" in the broad classical sense as the power to produce beautiful things. The products of this poetic activity he calls "ideas", though "ideas" in the Kantian sense, where they are "images" "symbols" of the rational or supersensible (II, 494). Given that religion consists in such images or symbols, it is only appropriate to measure them by aesthetic standards; cognitive or practical standards miss their purpose and meaning. Still, Lange's move from aesthetic standards to a "matter of taste" remains puzzling and surprising. After all, aesthetic criteria can be, or at least purport to be, universal and necessary, and so not a mere matter of taste depending upon the general spirit of the age.

Remarkably, Lange had posed the main objection to this position in the preface to the first edition of his *Geschichte des Materialismus*. After stating his theory that the essence of religion consists in creative activity, Lange introduces an hypothetical objector who declares that this too is subjective; it leaves only aesthetic criteria, which would allow for even forms of superstition and idolatry provided that they are aesthetically pleasing (vii). Was not the Catholic Mass, after all, an aesthetic experience? Though Lange admits that this objection weighs heavily upon him, he leaves us with the baffling confession: "I depend upon the correctness of the *signatura temporis*, as I understand it" (viii). This was essentially a surrender to relativism, to the whims of the *Zeitgeist*. As Lange well knew, the *signatura temporis*, the *Zeitgeist*, was sending conflicting signals, given that there was the greatest disagreement in the free community movement about the best ideals and values for the new age.

10. Philosophy as Poetry

In his *Geschichte des Materialismus* Lange was very clear that the ideas of metaphysics (viz. God, freedom, the soul) are based upon practical reason and that they have only a "poetic validity". He did not explain, however, just how they are based on practical

reason, or what exactly their poetic validity means. The net result: one half of the
entire *globus intellectualis*, the poetic half, and its relation to the other scientific half,
had been left in darkness. Lange finally confronted these issues in an unlikely place,
in a chapter for a book on Schiller's philosophical poetry. He had worked on this book
for nearly a decade but never published it, even though parts of it were already in
proof stage. The book was eventually published posthumously by his biographer,
A.O. Ellissen, as *Einleitung und Kommentar zu Schillers philosophischen Gedichten.*[82]

A book on Schiller's philosophical poetry seems an implausible place for reflection
on such issues. All the more so when we consider the book's purpose: to serve as a
teacher's guide to help Gymnasium students read Schiller's more difficult philosophical poems. For Lange, however, the introduction to this book was the best occasion
to raise just these philosophical questions. Schiller had always loomed large in his
philosophical thinking, and on just these issues. Regarding the relationship between
practical reason and the ideas, Lange told his friend Überweg on June 2, 1870, that
he was "more a Schillerian than a Kantian".[83] In the preface to the first edition of the
Geschichte des Materialismus he stated that the Kantian who came closest to his own
views was Schiller, and he regretted that he did not have space to explain the philosophy of "the great poet" (v). In general, Lange held up Schiller's philosophical poetry
as the model for where philosophy should go after it renounces its traditional metaphysical pretensions and realizes the crucial tasks that lie before it: the aesthetic education of the nation.

The first chapter of Lange's *Einleitung und Kommentar*, titled 'Philosophie und
Poesie',[84] contains his most detailed account of the relationship between the two
halves of the intellectual sphere. He first identifies these halves with the realms of
truth and beauty. They are distinct, Lange explains, because truth and beauty impose
different demands upon us. The scientist has to determine the truth, even if it is ugly;
the artist has to create the beautiful, even if it means ignoring the imperfections and
particularities of reality (1). Of course, we want the two to be united: we hate beautiful lies, we prize elegant exposition. Still, the standards of these realms remain
distinct, and the idea of their unity is only a fiction (2). Why, exactly, are they different? Lange provides no explicit explanation, but his underlying presuppositions
are plain enough. Truth and beauty are for him the objects of science and art, which
are distinct kinds of activity. All science strives for knowledge, which is limited to
the world of experience, where an object is given to us through the senses. Art, however, simply creates its own object; it can transcend experience, and is not limited
to reproducing something given to us. We confuse these realms, Lange warns us, if

[82] Friedrich Albert Lange, *Einleitung und Kommentar zu Schillers philosophischen Gedichten*
(Bielefeld: Velhagen & Klasing, 1897), ed. A.O. Ellissen. All references in parentheses above are to this
edition.
[83] Ellissen, *Lange*, p. 263.
[84] Lange, *Einleitung und Kommentar*, pp. 1–25. Though Ellissen says that the manuscript was already
in proof stage (p. x), this chapter seems to have been incomplete, because it ends in mid-sentence (25).

we assume that the beautiful is something that exists, as if it could somehow be an object of knowledge; to make such an assumption would be to hypostasize our own creations (5).

The most striking feature of Lange's map of the intellectual sphere is that it is dualistic, divided between the demands of truth and beauty, science and art, leaving no place for the realm of morality. Lange is implicitly departing from Kant's own topography, which divided the whole intellectual sphere into three realms: truth, beauty and goodness.[85] Lange was subordinating the moral realm to the aesthetic one—a not unnatural move for someone who had devoted much of his early career to Herbart's psychology. Why, though, this subordination of morality to art? Lange was simply taking some Kantian doctrines to their ultimate conclusion. First, he holds that the ideas of reason—the ideas of God, freedom and immorality— that play such a central role in morality are only our own creations, and that if we assume that there is some reality corresponding to them we indulge in hypostasis, the basic fallacy of pure reason according to the Transcendental Dialectic of the first *Kritik*. Second, like Kant, Lange thinks that moral principles are construc- tions, that the principles to which we are subject as autonomous agents should be also the principles that we create for ourselves as rational beings. Why, though, does the production of these principles not conform to *sui generis* moral stand- ards? Nowhere does Lange explicitly address this question. But the answer seems to lie in his rejection of Kant's deductions of moral principles. As we have already seen,[86] Lange does not think that we can provide an a priori deduction of a moral principle that will show it to be valid universally, necessarily, and for all times and places. The historicist strand in his thinking made him reject moral absolutes; the empiricist strand made him want to base moral principles upon sentiment, just as Smith had done. Justifying moral principles on sentiment brings them closer to the aesthetic sphere.

Whatever its ultimate rationale, Lange's subordination of the moral to the aes- thetic realm has an important result for his conception of practical reason and how it justifies metaphysical ideas. At first Lange seems to accept Kant's practical justifica- tion at face value: it means that although we cannot *know* the ideas are true, we are still allowed to proceed *as if* they were, or that we are permitted *to think* that they are true for the purposes of moral action (4). On this account, the practical justification of the ideas is based on morality: the ideas are justified when we show that believing in or acting upon them is necessary to fulfill the demands of moral principles. Thus, regarding the idea of freedom, Lange says that though we cannot know we are free, we are still justified in thinking that we are so for the sake of moral responsibility (4). Yet a little later Lange gives practical justification a very different twist, one that reflects the domination of the aesthetic in his thinking. Kant went astray, he argues,

[85] See Kant, *Kritik der Urteilskraft*, §5, AA V, 209–211.   [86] See Chapter 9, Section 1.

when he attempted to provide a logical deduction of the ideas from practical reason, a procedure just as illusory as that of the old metaphysics (8). There is indeed a neces-sity behind the ideas, Lange assures us, but it is not a logical but a strictly aesthetic necessity (8). What justifies the Kantian ideas, in other words, is not their morality but their beauty, or better yet their sublimity. It is ultimately the idea of the sublime, Lange argues, that proves to be the real standard and justification for the Kantian ideas: "Even if one does not want to place Kant's system under the idea of the beauti-ful, it still belongs all the more surely under the idea of the sublime." (8–9)

Where do we put philosophy on Lange's intellectual map? It seems to have no place at all because philosophy is neither natural science nor art. Traditional philosophy was metaphysics, which pretended to be a kind of science through pure reason, a demonstrative knowledge of the objects falling under the ideas. We know now, how-ever, that metaphysics is illusory, partly because it hypostasizes its own creations, and partly because it attempts to transcend experience, which determine the limits of knowledge. So Lange has a clear place for metaphysics on his intellectual map: since it is not a form of knowledge, and since it creates its own objects, it is really a form of art rather than science (8). More simply, metaphysics is poetry (*Dichtung*) (8). Lange does not draw the conclusion, however, that *all* philosophy is a form of art. He makes a distinction between two kinds of philosophy: *critical* philosophy, which is science, because it involves methods of empirical investigation; and *positive* philoso-phy, which is a form of art or poetry (7–8). Positive philosophy takes over the task of traditional metaphysics: it attempts to provide us with a general worldview; but rather than pretending to provide knowledge of apparent supersensible objects, it is self-conscious poetry.

Lange's conception of positive philosophy came with a drastic deflation of the ide-als and claims of traditional metaphysics. Metaphysics could no longer pretend to provide a worldview having universal validity. Since positive philosophy is a form of poetry, and so subject to aesthetic standards, there is no single form it should take; there is no single system of philosophy that will be valid for everyone alike, for there are all kinds of ways of constructing a system of philosophy, and which system we adopt will be a matter of taste (6). There is an obvious *non sequitur* involved in such reasoning: just because we apply aesthetic standards does not mean we are limited to personal taste. Why not *universal* aesthetic standards? For reasons best known to himself, Lange does not accept that possibility; the realm of universal validity is for him co-extensive with the realm of knowledge. Perhaps one reason he does not believe in the possibility of universal aesthetic standards is because of his historicism, his belief that philosophy, religion and art are subject to the *Zeitgeist*, that they are the expression of the values and ways of life of a particular nation. This historicism appears clearly when he writes that the principles of positive philosophy change with the times, that they differ from one generation to the next (8). We have already seen how the choice of religion is determined by the *signatura temporis*; the same now seems to be the case with philosophy itself.

The final result of Lange's reflections on the relationship between philosophy and poetry was a harsh dilemma: either hard science or poetry. There is no other legitimate form of intellectual discourse. Traditional philosophy, which was neither empirical science nor poetry, had been squeezed out, eliminated from the *globus intellectualis*. What Lange termed "critical philosophy" was really nothing more than a branch of empirical science, fully in accord with his conception of transcendental philosophy as psychological and physiological research. In short, Lange was making philosophy redundant, dissolving it into empirical science or poetry. This proved a severe challenge for his successors. The young Hermann Cohen and Wilhelm Windelband were determined to uphold the traditional conception of philosophy, to keep a place for philosophy between empirical science or poetry. We shall soon see what came of their efforts.

10

The Battle against Pessimism

1. Sources of Pessimism

Beginning in the mid-1860s, the neo-Kantians began to turn their attention to a new disturbing phenomenon on the cultural horizon: pessimism. There were two thinkers behind this phenomenon, two major champions of pessimism: Arthur Schopenhauer and Eduard von Hartmann. Schopenhauer's main work, *Die Welt als Wille und Vorstellung*,[1] first appeared in 1819 and, though ignored for decades, it had been rediscovered in the 1850s and had virtually become a cult classic by the 1860s. Hartmann's chief work, *Die Philosophie des Unbewussten*,[2] which was first published in 1869, was a huge and immediate hit, going through many printings and spawning a flood of polemical literature. The success of Schopenhauer's and Hartmann's work spoke for a new cultural phenomenon: pessimism was now the *Zeitgeist*.

This was a challenge the neo-Kantians could not afford to ignore. They soon rose to the occasion. Almost every major neo-Kantian had something to say about pessimism. From the mid-1860s until the early 1900s, Kuno Fischer, Otto Liebmann, Jürgen Bona Meyer, Friedrich Paulsen, Rudolf Haym, Alois Riehl, Johannes Volkelt, Hermann Cohen and Wilhelm Windelband wrote articles, essays, or book chapters about it. Such, indeed, was the interest in Schopenhauer that Fischer, Haym, Volkelt and Meyer wrote some of the first monographs on him.[3] By the late 1870s, pessimism had replaced materialism as the neo-Kantians' *bête noire*. Where there was once Büchner, Moleschott, Czolbe or Vogt, there now stood Schopenhauer and Hartmann.

But why were the neo-Kantians so troubled by pessimism? And why did it become so popular? Neither question is easy to answer.

---

[1] Arthur Schopenhauer, *Die Welt als Wille und Vorstellung* (Leipzig: Brockhaus, 1819).

[2] Eduard von Hartmann, *Philosophie des Unbewussten: Versuch einer Weltanschauung* (Berlin: Duncker, 1869). The book was reprinted eight times in the 1870s alone. Windelband referred to the *"meteorhaften Erfolg"* of Hartmann's work, 'Die Philosophischen Richtungen der Gegenwart', in *Grosse Denker*, ed. Ernst von Aster (Leipzig: Quelle & Meyer, 1911), II, 365. On Hartmann, see Otto Braun, *Eduard von Hartmann* (Stuttgart: Frommann, 1909).

[3] Rudolf Haym, *Arthur Schopenhauer* (Berlin: Reimer, 1864); Jürgen Bona Meyer, *Arthur Schopenhauer als Mensch und Denker* (Berlin: Carl Habel, 1872); Kuno Fischer, *Schopenhauers Leben, Werke und Lehre*, Zweite Auflage, Band IX of *Geschichte der neuern Philosophie* (Heidelberg: Winter, 1898); Johannes Volkelt, *Arthur Schopenhauer. Seine Persönlichkeit, seine Lehre, sein Glaube* (Stuttgart: Frommann, 1900).

Why pessimism should be a threat to neo-Kantians is not so obvious. *Prima facie* a good Kantian should not be especially concerned by Schopenhauer's or Hartmann's version of it. The central thesis of their pessimism is that life is not worth living because it brings far more suffering than happiness. A good Kantian, however, is a stoical soul who never expects life to bring him much happiness. He need not even contest the claim that life is not worth living if it is measured in *eudemonic* terms. Instead, he insists that the value of life has to be assessed in *moral* terms. So, even if life is suffering, the good Kantian still finds meaning in it by performing his moral duties and striving for the highest good. Progress towards a better world redeems all suffering and makes life worth living. This simple point should be enough, it seems, to disarm the threat of Schopenhauer's and Hartmann's pessimism.

Yet, on a deeper level, Schopenhauer's pessimism was very disturbing for the good Kantian.[4] For there was a quietistic message behind it that made all human endeavour meaningless, even when measured in strictly moral terms. The implication of Schopenhauer's argument in the final chapters of *Die Welt als Wille und Vorstellung* is that all striving for a better world is pointless. No matter how much we struggle to improve it, we make no progress towards the highest good. We are like Sisyphus pushing his rock up the hill only for it to roll back down again. Rather than striving to create a better world, we should renounce our will to live and attempt to escape the world in religious and aesthetic contemplation. It was chiefly this quietism, for reasons we shall soon see, that so troubled the neo-Kantians about pessimism.

The reasons for the popularity of pessimism are even less clear. The public obsession with pessimism puzzled neo-Kantians themselves. Fischer and Meyer offered the explanation that it expressed the spirit of the times after the defeat of the Revolution of 1848.[5] After the failure to achieve such basic liberal ideals as constitutional government and national unity, we are told, people lost faith in the old optimistic philosophies, which rested upon the hope of progress in history. Now that the forces of

---

[4] At least Schopenhauer's pessimism was disturbing. Whether Hartmann's pessimism was so is another question. Hartmann protested that his pessimism was *not* quietistic but only eudemonic, that is, it held that there is more suffering than happiness in life. See his *Philosophie des Unbewussten*, Zweite Auflage (1870), pp. 642–646, 675–76. Hartmann advocated what he called an "evolutionary optimism", according to which history is progressing towards greater moral perfection. He attempted to distance his own pessimism from Schopenhauer's quietism. See Hartmann's 'Mein Entwicklungsgang' in *Gesammelte Studien und Aufsätze* (Berlin: Duncker, 1876), pp. 38–40; and 'Mein Verhältnis mit Schopenhauer', in *Philosophische Fragen der Gegenwart* (Berlin: Duncker, 1885), pp. 25–37. In his 'Kant als Vater des Pessimismus', *Zur Geschichte und Begründung des Pessimismus* (Berlin: Duncker, 1880), pp. 1–64, Hartmann enlisted Kant into the pessimistic cause, arguing that he advocated the same eudemonic pessimism and evolutionary optimism as himself. The neo-Kantians were not convinced. See his dispute with them in *Philosophische Fragen der Gegenwart*, pp. 112–120.

[5] Fischer's explanation is in *Schopenhauers Leben, Werke und Lehre*, pp. 97–103, and in his *Der Philosoph des Pessimismus*, in *Kleine Schriften* (Heidelberg: Winter, 1898), II, 401. Meyer's explanation is in his essay 'Weltlust und Weltleid', in *Probleme der Weltweisheit*, Zweite Auflage (Berlin: Allgemeine Verein für Deutsche Literatur, 1887), pp. 293–295.

reaction had the upper hand, there seemed no way forward, so that idealism gave way to cynicism. This is how Fischer described the spirit of the times:

After the shipwreck of the attempts at national unity, after the days of Bronnzell and Olmütz, after the restoration of the alliance in Frankfurt am Main, there came the satyr song with its elegiac mood: "O, du lieber Augustin, everything is lost." The only consolation went: "*Ergo bibamus!*".[6]

So, on this reading, pessimism was a philosophy of disappointment and disillusionment, capturing a mood especially prevalent in the 1850s and 1860s. This interpretation cannot explain, however, why pessimism continued to be so popular in the 1870s, a decade which saw the fulfilment of liberal dreams. With the 1870s came the founding of the new Reich, victory over the French, the growth of representative government, and much technical and social progress. So, if political disappointment could explain the *origin* of pessimism, it could hardly account for its *persistence*. It was precisely the continuing popularity of pessimism, however, that puzzled neo-Kantians. Johannes Volkelt, a young neo-Kantian in Vienna, suggested this explanation for the phenomenon: the failure of social and political institutions to provide for the rising expectations of the masses.[7] "Who can blame the spectator for lapsing into pessimistic reflections," Volkelt wrote, "when he sees the spectre of mass poverty?" Volkelt, it seemed, had hit the nail on the head. For at least one prominent pessimist agreed with him. Agnes Taubert, the wife of Eduard von Hartmann, admitted that disappointment among the masses was indeed one reason for pessimism.[8] She disagreed with Volkert, however, that one should try to encourage optimism, to give the masses hope to change their situation. Pessimism was the best remedy for the disaffection of the masses because it would teach them to limit their expectations and to restrain their desires. These expectations and desires had become unrealistic, increasing far beyond any social, political and economic means of fulfilling them. From pessimism, at least the people could learn that suffering and misery is a constant of human life, and that it prevails as much in the nobleman's palace as in the peasant's hut.

Taubert's reactionary views reveal one crucial feature behind the controversy about pessimism: its political dimension.[9] Many neo-Kantians were suspicious of pessimism, because they saw it as more of a doctrine of reaction than disillusionment. They regarded it as a reactionary weapon for keeping in check the hopes and ideals of the masses, who believed that they could make progress and change the world through political organization and action. What better way to take the wind out of their sails than to tell them there is no progress in history, that life is inescapable

    [6]   Fischer, *Schopenhauers Leben, Werke und Lehre*, p. 101.
    [7]   Johannes Volkelt, 'Die Entwicklung des modernen Pessimismus', *Im neuen Reich* II (1872), 952–968, p. 967.
    [8]   Agnes Taubert, *Der Pessimismus und seine Gegner* (Berlin: Duncker, 1873), pp. 103–105, 114–117.
    [9]   This political dimension has been stressed by Klaus Köhnke, *Entstehung und Aufstieg des Neukantianismus* (Frankfurt: Suhrkamp, 1986), pp. 327–336.

suffering, that it is futile trying to change the world, which always remains the same? Schopenhauer probably never had these political intentions in mind in formulating his pessimism in the early 1800s. But it was also no accident that his pessimism later conveniently served reactionary ends. For Schopenhauer's political convictions were decidedly reactionary, and he had sided with the monarchy during the 1848 Revolution.[10] A clause in his will gave money to soldiers wounded in battle with radicals and workers in Frankfurt.

Against Schopenhauer's reactionary views, the neo-Kantians still upheld the old liberal faith, the old hope in social and political progress. It is in recognizing this political dimension behind pessimism that we can begin to see the motivation for the neo-Kantians' battle against it. That battle was directed primarily against Schopenhauer's quietism, which undermined all motivation to change and reform the world.

The neo-Kantian struggle against pessimism reveals one of its central and characteristic features as an intellectual movement: its faith in human autonomy, the power of human beings to change their world. We misunderstand this feature if we confuse it with optimism, which is for the neo-Kantian the belief in inevitable historical progress, the thesis that the laws of history are moving towards greater freedom and equality. For the neo-Kantian, optimism commits the same mistake as pessimism: by having us believe in the inevitablity of progress, in the necessity of historical development, it undermines the motivation of the individual to change his world. Optimism and pessimism are the two extremes to be avoided at all cost. The middle path between them is political realism, the recognition that each individual human being has the power and responsibility for political action to change his or her world.

To a scholar of Kant's philosophy, this political realism is not likely to seem Kantian at all. Kant's later writings on history make him into a cautious historical optimist, someone who believes that nature herself will bring forth a republican constitution. But, as we shall soon see, when it came to politics, the neo-Kantians were more neo-Fichtean than neo-Kantian. The revival of Fichte in the 1860s was a crucial force behind the revival of Kant himself. We shall examine the meaning of this Fichtean revival in Section 3.

Our task now will be to examine the neo-Kantian battle against Schopenhauer's pessimism.[11] We need to know the arguments as well as the motivations behind it. This will involve a survey of the highlights of the neo-Kantian polemic against pessimism.

---

[10] On Schopenhauer's political views, see Fischer, *Schopenhauers Leben, Werke und Lehre*, pp. 97–103.

[11] The neo-Kantians were also active in combating Hartmann's pessimism. See, for example, Rudolf Haym, *Die Hartmann'sche Philosophie des Unbewusstseins* (Berlin: Reimer, 1873); Johannes Volkelt, *Die Entwicklung des modernen Pessimismus* (Leipzig: Hirzel, 1872); and Jürgen Bona Meyer, *Weltelend und Weltschmerz. Eine Reden gegen Schopenhauer's und Hartmann's Pessimismus* (Bonn: Marcus, 1872). The dispute with Hartmann's pessimism would be, however, another chapter.

2. The Polemic against Pessimism

It was a bleak picture of human life that Arthur Schopenhauer painted in the fourth and final part of *Die Welt als Wille und Vorstellung*. The central thesis of his pessimism is simple: "all life is suffering" (I, 426; §56).[12] This suffering is inescapable, constant and unbearable. That is the hard fact of life, though few are willing to recognize it, because they are so caught in the snares of their desires that they never ask themselves where they lead, why they pursue them and what is the point of it all. The major premise of Schopenhauer's pessimism is his most basic metaphysical principle: that the heart of reality, the thing-in-itself, consists in the will, which consists in a blind, ceaseless striving without end or purpose.[13] This will determines, and appears in, all human thoughts, deeds and desires. Because we are forever willing, we are forever desiring; but all desire is by its very nature suffering, because it consists in a felt need or lack. To free ourselves from this pain, we struggle to satisfy our desires; but the satisfaction never lasts very long. No sooner have we satisfied one desire than we have another. While desire is long, satisfaction is short, lasting only for a moment. And while pain is a reality, a positive quality, whose presence is all too keenly felt, pleasure is only a privation, a negative quality, the momentary relief and release from suffering. So life is caught in a constant cycle of desire and desperation, a cycle whose only purpose is to prolong itself. Should this cycle pause for a moment between desires, then we suffer an even worst fate: boredom (428; §57). Boredom makes our very existence unbearable, and so we struggle to escape it. How? By restarting the cycle, of course. So, according to this grim picture, life is a grim struggle for existence, where existence serves no value or purpose at all. Life is ceaseless torment, inescapable suffering, only occasionally and briefly relieved when we satisfy our desires. No matter how many cliffs we avoid in the course of our struggle to survive, there is one we know that we cannot avoid, and that is the worst of all: death (429; §57).

As bleak as this picture was, Schopenhauer still held out the prospect of salvation. He painted life in such dire terms only in the hope that we, or at least a few among us, would see through it, renounce it, and finally escape it. Although he taught that all our thoughts, actions and feelings are manifestations of the will, he still held that we can stand outside and above the will through acts of intellectual insight which reveal to us the futility of desire and the source of suffering.[14] Once we gain such insight, we have the power to deny the will, to renounce all its promptings and urgings, and to lead an ascetic life of contemplation. Such a life will be serene and peaceful, Schopenhauer promised (I, 529; §68). This was his version of the stoic ideal of *atarxia,* of the Christian concept of "rebirth" and "grace", of the Buddhistic doctrine

---

[12] Cf. Schopenhauer, I, 436–437, §57. All references to Schopenhauer's works will be to *Arthur Schopenhauer. Sämtliche Werke*, ed. Wolfgang Freiherr von Löhneysen (Stuttgart: Insel, 1968), Roman numerals refer to volume numbers and Arabic numerals to page numbers. "§" indicates the chapter or section number. *WWV* stands for *Die Welt als Wille und Vorstellung.*

[13] *WWV*, I, 165, §20; 174, §23; 240, §29; 427, §57.   [14] *WWV*, I, 5 15, 540, §68; and I, 547, §70.

of nirvana or enlightenment. Of all these variants, Schopenhauer preferred most the Buddhistic one. According to Fischer, Schopenhauer was deeply serious about his Buddhism, which he hoped would become the new religion of the West.[15] He saw himself as its sage, his book as its gospel.

The neo-Kantians' response to Schopenhauer's pessimism could not have been more negative.[16] They scrutinized its every premise, presupposition and conclusion, and rejected them all. Such hostility is *prima facie* surprising, given that good Kantians are not prone to celebrating the joys of life, and given that they are ready to concede that the world is a miserable place when measured by eudemonic standards. What motivated their animosity, though, was less Schopenhauer's bleak portrait of life than the conclusions he wanted to draw from it. For political and ethical reasons, the neo-Kantians were utterly opposed to the very ethic that Schopenhauer wanted to promote: denunciation of the will, renunciation of life, resignation about the ways of the world. For the neo-Kantians, this was tantamount to surrender to the evil forces of this world; the point of our lives was not to escape the world but to change it. Since so much was at stake, Schopenhauer's pessimism would have to be defeated, eradicated root and branch. And so, nearly for four decades, stretching from the 1860s until the early 1900s, the neo-Kantians would fight Schopenhauer on many occasions, whenever energy and time permitted.[17]

One central strategy in the neo-Kantian campaign against Schopenhauer's pessimism was to undermine its claim to scientific or philosophical status. In one form or another, Windelband, Paulsen, Liebmann, Meyer and Riehl all followed this strategy.[18] They contended there could be no proof for Schopenhauer's doctrine, either empirical or a priori, and that it was ultimately more a statement about his personal attitude than a genuine metaphysical fact about the world. According to this line of argument, whether life is worth living is a question of value, and so it is a matter for each individual to decide on the basis of his or her own experience. Who was Arthur Schopenhauer to tell everyone that their lives are pointless or worthless? In advocating his pessimism as if it were some kind of deep metaphysical truth, Schopenhauer

[15] Fischer, *Schopenhauers Leben, Werke und Lehre*, p. 104. Some of Schopenhauer's hopes for a new Western Buddhism appear in *WWV*, I, 487; §64.

[16] Here the one exception is Johannes Volkelt's *Schopenhauer*, which attempts to provide a balanced appraisal of Schopenhauer's pessimism. See pp. 212, 229, 231, 246–247, 257. Volkelt found Schopenhauer's pessimism a worthwhile antithesis to optimism and the *"Fortschrittsphilister"*.

[17] In some respects the campaign against pessimism continued well into the 1920s. See Heinrich Rickert's *Die Philosophie des Lebens* (Tübingen: Mohr, 1920), which takes issue with Schopenhauer on several occasions, pp. 18, 21, 139, 162. Yet in other respects Schopenhauer had become less important by the 1920s, downgraded to a precursor of more dangerous figures, especially Nietzsche.

[18] See Windelband, 'Pessimismus und Wissenschaft' (1876), *Präludien*, ninth edition (Tübingen: Mohr, 1924), II, 218–243; Friedrich Paulsen, 'Gründen und Ursachen des Pessimismus', *Deutsche Rundschau* 48 (1886), 360–381; Liebmann, 'Trilogie des Pessimismus', in *Gedanken und Thatsachen* (Straßburg: Karl Trübner, 1902), II, 265–266; Jürgen Bona Meyer, *Arthur Schopenhauer als Mensch und Denker*, pp. 44–45; and Alois Riehl, *Zur Einführung in die Philosophie der Gegenwart*, Fünfte Auflage (Leipzig: Teubner, 1919), p. 187.

had made a fundamental confusion between fact and value. Questions of value cannot be determined on the basis of pure reason alone; we can use all kinds of ends or criteria to assess the value of life, all of which are perfectly rational; which conclusions we reach depends on which we apply. Windelband, who developed this line of argument most fully and rigorously,[19] contends that there could be only one way to make an objective thesis about the value of existence: if we knew the purpose for which the world was created, then we could tell whether it was good or bad; it would then be a matter of simply seeing whether the world fit its purpose or not. But there is no way of knowing, Windelband argued, what the purpose of life is in itself; because metaphysics is impossible, as Kant rightly taught, we have no means of knowing reality as a whole.

One variation on this strategy, which was pursued by Paulsen and Meyer,[20] is that Schopenhauer's pessimism could be scientific or philosophical only if there were a kind of hedonic calculus, that is, a method of comparing the pleasures and pains of this life and determining which outweighs the other. Although they knew that Schopenhauer never claimed to be in possession of such a calculus, they still maintained that it is a presupposition of his argument, because it is only by showing the predominance of suffering over happiness, of pain over pleasure, that he can justify his claim that life is not worth living. But such a presupposition, Paulsen and Meyer argued, is absurd, for the simple reason that it is impossible to make such comparisons. Pleasures and pains are very heterogeneous, and to determine their value we have to assess not only their quantities but also their qualities. Paulsen pointed out that it is impossible to determine for even a single ordinary day in a person's life whether pleasures or pains predominate. For that to work, we would have to assign numerical values to the most heterogeneous pleasures and pains. But how do we measure, Paulsen asked, the pleasure of a good breakfast against the displeasure from eating burnt soup for dinner? And how do we determine the pleasure of reading a good book against the displeasure of hearing disturbing background noise? If we cannot calculate the sum of pleasures and pains on a single day, then how are we to do that for a whole human life? And then for human life in general?

In his defence, it has to be said that Schopenhauer never intended to provide empirical justification for his theory.[21] His argument on behalf of pessimism was supposed to be a priori, based on general facts about human life, desire and pleasure. The case for pessimism rested for him more on metaphysics than on ordinary experience. It also has to be said, however, that the neo-Kantians were aware of Schopenhauer's intentions on this score, which they duly countered with a priori objections of their own. Schopenhauer's pessimism, Paulsen, Meyer and Volkelt contended, rests on a faulty

---

[19] Windelband, 'Pessimismus und Wissenschaft', pp. 23–33.
[20] Paulsen, 'Gründen und Ursachen des Pessimismus', pp. 361–362, 367; Meyer, 'Weltlust und Weltleid', pp. 263–264.
[21] *WWV*, I, 443, §59; 426, §56.

understanding of pleasure as well as desire. Schopenhauer assumes that pleasure is *extrinsic* to action, as if it were a reward attained at the end of an activity. But this fails to see that pleasure is often *instrinsic* to action, that it derives from its very doing.[22] There is a very big difference between the pleasure of gratification, which comes at the end of an action, and the pleasure of doing, which comes from acting itself. The sensation of satiety after a full meal, the feeling of rest after exertion, are pleasures of gratification; the enjoyment of playing the piano, or of reading a good book, are pleasures of doing. So Schopenhauer's concept of pleasure is too narrow, derived entirely from pleasures of gratification, as if they were the sole kind of pleasure. This mistake is a crucial premise to his pessimism, however, because it assumes that the active pursuit of pleasure has to be painful, a source of suffering, when it can be entirely enjoyable.

Schopenhauer also goes astray, Windelband, Riehl, Paulsen, Meyer and Volkelt charged,[23] in attributing solely a negative significance to pleasure, as if it were nothing more than freedom from the pain of desire. Schopenhauer's argument for this thesis is insufficient: the mere fact that desire attempts to eradicate some need does not mean that its satisfaction consists only in the removal of the need. There can still be some positive feeling in the satisfaction of the need. And, although we feel pleasure more intensely when we free ourselves from pain, we still have feelings of pleasure when we have not felt privation beforehand. Are there not pleasant surprises in life?

The most weighty objection against Schopenhauer's a priori argument for pessimism concerned the chief concept behind it, the will. The neo-Kantians doubted that this pivotal concept could be given any definite meaning at all. Schopenhauer's will did not have any definite motive or purpose. But what kind of will is that, Otto Liebmann asked, that does not have a motive or end?[24] If I have a will, I have to will something; my will needs a specific object. Liebmann found it strange that Schopenhauer's will is the source of the human body, when all the desires he ever knew presupposed the existence of the body. For his part, Meyer could not understand Schopenhauer's claim that the essence or inner nature of a human being consists in the will. We are supposed to know this through some kind of immediate intuition of ourselves. But though it is true that we are always conscious of ourselves as acting, it does not follow that this acting is always a form of willing; it might consist in thinking or feeling as much as willing.[25] Many years later Alois Riehl pressed home these kinds of criticisms.[26] He maintained that the concept of a will is only an abstraction, which we derive from particular acts of will, every one of which depends on a motive or purpose. In depriving the will of motives and ends Schopenhauer was confusing it with

[22] Thus Paulsen, 'Gründen und Ursachen des Pessimismus', p. 365; Meyer, 'Weltlust und Weltleid', p. 269; Volkelt, *Schopenhauer*, p. 214.

[23] Thus Windelband, 'Pessimismus und Wissenschaft', p. 237; Riehl, *Einführung*, pp. 182, 189; Paulsen, 'Gründen und Ursachen des Pessimismus', p. 363; Meyer, 'Weltlust und Weltleid', pp. 258, 270; Volkelt, *Schopenhauer*, p. 216.

[24] Otto Liebmann, *Kant und die Epigonen* (Stuttgart: Schober, 1865), pp. 191–192.

[25] Meyer, *Arthur Schopenhauer als Mensch und Denker*, p. 32.   [26] Riehl, *Einführung*, p. 177.

simple desire, because though desires have no conscious purpose, the will must have one by its very nature as a distinctively human form of volition.[27]

No less problematic was the metaphysics Schopenhauer based on his theory of the will. He had claimed that the will is the inner nature not only of human beings but of all things, whether animate or inanimate. Whoever knows that the will is his inner nature, Schopenhauer said, will want to generalize this for everything else, so that their inner nature too consists in the will.[28] For Liebmann, Meyer, Haym and Riehl, however, this was a speculative leap of astonishing proportion. "Never have the basic limits of speculation been treated with more nonchalance than with this inference", Liebmann wrote.[29] This was "a tightrope walker's leap over a metaphysical chasm". For his part, Meyer found Schopenhauer's inference to be bolder than anything undertaken by the *Naturphilosophen*.[30] And Riehl held Schopenhauer's concept of will to be so mysterious that he could not understand how it could explain the entire world: this was a true explanation *obscurum per obscurius*.[31]

Fischer, Meyer, Haym, Riehl and Volkelt were quick to point out the main difficulty in Schopenhauer's theory of redemption.[32] Schopenhauer had maintained that the will is the guiding force behind the intellect, which is essentially only a tool to determine the means for its ends.[33] But if this is so, how does human knowledge, which derives from the intellect, free itself from the will and allow us to stand above human striving? Somehow, the intellect is both bound by the will yet liberates us from it. Keenly aware of this difficulty, Schopenhauer tried to address it at the close of *Die Welt als Wille und Vorstellung*.[34] But his solution simply begged the question: he merely restated his conviction that knowledge could change the direction of the will (I, 547; §70). How it could do this was the very question at issue. In the end, Schopenhauer seems to put his trust in all the reports and stories about Christian and

---

[27] Riehl, *Einführung*, p. 178.   [28] *WWV*, I, 169–170; §21. Cf. *WWV*, I, 165, §19.
[29] Liebmann, *Kant und die Epigonen*, p. 194.
[30] Meyer, *Arthur Schopenhauer als Mensch*, p. 38.   [31] Riehl, *Einführung*, pp. 178–179.
[32] Fischer, *Schopenhauers Leben, Werke und Lehre*, p. 514; Meyer, *Arthur Schopenhauer als Mensch*, p. 45; Haym, *Schopenhauer*, pp. 31–32; Riehl, *Einführung*, pp. 183–184; and Volkelt, *Schopenhauer*, pp. 262–264.
[33] *WWV*, I, 225; §27. Cf. 245–246; §33. See especially Kap. 19, 'Vom Primat des Willens im Selbstbewußtsein', *WWV*, II, 259–316.
[34] Schopenhauer poses the difficulty on several occasions, admitting that the self-renunciation would involve a contradiction in the will itself. See *WWV*, I, 397, §55; 414, §55; 457, §62. He finally addresses it in sections §§68 and 70. At §70 he states that the core of the difficulty is resolved by noting that, according to his theory, the will does not have to deny itself because its direction is changed by an act of insight independent of the will. But this does not address the question of how there can be such insight independent of the will. Schopenhauer distinguishes between knowledge of the intellect following the principle of sufficient reason and the immediate knowledge involved in knowing my own inner nature. While the former kind of knowledge is directed by the will, the latter is not. This distinction, though, does not really help him. One still wants to know why such immediate knowledge, given the omnipotence and omnipresence of the will, is free from its direction. In the end, Schopenhauer wants us to accept at face value the claims of mystics and spiritualists about their transcendent, life changing experiences. But if these really are facts, they are not in accord with his metaphysical theory.

Buddhistic spiritual life. But it never seemed to have occurred to him, as it later did to Nietzsche, that even this apparently ascetic life could be just another subconscious form of the will, the ultimate expression of the will to power. Given this difficulty, it is hardly surprising that the neo-Kantians were sceptical whether, on Schopenhauer's premises, there could be any deliverance from suffering, any redemption from the striving of the will.

All that we have said above is an abstract of just some of the neo-Kantian polemic against Schopenhauer's pessimism. The polemic was much richer, subtler and more nuanced than we can recount here. We must keep in perspective, though, the second-ary importance of this polemic. Ultimately, it was only a means to an end: undercutting Schopenhauer's quietism, his attempt to sabotage the effort to change the world. Just why the neo-Kantians were committed to undermining this quietism, just how and why their own philosophy was deeply activitist, is a question that we must now address. Only when we understand the sources of their activism will we be fully in a position to understand the motives and rationale behind their attitude towards pessimism.

3. Neo-Kantianism as Neo-Fichteanism

Scholars of the 19th century tend to think of pessimism as a phenomenon peculiar to that century, one that begins in the 1860s with the rehabilitation of Schopenhauer and the publication of Hartmann's *Philosophie des Unbewussten* (1869). But pessi-mism was very much a problem of the 18th century too. Its most powerful spokesman was Jean Jacques Rousseau, who, in his first discourse (1750),[35] had put forward the provocative thesis that the progress of the arts and sciences is not improving but cor-rupting morals. That thesis was a great challenge to the Enlightenment, whose first article of faith had been that the progress of civilization, the growth of the arts and sciences, would improve life and morals.

Among those *philosophes* and *Aufklärer* shocked by Rousseau's thesis was Kant himself, who was devoted to the cause of Enlightenment. Though it is only implicit, Kant's response to Rousseau's pessimism is central to his mature philosophy. If Kant were to defend the cause of Enlightenment, and indeed the value and authority of reason itself, he had to respond to Rousseau's pessimism. Since the neo-Kantian cri-tique of Schopenhauer's and Hartmann's pessimism in the 19th century grew out of Kant's response to Rousseau's pessimism in the 18th century, we first need to take into account Kant's attitude towards Rousseau.

Kant's critique of Rousseau appears in his famous 1784 essay on world history, 'Idee zu einer allgemeinen Geschichte in weltbürgerlicher Absicht'.[36] Although Kant never

---

[35] Jean Jacques Rousseau, *Discours sur les sciences et les arts*, in *Œuvres complètes*, eds Bernard Gagnebin and Marcel Raymond (Paris: Gallimard, 1964), III, 1–30.
[36] Kant, *Schriften* VIII, 15–31.

mentions Rousseau in this essay, its thrust and content become fully meaningful only when we take into account its intended target: Rousseau's pessimism. The nub of Kant's critique is that the mechanism of nature leads inevitably towards the ideals of freedom and equality of a republican constitution, which is a better condition for mankind than the state of nature, where human beings never develop their natural powers. Kant's response is based upon his teleological theory of nature, according to which everything in nature works towards the full realization of all the natural capacities of man. The mechanism by which nature achieves this end is the "unsocial sociability" of mankind, which consists essentially in competition among individuals for power, property and prestige (*Herrschsucht, Habsucht, Ehrsucht*). Such competition forces people to develop their natural capacities. In competing for power, property and prestige, people are compelled to work hard, to use their wits, and to learn new skills and tools, all of which develops their natural powers and intelligence. Kant admits that without this mechanism "man would live an Arcadian pastoral existence of perfect concord, self-sufficiency and mutual love", which is the perfect portrait of Rousseau's state of nature. But in that idyll they would not develop their natural powers, so that they would be "as docile as the sheep they tended". So, though the price of civilization is the loss of pastoral happiness, the reward is the development of our natural powers. Kant pressed home his argument against Rousseau by claiming that the very same mechanism would eventually lead to the creation of a republican constitution, a state devoted to the ideals of freedom and equality. Sheer self-interest inclines everyone towards a republican constitution, because it alone gives everyone maximal freedom to pursue property, power and prestige without the interference of others. The republican constitution is for Kant a regulated or managed form of "unsocial sociability", which naturally leads to the maximum development of human powers. Thus Rousseau's lost freedom and equality would be regained through political means, through the creation of a republican constitution, which was the greatest task facing humanity. And so, with a brilliant twist of the dialectical knife, Kant had turned Rousseau's argument against him. The very mechanism that Rousseau saw as a source of civilizations's discontent—competition and the workings of *amour propre*—Kant saw as the source of its beneficence.

Implicit in Kant's argument against Rousseau is the concession that happiness would be lost with the progress of culture. Kantian agents would be more perfect, rational and self-realized than Rousseauian noble savages; but they would not be happy. This was not so much a lacuna in Kant's argument but the reflection of an important underlying principle. For Kant had disputed whether happiness is the proper measure of the value of life and existence. If nature gave us reason so that we could become happy, he had argued, then it has chosen a very ineffective instrument indeed, because we would actually be happier if we ran our lives by instinct alone.[37]

[37] See Kant, *Grundlegung zur Metaphysik der Sitten*, IV, 395–396.

An argument for pessimism based on eudemonic considerations alone, Kant was saying, would reduce human beings down to animals and fail to see the true purpose of their reason: acting not according to laws but for the sake of laws, that is, for the sake of moral principle.[38]

For Kant, then, the measure of the value of existence should be not eudemonic but moral. Or, as he famously put it, the purpose of life is not to be happy but to be *worthy* of happiness, that is, to live our lives for the sake of moral ideals.[39] There is one ideal to which all human beings have a duty to contribute: the highest good, the perfect proportion between personal happiness and moral merit. This ideal went hand-in-glove with Kant's ideal of a republican constitution, which would enshrine principles of distributive justice, which apportion reward with desert. The moral duty to realize the highest good, to strive for the ideals of a republican constitution, would seem to make political action the final answer to the Rousseauian pessimist. Kant seemed to be saying against Rousseau: if we only strive for the ideal of a republican constitution, we will achieve, or at least approach, the freedom and equality of the lost state of nature. Life will have a purpose after all, and all our struggles can make a difference, making life worthwhile after all.

Yet, as much as Kant seems to imply this, he had placed severe constraints on human political action. He did not believe in the powers of co-ordinated political action, in human beings coming together and achieving through their own efforts grand republican ideals.[40] Success in political endeavours depends too much on fortune, on the beneficent guiding hand of providence. That the republican constitution will eventually come into being depends not on us, Kant held, but the mechanism of nature, which ultimately involves providence, the divine design behind nature. In the end, then, Kant's response to pessimism rests on religious faith, the belief in the power of the creator to guide human beings towards their final end.

Philosophers in the neo-Kantian tradition shared Kant's basic optimism, even if they did not accept the details of his theory of history. They reaffirmed his belief in progress, his hope that humanity, through constant striving and effort, could at least approach, if not attain, the ideals of a republican constitution. They were less willing to accept, however, Kant's teleology and theology. Not ready to rest their faith in providence, which they saw as a residue of the old theology, they believed instead in the power of the human will and the efficacy of direct action. Man had to take control over his own fate, and he could not wait for providence or nature to do things for him. If people would only work together in political associations, they could transform the political order and make progress towards Kant's grand ideals.

---

[38] Kant, *Grundlegung zur Metaphysik der Sitten*, IV, 412.   [39] KrV, B 833–837.
[40] See Kant's 'Über den Gemeinspruch: Das mag in der Theorie richtig sein, taugt aber nicht für die Praxis', AA VIII, 308–312. On the ineliminable metaphysical and theological dimension of Kant's ideals, see my article 'Moral Faith and the Highest Good', in *The Cambridge Companion to Kant and Modern Philosophy*, ed. Paul Guyer (Cambridge: Cambridge University Press, 2006), pp. 588–629.

The *locus classicus* for this activist response to Rousseau's cultural pessimism is the fifth of Fichte's famous lectures on *Die Bestimmung des Gelehrten*,[41] which he delivered in Jena in 1794. Here Fichte argued against Rousseau that we should see moral corruption as the result of a *specific* culture and state—that of the *ancien régime*—and not as the result of culture and the state in general. While Rousseau pined for the lost golden age of nature, where men lived in peace, justice and harmony, he should have realized that this is achievable only in a republican constitution. What he saw behind us in the past, Fichte declared, we should now put ahead of us in the future as a goal for human striving. Fichte's remedy for Rousseau's pessimism was thus political activism. His lectures closed with a rousing call to political action: "Act! Act!, that is what we are here for."[42] No one believed more passionately than Fichte in the powers of the human will to transform its world.

It was Fichte's radical Promethean faith—not Kant's belief in providence—that entered into the mainstream of the neo-Kantian tradition.[43] The deep strain of Fichtean activism in the neo-Kantian tradition first became apparent in the early 1860s. It was in the beginning of this decade that several prominent neo-Kantians— Kuno Fischer, Jürgen Bona Meyer, Rudolf Haym and Eduard Zeller—celebrated Fichte for his political activism on behalf of the liberal-national cause. The occasion for their celebration lay in their own need to reassert their liberal and national ideals, which had been defeated in 1848, but which had forever remained in their hearts. After Kaiser Wilhelm I came to the throne in 1861, it was imperative to remind the new monarch of his potential future role in creating German unity. Who better than Fichte to remind his majesty of his duties? For in his *Reden an die deutsche Nation* Fichte, still very much the firebrand of 1794, called upon Germans to resist their French occupiers and demanded the creation of a single German nation.[44] In the early 1860s that Fichtean ideal seemed more timely than ever, especially for those liberals who never lost faith in German unity. Given that Fichte was the right messenger, the only question was when to call upon him. What better opportunity than the centenary of his birth, May 1862? Speakers could affirm their liberal-national cause through Fichte without raising the suspicions of censors. And so, on March 3, 1862, the Berlin chapter of the *Deutsche National Verein*—a liberal-national organization of some 25,000 members advocating

[41] Fichte, *Sämtliche Werke*, ed. I.H. Fichte (Berlin: Veit, 1845–1846), VI, 335–346.
[42] Fichte, *Sämtliche Werke*, VI, 345.
[43] On the enormous influence of Fichte on neo-Kantianism in the 1860s, see Köhnke, *Entstehung und Aufstieg*, pp. 186–194. For Fichte's importance for neo-Kantianism in the early 20th century, see Hermann Lübbe, *Politische Philosophie in Deutschland* (Munich: Deutscher Taschenbuch Verlag, 1974), pp. 194–205.
[44] It is noteworthy that Fichte's concept of national unity is more cultural than political; Fichte wants to realize a national German character; but he does not envisage a single national German state. What matters to him is simply that different German states have a common program of education to realize this character. He even states that it is indifferent to him whether there is one or many German states. See Fichte, *Reden an die deutsche Nation, Sämtliche Werke* VII, 397–398, 437–438. For the political purposes of the Fichte-Feier, however, this was an embarrassing nicety that it was better not to mention.

German unity under Prussian leadership—resolved to celebrate the centenary of Fichte's birth, leaving it to other local chapters to organize their own events. Those other chapters were more than happy to follow suit. Thus on May 19, 1862 there were celebrations of the Fichte centenary throughout Germany.[45] Some 2,500 individuals participated in the Berlin celebration alone. Among the neo-Kantians, Fischer, Meyer and Haym gave speeches.[46]

The *Fichte-Feier* of 1862 was of the greatest importance for the rehabilitation of Kant, who piggy-backed on Fichte's success.[47] For it was made clear through the many speeches that the father of Fichte's liberal ideals, and the founder of his philosophy, was Immanuel Kant. It was Fischer who spearheaded this Fichtean interpretation of Kant, for he had argued in the third volume of his *Geschichte der Philosophie* that Kant's philosophy was completed through Fichte.[48] This was true not only with respect to Kant's theoretical philosophy, Fischer argued, but also with regard to his practical philosophy. Just as Fichte eliminated the thing-in-itself from the theoretical philosophy, so he removed the last vestiges of religious hypostasis, namely, the belief in providence, from his practical philosophy. Fichte's great advance over Kant was in seeing that we could change the world through our own actions, and that we did not have to rely on or wait for providence. As Fischer described Fichte's activism in his centenary address: "Kant had reformed philosophy, Fichte wanted reform through the Kantian philosophy."[49]

It was with this optimistic Fichteanism that the neo-Kantians would confront the phenomenon of pessimism in the 1860s. Just as Fichte had refused to accept Rousseau's pessimism, so the neo-Kantians would react against Schopenhauer's and Hartmann's fashionable *Weltschmerz*. For all the differences between Rousseau's pessimism and its 19th-century German variants, there was still a common denominator: the belief that political action is futile, that we cannot remove the sources of human calamity through striving. The real problem with Schopenhauer's pessimism lay for the neo-Kantians in its quietism, its belief that it is necessary to resign to the evils of life because they are inescapable and irremediable. We now need to take a closer look at that quietism and see how the neo-Kantians reacted to it.

[45] On the extent of these celebrations, see the chart and map in Köhnke, *Entstehung und Aufstieg*, pp. 190–191.

[46] Jürgen Bona Meyer, *Über Fichte's Reden an die deutsche Nation* (Hamburg: Meissner, 1862); Rudolf Haym, *Eine Erinnerung an Johann Gottlieb Fichte* (Berlin: Reimer, 1861); Kuno Fischer, 'Johann Gottlieb Fichte', in *Akademischen Reden* (Stuttgart: Cotta, 1862), 1–75. Zeller wrote an appreciative account of Fichte only two years earlier, 'Johann Gottlieb Fichte als Politiker', *Historische Zeitschrift*, 40 (1860), 1–35.

[47] Here I follow Köhnke, *Entstehung und Aufstieg*, pp. 188,193.

[48] Kuno Fischer, *Immanuel Kant: Entwicklungsgeschichte und System der kritischen Philosophie*, Band III of *Geschichte der neuern Philosophie* (Mannheim: Bassermann, 1860), 344. Fischer's interpretation was extolled by Carl Fortlage in an enthusiastic review, 'Kuno Fischers Darstellung der Kant'schen Philosophie', in the *Blätter für literarische Unterhaltung* Nr. 16, April 18, 1861, pp. 285–291, esp. 288. Fortlage praised how this Fichteanized version of Kant's philosophy made "*der Mensch sein eigener Herr*".

[49] Fischer, 'Johann Gottlieb Fichte', p. 13.

4. Critique of Quietism

"Abandon all hope you who enter here" would have been a fitting motto for *Die Welt als Wille und Vorstellung*. For in every possible way Schopenhauer undermines his reader's hopes of making a difference to life and improving the world. In Book IV of his pessimistic masterpiece Schopenhauer builds his case, piece by piece, for why the only appropriate response to life lies in resignation, in the denial of the will to life. Why is all hope futile? Schopenhauer gives several reasons. First, even if we created the perfect state, there would still be many evils intrinsic to life itself (I, 478; §62). The only purpose of the state is to prevent people from harming one another; but it cannot provide them with happiness. And even if all conflicts between people were resolved within the state, there would still be conflicts between states. Second, virtue cannot be taught, because it rests upon inner disposition and innate character rather than external behaviour; all the constraints of the law and all the inducements of education act only upon external behaviour.[50] This means that all attempts to create virtue through political reform and education cannot succeed. Third, there is no progress in history, but everything stays the same. "The motto of history should be '*eadem sed aliter*' [the same but in a different way]."[51] The Hegelian doctrine of reason in history, the thesis that history conforms to ends and progressively realizes them, rests upon a confusion of the contingent realm of fact with the necessary truths of reason. Fourth, cosmic justice does not consist in an ideal world where happiness is in proportion to merit but in the real world just as we see it before us; whatever happens is right just because the will wills it, and whatever the will wills is just because it wills it (I, 480; §63). Hence world justice is the course of the world itself. Rather than judging the world by moral standards extrinsic to it, we should learn to adjust to its own immanent standards of justice. We should resign ourselves to whatever happens, however horrible, because it is just, a manifestation of that cosmic will which is the source of all justice.

Schopenhauer's quietism was essentially a rehabilitation of the old Christian and Buddhistic ethic, which preached salvation by self-denial and renunciation. No one was more aware of the historical provenance of his doctrine in this regard than Schopenhauer himself. "The true spirit and core of Christianity," he wrote, lay in "the recognition of the nothingness of earthly happiness, the complete contempt for it, and the turning towards a completely different, even opposed existence."[52] In the penultimate chapter of *Die Welt als Wille und Vorstellung* Schopenhauer went out of his way to stress the affinity of his teaching with the old Christian ethics.[53] No, Schopenhauer did not believe in God or the kingdom of heaven; but he did expressly rehabilitate the concepts of sin, grace, deliverance and

---

[50] *WWV*, I, 501–503, §66; and *WWV*, I, 405–406, §55.
[51] See 'Über Geschichte', *WWV*, II, 563–573, p. 570.
[52] *WWV*, II, 563–573, p. 569.
[53] *WWV*, I, 547–554, §70.

redemption, where redemption lay in withdrawal from the world and renuncia-tion of all striving of the will.[54]

Nothing could be more opposed to this quietistic Christian ethic than Fichte's Prometheanism. Rather than resigning oneself to the world and attempting to escape it, Fichte preached rebelling against it and striving to transform it. The very will Schopenhauer wanted to renounce Fichte wanted to enflame. While Schopenhauer saw the striving of the will as the chief source of mankind's problems, Fichte viewed it as the sole means for its redemption, because only through that striving could it achieve the ideals of a republican constitution. Nowhere is Fichte's opposition with the Christian tradition more apparent than in his claim that the unification of all striving Fichtean agents would be nothing less than God.[55] Of course, this is an ideal these agents would never reach; but they could make progress towards it, approach-ing it if not attaining it.

This Fichtean Promethianism was the ultimate motivating force, the guiding spirit, behind the neo-Kantian critique of Schopenhauer's pessimism. While it is con-stantly present and presupposed, it is not always made explicit. There are places in the neo-Kantian polemic, however, where it emerges explicitly and unmistakably. One of these places appears in one of the earliest reviews of Schopenhauer's *Die Welt als Wille und Vorstellung*: Herbart's justly appreciative yet highly critical review, which appeared in *Hermes* in 1820.[56] At the close of his review Herbart focuses on Schopenhauer's con-troversial remarks that optimism is not only an absurd but a pernicious way of thinking because it makes light of "the inexpressible suffering of humanity".[57] To this "declara-tion" Herbart responds with one of his own: that he regards himself as an optimist, not of the dogmatic theoretical kind that Schopenhauer rails against, but one of a more prac-tical kind. He confesses that he is an optimist "by disposition" (*der Gesinnung nach*), which means that, though the world is a bad place, he is disposed to do as much as he can to make it a better one. This practical optimist believes that the physical sufferings of humanity are bearable, but that the real source of human unhappiness lies in "social relations", which it is the duty of all humanity to address. Herbart then likens the fate of humanity to something very mundane that he has seen lately: an untended bean garden. The beans are growing out of the earth in great profusion; but because their growth is wild, only a few of the plants prosper, preventing others from growing to their full height or even suffocating them from lack of light. If these less fortunate beans had conscious-ness, they would become Schopenhauerian pessimists. They would whine about the useless urge to life, they would pity one another, and then they would find solace in the "denial of the will to life". But, Herbart asks, is their situation really so hopeless? What these beans are lacking is a few good gardeners who know how to place poles to direct

[54] See especially *WWV*, I, 520, §68; I, 548, §70.
[55] Fichte, 'Vorlesungen über die Bestimmung des Gelehrten', *Werke* VI, 310.
[56] Johann Friedrich Herbart, Review of *Die Welt als Wille und Vorstellung* (Leipzig, 1819), *Hermes*, Stück 3 (1820), 131–149, in *Sämtliche Werke* XII, 56–75.
[57] *WWV*, I, 447, §59.

their growth, so that all can grow to a great height. The moral is clear: what humanity needs is just a few good reformers who know how to regulate its affairs through wise laws and institutions. Though by the 1820s Herbart had long since outgrown Fichte's metaphysics, his response to Schopenhauer betrayed his lingering Fichtean activism. For his response was precisely that of a Fichtean educator of humanity, who believed that the world could indeed become a better place if we reformed its social and political institutions through the education of its youth. That old Fichtean faith never died in Herbart and it dictated in no small measure his reaction to Schopenhauer's pessimism.

Another revealing neo-Kantian response to Schopenhauer's quietism appears in Meyer's illuminating 1886 essay 'Weltlust und Weltleid'.[58] Meyer explicitly considers the quietistic implications of Schopenhauer's pessimism. What would most people do, he asks, if they were faced with the option of ending their life with all its burdens? They might choose to end it all, just as Schopenhauer predicts. But, Meyer then adds, they would also probably be like the overburdened man in the fable: as soon as he saw death approaching, he quickly picked up his load again. His one fervent wish is only for a little help in lightening his burden. The moral of the story is plain enough: there is nothing instrinsically insufferable about life; if people only help one another, they will find life bearable. Writing in the late 1880s, Meyer finds the persistent popularity of pessimism puzzling. He notes the great achievements of the times, the creation of national unity, victory on the battlefield, technical and social progress. These are no times for "a dark lament about the world", he claims, because we can now all have faith again in "the moral world order". But Meyer makes it clear that this faith ultimately rests not on the workings of providence, still less the laws of history, but in the power of our own individual actions. His Fichtean activism reveals itself loud and clear when he declares that we should now create this world order through our own deeds. Man is not born to suffer evil, to lament misery or to resign himself to the evils of the world; rather, the purpose of life is to fight evil and misery. Our greatest happiness lies in striving "to create and promote the welfare of humanity through service to the ideas of the good, beautiful and true." We can even derive pleasure from this striving, so that one day we can declare with Posa: "Life is still beautiful!"

The neo-Kantian attitude towards Schopenhauer's quietism is illustrated most beautifully and simply by a late essay of Otto Liebmann's, 'Trilologie des Pessimismus', which appeared in his *Gedanken und Thatsachen*.[59] The trilogy tells the story of three pessimists: Hegesias, an ancient philosopher, who teaches suicide as the only solution to life's problems; Timon the misanthrope, who, after becoming the victim of fraud and treachery, retires from humanity and decries its evil nature; and Buddha, who preaches renunciation of desire and the value of withdrawal from the world. Liebmann finds all these attitudes understandable but ultimately too extreme. Life is neither a heaven nor a hell. But we should not pretend to play the role of the ancient

[58] Meyer, 'Weltlust und Weltleid', pp. 253–295.
[59] Liebmann, *Gedanken und Thatsachen*, II, 235–267.

gods and to look down upon it as if it were a tragedy or comedy. "Rather, we should fight and we should act." (262). The pessimists and optimists of this world fail to see that life or existence in itself is neither good nor evil. These are relative qualities, depending on the attitude of human beings to things. And whether things are good or bad depends not only on how we look at them but upon what we do with them (266).

Although there are other instances of this Promethian faith in the neo-Kantian polemic, the examples we have chosen here make it especially clear, striking and piquant. By now it should be fully clear that the battle between neo-Kantianism and pessimism was indeed ultimately one between Fichtean activism and Schopenhauerian quietism. This is not to say, however, that this was the only source of friction between the neo-Kantians and Schopenhauer. One final issue remains. While this issue does not strictly concern Schopenhauer's pessimism, it does concern his politics and his relation to the post-Kantian tradition in general. Since this issue has been important for the reception of neo-Kantianism, it is important that we discuss it here.

5. University Philosophy

In the late 1840s Schopenhauer wrote an essay for his collection *Parerga und Paralipomena* on philosophy in the universities, 'Über die Universitäts-philosophie',[60] in which he called into question the whole practice of teaching philosophy at universities. Schopenhauer criticized professors of philosophy as servants of religion and the state, as modern sophists who were more interested in living *from* philosophy than living *for* it. Schopenhauer's chief targets were Fichte, Schelling and Hegel, but he also did not hesitate to take aim at some early neo-Kantians, most notably Fries and Herbart. Although Schopenhauer did not live to see the rise of the neo-Kantian movement in the 1860s, there could be little question what he would have thought of its members. Since most neo-Kantians were professors at universities, they too would have been victims of his wrath.

Thanks to its malicious tone and ferocious wit, Schopenhauer's essay proved very popular and became highly successful. Neo-Kantianism has been living under its shadow ever since. Schopenhauer's essay helped to solidify the reputation of neo-Kantianism as a conservative movement which endorsed the social, political and intellectual status quo.[61] Schopenhauer's criticism of university philosophy, which was later endorsed by Kierkegaard and the young Nietzsche,[62] has also been very influential in forming the conception that creative, innovative philosophy in the 19th century took place outside the university. To many, such philosophy seems to

---

[60] Schopenhauer, *Sämtliche Werke*, IV, 171–242.
[61] The *locus classicus* for this conception of neo-Kantianism is Karl Löwith's influential *Von Hegel zu Nietzsche* (Zurich: Europa Verlag, 1941), pp. 135, 136.
[62] See Section 8 of Nietzsche's 'Schopenhauer als Erzieher', which uncritically adopts Schopenhauer's entire position. *Sämtliche Werke*, ed. G. Colli and M. Montinari (Berlin: de Gruyter, 1980), I, 411–427.

have been the work of Schopenhauer, Marx, Nietzsche and Kierkegaard, who were not academics. These are the grand revolutionary thinkers of the 19th century, we are told, and they are enshrined today in the textbooks,[63] and written about *ad nauseum*. Since the neo-Kantians, as university philosophers, have fallen out of this scheme, they have been almost entirely neglected.

Because of the influence of Schopenhauer's essay, we do well to consider its claims and contents; and, in the interests of fairness, we should see what neo-Kantians had to say about it.

Schopenhauer's essay is for the most part a screed, lambasting and lampooning the university philosophers, who are chiefly Fichte, Schelling and Hegel. Schopenhauer refers to their work in the most scurrilous and derogatory tones. Since he condemns it wholesale and never subjects it to a detailed examination, it would be pointless to give any weight to his diatribes. The reader learns nothing about what is problematic in the philosophy of Fichte, Schelling and Hegel. What is obvious to all is Schopenhauer's motives in making this criticism, which he makes painfully apparent in several passages.[64] Desperate for literary fame, Schopenhauer feels that the university professors have completely ignored his work and that they have refused to give it the recognition it deserves. He writes as if there were a conspiracy against him, as if the whole academic establishment were scheming to deny a fair hearing to his writings. This raises the hypothetical question: what if Fichte, Schelling or Hegel had written favourable reviews of his work? In that case would Schopenhauer have railed against them?

It would be a mistake, though, to dismiss Schopenhauer's essay as a failed polemic.[65] For all its bombast, vitriol and wounded vanity, it put a finger upon a real problem with university philosophy. Schopenhauer's main point is that university philosophy is hopelessly compromised because it cannot teach anything contrary to religion and state. The philosopher is the employee of the state, which can exert censorship over him. We cannot expect the state to do otherwise, Schopenhauer argues, because it is not in its interests to employ someone to criticize, either implicitly or explicitly, its policies or its official religion. However, philosophy requires, Schopenhauer rightly insists, complete intellectual freedom, the right to take an investigation wherever it might lead, whatever the consequences for conventional morality, religion or state. Philosophy simply cannot serve two masters, truth and the world. In making this point Schopenhauer was taking on the mantle of Lessing, who had argued for such freedom of enquiry in the 18th century. But he was taking Lessing's campaign on behalf of free enquiry a step further, pointing out that the dangers to it lay as much in the university as in press censorship. It would be foolish to underrate the importance of

---

[63] The latest reference work to endorse this conception is *Nineteenth-Century Philosophy: Revolutionary Responses to the Existing Order*. Volume 2 of *The History of Continental Philosophy*, eds Alan Schrift and Daniel Conway (Chicago, IL: University of Chicago Press, 2010). See my review of this work in *The Notre Dame Philosophical Review*, August 25, 2011.

[64] See Schopenhauer, *Sämtliche Werke* IV, 176–177, 225–226.

[65] This is Fischer's assessment, *Schopenhauers Leben, Werke und Lehre*, pp. 493–494.

Schopenhauer's criticism, which points out a danger that continues to exist in state universities to this day, especially in Germany, where every professor is a civil servant.

Granted that there is some merit to Schopenhauer's criticism, the question remains whether it applies to the neo-Kantians. Were they university philosophers as Schopenhauer portrays them? It has to be said that Schopenhauer's portrait was not only unfair but contemptible. Schopenhauer writes as if all university philosophers were obedient and obsequious servants of the state, who would write their philosophy to suit government policy and religious dogma. Against this, we have to consider the harsh and blunt reality: that from the 1820s to the 1860s, the formative years of neo-Kantianism, *most* neo-Kantians were persecuted or even prosecuted by the state. They stood by their convictions and writings; and they were punished for it, often at great personal cost. This was the case for Fries, Beneke, Fischer, Zeller and Lange.

What was the neo-Kantian reaction to Schopenhauer's essay? Though they did not know the essay itself, the early neo-Kantians knew well enough the views that went into it. Even before its publication in the 1850s, Schopenhauer's tirades about Fichte, Schelling and Hegel were well known, sprinkled as they were throughout *Die Welt als Wille und Vorstellung*. As critical as they were of Fichte, Schelling and Hegel, the early neo-Kantians never once endorsed Schopenhauer's diatribes. They felt that his remarks went beyond the pale of civilized criticism, and that they were simple ventings of envy and sour grapes. The young Beneke censured Schopenhauer's diatribes as "unworthy of a philosopher"; and Herbart went out of his way to show how Schopenhauer's ideas resembled those of his old teacher, Fichte. That the world is the self-consciousness of the will, Herbart pointed out, was a central theme of Fichte's later philosophy.

Three later neo-Kantians, Haym, Paulsen and Fischer, responded explicitly to Schopenhauer's views on university philosophy. In his *Arthur Schopenhauer*,[66] one of the first monographs on the philosopher and surely one of the most savagely critical, Haym scoffed at Schopenhauer's claim that his essay was the greatest invective since Cicero's *In Verrem*. This piece was nothing more than arrogant bluster, "a series of noisy insults" (94). Haym reaffirmed Herbart's and Beneke's points about the uncivilized manner of Schopenhauer's diatribes. Never before and since had there been such unabashed rudeness in literary discourse. "Schopenhauer's crudity is pure, positive and undisguised crudity." (89) The tone in which he expressed his views about Fichte, Schelling, Herbart and Hegel was that in which sailors, coachmen, street ruffians and fishermen's wives cursed one another. This animosity had nothing to do with his opposition to their ideas but had everything to do with his personality, especially his arrogance, his belief in his own genius and the admiration it deserved (91). Schopenhauer's diatribes were at their most shameless when it came to his attacks on Fichte. Haym reiterated Herbart's point that Schopenhauer had failed to

---

[66] Haym, *Arthur Schopenhauer* (Berlin: Reimer, 1864). All references in parentheses are to this edition.

acknowledge his great debt to Fichte. After Plato and Kant, no philosopher influenced Schopenhauer more than Fichte (54–55). Haym implied that one reason for the bitterness of Schopenhauer's polemic against Fichte and Schelling is that he felt threatened by them: he knew their ideas were similar to his own, and to protect his originality he declared his contempt for them (93). Rather than agreeing with Schopenhauer about the dangers of university philosophy, Haym averred that nothing would have helped Schopenhauer more than employment at a university (87–88). If he had remained at the university, he would have learned to clarify and develop his ideas, because he would have to make his philosophy more comprehensible to students and to respond to the objections of colleagues. He would also have learned more about the different sciences, and would have adapted his ideas to the latest research. Instead of learning in these ways, Schopenhauer responded to university life with scorn and turned inwards and isolated himself, repeating over and over again the same ideas he had in his early years.

Paulsen and Fischer took the response to Schopenhauer's diatribe to a new level: their target was not the philosophy but the man. This approach, already implicit in Haym, was developed by Paulsen in an 1882 essay 'Arthur Schopenhauer', which was later republished as part of his 1901 book on pessimism, *Schopenhauer, Hamlet, Mephistoteles*.[67] Only when we consider Schopenhauer's pathology, Paulsen argued, can we begin to make sense of some of his opinions, especially those concerning university philosophers (53). No one can take seriously Schopenhauer's belief that there was a conspiracy of university professors against him (48–49). This belief becomes comprehensible only when we consider the two dominant characteristics of his personality: an extraordinarily high opinion of himself and his craving for recognition, especially through literary fame. What, Paulsen asks, did Schopenhauer really expect from these professors? Reviews, citations, refutations? Hardly. What he wanted was admirers, disciples and acolytes, people who would pay homage to his genius (51). The university professors, whose very intellectual independence he doubted, were in fact much too independent to give him the discipleship he wanted. While Haym thought that an academic career might have done Schopenhauer some good, taking off the rougher edges of his testy personality, Paulsen thought that Schopenhauer knew himself well enough not to persist in a career so unsuitable for his nature (32). Never would he have settled for the stuff of academic routine, setting exams, grading papers and sitting on committees. He thought too much of himself to bother with such routine and petty matters. Behind all Schopenhauer's contempt for university philosophers, Paulsen perceptively said, lay his class consciousness, his patrician self-esteem, which made him look down upon those from a lower social stratum who had to make their money from publications and lectures (21).

---

[67] Friedrich Paulsen, *Schopenhauer, Hamlet, Mephistopheles: Drei Aufsätze zur Naturgeschichte des Pessimismus*, Dritte Auflage (Stuttgart: Cotta Nachfolger, 1911). All references in parentheses are to this edition.

Kuno Fischer treated the problem of Schopenhauer's character in a short tract published in the 1890s, *Der Philosoph des Pessimismus*.[68] It is fair game to consider not only Schopenhauer's philosophy but also his character, Fischer argued, given that he saw himself as the leader of a new sect of Western Buddhism (416–417). He pointed out the great discrepancy between Schopenhauer's personal life and his own pessimism. Here was a man who preached the value of ascetism, but who lived the life of a *bon vivant*. And here was a man who prized humility and self-denial, but who was obsessed with his own literary fame. The discrepancy between Schopenhauer's philosophy and character disappear, however, if we measure his life by aesthetic rather than ethical standards. For Schopenhauer, as a child of the Romantic age, saw himself as a genius, and this was a role he played throughout his life (420–421). In his larger monograph, *Schopenhauers Leben, Werke und Lehre*,[69] Fischer applied the same kind of approach to Schopenhauer's views on university philosophy. Here he points out two very revealing discrepancies between Schopenhauer's life and philosophy. While these discrepancies do not undermine the validity of Schopenhauer's criticisms of university philosophy, they do cast serious doubts on his motives. The first discrepancy concerns Schopenhauer's own desire for a university career. Schopenhauer was himself a university philosopher, and on several occasions flirted with the idea of a university career, Fischer points out. Though he lectured for only one semester in Berlin, he remained inscribed as a *Dozent* for ten years, even making use of that formality to impress a prospective British publisher. Since Schopenhauer was no success as a university lecturer, and since he also sought, but failed to attain, a position in Heidelberg, it seems that his spleen about university philosophy was motivated by envy and resentment. The second discrepancy is more serious. In his essay Schopenhauer portrays himself as the 19th-century Lessing, whose fundamental ideal is freedom of enquiry. Yet when the reaction came in the 1850s, Schopenhauer was beside himself with joy when left-wing university professors had their *venia legendi* revoked.[70] To his reactionary mind, the materialists, the left-wing Hegelians and the liberals all got what they deserved. Rather than championing academic freedom and liberty of press, Schopenhauer turned out to be champion of censorship.

Fischer had an understandable reason for pursuing these *ad hominem* criticisms. For Schopenhauer's rant about university professors had impugned not only their integrity but also his own. He pointed out that insinuations about servility were completely unfair when it came to thinkers like Ludwig Feuerbach, David Friedrich Strauß, Theodor Vischer, Bruno Bauer and Arnold Ruge, who had all been victims of state persecution, and who had all abandoned their ambitions for a university career

[68] Kuno Fischer, *Der Philosoph des Pessimismus. Ein Charakterproblem.* (Heidelberg: Carl Winter, 1897). Reprinted in *Kleine Schriften* (Heidelberg: Winter, 1898), II, 389–446. All references are to this later edition.
[69] Kuno Fischer, *Schopenhauers Leben, Werke und Lehre*, pp. 87–88, 492–494.
[70] Fischer, *Schopenhauers Leben*, pp. 98–99.

because of their convictions and writings.[71] Fischer might well have included in that list two of his neo-Kantian contemporaries: Eduard Zeller and Friedrich Lange. Last but not least, though he was too modest to mention it, he could have added himself. While Schopenhauer did note that Fischer had been banished,[72] this hardly satisfied Fischer, who rightly believed that Schopenhauer's portrait of his contemporaries was a scandal that made light of the fact of their very real suffering and persecution.

But let us leave aside all these *ad hominem* points, which do nothing to address the main philosophical issue. In one of the few philosophically valuable passages of Schopenhauer's screed he complains that the university philosophers have been ignoring, for the sake of theology, the most fundamental question of all, the question of existence or whether life is worth living.[73] This complaint was later made by Karl Löwith against the neo-Kantians, who, he had argued, had lost sight of this problem, which later became so important for Kierkegaard, Nietzsche and the neo-Hegelians.[74] We will soon see that that there is some justice to this complaint, because the neo-Kantians originally defined philosophy as the logic of the sciences, leaving out of account its traditional ethical concerns.[75] It is necessary to add, however, that the neo-Kantians themselves became aware of this shortcoming and revised their definition accordingly. If in the 1860s and early 1870s they saw philosophy as nothing but the logic of the sciences, in the 1880s and 1890s they broadened the definition of philosophy to include ethics and the question of the value of life. Philosophy should no longer be simply science, the neo-Kantians believed, because it also had to be a worldview.

For the neo-Kantians, then, no less than Schopenhauer, Kierkegaard and Nietzsche, the question of the value of existence eventually became a central issue. But they differ from these 19th-century giants in one important respect: for them, the problem of the value of existence is fundamentally a *political* problem. Though the state is no remedy for all human suffering, the creation of a just state, based on principles of liberty, equality and fraternity, does make life much more bearable and so much more worth living. Schopenhauer, Kierkegaard and Nietzsche, in their view, had made suffering an eternal part of the human condition, neglecting the importance of society, the state and history in shaping the fate of human beings. The neo-Hegelians would make similar criticisms of these *Lebensphilosophen*, who they regarded as insufficiently historical. But the neo-Kantian position also differs from the neo-Hegelians in one important respect: it denies the Hegelian faith in historical inevitability and the rationality of history. For the neo-Kantians, the only thing that will make the world more rational is our own actions, taking the responsibility for our world into our own hands and striving to create better laws and institutions.

[71] Fischer, *Schopenhauers Leben*, p. 87.   [72] Schopenhauer, *Sämtliche Werke* IV, 176.
[73] Schopenhauer, *Sämtliche Werke* IV, 233.   [74] Löwith, *Von Hegel zu Nietzsche*, pp. 135, 136.
[75] See Part III Introduction, Section 2.

The great virtue of the neo-Kantian position is that it gave hope while avoiding the hypostases of providence or reason in history. It rightly admonishes us that existence can be worthwhile, that life can be worth living, but only if we make it so. That was the ultimate neo-Kantian *credo*, which emerged so clearly in their response to pessimism. This was the lesson handed down to the neo-Kantian socialists of the early 20th century, to Franz Staudiger, Eduard Bernstein and Karl Vorländer.[76]

---

[76] On these figures, see Hermann Lübbe, *Politische Philosophie in Deutschland* (Munich: deutscher Taschenbuch Verlag, 1974), pp. 111–123.

11

Encounter with Darwinism

1. The Rise of Darwinism in Germany

Writing at the end of the 19th century, John Theodore Merz, Nestor of 19th-century intellectual historians, remarked: "Germany may be said to have produced *Darwinismus* in this century as France created *Newtonianisme* in the last."[1] Merz's remark proved entirely accurate. Germany indeed became the homeland of Darwinism. It was in Germany where it was first established, where it spread widest, and where it struck deepest roots. Quite justifiably, Darwin himself saw Germany as the best hope for the triumph of his theory; thus he wrote his friend Wilhelm Preyer in March 1862: "The support which I receive from Germany is my chief ground for hoping that our views will ultimately prevail."[2] Darwin succeeded beyond his wildest dreams. Had he lived until the end of the century, he would have been astonished to learn the results of a readers' survey conducted by the *Berliner Illustrierte Zeitung* in 1899. Asked to list the three greatest thinkers of the 19th century, readers named Helmuth von Moltke, Immanuel Kant and Charles Darwin, in that order; but they deemed the most influential book of the century to be *The Origin of the Species*.[3]

Why had Darwin become so popular in Germany? There is no easy answer to this difficult question, and we can only indicate some central factors here.[4] Social and

---

[1] John Theodore Merz, *A History of European Thought in the Nineteenth Century* (Edinburgh: William Blackwood & Sons, 1904–1912), I, 251, n.4.

[2] Darwin to Wilhelm Preyer, March 1861, *The Life and Letters of Charles Darwin* (New York: Appelton, 1986), II, 270.

[3] As cited in Alfred Kelly, *The Descent of Darwin: The Popularization of Darwinism in Germany 1860–1914* (Chapel Hill, NC: University of North Carolina Press, 1981), p. 23.

[4] Of late, there has been much research on Darwin's reception and influence in Germany. See Mario Di Gregario, 'Under Darwin's Banner: Ernst Haeckel, Carl Gegenbaur and Evolutionary Morphology', and Dirk Backenköhler 'Only Dreams from an Afternoon Nap? Darwin's Theory of Evolution and the Foundation of Biological Anthropology in Germany 1860–1875', in *The Reception of Charles Darwin in Europe*, eds Eve-Marie Engels and Thomas F. Glick (London: Continuum, 2008) I, 79–97, 98–115; Eve-Marie Engels, *Die Rezeption von Evolutionstheorien im 19. Jahrhundert* (Frankfurt: Suhrkamp, 1995); Lynn Nyhart, *Biology Takes Form: Animal Morphology and the German Universities 1800–1900* (Chicago, IL: University of Chicago Press, 1995), pp. 105–142; William Montgomery, 'Germany' in *Comparative Reception of Darwinism*, ed. Thomas F. Glick (Austin, TX: University of Texas Press, 1972), pp. 81–115; P.J. Weindling, 'Darwinism in Germany', in *The Darwinian Heritage*, ed. David Kohn (Princeton, NJ: Princeton University Press, 1985), pp. 685–698; and Andreas Daum, *Wissenschaftspopularisierung im 19. Jahrhundert* (Munich: Oldenbourg, 2002), pp. 65–84, 300–324, 359–369. See also the study by Alfred Kelly cited in note 3.

political factors played a major role. Darwin meant different things to different political factions in Germany, and he was used to justify both right- and left-wing views. But if we ask about the social and political factors behind his *initial* reception, the reasons he *first* became popular, then we must consider his strong appeal to left-wing intellectuals. The collapse of the liberal and nationalist cause in the Revolution of 1848 had led to consternation and frustration among left-wing intellectuals, who would now have to fight for their cause through intellectual rather than political means. What they could not achieve through the barricades or ballot box, they would now attempt through science and philosophy. Left-wing intellectuals were intent on creating a humanist, secular and materialist worldview, one which would support human autonomy and democracy. Central to that objective was undermining the traditional alliance of throne and altar, whose ideology seemed to rest on hypostasis and heteronomy, the alienation of human autonomy through belief in supernatural forces. Darwin's theory, in eliminating the need for supernatural intervention in the universe, seemed to confirm the left's worldview, and so to be a useful weapon to undercut the alliance of throne and altar.

Although it is alien to our present understanding of Darwin,[5] the early German Darwinists associated Darwin's theory with social and political progress. What Darwin saw in nature—the increasing perfection of a species through the struggle for existence—they saw in social and political life. Darwin seemed to make social and political progress into a natural law, so that greater autonomy and democracy would inevitably triumph. Nowhere is this line of thinking more evident than in Ernst Haeckel's famous and influential lecture 'Ueber die Entwicklungstheorie Darwins', which he gave in Stettin on September 1863 at the *Versammlung deutscher Naturforscher und Ärtze*.[6] At the close of his lecture, Haeckel makes clear the political meaning of Darwinism for him, and later much of his generation:

Do we find the same law of progress [as found in nature] active everywhere in the historical world? Quite naturally so! For also in civil and social relations it is the same principles of the struggle for existence and natural selection that drive the people irresistably forwards and gradually to higher culture. Regression in state and social life, in moral and scientific life, which the self-serving efforts of priests and despots in all periods of world history have been intent on producing, can indeed temporarily hinder this universal progress or apparently repress it; but the more unnatural, the more anachronistic, these reactionary strivings are, the more quickly and forcefully will they create progress, which will follow hard on their [i.e. the despots' and priests'] heels. For this progress is a natural law, which no human force, neither

---

[5] Robert J. Richards has recently argued that we have reason to correct our understanding and to bring it more in line with Haeckel's interpretation. See his *The Meaning of Evolution* (Chicago, IL: University of Chicago Press, 1992), pp. 84–90.

[6] See Ernst Haeckel, *Gemeinverständliche Vorträge und Abhandlungen aus dem Gebiet der Entwicklungslehre*, Zweite Auflage (Bonn: Emil Strauß, 1902), I, 1–34. On Haeckel, see above all Robert J. Richards, *The Tragic Sense of Life: Ernst Haeckel and the Struggle over Evolutionary Thought* (Chicago, IL: University of Chicago Press, 2008).

the weapons of tyrants nor the curses of priests, can ever repress. Only through progressive movement is life and development possible. Even standing still is a retreat and every retreat carries the germ of death in itself. The future belongs only to progress![7]

There were also, of course, intellectual factors behind the triumph of Darwinism. Darwin's seed fell on fertile and well-prepared soil in Germany. In the 1840s the "bio-physics programme" of Helmholtz, Theodor Schwann (1810–1882), Ernst Brücke (1819–1892) and Emil Du Bois-Reymond (1818–1896), had advanced the cause of a purely mechanical explanation of life. And in the 1850s the rise of German materi-alism had gone a radical step futher in maintaining that all life and consciousness consists in nothing more than matter in motion. Vogt, Büchner and Moleschott had been especially active and successful in promulgating and popularizing the mate-rialist cause. Indeed, in 1851 Vogt had published a translation of Robert Chambers *Vestiges of Creation*,[8] an amateurish harbinger of Darwin's theory, which had appeared in Britian in 1844.[9] The biophysicists and materialists were, on the whole, extremely receptive of Darwin's theory, which seemed to provide strong empirical support for their views.[10] Even though Darwin himself was reluctant to express mate-rialist views, the German materialists were not so hesitant in enlisting him for their cause. Soon enough, Darwinism and materialism became closely associated among the German public. Darwin would never create scandal and shock in Germany as he had in England, because the materialists had already prepared the public for him. As Frederick Gregory puts it: "Once Germans had been told that man's mind could be compared to urine, it came as no shock that man was now supposedly related to apes."[11]

With these political and intellectual factors in its favour, Darwinism spread rapidly in Germany. Within weeks of the publication of *On the Origin of Species* in Britian in 1859, Heinrich Georg Bronn (1800–1862), professor of zoology at Heidelberg, offered to translate it into German.[12] His translation appeared in 1860, and then was reprinted in 1862. At first, the reception of Darwin was rather slow and cautious, leading Huxley

[7] Haeckel, *Vorträge und Abhandlungen*, I, 29–30.

[8] Robert Chambers, *Natürliche Geschichte der Schöpfung des Weltalls* (Braunschweig: Vieweg, 1851), trans. Karl Vogt; a second edition appeared in 1858.

[9] Chambers, *Vestiges of the Natural History of Creation* (London: Churchill, 1844). The work, which went through many editions, originally appeared anonymously.

[10] On the materialists' reception of Darwin, see Frederick Gregory, *Scientific Materialism in Nineteenth Century Germany* (Dordrecht: Reidel, 1977), pp. 175–188.

[11] Gregory, *Scientific Materialism*, p. 175.

[12] See Charles Darwin, *Über die Entstehung der Arten im Thier und Pflanzenreich durch natür-liche Züchtung* (Stuttgart: Schweizerbart, 1860). Bronn added a critical appendix, 'Schlusswort des Übersetzers', pp. 495–520, which was widely read and important for the early reception of Darwin. On Bronn, see Richards, *Tragic Sense of Life*, pp. 474–478, and Nyhart, *Biology Takes Form*, pp. 110–117. Because Darwin disliked the appendix, and because many saw it as interfering with the reader's own judgement, a new translation was undertaken by Viktor Carus, *Über die Entstehung der Arten im Thier und Pflanzenreich durch natürliche Züchtung* (Stuttgart: Koch, 1872). All references to Darwin's work in this chapter will be to the first edition, *On the Origin of Species* (London: John Murray, 1859).

to remark "Germany needs time to consider".[13] The real breakthrough for Darwin came with Haeckel's 1863 lecture. Speaking with all the zeal of a new convert, Haeckel inspired the public, sweeping it along with his enthusiasm. The *Stettinger Zeitung* for September 20, 1863 noted its effect on the assembly, stating how Haeckel "captivated the audience" and how "a huge applause followed this exciting lecture".[14] But Haeckel was only the first of many talented and spirited spokesmen for Darwin. In the 1860s Alfred Brehm, Carl Vogt, E.A. Rossmüller, Fritz Müller, Wilhelm Preyer, Friedrich Ratzel and Ludwig Büchner all rallied to advance Darwin's cause. Such was the swift ascent of Darwin that, by the late 1860s, he dominated discussion in the life sciences. Writing in 1875, Friedrich Albert Lange stated in the second edition of his *Geschichte des Materialismus* that the dispute over materialism had now morphed into a dispute over Darwin.[15] The old German materialists faded into the background, Lange said, so that a new edition of Büchner's *Kraft und Stoff* no longer created an outcry, and so that old Moleschott was nearly forgotten. Now all attention was focused on Darwin, and one had to be either for or against him.

It has been estimated that, already by the middle of the 1870s, Darwinism had triumphed in Germany.[16] The Darwinians were growing in numbers and influence— Haeckel and Carl Gegenbaur were now professors in Jena—and they had control over major journals, such as *Ausland* and *Kosmos*. The ranks of the anti-Darwinians, who belonged to an older generation, were dwindling in number and energies. Only Adolf Bastian, Albert Wigand and Rudolf Virchow mounted a rear guard action on behalf of the weakening anti-Darwinian cause.[17] Commenting on the rapid rise of Darwin in 1875, Otto Liebmann reckoned that, apart from religious bigots and a few crackpots like himself, almost all intelligent opinion in Germany was now on the side of Darwin.[18] "Sir Charles", as he now needed to be called, had so grown in prestige that he received institutional recognition: in 1867 he was made a knight of the Prussian order *Pour la Mérite*, and in 1878 he was elected to the Berlin *Akademie der Wissenschaften*.[19]

It is a remarkable fact that the rise of Darwinism coincides with that of neo-Kantianism in Germany. Both movements came into their own in the 1860s, and both became dominant forces in the 1870s and 1880s. The relationship between these movements very much depends on whether Darwinism was associated with materialism. Some neo-Kantians wanted to make a sharp distinction between Darwin's theory of natural selection and materialism: while his theory was founded

[13] Weindling, 'Darwinism in Germany', p. 686.
[14] As cited in Richards, *The Tragic Sense of Life*, p. 100.
[15] Friedrich Albert Lange, *Geschichte des Materialismus*, 2nd edn. (Iserlohn: Baedeker, 1873–1876), II, 240.
[16] Kelly, *Descent of Darwin*, p. 21.   [17] Kelly, *Descent of Darwin*, p. 21.
[18] Otto Liebmann, 'Platonismus und Darwinismus', in *Zur Analysis der Wirklichkeit*, 3rd edn. (Straßburg: Trübner, 1900), pp. 318–319.
[19] Kelly, *The Descent of Darwin*, p. 21.

on observation and experiment, materialism was a more general philosophical worldview that drew unfounded conclusions from it. If Darwinism meant simply the theory of natural selection, then the neo-Kantians were happy to endorse it. They encouraged the naturalism and mechanism of Darwin's theory, which they saw as a crucial step forward in the progress of the sciences. If, however, Darwinism was associated with materialism, and especially with the doctrines of Ernst Haeckel, the neo-Kantians were ready to fight it tooth and nail. They saw Haeckel as a disguised materialist, who needed to be exposed and refuted.

There was no party line in the neo-Kantian response to Darwinism. The three neo-Kantians of the 1860 generation who were most active in responding to Darwinism—Friedrich Albert Lange, Jürgen Bona Meyer and Otto Liebmann— had very different reactions to it. While Lange was completely enthusiastic, Meyer was totally sceptical, and Liebmann was lukewarm, ready to meet it only halfway. While Lange and Meyer were happy to see the end of the Aristotelian tradition, Liebmann was bent on preserving it and tried to combine it with Darwinism. Though very diverse, these reactions to Darwin are still describable as "Kantian" insofar as each emphasizes different aspects of the Kantian legacy. Lange represented Kant's naturalism and mechanism, Meyer his scepticism, and Liebmann his dualism.

It is only at the end of the century that the relationship between neo-Kantianism and Darwinism began to sour. The publication and popularity of Ernst Haeckel's *Die Welträtsel* in 1899 alarmed the neo-Kantians. Here was a very successful book which was, its author's disclaimers nothwithstanding, essentially materialist, and which claimed to be based upon Darwin's theory. For some neo-Kantians, Haeckel represented a resurrected materialism with a Darwinian face. Two later neo-Kantians, Friedrich Paulsen and Erich Adickes, were moved to write polemics against him. It is with Paulsen's and Adickes' polemics that another side of the Kantian legacy comes especially to the fore: its anti-materialism.

The rise of Darwinism, its remarkable success as a scientific hypothesis about the origin of species, raised a very important question for neo-Kantianism: Can biology be a science? Kant's own negative verdict on this question seemed to be antiquated by Darwin's success. Kant had denied that speculation about the origin of species could remain within the limits of experience; and biology hardly fit his own mathematical paradigm of science. The great challenge to neo-Kantianism in the second half of the 19th century would be in responding to the rise of the new sciences. Somehow, it would have to reconceive its paradigm of science to match the *de facto* progress of the sciences. Not to do so would be to relegate Kant's philosophy to an older scientific age and to undermine its credibility as a 19th-century philosophy. We shall see in this chapter how neo-Kantians responded to this challenge with regard to biology.

Our task now is to examine the neo-Kantian response to Darwin's theory, first in the 1870s in the work of Lange, Meyer and Liebmann, and then in the early 1900s in the polemics of Adickes and Paulsen against Haeckel.

2. Lange, the Naturalist

The first neo-Kantian to discuss Darwin at length and in detail was Friedrich Albert Lange. He wrote about Darwin in the first edition of his *Die Arbeiterfrage*, which appeared in 1865;[20] and he did so again in the first edition of his *Geschichte des Materialismus*, which was published in 1866.[21] In the second volume of the second edition of his *Geschichte*, which appeared in 1875, he added much new material about Darwin, so that the original twelve-page discussion evolved into a forty-four page chapter devoted to the topic of 'Darwinismus und Teleologie'.[22] In some retrospective passages from the second edition, Lange noted that Darwinism was a novel theme when he had discussed it in the first edition (II, 240).[23] The battle lines had not yet formed; Darwin's friends had still not organized themselves; and his foes had not fully absorbed the meaning of his teaching. By the time of the second edition, however, Darwin dominated the field. All discussion in the life sciences centred around his work. The debate had so advanced that Lange felt it necessary to go into much more detail if he were to say anything worthwhile.

Of all the neo-Kantians to treat Darwin, Lange was by far the most sympathetic. All his materialist leanings, which are usually implicit in his *Geschichte des Materialismus*,[24] become fully explicit in the case of Darwin. For Lange, Darwin was nothing less than the Empedocles of the modern world,[25] the greatest contemporary spokesman for scientific naturalism. Lange saw the theory of natural selection as the triumph of that naturalism, because it finally demonstrated that naturalism could explain the organic world as well as the inorganic. While Liebmann would later object to Darwin's theory on philosophical grounds, and while Meyer would quarrel with it on empirical grounds, Lange endorsed it both philosophically and empirically. Philosophically, Darwin had taken a great stride forward in creating a naturalistic worldview that could satisfy heart and intellect (243). And, empirically, his theory pulled off that rarest of feats: it was a unified explanation of the world not falsified by any facts (243). While Lange realized that many parts of Darwin's theory were hypothetical, he was fully confident that, with more research, confirmation was forthcoming.

Darwin's influence on Lange first appears in his political theory. In his *Die Arbeiterfrage*, a classical text of early German socialism, Lange gives a central role to

---

[20] Friedrich Albert Lange, *Die Arbeiterfrage in ihrer Bedeutung für Gegenwart und Zukunft* (Duisburg: Falk & Volmer, 1865), pp. 7–55. The first chapter, which contains long citations of Darwin's *Origin*, is entitled 'Der Kampf um das Dasein'.

[21] Friedrich Albert Lange, *Geschichte des Materialismus und Kritik seiner Bedeutung in der Gegenwart* (Iserlohn: J. Baedeker, 1866), pp. 398–409.

[22] Friedrich Albert Lange, *Geschichte des Materialismus und Kritik seiner Bedeutung in der Gegenwart*, Zweite Auflage (Iserlohn, J. Baedeker, 1875), pp. 240–284. Lange kept the original discussion from the 1866 edition, which appears on pp. 241–253.

[23] All references to Lange, *Geschichte des Materialismus* in parentheses are to the second edition.

[24] See Chapter 9, Section 4.   [25] Lange, *Geschichte des Materialismus* (2nd edn), I, 23.

the Darwinian theme of the struggle for existence. Lange takes this theme directly from Darwin's *Origin of Species*, "this epoch-making book", which he cites at length in his first chapter. Five years before Darwin's *Descent of Man*,[26] Lange maintains that this theme applies to human beings as much as it does to plants and animals. He sees the struggle for existence taking place chiefly in the market place of civil society (8). Just as in nature individuals of the same or different species struggle against one another for their survival, so in civil society workers have to compete against one another to earn the means of their subsistence; and just as nature produces an abundance of seed to create a single plant, so there is an enormous supply of workers where only a lucky few get a living wage. Natural selection and the struggle for existence mean that the strong will rule over the weak not only in nature but also in society, so that there will always be an elite to dominate the masses (66). Lange even imagines that if the present class differences persist for millenia, they will create racial differences between workers and bourgeoisie (70). Unlike Haeckel, then, Lange does not think the Darwinian mechanisms lead to greater progress and perfection; rather, he argues the very opposite: they will result in oppression and misery. It is a grim picture of human social life that Lange portrays in *Die Arbeiterfrage*, one so dire that he does not even allow his reader the little consolation that Darwin provides at the close of Chapter 3 of *Origin of Species*.[27] Man knows the terrors of annihilation that await him, he feels oppressed by the unrelenting struggle for survival, and there is no assurance that the virtuous survive and multiply (12).

So far Lange might sound like an early social Darwinist, that is, someone who believes that society *should be* organized on the principles of natural selection, as if the elite few who win out in the struggle for existence have a right to their social position on the grounds of their natural superiority. But Lange's use of Darwin is motivated with the very opposite intention: to show the plight of the workers and the need for drastic social and political reform, whose purpose is to cancel the effects of natural selection. Unlike the social Darwinist, Lange regards neither natural selection nor the struggle for existence as an inescapable fate: mankind can and should struggle against these natural forces to correct or ameliorate their effects through institutional and political means. There are two conflicting forces at work in Lange's social and political universe: natural ones, which work towards inequality and domination through the struggle for existence; and spiritual or moral ones, which strive towards equality and freedom for all. History consists in the eternal battle between these forces. If these conflicting forces appear to reflect Kant's dualism between the realms of freedom and nature, it is necessary to recall that Lange had questioned that

---

[26]   Darwin, *The Descent of Man and Selection in Relation to Sex* (London: John Murray, 1871).

[27]   Darwin wrote at the close of Chapter 3 of *Origin of Species*: "When we reflect on this struggle, we may console ourselves with the full belief, that the war of nature is not incessant, that no fear is felt, that death is generally prompt, and that the vigorous, the healthy, and the happy survive and multiply." *Origin of Species*, p. 79.

dualism in his *Geschichte des Materialismus*, placing all moral acts in the phenomenal world.[28] One might well question, however, how Langean man escapes the struggle for existence, how he can cancel its effects, without that dualism. Arguably, in his social and political theory, Lange presupposes the very Kantian dualism that he brings into question.

In the hope of collaborating with Marx and Engels, Lange had sent them copies of *Die Arbeiterfrage* in March 1865. They took issue with the book, however, chiefly because of its Darwinian theme. In a long letter to Lange written March 29, 1865,[29] Engels explained that the problem of modern civil society— the gross inequality in wealth—had its source not in nature but in social and economic relations, in the system of private ownership of the means of production and in the resulting class conflict. Economic laws are not eternal laws of nature but the product of human beings, of their social and political relations at a specific moment in history. Engels implied that Lange was making the same mistake as the classical political theorists: the hypostasis of social and political relations, making a natural law out of what is the result of society and history. Taking note of this criticism in a later edition of his *Die Arbeiterfrage*,[30] Lange replied that there would not be class conflict in the first place if workers were not compelled to compete against one another and to sell themselves on the marketplace to earn the means of their subsistence. Competition and the need to subsist were basic natural facts behind social conflict. The power of a captain of industry over his workers was simply an expression of his dominant position in the struggle for existence.

Darwin was crucial for Lange's worldview as much as his political theory. The modern Empedocles seemed to vindicate Lange's steadfast naturalism, mechanism and nominalism, his long-standing opposition to the teleology and (conceptual) realism of the Platonic-Aristotelian tradition. Because Darwin had aroused so much opposition, Lange felt called upon to defend him, and duly did so in his *Geschichte des Materialismus*. Much of his chapter on Darwin is a critique of his many foes, "our new Aristotelians", as Lange calls them. Opposition to Darwin, Lange maintains, chiefly comes from those who still cling to the old teleological conception of the world. Their defence of this teleology rests on the premise that there are gaps in natural explanation which can be filled only with the idea of purpose (245). They understand creation in nature on analogy with human creation of an artefact: just as we would make a machine, so God produces an organism according to intelligent design. But this anthropocentric conception of teleology, Lange argues, has been completely defeated

[28] See Lange, *Geschichte des Materialismus*, II, 58, 60.
[29] See Engels to Lange, March 29, 1865, in *Friedrich Albert Lange: Über Politik und Philosophie, Briefe und Leitartikel 1862–1875*, ed. Georg Eckert (Duisburg: Braun Verlag, 1968), pp. 79–83.
[30] Friedrich Albert Lange, *Die Arbeiterfrage. Ihre Bedeutung für Gegenwart und Zukunft*. Vierte Auflage (Winthur: Bleuler, Hausheer & Cie, 1879), pp. 217, 225, 227, 234–235. Great changes were made in later editions of this work. It is possible that Lange made this reply by the second edition, though this has not been available to me.

by the theory of natural selection (245). Putting aside all Darwin's analogies between natural and domestic selection, Lange stresses one important implication of the theory of natural selection: that nature does *not* create life in the same manner as we create an artefact (246–247). To produce an artefact, we choose the simplest and most effective means to our ends; there is no room for chance because we work to produce exactly what we intend. To create an organism, however, nature appears to work by chance, adopting a blunderbuss approach, spewing forth millions of seeds for only a few of them to survive and germinate. If we measure the production of a plant by human standards, it seems as if nature works by "blind chance" or "dumb luck". If a seed finds fertile soil and germinates, that is the exception rather than the rule. What succeeds in nature is therefore "the lucky special case in an ocean of birth and death" (248). The old model of teleology is deeply misleading, Lange concludes, because it makes this exception into the rule, as if nature somehow followed a norm or plan.

Much of Lange's opposition to teleology was based on his assumption that teleology means an interruption of, or intervention in, the mechanical processes of nature (272). But attacking that concept of teleology seemed like charging against open doors. For who, in the mid-19th century, held that supernaturalist concept of teleology anymore? The conception of teleology advanced by Schelling and Hegel in the early 1800s, and then revived by Trendelenburg and Lotze in the 1840s, stressed that purposes work *through* mechanism, which is the necessary means for their fulfilment. Lange duly notes this conception of teleology, which he even calls "correct teleology". But he immediately restricts the force of this concession by invoking Kant's regulative doctrines. Although we constantly use the idea of purpose in the life sciences, it has no metaphysical validity, that is, we cannot assume that it is true of nature but we can only proceed in our enquiries as if it were so. Kant, Lange explains, has two conceptions of teleology, both of which are compatible with a naturalistic worldview (276–277). One is the *formal* conception of purposiveness, according to which we proceed in our enquiries as if nature formed a system according to genera and species; the other is the *objective* concept of organic unity, according to which we treat natural products as if they were the result of design. In neither case, Lange notes, are we justified in assuming that there really is some purpose in nature. Kant's teleological principles mean not that mechanical explanation comes to an end, as if at some point purposiveness takes over, but only that the process of mechanical explanation is an infinite task (277). For Lange, then, the idea of purposiveness would prove superfluous with the complete mechanical explanation of the world. While he approves of Kant's regulative doctrine, he thinks that Kant went astray in thinking teleology to be a *necessary* manner of thinking for the human mind (276). The more science progresses, Lange is confident, the more it will eliminate this old pre-scientific manner of thinking.

Another topic in Lange's defence of Darwin was the concept of species. Some discussion of this topic was inevitable, given that the doctrine of fixed and eternal species was a major source of resistance against Darwin. The doctrine was so entrenched that even materialists like Carl Vogt clung to it.[31] Lange, though, has little patience for opposition on this score. There is no more conspicuous example of superstition and prejudice in science, he declares, than the still prevalent belief in the concept of a fixed and eternal species (241–242). The reason this concept is so prevalent and deep-rooted, he explains, is because of its ancient origins: it goes back to the Aristotelian tradition, according to which universals exist in things (301, n.54). As a convinced nominalist, Lange claims that the belief in eternal and fixed species is wrong in principle: it rests on the classical malady of hypostasis, which can be cured with a little conceptual surgery.

Though hypostasis motivated all his animus against the old Aristotelian doctrine, Lange does not stress this theme in his chapter on Darwin. Instead, he makes two points about the fixed species doctrine, both intended to demonstrate its obsolescence and redundancy (253–254). First, it is the result of doing biology *without* a microscope and starting from the *higher* end of the living scale. If, however, we begin our biology *with* that instrument to examine the *lower* end of the scale, we are utterly overwhelmed with the profusion and complexity of life forms, which do not easily fall into the Linnaean classificatory scheme of genus and species. Second, Darwin's theory can explain the relative permanence and stability of species, so it can account for the appearance of fixity so insisted upon by Darwin's foes.[32] When creatures establish themselves and adapt to their environment, they can live and breed for milennia, as long as their environment remains the same. We can account for the concept of a species, then, without all the metaphysical afflatus of a concrete universal or the theological baggage of a supernatural creator.

Another enduring aspect of the Aristotelian legacy, which Lange believed he had to eradicate, was the idea of organic form. Even hearty mechanists like Virchow and Vogt could not bear to part from this idea, which they used to explain the essence of an individual (250–251). For Lange, however, this idea is just another relic of scholasticism. Crucial to the idea of organic form are two old Aristotelian assumptions: that the whole is prior to its parts; and that every part plays a necessary role in the whole. Lange finds both assumptions utterly obsolete. "Not much can be done with the old mystical idea of the dominance of the whole over its part", he confidently informs us (251). As a mechanist, Lange holds just the opposite view: that the part is prior to the whole, which is only the sum of all its parts. Modern research has defeated Aristotelian holism, he argues, because it shows that a cell can live without the whole organism, just as the heart of a frog continues to beat after its dissection (252). Nowadays one takes parts of one body and attaches them to another; and there are

---

[31] On Vogt's complex views about species, see Gregory, *Scientific Materialism*, pp. 175–178.

[32] Although it is not explicit, Lange seems to be responding here to Bronn's objection, set forth in the widely read appendix to his translation of *Origin of Species*, that variation would result in a chaos of intermediate forms, where there would not be distinct groups. See Bronn, 'Schlusswort des Übersetzers', pp. 503–505.

creatures at the lower end of the organic scale which come together by the fusion of independent cells. Wisely, though, Lange did not push his mechanist assumptions too far. He admitted that the old Aristotelian assumption is valid "for the most part" and limited himself to denying that it is not a necessary metaphysical truth (252).

As part of his polemic against organic form, Lange also targets the assumption that there is a *natural* or *real* unity to things. The assumption seems natural because a plant or animal forms a unit, a single whole, which appears self-sufficient and independent of other plants and animals. But for Lange this assumption too is a lingering remnant of Aristotelianism. We think that there is a natural unity because we assume that there is a universal, a genus or species, existing in things and holding them together. For Lange, however, the unity of a universal is only due to an act of the mind, and there is no reason to assume that it is really inherent in things. What we see as a unity is entirely relative, because there is nothing unnatural or false about regarding each part of an organism as a unity (251). We can see not only the whole plant but also its stem, leaves and bud as one. Furthermore, the idea of an independent life can be applied as much to the part as to the whole. Much of Lange's argument here seems indebted to the latest research, especially to Haeckel's work on tiny marine invertebrates, the radiolarians.[33] Haeckel observed how these creatures could both lead an independent life but also could fuse together to form a single organism. Whether the radiolarians were a unit or a part, Haeckel concluded, was simply a matter of convenience, depending on the perspective of the scientist.

In his radical nominalism, and in his insistence upon the merely conventional and relative aspects of classification, Lange is not an entirely faithful Darwinian. In the *Origin of Species* Darwin retreats from a radical nominalism which would make all classification simply a matter of convention or convenience.[34] According to Darwin, classification should be neither Aristotelian nor conventional but "geneological", reflecting the origin of a species through its line of descent from primitive ancestors. We will leave aside here, however, the question to what extent Lange was a faithful Darwinian. It was never his intention to be a Darwinian bulldog or bard. His chapter on Darwin in his *Geschichte des Materialismus* is devoted not only to a defence but also a revision of Darwin's theory. For all his admiration of the English Empedocles, Lange finds problems with the formulation of his theory, problems which make it vulnerable to objections. To avoid these objections, revision and qualification are necessary, he advises (272).

Darwin's major mistake, Lange believes, is in putting too much emphasis on natural selection, as if this were the only mechanism behind the evolution of new species.

---

[33] Ernst Haeckel, *Die Radiolaren (Rhizopoda Radiara). Eine Monographie.* (Berlin: Georg Reimer, 1862), 2 vols. Though Lange does not explicitly cite this book, he was well-read in Haeckel's work, which he cites often in the notes to this chapter. Lange refers specifically to Haeckel's theory of individuality from Haeckel's *Generelle Morphologie der Organismen* (Berlin: Reimer, 1866), I, 265ff.

[34] See Darwin, *Origin of Species*, p. 413.

In stressing this mechanism alone Darwin is guilty of characteristic "English extremism" (263). Natural selection alone cannot explain the origin of a new species, Lange argues, because it determines only which organisms are actual, which are going to survive; it does not determine, however, which are possible in the first place, which are among the pool of contenders in the struggle for existence (266). Lange also finds Darwin's theory problematic on the standard grounds that it provides no clear explanation for the source of variation. Darwin gets into trouble because he separates variation from change in environment, as if there were no connection between "changes in form" and "changes in the conditions for existence" (257). This makes it seem as if the production of useful variations were entirely a matter of chance, so that it is hard to understand the creation of useful characteristics and adaption to the environment.

To remove these apparent problems with Darwin's theory, Lange proposes postulating what he calls "a law of development" for each organism, a law that determines its characteristic structure and distinctive stages of growth (263). Such a proposal had been advanced by several leading zoologists and anatomists in Germany—by Bronn, Karl Ernst von Baer (1792–1876), Albert von Kölliker (1817–1905) and Carl Nägeli (1817–1891)—and it was a common theme of their reaction to Darwin.[35] Lange explicitly endorses their proposal. What exactly is meant by this law of development is unclear, however, and its meaning varies from one writer to another. For Lange, it means that an organism has the inherent striving to survive and to adapt to new circumstances, so that if its environment changes, it has within itself the "disposition to variation" which generates new characteristics more adaptable to its altered world (255–256). This seems to inject a note of Lamarckianism into Darwin's theory, according to which an organism will inherit new characteristics from its attempt to adapt to its environment. Sure enough, Lange reads Darwin in this Lamarckian manner, praising him for having proved the inheritance of acquired characteristics (266).

In postulating a characteristic "law of development" for each kind of organism, Lange seemed to be falling into the old pitfall of substantial forms. Indeed, had not Leibniz attempted to explain the Aristotelian concept of an entelechy in just this manner, in terms of the distinctive laws of growth of an organism? Lange protested, however, that his law of development is not intended to be something "mystical" or "supernatural", still less something purposive. Rather, it is nothing more than "the unique combination of laws, thought as a unity, which produces the appearance of development [of an organism]" (265). These laws are completely mechanical, and each kind of organism consists in a unique combination of them. To arrest any doubts that he had in mind something "mystical" or teleological, Lange explores a suggestion of Haeckel's to the effect that "the plan" behind the growth of an organism consists in nothing more than the special way in which its carbon molecules combine with one another. Haeckel noted how carbon is constitutive of all life, and how the laws of

---

[35] On the reaction to Darwin among these thinkers, see Nyhart, *Biology Takes Form*, pp. 105–142. Lange endorses the views of Kölliker and Nägeli, *Geschichte des Materialismus*, II, 262–263.

combination of carbon create its *complex* structure. Hence Lange proposes that the law of development consists in nothing more than "the law of substitution for carbon combinations" (266).

On one important point Lange distances himself from an "extreme Darwinism": the theory of "monophyletic descent", that is, the derivation of all organisms from one and the same primal being (270). This hypothesis had been put forward by Haeckel as the final conclusion for Darwin's theory of descent.[36] Lange thinks that the theory might be true; but he is cautious about it and the whole doctrine of recapitulation. "*The simple forms that all organisms pass through are not necessarily essentially alike*", he stresses in an italicized passage (270). We must be careful for mistaking a mere morphological affinity for a real identity, he warns, because we need to take into account the finer microscopic structures and chemical elements of these apparently similar forms; these structures and elements could be very different, despite their morphological likeness. The theory of monophyletic descent is extreme and implausible, Lange finds, because it assumes all differences between organic beings arise from natural selection alone, not having to take into account any difference in inner development. It is more plausible to assume polyphyletic descent, according to which the basic types of organisms derive from different original seeds; such a hypothesis at least accounts for the great variety of different forms (271).

Much more could and should be said about Lange's reaction to Darwinism. His chapter on the subject in the *Geschichte des Materialismus* is rich, complex and nuanced, going into detail about many issues, which we cannot do justice to here. Here we have provided only a superficial summary of the major themes.

3. Meyer, the Sceptic

Of all the neo-Kantian critics of Darwin, the most critical yet best-informed was Jürgen Bona Meyer. Having been trained in medicine, Meyer was well-qualified to discuss issues in anatomy, zoology and embryology; and he was well-studied in recent French and German biological literature. No less important, he was well-versed in the history of the life sciences. As a student of Trendelenburg, Meyer wrote his habilitation thesis on Aristotle's biological writings. Remarkably, though, none of Trendelenburg's neo-Aristotelianism animus against Darwin affected Meyer's own judgement. Though he regarded Aristotle as the "the father of organic natural science", he did not regard his thinking as a model for future biology.[37]

As soon as Darwin's work appeared, Meyer devoted careful attention to it. He was a close reader of the *Origin of Species* and *The Variation of Plants and Animals*. In 1866

---

[36] Lange cites Ernst Haeckel, *Natürliche Schöpfungsgeschichte*, Vierte Auflage (Berlin: Reimer, 1873), p. 373

[37] See Meyer, 'Die Rangordnung der organischen Wesen', in *Philosophische Zeitfragen, Populäre Aufsätze* (Bonn: Adolph Marcus, 1870), pp. 104–119, esp. 105–107.

he wrote a long review for the *Preussische Jahrbücher* of the German translation of the second edition of the *Origin of Species*.[38] A few years later, in his *Philosophische Zeitfragen*,[39] he devoted a substantial chapter, some sixty-five pages, to an exacting examination of Darwin's work.

Although Meyer was harshly critical of Darwin, he also greatly respected him. His critique begins with a tribute. There should be no question in anyone's mind, he declared, that Darwin's work, in its thoroughness, exactitude and erudition, has contributed greatly to the advancement of science (44). Whatever one thinks of his specific conclusions, Darwin made a major contribution in raising questions that until recently had been regarded as settled (72). More specifically, he had forced naturalists to reconsider the doctrine of the fixity of species, which had become a virtual dogma in the early decades of the 19th century. George Cuvier (1769–1832), the head of the *Académie des Sciences*, had reaffirmed that doctrine with renewed zeal and energy in his *Règne animal* (1817).[40] Because he had insisted on exact observations, because he had condemned the speculations of *Naturphilosophie*, and because he amassed so many facts in its favour, Cuvier's doctrine seemed to represent the standpoint of exact science (42). The transformationist theories of Lamarck and Geoffrey Saint-Hilaire, by contrast, seemed speculative fantasies because they lacked empirical data to vindicate them. Fortunately, Darwin's questions came at just the right time because, by mid-century, newly-discovered paleontological facts had discredited much of Cuvier's doctrine. After Darwin, no one could question that species change, Meyer wrote, and the only questions had become how they do so and to what extent they do so (54, 86).[41] Writing in 1863, Karl Vogt, a new convert to species change, summarized Cuvier's embarrassment: "It was only thirty years ago that Cuvier said that there are no ape fossils and that there cannot be any—and today we speak of ape fossils as if they were old friends."[42]

It was one of Darwin's central contributions, Meyer maintains, to have questioned whether sterility is the most reliable criterion of a species. The old doctrine of the fixity of species had rested upon the fact that the interbreeding of species leads to either no result or sterility in the offspring. Sterility seemed to be nature's way of marking

---

[38] See Jürgen Bona Meyer, 'Der Darwinismus', *Preussische Jahrbücher* 17 (1866), 272–302, 404–452. In 1866 Rudolf Suchsland drew this review to Darwin's attention, arguing that Meyer had misunderstood Darwin at one point because of the Bronn translation. See Suchsland to Darwin, April 2, 1866, in *The Correspondence of Charles Darwin*, ed. David Burkhardt *et al.* (Cambridge: Cambridge University Press, 2004), XVII, 111. Unfortunately, the enclosure containing the passage from the review is lost, so it is not clear how Suchsland thought that Meyer misunderstood Darwin.

[39] 'Die Entstehung der Arten. Der Darwinismus', in Jürgen Bona Meyer, *Philosophische Zeitfragen. Populäre Aufsätze* (Bonn: Adolph Marcus, 1870), pp. 39–103. This chapter is in large parts a revised version of the original article in the *Preussische Jahrbücher*. All references in parentheses are to this later version.

[40] George Cuvier, *La Régne animal distribué d'après son organisation* (Paris: Déterville, 1817), I, 20.

[41] Meyer cites the opinion of Mattheus Schleiden from his *Ueber den Materialismus der neueren deutschen Naturwissenschaft* (Leipzig: Engelmann, 1863), p. 10n.

[42] Carl Vogt, *Vorlesungen über den Menschen* (Gießen: Ricker, 1863), II, 269. The entire passage is cited by Meyer, pp. 48–49.

a definite boundary between creatures by forcing mating to take place within a species. While there could be fertile breeding between varieties *within* a species, there
could be none *between* species themselves. Darwin had cast doubt on this criterion
in *Origin of Species,* asserting that many different species could unite with ease,
whereas many similar ones could not cross at all.[43] Fertility and sterility were matters
of degree, and it was impossible to decide where fertility ended and sterility began.[44]
In any case, disputations about whether something is a species or variety Darwin
regarded as "so much beating of the air", partly because the terms are so ill defined,
and partly because naturalists would forever argue in a circle, reasoning that successful interbreeding creatures *ipso facto* belong to the same species. While Meyer
complains that Darwin cites insufficient evidence for the successful interbreeding of
species (50), he praises Darwin for rejecting the value of fertility as a general criterion
to distinguish species and varieties (72). On the whole, he thinks that Darwin was
right to lay aside scholastic disputes about what constitutes a species and to submit
the whole question about change of species to empirical investigation (50, 61).

Although Meyer thinks that Darwin was correct to question the fixity of species, he
does not himself take a stand on the issue whether one species evolves into another. In
keeping with his general scepticism,[45] he adopted a neutral or agnostic position, neither affirming nor denying evolution. There was simply insufficient evidence to come
to a decision on these matters, and so, like a good sceptic, he would cultivate his equa-
nimity. As a critical philosopher, Meyer insisted that naturalists strictly observe the
limits upon knowledge, and that they refrain from speculation beyond experience. In
his opinion, both Darwin and his opponents had transcended these limits, drawing
conclusions that went well beyond empirical verification. Alexander von Humboldt
and George Cuvier had maintained the fixity of species on the slender grounds that
there had been no change in many species since the time of the ancient Egyptians—a
much too narrow time frame for such a broad generalization (57). Although Darwin
cited evidence for the fluidity of species from a much wider time frame, all his evidence showed is that species had changed, not that one had grown out of another (56,
96–97). While Meyer stressed that there is nothing intrinsically wrong with hypotheses in the sciences, he demanded that one know the difference between hypothesis
and fact, speculation and science.

It was in just this regard that Meyer deemed Darwin a great sinner. His chief criticism of Darwin is that he blurs these boundary lines, putting forward speculation as
if it were science, hypothesis as if it were fact. This was a controversial point, given that
Darwin, a schooled and scrupulous methodologist, was confident that he had stayed
within the limits of experience, and that his results gave the *vera causa* of things.[46]

[43] Darwin, *Origin of Species*, p. 257.   [44] Darwin, *Origin of Species*, p. 248.
[45] See Chapter 8, Section 2.
[46] On Darwin's methodological guidelines, see C. Kenneth Waters, 'The Arguments in the *Origin of
Species*' and David L. Hull, 'Darwin's science and Victorian philosophy of science', in *The Cambridge*

It was indeed supposed to be the great merit of his work that it brought many issues within the realm of science that had hitherto escaped it. Meyer is well-aware of this alleged virtue of Darwin's work, and to some extent is ready to agree with it (72, 90); but, in the end of the day, for reasons we shall soon see, he thinks that Darwin infracts his own methodological guidelines.

Noting a notorious ambivalence in Darwin's theory, Meyer complains that Darwin has failed to explain, and even to develop a consistent position on, the sources of variation. Darwin had laid great weight upon the reproductive system and inheritance in explaining the origin of species, and he laid less emphasis on the environment because children of the same parents differ greatly though exposed to the same "natural conditions".[47] But Darwin hedged and vascillated on the question of the environment affecting variation, stating on several occasions that "natural conditions" could have a great effect on the reproductive system.[48] On opposite pages he stated both that heredity was "by far the predominant Power" in variation, but also that "the conditions of life, from their action on the reproductive system" are "of the highest importance in causing variability".[49] Darwin's hesitation on this important issue did not escape Meyer, who chastened him repeatedly for his obscurity on such a fundamental issue (61, 64, 66, 67–68). Of course, Darwin himself had stressed the great lack of knowledge surrounding the laws of heredity, frankly admitting in the first chapter of the *Origin of Species*: "The laws governing inheritance are quite unknown".[50] Although Meyer duly praises Darwin's modesty on this score, he still finds that Darwin, given such an admission, goes too far in his speculations.

On the whole question of the role of heredity versus environment, Meyer, like Lange, did not see that much of a difference between Darwin and Lamarck. He was surprised by the number of Lamarckian explanations in *Origin of Species,* where Darwin would often refer to the role of use and habit in the formation of a species. In his one attempt to reconcile the role of heredity versus environment, Meyer argues, Darwin comes very close to Lamarck, so much so that their positions become virtually indistinguishable. Darwin stated that while "natural conditions" have an *indirect* influence on variation, heredity has a *direct* influence, that is, the environment affects the reproductive system, which in turn leads to the variation.[51] But this was very much Lamarck's position too, Meyer contends, because Lamarck would never have questioned that the natural conditions and the acquired habits have anything more than an indirect influence on variation through the reproductive system (64). Ultimately, Meyer finds, the only difference between Darwin and Lamarck is one of emphasis,

Companion to Darwin, second edition, eds Jonathan Hodge and Gregory Radick (Cambridge: Cambridge University Press, 2009), 120–146, 173–196. According to Waters, the entire structure of the *Origin of Species* revolves around Herschel's theory of explanation.

[47] Darwin, *Origin of Species*, p. 10.   [48] Darwin, *Origin of Species*, pp. 8, 82, 133–134.
[49] Darwin, *Origin of Species*, pp. 42–43. Cf. p. 8.   [50] Darwin, *Origin of Species*, p. 13.
[51] Darwin, *Origin of Species*, pp. 133–134.

with Darwin stressing the role of the reproductive system and Lamarck the role of the environment (67).

Although Darwin laid great weight on the role of inheritance and the reproductive system, Meyer insisted that his idea of the struggle for existence commits him to giving no less importance to the environment. "This new name [struggle for existence] comprises what one would otherwise call dependence of the organism on climate, nourishment, life's dangers and opportunities." (66) What Meyer suggests here is a complete revision of Darwin's theory, according to which one source of variation would be the struggle for existence itself. Although Darwin had treated variation and the struggle for existence as independent variables, Meyer wants to connect them, proposing that the struggle for existence should be a major source of how natural conditions affect heredity. If Darwin does the opposite, separating variation from the struggle for existence, Meyer contends, then he exposes his theory to a grave difficulty. For it means that whether a variation leads to adaptation is entirely a matter of accident or luck (80). If variation is strictly a matter of the laws of heredity, there is no reason to assume that variation will lead to greater adaptation; it will be possible for it to result in less adaptation or for it to be simply indifferent. It is indeed often the case, Meyer points out, that nature reproduces bad and indifferent variations, and for it to do so for generations (78). Furthermore, there is no reason to think that animals inheriting useful variations will survive in the struggle for existence, because they can be struck down by all kinds of circumstances, viz., disease, famine, competition, new changes in the environment.

On the whole, Meyer finds it hard to understand on Darwin's premises how, without an enormous degree of luck, a new useful trait ever establishes itself in a species. That trait needs to be passed down and inherited by a future generation; but for that to happen a long list of conditions has to be fulfilled, viz., that the parent does not perish before it reproduces, that it mates with another parent having the same characteristics, that their offspring inherit the same traits, that the offspring survive, and so on (94).

All this goes to show, Meyer contends, that if we are to explain the origin of new species on Darwin's theory, then we must take his guiding metaphor of natural selection literally (74–75). Darwin had based his theory on the analogy between artificial and natural selection, arguing that just as human beings can alter species through selective breeding, so nature herself could do so, and even in a more potent way by affecting the internal characteristics of an organism, or what Darwin called "the whole machinery of life".[52] The very idea of natural selection suggests, however, that there is some intelligent agent or design ensuring that useful variations will be chosen and adapt to their environments. Of course, Darwin does not want us to take that metaphor literally, and he goes to pains to explain that the selecting agency in

---

[52] Darwin, *Origin of Species*, pp. 83–84.

nature is nothing more than the struggle for existence itself.[53] But Meyer counters that only a literal reading of the metaphor explains the crucial fact that Darwin wants to explain: that natural selection results in the origin of a new species. Only the assumption of an intelligent agent or design removes the excessive role of chance in Darwin's theory, which makes it unlikely that any useful variation is preserved and inherited. For Meyer, unlike Lange, teleology could not be so easily removed from the body of Darwin's theory.

The great vice of Darwin's theory, on Meyer's final reckoning, consists in its grand speculations, its bold theorizing, for which there is hardly a shred of evidence. While Darwin avows empirical science in principle, he falls far short of it in practice. This is especially apparent, Meyer maintains, when Darwin fails to provide sufficient evidence for his central thesis: that it is possible for one species to evolve into another. Most of his hard evidence for change in species comes from his account of the domestic breeding of pigeons, where we learn that the more than 150 varieties of pigeons have a common ancestor in the rock pigeon. Yet all Darwin's argument shows, Meyer declares, is that a pigeon is still a pigeon (71). All the effects of breeding are only different varieties of a single species. Darwin still has not demonstrated that there is a change of one species into another.

If Darwin has little evidence for an actual change in species, he has even less evidence, Meyer added, for his theory of descent, according to which all species have derived from a few primitive ancestors. While the geological record does show that there were once living on earth animals very different from those today, it does not demonstrate that they have grown out of one another, still less that we have grown out of them (56). Some naturalists think that Darwin's theory of descent explains the great affinities in embryological and morphological structure; but these affinities too are only that: similarities in structure and geneology; they do not demonstrate that one species has actually *evolved into* another (96, 97).

Meyer's model for the scientific treatment of the origin of species came from a very predictable source: Kant. The great sage of Königsberg was cited as the appropriate *medicina mentis* to be administered against the malady of speculation and excessive theorizing represented by Darwin. Meyer refers to, and cites at length, Kant's 1785 essay on race,[54] which had laid down severe limits on speculation about the origins of life. Kant had declared that the limits of natural explanation lie within possible experience, and that we transcend these limits as soon as we speculate about the origins of life itself. But Kant went even further, proscribing speculation about the origins of species themselves. Experience shows us evidence, he argued, only for how one creature came from a similar one; but to engage in speculation about how one species arose from another different one, well that was "an adventure of reason". Darwin

---

[53] Darwin, *Origin of Species*, pp. 467–468.
[54] Kant, 'Bestimmung des Begriffs einer Menschenrace', AA VIII, 89–106. This essay was first published in the *Berlinische Monatsschrift* VI (1785), 390–417.

engaged in just such an adventure in speculating about the origin of species, Meyer implied, for he had failed to find sufficient evidence for an actual transformation in species, and for all species deriving from a few basic forms. All Darwin's hypotheses about the origins of species exceed, Meyer wrote, "the standard of science" (92). Although hypotheses are perfectly permissable to explain facts, they cease to have value when there are no facts for them to explain; in Darwin's case there really are no facts; all that we have are *presumed* facts to justify the hypotheses.

In coming to his verdict against Darwin, Meyer denied that he was applying stricter standards than Darwin himself, and he stressed that he and the English naturalist shared the same scientific ideals (90). Darwin too believed that scientific theories have to be tested by observation and experiment, and he too stressed that the problem of the origin of species has to be settled through these means. Meyer concedes that, to some extent, Darwin had succeeded in following his own guidelines. He had stayed within the limits of experience on several issues: in contesting fertility as a mark of a species, in showing that the degree of variability is much wider than assumed, and in consulting the geological record to support change of species. Still, he had gone well beyond experience in holding that species are transformable and that they are all derived from a few parent species.

Meyer's criticism had raised, however, questions of its own. It was one thing to criticize Darwin for going beyond the available evidence; it was quite another to criticize him for speculating about that for which there could be no evidence at all. In other words, it is necessary to distinguish scientific speculation from metaphysics. It is a serious weakness of Meyer's critique that he fails to make this distinction. This gave an opening for Darwin's defence. It was possible to respond to Meyer's criticisms: Darwin's speculations are scientific; though they lack sufficient evidence, it is still possible, at least in principle, to provide it; and further experiment and observation could perhaps even confirm them. Darwin knew all too well he was pushing the envelope when it came to his speculations about the origin of species; he was well aware that they went beyond the available evidence; still, he believed that more evidence would become available with further research. And had this not happened, even by Meyer's own reckoning? In any case, in the meantime, could his speculations not have value at least in providing direction for future enquiry?

It is a very tricky business setting the limits of knowledge. If we draw the boundaries too narrowly, we limit enquiry arbitrarily, which is dogmatism. If, however, we draw them too broadly, we admit metaphysics and its cousins, fantasy and enthusiasm. Meyer, it seems, had drawn the boundaries too tightly by forbidding even hypotheses or conjectures about the natural world. When he insisted that speculation has to be founded on already verified facts, he had virtually limited theory to what is already known. So scrupulous was Meyer that he had failed to see that a natural scientist does not play by the same rules as a philosophical sceptic. If Darwin had followed Meyer's sceptical guidelines, he would never have written the *Origin of Species*. That was the ultimate refutation of his entire sceptical approach.

4. Liebmann, the Matchmaker

The last neo-Kantian to discuss Darwin in some depth and at some length was Otto Liebmann. He wrote a long essay on the theme 'Platonismus und Darwinismus' for his *Zur Analysis der Wirklichkeit,* which first appeared in 1876,[55] and then several shorter essays on issues related to Darwin for his *Gedanken und Thatsachen,* which was published in 1899.[56] Liebmann occupies his own niche in the neo-Kantian response to Darwin. Unlike Lange and Meyer, he represents the old Aristotelian tradition, the very tradition that Darwin intended to overthrow. Yet Liebmann's aims were not counter-revolutionary; for his task was not to replace Darwinism with neo-Aristotelianism but to reconcile these warring parties, so that the English and Greek naturalists could live in harmony. This programme of reconciliation would be neo-Kantian in its own unique way, founded on the basis of Kant's dualism between the natural and normative, the phenomenal and noumenal.

When Liebmann first turned to Darwinism in the early 1870s, he felt himself to be swimming against the current. Darwin's theory was now so well-established in Germany that all discussions in the life sciences revolved around it. Liebmann wrote that "the great majority of the public", "unless it had some religious prejudices", had been converted to the new theory. He counted himself among the rare few who wanted to question it. While he did not want to contest Darwin's theory on empirical grounds, he did want to point out its limits on philosophical grounds. The crucial question for Liebmann was whether Darwin's theory could provide the basis for a materialist worldview. Were Büchner, Vogt and Haeckel right to see Darwin's theory as confirmation for their own materialist creed? Liebmann was sceptical of those materialists who had made Darwin's theory into their "philosophical gospel" (319). His critical objective was to limit Darwin's theory strictly to the empirical realm, undermining any attempts to draw broader metaphysical conclusions from it.

Liebmann's stance towards Darwin is almost the opposite of Meyer's. While Meyer measures Darwin's theory by the standards of empirical science and finds it wanting, Liebmann is concerned only with its metaphysical implications. Even if Darwin himself, forever the cautious scientist, was careful not to put forward metaphysical claims, his materialist apostles and acolytes in Germany were not so scrupulous; they saw Darwin's theory as evidence for their materialist worldview. It is these materialists, not Darwin himself, that are Liebmann's target. Unlike Meyer, then, Liebmann does not impugn the value of Darwin's theory as empirical science. He does not think that Darwin's theory sins against the standards of scientific method, and he even affirms that it is the best theory around about the origins of species. It was another

[55] Otto Liebmann, 'Platonismus und Darwinismus', in *Zur Analysis der Wirklichkeit* (Straßburg: J. Trübner, 1900), 3rd edition, pp. 317–361. All references in parentheses are to the third edition.
[56] Otto Liebmann, 'Idee und Entelechie', and 'Organische Natur und Teleologie', in *Gedanken und Thatsachen* (Straßburg: J. Trübner, 1899), I, 89–121, 230–275.

great contribution of Darwin, Liebmann adds, to have provided so much evidence for the theory of transformation (347). While Darwin did not invent that theory—it had been around for millennia—he succeeded in providing it with an exact formulation (347). At the very least, any impartial reader of Darwin's *Origin of Species* will find it highly illuminating (349). Indeed, it provides "the Ariadne's thread through the labyrinth of the organic realm". This does not mean, of course, that the theory is completely confirmed, that it is now incontestable doctrine. It is impossible to calculate the probability of Darwin's theory, Liebmann notes, because there is still insufficient evidence for it, and there is still so much research to do (350). Nevertheless, because there is so much evidence in its favour, and because it seems to explain so many facts, we have good reason to adopt it as a regulative principle to guide further empirical research.

Nowhere is the contrast between Liebmann and Meyer more extreme than in their use of Kant in the origin of species debate. While Meyer invokes Kant as a talisman to banish all speculation about the origin of species, Liebmann cites him as an example of just such speculation, indeed as a forerunner of Darwin himself. Liebmann cites a long passage from Kant's 1775 article 'Von den verschiedenen Racen der Menschen' to the effect that all species derive from a few prototypes.[57] "Indeed, a true programme for Darwinism!", he exclaims. If this were not enough, he then cites another passage from Kant's *Anthropologie* where Kant hypothesizes that human beings could have emerged from apes.[58] One is astonished to find, Liebmann exclaims, that Immanuel Kant, "the earnest idealist", is a forerunner of "the notorious ape theory" that got Carl Vogt into so much trouble.

To examine the metaphysical implications of Darwin's theory, Liebmann poses a single question: What is the relationship between Darwinism and Platonism? Are they compatible? Incompatible? Or complementary? By "Darwinism" and "Platonism" Liebmann means not the specific doctrines held by two historical individuals but two general worldviews (319). "Darwinism" stands for the attempt to explain life on mechanical principles, and more generally for the materialism of the Epicurean tradition. "Platonism" represents the attempt to explain life on idealist principles or on the basis of teleology. Behind these worldviews, on Liebmann's account, are two contrasting views about the reality of universals. While the Epicurean is nominalist, regarding universals as mere concepts in the mind, the Platonist is a "formalist", giving substantial reality to universals, whether above or beyond things. Liebmann uses the term "Platonism" in a broad sense, therefore, so that it includes any belief in the reality of universals. His own views commit him more to an Aristotelian than

---

[57] Immanuel Kant, 'Von den verschiedenen Racen der Menschen', AA II, 427–444. This article first appeared in an announcement for Kant's lectures on physical geography in the Summer Semester, 1775. *Von den verschiedenen Racen der Menschen zur Ankündigung der Vorlesungen der physischen Geographie im Sommerhalbenjahre 1775* (Königsberg: Hartung, 1775).

[58] See Immanuel Kant, *Anthropologie in pragmatischer Hinsicht* AA VII, 327–328n.

Platonic view about the reality of universals, because, as we shall soon see, his universals exist within animate things.

Liebmann's central contention in 'Platonismus und Darwinismus' is that these apparently clashing worldviews are ultimately reconcilable, that Platonism must begin where Darwinism leaves off, because each is necessary for a full explanation of life. Liebmann is in no doubt whatsoever about the value and importance of providing, as far as possible, a mechanical and material explanation of life. To understand life, we have to know how it works and in what it consists, which means knowing its mechanical causes and its chemical components. Liebmann is highly critical, therefore, of the old doctrine of a *"Lebenskraft"*, an *élan vital*, because it places vital forces outside and beyond the general laws of nature (337–338). The laws of physics, mechanics and chemistry are universal, and they should apply to organic as well as inorganic matter. It was one of Darwin's great merits, he recognizes, to have extended mechanical and material explanation beyond the traditional limits, and to have used them to account for the origin of species.

Nevertheless, despite his banishment of occult forces, Liebmann also believed that mechanical and material explanations have their limits. While they are indeed a *necessary* condition for the explanation of life, they are not a *sufficient* one. They can explain its mechanisms and material constituents; but they cannot explain its origins, how and why all these mechanisms and constituents came together to form a single living individual. The first causes of life, and its organic structure, remain inaccessible to mechanical and material explanation for the simple reason that such causes and such structures provide necessary conditions for any living phenomena. While natural science can explain any *particular* living phenomenon, it cannot account for why there are living phenomena in the first place (355). This is a metaphysical question which transcends the limits of all empirical science. In this respect Liebmann thinks that there is still some good sense to the old concept of a *Lebenskraft* after all. This concept serves to designate that aspect of life that is inexplicable according to mechanical and material explanation; it is that something more, that extra X, which mechanical and material explanation leave behind and fail to explain.

It was precisely with regard to this extra X, Liebmann contends, that Platonism enters the scene and goes beyond materialism and mechanism. This X is nothing less than the Platonic form, the universal inherent in a living thing that explains its constant structure and development. We need the idea of an organic form, Liebmann argues, to explain the difference between living and non-living things. For the organic, form is essential and necessary; for the inorganic, it is inessential and accidental (331). While the form of an organic thing grows out of it and is inherent in it, it is imposed upon an inorganic thing, which can take on a different form or structure. The form of an organic being stands for "all the characteristic, specific properties conceived together, such as habits, instincts, aptitudes, inclinations, degree of intelligence" (352). In stressing the idea of a substantial form as central to the concept of life, Liebmann went back immediately to the Leibnizian, and ultimately the Aristotelian, tradition, according to which the distinguishing feature of a living being is its characteristic form and energy (entelechy) to realize such a form (360). Liebmann saw no conflict between these traditions and Darwin's theory, chiefly because Darwin was not concerned with the metaphysical question of the distinction between the living and non-living. It was in raising that more general question that the old "Platonic" tradition showed its abiding value for the explanation of life.

Although Liebmann was eager to defend Platonic and Leibnizian metaphysics, he was careful not to grant a constitutive validity to its basic concepts. The idea of a substantial form, of an entelechy, remained for him, as a good Kantian, strictly regulative. They are ideas that have a subjective validity for us to help us make sense of life; but we have no reason to believe that they are objectively true. Metaphysics is, as Liebmann put it, "not a science but only a postulate and problem" (356). It is one thing simply to deny a problem, as the positivists did, but quite another to recognize it and admit the impossibility of answering it. Implicitly but unmistakably, Liebmann took issue with Lange's remark that metaphysics is only a poetic fiction, "*Begriffsdichtung*" (355–356). For Liebmann, teleology and organic form are more than poetry because they still have explanatory value, even if it is only regulative. Though Lange and Liebmann both stress the regulative status of teleology, they give a very different meaning to that status. Lange assumes that purposiveness will gradually and continually, though never completely, dissolve with the advance of mechanical explanations; for Liebmann, however, purposiveness is a completely irreducible and necessary concept, an indispensable device of the human understanding in coming to grips with organic phenomena.

Though bold and ingenious, Liebmann's reconciliation strategy has problems of its own. While Meyer assumes there is no distinction between science and metaphysics. Liebmann presupposes that there can be a rigid and absolute borderline between them. But is this possible? Does not a scientific theory like Darwin's have profound metaphysical implications? And is this not the reason why his theory is so important? Arguably, Liebmann never fully understood or appreciated the metaphysical implications of the Darwinian programme. It was a central thesis of Darwin's theory that varieties are "incipient species", that organic form grows and develops from natural selection and the struggle for existence. The net effect of such a theory is that the concept of a substantial form or entelechy is redundant for explaining life.

In going back to the Aristotelian and Leibnizian traditions, Liebmann was reinvoking the very tradition of fixed species that was Darwin's chief target. The Linnaean system, which Darwin had set out to vanquish, is profoundly Aristotelian, holding that a species is a concrete universal. In *Origin of Species* Darwin had explicitly taken issue with the Linnaean view that the species or genus is prior to living phenomena, not derivative from them.[59] The Linnaean system did not give the true causes of living

---

[59] Darwin, *Origin of Species*, p. 413.

phenomena precisely because it focused on formal or structural features, which are not basic but derivative. According to Darwin, a true system of classification has to be geneological, showing the common origins and parents of the various species; their formal or structural features would be the product or effect of the genetic potential of these parents in the struggle for existence. Thus Darwin had replaced an intellectualist or "formalist" worldview with a genetic or historical one. It was this fundamental fact that Liebmann failed to appreciate, and that ultimately doomed his well-intended but misconceived attempt to reconcile Darwinism and Platonism.

5. All Mysteries Solved!

In 1899 the weary and ageing Ernst Haeckel, now in his sixty-fifth year, published his last will and testament, *Die Welträthsel*.[60] He called himself a child of the 19th century, and he saw its close as a fitting time to end his life's work. *Die Welträthsel* was to be the final statement of his philosophy, the culmination of all his labours and reflections as a natural scientist.

Just as Haeckel wished, the book ended his career with a bang, giving him all the publicity and controversy that he could have ever wished. It sold 40,000 copies in its first year of publication, 400,000 by the time of the First World War. And, just as Haeckel expected, it aroused howls of protest and indignation. *Die Welträthsel* was one of the most aggressive statements ever of a scientific and naturalistic worldview. With all guns blazing, it charged the social, political and religious establishment, shooting down every dogma and sacred cow in sight. Now that Ernst Haeckel was leaving this world, he wanted to leave nothing of the old order standing behind him. The new world order of the 20th century had to be founded on a completely new scientific morality and religion.

Die Welträthsel was first and foremost an exposition of Haeckel's scientific worldview, which he called "monism". This is the doctrine that we would nowadays call "naturalism", that is, the thesis that everything in the universe is explicable (at least in principle) according to natural laws. The antithesis and enemy of monism Haeckel calls "dualism", that is, the doctrine that there are limits in principle to scientific explanation, limits set by life and the mind, which supposedly fall outside the sphere of nature and exist in a supernatural realm. Haeckel saw his monism as *the* philosophy of natural science, as the worldview confirmed by all the scientific developments of the 19th century, which could boast that it had achieved more in science than all centuries before it.

---

[60] Ernst Haeckel, *Die Welträthsel* (Bonn: Emil Strauß, 1899). All references in parentheses are to this edition. There is an old English translation of this work by Joseph McCabe, *The Riddle of the Universe* (New York: Harper & Brothers, 1900), though it is of questionable reliability. Even the translation of the title is misleading. Haeckel's title is pointedly in the plural, a reference to Emil Du Bois-Reymond's *Die Sieben Welträthsel*.

Such was Haeckel's confidence in the progress of science that he believed it could solve all the outstanding "mysteries" or "puzzles" of the universe. According to Emil Du Bois-Reymond, an erstwhile friend of Haeckel's and the president of the Academy of Sciences in Berlin, there are seven such puzzles: 1) the essence of matter or force; 2) the origin of motion; 3) the genesis of life; 4) the design of nature; 5) the origin of sensation; 6) the genesis of consciousess and language; and 7) free will.[61] Zealous and self-assured, Haeckel declared that natural science had already solved the first six of these, and that the seventh was not really a puzzle at all, because free will did not exist and could not be the object of scientific investigation (18–19). Seldom in the history of science has a major scientist expressed such extraordinary confidence.

But we have to place Haeckel's arrogance in context. It was his reaction to the treachery and timidty of old friends and colleagues. They had all renounced their faith in science, and they were now seeing irresolvable mysteries where they had once seen answerable questions. Although *Die Welträthsel* was meant to be a philosophy for the future, the worldview of the coming 20th century, its author knew all too well that it was really a rear guard action, the last stand of an old-fashioned naturalist who now felt himself to be alone in the world. Haeckel's book was written in self-vindication against his old friends and colleagues, who had once been proud naturalists themselves, but who had now renounced the errors of their mechanist ways and had become "dualists".[62] Rudolf Virchow (1821–1902), Karl Ernst Baer (1792–1876), Emil Du Bois-Reymond (1818–1896) and Wilhelm Wundt (1832–1920)—these were all old friends and colleagues of Haeckel, and they had conspired with him in their youth to create a world free of teleology and vital forces in embryology, physiology and psychology. But in their later years they had come to renounce their mechanical programme as unworkable. Haeckel saw them all as traitors to the scientific cause, which it was left for him alone to vindicate. Pointedly, Haeckel discusses all their cases as signal instances of premature despair and senility. Self-vindication appears in the very title of Haeckel's work, which was his counter to Emil Du Bois-Reymond's 'Die sieben Weltraethsel'. Du Bois-Reymond meant his enigmas to be limits to monism, warning signs to an overambitious naturalism. Haeckel wanted to expose them as hollow, arbitrary and artificial limits to the progress of the sciences.

Besides a statement of Haeckel's monism, *Die Welträthsel* was an attack on every aspect of dualism and the moral and religious interests behind it. Its chief target was "the three central dogmas of metaphysics", that is, the beliefs in the existence of God, freedom and immortality (267). All these beliefs are incompatible with monism,

---

[61] Emil Du Bois-Reymond, 'Die Sieben Weltraetsel. Nachtrag', *Monatsbericht der Koeniglich-Preussischen Akademie der Wissenschaften* (8 Juli 1880), 1045–1072. Reprinted in *Über die Grenzen des Naturerkennens. Die sieben Welträthsel, Zwei Vorträge* (Leipzig: Veit, 1882), pp. 83–110.

[62] Haeckel's reaction against his former allies and colleagues begins in his *Freie Wissenschaft und freie Lehre* (Stuttgart: E. Schweizerbart, 1878), which was a critique of Ernst Baer, Emil Du Bois-Reymond and his old teacher Rudolf Virchow.

Haeckel argued, because they presuppose the existence of some supernatural realm. All have been falsified by the advance of the sciences.

Science has shown that: 1) theism rests on anthropomorphism, the projection of human fantasies and wishes on reality; 2) freedom does not exist because everything happens of necessity according to natural laws; and 3) the soul is mortal because it depends on the brain and the body to exist. Monism is therefore atheistic, deterministic and "thanatistic" (Haeckel's term for the doctrine of the mortality of the soul). Haeckel had little objection to calling monism "pantheism", which he defined as the doctrine that God and the world are one and the same. Pantheism, he noted, had always been the worldview of modern science (333). But he pointedly reminded his readers of Schopenhauer's remark that pantheism was just a polite term for atheism (336).

Regarding the great conflict between science and religion, reason and faith, which had emerged from the materialism controversy, Haeckel took a firm stand on behalf of science and reason. There was no middle path where reason could justify faith. The more we take scientific investigation to its limits, he argued, the more we find not only that there is no evidence for the beliefs in the existence of God, freedom and immortality, but that the evidence actually goes against these beliefs, which can be shown to be simply false. Hence Haeckel is uncompromising that there can be no compromise: the old faith has to go, and it is high time for people to learn to live without the old gods. Faith, if it is incapable of scientific verification, is nothing more than superstition (348). While Haeckel readily conceded the moral and practical value of religious faith, he still insisted that such belief be based on reason. Rather than the church, there would now be "a palace of reason", which would preach no longer the old trinity of father, son and holy ghost but the new trinity of truth, goodness and beauty (388).

Not the least provocative side of *Die Welträthsel* was its attack on neo-Kantianism itself. Haeckel was highly critical of the limits that Kant had placed on the mechanical explanation of life. Little could Kant have foreseen that "the Newton of the blade of grass" would appear in Charles Darwin, who had now revealed that mechanism really could explain the origin of life (301). Kant's worst mistake, however, was his dualism, and especially his attempt to rescue the beliefs in God, freedom and immortality through practical reason (402). What Kant did not permit in the realm of theoretical reason—moral and religious faith—that he sneaked in through the back door of practical reason. For Haeckel, the distinction between theoretical and practical reason was just another dualism, a sneaky kind of dualism to preserve moral and religious faith. The faulty assumption behind Kant's attempt to rescue these beliefs, Haeckel argued, is that they are neither demonstrable nor refutable, that is that the evidence is neither for nor against them. But the advance of the sciences has unearthed mountains of evidence against these beliefs, and it has shown them to be simply false. In attempting to justify these beliefs in practical terms, the neo-Kantians have shown themselves to be out of touch with the sciences. The neo-Kantian movement, Haeckel claimed, was largely based on this failed strategy (403).

Since Haeckel found the respect for Kant among the neo-Kantians grossly exaggerated, he proceeded to demolish their idol in a long polemical footnote (453–455, n.11). Kant's lack of training in the medical sciences, his lack of experience with women, his failure to travel beyond the outskirts of Königsberg, all these showed the limits of his mental horizons. Was this the kind of philosopher who should be taken as the philosophical authority for the new century?

In advancing the cause of a scientific naturalism, and in insisting that the old dogmas had to go, Haeckel resembles nothing more than the old materialists of the 1850s. *Die Welträthsel* seems to be the latest materialist manifesto, a replacement for Büchner's *Kraft und Stoff,* which was now beginning to look dated after its 20th edition. It was not surprising that Haeckel's contemporaries saw his book in just this light. To the more elderly among them, *Die Welträthsel* was a nasty blast from the past, a throwback to the days of the materialism controversy. Yet it is important to see that Haeckel struggled to dissociate himself from the old materialists (23). After all, they knew nothing about Darwin, and the sciences had advanced mightily since their day. More importantly, Haeckel insisted that monism is not materialism. While materialism denies the existence of mind and dissolves the universe into a swirl of "dead atoms", monism affirms the existence of the mind and maintains that matter consists in living forces. Haeckel then went on to identify his monism with Spinoza's philosophy, according to which mind and body are distinct attributes of one and the same thing.

Yet the identification with Spinoza was something of a smokescreen, disguising the truly materialist dimension of *Die Welträthsel.* Haeckel had defended some defining materialist doctrines in his book, more specifically, the theory that the soul is nothing more than "a collective name for a sum of brain functions" (236). He thus undertook the classic materialist strategy of reducing the mental down to the physical. Such theories and strategies are hardly Spinozist, however. According to Spinoza's monism, the mental and physical are equal and independent attributes of a single infinite substance, so that neither attribute is more real or fundamental than the other. We can see the *whole* universe from an ideal or real, mental or physical perspective; but we must not "mix attributes", that is, make one reducible to another, given that both kinds of attributes are self-sufficient and independent.

There was, however, another kind of monism implicit in *Die Welträthsel,* a less materialist monism that came closer to vitalism, that is, the doctrine that everything in nature is alive and an expression or manifestation of life. For Haeckel, true to the vital materialist tradition, saw matter not as inert extension but as active living force, and he held that feeling and volition could be ascribed to the activity of all atoms.[63]

---

[63] See Haeckel, *Die Welträtsel*, pp. 206, 259.

Yet Haeckel did not develop this line of thinking, which would have brought him closer to Leibniz and the philosophy of identity of Schelling and Hegel. In the end, Haeckel never resolved the tension in his philosophy, which wavered between a complete materialism and a vitalistic monism. As we will now see, his neo-Kantian critics were relentless in pointing out this tension.

6. Restoring Mysteries

Given that Haeckel made a target of the neo-Kantians, it should not be surprising that they responded in kind. There were two major neo-Kantian polemics against *Die Welträthsel*, both published in 1901: Erich Adickes' *Kant contra Haeckel*; and Friedrich Paulsen's 'Ernst Haeckel als Philosoph', which appeared as part of his *Philosophia Militans*.[64] Both Adickes and Paulsen understood their polemics to be critiques of "natural scientific dogmatism", that is, the uncritical attempt to base metaphysics on natural science. This was to strike at the central nerve of Haeckel's philosophy, which claimed to be *the* philosophy of natural science. For the neo-Kantians, there is no such philosophy.

From a philosophical standpoint, Paulsen's polemic is a disappointment. It targets Haeckel's manner of thinking more than any of his ideas. The professed aim of his tract is to show that "Haeckel is not to be taken seriously as a philosopher" (125). Paulsen deplores Haeckel's tendentious reasoning, and his superficiality, ambivalence and confusion, which makes it difficult to ascribe any definite doctrine to him. He especially despises Haeckel's dogmatism, which makes him confident that he has completely solved problems which he has not really begun to investigate. Rather than examining the views of others in depth, Haeckel passes judgement on them without having really studied or understood them. Haeckel's worst sin, however, is that he does not fully recognize and appreciate the problems that he claims to solve (131).

While Haeckel is indeed guilty of all these sins, Paulsen's own polemic does not really take the discussion any further at all. So, arguably, it is Paulsen who does not take seriously the problems at stake. However sloppy and obnoxious Haeckel's reasoning, he still puts forward serious contentions to which any neo-Kantian worth his salt should respond. We want to know, for example, Paulsen's response to Haeckel's claim that Kant's distinction between theoretical and practical is untenable. Rather than tackling this important challenge, Paulsen spends his, and his reader's, time and energy showing that Haeckel was a poor Kant scholar. But would anyone have ever thought otherwise? Who would read Haeckel for his Kant scholarship?

At its close Paulsen confessed that he wrote his polemic in a fit of indignation. He was incensed that a public intellectual like Haeckel could be so dogmatic and arrogant

---

[64] Erich Adickes, *Kant contra Haeckel: Erkenntnistheorie gegen Naturwissenschaftlichen Dogmatismus* (Berlin: Reuther & Reichard, 1901); and Friedrich Paulsen, 'Ernst Haeckel als Philosoph', in *Philosophia Militans* (Berlin: Reuther & Reichard, 1901), pp. 119–192.

on such a flimsy basis. Sometime afterwards, however, Paulsen added a postscript, which examines Haeckel in a much cooler light and in a more generous spirit. He now gives credit to Haeckel for fighting for Darwinist ideas when they were new in Germany and when they were received with hostility and derision. This explains some of Haeckel's provocative style, which was simply responding to his enemies in kind. In this more reflective mood Paulsen also makes his one truly incisive comment about Haeckel's philosophy. He notes the deep tension in Haeckel's monism. On a superficial level, it is materialism pure and simple, a doctrine on par with Büchner's and Vogt's, though Haeckel lacked the courage to admit it. Yet, on another deeper level, it is not materialism at all but organicism or vitalism, that is, the thesis that the inner core of all reality is alive. This is the import of Haeckel's frequent statements that feeling and volition are inherent in all things, and that nothing is dead or inert. If the external nature of things consists in motion and extension, as the materialist insists, its internal nature consists in feeling and thought. This vitalistic monism put Haeckel in the tradition of Spinoza, Bruno and Goethe, and now and then he justifiably felt a solidarity with them. Had Haeckel followed through this tendency of his thinking, Paulsen argues, he would have come to conclusions like his great contemporary Theodor Fechner,[65] who saw all reality as alive. Yet Haeckel never developed this side of his thinking, and instead he lapsed back into his materialism by reducing life itself down to something material (190).

Adickes' polemic is very different from Paulsen's. Rather than just attacking Haeckel's intellectual style, Adickes focuses on the general issues and states his own position on them. *Kant contra Haeckel* is not simply a defence of Kant's philosophy against Haeckel's objections, and Adickes warns us that he does not accept everything in Kant (4). What he does take over from Kant is his critical epistemological standpoint, which he regards as fundamental for all modern philosophy. It is this standpoint that he will apply to assess Haeckel's metaphysics. Once one adopts that standpoint, Adickes argues, the verdict on Haeckel's book is clear: "Kantian criticism (or more generally: epistemological reflection) should have been the foundation for the whole work. But, of course, in that case, it would never have been written." (14) For Adickes, Haeckel's work was from start to finish nothing but dogmatic metaphysics—a new kind of dogmatism, of course, one that claimed to be based on natural science rather than pure reason, but a dogmatism all the same. Kant's old sentence, we are told, applies perfectly well to Haeckel: "The dogmatism of metaphysics, that is, the prejudice to make progress without a critique of pure reason, is the true source of all disbelief contrary to morality, which is always very dogmatic."[66] (114)

---

[65] Gustav Theodor Fechner (1801–1887) was the author of two books expounding a vitalist view of the universe, *Nanna: oder Über das Seelenleben der Pflanzen* (Hamburg: Voß, 1848) and *Zend-Avesta: oder Über die Dinge des Himmels und des Jenseits vom Standpunkt der Naturbetrachtung* (Hamburg: Voß, 1851). The former work maintains that plants have feelings and desires; the latter holds that even material things are animate.

[66] KrV B xxx. My translation follows Adickes' inexact citation.

No less than Paulsen, Adickes' reads Haeckel's book as a materialist manifesto. We can safely reject all of Haeckel's evasions, dementis and equivocations, he maintains, because Haeckel is perfectly clear in adopting the defining materialist doctrine that the mental is reducible to the physical. There are three ways in which one can reduce the mental to the material: 1) making thought and feeling properties of matter, which it manifests under specific circumstances; 2) identifying thought and feeling with movements and brain processes; and 3) deriving thought and feeling as effects of matter, which is their cause. It is a sure sign of Haeckels's materialism, but also evidence for his confusion, that he adopts all three of these reduction strategies (9–10, 21–23).

Given that Haeckel's philosophy is materialism, it is vulnerable to all the objections that have been made against that doctrine. Adickes finds it remarkable that Haeckel has learned so little from the materialism controversy of recent memory. All the weaknesses that Lange exposed in the materialism of Büchner, Vogt and Moleschott apply *mutatis mutandi* to Haeckel. The most important of these objections is that there is no evidence for the existence of matter in the materialist's sense, that is, an object that exists in space and time, having all the properties that we perceive it to have even when we are not perceiving it. All the evidence from physiology and psychology show how our cognitive processes condition and determine what we know, so that we cannot claim that the existence of matter is a simple given of our sense experience (35–39). Rather than saying reality in itself consists in matter, we should say the very opposite: *"everything physical is derived from the psychic, matter is a product of our mind, existing only as a state of consciousness"* (35; Adicke's stress). This proposition, Adickes reminds his readers, is the result of "epistemological idealism", which one now associates with Kant's name (36).

Though Adickes thinks that Haeckel is naive and dogmatic for ignoring the challenge of Kant's "epistemological idealism", he does not think this alone stands as the final refutation of Haeckel's metaphysics. While it is indeed fatal for Haeckel's materialism, that is not the only aspect or interpretation of Haeckel's philosophy. Adickes, like Paulsen, thinks that there is another secret vitalist or organicist side to Haeckel's philosophy. This vitalism becomes apparent whenever Haeckel claims that feeling and desire are inherent in all matter.[67]

For this vitalist thesis, Adickes argues, Haeckel can find no confirmation through observation or experiment; it is just as much an act of faith on his part as the Christian faith in God and immortality. But once we stress this vitalist side of Haeckel's philosophy, Adickes contends, we can make full sense of his professed Spinozism. For there are now two equal and independent sides to reality corresponding to Spinoza's two attributes. There is an inner side, in which each thing has feeling and desire; and there is an outer side, in which it appears as nothing more than movement and extension. This would be an acceptable version of Spinoza's dual attribute doctrine, because we

---

[67] See, for example, Haeckel, *Die Welträthsel*, pp. 182–183, 254, 259.

could see one and the same universal substance from either an internal or external perspective. Though Adickes' maintains that this doctrine is implicit in Haeckel's book, he regrets that Haeckel failed to develop it because of his attraction to materialism. For Adickes, like Paulsen, Haeckel's monism is a monster, a conflation of materialism with the vitalist philosophy of identity of Schelling and the *Naturphilosophen*. Haeckel is so far from refuting Kant's doctrine of practical faith, Adickes claims, that the old Kantian strategy of denying knowledge to make room for faith is as valid as ever (113). Had Kant lived through the materialism controversy, had he read Büchner's *Stoff und Kraft* and Haeckel's *Welträthsel*, he would have been astonished at how little people had listened to him. Kant would only have repeated what he said in the *Kritik der reinen Vernunft*: that beyond the world of our consciousness there is an empty space, and that whoever dared to leave the little island of experience for "the wide and stormy ocean of reality itself" could do so only on the little boat of faith (114). The existence of an unknowable thing-in-itself was for Adickes the inevitable result of Kant's transcendental idealism, and it provided a refuge for the entire realm of faith. Adickes denies that Haeckel has provided anything like a refutation of the beliefs in God, freedom and immortality. Because these beliefs are about the transcendent, they stand above and beyond refutation as well as demonstration, and so we are left with an agnosticism for the theoretical powers of reason. The realm of faith for Adickes is as broad as whatever cannot be demonstrated or refuted through reason or experience; it therefore includes all metaphysics, not least of all Haeckel's own metaphysics, which is as much a matter of faith as Christianity (88, 96–98). It is simply naive, Adickes argues, to think that these principles are the simple and straightforward result of experiment and observation, which never proves universality and necessity.

As much as Adickes defends Kant's doctrine of practical faith, he gives it an interpretation that hardly could be called Kantian. What we believe is for Adickes a matter of individual choice and feeling, and its justification is entirely personal and pragmatic: that I as an individual cannot get through life without it. There is no element of morality in Adickes' version of practical faith, no attempt to use the categorical imperative to justify the beliefs in God, freedom and immortality. The problem with Haeckel's rejection of practical faith is not that he ignored its moral dimension but that he failed to see how important faith is to individuals. Who was Haeckel to deprive people of their faith in immortality and God when it gave them comfort against the blows of fortune? (95) Haeckel's atheistic and materialistic worldview is no less an act of faith than Christian theism because it too goes beyond the limits of experience and therefore knowledge.

Adickes concludes his polemic with a brief account of why Haeckel's book has become so popular (115–129). He finds four reasons: 1) because people nowadays overestimate the powers of natural science; 2) because there is a philosophical need for a comprehensive worldview; 3) because of a trendy radicalism in all intellectual circles; and 4) because of an increasing anti-clericalism and anti-Christian tendency among intelligentsia. It was a plausible and exhaustive account of the reasons for Haeckel's success. But it leaves the reader wondering whether Haeckel, despite all Adickes' polemics, had won after all. From Adickes diagnosis of his success, it is easy to understand that the *Zeitgeist* was in Haeckel's favour. All these were indeed reasons why neo-Kantianism would prove less popular in the new century.

PART III

Introduction

The New Establishment

1. The Decade of Consolidation

If the 1860s mark the breakthrough of neo-Kantianism, the 1870s is its decade of consolidation. It was during the 1870s that neo-Kantianism began to emerge as the predominant philosophical movement in Germany. There are several telling facts, all carefully assembled by Klaus Christian Köhnke,[1] that attest this predominance. After 1862 the number of writings on Kant grew every year in geometric proportion, and the lecture courses on Kant in the 1870s (189) more than trebled from the 1860s (54). Indeed, more lectures were given on Kant than on all other modern philosophers. By the late 1870s there was also at least one neo-Kantian professor in ten major German-speaking universities, more than any other school or line of thought.[2] From the 1870s until 1900, Kant had become such a powerful presence in journals and lecture halls that Köhnke has referred to these years, with no exaggeration, as "the neo-Kantian period of German university philosophy".[3]

What accounts for the extraordinary success of the neo-Kantians? Naturally, political and social factors played an important role. Part of the reason lies with the more liberal political atmosphere of the 1870s. The *Maigesetze* of 1873 brought with them increasing separation of church and state, and the ensuing independence of academic life from church control gave academics greater freedom on the podium. Gone were the bad old days of the 1850s when even referring to David Friedrich Strauß, or

[1] See Klaus Christian Köhnke, *Entstehung und Aufstieg des Neukantianismus* (Frankfurt: Suhrkamp, 1986), pp. 314–317, 382–384.
[2] According to Köhnke, *Entstehung und Aufstieg*, p. 505, n.30, they were "Meyer (Bonn), Fischer (Heidelberg), Liebmann (Straßburg), Riehl (Graz), Windelband (Freiburg), Cohen (Marburg), Paulsen (Berlin), Volkelt (Jena), Erdmann (Kiel), Vaihinger (Straßburg)."
[3] Köhnke, *Entstehung und Aufstieg*, p. 385.

456

espousing pantheism, was enough to bring dismissal. What Fischer and Zeller went through in the 1840s and 1850s was now a thing of the past.

Another part of the reason rests with the growth of the German university system. Beginning with the *Reichsgründung* in 1871, there was a hiring spree in German universities, which Köhnke has referred to as a *"Berufungsboom"*.[4] There was a great demand for university teachers, partly as a result of the building of new universities, and partly as a result of the need to make up for the lack of hiring in the 1850s. These were years of opportunity for any talented young man intent on an academic career. While in the 1850s a candidate would have to wait, on average, fourteen years to become an ordinary professor, in the 1870s one would have to wait only eight years. Following this trend, from 1876 to 1878, Liebmann, Cohen, Riehl and Windelband all became ordinary professors.

Of course, these factors only go so far in explaining the rise of neo-Kantianism. They are reasons why *any* philosophical movement, or *any* academic discipline, would have flourished in the 1870s. The reasons for the success of neo-Kantianism specifically have to do with its intellectual or philosophical qualities in comparison with other intellectual movements of its day. The two selling points behind neo-Kantianism in the 1860s had lost none of their appeal in the 1870s.[5] Neo-Kantianism was not only a powerful bulwark against materialism but it also had the best account available about the role of philosophy in the modern scientific age. The thesis that philosophy should be first and foremost epistemology, the examination of the logic of the sciences, seemed to ensure the survival of philosophy. It not only gave philosophy a distinctive vocation, so that it could not be rendered obsolete by the sciences, but it also made it a valuable adjunct to the sciences. For these reasons, Windelband, Riehl and Paulsen will continue to advocate the conception of philosophy first worked out by Fischer, Zeller and Meyer in the 1860s.

Apart from these selling points, there was also the growing weakness of old adversaries. Hegelianism was a rapidly fading memory; and while Lotze and Trendelenburg struggled to preserve the idealist legacy, specifically its teleology and organic conception of nature, they were mainly fighting a rearguard action. Materialism too began to disappear as an intellectual movement by the 1870s. Lange tells us in the second edition of his *Geschichte des Materialismus* that discussion of Darwinism had completely overshadowed materialism.[6] There were still readers of Büchner's writings, but none of their latest editions roused the hue and cry they once did; Vogt was rarely mentioned, and Moleschott was almost completely forgotten. The old fearsome dragon of the 1850s now lay slain in a heap, presided over by two triumphant knights in shining armour (named Helmholtz and Lange).

But if the 1870s mark the establishment of neo-Kantianism, they also reveal flaws in its foundation and the first signs of its dissolution. There was an inherent tension

---

[4] Köhnke, *Entstehung und Aufstieg*, p. 310. [5] See Part II Introduction, Section 1.
[6] Lange, *Geschichte des Materialismus*, II, 240.

in the neo-Kantian conception of philosophy, which would become the source of controversy in the later 1870s and 1880s. That conception rested on two inconsistent ideals: the demand that philosophy be autonomous, a discipline in its own right; and the requirement that philosophy imitate the model of the natural sciences. The more philosophy imitated the sciences, the more it became like them, forfeiting its autonomy and hastening its obsolescence. This tension was especially evident in the case of psychology, which was meant to be the model of scientific epistemology; but the more psychology became scientific, the less it needed philosophy, which became superfluous. We have already seen this problem at work in the 1860s, but it became more apparent in the 1870s and 1880s.

Another greater challenge to the new orthodoxy concerned the tenability of the epistemological conception of philosophy. Though entrenched, salient and prevalent, this definition came under increasing stress during the late 1870s and thereafter. Granted that this definition was very strategic in helping philosophy overcome its crisis of obsolescence, nagging doubts remained that it was too narrow. If philosophy is simply epistemology in the strict intended sense, that is, the second-order examination of the logic of the sciences, then it has to forfeit its traditional role as a worldview, that is, an attempt to answer the most basic questions about the meaning and purpose of life. These questions had been placed at the centre of philosophy since antiquity, and were they to be simply ignored? Was it not the purpose of philosophy to answer them, to try to resolve "the riddle of existence"? That there was a price to ignoring them had been made clear by the great popularity of Schopenhauer and Hartmann in the 1870s. If the neo-Kantians were too strict and stern about limiting philosophy to epistemology, they were in danger of losing the interest of the public. Their philosophy would become esoteric, the preserve of a few trained specialists. But is not such esotericism a sign of irrelevance? And is not irrelevance the first step on the slippery slope to obsolescence?

2. A Fragile Alliance

One of the defining phenomena of neo-Kantianism in the 1870s was its close alliance with positivism. In the final quarter of the 19th century, positivism had become a force in German philosophy.[7] Among its leading exponents were Richard Avenarius (1843–1896), Ernst Laas (1837–1885), Ernst Mach (1838–1916) and Eugen Dühring (1833–1921). The mouthpiece for the new positivist movement was the *Vierteljahrschrift für wissenschaftliche Philosophie*,[8] which was edited by Avenarius, Karl Göring, Max Heinze

---

[7] On positivism in 19th-century Germany, see Gerhard Lehmann, *Geschichte der Philosophie*, Vol. IX *Die Philosophie des neuenzehnten Jahrhunderts* (Berlin: de Gruyter, 1953), pp. 114–126.

[8] *Vierteljahrschrift für wissenschaftliche Philosophie*, ed. R. Avenarius (Leipzig: Fues, 1877–1901), 24 vols. In 1902 the journal appeared under the new title *Vierteljahrschrift für wissenschaftliche Philosophie und Soziologie*, ed. Paul Barth (Leipzig: Riesland, 1902–1916). 15 vols.

and Wilhelm Wundt. The neo-Kantian alliance with the positivists, which was for the most part tacit and implicit, mainly took the form of their writing articles for the *Vierteljahrschrift*. Friedrich Paulsen, Hans Vaihinger, Otto Liebmann, Eduard Zeller and Wilhelm Windelband were among the contributors, and for a short while Alois Riehl even helped with its editing.

Prima facie the agenda of the *Vierteljahrschrift* was one the neo-Kantians would be happy to endorse. According to Avenarius's introductory article,[9] the journal would be devoted to "scientific philosophy", whose task is to investigate the logic of the sciences. Scientific philosophy would attempt to solve the traditional problems of philosophy, but only insofar as they were empirically refutable or verifiable. But many traditional problems were "pseudo-problems", Avenarius said using a redolent term, because they went beyond the limits of experience. Several themes of this agenda—hostility to metaphysics, experience as the limits of knowledge, philosophy as the logic of science—rang true to the Kantian conception of philosophy worked out in the 1860s.

Yet the alliance with the positivists was flawed, flimsy and fragile. It was more tactical than doctrinal. It served to keep at bay some of their common enemies: the protagonists of metaphysics (Lotze and Trendelenburg); the old reactionary forces of church and altar; and the new popular irrationalist forces (Schopenhauer and Hartmann). But this tactical alliance could work only by pretending to ignore fundamental philosophical differences. The neo-Kantians were highly critical of the positivist's extreme empiricism, their naive faith in given facts, and their belief in the complete autonomy of the sciences, as if they had no metaphysical presuppositions at all. These issues had begun to emerge in the late 1870s. In the first volume of his *Der philosophische Kriticismus*, which appeared in 1876, Riehl engaged in a tacit polemic against the positivists when he criticized the empiricism of Locke and Hume.[10] By 1878 they had become explicit when Carl Schaarschmidt declared positivism "false criticism" because of its naive and dogmatic empiricism.[11] And by the 1880s they had become explosive. We have already seen how, in 1884, Liebmann threw a bomb in the positivist camp with his *Die Klimax der Theorieen*.[12]

The most important issues dividing the neo-Kantians from the positivists were not, however, epistemological. They concerned the very identity of philosophy itself. In the late 1870s the neo-Kantians became more and more dissatisfied with the strictly epistemological definition of philosophy, which excluded enquiry about the

---

[9] Richard Avenarius, 'Zur Einführung', *Vierteljahrschrift für wissenschaftliche Philosophie* I (1877), 1–14.

[10] Alois Riehl, *Der philosophische Kriticismus* (Leipzig: Engelmann, 1876), I, 74, 84, 87. It is significant that Riehl regarded Hume as the father of positivism, so that his critique of Hume is intended to apply to positivism itself. Köhnke, *Entstehung und Aufstieg*, pp. 374–376, regards Riehl as a positivist and stresses his affinity with Dühring, and misses the implicit critique of positivism.

[11] Carl Schaarschmidt, 'Vom rechten und falschen Kriticismus', *Philosophische Monatshefte* 14 (1878), 1–12.

[12] See Chapter 7, Section 8.

meaning of life and ethical values. This dissatisfaction became apparent in several ways: in Volkelt's call for a renewal of Kant's ethics;[13] in Windelband's turn towards ethics;[14] in Riehl's recognition of, and increased interest in, practical philosophy;[15] and in the new agenda of the *Philosophische Monatsschrift*, which was now devoted to "the systematic knowledge of the highest and most general ideas, and thus the highest and most general goals of humanity."[16] The more neo-Kantians pushed against the narrow epistemological conception of philosophy and stressed the need for ethics and practical enquiry, the more they moved themselves outside the orbit of positivism. Of course, the positivists had their own ethics, which are empiricist in principle. But the neo-Kantians were even more dissatisfied with empiricism in ethics than in epistemology, because they were convinced that it leads down the slippery slope to relativism and nihilism. As Friedrich Paulsen summarized this common attitude: "Is it not a firm axiom that empiricism leads to materialism, and in the end to complete scepticism, which leads to moral nihilism?"[17]

According to Köhnke, there was one sudden dramatic event that took place in the late 1870s which precipitated the break between positivism and neo-Kantianism.[18] This was the assassination attempts on Kaiser Wilhelm I in May and June of 1878. These led to the anti-socialist hysteria of 1878, which was exploited by Bismarck, and which then led to anti-socialist legislation in the *Reichstag*. It was these events, Köhnke contends, that motivated the neo-Kantian concern with the practical, whose task was to create a new authoritarian ethics to keep the masses in control and to counter the dangers of democracy and socialism.

There are, however, serious problems with Köhnke's hypothesis. There is insufficient evidence about the political attitudes of the neo-Kantians in the 1870s. He generalizes from the cases of Meyer and Windelband, but, as we shall see,[19] it does not really apply to Windelband. But quite apart from this, the chief difficulty is that the neo-Kantian concern with the practical antedates the events of 1878. Rather than a response to the dangers of socialism, they were more a reaction to the alarming popularity of pessimistic doctrine in the 1860s and 1870s.[20] One of the reasons for

[13] See Johannes Volkelt, 'Wiedererweckung der kantischen Ethik', *Zeitschrift für Philosophie und philosophische Kritik*, 81 (1882), 37–48.
[14] Wilhelm Windelband, 'Vom Princip der Moral' (1883), *Präludien*, Neunte Auflage (Tübingen: Mohr, 1924) II, 161–194.
[15] See Chapter 14, Section 10.
[16] See Johannes Volkelt, Review of *Philosophische Monatshefte* 13 (1877), in *Jenaer Literaturzeitung* 5 (1878), 95–96.
[17] Friedrich Paulsen, 'Idealismus und Positivismus', *Im Neuen Reich* 10 (1880), 735–742, pp. 738–739.
[18] Köhnke, *Entstehung und Aufstieg*, pp. 404–433.   [19] See Chapter 13, Section 10.
[20] This is especially apparent from Johannes Volkelt's 'Wiedererweckung der kantischen Ethik', which Riehl cites as evidence for his own reading. This article was not a response to any political situation in the late 1870s, as Köhnke implies. Volkelt's call for a renewal of Kantian ethics grew out of his earlier encounter with pessimism and its decadent ethics. See his earlier articles 'Die Entwicklung des modernen Pessimismus', *Im neuen Reich* II (1872), 952–968, p. 967; and *Kant's Kategorischer Imperativ und der Gegenwart* (Vienna: Selbstverlag des Lesevereins der deutschen Studenten Wiens, 1875).

the popularity of Schopenhauer and Hartmann, as we have seen, was that they had directly addressed "the question of existence", the problems of the value and meaning of life. This problem had been ignored or neglected by neo-Kantians and positivists, who were recommending a more scholastic concern with the logic of the sciences. The neo-Kantian turn towards the practical, and the ensuing break with positivism, was more a response to the challenge of pessimism than the political events of the late 1870s. The motivation for this turn was mundane enough: if a philosophy does not appeal to the public and students, its books do not sell and its lecture halls do not fill; the income of *Dozenten*, and the reputation of professors, rested not least on book sales and full lecture halls.

3. From Psychology to Epistemology

The 1870s marks a sea change in the interpretation of Kant from the 1860s, and indeed from the entire neo-Kantian tradition hitherto. The three major neo-Kantians of the 1870s—Hermann Cohen, Alois Riehl and Wilhelm Windelband—reacted against the psychological interpretation of Kant, which had been first formulated by Fries in the 1790s and which had become virtual orthodoxy ever since. They all insisted *una voce* that the critical philosophy is primarily an epistemological enterprise whose main concern is with the validity rather than causes of synthetic a priori knowledge. The emphasis of Kant interpretation had shifted, therefore, away from the *quid facti?*—'What are the origins and causes of knowledge?'—to the *quid juris?*—'What makes judgements true and reasoning valid?' The psychological interpretation was now rejected as a misconception, a misinterpretation based on the mistaken assumption, flatly contrary to the texts, that Kant's main concern was to answer the *quid facti?* rather than the *quid juris?* This new orthodoxy declares that transcendental enquiry is *second-order*, concerned with our knowledge of the world rather than the world itself, while psychological enquiry is *first-order*, dealing with the world itself. After all, psychic events, like physical events, are still in the world; and there is a vast difference in logical type between talking about the world and talking about talk about the world.

What was the source of this change, this reversal in interpretation? We have already seen how, in the 1860s, cracks began to appear in the wall of the psychological interpretation.[21] Fischer and Liebmann had noted that Kant's transcendental philosophy could not be simply psychology, because its task was to investigate the possibility of *all* forms of empirical knowledge, of which psychology was just one form. If transcendental philosophy were only empirical psychology, then it would be circular, presupposing precisely that which it should investigate. It was only a matter of drawing the implications of these criticisms to see that transcendental philosophy could not

---

[21] See Introduction to Part II, Section 3.

be simply a matter of psychology, and that it was necessary to develop a new under-standing of its purpose and logical status. But such was the authority of the empirical sciences in this age that these implications were not drawn. These criticisms led to no open rebellion against the psychological interpretation, which was instead doomed to a slow and lingering death.

It also has to be emphasized that the break with the psychological interpretation was never clear, clean and dramatic. Cohen, Windelband and Riehl had been in their early years enthusiastic students of Herbart's psychology, and they had insisted that psychology too had a basic role to play in understanding the processes of cognition. It was no accident that they were contributors to Steinthal's and Lazarus's *Zeitschrift für Völkerpsychologie und Sprachwissenschaft*,[22] whose aim was to advance the psy-chological understanding of group interactions and culture. As much as Cohen and Windelband would stress the *sui generis* status of logical enquiry, they would also emphasize that logical rules regulate and refer to psychic events; and never would they forget Fries' old point about the distinction between the order of discovery and the order of justification. It was only later in the 1880s that Cohen, Windelband and Riehl dropped their interest in empirical psychology and would devote themselves to explaining the strictly logical or epistemological side of transcendental philosophy.

Much of the reason for the slow death of psychologism has to do with the ambigu-ous status of psychology itself. Some psychologists, namely, Fechner, Ernst and Eduard Weber, had understood their discipline as a straightforward natural science whose task was to determine, through observation and experiment, causal relation-ships between psychic or psycho-physical events. However, other psychologists, most notably Brentano and the young Dilthey, saw psychology as something more: as an attempt to investigate not only psychic events and their causes, but also psychic con-tents and their meanings. If psychology were understood in the latter sense, then its difference from epistemology was diminished, if not negligible. For were not the logic of these contents, these intentional objects, the essential subject matter of epistemol-ogy? The confusions engendered by this ambiguity are most visible in the case of the young Alois Riehl, who first defined philosophy in psychological terms as a science of consciousness, but who then turned around to insist that it was psychology in a new and different sense, the interpretation of psychic contents rather than causes.[23] He then went on to make a drastic distinction between philosophy and psychology understood as the attempt to determine the natural laws of psychic life.

These are all reasons for thinking that the change was gradual, but they still do not explain why it took place. But to give clear reasons for the change is no easy matter. Here the philosophical historian enters a murky realm, the dimly lit castle of the past where he or she is more likely to stumble than to see. The obscurity lies partly on the

---

[22] *Zeitschrift für Völkerpsychologie und Sprachwissenschaft*, eds Moritz Lazarus and Heymann Steinthal (Berlin: Dümmler, 1860–1890), 20 vols.
[23] See Chapter 14, Section 3.

individual level, with what particular thinkers thought in the late 1860s and early 1870s, and partly on the global level, with the philosophical and cultural *Zeitgeist* of the age. On neither level is there any clear vista, any hard and simple facts on which to build a solid case or even a likely story. Crucial for an understanding of this change was the thinking of the young Hermann Cohen in his happy and heady summer of 1870. It was during those inspired weeks that Cohen wrote the outlines of his *Kants Theorie der Erfahrung,* which laid down the basis for the new epistemological interpretation.[24] Yet what Cohen did and thought in that summer is poorly documented, and, given the destruction of his family archives, we are not likely to know more. What moved Windelband in the 1870s away from his originally syncretic approach to epistemology, which combined psychology with logic, to his more strictly logical approach, is also obscure. It is important, however, that we attempt, as best we can, to peer through the fog, for it was during the 1870s that Windelband developed one of his most important and influential concepts, a concept that has a redolent meaning in all contemporary philosophy: normativity.[25]

On the global level two factors deserve mention, though it is almost impossible to pinpoint and weigh their exact impact on the thinking of the neo-Kantians. One factor is the well-attested influence of Hermann Lotze on his age. In his 1874 *Logik,* but even before then in the third volume of his *Mikrokosmus* (1864), Lotze had made a clear distinction between matters of fact and validity.[26] It is one thing to determine whether something is a matter of fact, whether it exists or not in the world, but it is quite another to determine whether or not a proposition is true or reasoning is valid. A proposition could be true, or reasoning valid, even though they correspond to no matter of fact or anything existing in the world. This was the case for hypothetical propositions, counterfactual propositions, mathematical propositions, and even scientific generalizations. This realm of truth and validity, so different from the realm of fact and existence, Lotze called "the most wonderful thing in the world", and he hoped that philosophers would take it more into account. No vain hope, this. Lotze's distinction became part of the mainstream of German philosophy in the 1870s. Later generations fully recognized Lotze's role in changing the climate of thought.[27]

---

[24] See Chapter 12, Sections 2–6.   [25] See Chapter 13, Sections 7–9.

[26] On the distinction, see Hermann Lotze, *System der Philosophie: Erster Theil. Drei Bücher der Logik* (Leipzig: Hirzel, 1874), I, 465–497. See also *Mikrokosmos,* Vierte Auflage (Leipzig: Hirzel, 1888) Book VIII, Chapter 1, 'Die Wahrheit und das Wissen', III, 185–243.

[27] The neo-Kantians fully recognized Lotze's importance. Windelband had been the student of Lotze, to whom he paid full tribute as "the greatest thinker" of the post-idealist age. He praised Lotze for his distinction between being and value. See his article 'Die philosophischen Richtungen der Gegenwart', in *Große Denker,* ed. Ernst von Aster (Leipzig: Quelle & Meyer, 1911), II, 376. Erich Jaensch, a student of Riehl, tells us how Riehl enthusiastically endorsed his view that the decisive shift in 19th-century philosophy came with Lotze and his distinction between validity and existence. See his 'Zum Gedächtnis von Alois Riehl', *Kant-Studien* 30 (1925), i–xxxvi, pp. xix–xx. Also note the comment by Emil Lask: *"Lotzes Herausarbeitung der Geltungsphäre hat der philosophischen Forschung der Gegenwart den Weg vorgezeichnet."* See his *Logik der Philosophie und die Kategorienlehre,* in *Gesammelte Schriften* (Tübingen: Mohr, 1923), II, 15.

Psychologism, which seemed to conflate the realms of validity and matter of fact, had now become passé.

Another factor is the influence of Herbart. Although Herbart had jumped on the psychological bandwagon in the early 1800s, insisting that Kant's epistemology had to be refashioned as an empirical psychology, he had never ceased to distinguish between matters of logic and psychology.[28] He was always a good enough Kantian to insist that logic is a normative matter, about how we ought to think, and that it has nothing to do with psychology, how we as a matter of fact do think. It was an important, though too little appreciated or recognized, fact that Cohen, Windelband and Riehl had all been avid students of Herbart in their early days. They were as much Herbartians as they were Kantians. For them to make a sharp distinction between logic and psychology they only had to heed, and see the implications of, Herbart's teaching.

In the three chapters of Part III we will do our best to find our way through the castle of history, so dark and miasmic in its passageways, and so haunted with the ghosts of a glorious past. We will attempt to determine the sources of the revolution in neo-Kantian thinking by a detailed look at the philosophical development of Cohen, Windelband and Riehl. We will note the important effect that this revolution had on their conception of philosophy, and how they developed that conception in the course of their philosophical development.

---

[28] See Johann Friedrich Herbart, *Lehrbuch zur Einleitung in die Philosophie* (Königsberg: Unzer, 1813), §§34, 52 (*Sämtliche Werke*, IV, 67, 68, 78).

12

The Young Hermann Cohen

1. An Important Little Book

In 1871 the young Hermann Cohen, then only twenty-nine years old, published his *Kants Theorie der Erfahrung*.[1] Though now nearly forgotten, this little book was revolutionary in its day. It is indeed no exaggeration to say that it marks "a turning point in the history of the interpretation of Kant."[2] It laid down the foundation not only for the philosophy of the Marburg school but also for much of our contemporary understanding of Kant.

Why, more specifically, was Cohen's book so important? Part of its significance lay with its method of interpretation. In an age when Kant reception was very anachronistic, twisting Kantian texts to fit contemporary needs, Cohen strived for a proper historical understanding of Kant. A student of August Böckh and Adolf Trendelenburg, he applied the same philological and historical methods to Kant as his mentors had to classical texts. Thus in his preface he states that he intends to uncover "the historical Kant" and that he wants to interpret him in *his* own terms, contrary to the attempts of his contemporaries, who were bent on understanding Kant in *their* terms. And so, with all the love and care of a Talmudic scholar, Cohen read and re-read the Kantian texts, finding in their exact words depths and subtleties of meaning that Kant's critics had simply ignored.[3]

Another part of the significance of Cohen's book lay with his interpretation of Kant. Cohen emphasized aspects of the critical philosophy that had been much

---

[1] Hermann Cohen, *Kants Theorie der Erfahrung* (Berlin: Ferdinand Dümmler, 1871). This book has been reprinted as Volume 1.3 of *Hermann Cohen Werke*, ed. Helmut Holzhey (Hildesheim: Olms Verlag, 1987f).

[2] Andrea Poma, *The Critical Philosophy of Hermann Cohen* (Albany, NY: State University of New York, 1997), p. 6.

[3] Recently Klaus Christian Köhnke and Reinhardt Brandt have questioned Cohen's claim to provide an exact historical interpretation of Kantian texts. See Köhnke *Entstehung und Aufstieg des Neukantianismus* (Frankfurt: Suhrkamp, 1986), pp. 273–275; and Brandt, 'Hermeneutik und Seinslehre bei Hermann Cohen', in *Philosophisches Denken-Politisches Wirken: Hermann-Cohen-Kolloquium Marburg 1992*, eds Reinhardt Brandt and Franz Orlik (Hildesheim: Olms, 1993), pp. 37–54. Both Köhnke and Brandt interpret Cohen's early work as if it were the first formulation of his later thought, which was indeed much less historical in its approach to Kant's texts. But the early work did strive for a more accurate historical interpretation of Kant, and it must not be reduced to an anticipation of Cohen's later views. Cohen's reputation for careful scholarship, at least in his first work, deserves full restoration.

neglected in the neo-Kantian tradition, viz., the transcendental deduction of the concepts of understanding, the role of synthesis in constituting objects of experience, the place of empirical realism within transcendental idealism, and the principle behind Kant's "new method of thought". More important than all these particular points, though, was Cohen's general conception of Kant's aims and methods. He stressed the essentially *epistemological* purpose of Kant's enquiry. Kant's central question was not the *quid facti?*—"What are the causes of representations?"—but the *quid juris?*—"What is the justification of synthetic a priori judgements?" Cohen insisted upon the *transcendental* status of Kant's enquiry, drawing attention to how it is not *first-order*, about objects in the world, but *second-order*, about the conditions for *knowledge* of such objects. Accordingly, he understood the a priori neither in psychological terms, as innate ideas, nor in metaphysical terms, as Platonic archetypes, but in epistemological terms, as the general conditions for knowledge of experience. This was a sharp break with the neo-Kantian tradition since its inception with Fries. We have already seen how that tradition was essentially psychologistic, interpreting Kant's epistemology as a proto-psychology. Only at rare moments did Fischer and Liebmann question this interpretation, but then only to fall back into it. Though the young Cohen too was influenced by psychologism, he sharply distinguished it from epistemological questions. The psychological interpretations had pushed Kant's epistemological intent into the background; it was Cohen's great contribution to have pushed it again into the foreground.[4]

The great significance of Cohen's book for the Marburg school lay in its ideas about philosophical method. A crucial part of Kant's epistemological enterprise, Cohen taught, lay in his transcendental method. This method begins with the "fact of science", viz., Newtonian physics, and then determines the conditions of its possibility. It does not attempt to prove this fact from higher principles or to secure it against sceptical doubt; rather, it accepts it as a given and then determines its underlying conditions. Philosophy is thus the analysis of the logic of scientific enquiry rather than the foundationalist enterprise of demonstrating knowledge from first principles. In an article published in 1912, Paul Natorp stressed the importance of this method and conception of philosophy for the Marburg school.[5] Their germ lay forty years earlier in Cohen's little book.

Given its great historical importance, it is worthwhile to investigate the origins of Cohen's book. Such an investigation promises to shed some light on not only the genesis of Marburg neo-Kantianism but also on the profound turn in the neo-Kantian tradition, the turn away from psychology and towards epistemology proper. What led Cohen to his epistemological or transcendental interpretation of Kant? What

[4] This point was stressed long ago by Ernst Cassirer, 'Hermann Cohen und die Erneuerung der kantischen Philosophie', *Kant-Studien* 17 (1912), 252–273, esp. 254–255.

[5] Paul Natorp, 'Kant und die Marburger Schule', *Kant-Studien* 17 (1912), 193–221.

made him break with psychologism? *Prima facie* these seem to be sterile questions about the history of scholarship. But it is important to see that much more was at stake. The proper interpretation of Kant was for Cohen an issue of the greatest philosophical and cultural importance. For he saw Kant's philosophy, and specifically his interpretation of that philosophy, as the only solution to the cultural crises of his age. His neo-Kantian philosophy grew directly out of two major philosophical disputes of the mid-19th century: the materialism controversy and the Fischer–Trendelenburg debate. To understand his philosophy, we need to reconstruct how Cohen conceived it as a solution to the problems raised by these disputes.

There is another reason why we should re-examine Cohen's book. Although it has often been the subject of scholarly analysis, it has also been misinterpreted. All too often the book has been interpreted anachronistically, as if it were an anticipation of Cohen's later philosophy in his 1902 *Logik der reinen Erkenntnis*.[6] But Cohen's early work has to be understood in its own terms, not least because it is at odds in fundamental points with his later philosophy. Only when these points are fully taken into account will we have an accurate account of the origins of Marburg neo-Kantianism and Cohen's own philosophical development.

Our purpose here, then, is to reconstruct the genesis of Cohen's book, to restore its original purpose and meaning, removing the layers of anachronistic interpretation imposed upon it. This quickly proves to be a daunting undertaking. For there is a severe lack of documentation in trying to understand Cohen's intellectual development. Tragically, too many materials have been lost or destroyed.[7] As a result, we have a much more detailed knowledge of philosophers from the remote past than we do of Cohen. *Incredibile sed verum:* we can know much more about Leibniz than Cohen.

This is all the more a pity because, from the little we do know, Cohen's intellectual development is fascinating. The story is dramatic. For Cohen came into his own only by breaking with his three great teachers: Heymann Steinthal, Friedrich Lange and Adolf Trendelenburg. Though he revered them all, he also rebelled against them. If a teacher is somehow a father, as the German word *Doktorvater* has it, then Cohen came into his own only through a treble parricide.

The story is also mysterious. For when we go back to Cohen's early years we find that he was himself a staunch advocate of the very psychological approach to Kant that he would later repudiate. Indeed, Cohen championed this approach as late as 1870, the very year he wrote *Kants Theorie der Erfahrung*. Why did Cohen make such a *volte face*, and so suddenly?

---

[6] See the interpretations mentioned in note 3. See also Manfred Kühn, 'Interpreting Kant Correctly: On the Kant of the Neo-Kantians', in *Neo-Kantianism in Contemporary Philosophy*, eds Rudolf Makkreel and Sebastian Luft (Bloomington, IN: Indiana University Press, 2010), pp. 113–131, esp. 115–121.

[7] The Cohen family archives were destroyed in 1941 following the deportation of Cohen's widow, Martha Cohen neé Lewandowski, to Theresienstadt. The few surviving documents are in the *Hermann Cohen Archiv* in Zürich under the supervision of Helmut Holzhey.

2. The Young Volkpsychologist

Our story begins in May 1865 in Berlin. It was then and there that Cohen formed a friendship with Heymann Steinthal, who was a pioneer in the fledgling disciplines of linguistics and ethnology.[8] Along with his friend and brother-in-law, Moritz Lazarus, Steinthal had founded and edited a journal devoted to these new disciplines, the *Zeitschrift für Völkerpsychologie und Sprachwissenschaft*.[9] Seeing in Cohen a promising disciple, Steinthal decided to give the struggling young student the opportunity to prove himself by writing articles for his new journal. In commissioning articles Steinthal expected that Cohen would promote the intellectual cause behind the journal; and in this respect, he was not to be disappointed. The young Cohen soon became a champion of the new science of *Völkerpsychologie*.

Völkerpsychologie was the ancestor of modern anthropology or social psychology.[10] Its subject matter was the *Volksgeist*, the mind or spirit (*Geist*) of a nation or people (*Volk*).[11] Though it has vague and mystical connotations, Lazarus went to great pains to define the *Volksgeist* in clear and non-metaphysical terms as "what is common to the inner activity of all individuals of a nation".[12] The task of *Völkerpsychologie* was to examine how this *Volksgeist* appeared in, and affected the lives and psyches of, individuals. Its guiding assumption is that a community is an irreducible whole that affects the psychology of its individual members; in other words, we can fully understand the individual psyche only by seeing it within its historical and cultural context. While *Völkerpsychologie* has a Hegelian provenance and inspiration—it has an obvious debt to Hegel's category of objective spirit—both Lazarus and Steinthal insisted that the method of *Völkerpsychologie* should be utterly empirical and thoroughly mechanical.[13] They were indeed devotees of the psychology of Johann Friedrich Herbart, which was the dominant empirical psychology of their day. There are four salient characteristics of Herbart's psychology, most of which reappear in *Völkerpsychologie*: an emphasis on mechanical explanation; an insistence that the mind consists in processes rather than powers; the analysis of complex psychic

[8] On Cohen's early years as a collaborator with Steinthal, see Dieter Adelmann, 'H. Steinthal und Hermann Cohen', in *Hermann Cohen's Philosophy of Religion*, eds Stéphane Moses and Hartwig Wiedebach (Hildesheim: Olms, 1997), pp. 1–33; Ulrich Sieg, 'Hermann Cohen und die Völkerpsychologie', *Aschkenas* XIII (2004), 461–483; and Klaus Köhnke, '»Unser junger Freund« – Hermann Cohen und die Völkerpsychologie', in *Hermann Cohen und die Erkenntnistheorie*, eds Wolfgang Marx and Ernst Orth (Würzburg: Königshausen & Neumann, 2001), pp. 62–77.

[9] *Zeitschrift für Völkerpsychologie und Sprachwissenschaft* (Berlin: Dümmler, 1860–1890), 20 vols.

[10] For the influence of *Völkerpsychologie* on modern anthropology and social psychology, see Ivan Kalmar, 'The *Völkerpsychologie* of Lazarus and Steinthal and the Modern Concept of Culture', *Journal of the History of Ideas* 48 (1987), 671–690.

[11] Moritz Lazarus, 'Ueber den Begriff und die Möglichkeit einer Völkerpsychologie', *Deutsches Museum* I (1851), 112–126, pp. 112–113.

[12] Moritz Lazarus, 'Einleitende Gedanken über Völkerpsychologie', *Zeitschrift für Völkerpsychologie und Sprachwissenschaft* I (1860), 1–73, p. 35.

[13] See Moritz Lazarus, 'Einige synthetische Gedanken für Völkerpsychologie', *Zeitschrift für Völkerpsychologie und Sprachwissenschaft* III (1865), 1–94, esp. 85.

processes into more basic units, so that parts precede wholes; and the application of mathematics to explain the dynamics of mental events. It is noteworthy that, though Herbart advocated a mechanical and mathematical approach to the mind, he was no materialist himself, and he would often stress the *sui generis* status of the mental. Thus he found the concept of the soul indispensable in defining the subject matter of psychology.[14]

For better or worse, the young Cohen was very much a follower of this Herbartian psychology.[15] His devotion to Herbart's psychological programme appears in the first thesis of his doctoral promotion: "*Omnem philosophiae progressum in psychologia constitutum esse.*"[16] Two of his early articles for the *Zeitschrift für Völkerpsychologie* apply Herbart's psychology to the fields of religion and poetry.[17] Though he appropriates Kantian concepts—the a priori, the unity of apperception, form and content— Cohen interprets them in Herbartian or Steinthalian terms. His interpretation of these concepts is flatly at odds with Kant's transcendental psychology, the very psychology Cohen will defend in *Kants Theorie der Erfahrung*.

The contrast between Cohen's early and later psychology is striking, and in three specific respects. First, the early Cohen understands the a priori in terms of temporal rather than logical priority, that is, an a priori representation is prior in time to others, and it determines how the later or a posteriori ones appear to consciousness.[18] The later Cohen, however, will stress the importance of a strictly logical interpretation of the a priori, so that it is a necessary condition of knowledge of experience. Second, the early Cohen interprets the unity of apperception strictly in terms of a mechanism of association, so that earlier representations exert an attractive force on later ones, forming habits of association according to the degree that past sequences have been repeated in consciousness.[19] The later Cohen, by contrast, will interpret the unity of apperception in transcendental rather than mechanical terms, so that "the affinity of appearances", their universal and necessary form, is the precondition for their association. Third, the early Cohen accepts a distinction between the form and content

[14] See Johann Friedrich Herbart, *Psychologie als empirische Wissenschaft* §31, in *Sämtliche Werke*, eds Karl Kehrbach and Otto Flügel (Langensalza: Hermann Beyer & Söhne, 1887–1912), V, 253.

[15] See Cohen's review of Jürgen Bona Meyer's *Kants Psychologie, Zeitschrift für Völkerpsychologie und Sprachwissenschaft* VII (1871), 320–330, pp. 324, 328–329. For a more detailed account of Cohen's early psychology, see Winrich de Schmidt, *Psychologie und Transzendentalphilosophie: Zur Psychologie Rezeption bei Hermann Cohen und Paul Natorp* (Bonn: Bouvier, 1976), pp. 19–31.

[16] Hermann Cohen, *Schriften zur Philosophie und Zeitgeschichte*, eds Ernst Cassirer and Albert Görland (Berlin: Akademie Verlag, 1923), I, 29.

[17] See Cohen, 'Mythologische Vorstellungen von Gott und Seele, psychologisch entwickelt', *Zeitschrift für Völkerpsychologie und Sprachwissenschaft* V (1868), 396–434 and VI (1869), 113–131; and 'Die dichterische Phantasie und der Mechanismus des Bewusstseins', *Zeitschrift für Völkerpsychologie und Sprachwissenschaft* VI (1869), 171–263. This article also appeared independently, *Die dichterische Phantasie und der Mechanismus des Bewusstseins* (Berlin: Dümmler Verlag, 1869). All references to it will be to this independent publication.

[18] See Cohen, *Die dichterische Phantasie*, pp. 27–28.

[19] See Cohen, *Die dichterische Phantasie*, pp. 28–29; and Cohen, 'Mythologische Vorstellungen', pp. 406–407.

of representations that is entirely non-Kantian. According to this early distinction, the content is the intentional object, what we represent, while the form is the feeling or tone of consciousness in general, which consists in nerve movements.[20] If all these differences were not enough, there are passages in these early articles where Cohen adopts the language of Herbart's alleged realism, writing as if objects are simply given to us and our representations resemble them.[21] So in these passages we are very far from the transcendental idealism that Cohen will later advocate in *Kants Theorie der Erfahrung*.

The articles for the *Zeitschrift für Völkerpsychologie* that expound a Herbartian psychology were published between 1866 and 1869. It would seem, then, that Cohen had more than a year to grow out of these doctrines before writing *Kants Theorie der Erfahrung*, which appeared in 1871. But the truth of the matter is much more puzzling. For Cohen finished his Kant book in the autumn of 1870,[22] which would have given him much less time to reverse his thinking. Furthermore, some of his later articles for the *Zeitschrift*, which appeared in 1871, still advocate a psychological approach to the history of philosophy.[23] Recognizing the discrepancy between the early and later Cohen and the short time span between them, Klaus Christian Köhnke has postulated an abrupt "revolution" *(Umbruch)* in Cohen's thinking, one that took place in only one year.[24] But even allowing for generous lags in publication dates, the revolution must have been even more swift and sudden. It took place probably in a matter of months. In any case, it is safe to assume that Cohen had a very creative and inspired summer in 1870! For he wrote his book very quickly, in the course of a single summer.[25] But what happened in those heady months to reverse so drastically the course of his thinking?

Someone might object that we should not overproblematize or overdramatize, because the break in Cohen's thinking is not so sharp and clean.[26] It is not as if we suddenly have a psychological Cohen in the 1860s, and then an epistemological Cohen in 1870, who springs fully formed from a single inspiring summer. There are anticipations of the later Cohen in the early essays, and residues of the early Cohen in the later work. After all, it is not as if Cohen completely understood the full implications of his

[20] See Cohen, *Die dichterische Phantasie*, p. 53; and Cohen, 'Mythologische Vorstellungen', pp. 420–421. Kinkel's claim that Cohen already goes in a Kantian direction because of this distinction seems to me to come from a failure to examine its precise meaning. See Walter Kinkel, *Hermann Cohen: Eine Einführung in sein Werk* (Stuttgart: Strecker und Schröder, 1924), p. 44.

[21] See Cohen, *Die dichterische Phantasie*, pp. 29, 49.

[22] This is plain from Cohen's October 3, 1870 letter to Hermann Lewandowsky, *Briefe*, eds Bertha and Bruno Strauss (Berlin: Schocken, 1939), p. 28.

[23] See Cohen, Review of Jürgen Bona Meyer, *Kants Psychologie* and Cohen, 'Zur Kontroverse zwischen Trendelenburg und Kuno Fischer', *Zeitschrift für Völkerpsychologie und Sprachwissenschaft* VII (1871), 249–271, p. 292.

[24] Köhnke, *Entstehung und Aufstieg*, p. 282.

[25] See Cohen to Hermann Lewandowsky, August 2, 1870, *Briefe*, pp. 24–25.

[26] This point is made, perfectly correctly, by Ulrich Sieg, *Aufstieg und Niedergang des Marburger Neukantianismus* (Würzburg: Königshausen & Neumann, 1994), p. 110, n.225.

new epistemological approach in 1870, so that he abruptly changed course and repudi-ated Herbartian psychology. Rather, he gradually realized the results of his new thinking throughout the 1870s.

Though perfectly valid, these points do not make the problem go away. They should not be stretched to obscure the very real and very big differences between early and later Cohen, that is, Cohen before and after the summer of 1870. Two basic differences should not be underestimated. First, there is an important difference in emphasis. While prior to the summer of 1870 Cohen thinks that the psychological approach is the key to under-standing Kant, after that summer he insists that the epistemological approach is crucial; the earlier psychology is pushed into the background, and it is indeed regarded as mis-leading for an understanding of Kant. Why? Second, in *Kants Theorie der Erfahrung* Cohen repudiates the basic tenets of Herbart's psychology, more specifically its concep-tions of the a priori, apperception, and the form–content dualism. The many passages criticizing Herbart's psychological approach to Kant are indeed in striking contrast to his earlier work. The Herbartian empiricist and realist had become a Kantian transcen-dental idealist. Why?

To answer these questions we need to take a closer look at some of Cohen's early essays. These will reveal to us a budding transcendental philosopher, one ready to burst out of the confines of *Völkerpsychologie,* and one on the threshold of his later interpre-tation of Kant.

3. A Kantian Interpretation of Plato

Cohen's debut article for the Steinthal-Lazarus journal was his 'Die Platonische Ideenlehre psychologisch entwickelt', which appeared in 1866.[27] This article has been the source of some controversy among Cohen scholars, who quarrel about whether it should be placed close to, or far removed from, his later position in *Kants Theorie der Erfahrung.* Some have seen it as the source and inspiration for his later position.[28] Others, however, have regarded it as the very antithesis of that position, and they have even dismissed it as "of negligible interest from the standpoint of critical idealism".[29] Which of these inter-pretations is correct? Only a close examination of the article will tell.

The main questions Cohen intends to answer in his article are "What is the Platonic idea?" and "By what psychic process did it arise?" (405). His strategy for answering them, which he explains in the very beginning of the article, reveals his approach and intentions. Cohen states that he wants to complete "the literary investigation" that Kant began in the 'Dialektik' of the first *Kritik* where he proposed "a milder interpre-tation" of Plato's theory of ideas (405).[30] According to that interpretation, the theory

---

[27] Cohen, 'Die Platonische Ideenlehre psychologisch entwickelt', *Zeitschrift für Völkerpsychologie und Sprachwissenschaft* IV (1866), 403–464.

[28] Köhnke, *Entstehung und Aufstieg,* p. 280.   [29] Poma, *Critical Philosophy,* p. 22.
[30] Cohen explicitly cites KrV A 313–314, A 582–583.

of ideas should be read not in a metaphysical or constitutive sense but in a regulative one, so that ideas are understood not as entities or substances but as goals or ideals for enquiry. The chief purpose of Cohen's article is to defend this "milder" Kantian interpretation.

Though the regulative interpretation of Plato's theory of ideas brings this article close to Cohen's later views in *Kants Theorie der Erfahrung*, it also seems in another respect far removed from them. For Cohen still wants to give a "psychological" interpretation of Plato's theory. The very title of the article—'Platonische Ideenlehre psychologisch entwickelt'—shows that he is following the psychological programme of *Völkerpsychologie*–the very programme from which he will distance himself in his later work. The article originally appeared as part of a volume of the *Zeitschrift für Völkerpsychologie* devoted to the history of science, where the methods of *Völkerpsychologie* were to be applied to explain scientific discoveries. The aim of Cohen's article was to extend those methods into the domain of classical studies.

What, more precisely, did it mean to explain Plato's theory of ideas "psychologically"? Cohen tells us that he wants to identify the "psychic process" behind Plato's theory. By this he means not the motives behind the theory but the facts it intends to signify. Cohen thinks that Plato meant to refer to the psychic process behind intellectual and artistic creation. Plato identified this process with the act of intuiting or seeing something, with how the philosopher or artist saw "in his mind's eye" the object he intended to create. The idea was thus the artist's or philosopher's creative vision, his imagining what he intended to create (427). Cohen stresses that, in its original meaning, the idea signified more an activity than an entity. What Plato originally meant by the idea, we are told, is not an intelligible or substantial form but an act of "intellectual intuition" (*intellektuelle Anschauung*). He admits, however, that Plato sometimes wrote about his ideas as if they were things, and notes that in his later dialogues he fell into the habit of hypostasizing them. Rather than talking directly about the activities themselves, Plato would sometimes refer to them obliquely through their objects, so that "the original being of intuiting surreptitiously became the being of the intuited" (428). Because of his careless metaphoric language, and because of the influence of the Pythagoreans, Plato hypostasized his ideas, making them into a peculiar kind of entity (428–429, 440–441, 448).

The controversy surrounding this article arises from Cohen's interpretation of Platonic ideas in terms of intellectual intuition. In some puzzling and often cited lines, Cohen writes that if Plato only kept true to the original meaning of his theory, he would have been "the ancestor of Fichte's intellectual intuition, of transcendental idealism itself" (427). It is this striking equation of Fichte's intellectual intuition with transcendental idealism that has proven so troubling. Some see it as the source of Cohen's philosophy in *Kants Theorie der Erfahrung*, whereas others see it as a violation of that very philosophy. But, in either case, both parties to the dispute assume that Cohen, in attributing Fichtean intellectual intuition to transcendental idealism, is advocating a very metaphysical interpretation of Kant.

The shared premise behind both views is false. A closer examination of the texts reveals that Cohen is *not* advocating a metaphysical interpretation of Kant at all, and that he is really only following through with his original plan to defend Kant's "milder" regulative interpretation of the theory of ideas. It is of the first importance to note precisely how Cohen understands his act of intellectual intuition. He explains that the highest form of intellectual intuition—that which would grasp the totality of all things—consists in the idea of a purpose. "The unity of ideas is the idea of the good", we are told, where the good is the purpose behind all things, the ultimate reason for their creation (449). At this very point, Cohen admits, idealism loses its psychological character and appears to become teleological, even theological (450). So it now seems that we are on very metaphysical terrain indeed, and that Plato's intellectual intuition is still very far removed from Kant, who had notoriously repudiated all intellectual intuition.[31] But it is precisely here, Cohen argues, that Kant understood Plato better than Plato understood himself. Kant perceived the original meaning of Plato's idealism, which gives the ideas not a constitutive but a regulative meaning. He recognized that Plato's ideas should be read as "a regulative concept for reflective judgement" (451). Kant himself had famously discussed intellectual intuition in §77 of the *Kritik der Urteilskraft*, and stressed that it should be given a purely regulative meaning for our finite understanding. Cohen argues that this was the original meaning Plato intended to give to it all along, even though in his enthusiasm he was sometimes seduced to write about ideas as if they were things (450–454).

Now that we have seen the faulty common premise behind both interpretations—the assumption that Cohen understands intellectual intuition in a metaphysical or constitutive sense—we can cut through the controversy between them and place this article properly within Cohen's intellectual development. Since Cohen understands intellectual intuition in a regulative sense, this article does indeed anticipate his later more critical position, which interprets Plato's theory of ideas strictly methodologically. It is therefore a mistake to argue that this article is of no relevance to Cohen's later transcendental idealism. However, it is no less an error to assume that this article foreshadows the later Cohen because it anticipates an alleged metaphysics involved in *Kants Theorie der Erfahrung*. That presupposes not only a mistaken account of the later work, which is not metaphysical at all, as we shall soon see,[32] but also a false metaphysical interpretation of the early article.

The important but overlooked fact that Cohen is intent on a regulative reading of Kant in this early article shows us that, even in the 1860s, he was very much a Kantian philosopher, and indeed in just the ways he appears in *Kants Theorie der Erfahrung*.

---

[31] Kant repudiated intellectual intuition in a constitutive sense and as a method of philosophy in his 'Von einem neuerdings erhobenen vornehmen Ton in der Philosophie', *Schriften* VIII, 387–406. He also denounced Fichte's *Wissenschaftslehre* in the August 29, 1799, issue of the *Allgemeine Literatur Zeitung*, *Schriften* XII, 370–371. See also Kant's April 5, 1798, letter to J.H. Tieftrunk, XII, 240–241.

[32] See Section 7.

In 1868 Cohen was not Platonizing Kant; he was Kantianizing Plato. Realizing this helps us to bridge the gap between the Cohen of the 1860s and the Cohen of 1870. We can close it even more if we consider the next stage in his philosophical development.

4. The Nascent Transcendental Philosopher

Cohen's growing distance from the psychological programme of *Völkerpsychologie* appears in his next major article for the *Zeitschrift*, 'Mythologische Vorstellungen von Gott und Seele', which was published in 1868.[33] It now becomes perfectly plain that we cannot describe the young Cohen *only* as a budding anthropologist and psychologist along the lines of *Völkerpsychologie*. Of course, he is that, but he is also much more. For in the opening pages of the article he firmly and expressly casts himself in the role of a critical philosopher whose proper field is epistemology. That field is then explicitly distinguished from all empirical disciplines, including psychology and anthropology (400). The primary task of the critical philosopher, Cohen tells us, is to engage in "the identification and examination" of "the great ideas" of philosophy (400). Among these great ideas are God and the soul, which will be the subject of the article. Although Cohen intends to determine the psychological and ethnological origin of these ideas, he also distances himself from this enterprise, confessing that such an investigation is only an "excursion" (*Streifzug*) for him, a foray into "a field alien from his own" (399).

We learn from Cohen's introductory disquisition exactly how he understands the method of epistemology, which turns out to be very far from that of anthropology or psychology. He calls the method of epistemology "deductive critique", where it is "deductive" for the simple reason that "True thinking is deduction even in the realm of the inductive" (398). To claim that proper thinking is deduction, and that the business of epistemology is to examine such thinking, is to take epistemology outside the field of empirical enquiry. Cohen then goes on to explain in more precise terms the subject matter of deductive critique (398–399). It comprises two aspects of concepts: their "logical innerness" and their "metaphysical power". Their logical innerness consists in the logical consistency of their elements; and their metaphysical power consists in their capacity to solve problems.

After explaining the method of deductive critique, Cohen then sharply distinguishes it from that of psychology. While deductive critique determines "the metaphysical validity" of concepts, psychology engages in an analysis of their elements and origins, the "mechanism" from which they arose in the mind and in history (399). Despite the difference between these methods, Cohen reassures us that they are complementary, and that deductive critique has much to gain from psychology.

---

[33] Cohen, 'Mythologische Vorstellungen von Gott und Seele', *Zeitschrift für Völkerpsychologie und Sprachwissenschaften* V (1868), 396–434 and VI (1869), 113–131.

From the empirical analysis of concepts, deductive critique receives new materials and starting points for an investigation into their consistency and logical powers (399). Cohen even goes on to stress the great value of psychological analysis for philosophy: it shows us that ideas which appear eternal really arose from history, and that ideas which appear unanalysable grew from simpler primitive elements (400). Nevertheless, he is also perfectly clear about, and indeed insists upon, the limits of psychology: "psychological analysis decides nothing about the metaphysical validity of a concept" (399). Already here, then, we see the clear distinction between the *Quid juris?* and *Quid facti?* that will play a decisive role in *Kants Theorie der Erfahrung.*

Cohen's statement that deduction is the proper business of thinking, his careful explanation of the difference between the deductive and psychological methods, and his confession that his essay is only an "excursion" for him, all make it plain that he is distancing himself from the Lazarus-Steinthal programme. Though he stressed how that programme could be very illuminating for the philosopher, he also made it clear that was not where his true interests lay. He was first and foremost a philosopher, and his discipline had very different methods and goals from empirical psychology and anthropology.

It is no less plain from this early article that Cohen saw Kant as his model philosopher, for he sees him as the source of the method of deductive critique (398). Already in 1868, then, Cohen identified himself strongly with Kant's critical philosophy, and he distinguished its methods and concerns from those of psychology and anthropology. Thus the main idea for *Kants Theorie der Erfahrung* was already laid; the only remaining business was to develop it.

5.   Cohen and the Materialism Controversy

Thus Cohen's writings in the late 1860s show us a philosopher already sympathetic to Kant, and one who interpreted him in non-psychological terms. These conclusions take us part of the way towards understanding the origins of Cohen's first book; but they hardly take us the whole way. We still have to answer two basic questions: Why was Cohen sympathetic to Kant in the first place? And why did he interpret him non-psychologically? Unless we have some answers to these questions, our explanation has not even begun.

As elementary as they are, these questions permit no straightforward answer. There is simply not enough historical evidence to answer them with certainty. Cohen's surviving correspondence is very scanty, and his early writings leave few clues about his philosophical leanings outside *Völkerpsychologie*. It is necessary *to reconstruct*, then, the path of Cohen's development, using evidence from his historical context and later writings.

If we piece together information from these sources, it becomes clear that one event in particular played a decisive role in Cohen's intellectual development, both in moving him towards Kant and in making him interpret Kant in transcendental rather than psychological terms. That event was the materialism controversy.

We know that the young Cohen, like most men of his generation, was deeply preoc- cupied with the chief issue raised by the pantheism controversy: the conflict between reason and faith. From his earliest days, Cohen had been searching for some way to reconcile a scientific naturalism with his religious heritage.[34] It is noteworthy, how- ever, that, initially, Cohen did not find the solution to this problem in Kant but in a very different place. In a short anonymous article he wrote in 1868, 'Virchow und die Juden', Cohen described the modern worldview as "the position of scientific materialism and ethical idealism".[35] Rather than shirking back from materialism, Cohen seemed to embrace it. It is important to see, however, that by "scientific mate- rialism" he did not mean the materialism of Marx and Engels, still less that of Vogt, Moleschott, Czolbe or Büchner. Rather, what he had in mind was the materialism of Heinrich Heine, which was inspired by Spinoza's pantheism.[36] According to Heine, Spinoza's single infinite substance, which manifests itself in all of nature, sancti- fies the reality of matter, so that we have good reason to appreciate the things of this world, the joys of the senses, which are as divine as the most ethereal realm of the spirit.[37] To the young Cohen, Heine's pantheism seemed to promise the very synthesis of reason and faith he was so ardently seeking. After all, Spinoza had not only natu- ralized the divine: he had also divinized nature. Furthermore, Cohen saw Spinoza's pantheism as the developed and refined form of Jewish monotheism.[38]

So, as late as 1868, Cohen was still very far from embracing all aspects of Kant's philosophy. He had accepted Kant's interpretation of Plato; he had endorsed his criti- cal conception of philosophy; but he did not see the import of Kant's philosophy for the resolution of the all-important conflict between reason and faith. Like so many thinkers of the *Goethezeit,* he had seen Spinozism as the solution to that conflict. Before he could become a full-fledged Kantian, then, he would first have to abandon that pantheism. Someone would have to convince him that Heine's solution to the dilemma of reason versus faith does not work, and that ultimately only the Kantian solution is really viable. Who could this someone be?

We do not have to search long for an answer. It was the pied piper of Marburg, Friedrich Albert Lange. Like many young men in the late 1860s, Cohen had fallen

---

[34] On Cohen's early concern with this issue, and on his early education, see Michael Zank, *The Idea of Atonement in the Philosophy of Hermann Cohen* (Providence, RI: Brown Judaic Studies, 2000), pp. 48–107.

[35] 'Virchow und die Juden', in *Jüdische Schriften*, ed. Bruno Strauß (Berlin: Schwetschke, 1924), II, 457– 462, p. 461. First published in *Die Zukunft, Demokratische Zeitung* August 14, 1868.

[36] See Cohen's early essay 'Heinrich Heine und das Judentum', in *Jüdische Schriften*, II, 2–44. This arti- cle was first published in *Die Gegenwart,* I (1867).

[37] Heinrich Heine, *Zur Geschichte der Philosophie und Religion in Deutschland*, in *Sämtliche Schriften*, ed. Klaus Briegleb (Munich: Hanser, 1976), V, 568–571. Cohen cites these passages in 'Heinrich Heine und das Judentum'.

[38] Cohen, 'Heinrich Heine und das Judentum', pp. 6, 9, 18.

under the spell of Lange's *Geschichte des Materialismus*.[39] Lange had shown him that
Kant's philosophy offers a middle path between a rational materialism and an irrational fideism, that it alone can save the autonomy of our moral and religious ideals without metaphysics, and that it alone can uphold the principles of mechanism
and naturalism without jeopardizing morality and religion. But Lange's arguments
would have also taught Cohen the weaknesses in the traditional Spinozist position.
For all the attractions of Spinoza's divinized nature and naturalized divinity, his philosophy was still much too metaphysical, much too dogmatic. It just assumed that we
could have some knowledge of the infinite, that we could have some knowledge of the
thing-in-itself. Lange had shown all too well how the materialists were naive, how
they simply presupposed that we have knowledge of a material reality independent of
us, and how that presupposition did not square with the latest results of the natural
sciences. Even if Spinoza's refined and religious materialism was very different from
the coarse and crass materialism of *"Vogt und Consorten"*, it still shared the same
naive realism.

That the young Hermann Cohen was inspired by Lange's book we have no reason
to doubt. There is no direct evidence from the 1860s about its influence, no letters or fragments that tell us of its immediate impact. We do not even know when
Cohen read Lange, though it must have been sometime after he wrote 'Virchow und
die Juden', which was in 1868. Nevertheless, we have more than enough evidence
from the 1870s that Cohen had read Lange's book, and that it had a great impact
upon him. There is a letter to Lange from November 1871, in which Cohen praises
Lange's "noble work on materialism" and thanks him for its "liberating" effect.[40]
Such, indeed, were Cohen's debts to Lange that he dedicated the second edition of
Kants Theorie der Erfahrung to his memory, and in 1876 he wrote two appreciative
obituaries for him.[41] Fittingly enough, in 1898 Cohen wrote a preface and introduction for the sixth edition of Lange's *Geschichte des Materialismus*.[42] So the evidence
more than suggests that it was Lange who effected Cohen's final conversion to the
critical philosophy.

Yet, for all the importance Lange's book had for him, Cohen had his reservations
about it. He made two basic criticisms, both decisive for developing his own transcendental interpretation of Kant. First, he took issue with Lange's psychological and
physiological interpretation of Kantian epistemology. The problem with that interpretation is that it placed the Kantian subject firmly within the realm of phenomena
and nature. To Cohen, such a conception of the a priori showed that Lange had not
sufficiently liberated himself from the very materialism he denounced. Rather than

[39] See Chapter 9, Section 3.   [40] See Cohen to Lange, November 16, 1871, *Briefe*, pp. 34–35.
[41] See Cohen, 'Friedrich Albert Lange', *Philosophische Monatshefte* 12 (1876), 46–47; and Cohen,
'Friedrich Albert Lange', *Preussische Jahrbücher* 37 (1876), 353–381.
[42] Lange, *Geschichte des Materialismus*, Sechste (wohlfeile und vollständige) Auflage (Leipzig:
Baedeker, 1898).

seeing the a priori in terms of epistemological conditions, Lange had hypostasized them, as if they were physiological conditions, making them just another kind of phenomenon in the natural world. That seemed to open the back door to materialism, allowing it to enter into the most sacred chambers of transcendental philosophy itself. Second, Cohen took exception to Lange's sceptical attitude towards Kant's practical philosophy, which Lange regarded as the weakest side of Kant's system. Lange regarded the noumenal realm beyond the sphere of phenomena as spooky and mysterious, as a hypostasis of our rational activities. For the young Cohen, however, that attitude was simply unacceptable, characteristic of the very materialism Lange attempted to refute. Lange had failed to appreciate one of the central teachings of the critical philosophy: that morality and religion could be based on *practical* reason. It was to counter Lange's scepticism about morality and religion, Cohen later said, that he wrote *Kants Begründung der Ethik*.[43]

Lange's shortcomings in understanding Kant, Cohen believed, were ultimately traceable to one underlying cause: his failure to grasp the transcendental dimension of Kant's philosophy. Such is his assessment of Lange, in the first edition of *Kants Theorie der Erfahrung*, where he criticizes him for misunderstanding the epistemological purpose and status of Kant's discourse (207–208). In his later 1875 obituary in the *Preussische Jahrbücher* he expanded this point by saying that critical idealism is not a metaphysics but a method, a procedure whose task is to determine the validity of knowledge claims rather than any truths about the existence of things.[44] The idea, the stock-in-trade of idealism, is not a thing but "an epistemological symbol of value" (*ein erkenntnistheoretisches Werthzeichen*).[45] Lange would have had a more adequate understanding of idealism, Cohen maintained, if he had only appreciated another thinker, indeed the very father of the idealist tradition: namely, Plato.[46] Plato's realm of ideas, if it is only properly understood, is not about a special kind of transcendent thing, as Lange interpreted it, but about a realm of value and validity completely distinct from that of existence. It is only by appreciating the *sui generis* status of this realm, he taught, that we secure the place of value in the world and find its source in practical reason.

6. Cohen and the Fischer–Trendelenburg Dispute

It was Cohen's response to the materialism controversy, then, that had fully and finally converted him to Kant, and that had even pushed him in the direction of an anti-psychological interpretation of his philosophy. But the materialism controversy alone did not spawn *Kants Theorie der Erfahrung*. It needed a more direct stimulus

---

[43] See Cohen's 'Biographisches Vorwort des Herausgebers', to the sixth edition of Lange's *Geschichte des Materialismus*, p. xi.

[44] Cohen, 'Friedrich Albert Lange', *Preussische Jahrbücher*, p. 374.

[45] Cohen, 'Friedrich Albert Lange', p. 373.   [46] Cohen, 'Friedrich Albert Lange', pp. 370–377.

and occasion. This was provided by the Trendelenburg–Fischer dispute, of which Cohen became a major contributor.

It was impossible for the young Cohen to ignore the dispute which took place right on his doorstep, so to speak. For Trendelenburg had been his teacher in Berlin,[47] and he was so exactly when the dispute was at its very height in the mid 1860s. Now that Lange had converted him to Kant, he could hardly be indifferent to the controversy, which concerned such major issues of Kant interpretation. A contribution to the dispute would also be the perfect opportunity to show his intellectual mettle. And so Cohen wrote an article on the dispute, his 'Zur Kontroverse zwischen Trendelenburg und Kuno Fischer', which appeared in 1871 in the *Zeitschrift für Völkerpsychologie und Sprachwissenschaft*.[48] This sketched *in nuce* the position he took in *Kants Theorie der Erfahrung,* which was his chief contribution to the dispute.[49]

By July 1870 Cohen had already formulated the essence of his position. Though he felt greatly indebted to Trendelenburg, he decided to take issue with his former teacher. His resolve and stance could not be more explicit: "I must attack Trendelenburg. He has completely misunderstood Kant in my view. So much so, that Fischer was right to wonder how little he has been understood by his colleagues."[50] There is some irony in the fact that Cohen chose to show the internal coherence of Kant's philosophy against Trendelenburg, for this was to apply his master's own methods against him. It was a central doctrine of the "Trendelenburg school" to interpret each philosopher sympathetically and from within, to show how his thought formed a coherent whole from a few governing ideas.[51] That was just the lesson that Trendelenburg had failed to apply to his own interpretation of Kant, Cohen believed. Trendelenburg would now be getting a dose of his own medicine.

Cohen's article 'Zur Kontroverse zwischen Trendelenburg und Kuno Fischer' begins by acknowledging the great philosophical importance of the dispute. We are told roundly that its issues concern *all* philosophy (249). They raise the fundamental problem of whether "the nature of things depends on the conditions of our mind? or the laws of nature can and must confirm our thinking?" In other words,

[47] Regarding the young Cohen's relationship to Trendelenburg, see Ulrich Sieg, 'Hermann Cohen und die Völkerpsychologie', *Aschkenas* XIII (2004), 461–483, pp. 466–467. Little research has been done on Trendelenburg's influence on Cohen. For a brief discussion, see Gerhard Lehmann, *Geschichte der Philosophie: Die Philosophie des neunzehnten Jahrhunderts* (Berlin: de Gruyter, 1953), VII, 75–76; and for suggestions, see Peter Schulthess's introduction to *Herman Cohen Werke* (Hildesheim: Olms, 2005) V, 10* n.5, 25 *n.56, and 27* n.64. See also the article by Ernst Wolfgang Orth, 'Trendelenburg und die Wissenschaft als Kulturfaktum', in *Hermann Cohen und die Erkentnistheorie*, pp. 49–61.

[48] Cohen, 'Zur Kontroverse zwischen Trendelenburg und Kuno Fischer', 249–271.

[49] Cohen himself saw his book in these terms. In his article (p. 252) he announced his plans to write "*eine umfänglichere Monographie*" on the main issue raised by the dispute, an obvious reference to his later book.

[50] See the letter quoted by Kinkel, *Hermann Cohen*, p. 46.

[51] The importance of this approach for Cohen was first pointed out by Lange, *Geschichte des Materialismus* II, 130 n.35. Lange saw Cohen's work as an application of "Aristoteles-Philologie" to Kant.

at stake is the great dispute between idealism and realism. Having paid tribute to the issues at hand, Cohen then makes a decisive methodological claim about how to resolve them. All thinking about the dispute can go forward, he says, only if one accepts Kant's distinction between psychology and metaphysics (250). This distinction is between matters of psychological fact and matters of a priori principle, which can be settled only through deductive reasoning.[52] This was Cohen's way of saying that the dispute was fundamentally epistemological rather than psychological.

Cohen analyses the dispute into two central questions: 1) Has Trendelenburg proven that there is a gap in Kant's proofs for the exclusive subjectivity of space and time?, and 2) Has Trendelenburg shown that Fischer has taken up non-Kantian elements in his exposition of the Kantian theory of space and time? (251). Cohen complains that the first question, which is the really important one, has been obscured by all the dust raised by the dispute. Rather than examining the logic of Trendelenburg's arguments, Fischer has been more concerned to defend his interpretation of Kant. But this is just as well, Cohen says, because a complete answer to the first question would require nothing less than a full examination of Kant's theory of experience and the proofs of the Transcendental Aesthetic. Because this goes beyond the limits of a single article, he has decided to leave aside the first question, which he will treat in a more comprehensive monograph, what eventually became *Kants Theorie der Erfahrung*. The article will deal with only the second question and another subsidiary one: Whether Fischer has proven against Trendelenburg that there is no gap in Kant's reasoning?

Although Cohen, true to his word, devotes much of his article to these lesser questions, he still reveals the main lines of the position he later takes in *Kants Theorie der Erfahrung*. Regarding the first question, Cohen denies that Trendelenburg has shown that there is a gap in Kant's proofs for the exclusive subjectivity of space and time. The problem with Trendelenburg's interpretation, he argues, is that it begins with some very dogmatic assumptions—assumptions that Kant decisively rejects. Trendelenburg assumes that the a priori is a psychological faculty, and that the world as we experience it, as it appears to our senses, consists in things-in-themselves (255). He has his own concept of objectivity, which is essentially that of transcendental realism, according to which we know an object when our representations correspond to the thing-in-itself, which is given in experience. But it is just this concept of objectivity, Cohen argues, that Kant intends to overthrow with his transcendental idealism. The central argument of *Kants Theorie der Erfahrung* will consist in showing that Kant's Copernican Revolution involves a very different conception of objectivity, one according to which objectivity is constituted by our a priori forms of intuition and understanding.

---

[52] Cohen was using the term "metaphysics" in one of its peculiar Kantian senses, according to which it means a priori knowledge of the basic principles of reason. See KrV B 879.

It is noteworthy that, regarding the all-important first question, Cohen takes a firm and explicit stance with Fischer against Trendelenburg. It is sometimes said that this article sides more with Trendelenburg against Fischer because the young Cohen was reluctant to take issue with his venerable teacher.[53] But the very opposite is the case. Although Cohen does side with Trendelenburg regarding the lesser second question, he stands against him on the more important first one. He states firmly his agreement with Fischer that not a single sentence of Kant's philosophy would be true if Kant had not refuted the third possibility. Fischer was indeed right: the entire Kantian system, the central doctrines of transcendental idealism, would collapse if the a priori forms of subjectivity were also true of things-in-themselves (260). Though Fischer was correct in substance, he did not establish clear and convincing arguments for his interpretation. If he is to be a good advocate of Kant, Fischer must prove and not simply proclaim his interpretation (260). Cohen sees himself as taking on the mantle of an advocate of Kant, confident that he can succeed where Fischer has plainly failed. That task he will undertake in his forthcoming book.

We will leave aside here Cohen's response to the lesser questions and his long stance on behalf of Trendelenburg against Fischer. These concern matters that are peripheral to the main issues of the dispute, as Cohen himself acknowledged. Noteworthy, however, is Cohen's concluding disquisition on method in the history of philosophy (290–296). Here he distances himself from the methods of both Fischer and Trendelenburg. He agrees with Trendelenburg's critique of Fischer's "free reconstructive method", which introduces terms and ideas into a philosopher even when there is no textual evidence for them; but he also cannot accept Trendelenburg's view that the only interpretation of a philosopher should be "an intricate mosaic" where the scholar reconstructs a philosopher's meaning from a mass of fragments. A mosaic, no matter how finely reconstructed, is still not a single cohesive whole. The best interpretation of a philosopher is one that understands him according to his own "basic thought" (*Grundgedanke*) (292–293).

The crucial question remains, however, how one finds this basic thought? It is in his answer to this question that Cohen surprises us and reveals how much his thinking was still in flux. Having made a firm distinction between metaphysical and psychological questions at the beginning of the article, Cohen blurs it at the close. For it turns out that the means for discovering a philosopher's basic thought lies in the realm of psychology after all (293). The basic thought is a "psychic process", and the historian of philosophy has to discover it through "the method of psychology", which will show the process through which it arose. This closing passage reveals, therefore, Cohen's lingering loyalty to psychology and the methods of *Völkerpsychologie* even in the midst of his discovery of the transcendental dimension in Kant.

---

[53] See Poma, *Critical Philosophy*, pp. 4–5; and Ulrich Sieg, *Aufstieg und Niedergang*, p. 111.

7. Kant's Theory of Experience

Cohen was true to his word when he announced his plans to write a monograph on the Trendelenburg–Fischer dispute. For that is exactly what he did in the summer of 1870, finishing it even before his article appeared in 1871. Cohen seems to have been inspired in the summer of 1870, for he made rapid progress in writing his book. Sometime in mid-July 1870 he reported: "I am getting on with my work. The whole thing is alive in my head; it is only a matter of writing it down."[54] A few weeks later, on August 2, he told his friend Herman Lewandowsky that he had already completed his exposition of the Kantian theory of space and that he was now working on the transcendental logic.[55] By October 3, 1870, the book was as good as done, for Cohen told Lewandowsky that he had completed his defence of Kant, which was all he intended the book to be.[56] The publication of the manuscript seems to have been delayed a full year, however, because the preface is dated October 31, 1871.

The first edition of *Kants Theorie der Erfahrung* is a modest book, only 270 pages long, less than half the size of its more ambitious second edition. It is very much a different book than its successor, which introduces many new themes. Still, the first edition is not rendered obsolete by the second, and it is indeed in one respect the better version, for its lesser size means that its main message emerges much more clearly. The first edition is also much more revealing about the original context and intention behind the work. For purely historical reasons, our focus now will be upon the first edition.[57]

The preface reveals much about Cohen's aims and methods. We learn that his main aim is "to present the historical Kant"—"Kant as he is present in his sources" (*den urkundlich vorhandenen Kant*)—so that he could defend him against his critics (iv). Some of the most common objections against the critical philosophy can be easily removed, he believes, simply by the citation of the appropriate texts. As if he were a disciple of Ranke, Cohen declares that the scholar only fully understands his sources through a surrender to the material, by casting aside his own biases and entering into the world of the author (vii). To encourage that practice, and to ward off tiresome and superficial objections, it is best, Cohen advises, to proceed according to one popular notion: that Kant is a genius (vii). Cohen does not think that this is literally true, but he still believes that it is a useful regulative assumption in Kant interpretation, because it makes us think twice about our criticisms of Kant, which all too often prove superficial.

---

[54] Kinkel, *Hermann Cohen*, p. 46. Kinkel does not cite the source of this quotation. His source appears to have been lost.

[55] Cohen to Herman Lewandowsky, August 2, 1870, *Briefe*, pp. 24–25.

[56] Cohen to Herman Lewandowsky, August 2, 1870, *Briefe*, p. 28.

[57] Unless otherwise noted, all references in parentheses are to the first edition: Hermann Cohen, *Kants Theorie der Erfahrung* (Berlin: Ferdinand Dümmler, 1871).

Though he stresses the need to restore the historical Kant, Cohen also insists on understanding Kant in the light of enduring systematic issues or philosophical problems. Historical reconstruction ultimately has to be guided by philosophical issues. The scholar should have an understanding of these issues, and he needs to work out his own response to them, Cohen maintains, if he is to fully understand the text before him. For what one reads into a text crucially depends on one's stance towards these problems. Cohen says that the Fischer–Trendelenburg dispute has taught him that one's ultimate philosophical commitments also determine one's exegesis, and that there is no such thing as a completely neutral reading of the text. "One cannot deliver any judgement on Kant without betraying in every line the world in one's own head." (v)

There is a tension here in Cohen's account of the philosophical and historical aspects of interpretation: the philosophical demands, or at least permits, prior commitments; but the historical insists upon laying such commitments aside and delving into the mental world of the author. Exactly how these philosophical and historical aspects hold together Cohen does not explain. It would be a mistake, however, to see Cohen's emphasis on the philosophical as a covert or implicit license for a completely non-historical reading of Kant.[58]

If there were a single phrase to summarize the significance of *Kants Theorie der Erfahrung*, it would have to be Cohen's discovery of the transcendental. The concept of the transcendental is the key to Cohen's interpretation of Kant, and indeed the guiding thread for the later interpretation of the Marburg school. The transcendental is for Cohen co-extensive with the a priori, which consists in what he calls "the formal conditions for the possibility of experience". It therefore comprises the formal intuitions of sensibility, space and time, as well as the pure concepts of the understanding. Cohen understands the a priori neither in terms of innate ideas—that would be too psychologistic—nor in terms of Platonic archetypes—that would be too metaphysical. Rather, the a priori is strictly epistemological, consisting in the general conditions for *knowledge* of experience, where "experience" consists in the world as it is understood through mathematical physics.

True to its title, *Kants Theorie der Erfahrung* concerns what Cohen calls "Kant's theory of experience". Such a theory is a general account of the *formal* conditions of experience, that is, those conditions that hold regardless of the particular content of experience. Cohen maintains that there is a single central principle to explain all these formal conditions, which happens to be the main thesis behind Kant's Copernican Revolution: namely, "that we know a priori of objects only what we put into them".[59] Kant himself had emphasized the decisive role of this principle in the prefaces to the *Kritik*, and even called it the guiding idea behind "our new method of thought".[60] Cohen emphasizes these passages, repeating them constantly, and making

---

[58] *Pace* Köhnke, *Entstehung und Aufstieg*, pp. 273–275; and Brandt, 'Hermeneutik und Seinslehre bei Hermann Cohen', pp. 37–54.
[59] KrV B xviii.   [60] KrV B xviii.

them the basis for his reconstruction of Kant's theory of experience. All the mistakes of previous interpretations of Kant, he argues, come from failing to appreciate the decisive role of this principle.

This principle means first and foremost, Cohen explains, that the transcendental subject is the source of the a priori, that it generates or creates the formal conditions of experience. This is the basic principle behind the Copernican Revolution, because it implies, as Kant famously put it, "that concepts do not conform to objects but that objects conform to concepts."[61] In other words, we should think about knowledge not as the correspondence of representations with an object that exists independently of them, but as the conformity of representations to standards or norms imposed by the subject itself. This means that the subject determines the very standards of objectivity, that it creates, as Kant called it, "the concept of an object", so that there is no need for an object outside our representations to which they have to conform.

It was one of the great merits of Cohen's little tract that it went back to the basics of the critical philosophy, that it had stressed the importance of the meaning of the Copernican Revolution itself. By going back to Kant's original starting point, Cohen thought he could see through the errors of other interpretations, not least the problem behind Trendelenburg's interpretation of Kant. Once we recognize that the subject creates the very conditions of objectivity, we see that it is pointless to talk about the extra or "third" possibility of representations corresponding to things-in-themselves. We can now see that the thing-in-itself is not only superfluous to explain the possibility of knowledge, but also that it is completely contrary to the spirit of the Copernican Revolution, which demands that we explain objectivity entirely in immanent terms, that is, in terms of the conformity of representations with the formal conditions of experience created by us rather than their correspondence with a thing-in-itself beyond us. It follows from this, Cohen concludes, that the dualism between the subject and object now falls *within* the formal conditions of experience, *inside* the transcendental perspective itself (35–37, 52, 54). We must not conceive of the a priori as an innate subjective faculty that precedes experience, applying concepts and intuitions to given objects, as Trendelenburg did, because these objects are created and constituted by the a priori conditions of our knowing them (48–49, 63–64, 72–73).

Cohen's conception of the a priori or transcendental is not as simple as it seems, and it is necessary to be on guard against misinterpretations. One of these conceives the a priori or transcendental entirely in normative terms, so that it consists in nothing more than rules, laws or norms, so that the subject behind them disappears. The subject seems dispensable because, on Cohen's own showing, the dualism between subject and object falls *under* these norms. For these reasons Cohen's transcendental idealism has been described as "an idealism without a subject".[62] While this interpretation is perhaps correct for the later Cohen, who thematizes "pure thought" in his 1902 *Logik der*

[61] KrV B xvii.
[62] See Manfred Brelage, 'Transzendentalphilosophie und konkrete Subjektivität', in *Studien zur Transzendental Philosophie* (Berlin: de Gruyter, 1965), p. 97; and Siegfried Marck, 'Die Lehre vom

reinen Erkenntnis, it is incorrect for the young Cohen, the author of *Kants Theorie der Erfahrung.* Although the young Cohen understands the a priori in normative terms, and although he stresses how the dualism between subject and object falls within experience, he still does not intend to eliminate the transcendental subject. On the contrary, he insists on retaining it, seeing it as the fundamental ground of all experience. Throughout *Kants Theorie der Erfahrung,* in both the first and second editions,[63] Cohen insists on the ineliminable role of the transcendental subject, which is the ground of the formal conditions of experience. Thus he states that subjectivity is the sole ground of experience (49), that the subject knows experience a priori by constructing it (11), that the starting point of all knowledge lies within ourselves (35), and that the only objectivity is that produced or created by the subject (54). It is the *empirical* subject who falls within experience, not the *transcendental* subject who creates or posits the formal conditions of experience itself.[64]

Another misinterpretation reads Cohen's early text in more metaphysical terms. It maintains that *Kants Theorie der Erfahrung* is the product of Cohen's mystical Platonism. According to this interpretation, Cohen attributes vast creative powers to the transcendental subject, so that it produces not only the form but also the matter of experience, and so that the given intuitions of sensibility utterly disappear.[65] Cohen so radicalizes Kant's new method of thought that he makes the object of experience, in both its form and content, into an a priori construction, having no features beyond what we create in it. Kant's paradigm of a priori knowledge—we know only what we create—then becomes the paradigm of *all* knowledge, even empirical knowledge. The source of this interpretation of Kant, we are told, is Cohen's early interpretation of Plato in his 1866 essay 'Die Platonische Ideenlehre psychologish entwickelt'.[66] Supposedly, Cohen read Plato's theory of ideas in terms of Fichte's intellectual intuition, which he saw as the essence of transcendental idealism itself.

This interpretation seems plausible enough, especially when it *appears* to have historical evidence to support it.[67] But this interpretation too is deeply anachronistic, turning Cohen's early text into an anticipation of his later work. Starting with

---

erkennenden Subjekt in der Marburger Schule', *Logos* IV, (1913), 364–366. For a fuller discussion, see Poma, *Critical Philosophy,* pp. 61–64.

[63] There are indeed anticipations of Cohen's later position in the second edition, where Cohen stresses the primacy of thinking over sensibility in the concept of the infinitesimal. See Cohen, *Kants Theorie der Erfahrung* (1885), pp. 423–424, 433–434. However, Cohen is still critical of rationalist attempts to reduce the content of sensation to the understanding. See Cohen, *Kants Theorie der Erfahrung* (1885), pp. 40–41. On the difference between these editions, see Poma, *Critical Philosophy,* pp. 37–53.

[64] Though Cohen makes no clear distinction between the transcendental and empirical subjects, it is the presupposition of his argument. Only such a distinction could explain how the subject could both fall within experience and create its formal conditions.

[65] See Köhnke, *Entstehung und Aufstieg,* pp. 273–301. Sieg, *Aufstieg und Niedergang,* pp. 111–112, follows Köhnke's interpretation.

[66] Köhnke, *Entstehung und Aufstieg,* p. 280.

[67] We have already seen in Section 3 that the concept of intellectual intuition in this early essay should be read in regulative rather than constitutive terms. Hence it does not provide any real evidence for Köhnke's reading.

his 1896 *Einleitung mit kritischem Nachtrag zur Geschichte des Materialismus,* Cohen had indeed moved toward an interpretation of Kant that eliminates the dualism between understanding and sensibility and that completely removes the given content of experience.[68] But Cohen stoutly resists this interpretation in his earlier work, which is much closer to the letter of Kantian doctrine. In his earlier work, Cohen insists that the a priori consists in the *formal* conditions of experience alone, and that the creative power of the subject does not extend to the matter of experience, which has to be given (100, 101). Although Cohen stresses the creative role of the subject in creating the object of its experience, he limits that role to its *formal* constitution; the subject creates *the concept* of the object, not the object itself. Cohen is indeed explicit that the subject has a passive sensibility, so that its object is given to it (163), and that it does not create the *existence* of the object (127–128). In classic Kantian fashion he stresses the interdependence of the form and content of experience, so that it is a mistake for the rationalists to think that matter is created and for the empiricists to assume that form is given (4). The central fallacy of rationalism is that it reduces the object of experience down to a mere construction or noumenon (210). Rather than seeing the a priori construction of experience as an intellectual intuition, Cohen stresses the role of inner sense, for which content must be given (163). Throughout his book Cohen emphasizes Kant's opposition to an intellectual intuition, which would be an understanding that creates objects in the act of knowing them (149, 150, 159, 238). He notes that Kant attempted to undercut all need to postulate an intellectual intuition by locating the creative powers involved in mathematical construction in human sensibility rather than reason (243). Far from wanting to affirm intellectual intuition, Kant saw it as characteristic of material idealism, which he utterly repudiated (149, 150, 159, 243–244).

As one would expect, *Kants Theorie der Erfahrung* contains a critique of the psychological interpretation of Kant. Cohen's concept of the a priori and transcendental dictate nothing less. The psychological interpretation had construed Kant's concept of the a priori in terms of the psychic or physiological conditions of experience, and so it had failed to grasp Kant's epistemological intention: explaining the conditions for our *knowledge* of objects. Sure enough, Cohen criticizes Herbart, Lange and Meyer for their basic misunderstanding of Kant's epistemological enterprise. Cohen's critique of these authors is notable, not least because he had himself followed them so closely in his early articles for the Lazarus-Steinthal journal. Indeed, shortly before his book appeared he had given

---

[68] It is a mistake to see the starting point of Cohen's later views in his 1883 *Das Princip der Infinitesimal-Methode und seine Geschichte* (Berlin: Dümmler, 1883), as Sieg has done (*Aufstieg und Niedergang*, p. 141). Though there are indeed indications of later developments, Cohen continues to affirm the necessity of a dualism between understanding and sensibility. See, for example, p. 18, §24. On this whole question, see Helmut Holzhey's introduction to *Einleitung mit kritischem Nachtrag* in *Hermann Cohen Werke* Band V, 7*–18*.

a largely positive review of Meyer's *Kants Psychologie.*[69] There can be no doubt, however, that Cohen's position in *Kants Theorie der Erfahrung* amounts to a break with some of his own previous psychology. Notably, Meyer's work now comes in for a severe bashing (123).

That said, it is also noteworthy that Cohen did not completely turn his back on his psychological past. His old allegiances and habits lingered on, and they surface from time to time in *Kants Theorie der Erfahrung.* This is most evident when Cohen argues that Kant's theory of the a priori does not exclude using the methods of psychology to discover the conditions of experience (100, 164). Fischer had argued that Kant's a priori concepts had to be determined by a priori means, by some kind of logical reflection and deduction, because they would lose their universality and necessity if they were found in experience.[70] But Cohen finds that argument fallacious on the grounds that, although the *validity* of a synthetic a priori principle is independent of experience, we still learn its *existence* from experience. Following a line of thinking worked out by Fries and Meyer, Cohen maintains that psychology is still the best means *to discover* a priori concepts. His early psychology resurfaces in other important forms, namely, when Cohen continues to affirm some fundamental doctrines of Herbart's psychology, such as the primacy of mechanical explanation and the rejection of mental faculties.[71]

The first third of *Kants Theorie der Erfahrung* is devoted to an analysis of Kant's arguments in the Transcendental Aesthetic. Such a focus is entirely what we expect, given that the Fischer–Trendelenburg controversy revolved around that portion of text, and given that the psychological interpretations had concerned Kant's account of sense perception. It is all the more remarkable and interesting, therefore, that most of the book in fact concentrates on the Transcendental Analytic, which had been virtually neglected in the controversies of the 1860s. It was one of the great merits of Cohen's work that it saw the central role of the Transcendental Deduction in Kant's enterprise, and that it placed it once again in the centre of scholarly attention. This was entirely strategic, because the Deduction demonstrated so clearly Cohen's central thesis about the a priori. Kant had stated unequivocally in the beginning of the Analytic that his guiding question was not the *quid facti?*—What are the origins of the concepts of the understanding?—but the *quid juris?*—What right or justification do we have for these concepts? Cohen thinks that the *quid juris?* was the decisive and leading question of the critical philosophy as a whole, which applies to the Aesthetic no less than the Analytic.

In giving such central importance to the Transcendental Deduction, Cohen had to take issue with no less a figure than Schopenhauer, who had notoriously claimed that the entire Analytic was modelled around the Aesthetic and only an afterthought

---

[69] See note 15.   [70] See Cohen, *Kants Theorie der Erfahrung*, Chapter 8, Section 4.
[71] See Cohen, *Kants Theorie der Erfahrung*, Chapter 8, Section 4.

to it.[72] Cohen suggested the exact opposite: that Kant first formulated his central conclusions for the pure concepts of the understanding and only later applied them to the forms of space and time (109). Still, he did not insist on this point, which he considered only a historical hypothesis, and he focused instead on Schopenhauer's misunderstandings of Kant's project. Schopenhauer's chief chief mistake was that he assumed, much like Trendelenburg, that the object in space is simply given to us, and that the categories are later applied to it (179–181). What he failed to see is that for an object even to be given to us, the pure concepts of the understanding must already have done their work. We cannot perceive a *determinate* object in space and time prior to the application of the categories, which are necessary conditions for it to be even perceived as such an object (142, 181). It is of the first importance to see that the a priori forms of intuition of the Aesthetic are really only an abstraction for the purpose of isolating the role of sensibility in transcendental enquiry; in reality understanding and sensibility are completely intermeshed, and no object even appears to sensibility without the co-operation of understanding (90–91).

It is striking that Cohen's account of the Transcendental Deduction, unlike more modern interpretations, stresses the fundamental role of the activity of synthesis, that is, the creative role of the understanding in forming the conditions of experience (183).[73] The fundamental principle behind the Deduction, he tells us repeatedly, is Kant's new method of thought: that we know a priori of things only what we create in them (112, 127–128). Cohen stresses the leading role of this principle, advising his reader always to keep it in mind: "It is this thought that one must always keep before one's eye. From this thought everything begins in Kant." (112). On his account, the categories apply to experience because they are instruments of the unity of apperception, which synthesizes the manifold of sensations into comprehensible wholes. "Transcendental apperception, with its levers, the categories, supplies the transcendental affinity of appearances by which we grasp appearances." (135). It is thus ironic to find Cohen, the opponent of psychological interpretations, emphasizing a concept that some modern scholars find too psychologistic because it allegedly rests upon upon "the imaginary subject of transcendental psychology".[74]

While Cohen's interpretation is more textually accurate, it seems that he can advance it only at the cost of inconsistency, for the concept of synthesis seems essentially psychological, involving reference to a mental activity. But in fairness to Cohen it must be said that synthesis falls within the purview of his own concept of the transcendental, which is less narrow than modern accounts. While the transcendental is indeed second-order for him, concerning knowledge of objects rather than objects

---

[72] See Schopenhauer, 'Kritik der kantischen Philosophie', Anhang zu *Die Welt als Wille und Vorstellung*, Dritte Auflage, *Werke* (Stuttgart: Insel, 1968), I, 561–715, pp. 580–582.

[73] Cohen himself would later object to the Kantian concept on the grounds that it presupposed a given manifold. See Cohen, *Logik der reinen Erkenntnis*, p. 24.

[74] See P.F. Strawson, *The Bounds of Sense* (London: Methuen, 1966), pp. 32, 97.

themselves, he thinks that it should include more than the truth conditions for judgements. The transcendental also involves the activity of cognition itself, of which judgements are only the product. Any account of the conditions of knowledge would have to take account of this activity, its limits and powers. It never escaped Cohen, as it did some modern interpreters, that an account of *what* we know cannot be separated from an account of *how* we know. Since it takes into account the activity of cognition, Cohen's concept of the transcendental is broader than the merely logical.

The more serious issue concerning Cohen's account of the transcendental deduction concerns his attitude towards scepticism. Arguably, the deduction is Kant's response to Humean scepticism, not least because Kant himself tells us about the importance of Hume for his awakening from his "dogmatic slumbers". But Cohen does not reconstruct Kant's answer to Hume, because he does not think of the deduction as a response to sceptical doubt. The deduction for him begins with "the fact of science", that is, the acceptance of mathematical physics as a datum; it then explains how that fact is possible, specifying the conditions for a mathematical knowledge of nature. But it does not attempt to demonstrate that these conditions obtain, or to defend mathematical physics against sceptical doubts. In the second edition Cohen defended this interpretation by playing down the significance of Hume.[75] The Scottish philosopher, we are told, had little understanding of mathematics and how it is used in natural science; and his scepticism of causality, which would have been of concern only to the pre-critical Kant, targeted an antiquated scholastic conception of little relevance to modern science. We need to ask, however, whether Cohen's interpretation of Kant, by playing down Kant's response to Humean scepticism, deprives it of some of its philosophical interest. On Cohen's account, Kant, by beginning with the fact of science, simply begs the question against Hume.

8. The Metaphysics of the Transcendental

When Cohen wrote his article on the Trendelenburg–Fischer controversy in 1870, it will be recalled, he did not attempt to answer the main issue behind it, that is, whether Trendelenburg had demonstrated a gap in Kant's reasoning about the exclusive subjectivity of space and time. He promised an answer to this question in "a more comprehensive monograph", which turned out to be *Kants Theorie der Erfahrung*. But what, exactly, was Cohen's answer to this question? How, more specifically, did he attempt to resolve the controversy between Fischer and Trendelenburg? Only when we have an answer to this question will we understand Cohen's motivations and argument in *Kants Theorie der Erfahrung*. Now that we have a better general idea of the contents of that work, we are in a better position to answer these questions.

---

[75] Cohen, *Kants Theorie der Erfahrung* (1885), pp. 51–58.

The heart of Cohen's strategy against Trendelenburg in *Kants Theorie der Erfahrung* is to show that his reasoning is based on a false dilemma. According to that dilemma, either we accept transcendental realism or we surrender to a complete subjectivism. Trendelenburg had argued that if the forms of space and time are not valid of things-in-themselves, we are locked inside the circle of consciousness, so that we know only our representations. But Cohen points out that there is a middle path between the horns of this dilemma. That *via media* is laid down by Kant's fundamental principle: "that we know a priori of things only what we place into them." This principle means that we, as transcendental subjects, create our own standards of objectivity, so that we must not conceive of objectivity as a thing-in-itself, that is, as an object that exists independent of consciousness and to which it must conform. Since our self-created and self-imposed standards are constitutive of our experience, we do not *per impossibile* have to go outside our experience to see if our representations conform to things-in-themselves. Trendelenburg's fundamental error is that he had failed to grasp the full implications of Kant's fundamental principle, namely, that standards of objectivity are not given but posited. He could not bring himself to renounce a transcendental realist conception of objectivity, according to which our representations have to conform to a thing-in-itself.

We might well ask ourselves, though, whether Cohen's argument against Trendelenburg is effective as it stands. It works well enough against Trendelenburg's *stronger claim* that some kind of transcendental realism is *necessary* for objective knowledge. Cohen shows us that Kant's concept of the a priori undercuts such a necessity because it shows how objectivity is still possible within experience and how it is possible to have an empirical realism with a transcendental framework. However, it does not work well against Trendelenburg's *weaker claim* that some kind of transcendental realism is still *possibile*. For it is still open for Trendelenburg to argue that empirical realism, though sufficient for objectivity, does not rule out the possibility that a priori forms still apply to things-in-themselves. Though we could explain the entire structure of objectivity in terms of a priori principles, it is still possible that this structure conforms to an objective world outside it.

Cohen could counter even Trendelenburg's weaker claim, however, provided that he made one very bold move: namely, eliminating things-in-themselves entirely. In that case there simply would be no extra reality for a priori principles to apply to. Cohen does not hesitate to take this more drastic step. In his penultimate chapter he maintains that the thing-in-itself is simply a regulative or limiting concept of the understanding (252), and that, read in a constitutive sense, it is only an hypostasis of this concept (258). It is only when we take into account Cohen's position on things-in-themselves, then, that his reply to Trendelenburg becomes fully effective.

Whatever the ultimate merits of Cohen's argument, it is striking that he had charged Trendelenburg with the same basic failing as Lange: neither had understood the transcendental dimension of Kant's discourse. While Lange conceived the a priori in a *naturalistic* fashion, as if it consisted in physiological and psychological laws, Trendelenburg had understood it in a *subjectivist* fashion, as if it consisted in innate faculties which precede experience, and which are applied to an already given object. He did not seem to realize that the a priori makes the object of experience possible in the first place. It is not as if experience is given, and then we apply a priori forms to it; on the contrary, these forms *constitute* experience. Once we grasp the distinctive transcendental stature of the a priori, Cohen argued, we can easily see that it is neither naturalistic nor subjectivist; rather, it is that which makes knowledge of nature and subjectivity possible.

Ultimately, Cohen took issue with Trendelenburg's interpretation of Kant for the same reason that he had contested Lange's. Neither of his teachers had fully responded to the challenge of materialism; both had left open a foothold for materialism to re-enter the critical philosophy. By conceiving the a priori in psychological terms, Lange had allowed it to be explained naturalistically, as if it were like any other event in nature. And by insisting upon a transcendental realism to guarantee objectivity, Trendelenburg had reinstated matter itself with all its old nasty characteristics (viz. independent existence in space).

So, finally, we can now fully appreciate the motives for Cohen's discovery of the transcendental: by seeing the a priori in its *sui generis* transcendental terms, Cohen could shut the backdoors to materialism unwittingly left open by both his teachers. The full purport of Cohen's anti-materialist animus appears explicitly at the very end of *Kants Theorie der Erfahrung*:

Through the discovery of the apriority of space and time, of the apodictic in sensibility, the motives of all *material* idealism, and of all *materialism*, are destroyed . . . To dissolve the variety of things into the difference of ideas—that is the secret of idealism. The history of human thinking reveals this secret, and therefore itself as the history of *idealism*. (270)

If my account of Cohen's path towards the transcendental is correct, it leaves us with a rather rich irony. It now turns out that Cohen's motives were ultimately metaphysical, intended to undercut the last vestiges of materialism still clinging to Lange's and Trendelenburg's interpretation of Kant. But the very logic of Cohen's concept of the transcendental excludes the metaphysical no less than the psychological. After all, the transcendental deals not with things—whether material or mental—but only our knowledge of them. Thus for decidedly metaphysical motives Cohen developed a decidedly non-metaphysical interpretation of Kant.

This is not a criticism of Cohen, still less a refutation; but it should make us mistrust the anti-metaphysical façade behind his transcendental idealism, which tends to conceal his own metaphysical allegiances. It was only in his later years, I believe, that Cohen revealed, finally, fully and frankly, the deepest motives behind his allegiance to Kant. The spirit of Kant's philosophy and Judaism, it turns out, are really one and the same.[76] But what exactly that means is the subject for another occasion.

---

[76] 'Innere Beziehungen der kantischen Philosophie zum Judentum', in *Achtundzwanzigster Bericht der Lehranstalt für die Wissenschaft des Judentums in Berlin* (Berlin: Meyer und Müller, 1910), 39–61. Reprinted in *Werke* XV, 309–345.

13

Wilhelm Windelband and Normativity

1. Windelband and Neo-Kantianism

Hermann Cohen's little book of 1871 took neo-Kantianism in a new direction, moving it away from a psychological and towards a more logical conception of epistemology. But Cohen was not alone in pushing neo-Kantianism in this direction. In the early 1880s another thinker appeared on the scene to give this movement even more impulse and energy: Wilhelm Windelband (1848–1915).

Although best remembered today for his work on the history of philosophy,[1] Windelband was a major thinker in the history of neo-Kantianism. His significance for this movement is just as great as Cohen's. Just as Cohen became the leader of the Marburg school, so Windelband became the father of the Southwestern or Baden school of neo-Kantianism. Windelband was the teacher of Heinrich Rickert (1863–1936), who was in turn the teacher of Emil Lask (1875–1915). Together, Windelband, Rickert and Lask form the inner core of the Southwestern school.

In the 1870s and 1880s, Cohen and Windelband seemed to be working together in shaping a new conception of epistemology, and in forging a new understanding of Kant. Both were sharp critics of the Friesian tradition and Helmholtzian programme, which would base epistemology on psychology. Both were champions of a new conception of transcendental philosophy, according to which its chief focus should be the *quid juris?* rather than *quid facti?*, the reasons rather than causes of knowledge. Hand-in-hand with this new understanding of epistemology went their new interpretation of Kant. Cohen and Windelband understood Kant's philosophy as "critical idealism", that is, as a strictly immanent analysis of the conditions of experience which involves no transcendent dimension, whether that of the thing-in-itself or Platonic forms. Because of their leading roles in the neo-Kantian movement, Windelband's and Cohen's views on these issues became the new orthodoxy of the 1880s and 1890s.

---

[1] Windelband's best-known historical work is his *Lehrbuch der Geschichte der Philosophie* (Tübingen: Mohr, 1900). It has been through no less than nineteen printings since 1900 and was published as recently as 1995. His chief works on the history of philosophy are his *Die Geschichte der neueren Philosophie in ihren Zusammenhange mit dem allgemeinen Kultur und den besonderen Wissenschaften*

These affinities between Windelband and Cohen raise the question of their personal relationship. Although they were virtual contemporaries, the two men never seem to have met, though they had once clashed over academic politics.[2] Because of the destruction of his correspondence, Cohen's opinion of Windelband will probably remain forever unknown. We do know, however, Windelband's opinion of Cohen, because in a late article discussing recent developments in contemporary philosophy the elderly Windelband found the fitting occasion to pass judgement on his slightly older counterpart.[3] Windelband appreciated Cohen's role in defeating the psychologistic tradition and in stressing the more logical side of Kant's philosophy. It was Cohen's "great contribution to have again validated the strict rationality of the Kantian philosophy". But Windelband thought little of Cohen's commentaries on Kant, which had made "the obscure more obscure, the difficult more difficult, and the complicated more complicated." He also thought that Cohen had failed to get beyond the narrow Kantian paradigm of science, which limited it to mathematics and natural science; never did Cohen attempt to explain how there could be a science of history or culture. Whether Cohen's emphasis on the method of the infinitesimal as the model for science would prove fruitful in the natural sciences Windelband did not venture to say; but he was confident that this would prove to be a "straitjacket" for philosophy.

Windelband was a very different writer from Cohen. While Cohen wrote a systematic philosophy, modelled around Kant's three *Kritiken*,[4] Windelband never came close to a system of his own. Although he believed in the value of systematic philosophy, he did not find the occasion, opportunity or energy to write one. His chief philosophical legacy is fragmentary. It consists in his collection of lectures and essays, which were first published in 1884 under the title *Präludien*.[5] The final edition consists in essays and lectures spanning some forty years, from the late 1870s until the end of the first decade of the 20th century. The title was apt: it was Windelband's way of admitting that his work was more suggestive than complete, more tentative than final. For these preludes, there would be no symphony.

(Leipzig: Breitkopf & Härtel, 1878-80) and his *Geschichte der alten Philosophie* (Munich: Beck, 1894). Both works went through many editions.

[2] In 1894 Windelband supported Julius Bergmann and opposed Cohen and Natorp in the habilitation case of Ludwig Busse, and he did so by declaring Bergmann alone a competent judge of the candidate's qualities. In the early 1900s Windelband saw no place for Cassirer in Straßburg "on confessional grounds"; whether he opposed Cassirer personally on these grounds, or was simply reporting a fact about the administration, is difficult to determine from the context. On these facts, see Ulrich Sieg, *Aufstieg und Niedergang des Marburger Neukantianismus* (Würzburg: Königshausen & Neumann, 1994), pp. 192, 335.

[3] Wilhelm Windelband, 'Die philosophische Richtungen der Gegenwart', in *Große Denker*, ed. Ernst von Aster (Leipzig: Quelle & Meyer, 1911), II, 361–377, esp. 370–371.

[4] Hermann Cohen, *System der Philosophie. Erster Teil: Logik der reinen Erkenntnis*. (Berlin: Cassirer, 1902). *System der Philosophie. Zweiter Teil: Ethik des reinen Willens*. (Berlin: Cassirer, 1904). *System der Philosophie. Dritter Teil: Ästhetik des reinen Gefühls* (Berlin: Cassirer, 1912).

[5] Wilhelm Windelband, *Präludien. Aufsätze und Reden zur Philosophie und ihrer Geschichte*. Neunte Auflage. (Tübingen: Mohr, 1924), two volumes. All references to this work will be to this edition.

With the benefit of hindsight, it is safe to say that Windelband made two central contributions to the neo-Kantian movement: his investigation into the logic of history; and his conception of philosophy as a normative enterprise. The concern with history will stimulate the later investigations of Rickert and Lask;[6] and the normative conception of philosophy will be the basis for the philosophy of value, which will be a central interest of German philosophy in the later 19th and early 20th centuries.[7] Windelband's normative conception of philosophy remains one of the vital links between neo-Kantianism and contemporary philosophy, which has been no less concerned with the concept of normativity.[8]

The sources and origins of Windelband's neo-Kantianism are obscure. There are no published letters or documents that show when, where, how, why and because of whom, he became converted to the critical philosophy.[9] Kuno Fischer seems to have been the decisive influence. Windelband had been a student at Jena, where he heard Fischer's lectures on Kant. The influence of Fischer upon him can be inferred from the importance he gave to Fischer, whom he regarded as the decisive figure in the birth of the neo-Kantian movement.[10] Otto Liebmann also appears to have been important for Windelband's neo-Kantianism. In a late tribute he praised Liebmann for being the first scholar to develop a genuinely critical interpretation of Kant, one neither psychological nor metaphysical.[11] Windelband met Liebmann in Straßburg in 1882, after which they were in frequent correspondence.

Having treated Windelband's work on the logic of history elsewhere,[12] the focus of this chapter will be upon Windelband's other contribution to neo-Kantianism, his normative conception of philosophy. We will see in the first five sections the precise meaning and problems of that conception, and then in the final three sections the stages in which it took shape in Windelband's thinking. Windelband's intellectual development was no less twisted and turbulent than Cohen's. It was only after a long inner struggle that he arrived at his normative conception of philosophy. We will not consider, however, Windelband's intellectual development after he formed the

[6] Windelband's interest in the logic of history began with his famous Straßburger Rektoratsrede *Geschichte und Naturwissenschaft* (Strassburg: Heitz, 1894). It continued with Heinrich Rickert's *Die Grenzen der wissenschaftliche Begriffsbildung* (Tübingen: Mohr, 1902) and *Die Probleme der Geschichtsphilosophie*, Dritte Auflage (Heidelberg: Winter, 1924). The same interest appeared in Emil Lask's *Fichtes Idealismus und die Geschichte* (Tübingen: Mohr, 1902).
[7] On the philosophy of value, or so-called *Wertphilosophie*, see Herbert Schnädelbach, *Philosophy in Germany 1831–1933*. (Cambridge: Cambridge University Press, 1984), pp. 161–191.
[8] This is especially the case with regard to the so-called "Pittsburgh school". See Chauncey Maher, *The Philosophy of the Pittsburgh School* (London: Taylor & Francis, 2012).
[9] There are few sources on Windelband's life. The main source is Heinrich Rickert's *Wilhelm Windelband*, Zweite Auflage (Tübingen: Mohr, 1929).
[10] See his assessment of Fischer in *Kuno Fischer und sein Kant* (Halle: Ehrhardt Karras, 1897), pp. 10–11; and *Kuno Fischer: Gedächtnisrede* (Heidelberg: Winter, 1907), pp. 24–25.
[11] See Wilhelm Windelband, 'Otto Liebmanns Philosophie', in *Kant-Studien* XV (1910), iii–x.
[12] See my *The German Historicist Tradition* (Oxford: Oxford University Press, 2011), pp. 365–392; and my 'Historicism and neo-Kantianism', *Studies in History and Philosophy of Science* 39 (2008), 554–564.

outlines of his normative conception. That would be a much longer story, which we have no space to tell here.

2. A Science of Norms

Windelband first put forward his normative conception of philosophy in a lecture he gave in 1881 on the occasion of the centenary of the publication of the *Kritik der reinen Vernunft*.[13] This lecture, entitled simply 'Immanuel Kant', reveals the rationale for his neo-Kantianism as well as his normative conception of philosophy. To celebrate the centenary with a fitting tribute, Windelband proudly declares Kant's *Kritik der reinen Vernunft* to be "the Bible", or more literally "the founding book" (*Grundbuch*), of German philosophy (114). Much of the rest of his lecture is an attempt to explain why this is so, in both a historical and philosophical sense.

As the occasion required, Windelband ascribes great historical significance to Kant's philosophy. There are, we are told, only two basic philosophical systems: that of Kant and that of the ancient Greeks (viz. Plato and Aristotle) (117). With Kant's philosophy, there began "a whole new realm of thought", one which stands in marked contrast to that of the Greek world. Kant's philosophy was indeed a revolution, because, for the first time in Western culture, it broke with the legacy of classical Greece. Kant overthrew the intellectualism of Greek culture, which rested upon its naive faith in reason, its bold confidence that thinking alone could reveal the very essence of the world. Kant questioned this faith in reason in two ways: by teaching that reason cannot get beyond the limits of experience; and by separating morality and aesthetics from reason (in its theoretical sense) (121–122). *Prima facie* this seems to be a false account of philosophical history, because it seems to ride roughshod over the ancient Greek sceptics, who questioned faith in reason no less than Kant. But Windelband's claim on behalf of Kant's originality is not that he was the first sceptic, but that Kant and the Greeks represent "the two great philosophical systems". The sceptics, being "intellectual nomads", as Kant called them, have no resting place or system. Kant's system of philosophy is not sceptical, Windelband stresses, because its aim is to determine the basic principles of all science, art and morality, the foundations on which all those disciplines rest (122). Kant's system differs from the Greeks because it places these foundations in a different place than they: not in contemplation of being as being, still less in the intuition of the forms, but in experience and the autonomy of reason.

Part of the originality and importance of Kant's philosophy, Windelband adds, lies in its close alliance with the modern mathematical sciences. The first important intellectual development since the Greeks, he tells us, was the rise of these new sciences (116). The purpose of Kant's critique was to determine their foundations, to show the

---

[13] Wilhelm Windelband, 'Immanuel Kant. Zur Säkularfeier seiner Philosophie'. Ein Vortrag, 1881. *Präludien* I, 112–146.

conditions for the possibility of a mathematical knowledge of nature. Hence Kant, entirely in the spirit of the new sciences, had adopted mathematization as the precondition of science itself: "I maintain that in each doctrine of nature there is only so much science to be found in it as there is mathematics."[14] Of course, the Greeks too were firm believers in the mathematization of nature, and they were indeed the founders of this method. But Kant differed from them in one important respect: he limited mathematical knowledge of nature to appearances. Mathematics was a human construction, the creation of our forms of sensibility, and as such not the reason according to which God created the world.

Although Windelband stresses the close connection between Kant and the new sciences, he is also quick to distance Kant's philosophy from the new positivism (123). The positivists too wanted a close connection between philosophy and the sciences—so much so, that they wanted philosophy to disappear into them. That positivist elimination programme presupposes, however, their very naive conception of science. The positivists are naive about science, Windelband argues, because they do not recognize the intellectual preconditions for its possibility (123). They are simple empiricists who see knowledge as a collection of facts, as if these facts were simply given, and as if human sensing and thinking played no role in their constitution. It is one of Kant's great contributions to have shown that there are intellectual preconditions of science. We cannot determine any point in time, undertake any measurement, calculate any weight, or conduct a single experiment, without applying basic concepts and presupposing fundamental principles. The very presence of these concepts and principles means that philosophy cannot be reduced down to the sciences, because it takes a philosopher to bring them to self-consciousness and to investigate their possibility.

The core of Kant's philosophy, Windelband tells us, centres around the question how a priori representations relate to their object (134). That, at any rate, was Kant's first formulation of his problem in his famous 1772 letter to Marcus Herz.[15] But it is important to note, Windelband advises us, that Kant's later thinking about this question changed its very meaning. As first posed, the question seems to assume that: 1) there is some object existing independent of our representations; and that 2) knowledge consists in the correspondence between them and their object. But it was these very assumptions that Kant overturned in the course of his investigation. Kant explains the possibility of knowledge not through the correspondence of a representation with an object but through the conformity of representations with rules (135). He replaced the concept of an object with that of a rule. For Kant, then, objects turn out to be nothing more than "determinate rules for uniting representations" (137).

---

[14]   Kant, 'Vorrede' to *Metaphysische Anfangsgründe der Naturwissenschaft*, AA IV, 470.

[15]   See Kant to Marcus Herz, February 21, 1772, *Briefwechsel*, ed. Otto Schöndörffer (Hamburg: Meiner, 1972), pp. 99–106.

It is in this context that Windelband introduces his concept of a norm (138). For him "a rule" and "a norm" are essentially synonomous terms.[16] The analysis of truth into rules was one and the same as its analysis into norms. The new normative conception of truth appears explicitly in the general principle: "Truth is normativity of thinking" (138). Windelband did not invent the concepts "norm" or "normativity", for which there was ample precedent in the writings of Lotze, Herbart and Sigwart. What is original to, and characteristic of, Windelband, however, is the central importance he gives to the concept of normativity in philosophy. Philosophy was for him essentially a science of norms. The task of philosophy is to determine the basic norms that bestow value upon all human activity, whether thinking, willing or feeling (139). There are basic norms not only in science but also in morality and art. There are then three parts of philosophy: science, ethics and aesthetics.

What, though, are these norms? What ontological status do they have? Where do they exist? Where do they come from? Such questions, Windelband replies, Kant wisely refused to answer. "Kant declined any metaphysical interpretation of these rules" (137). The attempt to answer such questions was the enterprise of speculative idealism. But Windelband issues an embargo against all such speculation, insisting upon the strictly immanent status of Kant's philosophy, whose intent is to stay firmly within the limits of experience.

In forgoing all metaphysical speculation, Windelband was self-consciously and deliberately pushing philosophy away from its traditional function as a worldview. He tells us explicitly and emphatically that Kant's task was to provide not "a worldview" (*Weltbild*) but a theory of "normal consciousness" (*das normale Bewußtsein*), that is, consciousness insofar as it conforms to norms (141). Yet on no other issue did Windelband vascillate so much as the need for and value of a worldview. As a student of Lotze, he had grown to believe in the necessity of metaphysics, which, in his early years, he makes an integral part of his epistemology.[17] In his later years, however, he will come full circle, reaffirming the need for and value of metaphysics as one of the legitimate concerns of philosophy.[18] What indeed distinguished Kant's philosophy from a soulless positivism, Windelband would later teach, is precisely that it provides a complete worldview. With the later Windelband, "Kant's worldview" would enter into the discourse of the Southwestern school.[19]

The ultimate upshot of Kant's philosophical revolution, Windelband reckons, is that it overturned the traditional way of conceiving knowledge as "the mirror of

---

[16] Here is the decisive passage in the *ipsissima verba* of the German original: "*In der unendlichen Mannigfaltigkeit der Vorstellungsverbindungen gibt es solche, welche einer allgemeingiltigen [sic] Regel, einer Norm entsprechen. Wahrheit ist Normalität des Denkens.*" (*Präludien* I, 138).

[17] See Section 7.

[18] See his 1904 lecture 'Nach hundert Jahre. Zu Kants hundertjährigen Todestage', *Präludien* I, 149–150.

[19] Windelband's student, Richard Kroner, developed this interpretation in his *Kants Weltanschauung* (Tübingen: Mohr, 1914).

nature" (*Spiegel der Welt*) (127). According to that ubiquitous metaphor, representations are images of objects which they resemble, just like a mirror image resembles its object (123). We determine whether representations are true or false by comparing them with their prototypes, which are objects existing independently from them. The Kantian Revolution means, however, that the standard of knowledge is not in the object but inside the subject itself, residing in the basic norm for organizing its representations.

Such, in a nutshell, was Windelband's first statement of his normative conception of philosophy. For a 21st-century reader, it is remarkable to find Windelband explaining Kant's philosophical revolution in terms of replacing the metaphor of the mirror of nature with that of normativity. Since Richard Rorty, anglophone readers have grown accustomed to seeing that transformation taking place in the early 20th century with philosophers like Dewey, Wittgenstein and Heidegger.[20] But if Windelband shows us anything, it is that we have to place that transformation much earlier: with Kant, or at least with his interpretation of Kant.

3. The Rehabilitation of Philosophy

The conception of philosophy Windelband formulated in 'Immanuel Kant' was his solution to the obsolescence crisis which had troubled all neo-Kantians. Just how it resolves that crisis Windelband did not explain in his lecture, but he turned to that task only a year later in a long essay, his 1882 'Was ist Philosophie?'[21]

Windelband's account of the origin of this crisis differs in important ways from his predecessors. For Windelband, it was not the result of the collapse of speculative idealism in the 19th century, as it was for Zeller and Meyer. Rather, it began with the general scepticism about metaphysics in the 18th century. After philosophy declared its independence from theology during the Renaissance, it conceived its characteristic task to be metaphysics, a universal theory of being or "the general science of the cosmos" (*die Gesamtwissenschaft vom Weltall*). Each of the new empirical sciences lay claim to knowledge of a special part of the world; but philosophy found its unique calling in metaphysics, which would be a knowledge of the world as a whole (16). Philosophers of the 18th century, however, became very concerned with epistemological issues, with questions about the origins, powers and limits of knowledge; and the more they examined the aims and claims of metaphysics, the more they found them wanting (18). The crisis of philosophy then arose when metaphysics could no longer legitimate itself, when it could not prove its worth as a science. But if metaphysics is bankrupt, what is left for philosophy? There seemed to be nothing more for it to do. The entire realm of nature had been carved up by the particular sciences.

---

[20] Rorty places Kant within the epistemological tradition held captive to the mirror of nature metaphor. See his *Philosophy and the Mirror of Nature* (Oxford: Blackwell, 1980), p. 12.

[21] Windelband, *Präludien* I, 1–54.

Windelband summarizes the predicament of philosophy like this: "Philosophy is like King Lear, who gave all his goods to his children, and who now must be thrown on the street like a beggar." (19)

Though it seems purely historical, Windelband's account of the obsolescence crisis makes an important point against his neo-Kantian predecessors. Unlike Fischer, Zeller and Meyer, Windelband does not think that the solution to this crisis lies simply with epistemology; for him, epistemology is part of the problem rather than the solution, because it created the crisis by undermining metaphysics. Windelband sees epistemology, reflection on the powers and limits of knowledge, as a pursuit characteristic of *pre*-Kantian epistemology; and he is perfectly clear that philosophy cannot resolve its crisis if it becomes "a theory of knowledge", that is, "investigation into the nature of science, the process of knowledge" (18). This means that the neo-Kantian proposal to make philosophy into epistemology cannot be sufficient; we have to go on to specify something about the kind of epistemology. Though Fischer, Zeller and Meyer had noted Kant's debts to the epistemological tradition of Descartes, Locke and Hume, they saw his differences from them simply as a matter of greater focus and emphasis. But Windelband does not think that this goes far enough; it fails to sees a fundamental difference *in kind* between pre-Kantian and Kantian epistemology. To miss this difference has profound consequences: ignorance of the very nature of philosophy itself.

For Windelband, epistemology before Kant was essentially a psychological or historical enterprise. Its fundamental task was to explain the causes of knowledge (22). It would explain knowledge as it would any fact in the world: by deriving it from its causes or general laws. Here Windelband seems to have in mind especially Locke's "plain, historical method" or Hume's "science of human nature". But Kant broke profoundly with this tradition, Windelband explains, because he saw epistemology not as a psychological or historical investigation into the causes of knowledge but as a critical investigation into its value or validity (23). What was at stake was not the causes of representations but the foundation or justification of judgements (25). There is a fundamental difference in kind between these concerns, Windelband argues, because both true and false judgements have natural origins; both arise from a process of natural necessity and fall under natural laws. These natural laws do not provide, therefore, a criterion for the truth of judgements; so a complete explanation of their causes will not answer the question whether the judgement is true (23). It is solely this question, however, that is the special province of epistemology: "for the theory of knowledge it is only a matter of whether the representations are valid, i.e., whether they should be recognized as true." (25)

Implicit in Windelband's account of pre-Kantian epistemology there lay another critique of his neo-Kantian predecessors. Windelband was in effect saying: Fries, Herbart, Beneke, Helmholtz, Fischer, Zeller, Meyer and Lange have all misunderstood the essential nature of the Kantian enterprise. They have misunderstood it because, like their pre-Kantian antecedents, they have misconstrued it in psychological terms. They have failed to notice the basic distinction between explaining the causes of beliefs and assessing the reasons for them. What was fundamental about the Kantian Revolution in philosophy, Windelband maintains, is precisely this shift away from causes and explanation towards reasons and criticism. Although this criticism of Windelband's neo-Kantian predecessors is completely implicit in "Was ist Philosophie?", it became entirely explicit in a later work, *Die Philosophie im deutschen Geistesleben des XIX. Jahrhunderts,* where Windelband takes a long retrospective look at all the philosophical movements of the 19th century, not least the neo-Kantian movement, which he expressly takes to task for its psychological interpretation of Kant.[22]

The central argument of Windelband's "Was ist Philosophie?" is that *only* his normative conception of philosophy can overcome the obsolescence crisis. If we define epistemology in terms of psychology in the manner of my noble neo-Kantian predecessors, Windelband was saying, then we do not escape the crisis but remain caught in its snares. For, by the late 19th century, psychology had become a natural science of its own, independent of philosophy.[23] It now applies the same methods of observation and experiment as physics and physiology, and it now employs the same paradigms of explanation as these sciences by subsuming psychic events under general laws. Whatever Herbart might say, psychology gets verifiable results independent of metaphysics, which is not needed to guide its enquiries. But if psychology is now an empirical science like any other, then those who fail to distinguish epistemology from psychology virtually ensure the obsolescence of philosophy. Rather than being a distinct discipline apart from the empirical sciences, philosophy will just become one among them. Fries, Herbart and Beneke had all dreamed of psychology becoming a science. But now that their dream had become a reality, where does that leave philosophy? Their psychologistic answers to that question only leads to the obsolescence they are so eager to avoid.

Despite these criticisms of the neo-Kantians, Windelband still accepted the common neo-Kantian conception of philosophy as epistemology *(Erkenntnistheorie)*; its just that he understands epistemology in very different terms. It is not the explanation of knowledge according to the laws of psychology but the criticism of knowledge according to the standards of reason. More specifically, philosophy is the criticism of particular kinds of claims to knowledge, namely, synthetic a priori or universal and necessary claims. Philosophy is therefore "the critical science of universally valid values" (29). There are three domains where universally valid claims are made: in science, morality and art, corresponding to the realms of cognition, volition and

---

[22] Wilhelm Windelband, *Die Philosophie im deutschen Geistesleben des XIX. Jahrhunderts. Fünf Vorlesungen.* (Tübingen: Mohr, 1909), pp. 81–84.

[23] Windelband would argue this point in his 1875 inaugural lecture in Zurich, which we will examine in Section 9, and in his 1894 'Strassburger Rektoratsrede', 'Geschichte und Naturwissenschaft', *Präludien* II, 143.

feeling; and so there is accordingly a philosophy of science, morality and art. In a marked departure from his own earlier views, whose causes we will examine later, Windelband warns against confusing epistemology with two very kindred but still very different disciplines: psychology and metaphysics (28). The problem with conflating philosophy with these disciplines is that one reifies or hypostasizes values, making them into psychological processes or archetypes of reason. Psychology and metaphysics are theories about what is or must be; but as a science of value philosophy concerns what ought to be.

To define further the nature of philosophy, Windelband attempts to specify its precise subject matter. He makes a distinction between two different kinds of propositions: judgements (*Urtheile*) and appraisals (*Beurtheilungen*) (29). Although they have the same grammatical form, where a predicate is attributed to a subject, these propositions have a very different meaning. In a judgement we attribute a property to an object; but in an appraisal we add nothing more to the representation of an object (30). Appraisals concern not the object itself so much as the subject's attitude towards it; they are essentially acts of approval or disapproval (30). The task of an appraisal is therefore to determine the *value* of the object. This distinction is crucial for defining philosophy, Windelband maintains, because its special concern is appraisals (32–33). Philosophy does not *describe* appraisals, like the historical sciences; and it does not *explain* them, like psychology; it does not treat them as if they were objects in the world at all. Rather, it actually *makes* appraisals, determining what should be or have a value.

When a critical philosopher makes an appraisal, Windelband explains, he assumes that something should be recognized as valid for everyone; he makes, in other words, a universal and necessary claim to value. In doing so, he presupposes "a universal criterion that should hold for everyone alike" (37). It is the task of the critical philosopher to determine these criteria, to ascertain the highest standards of judgement in the fields of science, morality and art. These criteria are norms, laws or ideals about what ought to be; they have no reality themselves because by them we measure or appraise all reality. In each field we presuppose the concept of an ideal being who recognizes and follows these norms. This ideal being Windelband calls "normal consciousness" (*Normalbewußtsein*) (45). We do not assume that this normal being exists, only that it ought to do so (44). Understood in these terms, philosophy is "the science of normal consciousness" (46).

Despite all Windelband's efforts to clarify the task of philosophy, there remained major ambiguities about his programme. It is unclear whether the Windelbandian *Wertwissenschaftler* is making values, assessing things according to values already made, or simply describing values and pointing out the means to and consequences of them. Sometimes it seems that he is doing some combination of all three. Only the first is really an appraisal in the strict sense, because the other two tasks need not involve accepting the values on which the appraisal is made; one is really judging rather than appraising because one is simply drawing out the logical conclusion of holding a value, or one is pointing out certain empirical facts (viz. the means to ends, or the consequences of acting on a value). Windelband's confusions on this score proved a troublesome legacy for Rickert and Weber, who struggled to fight through them.[24]

4. The Normative and the Natural

Windelband's solution to the obsolescence crisis of philosophy in "Was ist Philosophie?" rested entirely upon his distinction between two very different intellectual domains, the normative and the natural. While the natural sciences concern themselves with the natural realm, determining laws about what is the case, philosophy deals with the normative realm, determining standards or ideals for judgement about what ought to be the case. The distinction has the advantage of clarity and firmness. It also seems to achieve precisely what it sets out to do: it makes philosophy autonomous, giving it a unique and separate domain apart from the empirical sciences. So far, so good.

Yet the very strength of the distinction is also its weakness: it makes such a strong and sharp separation that the two domains seem to have nothing to do with one another. If philosophy deals with norms about what ought to be the case, and if it is not at all concerned with laws about what is the case, then it seems doomed to irrelevance. Philosophers can talk and theorize all they want about their ideal world of truth, beauty and goodness, but if their ideals are not followed, if their norms are not realized in the actual world, their safe and secure domain turns into a fantasy world. Windelband, it seemed, had solved the problem of obsolescence only at the price of irrelevance.

No one was more acutely conscious of this problem than Windelband himself. Philosophy was never for him an entirely theoretical activity having no bearing on the world itself. It was an essential part of Kant's revolution in philosophy, in his view, that it rejected the classical Greek conception of philosophy as contemplation, and that it would attempt to determine the fundamental norms behind all human activities. Philosophy should actually make a difference to the world, Kant held, because self-consciousness of these norms determines how we follow them, how we really think, act and feel in the world. Windelband shared this Kantian belief in the powers of philosophy; but the problem was how to justify it, how to explain the relevance of philosophy to life and the world. This was an especially pressing problem for Windelband, given his own sharp and fast distinction between the normative and natural.

---

[24] Rickert and Weber made the distinction between value judgements (*Werturteile)* and reference to values (*Wertbeziehung*), which they used to distinguish between the cultural and natural sciences. On their distinction and its problems, see Beiser, *The German Historicist Tradition*, pp. 412–414, 532–533.

Windelband's first sustained effort to solve this problem is his 1882 essay 'Normen und Naturgesetze',[25] which first appeared in the 1884 edition of *Präludien*. Though he would often return to this problem in later years, this essay would set the agenda for all his later efforts to deal with it.

Windelband first sets the problem in the context of one classical philosophical conundrum: freedom of will. This seems to make the original problem all the more insolvable by tying it to one of the most intractable issues in all philosophy. But Windelband felt he had no choice, that the deeper issue was unavoidable. The very possibility of normativity hung in the balance. For if all events in the natural world are governed by laws, such that they must occur and cannot be otherwise, what is the value of having norms? What is the point in telling people what they ought to do? Norms have a point only if we have the choice to act or not act on them; but if everything is determined by natural laws, so that we act necessarily in one way or another, there seems to be no choice. Windelband then generalizes the problem, stressing that the same problem arises for other norms, for those of science and art as well as morality. In science we assume that we have the power to follow the norms of logic; and in art we suppose that we have the capacity to follow the norms of painting, composing, building, etc. If all thinking and feeling were determined by natural necessity, these norms would be just as pointless as those of morality. So Windelband poses his problem in the most general form: What is the relationship between norms and laws?

To understand their relationship, Windelband advises, we must first have a clear account of the difference between them. We must grasp the different activities involved in each, in applying laws and in making norms (65). The main difference is simple enough. A norm is not a principle of explanation; and a law is not a standard or criterion of judgement. This is because laws *explain* things, whereas norms *assess* or *appraise* them. With laws, we determine what *must be* the case by subsuming particular events under general relations of cause and effect; and with norms, we determine what *ought to be* the case. Through a norm we determine what something should be if it is to be true, good or beautiful (66–67).

Once we put the distinction this way, Windelband thinks, we can see that there is no conflict between norms and laws. They are just two different activities which treat their object from complementary perspectives (67). Although they are very different, they are also connected, because the norm prescribes what we ought to do in the world; since 'ought' implies 'can', it is valid only if we can follow it, only if we can act upon it (68). The problem of accounting for the relationship between norms and laws is then to explain the connection between them while still recognizing their differences. We must avoid, Windelband warns, two extreme views: completely separating norms and laws, as if they have nothing to do with one another; and conflating them, as if there is really no difference between them (68).

---

[25] Windelband, 'Normen und Naturgesetze', *Präludien* II, 59–98.

What is the middle ground between these extremes? Windelband attempts to plot it by stressing the *contingent* connection between norms and laws. All particular human actions, as events in nature, conform to laws, and they occur of necessity. But it is contingent whether these actions happen to follow norms. They might comply with norms; but they also might not comply with them. Although the mere fact that an action occurs of necessity does not exclude its compliance with norms, it also does not entail it. For even actions that violate norms still follow natural laws (69).

Although norms and laws are only contingently connected regarding whether a particular action complies with a norm, there is another respect in which they are necessarily connected. Norms are intended to be followed, to be acted upon in the world, and they assume that we have the power to act on them. They presuppose that there are many possible ways of acting in the world, that there are different forms of thinking, acting and feeling, and they select one from them as the right or correct way or form (72–73). Thus the laws of logic are a selection from the possible forms of association in consciousness; the laws of ethics a selection from the possible forms of motivation; and the laws of aesthetics a selection from the possible forms of feeling (73). From all the possibilities of thinking, willing and feeling, norms prescribe one as the best or most worthy.

Because norms are intended to be acted upon, and because they are conceived as one way of thinking, willing and feeling in the world, they have for Windelband a necessary connection with the natural processes that realize them. A norm is for him the realization of value through a natural law, which is the means for the actualization of its end. Windelband then states the following definition: "*Norms are those forms of actualization through natural laws which should be approved for the end of universal validity.*" (74)

The close connection between norms and laws appears even more clearly, Windelband thinks, once we recognize that norms are supposed to be reasons for our actions. They are, as he puts it, the "determining grounds" (*Bestimmungsgründe*) of human conduct (85). When we accept the validity of a norm, we adopt it, under the appropriate circumstances, as the reason or justification for an action; it serves as a constraint upon us, telling us the particular thing that we should do among the wealth of possibilities. When we resolve to act upon the norm, it then becomes part of the process of law-governed events in the world (87). In this way ethical and aesthetic norms become not only reasons that justify actions but also causes that produce them.

For all their apparent plausibility, Windelband's attempts to connect norms and laws raise serious difficulties. While it is indeed the case that a norm is conceived as a manner of action, it also cannot be simply defined in such terms. For there is more to a norm than any set of actual actions. A norm determines what we ought to do, and just because "ought" is not reducible to "is," so the norm cannot be reduced down to any particular matter of fact, in this case manner of action. But, leaving that difficulty aside, there is another no less serious one in assuming that norms are actualized through natural laws. For this begs the question whether we really can act on these norms, and whether they really can be actualized in a deterministic universe. If all actions occur of necessity, such that they cannot be done otherwise, then the norm becomes pointless. We are not acting on the norm but just following a natural law. Windelband has still not addressed, in other words, the problem of freedom on which normativity rests.

Windelband's solution to this second difficulty is his compatibilism regarding the grand question of the relationship between freedom and necessity. If an event happens according to natural laws, he argues, that does not exclude the possibility that the agent has adopted a norm as a reason for his action. We assume that natural necessity is incompatible with normativity only because we think that acting on norms involves the possibility of doing otherwise, where that possibility is defined in terms of acting countercausally, contrary to the laws of nature. But no such assumption is necessary, Windelband contends, because reasons can still be causes of actions even though they are determined according to natural laws. We need not parse phrases about doing otherwise in terms of some mystical power of acting countercausally because all that these phrases mean is that we would have done differently if we, or the circumstances, were different (88).

Given his compatibilist position, it should come as no surprise that Windelband is highly critical of Kant's own solution to the problem of freedom (62, 88, 97). Kant's thinking about this issue began from the false premise that moral responsibility and natural causality are incompatible, that we have a power of transcendental freedom that involves spontaneity, which is the power to act without any prior causes. In assuming that the will consists in such a power, Kant pushed the will into a spooky noumenal world, Windelband complains, where it is inaccessible to science as well as moral imputation. Hence, on Kant's own admission, the real morality of our actions are unintelligible to us.[26] Above all, we need to overcome Kant's dualism, Windelband advises, because its radical separation between normativity and nature makes the connection between them obscure and mysterious. "The realm of freedom is in the middle of nature; it is that province where only norms are valid; it is our task and happiness to settle in this province." (98)

Despite these criticisms of Kant, there was still one respect in which Windelband, like Liebmann,[27] remained a very stubborn Kantian about the whole question of freedom. He was a Kantian of 1787 rather than one of 1792, in that he adopted Kant's account of freedom in the second *Kritik* over that in his *Die Religion innerhalb der Grenzen der bloßen Vernunft*. Windelband accepted Kant's account of freedom as autonomy, as the power to act morally. "Freedom is the domination of conscience. That alone that deserves this name is *the determination of empirical consciousness according to the consciousness of norms* . . . Freedom means to obey reason." (87–88)

---

[26] KrV B579n.   [27] See Chapter 7, Section 3.

Windelband's attraction to this concept of freedom is readily understandable, because it connects normativity with laws and removes any power of doing otherwise that seems to contradict these laws. But there is a problem with this conception of freedom, a problem that Kant realized in the early 1790s and that Windelband seems to have forgotten: that defining freedom in terms of moral action makes it impossible for us to be free and immoral. To avoid this problem, Kant made his famous distinction between *Wille* and *Willkür*, between the will and choice, and stressed the importance of *Willkür* or choice for moral responsibility and freedom. But the price of such a doctrine is again making a dualism between the realms of freedom and nature.

Whatever their ultimate merits, it should be clear from the criticisms suggested here that Windelband was very far from a having an unproblematic account of the relationship between normativity and nature. This is hardly surprising, given that figuring out that relationship involved the classical problem of freedom. It was one of the merits of Windelband's discussion of this relationship that he had never lost sight of that basic problem. But just because that problem was so complex and imponderable Windelband would return to it again in his later years. We will eventually have to consider his later attempt to address this conundrum of conundrums.

5. Philosophical Method

Windelband returned to the question of the vocation of philosophy in another article of the early 1880s, 'Kritische und Genetische Methode?', which was written in 1883.[28] This was his most rigorous attempt yet to define the nature of philosophy and to provide it with a firm foundation independent of the empirical sciences. Windelband now approaches his problem in a completely new manner, attempting to distinguish philosophy from the empirical sciences through their different methods. Kant had already discovered the proper method of philosophy, Windelband tells us, though he did not develop it with sufficient clarity. As a result, there has been constant confusion about how its method differs from that of empirical science. To prevent that confusion, Windelband strives to explain the distinctive method of philosophy in the most simple and fundamental terms. This article too had a polemical point: it is directed against all those neo-Kantians who wanted philosophy to imitate the methods of the empirical sciences.

Windelband casts his discussion in strictly logical terms, beginning with a detailed explanation of the difference between the inductive and deductive methods. Both these methods, we are told, presuppose certain basic principles or axioms. Kant would call them "synthetic a priori principles", but to avoid the controversy surrounding Kant's doctrine of the synthetic a priori, Windelband prefers the simpler term "axiom". He then defines philosophy as the science of axioms (107–108). Logic

---

[28] Windelband, *Präludien* II, 99–135.

determines the axioms of the sciences, aesthetics the axioms of art, and ethics the axioms of morality. The main task of philosophy is to expound the complete system of these axioms.

The chief problem of philosophy, Windelband informs us, is "the validity of axioms (*die Geltung der Axiome*) (108). Somehow, philosopy has to assess or evaluate axioms. But how can it do this? Because they are the basis of all proof, axioms cannot be proven themselves. We cannot assess or evaluate them, it seems, because to do that already presupposes them. Any attempt to justify them would be circular, assuming them in order to prove them. Still, Windelband reassures us, these axioms have an immediate certainty, a self-evidence, that does not require proof or demonstration. The business of philosophy is not to prove (*beweisen*) but to show (*aufweisen*) this immediate certainty, to lay this evidence before our eyes (109).

Philosophy can show this immediate certainty in two ways. Either one reveals the "factual validity" (*tatsächliche Geltung*) of these axioms by showing how they are embedded in the practices of everyday life, by revealing how they are involved in all our ways of thinking, feeling and acting; or one reveals their "teleological necessity" by showing how accepting these axioms is necessary to achieve certain ends (109). The former procedure is the *genetic* method; the latter is the *critical* method. For the genetic method, the axioms are actual ways of understanding, feeling and acting; for the critical method, however, they are not facts at all; they are norms. Norms prescribe means to ends; they tell us what we should do so that our thinking is true, our willing is moral, and our feeling grasps the beautiful (109). The ultimate justification for them is that they prove to be efficient and necessary means of attaining these ends.

Although Windelband is not so explicit, it is clear that his distinction in methods presupposes his earlier distinction in 'Normen und Naturgesetze' between norms and natural laws. The central concern of the genetic method is to determine a specific kind of law, namely, those which explain why people adopt axioms on psychological and cultural-historical grounds. The main interest of the critical method, however, is to determine a specific kind of norm, namely, that which prescribes how we achieve certain ends. The difference between these methods also follows along the lines of Windelband's earlier distinction between judgement and appraisal. All the ambiguities about appraisal—whether it is making or prescribing values, assessing things according to values or simply describing values—hold for Windelband's critical method.

However we describe the critical method, Windelband thinks that it alone is characteristic of philosophy. The genetic method falls within the provinces of the empirical sciences. All those who want to push philosophy in the direction of the empirical sciences assume that it has a genetic method. But if we take philosophy in this direction, Windelband argues, we pay a terrible price: forfeiting the validity of axioms, their claim to universal and necessary worth (114). The genetic method shows only that axioms are "factually valid", that is, it shows how people adopt them in the practices of their ordinary life, how they as a matter of fact assume them in the sciences, arts and morality. But it is an old and basic logical truth: what happens as a matter of fact cannot be the basis of a universal and necessary principle. What is believed or assumed is so only now and then by this or that person; and even if everyone believes them all the time, it still does not prove that they are true. The genetic method ends with a causal theory about the origins of beliefs, showing them to be the necessary result of psychology and cultural history; but this causal necessity proves nothing about validity for the simple reason that it applies to invalid as well as valid beliefs (115). For the genetic method, all beliefs are on a par, all are equally necessary results of psychological and historical causes. Thus those who push philosophy in the direction of the empirical sciences, Windelband concludes, have to accept a very problematic consequence: a complete relativism (116).

Relativism, of course, is the great challenge to Windelband's conception of philosophy. If relativism is tenable, then there is no philosophy, no science of universal and necessary axioms, all for the simple reason that there really are no such axioms. Windelband, however, found it hard to take relativism seriously. He argues that a radical relativism is not sustainable because it is self-refuting, presupposing the very axioms that it attempts to bring into question (116). The relativist must assume, for example, that it is possible to ascertain certain basic facts (viz. cultural diversity), that it is possible to draw general conclusions from them (viz. that all principles are valid only for a specific time and place), and that these have a universal validity; but in assuming all this the relativist presupposes the very rules he disputes. As Windelband puts it: "The more the relativist tries to prove his doctrine, the more ridiculous he becomes; for he refutes all the more what he wants to prove." (117)

All this was much too quick and dismissive, however. Self-refutation is indeed a danger for those who would dispute the basic rules of logic. But what about the moral and aesthetic relativist? Where is the self-refutation in denying any proposed norm of morality and aesthetics? To deny them might be a case of bad behaviour and bad taste, but hardly logical absurdity. It is indeed questionable whether Windelband's critical method avoids relativism any more than the genetic method. The critical method attempts to show how certain axioms are means to ends; but what if one does not accept these ends themselves? What about the immoralist, who does not want to live according to universal laws? What about the dada artist, who does not want to feel beauty? What is to be said against these people? Here Windelband is at least clear and frank: there is no in talking with them (123). The presupposition of the critical method, he admits, is the *faith* that there are universally valid ends. Whoever does not share that faith should simply "stay at home"; the critical philosophy can do nothing for him (123).

The most serious difficulty facing the critical method, Windelband acknowledges, is how the individual comes to know the standpoint of normal consciousness. There is a danger, which Windelband fully admits, that the individual confuses his individual, empirical opinions, desires and tastes with universal and necessary norms (124). The same problem appears on a more general cultural level when a particular nation or people elevates its own mores into universal norms, as if they should be binding on all people. It was the very purpose of the genetic method to expose this kind of specious universality and necessity, to show how the apparently universal and necessary really arises from a particular people at a particular time. What is to prevent the philosopher from making these kinds of specious generalizations, from making his own private views, or the customs and fashions of his own culture, into universal laws for all mankind?

Despite these dangers, Windelband is confident that the critical philosopher, if he is only careful enough, can avoid this fallacy. Since his norms prescribe means to ends, his task is only to determine the necessary means for the realization of ends; and to do this, he does not have to refer to any data of his own individual or empirical consciousness (125). All that he has to show is that the means are really effective for achieving the ends. But this response too was very hasty. Granted, it is a straightforward matter to determine means to ends, it is so only once we know the ends; but this begs the question of how the critical philosopher is to know these ends in the first place. That was the very problem to be solved. Windelband seems to assume that nothing more is involved than knowing the general ends of science (acquiring knowledge), morality (doing the good) and aesthetics (feeling the beautiful). But this account is simply too abstract to be of much help, because the critical philosopher still needs to know in what, specifically, knowledge, goodness and beauty consists. It is precisely in attempting to provide a more specific account of knowledge, goodness and beauty that controversy arises.

An even greater problem arises in trying to solve this difficulty. Windelband admits that the critical philosopher cannot simply spin the universal and necessary principles of reason out of his own head. To know these principles, he has to see how they are embodied in particular ways of thinking, acting and feeling. Just as the linguist knows the rules of grammar from seeing how people actually speak, so the critical philosopher knows the norms of logic, aesthetics and ethics from seeing how people actually think, feel and act. As Windelband puts it: "Teleological construction requires not only the determination of ends, but also the consideration of the material in which these ends should be realized." (127) But now we face the same problem that Windelband raised against the genetic method. Namely, from all these particular facts about actual thinking, feeling and acting we cannot draw universal and necessary conclusions. Windelband is very clear that "consideration of the material" should be only a means of *discovering* the principles of reason and not a means of *justifying* them (127). This is an important distinction to make, and we have seen how it had been applied with good effect by Fries and Meyer; but it does not help Windelband in this case. For it still does not tell us how from this material we can even discover the principles of reason. The problem is that there are many ways of thinking, feeling and acting; and which ways are the instances of the rules? The gap between "is" and "ought", between natural laws and norms, once again lurks in the background.

In the course of thinking about how the critical philosopher knows the principles of reason Windelband began to wrestle with another thinker who had considered this very problem some eighty years before him: Hegel. Rather than condemning Hegel, as so many neo-Kantians before him, Windelband pays tribute to him. He praises Hegel's "deep wisdom" in recognizing that rationality reveals itself only through history (133). There is no escaping the fundamental importance of history in knowing the principles of reason, Windelband realizes. The particular ways of thinking, willing and feeling that embody human rationality are intrinsically historical phenomena, appearing in a specific time, place and culture. The individual's awareness of the principles of reason is also, as a psychological event, a phenomenon that takes place in history. Windelband makes an even greater concession to Hegel when he claims that history provides more suitable material to know the content of reason than psychology. While psychology informs us only about broad formal or structural features of the mind, namely, that it appears in willing, thinking and feeling, history shows us the actual content of reason, namely, what we will, think and feel (131–132). For all these reasons, Windelband concludes that "knowledge of all the content of rational values grows out of the critical illumination of history" (134).

Having paid his homage to Hegel and having recognized the importance of history for rationality, Windelband still fell short of adopting a genuine Hegelian position. While Hegel strived to overcome the gap between the normative and natural through his concept of reason in history, Windelband insists that there is, always was and forever will be, a gap between the normative and the natural, the rational and the historical. There is simply no catapulting over Lessing's broad and ugly ditch, because it is impossible to infer universal and necessary validity from the facts of history. For Windelband, unlike Hegel, history is essentially contingent in the sense that none of its facts are logically necessary; history conforms to causal laws, to be sure, but not necessarily to logical ones, because the non-existence of its laws would not be self-contradictory. And so Windelband concludes: "For the critical method, the historical course of development, in its essentially empirical and contingent determinacy with respect to 'the idea', cannot have a systematic meaning." (133)

Windelband's interactions with Hegel would continue in his later years. The more he thought about "the old man", the more he admired him. The attraction grew to such an extent that the older Windelband nearly became a Hegelian. It was Hegel who helped to convince him that history should be "the organon" of the critical philosophy (i.e. the instrument by which it comes to know the principles of reason),[29] and that the critical philosophy should become a philosophy of culture.[30] It was also Hegel who taught him that the philosophy of history is the means to overcome the

---

[29] See Windelband, 'Über die gegenwärtige Lage und Aufgabe der Philosophie', *Präludien* II, 1–23, esp. 21.
[30] See Windelband, 1910 essay 'Kulturphilosophie und transzendentaler Idealismus', *Präludien* II, 279–294.

dualism between the normative and natural, a goal that seemed more and more desirable to the ageing Windelband. His late philosophy of history is indeed pure Hegel, making the self-consciousness of freedom into the *telos* of history.[31] In an article he wrote in 1910 on the nascent Hegel revival in Heidelberg, Windelband announced that, as long as they refrained from "historicism", the neo-Hegelians had nothing to fear from the neo-Kantians.[32] There was some sweet irony in this declaration of Kantian-Hegelian friendship, given how much the neo-Kantians once loved to hate Hegel. But at the dawn of the new century the old neo-Kantian animus had grown old and cold. A neo-Hegelian movement was in the making.[33] The owl of Minerva had flown back to her home along the banks of the Neckar.

6. The Problem of Freedom

The fundamental business of philosophy, according to Windelband's normative conception of this discipline, is to explain the possibility of norms. Philosophy has to be able to explain how it is possible for people to follow or act upon them. Nothing seems simpler, though, than the fact that people can act on norms, because they do this all the time. They follow instructions, they play games, they observe ancient customs. But, as happens so often in philosophy, what at first seems perfectly obvious later turns out upon reflection to be problematic, if not downright impossible. The possibility of following norms becomes problematic not least because they presuppose choice, that we might decide not to act on them, that we have the possibility of not following them; if we acted on them immediately, automatically and necessarily, it seems there would be no point in making them. Norms would be not imperatives but predictions. So, given that we must have the choice to follow them, the thorny question arises: How are norms possible in a deterministic universe?

We have already seen how, in his early 1882 essay 'Normen und Naturgesetze', Windelband raised and struggled with this question. He wanted to build a bridge between the normative and natural realms, and he made their connection dependent on the problem of freedom, which he had generalized so that it concerned all forms of norm following, whether the norms were moral, logical or aesthetic. But Windelband's first attempt to deal with this question was at best sketchy and provisional, and so it became necessary for him to return to it in later years. His final and most systematic effort to deal with it is his *Über Willensfreiheit*, which consists in twelve lectures which he first gave in Heidelberg in the Winter of 1903.[34] Because of

---

[31] See Wilhelm Windelband, *Geschichtsphilosophie. Eine Kriegsvorlesung. Fragment aus dem Nachlaß.* *Kant-Studien Ergänzungsheft* 38 (1916).

[32] Windelband, 'Die Erneuerung des Hegelianismus', *Präludien* I, 273–289, esp. 281, 284.

[33] On the neo-Hegelian movement, see Paul Honigsheim, 'Zur Hegel Renaissance im Vorkriegsheidelberg', *Hegel-Studien* II (1963), 291–301.

[34] Wilhelm Windelband, *Über Willensfreiheit. Zwölf Vorlesungen.* Zweite unveränderte Auflage (Tübingen: Mohr, 1905). All references in parentheses are to this edition.

the importance of freedom for Windelband's normative conception of philosophy, we do well to examine the main ideas behind these lectures.

In his first lecture Windelband defines the nature of his problem and his strategy for tackling it. When we consider the question of freedom we should realize, he advises, that it is never just a matter of affirming or denying freedom of will (6). The concept has too many meanings and whether one affirms or denies it depends on the particular sense. We also need to keep in mind that freedom is a relative concept (11–12). We are never free absolutely but always in some respect. In applying the concept we need always to ask 'free from what?' We can be free in one respect and not in another. The question of freedom also depends on the particular kind under discussion. There are for Windelband three kinds of freedom, each of which corresponds to three phases of volition (17). The first phase is the genesis of desire or the act of will; the second is the choice between different desires; and the third is the action itself (18). The whole question of freedom divides accordingly into freedom of will, freedom of choice and freedom of action. Windelband's discussion of freedom takes each of these aspects separately.

Windelband begins with freedom of action, the third and simplest form of freedom (19). Freedom of action is simply a movement of the body caused by the will, so that it is some purposive movement (19). We can separate, at least conceptually, will and action (20), Windelband maintains. This is because many of our reflex movements are involuntary, and many impulses of will do not result in action (20). Freedom of action, however, joins the will and action, so that it means simply that we do what we will (20–21). Freedom of action therefore extends only as far as I can execute my will through physical motion (25). No one has the power to touch the moon; and someone with a spinal injury cannot lift a cup.

Having dispatched freedom of action in his second lecture, Windelband moves on to freedom of choice, a much more complex and controversial topic, which takes up the next four lectures (lectures 3–6). The belief in freedom is pre-eminently a matter of the feeling that we have a choice, that we could choose equally between different courses of action, and that it is entirely up to me what I choose (33). Freedom of choice demands that I have the capacity not only to will but also to act on all options; if I am constrained so that I cannot do one or the other, or both, my freedom is limited accordingly (34). Nevertheless, Windelband observes, I can still choose one thing over another even if I cannot act on my choice; I can have preferences even if cannot act on them; it's just that choosing loses its point or purpose—what Windelband calls its *Zweckbedeutung*—if I do not have the power to act on it (34).

Windelband distinguishes freedom of choice from moral freedom. Freedom of choice is a *psychological* concept; it refers to our unconstrained choosing and acting. It is a formal concept because it is irrelevant what we choose (93). The concept of freedom in a moral sense, however, is a *normative* concept; it concerns not what is but what ought to be (96). In this moral sense freedom has a negative meaning because it means independence from desire and passion; but it also has a positive sense because it signifies acting according to reason (95). These senses of freedom are plainly distinct from one another, Windelband insists, because a person can have freedom of choice but not moral freedom (96). This is the case when he or she acts immorally with perfect resolve and through reflective choice. Though they are plainly distinct, these senses of freedom are confused constantly, Windelband complains. We call a person unfree if he acts on base passions, and free if he acts on higher ones. But in both cases we are equally free in terms of freedom of choice. Windelband's complaints about this confusion applied to no one more than himself, because, as we have seen,[35] he was guilty of it in 'Normen und Naturgesetze'.

The question of freedom of choice raises the hoary conundrum of whether there can be acts of choice without causes, motives or reasons? Windelband admits the possibility of a choice between equal options when there is no sufficient reason for choosing one over another (42). He gives this example: one comes to a round surface of grass in the middle of one's path; one can go around it by moving right or left; there is no sufficient reason for going one way or the other.

In this sense it is necessary to admit "the reality of a *liberum arbitrium indifferentiae*" whose basis lies in a "so to speak *principium rationis deficientis*" (42). But if Windelband accepts the possibility of a choice where there are no sufficient *reasons* for one option or another, he denies that there is such a possibility in the sense of an act of will for which there is no *cause*. He distinguishes between reasons and causes, so that even if there is no *reason* for moving right or left, or choosing one lottery number over another, there is still a *cause* for such an action (52). The principle of sufficient reason holds without exception if by "reason" one means simply a cause. Even in the cases where we are not self-conscious of the cause, there is still one there. In cases like moving to right or left or the lottery number, we allow something within ourselves to make the decision for us, namely, our motor mechanism, which has nothing to do with motives of will (45, 47).

Regarding the causes rather than just reasons for actions, Windelband is happy to affirm the central thesis of the determinist, that is, that there are causes for all human actions and decisions, such that if the causes are present, the action or decision happens of necessity (75). All philosophers are determinists, he asserts somewhat boldly, insofar as they hold what we will and do is the necessary product of our momentary and constant motives, where these constant motives make up what we call "character". Such determination of action through character Windelband calls self-determination (*Selbstbestimmung*) (76). When we say that we are the cause of our own actions, we mean that we are self-determining in just this sense, that is, that the actions follow from our character.

Freedom of choice (*Wahlfreiheit*), Windelband goes on to say, just means that we choose to act according to our characters (76). If this is so, he argues, then the whole dispute between determinist and indeterminist is in the end a verbal matter, because

---

[35] See Section 4.

all the indeterminist wants to say is that the will itself, in addition to all other motives, gives one motive (i.e. cause) for the action; he wants us to recognize something constant in our character as at least one of the motives or causes for the action. The indeterminist is opposed to determinism only because he thinks that all motives have to be *external* to character. But once we recognize that motives can also be *internal* to the character, belonging to his or her very nature or self, then the quarrel between determinist and indeterminist vanishes (78).

In attempting to resolve the dispute between determinism and indeterminism in this manner, Windelband adopts the classical compatibilist position, according to which freedom is possible within a completely determined universe. This was the position that he had already advanced in 'Normen und Naturgesetze', so it seems as if he has done little more than arrived, through a more circuitous route, where he already stood. It seems as if Windelband thinks the whole dispute about freedom has already been settled simply by adopting his compatibilism. His lectures might as well have ended, it seems, with the sixth lecture where he resolves the dispute between determinist and indeterminist.

But Windelband does not leave matters here. The whole issue of freedom becomes much more complicated for him when he comes to the third concept of freedom, freedom of the will. Now Windelband seems to put on hold his earlier compatibilism and to consider a more refined and qualified position. His analysis becomes more intricate and involved, partly because he now breaches the issue of responsibility, and partly because he enters the field of metaphysics. Windelband now distinguishes the three concepts of freedom along the following lines. While freedom of action is a *psychophysical* concept, and while freedom of choice is a *psychological* one, freedom of will is a *metaphysical* concept (123). Into the dark woods of metaphysics Windelband now enters. And the deeper into it he goes, the more murky his account becomes.

The metaphysical aspect of the problem of freedom begins for Windelband with the idea of first causes or causeless willing (123). We find ourselves presupposing this idea, he says, because of the concept of responsibility, which seems to demand that there are causes that are not the effects of other causes (122). This idea is problematic, however, because it appears incompatible with the principle of causality, which holds for all events in nature, whether psychological or physical (125). To resolve this apparent problem, Windelband advises caution, and more specifically noting different senses of causality. It is necessary to distinguish, he argues, between two senses of causality: that which holds between different events, and that which holds between a substance and individual events (126). When we talk about the determinism of nature we are referring to the first sense; but when we speak of metaphysical freedom we mean the second. While first causes or causeless willing is incompatible with the first sense, it is still compatible with the second. The principle of causality that holds sway over nature holds only for events, and it does not pretend to hold for some substance that is not within the series of events. For this substance, Windelband says, we can apply the concept of a first cause or causeless willing (127).

The metaphysical concept of freedom makes sense, Windelband explains, only when we apply it to the whole personality, not to individual acts of will and the events that are their effects (154). A person himself with his character stands outside all the series of events, even if all his individual acts fall inside it (155). The person or character as a substance is contingent, having no necessary causes, whereas the occurrence of all events is necessary (155). Windelband says that we can explain this concept of personality with the scholastic concept of *aseïtas,* that is, existing for onself as opposed to existing from or because of others (155). The concept of aeseity is essentially that of self-determination, where the self-determining is that which determines itself into action alone and is not determined into action by anything else (158). Spinoza had formulated this concept with his *causa sui* and Fichte with his self-positing ego.

Having taken his reader deep into the metaphysical woods in his tenth lecture, Windelband then struggles to take him out of them in his final two lectures. The concept of metaphysical freedom, which he seemed to endorse, is now suspended and rendered superfluous. We are now reminded that if the will were really without a cause, then we could not hold someone responsible (199–200, 210). Attributions of responsibility imply that we can act on someone's feelings and dispositions (through admonition or punishment) to make them act differently, so that it ultimately presupposes the principle of causality (210). "The whole procedure of making someone responsible is completely bound up with, both backwards and forwards, knowledge of empirical causality." (211) When we hold a particular person responsible, all we have to presuppose is the concepts of freedom of action and freedom of choice; but we do not have to presuppose that the person has some metaphysical power of will, that he or she had the power to act countercausally, so that they could have done otherwise on this particular occasion. To say that a person could have done otherwise really means that he or she *should have* done so, or that they would have done so if their character had been different and the way it should have been (212).

Windelband attempts to remove the metaphysical connotations of moral responsibility by talking about two ways of considering (*Betrachtungsweise*) human actions (195). We can consider human actions according to norms, where we appraise their value or worth; and we can consider them under laws, where we explain their occurrence. When we consider these actions under norms, we abstract from their causal explanation and focus on their compliance with rules, customs or laws. The concept of freedom of the will, of a causeless willing, is simply the result of abstracting from the causal explanation of the action; it is a way of saying that treating the causes of the action is irrelevant to its moral appraisal; but it does not mean that the action really has no causes, or even worse that it has mysterious causes that operate only by interrupting the continuity of nature (197). When we consider someone responsible for an action that he or she should not have done, this does not mean that we have some retrospective metaphysical knowledge of the action but only that we are justified in judging it according to norms, and that we are going to do something to the person so that he or she does not commit the offence again (218).

So, in the end, Windelband interprets the normative and the natural not as different ontological domains but simply as different methods or perspectives for regarding human actions. The difference between the normative and natural is not that between kinds of entity—something noumenal and phenomenal—but between different discourses about human actions. Just as we abstract from the causes of a belief when we judge its truth, so we abstract from the causes of action when we ponder its morality. While everything that exists falls under the natural perspective, it is not the only valid perspective on human action, the only method of dealing with it (195). There is not only the realm of existence but also the realm of norms, which have a *sui generis* logical status that does not imply the existence of anything. The problem with the metaphysical conception of freedom is that it treats the normative dimension as if it were somehow ontological, implying the existence of a distinct kind of will and soul. But once we grasp the *sui generis* discourse of norms, we realize that we are not bound to special ontological assumptions. We can proceed to evaluate human actions and assess responsibility with perfect legitimacy without metaphysics.

7. Early Epistemology

The origins and development of Windelband's normative conception of philosophy is a complicated and, as we shall soon see, controversial tale. Still, it is worthwhile to tell it because it alone fully explains the purpose and meaning of his mature philosophy. Windelband did not always define philosophy in exclusively normative terms, and he came to his later views about philosophy only by gradually working his way through earlier ones. We need to know why he kept, and why he discarded, elements of his earlier views to understand the rationale behind his later ones.

Windelband's first foray into the territory of epistemology was his habilitation thesis, his *Über die Gewißheit der Erkenntnis*, which first appeared in 1873.[36] The central purpose of this little tract is to answer some big questions: "What is certainty?", "How is it possible?" and "By what means is it attainable?" (16) Windelband raises these questions because he thinks they concern all of us as moral and practical beings. We all have "the thirst for certainty" because we fear that our most important beliefs—those by which we lead our lives—could be false. The sceptic arouses this fear in us because he brings all beliefs into question. We therefore turn to philosophy, which is the only discipline to address these doubts and to offer us deliverance from them.

In raising the classical problem of certainty, and in posing the dangers of scepticism, Windelband was deliberately, but cautiously, nudging philosophy towards foundationalism again. He defines philosophy as "the investigation into the ultimate grounds of being and thinking" (15). He then declares explicitly—as if he were Descartes or

---

[36] Wilhelm Windelband, *Über die Gewißheit der Erkenntnis. Eine psychologisch-erkenntnistheoretische Studie* (Berlin: F. Henschel, 1873). There is a new edition of this text produced by Adlibri Verlag, Hamburg, 2005. All page references are to this new, more accessible edition.

Reinhold—that there is still "the deep need for a deductive foundation of knowledge" (17). Philosophy has to proceed in this direction, Windelband assumes, because only such a foundation will slake the thirst for certainty and respond to the sceptic's doubts. Windelband is also taking issue with those of his contemporaries who maintain that philosophy should be nothing more than an investigation into the logic of the sciences. In his view, there are two problems with such a conception of philosophy: it accepts the methods and results of the empirical sciences as if they were dogmas; and it ignores the more general philosophical questions central to all cultural life (17).

Still, though foundationalism has its merits, Windelband makes it clear that he is not calling for a rehabilitation of the speculative idealist tradition. Although the great idealists were correct to address basic questions, they went too far in attempting to answer them entirely on an a priori basis. The time is over, he declares, when philosophy can chase "the phantom of a completely creative knowledge in the blue air of the imagination" (18). "The wax on the wings of Icarus has melted", so that philosophy has crashed to earth where it must learn to dwell among "the realm of facts". Philosophy has to orient itself around the results of the exact natural sciences, and it has to walk hand-in-hand with them.

Having made this concession, Windelband goes no further. We are told in no uncertain terms that there are different ways for philosophy to collaborate with the sciences, and that it must never let down its critical guard by simply accepting the methods, presuppositions and results of the sciences as if they were the only possible. The positivists are guilty of making a dogma out of the sciences, as if they stood above all criticism. Without mentioning names, Windelband takes issue with the likes of Helmholtz and Lange, who too readily place their trust in the empirical sciences, especially the latest psychophysical research. That research, he does not doubt, has confirmed one of the main results of the critical philosophy: that the content of perception is the result of our perceptual and intellectual functioning. But the advocates of such an approach, Windelband protests, have not taken into account its implications for natural science itself. Namely, if all the content of our perceptual world is created by the mind, how can we claim objective truth for science itself? The results of psychophysical research have posed yet again the question of the foundation of the sciences, and it is necessary for philosophy to deal with it (20).

Windelband was not to remain entirely true to the foundationalist conception of philosophy outlined in *Über die Gewißheit*. Never would he attempt to provide anything like a deductive foundation of the sciences along the lines of Reinhold and Fichte. In 'Was ist Philosophie?' he is clear that we cannot prove the basic principles of logic or ethics without presupposing them. But, to an extent, Windelband never lost his foundationalist concerns, insofar as he always insisted, until his very last breath, that philosophy should determine and assess the basic principles of knowledge, morality and art.

The central and characteristic feature of Windelband's early conception of philosophy, in contrast to his later conception, is its syncretism, its holistic approach to epistemology. In *Über die Gewißheit* Windelband stresses that philosophy should be not only a logical but also a psychological and metaphysical enterprise (32). This inclusion of psychology and metaphysics within the domain of epistemology is in marked contrast to his later strictly logical conception. Windelband not only preaches but practises this holistic approach. The account of certainty in *Über die Gewißheit* is pursued in not only logical but also psychological and metaphysical terms. We bring all these disciplines together, Windelband proposes, when we show "how a psychological process, by means of logical functions, is able to grasp metaphysical truths" (32). And with that as his goal, Windelband tries to show the interweaving of these logical, psychological and metaphysical factors.

In sharp contrast to his later conception of epistemology, the young Windelband is very emphatic about the need for psychology in epistemology. Any epistemological account of knowledge ultimately presupposes a psychological one, he argues in *Über die Gewißheit*, for the simple reason that thinking and knowing are mental activities. The limits, worth and justification of knowledge has to be determined by its purposes, which are the result of some psychological process (22). Although we can abstract the forms of judgement and reasoning from the psychic activities that create them, we need psychology to grasp "the actual driving mechanism behind knowing" (23). Formal logic tells us *how* we think; but it cannot tell us *why* or *that* we think, and even less *what* we think (24). It cannot even tell us why (i.e. the causes or mechanism) we draw the inference S=P from the premises M=P and S=M (23). The motive and power to do that comes from our psyche, about which logic tells us nothing.

As much as the young Windelband insists on the importance of psychology, he is very far from reducing epistemology down to psychology alone. The logical aspect of epistemology is of no less importance to him. Logic and psychology are for him two very different yet complementary approaches to knowledge. Windelband explains the difference between logic and psychology through two different senses of necessity. There is a causal or psychological sense of necessity, according to which a process of thinking is necessary because it conforms to natural laws. In this sense *all* thinking, whether valid or invalid, is necessary, simply because it is a natural event and all events conform to laws. But this is not the sense of necessity we have in mind in logic, because in logic we are concerned not with all thinking but solely with *valid* thinking (82). While both correct and incorrect thinking obey psychological laws, only correct thinking complies with logical ones. The kind of necessity involved in logical laws, which is more akin to the laws of ethics than psychology, is that of an imperative: they tell us what we *ought* to do, or how we *should* proceed, if we are to think correctly (85). We can make these logical laws into our habits, so that we learn to comply with them in all our thinking, and so that they become firm psychological realities; but we must not let this fact confuse us, so that we think that logical laws are only psychological in meaning and purpose (86).

In *Über die Gewißheit* Windelband provides an explanation of logical necessity that sheds much light on his later concept of normativity. The laws of logic turn out to be hypothetical imperatives: they prescribe means to ends. They tell us what we ought to do if we are to achieve a certain end: namely, the acquisition of knowledge. The laws of logic therefore lay down the necessary formal conditions for the acquisition of knowledge. They are, as Windelband calls them, "laws of ends, norms" (*Zweckgesetze, Normen*). This is the first instance in which Windelband uses the redolent term "norms", which will later become a mantra for him and the Southwestern neo-Kantians. We can see now why Windelband talks about a "teleological" justification of norms: they are the means by which we attain ends. If they prove to be effective means for these ends—if they are sufficient and necessary to achieve them—then they we have all the justification we could give for them.

Only at the close of *Über die Gewißheit* does Windelband introduce the third dimension of his epistemology: the metaphysical. As a student of Lotze, Windelband was fully convinced of the importance and necessity of metaphysics for epistemology, and he reaffirms his teacher's thesis that the problems of epistemology are ultimately resolvable only through metaphysics. "The question of the essence and possibility of knowledge conceals within itself," he writes in his foreword, "the whole puzzle of existence". For Windelband, it is the psychological dimension of epistemology that leads straight to the metaphysical, for that dimension regards knowing as an event, as a coming-into-being, as Aristotle would say, and to understand an event we need metaphysics (119). Herbart had always said that his psychology presupposes metaphysics, and Windelband heartily agrees, making it the foundation of psychology.

Windelband gives another reason for adding metaphysics to epistemology. The task of epistemology is to explain the relationship between the subject and object. But its analysis of that relationship always bumps up against something ultimately given—the particular content of sensation—that cannot be derived from the laws of our subjectivity. What this given is, and in what relations it stands to experience and other things, is the concern of metaphysics (105). Here again Windelband was gesturing towards Herbart, who made the ultimate simples of experience into the object of metaphysics. He expressly approves Herbart's view that metaphysics culminates in the theory of knowledge, because that theory treats the highest form of being, which is knowledge (119). On this account, the theory of knowledge virtually became a special form of metaphysics.

Already by the early 1870s, then, Windelband had worked out a conception of philosophy that was deliberately syncretic, combining logic, psychology and metaphysics. There was a normative element in his early conception of philosophy, because he explicitly conceived of the disciplines of logic and ethics in normative terms. But this normative element was only one part of a much broader epistemological programme, which included psychology and metaphysics as integral components. Before he could arrive at his later conception of philosophy, then, he had to abandon his earlier syncretism, dropping psychology and metaphysics from his epistemological programme.

8. A Normative Logic

The first sign of a shift in Windelband's syncretic position appears in a review he published in 1874 of Christoph Sigwart's *Logik*.[37] Here Windelband shows himself to be sympathetic to Sigwart's project for a purely formal logic. The question for him now is how logic can be autonomous, a discipline in its own right, independent of psychology and metaphysics. Psychology and metaphysics are now presented as the Scylla and Charybdis that logic should avoid if it is to be an autonomous discipline. On the one hand, logic has to avoid conflation with psychology, which gives no place to the concept of truth. From a purely psychological standpoint there is neither truth nor error because all thinking, whether true or false, conforms to natural laws. The distinguishing feature of logic from psychology is precisely that it retains the concept of truth and shows the means to attain it. On the other hand, logic should also steer clear of metaphysics, which poses too many unsolvable problems. As soon as we raise the epistemological question of the meaning of truth, we are caught in metaphysics; hence logic should avoid epistemology as much as psychology. The key to a purely formal logic, Windelband explains, is a strictly normative conception of truth, according to which truth consists in normative necessity, that is, in the need to follow norms to attain the ends of knowledge. This normative necessity, which is about what we *ought to* think, is very different from the natural or psychological necessity, which is about what we *must* think. If logic is understood as such a normative discipline, Windelband argues, then we steer clear of psychological questions about how we must think as well as metaphysical questions about whether logic conforms to being itself. The question will be only whether thinking conforms to its own immanent laws, whether it is consistent with itself. Whether it corresponds to a higher metaphysical truth can be left aside as unnecessary to determine the validity of thinking in particular cases.

The review of Sigwart's *Logik* shows Windelband concerned to separate rather than unify the disciplines involved in his syncretic project. It was significant that Windelband saw the normative dimension of logic as the means to separate it from psychology and metaphysics: he will later make the same point to provide an autonomous conception of philosophy. Still, it would be a mistake to assume that the syncretic project has fallen apart, that Windelband now thinks that logic, psychology and metaphysics should be separated. After all, Windelband is concerned in the Sigwart review only with formal logic, which is only one part of epistemology. While logic should separate itself from psychology and metaphysics, the same does not hold for epistemology, a more general discipline which attempts to unite logic, metaphysics

---

[37] Wilhelm Windelband, 'Zur Logik', *Philosophische Monatshefte* 10 (1874), 33–42, 85–91, 103–110. Although this article appeared one year after the *publication* of *Über die Gewißheit*, it appeared nearly two years after its *composition*, because, as Windelband tells us in the 'Vorwort' to that work, the publication of the almost printable manuscript was delayed for "personal reasons" for "almost a year".

and psychology. Indeed, even in the Sigwart review Windelband stresses that formal logic should not completely isolate itself from epistemology and psychology, because it is only by constant reference to them that it will be able to show how logic is applicable and relevant to attaining knowledge of the actual world.

That Windelband was far from relinquishing his syncretic project becomes clear from an article he published a year after the Sigwart review, 'Die Erkenntnislehre unter dem völkerpsychologischen Gesichtspunkte', which appeared in 1875 in *Zeitschrift für Völkerpsychologie und Sprachwissenchaft*,[38] the very organ in which Cohen made his intellectual debut a few years earlier. This article very much reaffirms the syncretic approach of *Über die Gewißheit*. Following the standpoint of its editors, Windelband's article endorses the value of having a psychological, and indeed anthropological or "historical-cultural", perspective in epistemology. Although the laws of logic and ethics appear eternal and immutable, one must not assume, he argues, that they exist in some self-sufficient noumenal realm, as if they could be isolated from social and historical change. These laws too are the product of history and culture, and we become aware of them only through education into a cultural tradition and only through the growth of language and linguistic sensibility (174). It is also a serious mistake, Windelband adds, to assume that the forms of logic have no reference to human psychology. The very opposite is the case: these forms have "sense and meaning" (*Sinn und Bedeutung*) only with reference to psychic activities (167). They are norms that make sense only if they direct and regulate the activity of thinking, so that if there were no thinking they would completely lose their point and purpose. All the basic laws of logic presuppose the ends of discourse (viz. persuasion, correction and criticism), the basic human activities of communication. Even the law of contradiction rests on a psychological foundation, because it makes sense only in the context of affirming and denying, which are speech acts (170). The principle of sufficient reason too presupposes a psychological activity, because its demand for reasons serves the purpose of human persuasion, which is trying to get someone to have the same thought processes as myself (171).

The psychologism and historicism of this early article are clear and emphatic, so much so that it has been seen as the work of "a relativist and pragmatist of the first rank".[39] But it is important to see that Windelband never departs from his earlier belief in the universality and necessity of logical norms. He closes his article by reassuring the logician that explaining the genesis of logical laws is perfectly compatible with their universal and necessary validity. "The dignity of logical laws as absolute authoritative norms remains entirely intact." (177) Still, there can be no doubt that, in this early article, Windelband is bent on *avoiding* a strictly logical or normative

[38] Wilhelm Windelband, 'Die Erkenntnislehre unter dem völkerpsychologischen Gesichtspunkte', *Zeitschrift für Völkerpsychologie und Sprachwissenschaft* VIII (1875) 166–178.
[39] Klaus Christian Köhnke, *Entstehung und Aufstieg des Neukantianismus: Die deutsche Universitätsphilosophie zwischen Idealismus und Positivismus.* (Frankfurt: Suhrkamp, 1986), p. 362. We will examine Köhnke's interpretation of the young Windelband in detail in Section 10.

approach to epistemology, and intent on complementing it with psychology, anthropology and even cultural history. Nothing, it seems, could lead Windelband away from his syncretic conception of epistemology. But, little did he know, there were strong centrifugal forces lying just around the corner.

9. Centrifugal Forces

The first cracks in the syncretic project appear shortly after Windelband's article in the *Zeitschrift für Völkerpsychologie*. On May 20, 1876, he gave his inaugural lecture as ordinary professor in Zurich, *Über den gegenwärtigen Stand der psychologischen Forschung*.[40] Windelband chose as the topic for his lecture the question of the relationship between philosophy and the empirical sciences. The topic seemed especially appropriate for his new position, because his chair was devoted to "inductive philosophy", an attempt to modernize philosophy by aligning it with the new empirical sciences. True to that spirit, Windelband reaffirmed his position in *Über die Gewißheit* about the importance of close collaboration between the empirical sciences and philosophy. The bad old days, when philosophers believed that they could achieve meaningful results simply through a priori speculation, were long over and should never return.

Having paid his homage to the new sciences, Windelband then turns around and insists that philosophy has to guard its borders from them. Philosophy and the empirical sciences, we are now told, need to respect their proper boundaries, and this is especially the case for philosophy and psychology (3–4). If these disciplines are to collaborate, each must know its special task, so that it is more effectively pursued. Windelband was thus reasserting the very academic division of labour that his syncretic approach was designed to overcome.

In stressing the importance of proper boundaries between philosophy and psychology, Windelband was addressing an issue that especially concerned German academic philosophy in the late 19th century: that because of the porous border between philosophy and psychology, positions once intended for philosophers were becoming increasingly filled by psychologists. This was the ultimate humiliating outcome of the identity crisis. If philosophers did not know themselves and set firm boundaries, they were going to be replaced by psychologists.

Windelband's strategy in responding to the crisis is the very opposite of what we might first expect. Rather than declaring the independence of philosophy from psychology, he recommends the independence of psychology from philosophy. Windelband chose this strategy, partly because it was more appropriate for a chair in "inductive philosophy", and partly because it was more effective in achieving his ultimate end: autonomy for philosophy. If you advocate the autonomy of psychology,

[40] Wilhelm Windelband, *Über den gegenwärtigen Stand der psychologischen Forschung. Rede zum Antritt der ordentlichen Professur der Philosophie an der Hochschule zu Zürich am XX. Mai MDCCCLXVI* (Leipzig: Breitkopf & Härtel, 1876).

psychologists will cease to compete with you; instead, they will lobby for their own positions independent of philosophy, which is what philosophers want too.

Windelband's argument for a sharp boundary line is simple and straightforward. Psychology will make progress, and be assured of achieving verifiable results, only to the extent that it becomes completely independent of metaphysics. Psychology must free itself from metaphysics for two reasons: first, because co-operation requires agreeing about the basics, and no one agrees about the basics in metaphysics; and, second, because metaphysics has all too often resorted to hypothetical explanations and abstract concepts (viz. the soul and *Lebenskraft*) which impede further empirical enquiry (6–10).

Assuming that philosophy should leave psychology to its own pursuits, what is left for it to do? Windelband only suggests his answer at the very end of his lecture. He now conceives the task of philosophy chiefly in logical terms: "the justification of the methods of scientific research and the foundation of the principle forms of conceiving and explaining" (24).

The implications of this lecture for Windelband's conception of philosophy are plain enough: the syncretic conception explodes, falling into three distinct pieces, logic, psychology and metaphysics. Honouring the academic division of labour means these should be separate disciplines, each pursuing their distinct concerns. Psychology should be separate from metaphysics, which violates its autonomy; and philosophy should be logic alone, leaving psychology to pursue its own empirical enquiries. Windelband did not draw all these implications immediately or explicitly; but their latent presence made them cracks in the wall of his fragile syncretic project.

That project came under further stress in an article Windelband wrote in the following year, his 'Ueber die verschiedenen Phasen der kantischen Lehre vom Ding-an-sich', which appeared in 1877 in the second issue of the *Vierteljahrschrift für wissenschaftliche Philosophie*.[41] This article is primarily historical in content, dealing with Kant's intellectual development, and more specifically the evolution of his doctrine of the thing-in-itself. One might think, therefore, that it holds little of interest for Windelband's philosophy. But, given Windelband's growing identification with Kant's philosophy, its implications for his own position prove to be considerable. We need not consider here all the details of Windelband's interpretation. Suffice it to say that he thinks that Kant, during his critical phase, held three incompatible views about the thing-in-itself: 1) that the thing-in-itself is something unthinkable and therefore impossible; 2) that it is something that we *can* assume even though we cannot know it; and 3) that it is something that we *must* assume to explain the world of appearances (256–257). Anticipating the patchwork theory, Windelband thinks that Kant held these views at different times, that they were written down in distinct fragments, which he then stitched together in the final months of the composition of the

[41] Wilhelm Windelband, 'Ueber die verschiedenen Phasen der kantischen Lehre vom Ding-an-sich', *Vierteljahrschrift für wissenschaftliche Philosophie* Jahrgang I, Heft II (1877), 224–266.

Kritik der reinen Vernunft (231–232). We can now see why Windelband famously said understanding Kant means going beyond him. We simply cannot, like Kant, hold all these views; consistency alone demands moving beyond the confusions inherent in the texts. One view alone can represent the spirit of the critical philosophy.

Which view should that be? Windelband is under no doubt about it. He thinks that the first view represents Kant's deepest intentions. The proper conclusion to draw from Kant's transcendental deduction, and the limits he places on knowledge, he argues, is that the thing-in-itself is a complete impossibility. The central thesis of the transcendental deduction is that objectivity derives not from the correspondence of representations to some entity that exists independent of them, but from the conformity of sensations to the rules of synthesis of the understanding. On this reading, the idea of a thing-in-itself is simply the hypostasis of the concept of an object, which really derives from the synthesizing function of the understanding (254). And the limits Kant places on knowledge—possible experience—mean that it is not possible to assume the existence of anything that exists beyond it (254). For these reasons, Windelband comes to the conclusion that the real spirit of Kant's critical idealism lies in the abolition of the thing-in-itself, which is only a hangover from a naive realistic view of the world that Kant intended to overthrow. And so Windelband declares his death sentence: "From the standpoint of epistemology, the thing-in-itself is a completely meaningless and useless, confusing and annoying, fiction" (258). The spirit of the critical philosophy resides in its principle, which is presupposed but never fully expressed, that knowledge must be explained completely within itself and not by transcendent postulates about something outside itself (260). "The divine gift of Kant to humanity," Windelband adds, lies in "this thought that there is nothing beyond representations" (261). He admits that there is no particular text that unambiguously expresses the spirit of Kant's philosophy. Kant comes closest to it in the chapter 'On the Distinction between Phenomena and Noumena' where he states that the very distinction between appearances and things-in-themselves is untenable; but even that text was altered in the second edition to make it accord with the hypothetical existence of things-in-themselves (248 n.10).

The implications of Windelband's interpretation of Kant for his general conception of philosophy are immediate and striking. Since Windelband stresses Kant's "critical idealism", which limits all knowledge to experience, epistemology is now purged of metaphysics. The pivotal role Windelband was ready to assign to metaphysics in *Über die Gewißheit* vanishes. Perhaps there is "a secret of being" lying in the depths of epistemology, as he once said; but he now realizes that the epistemologist is in no position to tell it.

There is another crucial implication of Windelband's interpretation, though it is less obvious. Towards the end of his article he insists upon connecting two aspects of Kant's philosophy that are apparently distinct: the postulate of the thing-in-itself and his psychology. When we drop the former, Windelband argues, the latter too disappears. Why? The explanation is perfectly straightforward. Kant's investigation into the possibility of knowledge originally arose from the question how a priori representations correspond to an object that exists independent of them. If these representations arise from the mind, if they are not the effect of the object itself, then how do they correspond to objects? This question assumes a thing-in-itself which exists independent of representations; and it is posed in psychological terms, because it deals with the causal relations between representations and their objects. If, however, we drop the thing-in-itself entirely, insisting upon explaining knowledge in entirely immanent terms, then the focus of enquiry is no longer on the *causes* but the *content* of knowledge. In other words, logical enquiry replaces psychological (259). The more Kant became involved in the argument of the transcendental deduction, Windelband argues, the more he could see that all the assumptions about the dualism between subject and object, and the causal relations between them, should not be the starting point but the subject matter of investigation. Seen properly, then, psychology cannot be the key to epistemology, as Fries, Beneke and Meyer preached, because it is really part of the problem. Kant himself, Windelband thinks, saw this point, even if through a glass darkly. It explains why, in the preface to the second edition of the *Kritik*, he demoted the importance of psychology, and why, in the *Prolegomena*, he formulated his problem in the terms of the possibility of synthetic a priori judgements. A purely immanent explanation of the possibility of knowledge thus became an essentially logical enquiry, an examination of the content of representation rather than its causes, of the *quid juris?* rather than the *quid facti?*

And so not only metaphysics but also psychology was ejected from Windelband's conception of epistemology. Already by 1877, then, we find Windelband close to the strictly normative conception of philosophy that he will preach in the early 1880s. Windelband came to this conception chiefly from two considerations: first, the academic division of labour, which demanded separating philosophy from psychology and metaphysics; and, second, his interpretation of Kant's philosophy as critical idealism. From these considerations alone, it seems that Windelband's normative conception was utterly overdetermined, the necessary result of his thinking *before* 1878.

As plausible as all this sounds, not everyone agrees with it. One scholar finds Windelband's crucial turning point *after* 1878; and, worse still, he sees all our reasoning as suspect. We must now give him a fair hearing.

10. The Politics of Normativity

According to Klaus Christian Köhnke, the account we have given so far of Windelband's intellectual development is naive.[42] It places Windelband in "a stage of innocence" that would explain his intellectual development entirely from systematic

---

[42] See Köhnke, *Entstehung und Aufstieg*, p. 421.

and philosophical considerations, as if he were a pure intellect who moved entirely in aetherial orbs. This is naive, Köhnke implies, because it abstracts Windelband from his social and political context, underestimating the political motives behind the formation of his philosophical views. Köhnke is convinced that there is one political event in particular that was decisive for Windelband's intellectual development, and that was the source of his normative conception of philosophy: the two assassination attempts on the life of Kaiser Wilhelm I in 1878.[43] This aroused a hysterical reaction among conservative politicians and the bourgeoise, who abhorred the growing threats of socialism and democracy. This reaction eventually led to Bismarck's introduction of an Anti-Socialist Bill in the Reichstag, which prohibited working class associations and meetings. Windelband, Köhnke believes, was among those "German mandarins" who feared working class agitation and universal suffrage,[44] which were alarming developments that threatened his entire world, not only elite rule but German culture itself. Socialism and democracy meant "levelling", the decline of moral, aesthetic and cultural standards to meet the demands of the ignorant masses. Windelband's chief defence against these dangers, Köhnke maintains, was nothing less than his normative conception of philosophy. It was philosophers alone who could and should be the standard bearers of culture by representing its universal and necessary values. The concept of "normal consciousness", as Köhnke puts it, was "a weapon (*Kampbegriff*) against democrats, republicans and socialists alike".

Dwelling in our stage of innocence, we might well be astonished that a philosophy that pretends to preserve and promote universal and necessary values somehow serves as a bulwark for "the interests of the authoritarian Bismarckian state".[45] This seems unduly partisan and partial, given that universal values should represent everyone alike, all intelligent or rational beings, whether they be stout Bismarckians or rabid socialists. But, arguably, this too is naive, because so much depends on *who* knows, and *who* administers, these values. If the Windelbandian state is ruled by philosophers, or at least princes advised by philosophers, then knowing universal values demands intelligence, education and talent. The masses, who lack such merits, cannot know these principles, and so they should not govern; or, in more concrete political terms, they should not have the right to vote.

So Köhnke's political account of Windelband's development is more plausible than it might first seem. The case for his theory ultimately depends on the concrete historical evidence he marshals for it, more specifically, evidence concerning Windelband's

---

[43] On the historical and political background, see James J. Sheehan, *German Liberalism in the 19th Century* (Chicago, IL: University of Chicago Press, 1978), pp. 182–184.

[44] Though it nicely fits with his analysis, Köhnke does not refer to Fritz Ringer's *The Decline of the German Mandarins: The German Academic Community, 1890–1933* (Cambridge, MA: Harvard University Press, 1969). Ringer includes Windelband among his German mandarins. Unfortunately, he offers no evidence about his social and political views. It seems that to be a mandarin one only needs to have been an academic during these years.

[45] Köhnke, *Entstehung und Aufstieg*, p. 427.

political views in the late 1870s and early 1880s. But before we examine that evidence, we need to consider Köhnke's argument for resorting to a political explanation in the first place.

Ironically, Köhnke turns to Windelband's politics and the events of the late 1870s because he finds a systematic or purely logical need to do so. There is, he argues, "a break" in Windelband's intellectual development in the late 1870s, indeed "a conversion from Saul to Paul".[46] The break is away from a psychological-historical approach to logic, ethics and aesthetics to a normative one. In *Über die Gewißheit* and the article for the *Zeitschrift der Völkerpsychologie* Windelband is "a relativist of the first order", Köhnke thinks, because he advocates a radical psychological and historical standpoint, according to which the norms of logic, ethics and aesthetics derive from psychology and history. But this relativist Saul became an absolutist Paul in the late 1870s. Why the sudden conversion? Politics, it seems, is the only plausible answer. This alone explains the shift from a champion of psychologism and historicism to an advocate of universal values and absolute norms.

Something can be said on behalf of Köhnke's account of Windelband's intellectual development. We have seen that there was indeed a break in Windelband's development in the 1870s, a move away from a syncretic conception of philosophy to a strictly normative one. But, apart from this very general point, Köhnke's account of this break is inaccurate, on both historical and philosophical grounds. Historically, the break took place not in 1878, the year of the assassination attempts, but earlier, in 1876 with Windelband's inaugural lecture in Zurich, and in 1877 with his article on the Kantian thing-in-itself. Philosophically, Windelband's break was not a black-or-white affair, a move away from a completely historical and psychologistic conception of epistemology to a totally normative one. Windelband's normative conception of philosophy was already fully in place in the early 1870s in *Über die Gewißheit*; it's just that it was also mixed with psychological and metaphysical elements. Never was Windelband the radical historicist and psychologist, the total relativist, that Köhnke makes him out to be. We have already seen how, at the end of the article in the *Zeitschrift für Völkerpsychologie*, Windelband reaffirmed the absolute status of logical and ethical truths. Behind Köhnke's entire account there lingers a false assumption. Namely, that Windelband's normative and historical-psychological approaches to epistemology are contradictory. It is for this reason that he has to portray Windelband's development in such black-or-white terms. But the assumption would have been rejected by Windelband, who always insisted that these approaches are complementary rather than contradictory. Because we have to distinguish between validity and fact, norms can have a universal and necessary validity even though they arise from particular and contingent psychological and historical causes.

Granted that Köhnke's account of Windelband's break is mistaken, it is still possible to rescue a weaker version of it. For even if the normative conception of philosophy

---

[46] Köhnke, *Entstehung und Aufstieg*, p. 421.

was already present in the early 1870s, it was not *entirely* or *exclusively* normative, and that entirety and exclusivity might well have a political explanation. Perhaps there were political reasons that motivated Windelband to advance a purely or strictly normative conception of philosophy? We have seen that Windelband had systematic reasons for developing that conception: the sharp distinctions he had drawn between philosophy and psychology are sufficient to explain its genesis. But they do not exclude a political explanation as well. So perhaps there were indeed political motives after all?

At this point everything rests on the evidence Köhnke provides about Windelband's political views in the late 1870s. Köhnke rests his case chiefly on two lectures that Windelband gave around 1878: 'Über Friedrich Hölderlin und sein Geschick' and 'Über Sokrates'.[47] Both these lectures show Windelband to be a staunch political conservative. In them his opposition to democracy, to a universal franchise, is especially apparent. In 'Über Friedrich Hölderlin' Windelband laments the specialization, fragmentation and atomism of modern civil society, which stands in sharp contrast to the unity of the ancient world, where each individual could understand and feel part of his entire culture. The paltry surrogate for this modern malady, Windelband says, is "dilettantism", the attempt to recapture a sense of wholeness by knowing a little bit about everything. This dilettantism appears in the salons and the alleyways. If it is comic in the salons, it is tragic in the alleyways, because those who practise it there are the demagogues, who use scientific themes to preach to the people. The political form of this dilletantism, Windelband then declares in a revealing passage, is "Parliamentarianism", which would give everyone a right to speak about public matters (256). In 'Über Sokrates' the same contempt for democracy emerges. Windelband paints a picture of Socrates as a spokesman for the authority of reason against the shallow enlightenment of the sophists, who popularized the democratic idea that everyone should express their opinion about everything. That idea was dangerous because it undermined cultural unity and the authority of the laws. "There follows from the democratization of knowledge", Windelband tells us in no uncertain terms, "the demoralization of culture." (61) Windelband's Socrates was a "*Wertwissenschaftler*" *avant la lettre* because he recognizes that there is a standpoint of a universal reason that stands above the individual and to which his judgement must submit (67–68). That standpoint thus serves as a bulwark against a rampant relativism and democratization, which would level all opinions and values.

So, much as Köhnke says, these lectures show Windelband to be a political conservative, and indeed during the social hysteria of 1878. But the crucial questions remain whether Windelband's political beliefs have the meaning Köhnke reads into them, and whether as such they were the chief motive for his normative conception of philosophy. And here it is necessary to be sceptical. Köhnke tells us that Socrates' standpoint

---

[47] 'Über Friedrich Hölderlin und sein Geschick', *Präludien* I, 230–259; and 'Über Sokrates', *Präludien* I, 55–87.

of reason, as portrayed by Windelband in 'Über Sokrates', was meant to be "utterly authoritarian" (*durch und durch autoritär gemeint*).[48] But Windelband stresses that Socrates' standpoint is accessible to everyone alike, that it has to be confirmed by the judgement of each individual, and that it will appear as an external authority only for that individual who has not sufficiently reflected and engaged in a full enquiry. Köhnke ignores the fact that Windelband's Socrates represents the standpoint of moral auton-omy no less than rational authority, and that, like a good Kantian, he encourages every individual to think for himself. On Windelband's interpretation, Socrates was not an opponent of enlightenment as such but only of a half-enlightenment which did not go far enough and stood only half way. There were three stages each individual went through, Windelband held, in his journey to philosophical enlightenment: blindly fol-lowing external authority; liberation from that authority; and then rediscovering that authority from within through the exercise of one's own reason (75). All this suggests that Windelband was not opposed to democracy or republicanism as such, but only to granting it to a public who were not ready for it because they lacked sufficient educa-tion—an all too common conservative belief in the 1870s and 1880s.

All the plausibility of Köhnke's reading of 'Über Sokrates' rests on a notorious but mysterious fact: that Socrates preferred aristocracy as his ideal form of government. The precise role of this fact in Socrates' trial has always been obscure. But to many it was decisive, making the trial into a contest between an aristocratic Socrates and a democratic Athens. This fact then makes it seem as if Socrates' stand on behalf of reason was meant to be aristocratic, indeed authoritarian. But it is striking and tell-ing that Windelband does not present Socrates' trial in this light. It was a mistake of Socrates' judges, he tells us, that they read his contempt for their tribunal as a con-tempt for democracy itself (84). The trial was not a contest between aristocracy and democracy but between individual autonomy and tradition (75–76). It is significant, Windelband points out, that Aristophanes, Socrates' most passionate critic, never gave any importance to Socrates' aristocratic beliefs (79–80). For Aristophanes, the issue was the social and political dangers of giving each individual the right to ques-tion the laws and traditions. Where Aristophanes misunderstood Socrates was in lumping him together with the sophists, whose shallow half-enlightenment he too regarded as dangerous.

The upshot of this closer reading of the text should be clear: that if Windelband intended Socrates' standpoint of reason to be "a weapon" against all democratic ten-dencies, it was not very effective at all. For this standpoint was not meant to be eso-teric, the preserve of philosophers alone. All were supposed to see its evidence and authority, if they were only properly prepared and educated. The point at issue then becomes whether Windelband was liberal enough to advocate equal opportunity for all to have a general education. And here there can be no doubt. In 'Über Friedrich

---

[48] Köhnke, *Entstehung und Aufstieg*, p. 427.

Hölderlin' Windelband expressly advocates an education "for all classes and individuals" which ensures "equality in [its] intellectual foundations" (257).

The ultimate irony is that in diagnosing the problems of modern education and culture Windelband proposes moving philosophy in a direction opposed to his purely normative conception of philosophy. For at the close of 'Über Friedrich Hölderlin' Windelband laments the fact that there is no longer a general philosophy that can forge all the results of the sciences into a single worldview (259). Only such a philosophy would help to overcome the fragmentation and specialization of modern life. This was the true student of Lotze speaking, whose *Mikrokosmus* was an attempt to provide just such a worldview. But this demand for a worldview would eventually push Windelband away from the exclusively normative conception of philosophy and back towards his more syncretic approach.

Now, at the end of our foray into Windelband's politics, we can perhaps rest content that our original explanation was not so naive after all. Köhnke's political account does not begin to explain the nuances, details and complexities of Windelband's philosophical development. To do that, we need to resort to systematic and internal philosophical considerations. The attempt to determine the rationale for a philosophical position through politics alone will never take us very far. The German mandarins, who might all have shared the same political interests, still held the most diverse philosophical positions.[49]

[49] I have to express my scepticism, therefore, about Ringer's attempt "to derive the opinions of the German academic intelligentsia from its peculiar role in German society." Ringer, *The German Mandarins*, p. 4. All that Ringer shows us is that many German academics shared a belief in the need for and value of elite rule. This is far from explaining their social and political views, let alone their epistemological and metaphysical ones, which were very diverse. Ringer's summaries of the more philosophical views of his mandarins are so clumsy and crude that it is questionable he understands their meaning or purpose.

14

The Realism of Alois Riehl

1. A Realist from the Tirol

The third major neo-Kantian thinker to emerge in the 1870s is Alois Riehl (1844–1924). Unlike Cohen and Windelband, Riehl never became the leader of a major neo-Kantian school, though he was a renowned teacher and lecturer. Among his students were Eduard Spranger (1882–1963), Heinrich Scholz (1884–1956), Max Frischeisen-Köhler (1978–1923), Oswald Spengler (1880–1936), Hans Reichenbach (1891–1953) and Richard Hönigswald (1875–1947), all of whom became noteworthy scholars or philosophers in their own right.[1] Last but not least, though not among his students, the young Herbert Feigl (1902–1988) and Moritz Schlick (1882–1936) were much influenced by Riehl.[2]

Riehl was born in Bozen (Bolzano), which is now part of Italy, though it was then part of Austria. Since he grew up in the Tirol mountains, he liked to call himself a *"Tiroler Bauer"*.[3] All his life he loved to hike in the hills, and it was after one such excursion, when he was only 12, that he discovered in a *Weingarten* a friend's copy of the *Kritik der reinen Vernunft*.[4] He started reading it, and never really stopped for the rest of his days. After attending Gymnasium in Bozen, Riehl studied philosophy, history and geography at the universities of Vienna, Munich, Innsbruck and Graz. Though he left Austria in 1882, a little bit of Austria went with him. He was the only neo-Kantian to be raised a Roman Catholic; and during his university days in Vienna, he came under the influence of Austria's "official philosopher": Johann Friedrich Herbart.[5] It was Herbart who planted the seeds of realism in Riehl's thinking. Through Riehl we can still hear the last faint echoes of the lost tradition.

---

[1] On Frischeisen-Köhler, Scholz and Spranger, see Volker Gerhardt, Reinhard Mehring and Jana Rindert *Berliner Geist: Eine Geschichte der Berliner Universitätsphilosophie bis 1946* (Berlin: Akademic Verlag, 1999), pp. 153–154, 217–218, 229–236, 315–317. On Hönigswald, see Hans Ludwig Ollig, *Der Neukantianismus* (Stuttgart: Metzler, 1979), pp. 88–93.

[2] On Riehl's influence on Schlick, Feigl and Reichenbach, see Michael Heidelberger, 'Kantianism and Realism: Alois Riehl (and Moritz Schlick)', in *The Kantian Legacy in Nineteenth-Century Science*, eds Michael Friedman and Alfred Nordmann (Cambridge, MA: MIT Press, 2006), pp. 211–226.

[3] See Heinrich Rickert, 'Alois Riehl', *Logos* 13 (1924/25), 162–185, p. 166.

[4] See Erich Jaensch, 'Zum Gedächtnis von Alois Riehl', in *Kant-Studien* 30 (1925), i–xxxvi, p. xxi–xxii.

[5] During his university days in Vienna, Riehl was the student of Robert Zimmermann, who in turn was the student of Franz Exner, who was a student of Herbart's. Franz Exner and Karl Lott were especially

For most of his career, Riehl was an academic nomad. He held posts in Graz (1873), Freiburg (1882), Kiel (1895) and Halle (1898). Finally in 1904, at the ripe age of sixty, he reached the pinnacle of success with an appointment in Berlin. He taught there until 1921, retiring to a house, designed for him by the up-and-coming Walter Gropius, in Neubabelsberg. Of all the neo-Kantians, Riehl had the greatest international stature. In 1913 he received an honorary doctorate from Princeton University; in 1917 he went to the Baltic states on a lecture tour; and in 1923 he was invited to give a lecture at the University of London, though he had to decline because of his age. Despite his illustrious career, Riehl, like so many neo-Kantians, suffered for his political and religious convictions. An early writing on religion had incurred the disfavour of the Catholic authorities,[6] so that Catholic theology students and faculty in Freiburg were prohibited from attending his lectures. Indignant, Riehl's response was to convert to Protestantism and to leave Freiburg for Kiel, which had a freer atmosphere for him.

Riehl's major work was his *Der philosophische Kriticismus*, which appeared in three volumes from 1876 to 1887.[7] Its chief aim was to criticize and develop Kant's philosophy, to re-interpret and revise it so that it was more in accord with the positive sciences.[8] Volume I treats the history of the critical philosophy and the interpretation of Kant's method. Volume II/1 examines the foundations of knowledge, and volume II/2 concerns issues in metaphysics and the philosophy of science. This tome is one of the classics of the neo-Kantian tradition, deserving to stand alongside Cohen's *Kants Theorie der Erfahrung* and Lange's *Geschichte des Materialismus*. Though its sheer length places great demands on the reader's time and energy, it also rewards his efforts with its many insights and ideas. Riehl wrote with great clarity and vigour, and took an original and interesting stand on all the central questions facing the critical philosophy. The book was quite successful in its day, and it was a token of its success that it was translated into English, Dutch, Japanese, Russian and Hungarian. Riehl rewrote many parts of the work for a second edition, though it was published in its complete form only posthumously, from 1924 to 1926.[9]

Riehl was very much a champion of the new epistemological approach to Kant characteristic of the 1870s. He agreed with Cohen and Windelband about the essentially epistemological nature of Kant's enterprise, and joined them in helping to

---

responsible for importing Herbart into Austria. See Carl Siegel, *Alois Riehl. Ein Beitrag zur Geschichte des Neukantianismus* (Graz: Leuschner & Lubensky, 1932), p. 21.

[6] See Alois Riehl, *Moral und Dogma* (Vienna: Carl Gerold, 1872), reprinted in *Philosophische Studien aus Vier Jahrzehnten* (Leizpig: Quelle & Meyer, 1925), pp. 61–90. On the content and reaction to this early writing, see Klaus Christian Köhnke, *Entstehung und Aufsteig des Neukantianismus* (Frankfurt: Suhrkamp, 1986), pp. 340–343.

[7] See Alois Riehl, *Der philosophische Kriticismus und seine Bedeutung für die positive Wissenschaft* (Leipzig: Wilhelm Engelmann, 1876–1887). Volume I appeared in 1876; Volume II/1 in 1879; and Volume II/2 in 1887. Since Volume II appeared in two separate halves, eight years apart from one another, it is customary to refer to three volumes. Here, following Riehl's own practice, we will designate the two parts of Volume II as II/1 and II/2. The work will be designated in footnotes with the abbreviations PK.

[8] See the preface to Volume I, iv.

[9] Alois Riehl, *Der philosophische Kriticismus* (Leipzig: Kroner, 1924–1926).

defeat the psychological interpretation that was so predominant in the 1860s. There was, however, something new and distinctive about Riehl's approach to Kant, something that sets him apart from Cohen and Windelband. Namely, Riehl stresses the realistic dimension of Kant's philosophy. He maintains that Kant's philosophy is a form of realism insofar as it affirms the existence of things-in-themselves, which we know to be the ground of appearances, and insofar as it affirms the existence of a given manifold of sensation. The very thing-in-itself that Cohen and Windelband were so desperate to remove from the body of Kant's philosophy, Riehl was equally determined to retain; he argued that the thing-in-itself is not inconsistent with but the very foundation of Kant's philosophy. The heir of Riehl's interpretation, though it was never acknowledged, was Martin Heidegger.

Realism was the leitmotif of Riehl's philosophy, its signature theme. Riehl first expounded his realism in his first philosophical writing, his *Realistische Grundzüge* of 1870. One of the main tasks of *Der philosophische Kriticismus* is to explain and defend his early stand on behalf of realism. We shall soon see, however, that Riehl's realism has no simple and straightforward meaning, and that he vacillated between a weaker and stronger form of the doctrine. It should come as no surprise, therefore, that the doctrine has often been misinterpreted, either as a form of materialism or identity philosophy.

Concerning Riehl's relationship with Cohen and Windelband, his two great contemporaries, very little is known. In the early 1870s he wrote positive reviews of Cohen's *Kants Theorie der Erfahrung* and Windelband's *Über die Gewißheit*.[10] Windelband thought enough of Riehl to recommend him as the successor to his post in Freiburg; but Heinrich Rickert, Windelband's student, tells us that Riehl, for reasons best known to himself, did not like Windelband and thought little of him.[11] What Cohen thought of Riehl is unknown.[12]

The most controversial question surrounding Riehl concerns his complex and tricky relationship to positivism. After his death, Riehl's friends and students were divided. Heinrich Rickert, a friend from Freiburg days, insisted that Riehl was no positivist: his realism demanded belief in the existence of a thing-in-itself, which could not be resolved into the positivist's facts of experience.[13] But Heinrich Maier, a student, thought Riehl more a positivist than a neo-Kantian: he taught respect for facts and he surrendered all claims to knowledge to the positive sciences.[14] Indeed, Riehl outdid the positivists themselves, because, unlike Comte and Spencer, he saw

[10] Review of Cohen's *Kant's Theorie der Erfahrung, Philosophische Monatshefte* 8 (1872), 212–215; and Riehl's review of Windelband's *Über die Gewißheit, Philosophische Monatshefte* 9 (1874), 292–296.
[11] Rickert, 'Alois Riehl', in *Logos* XIII (1924/25), p. 172.
[12] The only references to Riehl in Cohen's writings is three short footnotes in the third edition of *Kants Theorie der Erfahrung* (Berlin: Cassirer, 1918), pp. 128, 567, 585. These concern minor technical matters.
[13] Cohen, *Kants Theorie der Erfahrung*, p. 169.
[14] Heinrich Maier, 'Alois Riehl. Gedächtnisrede, gehalten am 24. Januar 1925', *Kant-Studien* 31 (1926), 563–579, p. 573.

no role for philosophy as a conspectus or system of the individual sciences. Even today, Riehl is readily classified as a positivist, and he is often cited as one of the main figures in forging an alliance between neo-Kantianism and positivism in the late 1870s and early 1880s.[15]

There is no simple answer to this question. Since Riehl accepted and rejected important strands of positivism, his philosophy is neither entirely positivist nor anti-positivist. There are indeed important positivist themes in his philosophy. Riehl rejected the metaphysics of classical philosophy, and he indeed insisted that all knowledge of the world lies with the positive sciences. He even declared criticism to be "the foundation of positive philosophy".[16] For many years Riehl was an editor of the *Vierteljahrschrift für wissenschaftliche Philosophie*, a journal promoting the positivist agenda of "scientific philosophy". He also acknowledged the influence upon him of Eugen Dühring, the arch German positivist.[17]

However, these positivist strands have to be balanced against even weightier anti-positivist ones. Riehl protested against positivist attempts to replace philosophy with science as well as positivist attitudes towards the history of philosophy. If he held that the sciences alone give us knowledge of the world, he also insisted that philosophy still plays a crucial role in helping the sciences understand philosophical issues. And, like a good Kantian, Riehl had no time for positivist naivety about facts, which for him were never simply given but the product of conceptual interpretation.[18] It is decisive against the positivist interpretation that Riehl himself, in a late essay,[19] contrasted the Kantian approach to epistemology with the positivist, and came down firmly on the Kantian side. He conceived his own realism in opposition to positivist phenomenalism, which would reduce an object down to the sum total of its sensations. The existence of an object independent of sensation—the central principle of his own realism—he made into a condition for the possibility of knowledge itself.[20]

Of all the neo-Kantians of the late 19th century, Riehl was the most challenged by the popular demand for reflection on the mystery of existence. The positivist strands of his thought did not fit well with that demand. Riehl had been very strict and adamant in stressing the purely epistemological role of philosophy, in handing over all knowledge of the world to the positive sciences, and in banishing worldviews from philosophy. He realized all too well, however, that he could not simply turn his back

---

[15] Klaus Christian Köhnke regards Riehl as a positivist. See Köhnke, *Entstehung und Aufstieg*, pp. 42, 375–376, 431.

[16] See the 'Vorrede' to the first volume of Riehl, *Der philosophische Kriticismus*, p. iii.

[17] See the 'Vorrede' to the first volume of *Der philosophische Kriticismus*, p. vi, and Riehl's review of Dühring's *Kritische Geschichte der Philosophie*, in *Philosophische Monatshefte* 11 (1875), 165–179.

[18] See Riehl's critical remarks on Avenarius in *Zur Einführung in die Philosophie der Gegenwart*, fünfte Auflage (Leipzig: Teubner, 1919), p. 212.

[19] See Alois Riehl, 'Logik und Erkenntnistheorie', in *Die Kultur der Gegenwart*, Teil I, Abteilung VI, *Systematische Philosophie*, ed. Paul Hinneberg, Zweite durchgesehene Auflage (Leipzig: Teubner, 1908), pp. 73–102, esp. 92–94.

[20] Riehl, 'Logik und Erkenntnistheorie', p. 94.

on the question of existence, because this would have indeed doomed *his* philosophy to obsolescence. Riehl's response to the crisis was drastic and dramatic: to divide philosophy into a scientific and non-scientific half. Beginning in the late 1880s, Riehl devoted much of his time and energy to this "non-scientific" philosophy. Yet that begged the question how this aspect of philosophy could be intellectually rigorous and respectable. Riehl seemed to have hoisted himself on his own petard. It was more his reputation as a hard positivist, rather than his neglect of the latest developments in the sciences, that explains the rapid demise of his philosophy after his death.[21]

It is clearly impossible in a single chapter to do justice to the many aspects of Riehl's philosophy. Our task therefore will be a very limited one: to understand the sources and meaning of Riehl's realism, his signature doctrine and his chief contribution to the neo-Kantian tradition. The account we give here of Riehl's philosophical development, which is based only on his published writings, will be crude and sketchy, the result of a lack of documentary materials.[22]

2. Early Realist Tendencies

The origins of Riehl's thought lie in a little tract he published in 1870, *Realistische Grundzüge*.[23] Though he later dropped some of its themes, this tract still anticipates doctrines of his mature philosophy, especially his realism and interpretation of Kant.[24] From it, we can understand much about the motives and reasoning behind them.

In his 'Vorwort' Riehl describes his philosophy as "syncretic", an attempt to combine the best in the philosophies of Leibniz, Herbart and Kant. We do well to take Riehl at his word here and to see his philosophy as a *synthesis* of these three philosophers; it would be onesided to interpret it only as a Herbartian metaphysics.[25] If Riehl corrects Kant through Herbart, he also completes Herbart with Leibniz, who

---

[21] Michael Heidelberger, 'Kantianism and Realism', p. 246, maintains that one of the chief reasons for Riehl's lapse into oblivion is that he did not "manage to connect his philosophy of science to the natural sciences, especially physics, of his day after about 1905." While this would have indeed undermined Riehl's prestige among positivist circles, it would not have been a problem for the larger public.

[22] The best and only biographical sources on Riehl are the articles by Rickert, Maier, Jaensch and Siegel, all cited above. Siegel, though not a student of Riehl, had access to his manuscripts and personal contact with his widow; however, the biographical part of his study is very brief and sketchy.

[23] Alois Riehl, *Realistische Grundzüge. Eine philosophische Abhandlung der allgemeinen und nothwendigen Erfahrungsbegriffe* (Graz: Leuschner & Lubensky, 1870). This tract was reprinted in *Philosophische Studien aus Vier Jahrzehnten* (Leipzig: Quelle & Meyer, 1925), pp. 1–60. All references in parentheses above are to the original edition.

[24] I disagree entirely with Heinrich Rickert's judgement that the early works do not represent his later position. See Rickert, 'Alois Riehl', in *Logos* XIII (1924/25), 162–185, p. 167. He says that the decisive change in Riehl's development came with his study of Kant and the natural sciences, though there is plenty of evidence for that already in the *Grundzüge*.

[25] *Pace* Steiger, *Riehl*, p. 27.

plays the central role in his synthesis. Riehl's early work might well be described as a neo-Leibnizian metaphysics, though much of that metaphysics would disappear in his mature philosophy.

The young Riehl would have bristled at the label "neo-Leibnizian metaphysics". That is first and foremost because he never expressly intended to rehabilitate metaphysical dogmatism. He professed to abhor metaphysics, and he understood his project chiefly in *critical* terms, as a second-order investigation into the fundamental concepts by which we understand and interpret experience, viz., matter, force, cause, change and motion. Any philosopher who built his system without a prior critique of these concepts, Riehl warned, was in danger of having his edifice torn down by the critical philosopher, "this intellectual building inspector" (*dieser wissenschaftlichen Baupolizei*) (3).

Yet, the more closely we examine Riehl's project, the more metaphysical it reveals itself to be. He first describes it as a "critique of concepts", as a "fundamental science" (*Fundamental-Wissenschaft*), whose basic task is to create a system of concepts (3, 6). But this system is not, as these descriptions suggest and as Riehl would like us to think, simply a second-order account of the logic of concepts. For we soon learn that the ultimate goal of any such investigation is "to reach the real (*das Reale*) through its sensible appearance and disguise", and that "the aim of enquiry" is "knowledge of the real" (6). Philosophy seeks to acquire, Riehl tells us in no uncertain terms, "a realistic concept of the world" (*einen realistisch ausgebildeten Weltbegriff*) (6). So, as much as Riehl professes to abhor metaphysics, his project proves to be nothing but that under a critical disguise. Its basic aim is to provide not a second-order knowledge of concepts but a first-order knowledge of the world, and indeed a knowledge of reality in itself. Here is indeed the starting point of Riehl's later realism.

We would be selling Riehl short, however, if we exaggerate the dogmatic or metaphysical dimension of his early project. It is not as if he, like Schelling, were "shooting absolute knowledge out of a pistol".[26] Though Riehl is indeed engaging in a metaphysics, it is meant to be a *critical* metaphysics, one which takes its path through the critical philosophy itself. The realistic elements in his project will emerge from a close examination of the chief presuppositions of Kant's epistemology. Hence Riehl immediately warns his sceptical reader that "there are more *realistic* elements in the critical philosophy than one would think" (7).

The starting point of Riehl's realism was Herbart's observation that there is a startling gap in the critical philosophy between the general forms of possible experience and the given content of sensation. However much the critical philosophy is idealistic about these general forms, ascribing their origins to the self-conscious subject, it has to admit a kind of realism about the particularities and determinate

---

[26] As Hegel described Schelling's attempt to acquire knowledge of things-in-themselves immediately through an intellectual intuition. See Hegel's preface to *Phänomenologie des Geistes* (Hamburg: Meiner, 1952), p. 26.

relations between sensations, which must be just given to us. What these particu-larities and relations are, when, where and how they appear, is independent of our self-conscious activity, our will and imagination. From the general a priori forms of intuition and the understanding we cannot derive the particular facts of experience, more specifically, how one particular kind of sensation stands in relation to another particular kind. As Kant himself put it, the particular empirical laws of nature are "contingent for the human understanding", given that they are only one possible form to instantiate its general categories.[27] The foothold for Riehl's realism lay pre-cisely here: that these determinate relationships, these particular truths, are given for the forms of understanding and sensibility. They have their source not inside but outside us. Riehl rejected Fichte's attempt to deduce the manifold from the ego as well as Schopenhauer's attempt to explain it as the product of a blind will (6). If these projects are indeed impossible—and few philosophers in the 1870s believed they were feasible—then philosophy had to begin by explaining the hard facts of experience. These, and nothing less, would be the basis of Riehl's "realistic worldview".

Despite his critical starting point, Riehl's metaphysical intentions are still plain and brazen, even if he does not want to describe them as such. For the subject matter of his realistic philosophy is nothing less than things-in-themselves! Riehl was eager to trespass and explore the very terrain prohibited and posted by Kant. Sure enough, the very first chapter of the *Grundzüge* begins with a theory about the most basic entities of the world, which we can call monads with Leibniz, reals with Herbart or things-in-themselves with Kant. Riehl postulates these entities to explain the objec-tive component of sensation, that is, the component that does not depend upon the subject's will and imagination, and that is the cause of its sensation (11). Though this being cannot be known directly, though we know it only through its appearances, we can still know it indirectly, by making inferences from appearances (17). This is because, Riehl later explains, sensations correspond to their stimuli in a law-like manner, so that from the constant determinate relations between particular sensa-tions we can infer constant determinate relations between things themselves. Even though the sensations are qualitatively distinct from their stimuli, depending on the sense organs, the particular relations between them depend on objects themselves (27–28). Unabashedly, Riehl is willing to apply the categories beyond appearances to things-in-themselves. Beginning from the assumption that they are the causes of the content of experience, we can begin to develop an entire theory about them.

Quickly, perhaps all too quickly, however, the reader of the *Grundzüge* soon finds him/herself launched into the wonderland of Herbart's metaphysics, which pro-vides much of the contours of Riehl's ontology. Our passport into this world is not any empirical or analytic method but the ways and means of sheer a priori excogi-tation. We do not make careful and gradual inferences about things-in-themselves

---

[27] See Kant, *Kritik der Urteilskraft*, 'Einleitung', V, 183–184.

from the structure of appearances; rather, we reflect on what is meant by a thing-in-itself, and it turns out that we can know much about them through sheer a priori reflection. The most simple concept we apply to reality in itself, Riehl informs us, is being (*Sein*). But being in itself means something absolute and simple. It is absolute in the sense that it has an independent reality, depending on nothing else to exist; and it is simple in the sense that it is an indivisible unity, resisting all partition in thought. Since these things are the grounds of appearances, and since there are a multitude of different appearances, we are justified in assuming, Riehl argues, that there is a variety of simple basic entities (11). From this simple analysis weighty consequences follow. We can think of these simple entities as atoms, perfectly in accord with modern physics. But we need to realize, Riehl declares with the ghost of Leibniz speaking through him, that these atoms are non-physical and non-spatial beings (18).[28] The physicality and spatiality of things is entirely due to the *composition* and *aggregation* of atoms, so that the simple things themselves cannot be spatial or physical at all. It follows from this point, Riehl further contends, that there is no such thing as matter as such. Matter is a composite or aggregate of more simple things, so that to believe that it is a thing itself is simply the hypostasis of an abstraction (20).

Nothing better shows the depth and extent of Riehl's new realism than his response to Kant's theory of space and time (21–42). The Transcendental Aesthetic, which Fischer, Meyer, Lange and Schopenhauer regarded as the model of philosophical reasoning, Riehl finds deeply problematic. He cannot accept the central idealist thesis behind the Aesthetic: that space and time are *only* subjective a priori forms of intuition, such that space and time would disappear if there were no human beings with their characteristic sensibility. He maintains, however, that there are realist elements or tendencies to Kant's theory which only need to be developed to explode its idealist thesis. Thus Riehl points out that Kant never intended to derive the determinate spatial relations between things from the a priori intuition of space in general, and that he even attempted to derive spatial relations from dynamic ones, from the attraction and repulsion between bodies (23). Furthermore, he notes that Kant expressly denied that space is an innate idea that precedes our perception of things in space, and that he held that we develop our idea of space by our reaction to determinate spatial relations (23). All that Kant's arguments forbid, Riehl insists, is that our subjective idea of space is *qualitatively* like real space (23). Kant, however, did not expressly limit his conclusions in this way. His intention was to uphold the strictly subjective status of space and time; hence he explicitly stated that space and time are *only* a priori intuitions, and that they would completely disappear if there were no human beings (23). There was a reason for this Kantian subjectivism, Riehl explains, which derives from Kant's intention to save faith. Kant did not want the world of things-in-themselves to

---

[28] See Leibniz, *Monadologie*, §3.

be spatial or temporal because he needed a distinct kind of noumenal world to save transcendental freedom (24).

Whatever the implicit realist tendencies of Kant's Transcendental Aesthetic, Riehl does not think that they are enough to save his theory. The theory of space and time he goes on to sketch in the *Grundzüge* is the virtual reversal of Kant's. Rather than holding that spatial and temporal order depend on human perception, Riehl argues just the opposite: that we human beings perceive things temporally and spatially only because we have been conditioned to do so by the spatial and temporal order of things themselves (24, 25–26). There is an objective order of space that arises from the inter-relations between things. Space does not precede these things as a vast receptacle in which they are placed; rather, these things are the basis of space itself. In other words, if there were no things, there would be no relations between them; and if there were no such relations, there would also be no subjective space (33–34). Space, as the interrela-tions between things, arises from the aggregation or composition of simple entities, an order that Riehl, following Herbart, calls "intelligible space". We do not perceive this intelligible space directly, but we know it though pure thinking, by inferring it from the correspondence between the order of things in our sensible space and their causes (28).

Thus far, Riehl's theory of space closely follows Herbart and Leibniz, and it seems to have no Kantian element at all. Riehl maintains, however, that there are two orders of space, one objective and another subjective, and that the Kantian theory is broadly correct about subjective space. Riehl agrees with Kant that there is an a priori dimen-sion to our concept of space and time. We must not understand this a priori dimen-sion as an innate idea, however, but simply as a universal psychological disposition to construct the idea of space as a single infinite magnitude. There is no such infinite space in nature, but we proceed as if it exists because we can naturally extend our idea of place beyond any given magnitude (32–33).

Given the importance of Kant's theory of space and time for his transcendental idealism, and given Riehl's sharp criticism of that theory, we are left wondering if there is much of Kant left in Riehl's "syncretic" philosophy. The Kantian dimension of his philosophy seems limited to its methodology, to the critical investigation of knowledge, and nothing more. But Riehl himself carefully corrects this impression in the final chapter of the *Grundzüge*, which discusses the relationship between appear-ances and things-in-themselves along Kantian lines. He very much wants to uphold Kant's distinction between appearances and things-in-themselves, and is very far from wanting to affirm a kind of direct or transcendental realism, according to which how things appear to us is the same as they are in themselves. Although Riehl does not accept Kant's theory of space and time, he still affirms the central Kantian thesis that our cognitive faculties condition what we know, so that what we know are the appear-ances of things-in-themselves. His only worry with the distinction between appear-ances and things-in-themselves is that it is used to defend a two-worlds doctrine like that of Schopenhauer, which would place appearances in the realm of phenomena and things-in-themselves in the realm of noumena (64). Appearances are not a distinct kind of entity apart from things-in-themselves, Riehl explains, because they are simply those things as they appear to us, as they are perceived by us. We are perfectly correct in our normal speech when we say 'This is red' rather than 'I see this as red' because the object is indeed red; it is just an objective fact about it that it is red in relation to human beings (65). The relation of things-in-themselves to appearances, Riehl explains, has to be understood along the lines of the relation of simple things to their composite products (65). Although what exists are masses of independent substances, what we perceive is joined together by the senses to form a single appearance. This analogy brought Riehl's theory very close to Leibniz's, who understood appearances as confused representations of things-in-themselves. That this was hardly orthodox Kant goes without saying, and it reveals again the Leibnizian dimension of Riehl's early metaphysics.

There are three salient principles or ideas that determine the contours of Riehl's early philosophy, all of which are more or less explicit in the *Grundzüge*. The first principle is Riehl's *nominalism*, which appears in his statements that everything in nature is individual, and that the universal exists only in and for thinking (13). This principle has significant consequences for Riehl, which he does not hesitate to draw and explain. First of all, it means that there is no such thing as power or force in nature, because that concept is only a general term that we use to designate similar appearances in nature (15). Secondly, it means that there is no sense to teleology in the classical sense, which ascribes causal efficacy to mere ideas or forms (57). Hence Riehl's model of explanation is essentially mechanical. Thirdly, it implies that there is no such thing as empty absolute space or time, which is only an abstraction from the particular relations between things. The second fundamental principle is Riehl's *naturalism*, which comes to the fore in his statement that "Knowing too has its historical origins on earth." (26) Riehl was fundamentally opposed to dualism, any doctrine that would postulate a noumenal, spiritual or intelligible realm independent of the natural world. All things were, at least in principle, explicable according to natural laws. It was this naturalism that was driving Riehl's realism: because he saw human thinking and willing as parts of nature, he was committed to giving an independent reality to nature. The third basic principle of Riehl's early philosophy is its *vitalism*, which here means the doctrine that everything in nature is essentially alive or psychic. It does not mean the doctrine that life is inexplicable in natural or mechanical laws, which is incompatible with Riehl's naturalism; still less does it mean that there is some vital force behind all natural or organic phenomena, which violates his nominalism. Rather, Riehl was moved towards the metaphysical doctrine of vitalism by the reflection that simple basic entities must be active and dynamic and cannot be inert and static. Since matter arises only from composition, Riehl argues, the distinction between the physical and psychic is not original or primitive (20). We must understand atoms according to "the analogy of psychic beings" that are endowed with an original striving or *nisus*. We must postulate a continuum in nature, according to the extent or degree this striving is realized; its highest state of development would be consciousness itself (20–21, 54). This vitalistic aspect of Riehl's early philosophy shows his great debt to Leibniz. It was, however, that aspect that completely disappears in his later work.[29]

It was altogether a heady concoction, this syncretic philosophy of the young Riehl. It was a combination of Kant's transcendental idealism with Leibniz's monadology, all under the direction and discipline of Herbart's nominalism and naturalism. Although Riehl never claimed originality for his philosophy, generously acknowledging how these three philosophers provided its essential components, he did claim that he had reconciled them, bringing them together into a single coherent system. But had he achieved even this? Despite all his efforts, there were still tensions. Although Riehl had thrown out teleology, he had to admit that there was something to it, because the fundamental elements of the world were endowed with striving, which makes no sense without the concept of a purpose (58–60). But, even more problematically, Riehl's ontology of monads, of simple independent atoms, made it difficult to explain the interaction between them. How and why do they interact if each of them is self-sufficient, a universe unto itself? That was Leibniz's classic problem, which Riehl resolved only by the question-begging assumption that each monad causes the sensations of others (48). The problem of explaining the interaction between monads raised broader issues about whether Riehl's ontology could support his naturalism, which, like all naturalism worthy of the name, has to assume the reality of change and interaction. Finally, Riehl had really given very little justification for the central assumption of his realism: that, somehow, we could know things-in-themselves. He simply assumed that we could make accurate inferences from the order of our sensations to the order of things-in-themselves. But can we? What warranted such a bold practice, especially in the face of Kantian objections? It should come as no surprise that these tensions and unanswered questions set much of the agenda for Riehl's later philosophy.

3. An Early Discourse on Method

Riehl, like all the neo-Kantians, was worried by the obsolescence of philosophy in the modern scientific age. To ensure its survival, he had to explain how philosophy differs from the natural sciences, and how it too has its own unique vocation. Such was the purpose of a little book Riehl published in 1872, *Über Begriff und Form der Philosophie*.[30] In it Riehl stakes out his own position on the obsolescence crisis, which

---

[29] In Volume II/2, 180–181, of *Der philosophische Kriticismus*, Riehl repudiates the panpsychic atomism of Haeckel and Nägeli, which he describes in similar terms to his own earlier doctrine. Riehl now argues that the very idea of feeling depends on that of consciousness, the very opposite of what he held in the *Grundzüge*.

[30] Alois Riehl, *Über Begriff und Form der Philosophie* (Berlin: Carl Duncker, 1872). Reprinted in *Philosophische Studien*, pp. 90–175, 332–339. All references in parentheses above are to the original edition.

differs in important ways from that of Fischer, Zeller, Meyer and Windelband. Most of his later views about the purpose and method of philosophy are contained in this little book, though it also has ideas which were later discarded.

Only two years separate Riehl's *Grundzüge* from *Über Begriff und Form der Philosophie* yet a marked conceptual distance lies between them. Riehl is no longer a syncretist who wants to combine the best from the great systems of the past. He is much more critical of Herbart, whose method and metaphysics he now rejects, and he no longer gives Leibniz a central role in his thinking. Kant, however, has become more important for Riehl, who praises his transcendental method for having made "the greatest progress towards the resolution of epistemological problems since Aristotle" (61).[31] This is not to say, however, that the young Riehl had become a Kantian. As we shall soon see, he distances himself from Kant in important ways.

Riehl begins *Über Begriff und Form der Philosophie* by sketching a broad historical picture of the relationship between philosophy and science (1–16). Since antiquity, he writes, there have been two basic philosophical traditions (2). There has been the *scientific* tradition, which is exemplified by Aristotle, and there has been the *aesthetic-religious* tradition, which is represented by Plato. The Aristotelian tradition had a discursive paradigm of knowledge, according to which we know things through following strict methodological procedures, whose results we elaborate in concepts, judgements and inferences. The Platonic tradition, however, had an intuitive paradigm of knowledge, according to which we know reality through an act of intellectual insight. Such insight transcends all discursive exposition, and we acquire it through inspiration, by cultivating the right feelings and dispositions. By no means a thing of the past, this ancient tradition has its modern protagonists in Schelling and Schopenhauer.

To determine the right method of philosophy, Riehl says, we must choose between these traditions. Not for a moment does Riehl hesitate to decide for the scientific tradition, and he even describes his tract as a polemic against the aesthetic-religious tradition (iv–v). It is a big mistake, Riehl warns us, to confuse aesthetic and religious feeling with scientific knowledge, and it is an even bigger mistake to think it is superior to science or even to rank it alongside science (12). The proper criterion to decide between these traditions is purely pragmatic: we judge them by their fruits. We all know the rewards of the scientific method, whose successes have been spectacular. But what have we gained by the aesthetic-religious approach? All the systems of philosophy that have followed it have met the same fate: they cannot derive the concreteness and determinacy of the actual world from a vague and obsure intellectual intuition (14–15). The aesthetic-religious tradition leaves us with an insurmountable

<hr>

[31] It is misleading to describe this tract as revealing a transition from Herbart to Kant. See Hans-Ludwig Ollig, *Der Neukantianismus*, p. 23. While Riehl is indeed more critical of Herbart, his debts to Kant are already apparent in his earlier work; and the later work also distances itself from Kant in ways uncharacteristic of Riehl's *Der philosophische Kriticismus*.

dualism between its pretended knowledge of reality and the hard facts of the empirical world.

In affirming the scientific tradition, and in repudiating the aesthetic-religious one, Riehl reveals his positivist leanings. The positive sciences had now become for him the model of intellectual excellence. If philosophy claims to be a science rather than just an art, then it should follow the methods and standards of the positive sciences (17). It should follow rigorous procedures of induction and deduction; it should strive for clarity in the definition of concepts; and it should consult the facts of experience.

It would be a mistake, however, to see Riehl's tract as a positivist manifesto. The very opposite is the case: its central argument is directed against positivism, specifically its attempt to dissolve philosophy into science. Riehl's intent is to save philosophy from its positivist and materialist detractors, to provide it with its own vocation distinct from the sciences. How, one might ask, is this possible if philosophy is to adopt the methods and standards of the positive sciences? *Prima facie* this seems a recipe for obsolescence rather than survival.

Riehl's strategy for dealing with this problem is to distinguish philosophy from natural science through their different subject matters. The difference between them lies not in their form or method but in their content or object. What, then, is the distinctive subject matter of philosophy? The proper object of philosophy, Riehl declares, is consciousness (*Bewußtsein*), so that philosophy is "the doctrine of consciousness" (*Bewußtseinslehre*) (27). While the proper subject of science is the natural world, the true subject of philosophy is the consciousness of that world. The natural sciences simply remove consciousness from their purview, while history examines it only in its particular instances with no concern with its general structure (27–28). Although the traditional disciplines of philosophy—epistemology, ethics and aesthetics—concern the true, good and beautiful, we need to remember that these objects exist only for some consciousness (28). Hence Riehl thinks that we should define philosophy as *"the scientific investigation of consciousness, its objects and laws"* (28).

Such a definition immediately raises the question: How does philosophy differ from psychology? Riehl seems to be working with a very narrow definition of natural science, one which limits its subject matter to the natural world. Why, though, adopt such a narrow definition? If we extend the method of science to the psychic world, then it seems we have Riehl's idea of philosophy, which is indistinguishable from psychology. By conflating philosophy with psychology, Riehl seems to be hastening the demise of philosophy.

A closer look at Riehl's texts, however, shows that he can avoid this dire conclusion. Riehl has in mind a very specific kind of psychology, one so unlike the usual or normal kind that he might as well call it philosophy. He explains that philosophy differs from psychology in that it deals with psychic *content* or the *objects* of consciousness, whereas psychology concerns the *origins* or *causes* of consciousness (31). Alternatively: philosophy studies psychic *products* while psychology examines psychic *processes*.

Riehl's distinction between philosophy and psychology is strategic and significant. It is strategic because it is sufficient to secure philosophy a distinctive domain and to save it from obsolescence at the hands of psychology, which really is more concerned with psychic processes. And it is significant for several reasons: because it precedes Brentano's psychology,[32] which will not appear until two years later; because it anticipates the later interpretative psychology of Dilthey, which will not emerge for at least another two decades;[33] and because it marks a sharp break with Herbart's psychology, which had limited itself to psychic processes instead of contents.[34] So the young Riehl, if rashly and confusedly, was pushing philosophy in a new and interesting direction.

But as promising as this direction might seem, Riehl had failed to grasp its problems and implications. For the question immediately arose: What method should philosophy use to grasp the contents of consciousness? Riehl had assumed that the methods of philosophy and natural science are the same. But can we use the methods of natural science to analyse, understand and interpret the contents of consciousness? Dilthey would famously argue that this is impossible, and that it is necessary to make a firm distinction between an *interpretative* psychology, which deals with content, and an *explanatory* psychology, which concerns origins and laws. Riehl, however, was not ready for such a major distinction. Unlike Dilthey, he had no appreciation of the hermeneutical tradition with its very different methods of interpretation of psychic content. Riehl's difficulties are compounded by the fact that he agreed with Dilthey about the limits of natural science in explaining the contents of consciousness. While he insisted that the methods of philosophy and science are the same, he went on to argue that consciousness, insofar as it concerns content, is really inaccessible to natural science. The contents of consciousness are too heterogeneous with the laws of motion for them to be explained by, or reduced down to, natural laws (38).

This points towards a larger tension in Riehl's position. While he insists on aligning philosophy with the sciences, so that they have one and the same method, he also, as his argument unfolds, distinguishes philosophy from the sciences. "No border is more clearly drawn than that between the investigation of nature and consciousness, if by nature we understand the object of physical investigation and not the totality of phenomena" (39). Riehl stresses that the methods of natural science are "patently insufficient" for epistemology, ethics and aesthetics, and that these disciplines need a completely different kind of enquiry whose presuppositions are different from those of natural science (39). What kind of enquiry should this be? To such a basic question Riehl had no answer.

[32] Franz Brentano, *Psychologie vom empirischen Standpunkt* (Leipzig: Duncker & Humblot, 1874).
[33] Wilhelm Dilthey, *Ideen über eine Beschreibende und Zergliedernde Psychologie, in Sitzungsberichten der Berliner Akademie der Wissenschaften*, (1894), 1309–1407. See *Gesammelte Schriften* (Stuttgart: Teubner, 1964), V, 139–240.
[34] See Herbart, 'Ueber die Möglichkeit und Nothwendigkeit Mathematik auf Psychologie anzuwenden', in *Sämtliche Werke*, ed. Karl Kehrbach and Otto Flügel (Langensalza: Hermann Beyer & Söhne, 1887–1912) V, 91–122, 107.

We should not, however, stress this shortcoming. Riehl's little tract has much more to offer, and we need to do justice to some of its other themes. One of its more striking and important motifs is its compelling defence of philosophy against its positivist or scientistic detractors.[35] Riehl strikes a new chord, insisting that the relationship between philosophy and natural science needs a complete rethinking. The commonplace depreciation of philosophy in comparison with the natural sciences rests upon false premises, he argues. It assumes that philosophical method is a priori and deductive, whereas the proper method of the sciences is a posteriori and inductive. All the excesses of Hegelian speculation and Schellingian *Naturphilosophie* are attributed to the a priori and deductive method of philosophy. The proper scientific method, these critics contend, rests on slow and patient induction, experiment and observation. This position seemed confirmed by Mill's *Logic*, which stressed the importance of induction and generalization in natural science. Riehl, however, is highly critical of such empiricism. A purely inductive science is for him a "*contradictio in adjecto*" (viii). The more we examine the method of the sciences, he argues, the more we see the role of pure thinking, of deductive reasoning, which is vital in formulating the ends of enquiry, in posing questions, and in formulating laws in mathematical terms. If science were mere induction, the enumeration of facts, we would arrive at no general laws at all (51–52). Induction by itself is only an aid in collecting facts but it is not really involved in the proof or verification of a theory. Riehl agrees with the critics of Hegelian speculation and Schellingian construction that they have relied too heavily on pure thinking and that they have imposed constructions on the facts. But he finds that the problem with the speculative tradition does not lie simply with its use of deductive or a priori methods. Such methods are as vital to natural science as philosophy, he insists. To understand the method of science as well as that of philosophy, he recommends that we get beyond a one-sided empiricism and rationalism.

Riehl's account of scientific method stresses how it rests on the combination of several procedures. "Human knowledge is no simple product that can be produced in one way and according to one formula. The scientific course of proof needs different methods and aids for its completion. Mere induction does not exhaust its nature." (49) We cannot acquire knowledge through deduction alone, because everything rests on the truth of its premises (50). We need to resort to experience to determine whether premises are true. But to formulate a scientific law, the scientist does not normally wait for a long induction, an enumeration of all the instances. Rather he begins from one example taken as typical, and then generalizes on the basis of intuition. "Intuition is the productive element of each scientific discovery, and the way to

---

[35] Riehl, *Realistische Grundzüge*, pp. 1–2, already began with a defence of philosophy on these grounds. Riehl, *Über Begriff und Form*, pp. 49–56, takes this critique a step further. Riehl explains (p. 56) that this whole section, Section 9, 'Zur Methodik überhaupt', was written to counter objections against the scientific stature of philosophy.

discover new truths" (53). There are, then, three fundamental components to scientific method: 1) the use of a priori intuition in the formulation of laws; 2) the use of deduction in determining the consequences of these laws; and 3) the construction of an experiment according to this deduction (54). This procedure confirms, Riehl maintains, Kant's dictum that we know only what we a priori create. To this extent he cites a maxim of Schelling: "every experiment is a question to nature, to which she is forced to answer; but each question contains a hidden a priori judgment." That Riehl should cite Schelling approvingly is a sea change from the 1860s and marks the beginning of a reappraisal of the speculative tradition.

Not the least important contribution of Riehl's tract is its interpretation of Kant (61–71). Only a year after Cohen's little book and before Windelband, Riehl attacks the psychological interpretation of the critical philosophy and advances a logical account of Kant's critical enterprise.[36] Although the question of the origins and limits of knowledge seems to be psychological, there are two very different ways of approaching it, Riehl maintains. We can attempt to understand the origins or genesis of knowledge, and we can attempt to analyse its essential constituents or content (64). Kant's primary task was the second one, and only incidentally or occasionally was he concerned with the first. Kant reached his conclusions about the structure of experience not through introspection but through logical analysis (65). His primary concern was not to understand psychological activities or forms of consciousness but to investigate the reasons for and kinds of judgements we make in science, art and morality (65, 70). The psychological interpretation of Kant is especially misleading, Riehl charges, when it comes to the analysis of the a priori. It understands the a priori as if it were some kind of innate idea, some form inhering within consciousness; but Kant himself expressly denies the doctrine of innate ideas. The a priori concerns not some innate structure of consciousness but the necessary and universal conditions of empirical knowledge.

Anticipating some contemporary interpreters of Kant, Riehl wants to distinguish Kant's method from his transcendental idealism. While he finds the subjectivism of transcendental idealism objectionable, he thinks that Kant's method was the most important advance in epistemology since Aristotle (61). The great step forward of Kant's method consists in its logical investigation of the conditions and limits of experience. This analysis was not intended to be psychological, as it is in Locke and Hume, but to be logical, an account of the content rather than causes of our representations. The problem with Kant's transcendental idealism, however, is that "it ripped consciousness from its place in the totality of nature" (62). Kant created a transcendental

[36] It is likely that Riehl was influenced by Cohen. See Riehl, 'Zur Aprioritätslehre', his appreciative review of *Kants Theorie der Erfahrung* in *Philosophische Monatshefte* 8 (1872), 212–215. He also notes Cohen's influence upon him in the preface to the first volume of *Der philosophische Kriticismus*, I, v. Köhnke discusses in more detail the influence of Cohen on Riehl in *Entstehung und Aufstieg*, pp. 351–356.

subject who stands above and beyond the sphere of nature, and who is the origin of the necessary forms of experience. "Since man is not natureless, he plainly cannot be torn from the ground of nature." (62) Kant also assumed, arbitrarily, that the a priori forms of consciousness hold only for the subject, excluding the possibility that they are also true of the world itself. Helmholtz was right, Riehl thinks, in holding that the law of causality is a priori yet still valid beyond the strictly subjective sphere (62).

However salutary in itself, Riehl's rejection of the psychological interpretation of Kant leaves us with some nagging doubts about his general definition of philosophy. Riehl saw Kant's critical method as central to and paradigmatic for philosophy itself. But if this method is non-psychological, what sense does it make to define philosophy in terms of psychology, as "an investigation into consciousness, its objects and laws"? The psychological connotations of Riehl's definition of philosophy did not sit well with his purely logical, indeed anti-psychological, account of the method of transcendental philosophy.

Riehl's tract closes with a remarkable salute to the history of philosophy. Nothing earlier in the tract prepares the reader for what comes in two closing sections: Riehl makes the history of philosophy central to philosophy itself.[37] This is surprising even to the closest reader because Riehl had proscribed genetic enquiries from philosophy, and he had banished psychology from the critical philosophy. But now the psychological definition of philosophy returns, and its method is made genetic. Since the central object of philosophy is consciousness, and since consciousness cannot be separated from its development, Riehl reasons, the history of philosophy is integral to philosophy itself (86, 90). Philosophy, Riehl goes as far to say, should be an historical science, and it should adopt an historical method (90). "A phenomenology of spirit, a history of consciousness, development of the ethical, aesthetic and logical spirit, are its [philosophy's] tasks." (91) The history of philosophy is now even made into a touchstone of philosophical truth: what proves to be enduring and common to all the systems of the past can serve as a test for the value of new thinking (86). The hero of Riehl's new historicist conception of philosophy is Hegel, whose historical sense points philosophy towards the future (91). Kant's philosophy, however, cannot help philosophy in moving in this new and exciting direction because it is fundamentally non-historical (89, 90–91).

What motivated this historicist frenzy? It is not surprising to find that Riehl returned to sobriety and never attempted to realize the programme he had dreamed up in these final sections. Yet his enthusiasm for history is all too understandable if we see it as a reaction against positivism. With an almost indignant fervour, Riehl was assaulting the positivist dogma that the history of philosophy before natural science is only a history of delusion and superstition. The historicist sections were just another respect, then, in which Riehl's thinking proves to be profoundly anti-positivist.

---

[37] See Section 13, Riehl, 'Die Geschichte der Philosophie in ihrer Bedeutung für die Philosophie', pp. 84–87, and Section 14, Riehl, 'Die Philosophie als Geschichte', pp. 87–93.

4. Arrival of a Neo-Kantian

In 1876, some four years after his tract on method, Riehl published the first volume of his *Der philosophische Kriticismus*.[38] With this volume Riehl's conversion to Kant is complete. There is no longer any dream of taking philosophy in a historical direction, and there are no longer any qualms about Kant's unhistorical thinking. Philosophy now means for Riehl first and foremost *critical* philosophy, that is, the criticism of metaphysics and the investigation of the logic of the sciences (1). The psychological definition of philosophy, which played such a leading role in the tract on method, has now been pushed into the background.[39] Riehl now tells us in no uncertain terms: "*The critical philosophy of Kant knows no psychology.*" (8)

Just what this conversion meant was spelled out by Riehl in his preface. Critical philosophy, Riehl is emphatic, does not mean exclusively the philosophy of Kant. Although Kant was the greatest representative of the spirit of criticism, "the critical manner of thinking" is not exhausted by, or dependent on, Kant's system (iii). It was one of Kant's great achievements to have allied philosophy with the natural sciences of his day; but the progress of the sciences since then makes it impossible to remain on Kant's standpoint (iv). To think in the spirit of Kant, Riehl would have agreed with Windelband, means to go beyond him. And so Riehl says: "My aim is directed toward the critique and continual development of Kant's philosophy." (iv)

What makes it necessary to go beyond Kant, Riehl explains, are some fundamental ambiguities in Kant's system. While one part of Kant's system is oriented towards the positive sciences, the other part is directed towards "a practical metaphysics" whose chief goal is the moral justification of religious belief. This ambiguity corresponds to another in the Kantian system: things-in-themselves are either the basis of appearances or noumena, the objects of intellectual intuition (iv). We must resolve the first ambiguity, Riehl thinks, by developing the orientation towards the natural sciences and by dropping the practical metaphysics, which has only a reactionary meaning in our present age. We must resolve the second by preserving the ground of appearances and by proscribing noumena, which are spooky speculative entities. After executing both these manoeuvres, we are left with a philosophy that is critical in spirit but one that corresponds only partly with the historical Kant.

As Riehl's critical attitude towards Kant's "practical metaphysics" suggests, there was a moral and political agenda behind his new philosophy. This new critical

[38] Alois Riehl, *Der philosophische Kriticismus und seine Bedeutung für die positive Wissenschaft* (Leipzig: Engelmann, 1876). All references in parentheses above are to this edition. The preface is dated November 1875. Riehl indicates in the preface (p. vi) that the printing of the work had been completed "for a long time" (*seit geraumer Zeit*), but that its publication was delayed from "an unforeseen accident" (*ein unvorhergesehenes Missgeschick*). The composition of the work was therefore probably completed well before the autumn of 1875.

[39] It is pushed into the background, though not completely pushed aside, because Riehl still writes of "*eine Philosophie des Bewusstseins*" that is not "a mere psychology and physiology" (v). This earlier formulation plays no role, however, in Riehl's account of philosophy in *Der philosophische Kriticismus*.

philosophy was meant to be humanist, a philosophy for man, who is urged to build his heaven on this earth, and who is warned not to squander his riches on an imaginary heaven beyond it. "Criticism is the destruction of the transcendent, the foundation of the positive philosophy . . . It rouses the spirit out of its metaphysical dreams and toward the waking life of the day and reality." (iii)

The identification of criticism with "the foundation of positive philosophy" reveals Riehl's sympathy with positivism. It is not least because of this sentence that Riehl's philosophy has been identified with positivism.[40] We must be careful, however, not to lump Riehl under the positivist label, as if it described the essence or whole of his philosophy. Sympathy with some aspects of positivism does not alone make a positivist. There are too many passages in Riehl's work where he is critical of the positivists for him to be described as a loyal disciple of the positivist cause. Riehl was critical of Comte's crude empiricism, which gave no place to the form of cognition.[41] He disapproved of Dühring's naive realism, which could not account for the role of the cognitive subject in forming experience.[42] And he rejected Laas's idealism, which ended out in an extreme subjectivism.[43] While Riehl, like any good positivist, recommends that philosophy orient itself around the positive sciences, he also preaches that the sciences sometimes lapse into dogmatism and need to learn from philosophy.[44]

While Riehl goes to some pains to distinguish his critical philosophy from the historical Kant, it would be a mistake to think that the historical Kant is irrelevant to formulating his own position. Some scholars have gone too far in distancing Riehl's philosophy from the historical Kant.[45] The truth of the matter is that Riehl orients his own critical philosophy around "the spirit" of Kantian doctrine, and he does his best to read that spirit into the Kantian letter. Of course, Riehl regards his own philosophy as a species of realism; but this is a form of realism that he finds in Kant's own system, and which he thinks is the proper interpretation of Kant. He also describes Kant's philosophy as "an idealism of appearances on a realistic foundation" (10), which is very much, as we shall soon see, an accurate account of his own philosophy. Riehl, like many neo-Kantians, never broke with the habit of conflating what Kant ought to have said with what he really meant and, in his better moments, did say.

This habit is very much in evidence in Riehl's account of the two major misinterpretations of Kant's philosophy. The first volume of his work is devoted to rooting out

---

[40] See, for example, Köhnke, *Entstehung und Aufstieg*, p. 376.

[41] See Riehl, *Der philosophische Kriticismus*, I, 79.

[42] Riehl, *Der philosophische Kriticismus*, II/2, 42.

[43] Riehl, *Der philosophische Kriticismus*, II/2, 133, 149–150.

[44] See, for example, Riehl, *Der philosophische Kriticismus* I, 31 and II/2, 182.

[45] See, for example, Siegel, *Alois Riehl*, p. 10. I also disagree with Michael Heidelberger's claim, 'Kantianism and Realism', p. 233, that in Riehl's main work "the Kantian element is comparatively limited", and that Riehl's interpretation was "very idiosyncratic and inventive". One might regard Riehl's interpretation in this light if one disagrees with it on textual and historical grounds; but the fact remains that Riehl himself saw his realism as the proper interpretation of Kant. We shall see in Section 8, how closely Riehl cleaved to Kant in some of the fundamental philosophical issues of his day.

the two most prevalent "prejudices" of Kant exegesis. The first is the psychological prejudice, according to which the main purpose of Kant's philosophy is the investigation into our mental faculties and the origins of knowledge. Riehl insists that the critical philosophy has nothing to do with psychology, and that it is only an investigation into the grounds for our knowledge (8, 310). The second prejudice is the idealist prejudice, which would conflate Kant's idealism with Berkeley's, and which maintains that idealism is both the method and result of Kant's philosophy (311). Riehl thinks that describing Kant's philosophy as idealist is completely misleading because Kant never intended to deny the existence of things independent of our consciousness, which he regarded as the grounds of appearances (9, 311). In thus attempting to root out all psychology and idealism from Kant's philosophy, Riehl shows how far he was from fully distinguishing what he thought Kant should say from what Kant really did say. The historical Kant never intended to purge all psychology from his philosophy, and he described his own doctrine as a species of idealism, calling it "transcendental", "critical" or "formal" idealism. The mere fact, however, that Riehl thinks his own interpretation is true of the historical Kant shows how closely he wants to follow him.

So much is Riehl concerned with understanding the actual historical Kant that Volume I of *Der philosophische Kriticismus* is devoted to an accurate account of the origins, context and content of Kant's first *Kritik*. The first part, which has chapters on Locke, Hume and Wolff, concerns Kant's broader historical context. The second part deals with Kant's intellectual development and the proper interpretation of the *Kritik der reinen Vernunft*. It is striking that Riehl finds the origins of the critical philosophy in the empiricist tradition of Locke and Hume, which he regards as the most important influence on Kant.[46] This is in stark contrast with Cohen's account, which stresses the role of the rationalist tradition, of Descartes, Leibniz and ultimately Plato. Although Riehl agrees with Cohen in distinguishing Locke's and Hume's psychological method from Kant's critical one, he still thinks that Locke and Hume set the agenda that Kant was intent on following. While Locke and Hume were wrong about method, they were still right about the basic goals of epistemology: the critical examination of the powers and limits of knowledge.

Riehl's discussion of Locke and Hume in Volume I of *Der philosophische Kriticismus* reveals his critical view of empiricism, and with it his stance towards positivism itself. As Riehl sees it, Locke and Hume have the same fundamental shortcoming: they have a much too narrow empiricist criterion of knowledge, which judges claims to knowledge strictly according to whether it corresponds to ideas or impressions given in experience.[47] While this is a good test for the *content* of knowledge, it is inadequate for its *form*. If we adopt their criterion alone, then we have no justification for the universality and necessity involved in the fundamental principles of the natural sciences and common life. Anticipating a later theme of Ernst Cassirer,[48] Riehl notes how Locke's and

---

[46] On the background of Riehl's interpretation, see Köhnke, *Entstehung und Aufstieg*, pp. 373–376.
[47] See Riehl, *Der philosophische Kriticismus*, I, 61, 74, 78.
[48] Ernst Cassirer, *Substanzbegriff und Funktionsbegriff* (Berlin: Cassirer, 1910).

Hume's criticism fails to understand the mathematical dimension of natural science.[49] Locke's nominalism made him equate concepts with mere names or generic concepts; and he failed to see how concepts in the natural sciences have an essentially mathematical meaning. Hume's critique of causality suffers for the same reason: it does not appreciate that in modern science cause and effect stand for the two sides of an equation. The lesson that emerges from Riehl's treatment of Locke and Hume in Volume I is a negative one for positivism: that if philosophy is to justify the natural sciences, then it has to get beyond empiricism.

5. Aims and Varieties of Realism

A central task of the systematic part of Riehl's *Der philosophische Kriticismus,* Volumes II/1 and II/2, was to explain and justify the realism that he had first sketched in 1870 in his *Realistische Grundzüge.* If that realism was promising and original, it was also problematic and controversial. Riehl had to defend it against not only sceptical or dogmatic idealism but also common sense or naive realism. Riehl's realism, in its most basic and weak form, stood for two theses: 1) that we have knowledge of the *existence* of a thing that exists independent of our consciousness of it; and 2) that our knowledge of the *essence* or *nature* of a thing depends (at least partly) on our conscious activity, so that we know it only as an appearance.[50] The first thesis was at odds with *dogmatic* idealism, which claims that only ideas exist, so that there is no independent reality for us to know, as well as *sceptical* idealism, which holds that we *know* only ideas and can only make uncertain inferences beyond them. The second thesis was in conflict with common sense or naive realism, according to which we know the essence or nature of things as they exist in themselves. The stumbling block of this realism, Riehl maintained, is its naive assumption that representations simply mirror things as they are, that the world is just as it appears to us; this completely failed to take into account the contribution of the knowing subject in forming the object of knowledge.[51] While idealism fully recognized that contribution, it took that point to such an extreme that it made it impossible to know an independent reality. After all, if all knowledge is only our own product or construction, how do we see around it to the things themselves? With his realism Riehl wanted to combine the strength of idealism—recognition of the knowing subject's role in forming the object of knowledge—with the benefit of common sense realism—knowledge of a reality independent of consciousness. But how could we acknowledge that strength without admitting the drastic conclusion that we know only the appearances of things? That was the question.

---

[49] Cassirer, *Substanzbegriff und Funktionsbegriff,* I, 21, 87. See also PK II/1, 243, 248, 257.
[50] See Riehl's statement of the general principles of his realism in *Der philosophische Kriticismus,* II/2, 152–153, 174, 190.
[51] Riehl, *Der philosophische Kriticismus,* II/2, 174.

The central role of realism in Riehl's book becomes clear from his introductory account of epistemology. The aims and problems of epistemology, as he explains them in the introduction to Volume II/1, revolve entirely around his realism. Riehl states that he is beginning with "the realist hypothesis" that "something exists independent and different from consciousness", and that the problem of knowledge acquires its meaning and significance from this hypothesis (II/1, 18). The problem of knowledge, Riehl explains, is to answer the question "Under what presuppositions does knowledge have real significance?" (4) The "real significance" (*reale Bedeutung*) of knowledge means that it is true not only of our representations about the world but of the world itself, that is, the world as it exists independent from these representations.

Riehl understood his formulation of the problem of knowledge to be a move beyond Kant. The central concern of Kant's critical philosophy, he held, was the critique of metaphysics. This is why Kant wrote a critique of *pure* reason: *pure* reason was the *modus vivendi* of classical metaphysical rationalism (II/1, 17).[52] It was not Kant's main intention to investigate the possibility of knowledge in general or even empirical knowledge in particular. The aims and methods of empirical science were really not a theme in the first *Kritik*. The Transcendental Deduction demonstrated at best only that the most general a priori concepts are valid of experience; but it did not explain how we acquire knowledge of particular matter of fact, still less empirical laws. This gap in Kant's transcendental project Riehl now intends to fill. His epistemology will be less about the possibility of metaphysics than empirical science (17).

In attempting to justify his realism, Riehl believed that he was also defending the metaphysical presuppositions of natural science itself. Natural science presupposes that there is an objective world outside our awareness of it, and that furthermore it can provide us with knowledge of this world.[53] But how can we begin to justify such an assumption? Riehl immediately notes a major problem for such a project. We cannot prove or disprove the existence of anything; and we determine whether something exists only by experience. Whether that experience is veridical also cannot be demonstrated, because the same empirical content can be in dreams and hallucinations. So Hume was right, Riehl admits, that we can only have faith in the existence of the external world (II/1, 3). He even concedes that his enquiry is caught in a circle. It must justify yet assume the existence of reality in itself (3). Riehl reassures us, though, that the circle is not vicious: the presuppositions of the enquiry will be justified as it proceeds.

Though Riehl recognizes that he cannot prove realism, he still thinks that he can provide an indirect proof for it by considering the problems of idealism. Although idealism is not self-contradictory, it cannot be proven, and even worse it cannot be fully carried out to explain appearances, that is, the apparent independent reality of the external world (II/1, 19–21). Neither Berkeley nor Fichte were successful in

[52] Cf. Riehl, *Der philosophische Kriticismus* I, 12, 337.
[53] Riehl, *Der philosophische Kriticismus*, II/2, 128.

pushing through their idealism. To explain the tree in the quad, Berkeley had to postulate the mind of God; and to account for the finitude of the ego, Fichte had to posit
an obstacle to its infinite striving. Even Mill's phenomenalism, which did not deny
the existence of things but analysed them into permanent possibilities of sensation,
had a similar problem. For Mill had to assume that these permanent possibilities,
which are constant and hold for all observers, are based on the permanent and independent reality of some external object. Although the existence of the external world
cannot be demonstrated, Riehl does think that it provides us with the simplest and
most plausible hypothesis about the recurrence of the same sensations to different
observers (21). It is more plausible to assume that these sensations arise from some
reality independent of the observers' perceptions than that they arise from some
mysterious pre-established harmony between them.

The crucial question for Riehl, then, was not *whether* we should be a realist but
Assuming that this is the sole justification of realism, it would seem that the philosopher's task is already complete. There is little point in doing more epistemology,
at least on Riehl's understanding of that discipline. If providing that justification is
the chief task of epistemology, as Riehl says, and if we now already have all the justification we are going to get, as Riehl also says, why go any further? Riehl, it seems, need
not have written anymore than his introduction. Of course, Riehl had not begun to
answer his real problem, which went much deeper. The real problem was not simply to show *that* there are external objects; it was to determine how, to what extent,
and indeed whether, we *know* them. This deeper problem arose chiefly because Riehl,
despite all his criticisms of idealism, was something of an idealist himself. He stresses
that the world we know is not only the product of things outside us but also the result
of the activities by which we know them (II/1, 4–5). Like a good Kantian, he holds
that there are certain a priori laws of consciousness, and that these laws are the precondition of our thinking and perceiving things (11). Hence, to take account of these
Kantian assumptions, Riehl reformulates his conception of epistemology. Its task is
to determine whether and how a priori concepts are true not only of appearances but
also of reality itself (11–12).

The crucial question for Riehl, then, was not *whether* we should be a realist but
what kind of realist we should be. It seemed to him clear *that* the world exists; but
the problem was *how,* and the *extent to which* we could know that existing world.[54]
To solve that problem it was necessary, somehow, to separate the contribution of the
knowing subject to experience from its given content—a seemingly impossible task,
given that these were completely intertwined. Another part of the problem was that
Riehl himself was uncertain about how far to push his realism. The two theses above
represent its basic and minimal form; but sometimes Riehl was tempted to push his
realism further, so that we have some knowledge of the essence or nature of things
themselves. In the *Grundzüge* he had maintained that though the qualities of things

---

[54] Riehl, *Der philosophische Kriticismus*, II/2, 130.

depend upon us, we can still have knowledge of their relations and mathematical form. This stronger form of realism reappears in the Volume II/1 of *Der philosophische Kriticismus,* though, as we shall eventually see, it disappears again in Volume II/2. The reason for this vascillation we shall examine later.

To clarify Riehl's realism, we will have to examine closely the details of his epistemology, especially his theory of sensation and space and time. Before we turn to these tasks, however, we can get a better preliminary picture of Riehl's realism by distinguishing it from two common forms of realism that were close to his own. One was Kant's empirical realism, the other Locke's scientific realism. The similarities between them are striking. Both shared a common goal with Riehl: attempting to combine the existence of things outside us with the recognition that the world is, if only partly, the creation of consciousness itself. Yet each form of realism was unique.

According to Kant, transcendental idealism is not only compatible with, but presupposes empirical realism, according to which reality consists in the intersubjective order of consciousness. Although empirical realism teaches that we know only appearances, it still thinks that these appearances amount to reality because they conform to the universal and necessary forms of experience which hold for all observers alike. An appearance should not, therefore, be conflated with an illusion, which violates these rules.

However plausible and appealing, empirical realism was simply not enough for Riehl. He complained that it still leaves us caught inside the circle of appearances, so that we cannot make any claim to knowledge of reality itself. "The mere agreement of representations among themselves, a play of the mind," he wrote, "can satisfy only a subjective interest."[55] This empirical realism, he insisted, required a deeper and stronger realism to support it.

It would seem that Riehl's realism is closer to something like Locke's scientific realism than Kant's empirical realism. The scientific realist maintains that we have knowledge of a world independent of consciousness; and he avoids the naivity of common sense realism because he does not simply equate our perceptions of the world with the world itself. The scientific realist makes a distinction between secondary qualities, which depend entirely on the perceiver, and primary qualities, which exist in the world itself. These primary qualities are those which we can measure, and which we can formulate in general quantitative laws.

Despite the apparent affinity of their positions, Riehl is a very harsh critic of scientific realism. There is no tenable distinction, he argues, between secondary and primary qualities, because the content of each depends as much on the subject having them as the stimulus that excites them.[56] As far as the qualitative aspect of sensations goes, Berkeley was entirely correct in criticizing Locke's distinction.[57] The scientific realist's attempt to explain sensation was no better than his distinction between

[55] Riehl, *Der philosophische Kriticismus,* II/2, 128.
[56] Riehl, *Der philosophische Kriticismus,* II/1, 64–65. Cf. I, 27–35.   [57] PK I, 23, 31.

primary and secondary qualities. He attempts to explain sensation on the basis of physiological laws, holding that there are strict correlations between sense qualities and the motions of particles or waves striking our sense organs. Riehl objects that these kinds of explanations put the cart before the horse, reversing the true course of ontological priority.[58] What we know for certain is the content of sensation, and what we construct on their basis are motions, particles and laws. Rather than explaining sensations on the basis of particles and motions, we need to explain particles and motions on the basis of sensations. The belief in motion, Riehl further contends, is not primitive but constructed, arising from perceiving an object in different places at different times and then postulating a continuum between these perceptions. "To want to observe a movement in itself," as Riehl ironically puts it, "is to demand to be able to observe without the senses themselves."[59] The last refuge for the scientific realist is his belief in the reality of laws themselves, which seem to hold sway over all the phenomena, whatever these might be. But, for Riehl, this belief is sheer hypostasis. There are no scientific laws as such existing in some realm governing the phenomenal world; we discover in nature only the laws that we make (II/2, 44).

Given Riehl's rejection of dogmatic and sceptical idealism, of empirical and scientific realism, we are left wondering what kind of realism his could possibly be. Somehow, it would have to walk the middle path between the extremes of idealism and realism. But what is that middle path? And can we really go down it without falling into the precipices on either side? For Riehl, explaining true realism was no easy task. It could come only at the end of enquiry, after investigating the fundamental factors involved in all knowledge, sensation, space and time, and the basic principles of the understanding. Our task now is to see how Riehl's realism grew out of his analysis of these factors.

6. Analysis of Sensation

Fundamental to Riehl's realism was his analysis of sensation, which takes place in many places in *Der philosophische Kriticismus,* primarily in Chapters 1 and 3 of Volume II/1 and Chapter 2 of Volume II/2. Our most basic contact with external reality, Riehl holds, happens in sensation. It is primarily through sensation that we know of the reality of things independent of our consciousness. Hence Riehl writes:

Only following the guiding thread of sensation do we achieve knowledge of the external world; and what we should validate as real must connect with sensation. To verify hypotheses that we form about events in the external world means to demonstrate their connection with sensation and direct perception. (II/2, 34)

How is it that sensation gives us knowledge of an external reality? Riehl thinks that the sense of touch is the most basic in giving us an awareness of an external world

---

[58] See the arguments in PK II/2, 32–44.   [59] PK, II/2, 34.

(II/1, 203). When we attempt to touch an object, when we try to push or pull it, we feel resistance; the source of this resistance is something external to ourselves. The basic fact that sensations come and go independent of our will and imagination, Riehl also argues, makes it evident that they have a source independent of our own conscious activity (II/1, 188). Descartes imagined that these sensations could be created by some deep subconscious activity within us. But Riehl finds this hypothesis implausible: it cannot explain why this world clashes with our will, and why we have to adjust to it (II/2, 151). If this activity is so powerful as to create the whole world, why does it not make one we like? Riehl also argues that the sheer heterogeneity of sense contents, the very different qualities of the different senses, is evidence for an external world (II/1, 194–195). We would not unite such different contents if there were not one object in which they inhere.

Sensation, for Riehl, gives not only the most certain knowledge of external reality, but also the most certain knowledge in general (II/1, 46). All knowledge has to be based ultimately upon sensation. If we insist with Kant that all knowledge has to be grounded in experience, he argues, then we have to go the further step and hold that it is based on sensations, which are the ultimate elements of experience (26, 47). "The norm of positive knowing, of material truth", Riehl tells us, "is the guiding thread of sensation." (47) Since the most certain knowledge is that based on direct concrete sensation, knowledge becomes less certain the more abstract it becomes, the more removed from sensation (46).

What makes knowledge through the senses so certain? One reason, Riehl explains, is that it is immediate, that is, it is not based on inference (II/1, 196). There is no causal inference that takes place when we sense things, as if we tacitly or subconsciously infer that the sensation is the effect of an object which serves as its cause. If that were so, we could make an error by inferring the wrong cause of a sensation. But we make no such inferences. What we sense are real objects, and not simply the ideas, representations or images of them, from which we then infer their causes. Riehl is therefore critical of Helmholtz's theory of subconscious reasoning,[60] according to which the perception of external objects consists in subconscious inferences that are based on visual, tactual and motor cues; he thinks that Helmholtz simply reads his own reconstructions into experience (II/2, 47–49; I, 126). We do not see images on our retina, or feelings at the end of our fingertips, and then construct an object out of them. Where we perceive the object is outside us in space and not inside us in our head through images and feelings (II/2, 56). These images and feelings too are fictions of the physiologist, the product of his analysis of sensation that he hypostasizes and reads into the phenomena (II/2, 56).

So far Riehl's analysis of sensation seems to be very empiricist. It emphasizes the importance of sensation as the basis of knowledge, and it stresses the passivity of the

---

[60]   See Chapter 4, Sections 5 and 6.

senses in perceiving things. Yet this is only one half of his theory, which, like Kant's, is intended to be a fusion of the empiricist and rationalist traditions. True to his Kantian roots, Riehl insists that sensation is not a purely passive response to stimuli, but that the subject plays an important role in shaping even the quality of sensation, which is never simply given (II/1, 50, 59). It is in virtue of this active element, he maintains, that sensation is cognitive, making a claim to knowledge of reality itself. All sensation involves a tacit reference to an object, a localizing of its source to something outside us that is not a sensation (II/1, 34, 42). To that extent it also involves an implicit judgement that something exists, that there is a thing outside us (I, 148; II/1, 32, 42–43). Because we cannot prove such a judgement, sensation involves an element of faith (*Glaube*), as Hume said, the belief that there is something out there to which we are responding, and that we are not simply imagining things (46).

It seems remarkable that Riehl maintains both that sensation is the most certain form of knowledge and that it is a form of faith. But Riehl's position is perfectly consistent. He is following Hume, who held that all belief in the external world is certain even though it is indemonstrable. In Volume I he had often discussed Hume's doctrine, although then he stopped short of approving it (I, 156). Now, in Volume II, he seems to endorse it.

Riehl's analysis of sensation is partly a reaction against the idealist interpretation, which would deprive sensation of any reference to the existence of something outside it. It is interesting to see how Riehl takes issue with Johannes Müller's theory of specific nervous energies, which had been cited by Liebmann, Lange and Helmholtz as evidence for this interpretation. According to Müller's theory, the quality of a sensation depends not on the stimulus but the nerves that perceive it. Riehl counters that the nerves have no specific energies at all, that they are not conditioning factors that determine the quality of a sensation (II/1, 51–53). Basing his argument partly on Wundt's psychology, Riehl maintains that the nerves are really nothing more than conductors of stimuli that they cannot produce or alter (52). It is a new finding of anatomy, he points out, that all nerves are basically alike and that the differences in their cells are not great enough to account for a change in their function (II/1, 53). Riehl also appeals to the theory of evolution to bolster his case against Müller's theory (II/1, 56–57, 58).[61] Our specific senses are adaptations, evolving in response to different stimuli in the environment. By giving us direct awaress of reality, they help the species to survive by informing it about the threats and opportunities of its world. Müller's sensations, which inform a creature only about itself, make no sense from an evolutionary standpoint.

Attempting to strike a balance between idealism and empiricism, Riehl maintains that there is both an objective and subjective component involved in sensation. A sensation has an objective component insofar as it refers to some object, to something

---

[61] See PK II/2, 48–49. But see also I, 29–30, where Riehl cited the theory of evolution to explain the doctrine of specific nervous energies.

distinct from sensation; but it also has a subjective component in feeling, which accompanies each sensation (II/1, 37). To sense something is also to feel it, and that feeling means that it never consists of a completely indifferent state of consciousness. Riehl thinks that it is a mistake to make a distinction between subjective and objective sensations along the lines of Locke's distinction between primary and secondary qualities (II/1, 62–63). Each sensation has a subjective and objective component, and it is as false to regard size and shape as completely objective as it is to hold colour and sound as completely subjective.

The fact that sensations are both subjective and objective means for Riehl that appearances are the product of both the subject who is aware of them and the object that stimulates them (II/2, 30). The content of the sensations is both a psychic as well as a physical fact, and we have to recognize that the facts of experience are "psychophysical". The result of the interaction between subject and object in perception is appearance, and not merely representation (II/2, 152). It is appearance in the proper sense of the word, that is, the appearance of something. All our knowledge of things is therefore relative, depending on our sense organs as well as the objects that stimulate them. What is not relative to our physiology, however, is the sheer existence of things, which remains the same no matter how many different ways that we perceive it (II/2, 153, 130).

What ultimately emerges from Riehl's analysis of sensation, then, is a very qualified realism, one so qualified that we can even regard it—*horribile dictu!*—as a species of idealism. According to this version of realism, all that we know of reality in itself is only its existence, not its nature or essence. What we know of reality depends so much on our cognitive activity that we can say that it does not represent or reflect the nature or essence of reality itself. Still, even though we know only the appearances of things, these appearances are not simply representations or ideas floating in our mind; rather, they are how real things exist relative to us. Appearances are properties of real existing things-in-themselves, it's just that they are relative properties, how those things exist for human beings with the cognitive faculties that they have. This theory could be described as idealism, because it holds that all the appearances of things exist only relative to our consciousness; but it is also a *qualified* form of idealism because it insists that the real existence of things is independent of our consciousness. In the *Prolegomena* Kant himself had described his idealism in just such terms. He called it "formal idealism" because it made only the formal dimension of things depend on consciousness; and he distinguished it from Berkeley's idealism because it affirmed the existence of things-in-themselves, which Berkeley's idealism denied.[62] Simply because it allowed for the existence of things-in-themselves, Riehl took issue with the tag "formal idealism", claiming that Kant's doctrine should not be called an idealism at all (II/2, 137). But this was more a matter of nomenclature than substance.

---

[62] Kant, *Prolegomena*, IV, 293, 375.

7. A Realist Theory of Space and Time

We are still very far, however, from a complete analysis of Riehl's realism. If the realism we get at the end of his analysis of sensation is very thin and flimsy, limited to affirming only the existence of things-in-themselves, the realism we obtain from his theory of space and time is thicker and firmer. For now we learn that spatial and temporal relations are objective, properties of things-in-themselves. The apparently conflicting conclusions can be easily resolved when we consider that sensations account for the *qualitative* dimension of experience, whereas space and time constitute its *quantitative* dimension. If this quantitative dimension is true of things-in-themselves, then Riehl's realism comes close to a scientific realism after all.

This stronger and more robust realism is the chief result of Riehl's theory of space and time, which is expounded in the longest chapter of *Der philosophische Kriticismus*, Chapter 2 of Volume II/1.[63] The special task of this chapter is to determine which properties of space and time, if any, are objective, and which, if any, are subjective (II/1, 80). It turns out that relations of sucession, simultaneity and co-existence are indeed objective, and that we can have precise scientific measurements of them.

Much of Riehl's chapter on space and time is devoted to a searching examination of Kant's theory of space and time in the Transcendental Aesthetic, which is a great challenge to Riehl's realism. Its central thesis is that space and time have a merely subjective status, that they are the product of the a priori forms of human sensibility, so that if there were no such forms, space and time would cease to exist. Although Riehl was determined to resist this conclusion, he still found much to accept and applaud in Kant's analysis of space and time. He admits that we need the ideas of absolute space and time to measure motion (II/1, 94); and he stresses that the purely formal features of space and time are a priori, having a subjective source in the mind itself (102, 115, 133). These purely formal features are the *homogeneity, continuity* and *infinitude* of the spatial and temporal manifolds. It is just a fact that these purely formal features cannot be derived from experience, and that we can make all kinds of mathematical theorems about them whose truth is strictly a priori. We construct these features of space and time a priori in thought, by reiterating numerically the pure concepts of unity and identity (116, 132).

While Riehl thinks that Kant is right that these formal aspects of space and time are a priori, he also maintains that he is wrong to conclude that space and time have a strictly subjective status, as if they were true of appearances alone. Kant went astray, Riehl argues, in conflating purely formal or mathematical space and time with true or real space and time (115). Homogeneity, continuity and infinitude are true of our idea of mathematical space and time, which we construct in our imagination and according to the concepts of the understanding. Real space and time, however, are based upon particular relations of co-existence and succession, which cannot be determined by the pure forms of space and time, and which we have to learn entirely from experience (116, 128, 129). Kant himself had admitted, Riehl notes, that these purely formal features on their own, which are general and indeterminate, cannot explain or derive the empirical ones, which are particular and determinate (90). This concession gave Riehl the crucial foothold necessary for his own realism.

Among the purely empirical features of space, according to Riehl, is its three-dimensionality. Kant was wrong to think that the three-dimensionality of space is a universal and necessary property of it. The three-dimensionality of space, Riehl insists, is a fact about its content, not its form. Alluding to the new non-Euclidean geometries, Riehl insists that there are no a priori limits to the number of dimensions of space. Though three-dimensionality is true of our experience, it is not the only thinkable or conceivable form of space (166–167). The proposition that space has three dimensions is what Riehl calls an "axiom of experience" because, though it is certain and a basic fact about our world, it is still based on experience (173). Though Riehl is happy to take into account non-Euclidean geometries, it is still noteworthy that he is rather conservative in his view about their application. He thinks that Euclidean space is at the basis of every empirical concept of space (179–180), and he foresees no value in the use of non-Euclidean spaces in physical theory (180).

Regarding the origins of our representations of space and time, Riehl maintains that we acquire them partly from experience, by learning how to co-ordinate our tactual and visual sensations, and partly from applying and exercising our original innate powers. He suggests, however, that the whole dispute between empiricists and nativists is a mistake, because these concepts are acquired both from experience and native activities and dispositions. Although there are no innate ideas of space and time, we could not learn them from experience if we did not already have dispositions to perceive things in certain ways (112–115).

It is striking that Riehl throws out Trendelenburg's "third possibility" in developing his own realistic theory of space and time (107, 108). If all the particular relations between space and time were determinable a priori, Riehl argues, then we would indeed have to admit that they are only subjective, having no correlate in things themselves. It is not possible for space and time to be completely a priori and subjective in origin and for them to still correspond with things-in-themselves. The problem with Trendelenburg's third option seems to be—though Riehl does not fully explain—that there would not be a sufficient reason to assume objectivity if the representations of space and time were entirely a priori. Why assume that they are still objective if all relations originate in the mind?

Fortunately, Riehl thinks, we do not have to go down Trendelenburg's twisted path, simply because spatial and temporal relations themselves do not have an entirely a priori origin. The particular relations of co-existence and succession cannot be derived from the a priori formal and general features of space and time. These particular relations have to be given in experience, and the simplest explanation for their existence and order is that things themselves exist and are ordered in these ways. They appear to be in just these relations independent of our will and imagination just because they exist in these relations, whether or not we perceive them. It was a mistake on Kant's part, Riehl argues, to claim that what orders sensations in certain relations—the form of experience—cannot be given in sensation itself, because these relations of succession and co-existence are given to us, independent of our will and imagination, just as much as the sensations themselves (II/1, 104). Riehl also gives "realistic significance" to measurement in determining exactly the size of objects themselves and the real distance between them (165). We have good reason to assume that their measured size and distance are properties of the objects themselves, because the reason we must apply the measuring rod or stick exactly so many times lies with the objects themselves and not simply the activity of our measuring them (165).

It now seems, at the end of Riehl's theory of space and time, that we really have a robust realism worthy of the name. It is not only the existence of things that we know to exist independent of our consciousness of the world. We also know the spatial and temporal relations of these things, and we are even able to measure them precisely. Whatever Riehl's qualms about the distinction between primary and secondary qualities, we are now fully in a position, it seems, to say with scientific realism that we know the world in itself through its quantitative dimension.

And yet what Riehl gives he also takes away. We shall soon see that Riehl retreated from this bolder realism, and that he did so for all too Kantian reasons. But this will require a little explanation.

8. Retreat from Realism

Riehl's *Der philosophische Kriticismus* was a work in progress. Its three volumes appear years apart from one another—Volume I in 1876, Volume II/1 in 1879 and Volume II/2 in 1887—and during these intervals Riehl's thinking evolved, and so much so that what he writes in an earlier volume he sometimes contradicts in a later one.[64] With the end of Volume II/1 we have the robust realism of his theory of space and time; by the end of Volume II/2, however, we lose that very realism. The reason for the loss concerns Riehl's theory on the classical mind–body issue. In developing his theory Riehl finds it necessary to distance himself from materialism; but in keeping materialism at bay he also undermines his robust realism.

Riehl develops his mind–body theory, which he expounds mainly in Chapter 2 of Section 2 of Volume II/2,[65] to resolve an apparent antinomy in the life sciences. Developmental biology and physiology have completely antithetical assumptions and approaches, yet both seem to be vindicated by experience (II/2, 178–9, 181, 203).

[64] This is especially clear with regard to Riehl's attitude towards the theory of specific nerve energies. Cf. Riehl, *Der philosophische Kriticismus*, I, 29–30 and II/1, 51–58.
[65] Riehl, 'Ueber das Verhältniss der psychischen Erscheinungen zu den materiellen Vorgängen', *Der philosophische Kriticismus* II/2, 176–216.

Biology assumes that function follows use, and it assigns a great role to consciousness in the survival of an organism; its theory of natural selection works only if we assume that an organism's consciousness responds effectively to dangers and opportunities in its environment. Physiology, however, sees everything in an organism as the result of physical and chemical processes, where consciousness is the result of nervous processes, which are the result of physical and chemical interactions. While biology assumes the efficacy of consciousness as an agent in nature, physiology regards consciousness as something completely epiphenomenal, the result of physical and chemical interactions. Because both approaches seem necessary and true of experience, Riehl calls this conflict between the disciplines "the physiological antinomy".

The only reason that the life sciences are caught in this predicament, Riehl claims, is that they have relapsed into a kind of scientific dogmatism, as if the naturalistic view of the world were true of reality in itself (II/2, 182). They assume that the world as analysed by science exists in itself, independent of our consciousness, and they do so because they reify the concept of matter, as if it designated an entity independent of our experience. The natural scientists have therefore failed to heed the chief lesson of Kant's 'Paralogismus' chapter in the *Kritik der reinen Vernunft*: that both the mental and the physical are aspects of a single experience, and that the idea of matter as an entity existing on its own independent of consciousness is only an hypostasis. The antinomy appears, Riehl argues, only under a certain presupposition: the absolute reality of mechanical events in nature; it disappears as soon as we assume the opposite: that these events are only appearances of the real, whose properties are known to us only by their effects on consciousness (II/2, 181).

Riehl provides several formulations for his solution to the physiological antinomy, though only the most prominent formulation concerns us here. According to that formulation, biology and physiology are two different approaches to, or perspectives upon, one and the same reality (II/2, 191, 196, 199). They do not explain distinct kinds of entity but are simply distinct explanations for one single entity. The activity of consciousness and the will, and the chemical and the mechanical interactions underlying them, are really one and the same activity, though seen from two standpoints (199, 200). When we assume the efficacy of consciousness and the will, we are speaking from a first-person and qualitative standpoint, where we attempt to explain the agent from within; and when we explain consciousness and the will by chemical and physical processes we are taking a third-person and quantitative standpoint (193, 201, 211). To avoid the antinomy, Riehl argues, we must replace a metaphysical dualism with a methodological one (191). Riehl called his own doctrine "critical monism" because it saw a single entity explained by different methods, in opposition to dogmatic dualism which assumed different entities as objects of these different methods.

Whatever its intrinsic merits, Riehl's critical monism raises the most profound questions about his own realism. For it is a consequence of his critical monism, as he understands it, that the mechanisms of the spatial and temporal world belong only to the appearances of things, not to things-in-themselves. Riehl is perfectly explicit in spelling out this consequence, when he insists that the mechanical explanations of physiology are valid only for appearances and not nature in itself (II/2, 194, 200, 216). After stressing this point, Riehl retreats to his thinner and more anemic conception of realism, according to which we know only the existence but not the essence of things-in-themselves: "And so the proposition still holds: knowledge of our self and things outside us is, although real, still relative regarding the reality of its objects. It is the knowledge of the relations of things to our consciousness, of consciousness to things." (II/2, 190)[66] This point is meant to apply not only to our qualitative knowledge of things in sensation, but also to the quantitative knowledge of things through the measurement of their spatial and temporal relations.

The reason for Riehl's retreat to the weaker form of realism is not difficult to surmise. It is his fear of materialism. If we assume that knowledge of spatial and temporal relations gives us knowledge of things-in-themselves, as the stronger form of realism wants, then we grant one of the most important premises of materialism: namely, that the spatial and temporal world is valid of things-in-themselves. Riehl defines materialism as "the doctrine of the congruence of external appearance with the external cause of appearance" (II/2, 188), which is exactly what one must accept if one assumes that spatial and temporal relations are true of things-in-themselves. As a good Kantian, Riehl is not willing to allow the materialist the slightest quarter; he insists that his belief in the reality of matter as an independent entity is the result of hypostasis, just as Kant had taught in the first *Kritik*.

The final result of Riehl's theory of critical monism, then, is the evisceration of his realism. Rather than the robust doctrine that we know not only the existence but also the spatial and temporal relations of things, his realism again becomes the anemic thesis that we know only the existence of things. That more feeble doctrine, as we have seen, could just as well be described as a form of idealism. But, in the end, Riehl had no choice but to retreat to his weaker realism. He faced a terrible dilemma: hold the critical monism and weaken the realism; or strengthen the realism and support materialism. Riehl chose the former option, though that left him with a very weak form of his signature doctrine. So when all is said and scrutinized, Riehl's realism proves itself to be only another name for Kant's formal idealism. Again, this was more a matter of emphasis than substance.

9. How to Keep Things-in-Themselves

Throughout the history of neo-Kantianism, the greatest stumbling block to the interpretation of Kant's transcendental idealism had been its concept of the thing-in-itself. Ever since Jacobi's famous statement that he needed this concept to enter Kant's system but had to drop it to stay inside it, it has proved to be a great challenge for all

---

[66] Cf. II/2, 152–153, 174.

neo-Kantians. We have seen how many neo-Kantians—Fischer, Liebmann, Lange, Cohen and Windelband—did their best to dismiss this concept or to re-interpret it in strictly regulative terms. Yet what was for them the greatest weakness of Kant's philosophy was for Riehl its greatest strength. His realist interpretation of the critical philosophy depends first and foremost on giving full and robust reality to things-in-themselves. Riehl rejected interpretations of the thing-in-itself that construed it in a strictly regulative sense or that made it an ideal of enquiry.

Yet Riehl's willingness to defend the existence of things-in-themselves placed a great burden upon him. How could he defend their existence in the face of the apparently telling objections against them? Riehl took up these interpretative challenges in the last and longest chapter of the first volume of his *Der philosophische Kriticismus*,[67] to which we must now turn.

Although Riehl is never so explicit, it is fair to say that the starting point for his realist interpretation lies in Kant's statements that his philosophy is *critical* or *formal* idealism. In the *Prolegomena* Kant had described his philosophy as critical and formal idealism to distinguish it from Berkeley's idealism, with which it had been conflated.[68] A critical idealism is one that sets limits to knowledge, and that forswears all claims about reality in itself. A formal idealism is one that ascribes ideality to the forms of experience, but which maintains that the matter of experience is given to us. In both respects Kant meant to contrast his idealism with Berkeley's, which is *metaphysical*, because it claims to know the essence of things, and which is *material*, because it dissolves the content of experience entirely into ideas. For Riehl, Kant's statements about his idealism show not only that it is compatible with the reality of things-in-themselves but that it even presupposes them (9–10, 311). It was only by assuming the reality of things-in-themselves that Kant could distinguish his idealism from Berkeley's (423–424). This was a point on which Kant himself had insisted, which we therefore have to take into account in any proper interpretation.

It might seem, on one plausible interpretation of Kant's critical idealism, that we should give a strictly hypothetical status to things-in-themselves. After all, if we limit knowledge to experience, we cannot know whether these entities exist or not. As we have seen, this was the interpretation of Kant's critical idealism set forth by Meyer.[69] Riehl, however, rejects this interpretation from the outset, mainly on textual grounds. It was beyond all doubt for Kant, he writes, that things-in-themselves exist and that they are the ground for appearances (9). It never occurred to him that there could be appearances floating on their own, without something that appears (10, 311). Here Riehl cites Kant's statements to the effect that the very concept of an appearance requires something that appears. In conceiving his idealism as a formal idealism Kant naturally presupposed and expressly assumed that there is something-in-itself that is the cause of its matter. Formal idealism means that it is only

---

[67] Riehl, 'Die Methode der Vernunftkritik', *Der philosophische Kriticismus*, pp. 315–447.
[68] Kant, *Prolegomena* IV, 293, 337, 373, 375.   [69] See Chapter 8, Section 2.

the forms of experience—the a priori forms of sensibility and the a priori concepts of the understanding—that arise from the knowing subject, so that the content of experience is given. But the very givenness of that content means for Kant, that it has a source that lies beyond the subject and in some object existing independent of it (433). Thus Kant's philosophy was an idealism in form and a realism in content (10, 312). Or, as Riehl also put it: "Kant's doctrine is an idealism of appearances on a realistic basis." (10)

Riehl is highly critical of any strictly dualistic account of the distinction between appearances and things-in-themselves. Appearances and things-in-themselves are simply two aspects of one reality (10, 313). Appearances are things-in-themselves as they happen to appear to us, whereas things-in-themselves are things considered apart from how they affect and appear to human sensibility and understanding. There are two sides or aspects to the concept of appearance, Riehl maintains (425). One side is turned towards the subject, which provides the form of representation; the other side is turned towards the object, which provides the particular material for the form of representation. With these two aspects, Kant walks a middle path between a realistic dogmatism, which just assumes that objects are in themselves just as they appear to us, and an extreme idealism, which reduces appearances down to representations alone.

Riehl felt it necessary to defend his own realist interpretation of the appearance/thing-in-itself distinction against Schopenhauer's popular idealist interpretation, which converted the realm of appearance into mere representations, "the veil of Maya" or realm of illusion.[70] In a passage from his *Parerga*, Schopenhauer had argued that Kant had no reason to assume an independent material component of experience because even the content of sensation is determined by the subject and exists only for it.[71] Picking on this passage, Riehl finds its reasoning tendentious. Schopenhauer, he argues, failed to observe the strictly formal limits of sensibility, which can no more determine the details and determinacy of sensation than the categories of the understanding (431). All that depends on sensibility, apart from its a priori forms, is simply feeling, the awareness that we are passive and that things act upon us. Sensibility does not have it within itself, however, to determine when, where, how and which sensations appear to us.

Granted that there is an independent material component to experience, how does Riehl justify the assumption that it has for its cause things-in-themselves? This was the very assumption that Jacobi had found hard to justify according to the

---

[70] Schopenhauer, *Die Welt als Wille und Vorstellung, Sämtliche Werke*, Wolfgang von Löhneysen (Stuttgart: Insel, 1968), I, 48–49, §5.

[71] Schopenhauer, 'Fragmente zur Geschichte der Philosophie', in *Parerga, Sämtliche Werke*, IV, 114–118. Riehl cites large extracts from this passage and comments upon it, *Der philosophische Kriticismus*, I, 429–431. I leave aside the question here whether Riehl's interpretation of this passage is accurate and whether it holds for Schopenhauer's position in general. The interpretation is interesting more for what it reveals about Riehl rather than Schopenhauer.

critical philosophy, which expressly limits the category of causality to experience. If things-in-themselves are not in experience, then we transcend the limits of knowledge in assuming that things-in-themselves are the causes of appearances. Riehl's response to this classic difficulty is to make a distinction between the *principle* and *concept* of causality (432). While the principle is indeed limited to experience, because it applies only to temporal sequences, the concept can be extended beyond experience. Here Riehl was relying on Kant's important distinction between *knowing* and *thinking* according to the categories. The restriction of the categories to experience holds only for knowing but not thinking. While this distinction indeed goes some way towards obviating Jacobi's difficulty, it does not go far enough for Riehl, who claims not only that we can *think of* things-in-themselves as the cause of experience, but also that we can *know* this.

It was probably because he was aware that this simple distinction did not go far enough that Riehl insisted that Kant's justification for assuming the thing-in-itself did not lie in a causal inference (432). To arrive at the existence of things-in-themselves, Kant did not make an inference from effect (the given sensations of experience) to cause (things-in-themselves) but he simply analysed the content of experience itself. If we analyse our representations, then we find that they have a formal and material element, and that while the formal element arises from our mental activity, the material element has to arise from a source independent of it (433). This manoeuvre made it seem as if Kant's method were purely phenomenological, limited to an analysis of the content of representation. Yet it too did not remove the sting of Jacobi's difficulty, because it tacitly postulated some cause for the content of representations, a cause that lies outside and not inside them.

Riehl's realist interpretation of things-in-themselves stood in stark contrast to the idealist interpretations of Cohen and Windelband, which attempted to formulate the thing-in-itself in strictly regulative terms as a limiting concept or goal of enquiry. Though Riehl never engages in explicit polemic against their interpretations, it is plain that he feels constantly challenged by them. The constant citations of texts for his realist interpretation were doubtless made to counter Cohen's interpretation, of which Riehl was well aware.[72] It is at least very striking that he addresses that textual passage that seems to provide the most compelling evidence for Cohen's view: namely, Kant's statement at the end of the 'Noumena and Phenomena' chapter that the concept of the noumenon is a mere limiting concept and that the division of

---

[72] Riehl reviewed Cohen's *Kants Theorie der Erfahrung* for the *Philosophische Monatshefte* 8 (1872), 212–215. Though Riehl praised the virtues of Cohen's book, he also took issue with Cohen's interpretation of the thing-in-itself, which he felt made Kant's transcendental idealism into an absolute idealism (p. 215). Some six years later, in the preface to first volume of *Der philosophische Kriticismus*, Riehl acknowledges that he has made use of all recent Kant literature, and he especially mentions the stimulation he has received from the work of Cohen and Zimmermann (v). Riehl also makes an unnamed reference to Cohen on p. 423, which is probably to the passage he had taken issue with in his earlier review. On Cohen's account of the thing-in-itself, see Chapter 12, Section 8.

the world into noumena and phenomena is inadmissable (B 310–311). Riehl deals with this passage by making an important distinction between a noumenon and thing-in-itself: the former is only a specific form of the latter. A noumenon is a distinct kind of intelligible entity, the object of an intellectual intuition. This is indeed a purely problematic concept, just as Kant tells us, because there is no evidence for the existence of such an object. The thing-in-itself, however, can be taken in another sense to mean the thing that is the basis of appearance, and in that sense its reality is not problematic at all, because we must assume the existence of such things to explain our experience.

Although Riehl advocates a realist interpretation of things-in-themselves, he also acknowledges that Kant's concept is ultimately ambiguous. There is not only the thing-in-itself as the thing that appears to human sensibility, but also the thing-in-itself that is a pure noumenon, the thing that is created by an intellectual intuition (438). The reason for this ambiguity, Riehl explains, lies with Kant's moral motivations: to save moral and religious faith, he postulated a noumenal realm completely distinct from phenomena. Riehl is just as anxious as Cohen and Windelband to remove this purely noumenal realm. He questions whether it really would provide the foundation for the moral and religious belief that Kant intends, given that it has a strictly hypothetical or problematic status. In basing moral and religious belief upon this realm Kant was making it rest on a mere logical possibility (435). "Can the empty possibility of a realm of transcendent things be the true support for our moral ideals, which are inescapable and demand realization?" (438), Riehl asks. He was convinced that realism alone could provide the proper foundation for ethics.[73] But just how this is so he did not explain.

10. Redefining Philosophy

The meaning and purpose of philosophy in the modern world never ceased to concern Riehl, who thought about it until his last days. Some ten years after his *Über Begriff und Form der Philosophie* Riehl returned to the topic in his inaugural lecture in Freiburg, his 1883 *Ueber wissenschaftliche und nichtwissenschaftliche Philosophie*.[74] This lecture is one of the classic statements of the neo-Kantian conception of philosophy, reaffirming unequivocally Fischer's and Zeller's standpoint expounded two decades earlier. Yet Riehl's lecture takes into account something new and troubling, a problem that threatened the entire neo-Kantian programme. His response to this problem will force him to rethink that programme and redefine philosophy itself.

The Freiburg lecture shows Riehl at his most positivist. His chief message is that the positive sciences alone give us knowledge of the world, and that traditional philosophy should surrender all claims to such knowledge. What is philosophy? We are told

[73] See Riehl, *Realistische Grundzüge*, p. 63.
[74] Alois Riehl, *Ueber wissenschaftliche und nichtwissenschaftliche Philosophie. Eine akademische Antrittsrede* (Tübingen: Mohr, 1883). All references in parentheses are to this edition.

that it is nothing but Greek science (18). That means that it was the primitive form of what we now know today as natural science, whose many different sub-disciplines have realized and surpassed all the wildest dreams of Greek philosophy. In short, philosophy, in its classical form, has become obsolete. This theme is hammered home constantly in Riehl's lecture, whose first half is devoted to a withering critique of traditional philosophy.

Riehl's first target is the foundationalist ideal of philosophy, its attempt to be systematic, to create a complete system derived from a single self-evident first principle (3, 8). This ideal proved to be impossible to realize. We cannot derive the concrete content of experience from first principles; and applying them to different kinds of content is only to force them into a straitjacket (4). The idea of a complete system should be reformulated as a regulative ideal, Riehl advises, so that it is a goal for future enquiry. But this ideal or goal, he insists, cannot be achieved by philosophy itself. Since all theoretical knowledge is acquired by the sciences themselves, they should take over the traditional systematic ideal of philosophy. Hence Riehl declares: "The true system of knowledge ... is the totality of the sciences themselves." (7).

Riehl also takes issue with the popular conception of philosophy as a worldview (*Weltanschauung*). This conception had been made popular by Dilthey, and it had been proposed as a substitute for and antidote to the positive sciences. A worldview is meant to be something more than a system of knowledge, because it attempts to provide us with an orientation towards the world, to address not only our intellects but also our souls (8–9). But even here, Riehl contends, traditional philosophy fails us. There are two elements to a worldview: an objective element, which involves knowledge of the world; and a subjective element, which contains a person's attitudes or feelings about the world. But the objective element is provided best by the sciences themselves; and the subjective element is a matter of faith and personal experience, which is no matter for scientific discussion at all (10–12).

Given the obsolescence of traditional philosophy, either as a system of knowledge or a worldview, it would seem that Riehl is close to announcing the death of philosophy itself. But Riehl does not take this last drastic step, and in this respect he resists positivism. He attempts to give a definition of philosophy that provides it with a vocation and method distinct from the sciences. Philosophy is for Riehl first and foremost epistemology (*Erkenntniswissenschaft*) (38). Rather than directly investigating things, as the positive sciences do, it investigates the understanding that knows things (37). Its fundamental task is therefore an examination of the logic of the sciences themselves (38). Such a definition means that philosophy can maintain its independence from the positive sciences while also not competing with them. As epistemology, philosophy is still a form of knowledge, and indeed a science, but it does not attempt to be a form of knowledge or science about the world. It is a second-order knowledge, knowledge of knowledge, which is distinct from the first-order knowledge of the sciences themselves. Riehl does not shirk from the conclusion that his conception of philosophy essentially makes it an underlabourer to the sciences. Philosophy must

THE REALISM OF ALOIS RIEHL   569

abandon its old claim to stand above the sciences, and it must learn to stand below them, recognizing its more humble role of a servant (38).

The final message behind Riehl's Freiburg lecture is that philosophy can survive in the modern world only as a footman to the sciences. The examination of the logic of the sciences ensures philosophy its autonomy and its claim to be a science; but it has to abandon its pretensions to be a system or worldview. That was, in essence, the same doctrine proclaimed by Fischer and Zeller in the 1860s. It was all very simple and very strategic, seeming to provide the ultimate solution to the obsolescence crisis.

So far, so good. Yet it was not really good enough. As Riehl could well see, the whole position had a deep fatal flaw. It saved one half of philosophy only at the price of forfeiting its most noble and important half: namely, the enquiry into human values. Philosophy had always been more than epistemology and logic; it had also been ethics, politics and aesthetics, the enquiry into the good, the just and beautiful. Its task was not only theoretical but also practical. Since antiquity, it had been central to philosophy to determine the basic goals of human life, to be an *ars vivendi* or a guide to life (*Lebensführung*) (50). In short, the definition of philosophy in terms of epistemology was simply too narrow, allowing no place for these traditional disciplines or the enquiry into values.

What was Riehl to do in the face of this difficulty? Should he abandon his narrow definition or one half of philosophy? To his credit, Riehl takes the former option. He decides to expand his original definition, so that there will now be two sides to philosophy. There will be not only the theoretical or *wissenschaftliche* side, which is logic and epistemology, but also the practical or *nichtwissenschaftliche* side, which treats ethics, politics and aesthetics. The practical side has the task of laying down "the plan for a truly human conduct of life" or a "teleology of human life" (51). This task is "non-scientific" because its ultimate aim is not to know but to achieve the good life. It not only describes values but also prescribes them, telling us how we should think, act and feel. Such is Riehl's concession to this practical side of philosophy that he even regards it as its nobler side. If epistemology is below the positive sciences, ethics, politics and aesthetics stand above them (50).

Why did Riehl make this decision? Why did he not simply stick to his more narrow definition, leaving ethics, politics and aesthetics to the particular sciences and arts? Part of the answer is that Riehl was playing to the *Zeitgeist*, adapting to the new interests and tastes of his age. According to Heinrich Rickert, a close friend during his Freiburg years, Riehl had come to see in the early 1890s, after finishing his *Der philosophische Kriticismus*, that his own ideal of a scientific philosophy no longer suited the needs of the age, that it failed to address the interests of the youth, who longed for some spiritual guidance from philosophy.[75] Now that religion was losing its

---

[75] Rickert, 'Alois Riehl', pp. 179–180. Rickert's view is confirmed by Riehl's 1913 Princeton lecture, 'The Vocation of Philosophy at the Present Day', in *Lectures delivered in Connection with the Dedication of the Graduate College of Princeton University in October 1913* (Princeton, NJ: Princeton University Press,

authority and attraction, students were turning to philosophy. Since they could not find answers in epistemology and logic, they were turning towards philosophers like Nietzsche and Schopenhauer.

So Riehl, in the early 1890s, faced another uncomfortable choice: change with the times or become an irrelevance. Riehl moved with the times, and in no half-hearted or begrudging manner. His interests moved more towards ethics and aesthetics. In 1897 he published an essay on poetics,[76] and one of the first monographs on Nietzsche.[77] The greater attention to practical philosophy is most evident in Riehl's 1904 introductory lectures on philosophy, which were published as *Zur Einführung in die Philosophie der Gegenwart*.[78] Now Riehl solves the obsolescence crisis by stressing the role of philosophy as a guide to life. While he does not abandon his old view about the central role of epistemology, Riehl now gives pride of place and greater emphasis to the practical tasks of philosophy. However much the sciences take over the theoretical side of philosophy, they cannot compete with its practical side. The former critic of "worldviews" (*Weltanschauungen*) now becomes an enthusiast for "life-views" (*Lebensanschauungen*), whose chief function is to provide a general view of life and the basic values needed to get through it. Riehl's lectures conclude with a long critical discussion of Schopenhauer's and Nietzsche's views on the value of life. The *Einführung* was Riehl's chief attempt to address the new interests of the youth, and in that it proved to be very successful, going through six editions from 1904 to 1921.

Now that Riehl had given such importance to the practical side of philosophy he needed to provide it with a foundation no less than the theoretical side. The foundation for the theoretical side was easy: we simply refer the philosophers to the natural sciences, who should begin their work of logical analysis and commentary. But what about the practical side? The simple positivist answer is to refer the philosopher to the social sciences, to jurisprudence, history and sociology. But it is striking that Riehl never took this easy route. For he insists that the practical philosopher should be something of a moral legislator and guide. He does not simply describe the values embedded in social, political and legal life but he also prescribes them. "To discover values, and thus to create them, is the vocation of that philosophy that is not a science but a life view and guide to the spirit." (195) Fitting that practical task, Riehl sometimes refers to Kant's doctrine of ideas, which, he reminds us, is properly founded strictly on practical reason (168). But just how ideas are based on practical reason

1914), pp. 43–63, esp. p. 47. Rickert maintains (p. 172) that this turn towards practical philosophy became apparent after completing *Der philosophische Kriticismus* in 1887, therefore decades before the Princeton lecture.

[76] Alois Riehl, 'Bemerkungen zu dem Problem der Form in der Dichtkunst', *Vierteljahrschrift für wissenschaftlichen Philosophie* 21 (1897), 283–306; reprinted in *Philosophische Studien*, pp. 266–303.

[77] Alois Riehl, *Friedrich Nietzsche. Der Künstler und der Denker* (Stuttgart: Frommann, 1897). The book went through four editions.

[78] Alois Riehl, *Zur Einführung in die Philosophie der Gegenwart*, fifth edition (Stuttgart: Teubner, 1919). All references are to this edition.

Riehl did not explain; and it is difficult to understand how his faith in Kantian ideas squared with his scepticism about the Kantian categorical imperative, which questioned its power to provide specific maxims for conduct (169). Just how far Riehl was from thinking through the foundation of practical philosophy becomes clear from his wavering about the logical status of value itself. He insisted that values are a matter of volition and feeling, and that they are not objects of knowledge (149); but he also stressed that values are not created but discovered, as if they were somehow facts in the world to be known (153).

In 1904 Riehl still had a long way to go towards a foundation for practical philosophy. Rickert informs us that, even in his final years, Riehl was willing, even struggling, to provide one.[79] He planned to write a book on value theory, which he was going to call *Kritik der allgemeine geltenden Werte*. But it never came to that, because his powers were gradually fading. Though his plans were great, his flesh was weak. Riehl died November 21, 1924, never having completed his work on value theory. He left his conception of philosophy divided into theoretical and practical halves with no unifying force between them.

---

[79] Rickert, 'Alois Riehl', p. 176.

Bibliography I: Primary Literature

Adelung, Johann Christian

Grammatisch-Kritische Wörterbuch der hochdeutschen Mundart. Vienna: Bauer, 1811.

Adickes, Erich

Kant contra Haeckel: Erkenntnistheorie gegen naturwissenschaftlichen Dogmatismus. Berlin: Reuther & Reichard, 1901.
'Erich Adickes', in *Die deutsche Philosophie der Gegenwart in Selbstdarstellungen,* ed. Raymund Schmidt. Leipzig: Felix Meiner, 1921. II, 1–30.
Kant als Naturforscher. Berlin: de Gruyter, 1924.
Kants Lehre von der Doppelten Affektion unseres Ich als Schlüssel zu seiner Erkenntnistheorie. Tübingen: Mohr, 1929.
Kant und das Ding an sich. Berlin: Pan, 1924. Reprint: Hildesheim: Olms, 1977.
German Kantian Bibliography. New York: Burt Franklin, 1970.

Apelt, E.F., Schmid, Heinrich and Schlömilch, Oskar, eds

Abhandlungen der Fries'schen Schule. Leipzig: Engelmann, 1847–49. 2 vols.

Arnold, Gottfried

Unparteiische Kirchen- und Ketzerhistorie. Frankfurt: Fritsch, 1729.

Avenarius, Richard

Philosophie als Denken der Welt gemäss dem Princip des kleinsten Kraftmasses. Prolegomena zu einer Kritik der Erfahrung. Leipzig: Fues, 1876.
'Zur Einführung', *Vierteljahrschrift für wissenschaftliche Philosophie* I (1877), 1–14.
Kritik der reinen Erfahrung. Leipzig: Fues, 1888–90.

Beneke, Friedrich Eduard

De veris philosophiae initiis. Berlin: Mittler, 1820.
Erkenntnißlehre nach dem Bewußtsein der reinen Vernunft in ihren Grundzügen. Jena: Frommann, 1820.
Erfahrungsseelenlehre als Grundlage alles Wissens, in ihren Hauptzügen dargestellt. Berlin: Mittler, 1820.
Review of 'Arthur Schopenhauer, *Die Welt als Wille und Vorstellung*', *Jenaische Allgemeine Literatur-Zeitung,* Nr. 226–229 (1820), 377–403.

Review of 'J.F. Herbart, *Lehrbuch zur Einleitung in die Philosophie*', *Jenaer Allgemeine Literatur-Zeitung*, Nr. 225–226 (1821), 353–363.

Grundlegung zur Physik der Sitten. Berlin: Mittler, 1822.

Neue Grundlegung zur Metaphysik. Berlin: Mittler, 1822.

Schutzschrift für meine Grundlegung zur Physik der Sitten. Leipzig: Karl Heinrich Reclam, 1823.

Beiträge zu einer reinseelenwissenschaftlichen Bearbeitung der Seelenkrankheitskunde. Leipzig: Karl Heinrich Reclam, 1824.

Review of J.F. Herbart, 'Ueber die Möglichkeit und Notwendigkeit, Mathematik auf Psychologie anzuwenden', *Jahrbücher der Literatur* 27 (1824), 168–180.

Psychologische Skizzen. Göttingen: Vandenhoeck & Ruprecht, 1825. 2 vols.

Allgemeine Einleitung in das akademische Studium. Göttingen: Vandenhoeck & Ruprecht, 1826.

Das Verhältnis von Seele und Leib. Göttingen: Vandenhoeck & Ruprecht, 1826.

Review of: 'J.F. Herbart, Psychologie als Wissenschaft', *Jahrbücher der Literatur*, 37 (1827), 75–140.

Grundsätze der Civil- und Kriminalgesetzgebung. Berlin: Amelang, 1830.

Kant und die philosophische Aufgabe unserer Zeit. Berlin: Mittler, 1832.

Die Philosophie in ihrem Verhältnisse zur Erfahrung, zur Spekulation und zum Leben. Berlin: Mittler, 1833.

Lehrbuch der Psychologie als Naturwissenschaft. Berlin: Mittler, 1833.

Grundlinien des natürlichen Systems der praktischen Philosophie. Berlin: Mittler, 1837–1840. 3 vols.

System der Metaphysik und Religionsphilosophie. Berlin: Dümmler, 1840.

System der Logik als Kunstlehre des Denkens. Berlin: Dümmler, 1842.

Die neue Psychologie. Erläuternde Aufsätze zur zweiten Auflage meines Lehrbuches der Psychologie als Naturwissenschaft. Berlin: Mittler, 1845.

Lehrbuch der pragmatischen Psychologie. Berlin: Mittler, 1853.

Ungedruckte Briefe, eds Renato Pettoelle and Nikola Barelmann. Aalen: Scientia Verlag, 1994.

Brentano, Franz

Psychologie vom empirischen Standpunkt. Leipzig: Duncker & Humblot, 1874.

Büchner, Ludwig

Kraft und Stoff. Frankfurt: Meidinger, 1855; Einundzwanzigste durchgesehene Auflage. Leipzig: Thomas, 1904.

Natur und Geist. Gespräche zweier Freunde über den Materialismus und über realphilosophischen Fragen der Gegenwart. Frankfurt: Meidinger Sohn & Comp, 1857.

Im Dienste der Wahrheit. Ausgewählte Aufsätze aus Natur und Wissenschaft. Gießen: Verlag von Emil Roth, 1900.

Cabanis, P.J.G.

'Rapports du Physique et du Moral de l'Homme', in *Œuvres complètes de Cabanis*. Paris: Bossange, 1823.

Chambers, Robert

Vestiges of the Natural History of Creation. London: Churchill, 1844.
Natürliche Geschichte der Schöpfung des Weltalls. trans. Karl Vogt. Braunschweig: Vieweg, 1851; 2nd edn, 1858.

Cohen, Hermann

Philosophorum de antinomia necessitatis et contingentiae doctrinae. Halle: Kautzleben, 1865.
'Die Platonische Ideenlehre psychologisch entwickelt', *Zeitschrift für Völkerpsychologie und Sprachwissenschaft* IV (1866), 403–464.
'Heinrich Heine und das Judentum', *Die Gegenwart* I (1867). *JS* II, 2–44.[1]
'Virschow und die Juden', *Die Zukunft, Demokratische Zeitung*, August 14, 1868. *JS* II, 457–462.
'Mythologische Vorstellungen von Gott und Seele, psychologisch entwickelt', *Zeitschrift für Völkerpsychologie und Sprachwissenschaft* V (1868), 396–434.
'Die dichterische Phantasie und der Mechanismus des Bewusstseins', *Zeitschrift für Völkerpsychologie und Sprachwissenschaft* VI (1869), 171–263.
Die dichterische Phantasie und der Mechanismus des Bewusstseins. Berlin: Dümmler, 1869.
Kants Theorie der Erfahrung. Berlin: Dümmler, 1871.
Review of Jürgen Bona Meyer *Kants Psychologie, Zeitschrift für Völkerpsychologie und Sprachwissenschaft* VII (1871), 320–330.
'Zur Kontroverse zwischen Trendelenburg und Kuno Fischer', *Zeitschrift für Völkerpsychologie und Sprachwissenschaft* VII (1871), 249–271.
Kants Theorie der Erfahrung. Berlin: Ferdinand Dümmler, 1871. 2nd enlarged edition 1885.
Die systematische Begriffe in Kants vorkritischen Schriften nach ihrem Verhältnis zum kritischen Idealismus. Berlin: Dümmler, 1873.
Review of Windelband *Über die Gewißheit, Philosophische Monatshefte* 9 (1874), 292–296.
'Friedrich Albert Lange', *Philosophische Monatshefte* 12 (1876), 46–47.
'Friedrich Albert Lange', *Preussische Jahrbücher* 37 (1876), 353–381.
Kants Begründung der Ethik. Berlin: Dümmler, 1877. 2nd enlarged edition 1910.
Platos Ideenlehre und die Mathematik. Marburg: Elwertsche Verlagsbuchhandlung, 1879.
Das Princip der Infinitesimal-Methode und seine Geschichte. Berlin: Dümmler, 1883.
'Biographisches Vorwort' to F.A. Lange, *Geschichte des Materialismus*, 4th edition. Leipzig: Baedeker, 1887.
'Biographisches Vorwort und Einleitung mit kritischem Nachtrag' to F.A. Lange, *Geschichte des Materialismus.* Leipzig: Baedeker, 1896. Buch I, pp. V–xiii. Buch II. Xv–llvi.
System der Philosophie. Erster Teil: Logik der reinen Erkenntnis. Berlin: Cassirer, 1902.
System der Philosophie. Zweiter Teil: Ethik des reinen Willens. Berlin: Cassirer, 1904.
Kommentar zu Immanuel Kants Kritik der reinen Vernunft. Leipzig: Meiner, 1907.
Philosophische Arbeiten, eds Cohen and Paul Natorp. Giessen: Töplemann, 1907.
'Innere Beziehungen der kantischen Philosophie zum Judentum. *Achtundzwanzigster Bericht der Lehranstalt für die Wissenschaft des Judentums in Berlin* 28 (1910), 39–61. Reprinted in *Werke* XV, 309–345.
System der Philosophie. Dritter Teil: Ästhetik des reinen Gefühls. Berlin: Cassirer, 1912.

---

[1] JS signifies *Jüdische Schriften,* ed. Bruno Strauß. Berlin: Schwetschke, 1924. 2 vols.

Schriften zur Philosophie und Zeitgeschichte, eds Ernst Cassirer and Albert Görland. Berlin: Akademie Verlag, 1923. 2 vols.

Jüdische Schriften, ed. Bruno Strauß. Berlin: Schwetschke, 1924. 2 vols.

Briefe, eds Bertha und Bruno Strauss. Berlin: Schocken, 1939.

Werke, eds Helmut Holzhey and Hartwig Wiedenbach. Hildesheim: Olms, 1987–2002. 17 vols.

Cuvier, George

La Régne animal distribué d'apres son organization. Paris: Déterville, 1817. 2 vols.

Czolbe, Heinrich

Neue Darstellung des Sensualismus. Leipzig: Costenoble, 1855.

Darwin, Charles

On the Origin of Species. London: John Murray, 1859.

Über die Entstehung der Arten im Thier und Pflanzenreich durch natürliche Züchtung. Trans. Heinrich Georg Bronn. Stuttgart: Schweizerbart, 1860.

The Descent of Man and Selection in Relation to Sex. London: John Murray, 1871.

Über die Entstehung der Arten im Thier und Pflanzenreich durch natürliche Züchtung. Trans. Viktor Carus. Stuttgart: Koch, 1872.

The Life and Letters of Charles Darwin. New York: Appelton, 1986. 2 vols.

The Correspondence of Charles Darwin, ed. David Burkhardt, *et al.* Cambridge: Cambridge University Press, 1985. 20 vols.

Descartes, René

Oeuvres de Descartes, eds C. Adam and P. Tannery. Paris: Vrin, 1964–1976.

Dilthey, Wilhelm

Einleitung in die Geisteswissenschaften. Versuch einer Grundlegung für das Studium der Gesellschaft und der Geschichte. Leipzig: Duncker & Humblot, 1883.

Dressler, Johann Gottlieb

Ist Beneke Materialist? Berlin: Mittler, 1862.

'Friedrich Eduard Benekes Leben', in *Pädagogisches Jahrbuch für Lehrer und Schulfreunde–1856.* Berlin: Diesterweg, 1856, pp. 1–105.

Drobisch, M.W.

Empirische Psychologie nach naturwissenschaftlicher Methode. Leipzig: Voß, 1842.

Droysen, Johann Gustav

Grundriß der Historik. Leipzig: Veit, 1868.

Du Bois-Reymond, Emil

Ueber die Grenzen des Naturerkennens. Ein Vortrag in der zweiten öffentlichen Sitzung der 45. Versammlung deutscher Naturforscher und Ärtze zu Leipzig 14 August 1872. Leipzig: Veit & Co., 1872.
'Die sieben Weltraetsel. Nachtrag', *Monatsbericht der Koeniglich-Preussischen Akademie der Wissenschaften zu Berlin* (1880), 1045–1072. Öffentliche Sitzung zur Feier des Leibnizischen Jahrestages.
Reden von Emil Du Bois-Reymond. Leipzig: Veit & Comp., 1886.
Über die Grenzen des Naturerkennens. Die sieben Welträthsel. Zwei Vorträge. Leipzig: Veit, 1882.

Engels, Friedrich

Ludwig Feuerbach und der Ausgang der klassischen deutschen Philosophie. Stuttgart: Dietz, 1888.

Fechner, Gustav Theodor

Nanna: oder Über das Seelenleben der Pflanzen. Hamburg: Voß, 1848.
Zend-Avesta: oder Über die Dinge des Himmels und des Jenseits vom Standpunkt der Naturbetrachtung. Hamburg: Voß, 1851.

Feuerbach, Ludwig

'Zur Kritik der Hegelsche Philosophie', *in sechs Bänden.* Ed. Erich Thies. Frankfurt: Suhrkamp, 1975. II, 7–53.
Das Wesen des Christenthums. Leipzig: Wigand, 1841.
'Vorläufige Thesen zur Reformation der Philosophie', in *Werke in sechs Bänden.* Ed. Erich Thies. Frankfurt: Suhrkamp, 1975. II, 223–243.

Fichte, Johann Gottlieb

Grundlage der gesamten Wissenschaftslehre. Leipzig: Gabler, 1794.
Ueber den Begriff der Wissenschaftslehre oder der sogenannten Philosophie. Weimar: Industrie-Comtoir, 1794.
Einige Vorlesungen über die Bestimmung des Gelehrten. Leipzig: Gabler, 1794.
'Erste Einleitung in die Wissenschaftslehre', *Philosophisches Journal* V (1797), 1–47.
'Zweite Einleitung in die Wissenschaftslehre', *Philosophisches Journal* V (1797), 319–378 and VI (1797), 1–40.
Appelation an das Publicum gegen die Anklage des Atheismus. Jena: Gabler, 1799.
Bestimmung des Menschen. Berlin: Voß, 1800.

Sämtliche Werke, ed. I.H. Fichte. Berlin: Veit, 1845–1846.
Briefwechsel, ed. Hans Schulz. Leipzig: Haessel, 1930. 2 vols.

Fisscher, Kuno

'Philosophie der Geschichte in der Geschichte der Philosophie', *Literatur- und Kunstbericht*, ed. Oswald Marbach, Leipzig: Wigand, Nr. 20 (1846), 78–79; Nr. 21 (1846), 81–84; Nr. 22 (1846), 85–87; and Nr. 23 (1846), 90–92.
'George Sand und Ida Gräfin Hahn-Hahn', *Literatur- und Kunstbericht*, ed. Oswald Marbach, Leipzig: Wigand, Nr. 27 (1846) 109–112; and Nr. 29 (1846), 113–115.
'Die Autorität', *Literatur- und Kunstbericht*, ed. Oswald Marbach, Leipzig: Wigand, Nr. 43 (1846), 169–170; and Nr. 44 (1846), 174–176.
'Philosophische Literatur', *Literatur- und Kunstbericht*, ed. Oswald Marbach, Leipzig: Wigand, Nr. 58 (1846), 229–232; Nr. 59 (1846), 233–235; and Nr. 60 (1846), 237–239.
'Theologische Fragen', *Literatur- und Kunstbericht*, ed. Oswald Marbach, Leipzig: Wigand, Nr. 73 (1846), 289–292; Nr. 74 (1846), 293–295; and Nr. 75 (1846), 298–299.
'Moderne Sophisten', *Leipziger Revue* Nr. 3 (1847), 9–11; Nr. 4 (1847), 13–14; Nr. 5 (1847), 17–20; Nr. 6 (1847), 21–23; Nr. 8 (1847), 30–32; Nr. 12 (1847), 45–48; and Nr. 13 (1847) 50–52.
'Ein Apologet der Sophistik und ein „philosophischer Reactionär"', *Die Epigonen* IV (1847), pp. 152–165.
'Arnold Ruge und der Humanismus', *Die Epigonen* IV (1847), 95–140.
'Das Wesen der Religion von Carl Schwarz', *Die Epigonen* V (1848), 177–208.
'Ludwig Feuerbach und die Philosophie unserer Zeit', *Die Akademie. Philosophische Taschenbuch* I (1848), 128–190.
Diotima. Die Idee des Schönen. Philosophische Briefe. Pforzheim: Flammer und Hoffmann, 1849.
De Parmenide Platonico. Stuttgart: Scheitlin, 1851.
Vorlesungen über Geschichte der neueren Philosophie. Abtheilung I: Einleitung in das Studium der Philosophie. Stuttgart: Scheitlin, 1852.
Logik und Metaphysik oder Wissenschaftslehre. Lehrbuch für akademische Vorlesungen. Stuttgart: C.P. Scheitlin, 1852.
Geschichte der neuern Philosophie: Erster Band, Das classische Zeitalter der dogmatischen Philosophie. Mannheim: Bassermann & Mathy, 1854.
Das Interdict meiner Vorlesungen und die Anklage des Herrn Schenkel. Mannheim: Bassermann & Mathy, 1854.
Apologie meiner Lehre. Mannheim: Bassermann & Mathy, 1854.
G.W. Leibniz und seine Schule. Mannheim: Bassermann, 1855.
Francis Bacon und seine Nachfolger. Leipzig: Brockhaus, 1856.
Clavis kantiana. Qua via Immanuel Kant philosophiae criticae elementa invenerit. Jena: Schreiber, 1858.
Geschichte der neueren Philosophie. Dritter Band: Immanuel Kant: Entwicklungsgeschichte und System der kritischen Philosophie. Mannheim: Bassermann, 1860.
Kant's Leben und die Grundlage seiner Lehre. Mannheim: Bassermann, 1860.
Die beiden kantische Schulen in Jena. Stuttgart: Cotta, 1862.
Johann Gottlieb Fichte. Stuttgart: Cotta, 1862.

Akademische Reden. Stuttgart: Cotta, 1862.

Geschichte der neuern Philosophie. Erster Band. Descartes und seine Schule. Erster Teil. Allgemeine Einleitung. Rene Descartes. Mannheim: Bassermann, 1865.

Geschichte der neuern Philosophie. Erster Band, Zweiter Teil. Descartes Schule. Geulinck. Malebranche, Baruch Spinoza. Zweite völlig umgearbeitete Auflage. Heidelberg: Winter, 1865.

System der Logik und Metaphysik oder Wissenschaftslehre. Heidelberg: Friedrich Bassermann, 1865.

Geschichte der neuern Philosophie. Zweiter Band. Leibniz und seine Schule. Zweite neu bearbeitete Auflage. Heidelberg: Winter, 1867.

Geschichte der neueren Philosophie. Dritter Band. Kants Vernunftkritik und deren Entstehung. Zweite revidierte Auflage. Heidelberg: Winter, 1869.

Geschichte der neuern Philosophie. Vierter Band. Kants System der reinen Vernunft auf Grund der Vernunftkritik. Zweite revidierte Auflage. Heidelberg: Winter, 1869.

Schiller als Philosoph. Leipzig: Fues, 1868.

Kritik der kantischen Philosophie. Munich: Bassermann, 1883.

Anti-Trendelenburg. Eine Gegenschrift. Jena: Hermann Dabis, 1870.

Ueber die menschliche Freiheit. Heidelberg: Winter, 1875.

'Die Hundertjährige Gedächtnisfeier der kantischen 'Kritik der reinen Vernunft', *Nord und Süd.* 17 (1881), 320–336.

Kleine Schriften. Heidelberg: Winter, 1896. 2 vols.

Der Philosoph des Pessimismus. Ein Charakterproblem. Heidelberg: Winter, 1897.

Geschichte der neuern Philosophie. Neunter Band. Schopenhauers Leben, Werke und Lehre. Zweite neu bearbeitete und vermehrte Auflage. Heidelberg: Winter, 1898.

Über David Friedrich Strauß. Heidelberg: Winter, 1908.

Fortlage, Carl

Die Lücken des Hegelschen Systems der Philosophie. Nebst Andeutung der Mittel, wodurch eine Ausfüllung derselben möglich ist. Heidelberg: Karl Groos, 1832.

'Die Stellung Kants zur Philosophie vor ihm und nach ihm', *Deutsche Vierteljahrsschrift* Heft IV (1838), 91–123.

Genetische Geschichte der Philosophie seit Kant. Leipzig: Brockhaus, 1852.

'Kant'sche Philosophie', *Blätter für literarische Unterhaltung* Nr. 29 (19. Jan. 1860), 525–529.

'Kuno Fischers Darstellung der Kant'schen Philosophie', *Blätter für literarische Unterhaltung* Nr. 16 (18. April 1861), 285–291.

Fries, Johann Friedrich

'Ueber das Verhältniß der empirischen Psychologie zur Metaphysik', *Psychologisches Magazin* III (1798), 156–202.

'Propadeutik einer allgemeinen empirischen Psychologie', *Psychologisches Magazin* III (1798), 203–267.

'Von der rationellen Seelenlehre', *Psychologisches Magazin* III (1798), 268–293.

'Abriß der Metaphysik der inneren Natur', *Psychologisches Magazin* III (1798), 294–353.

'Allgemeine Uebersicht der empirischen Erkenntnisse des Gemüths', *Psychologisches Magazin* III (1798), 354–402.

'Versuch einer Kritik der Richterischen Stöchymetrie', *Archiv für theoretische Chemie* I (1800), 315–446.

Dissertatio philosophica de intuitu intellectuali. Jena: Praeger, 1801.

'Versuch einer neuen Darstellung der Theorie des Lichts und der Wärme', *Archiv für theoretische Chemie* II (1802), 25–96.

Regulative für die Therapeutik nach heuristischen Grundsätzen der Naturphilosophie. Leipzig: J.C. Hinrichs, 1803.

Reinhold, Fichte und Schelling. Leipzig: August Lebrecht Reineicke, 1803.

Philosophische Rechtslehre und Kritik aller positiven Gesetzgebung. Jena: Johann Michael Mauke, 1803.

System der Philosophie als evidente Wissenschaft. Leipzig: Johann Conrad Hinrichs, 1804.

Wissen, Glaube und Ahndung. Jena: J.C.G. Göpferdt, 1805.

Neue Kritik der Vernunft. Heidelberg: Mohr und Zimmer, 1807. 3 vols.

Fichte's und Schelling's neueste Lehren von Gott und der Welt. Heidelberg: Mohr und Zimmer, 1807.

Julius und Evagoras oder Die neue Republik. Heidelberg: Mohr und Zimmer, 1814.

Von deutschen Bund und deutscher Staatsverfassung. Allgemeine staatsrechtlichen Ansichten. Heidelberg: Mohr und Winter, 1816.

'Über die Gefährdung des Wohlstandes und Charakters der deutschen durch die Juden', *Heidelberger Jahrbücher* 16–17 (1816), 241–264.

Beyträge zur Geschichte der Philosophie. Heidelberg: Mohr und Winter, 1819.

Handbuch der Psychischen Anthropologie. Jena: Cröker, 1820–1821. 2 vols.

Die mathematische Naturphilosophie nach philosophischer Methode bearbeitet. Heidelberg: Mohr und Winter, 1822.

System der Metaphysik. Heidelberg: Christian Friedrich Winter, 1824.

Neue oder anthropologische Kritik der Vernunft. Heidelberg: Winter, 1828–1831. 3 vols.

Handbuch der praktischen Philosophie oder der philosophischen Zwecklehre. Heidelberg: Christian Friedrich Winter, 1832. 2 vols.

System der Logik. Heidelberg: Winter, 1837.

Die Geschichte der Philosophie dargestellt nach den Fortschritten ihrer wissenschaftlichen Entwicklung. Halle: Waisenhaus, 1840.

Versuch einer Kritik der Principien der Wahrscheinlichkeitstrechnung. Braunschweig: Vieweg, 1842.

Sämtliche Schriften, eds Gert König and Lutz Geldsetzer. Aalen: Scientia Verlag, 1967-. 32 vols.

Dialogues on Morality and Religion, translated by D.Z. Phillips. Oxford: Blackwell, 1982.

Gruppe, Otto Friedrich

Antäus. Ein Briefwechsel über speculative Philosophie in ihrem Conflict mit Wissenschaft und Sprache. Berlin: Nancke, 1831.

Wendepunkt der Philosophie im Neunzehnten Jahrhundert. Berlin: Reimer, 1834.

Gegenwart und Zukunft der Philosophie in Deutschland. Berlin: Reimer, 1855.

Haeckel, Ernst

Die Welträthsel. Bonn: Emil Strauß, 1899.
Freie Wissenschaft und freie Lehre. Stuttgart: Schweizerbart, 1878.
Die Radiolaren (Rhipzopoda Radiara). Eine Monographie. Berlin: Reimer, 1862.
Generelle Morphologie der Organismen. Berlin: Reimer, 1866.
Gemeinversändliche Vorträge und Abhandlungen aus dem Gebiet der Entwicklungslehre, Zweite Auflage. Bonn: Emil Strauß 1902. 2 vols.
Natürliche Schöpfungsgeschichte. Vierte Auflage. Berlin: Reimer, 1873.

Hartmann, Eduard von

Philosophie des Unbewussten: Versuch einer Weltanschauung. Berlin: Duncker, 1869.
Gesammelte Studien und Aufsätze. Berlin: Duncker, 1876.
Zur Geschichte und Begründung des Pessimismus. Berlin: Duncker, 1880.
Philosophische Fragen der Gegenwart. Berlin: Duncker, 1885.

Haym, Rudolf

Eine Erinnerung an Johann Gottlieb Fichte. Berlin: Reimer, 1861.
Arthur Schopenhauer. Berlin: Reimer, 1864.
Die Hartmann'sche Philosophie des Unbewusstseins. Berlin: Reimer, 1872.

Hegel, G.W.F.

Differenz der Fichte'schen und Schelling'schen Systems der Philosophie. Jena: Seidler, 1801.
Phänomenologie des Geistes. Bamburg: Goebhardt, 1807; Hamburg: Meiner, 1952.
Grundlinien der Philosophie des Rechts. Berlin: Nicolaischen Buchhandlung, 1821.
Wissenschaft der Logik, ed. Georg Lasson. (Hamburg: Meiner, 1971).
'Neueste deutsche Philosophie', *Vorlesungen über die Geschichte der Philosophie*, in *Werke in zwanzig Bänden*, eds E. Moldenhauer and K. Michel. Frankfurt: Suhrkamp, 1971, XX, 314–462.
Werke in zwanzig Bänden, eds E. Moldenhauer und K. Michel. Frankfurt: Suhrkamp, 1971. 20 vols.

Helmholtz, Hermann

Über das Sehen des Menschen. Ein Populär wissenschaftlicher Vortrag gehalten zu Königsberg in Preussen. Zum Besten von Kant's Denkmal. Am 27. Februar, 1855. Leipzig: Voß, 1855.
Über das Verhältniss der Naturwissenschaften zur Gesammtheit der Wissenschaft. Akademische Festrede gehalten zu Heidelberg beim Antritt des Prorectorats, 1862. Heidelberg: Mohr, 1862.
Die Thatsachen in der Wahrnehmung. Rede gehalten zur Stiftungsfeier der Friedrich Wilhelms Universität zu Berlin am 3. August 1878. Berlin: August Hirschwald, 1879.

Vorträge und Reden. Vierte Auflage. Braunschweig: Vieweg und Sohn, 1896. 3 vols.
Wissenschaftliche Abhandlungen. Leipzig: Johann Ambrosius Barth, 1882. 3 vols.
Königsberger, Leo, *Hermann von Helmholtz.* Braunschweig: Vieweg & Sohn, 1902–1903. 3 vols.

Herbart, Johann Friedrich

Sämtliche Werke, eds Karl Kehrbach and Otto Flügel. Langasalzen: Hermann Beyer & Söhne, 1887–1912. 19 vols. (Henceforth abbreviated as SW).
'Etwas über die allgemeinsten Ursachen, welche in den Staaten den Wachstum und den Verfall der Moralität bewirken', *Blätter vermischten Inhalts.* Oldenburg: J.F. Thiele, 1787. (SW I, 351–361).
Ideen zu einem pädagogischen Lehrplan für höhere Studien. Oldenburg: Realschulbibliothek, 1801.
Pestalozzi's Idee eines ABC der Anschauung. Göttingen: Johann Friedrich Röwer, 1802. (SW I, 137–150).
'Über Pestalozzi's neueste Schrift: Wie Gertrud ihre Kinder lehrte', *Irene* I (1802) 15–51. (SW I, 137–151).
Ueber den Standpunct der Beurtheilung der Pestalozzischen Unterrichtsmethode, eine Gastvorlesung gehalten im Museum zu Bremen. Bremen: Carl Seiffert, 1804. (SW I, 301–309).
Kurze Darstellung eines Plans zu philosophischen Vorlesungen. Göttingen: Röwer, 1804. (SW I, 291–299).
De Platonici systematis fundamento commentatio. Göttingen: Roewer, 1805. (SW I, 311–348).
Hauptpuncte der Metaphysik. Göttingen: J.C. Baier, 1806. (SW II, 175–226).
Allgemeine Pädagogik. Göttingen: Röwer, 1806. (SW II, 1–139).
Ueber philosophisches Studium. Göttingen: Heinrich Dieterich, 1807. (SW II, 227–296).
Allgemeine praktische Philosophie. Göttingen: Danckwerts, 1808. (SW II, 329–515).
'Rede, gehalten an Kants Geburtstag, den 22. April 1810', *Königsberger Archiv* I (1812), 1–21. (SW III, 59–71).
Theoriae de attractione elementorum principia metaphysica. Regiomonti, typis academicis, 1812. (SW III, 155–200).
Ueber die Unangreifbarkeit der Schellingschen Lehre. Königsberg: Degen 1813. (SW III, 241–258).
Lehrbuch zur Einleitung in die Philosophie. Königsberg: Unzer, 1813. (SW IV, 1–294).
Ueber meinen Streit mit der Modephilosophie dieser Zeit. Königsberg: Unzer, 1814. (SW III, 311–352).
Lehrbuch zur Psychologie. Königsberg: August Wilhelm Unzer, 1816. (SW IV, 295–436).
Über die Möglichkeit und Notwendigkeit, Mathematik auf Psychologie anzuwenden. Königsberg: Gebrüder Bornträger, 1822. (SW V, 91–122).
Psychologie als Wissenschaft, neu gegründet auf Erfahrung, Metaphysik und Mathematik. Königsberg: Unzer 1824. (SW V, 177–434; and VI, 1–338).
Allgemeine Metaphysik. Königsberg: A.W. Unzer, 1828. (SW VII and VIII).

Herder, Johann Gottfried

Werke, eds M. Bollacher, *et al.* Frankfurt: Deutsche Klassiker Verlag, 1985–2000. 11 vols.

Hoffbauer, Johann Christoph

Allgemeine Betrachtungen über Seelenkrankheiten und eine Klassifikation derselben.
Halle: Hahn, 1802.
Naturlehre der Seele. Halle: Renger, 1796.

Hugo, Gustave

Lehrbuch des Naturrechts als Philosophie des positiven Rechts. Berlin: Mylius, 1799.

Hume, David

A Treatise of Human Nature. London: John Noon, 1739.
Enquiry Concerning Human Understanding, in *Essays and Treatises on Several Subjects.*
London: Cadell, 1777.

Jacobi, Friedrich Heinrich

Werke. Leipzig: Fleischer, 1815. 6 vols.

Jakob, Ludwig Heinrich

Grundriß der Erfahrungs-Seelenlehre. Halle: Hemmerde und Schwetschke, 1791.

Kant, Immanuel

Immanuel Kant's Sämtliche Werke, eds Karl Rosenkranz and Friedrich Wilhelm Schubert.
Leipzig: Voß, 1838–1842. 12 vols.
Kant's gesammelte Schriften, ed. Königlich Preußischen Akademie der Wissenschaften. Erste
Abteilung: Werke. 9 vols. Berlin: de Gruyter, 1902–1923.
Briefwechsel, ed. Otto Schöndörffer. Hamburg: Meiner, 1972.

Krug, Wilhelm

Review of Schopenhauer *Die Welt als Wille und Vorstellung* in *Leipziger Literatur-Zeitung,*
No. 21 (January 24, 1821), pp. 158–175.

Lange, Friedrich Albert

*J. St. Mills Ansichten über die sociale Frage und die angeblich Umwälzung der Sozialwissenschaft
durch Carey.* Duisburg: Falk & Lange, 1866.
Die Arbeiterfrage. Ihre Bedeutung für Gegenwart und Zukunft. Duisburg: Falk & Volmer, 1865.
Fourth edition: Winterthur: Bleuer-Hausheer & Co., 1879.
*Die Grundlegung der mathematischen Psychologie. Ein Versuch zur Nachweisung des funda-
mentalen Fehler bei Herbart und Drobisch.* Winterthur: Bleuer-Hausheer & Co., 1865.

Logische Studien. Ein Beitrag zur Neubegründung der formalen Logik und der Erkenntnistheorie. Iserlohn: Baedeker, 1877.

Geschichte des Materialismus und Kritik seiner Bedeutung in der Gegenwart. Iserlohn: Baedeker, 1866; 2nd edn: Iserlohn: Baedeker, 1873–1875, 2 vols; sechste (wohlfeile und vollständige) Auflage: Leipzig: Baedeker, 1898.

Einleitung und Kommentar zu Schillers philosophischen Gedichten. Bielefeld: Velhagen & Klasing, 1897.

Über Politik und Philosophie, Briefe und Leitartikel, 1862–1875, ed. Georg Eckert. Duisburg: Walter Braun Verlag, 1968.

Lask, Emil

Fichte's Idealismus und die Geschichte. Tübingen: Mohr, 1902.

Logik der Philosophie und die Kategorienlehre, Tübingen: Mohr, 1911; 2nd edn 1923.

Gesammelte Schriften. Tübingen: Mohr, 1923. 3 vols.

Lazarus, Moritz

'Ueber den Begriff und die Möglichkeit einer Völkerpsychologie', *Deutsches Museum I* (1851), 112–126.

'Einleitende Gedanken über Völkerpsychologie', *Zeitschrift für Völkerpsychologie und Sprachwissenschaft I* (1860), 1–73.

'Einige synthetische Gedanken für Völkerpsychologie', *Zeitschrift für Völkerpsychologie und Sprachwissenschaft III* (1865), 1–94.

Grundzüge der Völkerpsychologie und Kulturwissenschaft, ed. Klaus Christian Köhnke. Hamburg: Meiner, 2003.

Moritz Lazarus und Heymann Steinthal: Die Begründer der Völkerpsychologie in ihren Briefen, ed. Ingrid Belke. Tübingen: Mohr, 1971.

Lichtenberg, Georg Christoph

'Einfälle und Bemerkungen', Heft F 1776–1779, No. 485, in *Lichtenbergs Werke in einem Band*, ed. Hans Frederici. Berlin: Aufbau, 1982.

Liebmann, Otto

Kant und die Epigonen: Eine Kritische Abhandlung. Stuttgart: Carl Schober, 1865. Reprinted in Neudrucke seltener philosophischer Werke, Herausgegeben von der Kantgesellschaft. ed. Bruno Bauch. Berlin: Reuther & Reichard, 1912.

Ueber den individuellen Beweis für die Freiheit des Willens. Ein kritischer Beitrag zur Selbsterkenntniß. Stuttgart: Carl Schober, 1866.

Ueber den objectiven Anblick. Eine kritische Abhandlung. Stuttgart: Carl Schober, 1869.

Vier Monate vor Paris:1870–1871. Belagerungstagebuch eines Kriegsfreiwilligen im Gardesfüsilierregiment. Stuttgart: Carl Schober, 1871. 2nd edn: Munich: Beck, 1896.

'Eine neue Art von Kriticismus'. Review of Carl Göring: *System der kritischen Philosophie. Zeitschrift für Philosophie und philosophische Kritik* 65 (1874), 81–103.

Zur Analysis der Wirklichkeit. Philosophische Untersuchungen. Straßburg: Karl J. Trübner, 1876. 2nd edn: 1880. 3rd edn: 1900. 4th edn: 1911.

Ueber Philosophische Tradition. Eine akademische Antrittsrede. Straßburg: Karl. J. Trübner, 1883.

Die Klimax der Theorieen. Eine Untersuchung aus dem Bereich der allgemeinen Wissenschaftslehre. Straßburg: Karl J. Trübner, 1884.

Gedanken und Thatsachen: Philosophische Abhandlungen, Aphorismen und Studien. Straßburg: Trübner, 1899–1904. 2 vols.

Locke, John

An Essay concerning Human Understanding, ed. Peter Nidditch. Oxford: Clarendon Press, 1975.

Lotze, Hermann

Metaphysik. Leipzig: Weidmann, 1841.

Logik. Leipzig: Weidmann, 1843.

Medicinische Psychologie oder Physiologie der Seele. Leipzig: Weidmann, 1852.

Mikrokosmus. Ideen zur Naturgeschichte und Geschichte der Menschheit. Versuch einer Anthropologie. Leipzig: Hirzel: 1856–1864. 3 vols.

Streitschriften. Leipzig: Hirzel, 1857.

System der Philosophie: Erster Theil: Drei Bücher der Logik. Leipzig: Hirzel, 1874.

Briefe und Dokumente, ed. Reinhardt Pester. Würzburg: Königshausen & Neumann, 2003.

Luther, Martin

Kritische Gesamtausgabe Weimarer Ausgabe. Weimar: Hermann Böhlaus Nachfolger, 1883, XXXIX/2, 3–33.

Meyer, Jürgen Bona

De principiis Aristotelis in distributione animalium adhibitis. Berlin: Friedrich Wilhelm Universität, 1854.

Aristoteles Thierkunde, ein Beitrag zur Geschichte der Zoologie, Physiologie und alten Philosophie. Berlin: Reimer, 1855.

'Ueber Julius Schaller's »Leib und Seele«', *Deutsches Museum,* Nr. 4 (24. Jan. 1856), 121–128.

Zum Streit über Leib und Seele. Worte der Kritik. Sechs Vorlesungen am Hamburger akademischen Gymnasium gehalten. Hamburg: Perthes-Besser & Mauke, 1856.

Voltaire und Rousseau in ihrer socialen Bedeutung. Berlin: Reimer, 1856.

'Zum neuesten Stand des Streits über Leib und Seele: I. Kann Materie denken?', *Deutsches Museum,* Nr. 49 (4. Dez. 1856), 826–834.

'Zum neuesten Stand des Streits über Leib und Seele: II. Die Lehre von der Willensfreiheit im Materialismus und Idealismus', *Deutsches Museum,* Nr. 51 (18. Dez. 1856), 906–916.

'Zum neuesten Stand des Streits über Leib und Seele: III. Willensfreiheit und Sittengesetz',*Deutsches Museum,* Nr. 10 (5. März,1857), 345–358.

'Zum neuesten Stand des Streits über Leib und Seele: IV. Ueber den Sinn und Werth des Kriticismus', *Deutsches Museum*, Nr. 11 (11 März 1857), 395–402.

'Ueber Teleologie und Naturwissenschaft', *Deutsches Museum*, Nr. 42 (15. Okt. 1857), 572–579.

'Ueber den Kriticismus mit besonderer Rücksicht auf Kant', *Zeitschrift für Philosophie und philosophische Kritik* 37 (1860), 226–263 and 39 (1861), 46–66.

Über die Idee der Seelenwanderung. Hamburg: Meissner, 1861.

Über Fichte's Reden an die deutsche Nation. Hamburg: Meissner, 1862.

'Der Darwinismus', *Preußische Jahrbücher* 17 (1866), 272–302, 404–452.

Kant's Ansicht über die Psychologie als Wissenschaft. Einladungsschrift zum Amtsantritt der ordentlichen Professur der Philosophie an der Rheinischen Friedrich-Wilhelms-Universität am 9 Januar 1869. Bonn: Adolph Marcus, 1869.

Kant's Psychologie, Dargestellet und Erörtert. Berlin: Wilhelm Hertz, 1870.

Philosophische Zeitfragen. Populäre Aufsätze. Bonn: Adolph Marcus, 1870.

Index Aristotelicus. Berlin: Reimer, 1870.

'Neue Versuche einer Philosophie der Geschichte', *Historische Zeitschrift* 25 (1871), 303–378.

Arthur Schopenhauer als Mensch und Denker. Berlin: Carl Habel, 1872.

Weltelend und Weltschmerz: eine Rede gegen Schopenhauer's und Hartmann's Pessimismus gehalten im wissenschaftlichen Verein zu Berlin. Bonn: Adolph Marcus, 1872.

Die Fortbildungsschule in unserer Zeit. Berlin: Luderitz, 1873.

Der alte und neue Glaube. Betrachtungen über D.F. Strauß Bekenntniß. Bonn: Adolph Marcus, 1873.

Deutsche Universitätsentwicklung: Vorzeit, Gegenwart und Zukunft. Berlin: Carl Habel, 1874.

Zum Bildungskampf unserer Zeit. Bonn: Adolph Marcus, 1875.

Friedrichs der Grossen pädagogischen Schriften und Ausserungen. Langensalza: Beyer & Söhne, 1875.

Fichte, Lasalle und der Sozialismus. Berlin: Carl Habel, 1878.

Probleme der Weltweisheit. Berlin: Allgemeine Verein für deutsche Literatur, 1884.

Wahrheitskampf, Gelehrtenzank und Parteizwist. Berlin: Habel, 1890.

Mill, John Stuart

System der induktiven und deduktiven Logik, aus dem Englischen von J. Schiel. Braunschweig: Vieweg, 1862–1863.

Mirbt, Ernst Sigismund

Was heisst Philosophieren und was ist Philosophie? Sieben einleitende Vorlesungen. Jena: Hochhausen, 1839.

Kant und seine Nachfolger oder Geschichte des Ursprungs und der Fortbildung der neueren deutschen Philosophie. Jena: Hochhausen, 1841.

Moleschott, Jakob

Der Kreislauf des Lebens. Gießen: Emil Roth, 1852.

Moritz, Karl Phillip

Gnothi sauton oder Magazin zur Erfahrungsseelenlehre als eine Lesebuch für Gelehrte und Ungelehrte. Berlin: Mylius, 1783–1793. 10 vols.

Müller, Johannes

Zur vergleichende Physiologie des Gesichtsinnes des Menschen und der Thiere. Leipzig: Knobloch, 1826.
Handbuch der Physiologie des Menschen. Coblenz: Hölscher, 1838–1840. 2 vols.

Nietzsche, Friedrich

Sämtliche Werke, eds G. Colli and M. Montinari, Berlin: de Gruyter, 1980. 15 vols.

Noack, Ludwig

Immanuel Kant's Auferstehung aus dem Grabe. Leipzig: Wigand, 1861.

Novalis

Glauben und Liebe, in *Novalis Schriften,* ed. Richard Samuel. Stuttgart: Kohlhammer, 1960, II, 485–498.

Paulsen, Friedrich

'Gründen und Ursachen des Pessimismus', *Im neuem Reich* 48 (1866), 360–381.
'Idealismus und Positivismus', *Im neuem Reich* 10 (1880), 735–742.
Schopenhauer, Hamlet, Mephistopheles. Drei Aufsätze zur Naturgeschichte des Pessimismus. Dritte Auflage. Stuttgart: Cotta Nachfolger, 1911.
Philosophia Militans: Gegen Klerikalismus und Naturalismus. Fünf Abhandlungen. Zweite Auflage. Berlin: Reuther & Reichard, 1901.

Rickert, Heinrich

Die Grenzen der wissenschaftliche Begriffsbildung. Tübingen: Mohr, 1902.
Die Philosophie des Lebens. Tübingen: Mohr, 1920.
Die Probleme der Geschichtsphilosophie. Dritte Auflage. Heidelberg: Winter, 1924.
Wilhelm Windelband. Zweite Auflage. Tübingen: Mohr, 1929.

Riehl, Alois

Realistische Grundzüge. Eine philosophische Abhandlung der allgemeinen und nothwendigen Erfahrungsbegriffe. Graz: Leuschner & Lubensky, 1870.
Moral und Dogma. Vienna: Carl Gerold, 1872.
Über Begriff und Form der Philosophie. Berlin: Carl Duncker, 1872.

'Zur Aprioritätslehre'. Review of Hermann Cohen *Kants Theorie der Erfahrung*. *Philosophische Monatshefte* 8 (1872), 212–215.

'Zur Erkenntnistheorie'. Review of Wilhelm Windelband *Über die Gewißheit der Erkenntnis*. *Philosophische Monatshefte* 9 (1874), 292–296.

'Zur Geschichte der Philosophie'. Review of Eugen Dühring *Kritische Geschichte der Philosophie*. *Philosophische Monatshefte* 11 (1875), 165–179.

Der philosophische Kriticismus und seine Bedeutung für die positive Wissenschaft. Leipzig: Wilhelm Engelmann, 1876. Band I. Geschichte und Methode des *philosophischen* Kriticismus.

Der philosophische Kriticismus und seine Bedeutung für die positive Wissenschaft. Leipzig: Wilhelm Engelmann, 1879. Band II/1. *Die sinnlichen und logischen Grundlagen der Erkenntnis*.

Ueber wissenschaftliche und nichtwissenschaftliche Philosophie. Eine akademische Antrittsrede. Tübingen: Mohr, 1883.

Der philosophische Kriticismus und seine Bedeutung für die positive Wissenschaft. Leipzig: Wilhelm Engelmann, 1887. Band II/2. *Zur Wissenschaftstheorie und Metaphysik*.

'Bemerkungen zu dem Problem der Form in der Dichtkunst', *Vierteljahrschrift für wissenschaftlichen Philosophie* 21 (1897), 283–306.

Friedrich Nietzsche. Der Künstler und der Denker. Stuttgart: Frommann, 1897.

Zur Einführung in die Philosophie der Gegenwart. Leipzig: Teubner, 1902.

Hermann von Helmholtz in seinem Verhältnis zu Kant. Berlin: Reuther & Reichard, 1904.

Immanuel Kant. Rede zur Feier des Hundertjährigen Todestages Kants gehalten in der Aula der Universität Halle-Wittenberg. Halle: Max Niemyer, 1904.

'Logik und Erkenntnistheorie', in *Die Kultur der Gegenwart, Ihre Entwicklung und Ihre Ziele*. Teil I, Abteilung VI: *Systematische Philosophie*. Ed. Paul Hinneberg. Zweite durchgesehene Auflage. Leipzig: Teubner, 1908, pp. 73–102.

Beiträge zur Logik. Zweite durchgesehene Auflage. Leipzig: O.R. Reisland, 1912.

'The Vocation of Philosophy in the Present Day', in *Lectures Delivered in Connection with the Dedication of the Graduate College of Princeton University*. Princeton: Princeton University Press, 1914, pp. 45–63.

Führende Denker und Forscher. Leipzig: Quelle & Meyer, 1922.

Der philosophische Kriticismus. Leipzig: Kroner, 1924–1926.

Philosophische Studien aus vier Jahrzehnten. Leipzig: Quelle & Meyer, 1925.

Rist, Johann Georg

Lebenserinnerungen. ed. G. Poel. Gotha: Perthes, 1880.

Rosenkranz, Karl

Geschichte der kant'schen Philosophie. Leipzig: Voß, 1840.

G.W.F. Hegels Leben. Berlin: Duncker & Humblot, 1844.

Die Modifikation der Logik abgeleitet aus dem Begriff des Denkens. Berlin: Jonas, 1846.

Rousseau, Jean Jacques

Discours sur les sciences et les arts, in *Œuvres complètes*, eds Bernard Gagnebin and Marcel Raymond. Paris: Gallimard, 1964.

Ruge, Arnold

Briefwechsel und Tagebuchblätter. Berlin: Weidmann, 1896.

Savigny, Friedrich

Der junge Savigny: Kinderjahre, Marburger und Landhuter Zeit, ed. Alfred Stoll. Berlin: Carl
  Heymanns Verlag, 1927.
Vorlesungen über juristische Methodologie, ed. Aldo Mazzacane. Frankfurt: Klostermann, 1993.

Schaller, Julius

Die Philosophie unserer Zeit: Zur Apologie und Erläuterung des hegelschen Systems.
  Leipzig: Hinrichs, 1837.

Schaarschmidt, Carl

'Vom rechten und falschen Kriticismus', *Philosophische Monatshefte* 14 (1878), 1–12.

Schelling, Friedrich Wilhelm Joseph

Über die Möglichkeit einer Form der Philosophie überhaupt. Tübingen: Heerbrandt, 1795.
Bruno, oder über das göttliche und natürliche Prinzip der Dinge. Berlin: Unger, 1802. (SW 1/4,
  213–332).
Vorlesungen über die Methode des akademischen Studiums. Tübingen: Cotta, 1803. (SW V,
  211–352).
Sämtliche Werke, ed. K.F.A. Schelling. Stuttgart: Cotta, 1856–1861. 14 vols.

Schenkel, Daniel

Abfertigung für Herrn Kuno Fischer in Heidelberg. Heidelberg: Akademie Anstalt für Literatur
  und Kunst, 1854.

Schiller, Friederich

Schillers Werke, Nationalausgabe, eds Julius Petersen und Friedrich Beißner. Weimar:
  Hermann Böhlaus Nachfolger, 1943. 33 vols.

Schmid, Carl Christian Erhard

Empirische Psychologie. Jena: Cröker, 1791.
Review of K.L. Reinhold, *Fundament des philosophischen Wissens*, *Allgemeine Literatur
  Zeitung*, Nr. 92–93, April 9–10, 1792, pp. 49–60.
Grundriß einer Moralphilosophie für Vorlesungen. Jena: Cröker, 1793.
Critik der reinen Vernunft im Grundrisse. Jena: Cröker, 1794.
Wörterbuch zum leichtern Gebrauch der kanischen Schriften. Jena: Cröker, 1795.
Grundriß des Naturrechts. Jena: Gabler, 1795.

Schopenhauer, Arthur

Die Welt als Wille und Vorstellung. Leipzig: Brockhaus, 1819.
'Die Zeitgenössischen Rezensionen der Werke Arthur Schopenhauers', ed. Reinhard Piper, *Jahrbuch der Schopenhauer-Gesellschaft* VI (1917), 47–178.
Gesammelete Briefe, ed. Arthur Hübscher. Bonn: Bouvier, 1978.
Sämtliche Werke, ed. Wolfgang Freiherr von Löhneysen. Stuttgart: Insel, 1968. 5 vols.

Schlegel, Friedrich

1800–1801 lectures on *Transcendentalphilosophie* in *Friedrich Schlegel Kritische Ausgabe,* ed. Ernst Behler. Munich: Schöningh, 1958, XII, 1–264.

Schleiden, Mattheus

Ueber den Materialismus der neueren deutschen Naturwissenschaft. Leipzig: Engelmann, 1863.

Schulze, Gottob Ernst

Aenesidemus, oder über die Fundamente der von dem Herrn Professor Reinhold in Jena gelieferten Elementarphilosophie, ed. A. Liebert. Berlin: Reuther & Reichard, 1912.

Strauß, David Friedrich

Das Leben Jesu, kritisch bearbeitet. Tübingen: C.F. Osiander, 1835.
Die christlichen Glausbenslehre. Tübingen: C.F. Osiander, 1840.
Der Alte und Neue Glaube. Leipzig: Hirzel, 1872.
Ausgewählte Briefe von David Friedrich Strauß, ed. Eduard Zeller. Bonn: Verlag von Emil Strauß, 1895.

Taubert, Agnes

Der Pessimismus und seine Gegner. Berlin: Duncker, 1872.

Trendelenburg, Adolph

Logische Untersuchungen. Berlin: Bethge, 1840. Second edition: Leipzig: Hirzel, 1862. Third edition: Leipzig: Hirzel, 1870.
Die Logische Frage in Hegel's System. Zwei Streitschriften. Leipzig: Brockhaus, 1843.
Geschichte der Kategorienlehre. Berlin: Bethge, 1846.
Über Herbarts Metaphysik und neue Auffassungen derselben. Erster und Zweiter Artikel. Berlin: Bethge, 1854, 1856.
'Der Widerstreit zwischen Kant und Aristoteles in der Ethik', in *Historische Beiträge zur Philosophie.* Berlin: Bethge, 1867, III, 171–214.
Kuno Fischer und sein Kant: Eine Entgegnung. Leipzig: Hirzel, 1869.

Vogt, Carl

Ocean und Mittelmeer: Reisebriefe. Frankfurt: Literarische Anstalt, 1848.

Bilder aus dem Thierleben. Frankfurt: Literarische Anstalt, 1852.

Physiologische Briefe für Gebildete aller Stände. Zweite vermehrte und verbesserte Auflage. Gießen: Ricker, 1854.

Werke. Cassel: Balde, 1854.

Köhlerglaube und Wissenschaft: Eine Streitschrift gegen Hofrath Wagner in Göttingen. Gießen: Ricker, 1856.

Vorlesungen über den Menschen, seine Stellung in der Schöpfung und in der Geschichte der Erde. Gießen: Ricker, 1863. 2 vols.

Aus meinem Leben: Erinnerungen und Rückblicke. Stuttgart: Nägele, 1896.

Volkelt, Johannes

'Die Entwicklungen des modernen Pessimismus', *Im neuen Reich* II (1872), 952–968.

Kant's Kategorischer Imperativ und der Gegenwart. Vienna: Selbstverlag des Lesevereins der deutschen Studenten Wiens, 1875.

'Wiedererweckung der kantischen Ethik', *Zeitschrift für Philosophie und philosophische Kritik* 81 (1882), 37–48.

'Philosophische Monatshefte', *Jenaer Literaturzeitung* 5 (1878) 95–96.

Erfahrung und Denken: Kritische Grundlegung der Erkenntnistheorie. Hamburg: Voß, 1886.

Arthur Schopenhauer. Seine Persönlichkeit, seine Lehre, sein Glaube. Stuttgart: Frommann, 1900.

Walch, Johann Georg

Philosophisches Lexikon. Leipzig: Gleditsch, 1775.

Wagner, Rudolph

Menschenshöpfung und Seelensubstanz. Ein anthropologischer Vortrag. Göttingen: Wigand, 1854.

Ueber Wissen und Glauben. Forsetzung der Betrachtungen über Menschenschöpfung und Seelensubstanz. Göttingen: Wigand, 1854.

Weiße, Christian Hermann

Ueber den Gegenwärtigen Standpunct der philosophischen Wissenschaft: In Besonderer Beziehung auf das System Hegels. Leipzig: Barth, 1829.

Die Idee der Gottheit. Dresden: Grimmer, 1833.

Grundzüge der Metaphysik. Hamburg: Perthes, 1835.

Die philosophische Problem der Gegenwart. Leipzig: Reichenbach, 1842.

In welchem Sinn die deutsche Philosophie jetzt wieder an Kant sich zu orientiren hat. Leipzig: Dycke, 1847.

Windelband, Wilhelm

Die Lehren vom Zufall. Berlin: Henschel, 1870.

'Zur Charakeristik Ludwig Feuerbachs', *Im neuen Reich* II (1872), 735–743.

'Aus den romantischen Tagen der Philosophie', *Im neuen Reich* III (1873), 879–889.

Über die Gewißheit der Erkenntnis. Eine psychologisch-erkenntnistheoretische Studie. Berlin: Henschel, 1873. Reprint: Hamburg: Adlibri Verlag, 2005.

'Zur Logik', *Philosophische Monatshefte* X (1874), 33–42, 85–91, 103–110.

'Die Erkenntnislehre unter dem völkerpsychologischen Gescichtspunkte', *Zeitschrift für Völkerpsychologie und Sprachwissenschaft* VIII (1875), 166–178.

Über den gegenwärtigen Stand der psychologischen Forschung. Rede zum Antritt der ordentlichen Professur der Philosophie an der Hochschule zu Zürich am XX. Mai MDCCCLXVI. Leipzig: Breitkopf & Härtel, 1876.

'Pessimismus und Wissenschaft', *Der Salon* II (1877), 814–821, 951–957. *Präludien* II, 218–243.

'Ueber die verschiedenen Phasen der kantischen Lehre vom Ding-an-sich, *Vierteljahrschrift für wissenschaftliche Philosophie*, Jahrgang I, Heft II (1877), 224–266.

'Zum Gedächtnis Spinozas', *Vierteljahrschrift für wissenschaftliche Philosophie* I (1877) 419–440. *Präludien* I, 88–111.

Die Geschichte der neueren Philosophie in ihrem Zusammenhange mit der allgemeinen Cultur und den besonderen Wissenschaften. Band I: Von der Reniassance bis Kant. Leipzig: Breitkopf & Härtel, 1878–80; sixth edition Leipzig: Breitkopf & Härtel, 1919.

'Ueber experimentale Aesthetik', *Im neuen Reich* VIII (1878), 601–616.

'Ueber den Einfluss des Willens auf das Denken', *Vierteljahrschrift für wissenschaftliche Philosophie* II (1878), 265–297. Under the new title 'Denken und Nachdenken' in *Präludien* II, 24–58.

'Über Friedrich Hölderlin und sein Geschick'. Nach einem Vortrage in der akademischen Gescellschaft zu Freiburg am 29 November 1878. *Präludien* I, 230–259.

Die Geschichte der neueren Philosophie in ihrem Zusammenhange mit der allgemeinen Cultur und den besonderen Wissenschaften. Band II: Von Kant bis Hegel und Herbart. Leipzig: Breitkopf & Härtel, 1880.

'Über Sokrates' (Ein Vortrag gehalten 1880). *Präludien* I, 55–87.

'Immanuel Kant. Zur Säkularfeier seiner Philosophie'. (Ein Vortrag 1881), *Präludien* I, 112–146.

'Normen und Naturgesetze'. (Written 1882). *Präludien* II, 59–98.

'Kritische oder genetische Methode?' (Written 1882). *Präludien* II, 99–135.

Präludien. Aufsätze und Reden zur Einleitung in die Philosophie. Tübingen: Mohr, 1884.

'Ueber den teleologischen Kriticismus. Zur Abwehr', *Philosophischen Monatshefte* XX (1884), 161–169.

Geschichte der alten Philosophie. Munich: Beck, 1894.

Geschichte und Naturwissenschaft. Strassburg: Heitz, 1894. *Präludien* II, 136–160.

Kuno Fischer und sein Kant. Halle: Ehrhardt Karras, 1897.

'Kuno Fischer und sein Kant', *Kant-Studien* II (1898), 1–10.

Lehrbuch der Geschichte der Philosophie. Tübingen: Mohr, 1900.

'Nach hundert Jahren. Zu Kants hundertjährigem Todestage'. (Lecture 1904). *Präludien* I, 147–167.

'Kuno Fischer', *Die Woche*, XXIX (July 16. 1904), 1259–1261.

Über Willensfreiheit. Zwölf Vorlesungen. Tübingen: Mohr, 1905.

Kuno Fischer. Gedächtnisrede bei der Trauerfeier der Universität in der Stadthalle zu Heidelberg am 23. Juli 1907. Heidelberg: Winter, 1907.

Die Philosophie im deutschen Geistesleben des XIX Jahrhundert. Tübingen: Mohr, 1909.

Der Wille zur Wahrheit. Heidelberg: Winter, 1909.

'Otto Liebmanns Philosophie', *Kant Studien* XV (1910), iii–x.

'Die Philosophische Richtungen der Gegenwart', in *Große Denker,* ed. Ernst von Aster. Leipzig: Quelle & Meyer, 1911. II, 361–377.

Die Prinzipien der Logik. Tübingen: Mohr, 1913.

Einleitung in die Philosophie. Tübingen: Mohr, 1914.

Geschichtsphilosophie. Eine Kriegsvorlesung. Fragment aus dem Nachlass. Kant-Studien Ergänzungsheft 38 (1916).

Beiträge zur Lehre vom negativen Urtheil. Tübingen: Mohr, 1921.

Vom System der Kategorien. Tübingen: Mohr, 1924.

Präludien. Aufsätze und Reden zur Philosophie und ihrer Geschichte. Neunte Auflage. Tübingen: Mohr, 1924.

Zeller, Eduard [2]

'Vorwort', *Theologische Jahrbücher* I (1842), iii–viii.

'Erinnerung an Schleiermachers Lehre von der Persönlichkeit Gottes', *Theologische Jahrbücher* I (1842), 263–297. KS III, 47–70.

Die Philosophie der Griechen. Eine Untersuchung über Charakter, Gang und Hauptmomente ihrer Entwicklung. Teil 1–2 Tübingen: Fues, 1844–1846.

'Ueber das Wesen der Religion', *Theologische Jahrbücher* IV (1845), 26–75, 393–430. KS III, 71–152.

'Die Theologie der Gegenwart und die theologischen Jahrbücher. Vorwort des Herausgebers', *Theologische Jahrbücher* V (1846), 1–28.

'Ueber historische Kritik und ihre Anwendung auf die christlichen Religionsurkunden', *Theologische Jahrbücher* V (1846), 288–321. KS III, 153–187.

'Ueber die Freiheit des menschlichen Willens, das Böse und die moralische Weltordnung', *Theologische Jahrbücher,* V–VI (1846–1847), 384–447, 28–89, 191–258. KS II, 357–487.

'Ueber das Verhältniß der Theologie zur Wissenschaft und zur Kirche', *Theologische Jahrbücher,* IX (1850), 93–110. KS III, 249–266.

Die Philosophie der Griechen in ihrer geschichtlichen Entwicklung dargestellt. Tübingen: Fues, 1856–1869. 3 vols.

'Die Tübinger historische Schule', *Historische Zeitschrift* IV (1860), 90–173. VA I, 267–353.

'Johann Gottlieb Fichte als Politiker', *Historische Zeitschrift* 40 (1860), 1–35.

'Die historische Kritik und das Wunder. Ein Sendschreiben an den Herausgeber', *Historische Zeitschrift* VI (1861), 356–373. KS III, 348–365.

---

[2] There is an excellent complete bibliography of all Zeller's writings by Otto Leuze. See his 'Chronologisches Verzeichnis aller Literarischen Arbeiten Eduard Zellers', at the close of Volume III of his edition of *Eduard Zellers Kleine Schriften* (Berlin: Reimer, 1910–1911), III, 512–558.

Many of Zeller's writings are reprinted in two collections: Leuze's edition and Zeller's own, *Vorträge und Abhandlungen* (Leipzig: Fues, 1865–1884), 3 vols. All references to Leuze's edition will be designated KS; and all references to Zeller's will be designated VA.

Ueber Bedeutung und Aufgabe der Erkenntnistheorie. Heidelberg: K. Groos, 1862. VA II, 479–496.

'Über die Aufgabe der Philosophie und ihre Stellung zu den übrigen Wissenschaften', VA II, 445–466.

'Lessing als Theolog', *Historische Zeitschrift* 23 (1870), 343–383. VA II, 283–327.

'Über die gegenwärtige Stellung und Aufgabe der deutschen Philosophie', *Im neuen Reich* II (1872), 921–928. VA II, 467–478.

David Friedrich Strauss. Bonn: Verlag von Emil Strauss, 1874.

Geschichte der deutschen Philosophie seit Leibniz. 2nd edn. Munich: Oldenbourg, 1875.

'Zusätze zu: Über Bedeutung und Aufgabe der Erkenntistheorie', (1877) VA II, 496–526.

'Zum Jubiläum der Kritik der reinen Vernunft', *Nationale Zeitung.* June 10, 1881, Nr. 266. KS I, 239–251.

'Ueber Kants Moralprinzip und den Gegensatz formaler und materialer Moralprinzipien', *Abhandlungen der Akademie der Wissenschaften zu Berlin*, Philosophische-Historische Classe, Abhandlung V (1879) 32pp. VA III, 151–188.

'Ueber Begriff und Begründung der sittlichen Gesetze' *Abhandlungen der Akademie der Wissenschaften zu Berlin*. Philosophische-Historische Classe. Abhandlung II (1882) 35pp. VA III, 189–224.

Grundriss der Geschichte der griechischen Philosophie. Leipzig: Reisland, 1883.

Friedrich der Grosse als Philosoph. Berlin: Weidmann, 1886.

Outlines of the History of Greek Philosophy, translated by S.F. Alleyne and Evelyn Abbott. London: Longmans, Green & Co., 1886.

Staat und Kirche. Vorlesungen an die Universität zu Berlin. Leipzig: Fues, 1893.

Erinnerungen eines Neunzigjährigen. Stuttgart: Uhland, 1908.

Die Geschichte der neueren Philosophie. Sechste Auflage. Leipzig: Breitkopf & Härtel, 1919. 2 vols.

Heinrich von Sybel and Eduard Zeller, Briefwechsel (1849–1895). ed. Margret Lemberg. Marburg: N.G. Elwert Verlag, 2004.

Bibliography II: Secondary Literature

Intellectual Background and General Historical Studies

Barkhoff, Jürgen and Eda Sagarra, eds, *Anthropologie und Literatur um 1800*. Munich: Judicium Verlag, 1992.

Beiser, Frederick, *The Fate of Reason: German Philosophy between Kant and Fichte*. Cambridge, MA: Harvard University Press, 1987.

Beiser, Frederick, 'Schleiermacher's ethics', *The Cambridge Companion to Schleiermacher*, ed. Jacqueline Marina. Cambridge: Cambridge University Press, 1995, pp. 53–71.

Beiser, Frederick, *The Sovereignty of Reason*. Princeton, NJ: Princeton University Press, 1996.

Beiser, Frederick, *German Idealism: The Struggle against Subjectivism, 1781–1801*. Cambridge, MA: Harvard University Press, 2002.

Beiser, Frederick, 'Moral Faith and the Highest Good', in *The Cambridge Companion to Kant and Modern Philosophy*, ed. Paul Guyer. Cambridge: Cambridge University Press, 2006, pp. 588–629.

Beiser, Frederick, Review of 'Nineteenth-Century Philosophy: Revolutionary Responses to the Existing Order', *The Notre Dame Philosophical Review*, August 25, 2011.

Beiser, Frederick, *Late German Idealism: Trendelenburg and Lotze*. Oxford: Oxford University Press, 2013.

Beiser, Frederick, *After Hegel: German Philosophy from 1840 to 1900*. Princeton, NJ: Princeton University Press, 2014.

Bergmann, Julius, *Die deutsche Philosophie von Kant bis Beneke, Volume II of Geschichte der Philosophie*. Berlin: Mittler, 1893. 2 vols.

Blackburn, Simon, *The Oxford Dictionary of Philosophy*. Oxford: Oxford University Press, 1994.

Carhart, Michael, *The Science of Culture in Enlightenment Germany*. Cambridge, MA: Harvard University Press, 2007.

Cassirer, Ernst, *Der kritische Idealismus und Philosophie des "gesunden Menschenverstandes"*. Giessen: Töpelmann, 1906.

Cassirer, Ernst, *Substanzbegriff und Funktionsbegriff*. Berlin: Cassirer, 1910.

Cassirer, Ernst, *Das Erkenntnisproblem in der Philosophie und Wissenschaft der neueren Zeit. Band III: Die nachkantische Systeme*. Zweite Ausgabe, Berlin: Cassirer, 1923; Stuttgart: Kohlhammer, 1957.

Copleston, Frederick, *A History of Modern Philosophy: Fichte to Hegel*. New York: Doubleday, 1963. Volume 7.

Davies, Martin, 'Erfahrungsseelenkunde: Its social and intellectual origins'. *Oxford German Studies* 16 (1985), 13–35.

D'Hondt, Jacques, *Hegel in his Time*. Lewiston, NY: Broadview Press, 1988.

Dilthey, Wilhelm, *Die Jugendgeschichte Hegels, Volume 4 of Gesammelte Schriften*. Leipzig: Teubner, 1921; Stuttgart: Teubner, 1964.

Erdmann, Johann Eduard, *Versuch einer wissenschaftlichen Darstellung der Geschichte der neuern Philosophie*. Riga and Dorpat: E. Frantzen, 1834–1853. 7 vols; Leipzig: Vogel, 1848.

Erdmann, Johann, *Die Entwicklung der deutschen Spekulation seit Kant*, volume 5 of *Versuch einer wissenschaftlichen Darstellung der Geschichte der Philosophie*. Stuttgart: Frommann, 1977.

Ermath, Michael, *Wilhelm Dilthey: The Critique of Historical Reason*. Chicago: University of Chicago Press, 1978.

Faull, Katherine, ed., *Anthropology and the German Enlightenment*. Lewisburg, PA: Bucknell, 1995.

Fink, Karl, 'Storm and Stress Anthropology', *History of the Human Sciences* 6 (1993), 51–71.

Garrett, Aaron, 'Anthropology: the 'original' of human nature', in *The Cambridge Companion to the Scottish Enlightenment*, ed. Alexander Broadie. Cambridge: Cambridge University Press, 2003, pp. 79–93.

Gerhardt, Volker, Mehring, Reinhard and Rindert, Jana, *Berliner Geist: Eine Geschichte der Berliner Universitätsphilosophie bis 1946*. Berlin: Akademie Verlag, 1999.

Glockner, Hermann, 'Einführung in Johann Eduard Erdmanns Leben und Werke' in Volume I of the new edition of his *Versuch*. Stuttgart: Frommann, 1932, pp. 1–200.

Görtemaker, Manfred, *Deutschland im 19. Jahrhundert*. Opladen: Leske, 1983.

Gregory, Frederick, *Scientific Materialism in Nineteenth Century Germany*. Dordrecht: Reidel, 1977.

Hamerow, Theodore, *Restoration, Revolution, Reaction. Economics and Politics in Germany, 1815–1871*. Princeton: Princeton University Press, 1980.

Hammer, Espen, ed., *German Idealism: Contemporary Perspectives*. Abingdon: Routledge, 2007.

Hatfield, Gary, *The Natural and the Normative: Theories of Spatial Perception from Kant to Helmholtz*. Cambridge, MA: MIT Press, 1990.

Heine, Heinrich, *Zur Religion und Philosophie in Deutschland*, in *Sämtliche Schriften*, ed. Klaus Briegleb. Munich: Hanser, 1976. Volume V.

Hufbauer, Karl, *The Formation of the German Chemical Community* (1720–1795). Berkeley, CA: University of California, Press, 1982.

Kroner, Richard, *Kants Weltanschauung*. Tübingen: Mohr, 1914.

Kroner, Richard, *Von Kant bis Hegel*. Tübingen: Mohr, 1921. 2 vols.

Kuehn, Manfred, *Scottish Common Sense in Germany*, 1768–1800. Kingston, ON: McGill-Queen's University Press, 1987.

Kusch, Martin, *Psychologism: A Case Study in the Sociology of Philosophical Knowledge*. London: Routledge, 1995.

Léon, Xavier, *Fichte et son temps*. Paris: Armand Colin, 1954. 3 vols.

Lehmann, Gerhard, *Geschichte der nachkantischen Philosophie*. Berlin: Junker und Dünnhaupt, 1931.

Lehmann, Gerhard, *Geschichte der Philosophie: Vol. VIII: Die Philosophie des neunzehnten Jahrhunderts*. Berlin: Walter de Gruyter, 1953.

Lehmann, Gerhard, *Geschichte der Philosophie: Vol. IX: Die Philosophie des neunzehnten Jahrhunderts*. Berlin: Walter de Gruyter, 1953.

Lehmann, Gerhard, *Geschichte der Philosophie. Vol X: Die Philosophie im ersten Drittel des zwanzigsten Jahrhunderts*. Berlin: Walter de Gruyter, 1957. 2 vols.

Lenoir, Timothy, *The Strategy of Life: Teleology and Mechanics in Nineteenth Century German Biology*. Chicago, IL: University of Chicago Press, 1989.

Linden, Mareta, *Untersuchungen zum Anthropologiebegriff des 18. Jahrhunderts*. Frankfurt: Lang, 1976.

Löwith, Karl, *Von Hegel zu Nietzsche. Der revolutionäre Bruch im Denken des 19. Jahrhunderts*. Zurich: Europa Verlag, 1941.

Lübbe, Hermann, *Politische Philosophie in Deutschland*. Munich: Deutscher Taschenbuch Verlag, 1974.

Merz, John Theodore, *A History of European Thought in the Nineteenth Century*. Edinburgh: William Blackwood & Sons, 1904–1912. 4 vols.

Neubauer, John, 'Dr. John Brown (1735–1788) and Early German Romanticism', *Journal of the History of Ideas* 28 (1967), 367–382.

Nipperdy, Thomas, *Deutsche Geschichte 1800–1866*. Munich: Beck, 1983.

Otis, Laura, *Müller's Lab*. Oxford: Oxford University Press, 2007.

Pinkard, Terry, *Hegel: A Biography*. Cambridge: Cambridge University Press, 2000.

Richards, Robert, *The Romantic Conception of Life*. Chicago, IL: University of Chicago Press, 2002.

Ringer, Fritz, *The Decline of the German Mandarins. The German Academic Community, 1890–1933*. Cambridge, MA: Harvard University Press, 1969.

Rorty, Richard, *Philosophy and the Mirror of Nature*. Oxford: Blackwell, 1980.

Sagarra Eda, *A Social History of Germany 1648–1914*. London: Methuen, 1977.

Sagarra Eda, *An Introduction to Nineteenth Century Germany*. Harlow: Longman, 1980.

Schrift, Alan and Conway, Daniel, eds, *Nineteenth-Century Philosophy: Revolutionary Responses to the Existing Order*. Volume 2 of *The History of Continental Philosophy*. Chicago, IL: University of Chicago Press, 2010.

Sheehan, James, *German Liberalism in the 19th Century*. Chicago, IL: University of Chicago Press, 1978.

Sheehan, James, *German History 1770–1866*. Oxford: Oxford University Press, 1989.

Schings, Hans-Jürgen, ed., *Der ganze Mensch: Anthropologie und Literatur im 18. Jahrhundert*. Stuttgart: Metzler, 1992.

Schlegel, Friedrich, 'Fragmente', *Athenaeum* I (1798), 202.

Schnädelbach, Herbert, *Philosophy in Germany 1831–1933*. Trans. Eric Matthews. Cambridge: Cambridge University Press, 1984.

Schrimpf, Hans Joachim, 'Das Magazin zur erfahrungsseelenkunde und sein Herausgeber', *Zeitschrift für deutsche Philologie* 99 (1980), 161–187.

Schwegler, Albert, ed., *Jährbücher der Gegenwart*. Tübingen: Fues, 1843–1847. 6 vols.

Siebert, Otto, *Geschichte der neueren deutschen Philosophie seit Hegel*. Göttingen: Vandenhoeck & Ruprecht, 1898.

Simon, Ernst, *Ranke und Hegel: Beiheft der Historische Zeitschrift* 15 (1928), 16–119.

Stöckl, Albert, *Geschichte der neueren Philosophie von Baco und Cartesius bis zur Gegenwart*. Mainz: Kirchheim, 1883.

Toews, John Edward, *Hegelianism: The path toward dialectical humanism, 1805–1841*. Cambridge: Cambridge University Press, 1980.

Überweg, Friedrich, *Die Philosophie seit Beginn des neuenzehnten Jahrhunderts*, Volume IV of *Grundriss der Geschichte der Philosophie*. Tenth Edition. Berlin: Mittler 1906.

Wittkau-Hogby, Annette, *Materialismus: Entstehung und Wirkung in den Wissenschaften des 19. Jahrhunderts.* Göttingen: Vandenhoeck & Ruprecht, 1998.

Wood, Allen, *Kant's Ethical Thought.* Cambridge: Cambridge University Press, 1999.

Wundt, Max, *Die deutsche Schulphilosophie im Zeitlater der Aufklärung.* Tübingen: Mohr, 1945.

Zammito, Kant, *Herder & the Birth of Anthropology.* Chicago, IL: University of Chicago Press, 2002.

Neo-Kantianism in General

Adair-Toteff, Christopher, 'The Neo-Kantian Raum Controversy', *The British Journal for the History of Philosophy* II (1994), 131–148.

Beck, L.W., 'Neo-Kantianism', in *The Encyclopedia of Philosophy*, ed. Paul Edwards. New York: Macmillan, 1967. V, 468–473.

Boyle, Nicholas, Disley, Liz and Cooper, Ian, eds, *The Impact of Idealism: The Legacy of Post-Kantian German Thought.* Cambridge: Cambridge University Press, 2013, 4 vols.

Braun, Otto, *Eduard von Hartmann.* Stuttgart: Frommann, 1909.

Brazill, William, *The Young Hegelians.* New Haven, CT: Yale University Press, 1970.

Chignell, Andrew, Irwin, Terence and Teufel, Thomas, eds, *Back to Kant: Neo-Kantianism and its Relevance Today, The Philosophical Forum* 39 (2008).

Frank, Manfred. *»Unendliche Annäherung«, Die Anfänge der philosophischen Frühromantik.* Frankfurt: Suhrkamp, 1997.

Frank, Manfred, *Unendliche Annäherung: Die Anfänge der philosophischen Romantik.* Frankfurt: Suhrkamp, 1998.

Friedman, Michael and Nordmann, Alfred, eds, *The Kantian Legacy in Nineteenth-Century Science.* Cambridge, MA: MIT Press, 2006.

Holzhey, Helmut, 'Neukantianismus', in *Historisches Wörterbuch der Philosophie.* Basel: Schwabe, 1984. VI, 747–754.

Holzhey, Helmut, ed. *Ethischer Sozialismus.* Frankfurt: Suhrkamp, 1994.

Köhnke, Klaus Christian, *Entstehung und Aufstieg des Neukantianismus: Die deutsche Universitätsphilosophie zwischen Idealismus und Positivismus.* Frankfurt: Suhrkamp, 1986.

Lehmann, Gerhard, *Geschichte der nachkantischen Philosophie.* Berlin: Junker und Dünnhaupt, 1931.

Linden, Harry van der, *Kantian Ethics and Socialism.* Indianapolis, IN: Hackett, 1968.

Luft, Sebastian and Makkreel, eds, *Neo-Kantianism in Contemporary Philosophy.* Bloomington, IN: Indiana University Press, 2010.

Ollig, Hans-Ludwig, *Der Neukantianismus.* Stuttgart: Metzler, 1979.

Riley, Patrick, *Kant's Political Philosophy.* Totowa, NJ: Rowan and Littlefield, 1983.

Seung, T.K., *Kant's Platonic Revolution in Moral and Political Philosophy.* Baltimore, MD: Johns Hopkins University Press, 1994.

Sieg, Ulrich, *Aufstieg und Niedergang des Marburger Neukantianismus.* Würzburg: Königshausen & Neumann, 1994.

Vaihinger, Hans, *Kommentar zu Kants Kritik der reinen Vernunft.* Stuttgart: Deutsche Verlags Anstalt, 1922.

Willey, Thomas E., *Back to Kant: The Revival of Kantianism in German Social and Historical Thought,* 1860–1914. Detroit, MI: Wayne State University Press, 1978.

Beneke, Friedrich

Avineri, Shlomo, *Hegel's Theory of the Modern State*. Cambridge: Cambridge University Press, 1972.

Brandt, Francis, *Friedrich Eduard Beneke: The Man and his Philosophy*. New York: Macmillan, 1895.

Gramzow, Otto, *Friedrich Eduard Benekes Leben und Philosophie*. Bern: Steiger, 1899.

Murtfeld, Rudolf, 'Vergeblicher Kampf gegen den Idealismus. Friedrich Eduard Benekes Schicksal und seine Wissenschaftstheorien', *Zeitschrift für Geschichte der Erziehung und des Unterrichts* 26 (1936), 1–48.

Cohen, Hermann

Adelmann, Dieter, 'H. Steinthal und Hermann Cohen', in *Hermann Cohen's Philosophy of Religion*, eds Stéphane Moses and Hartwig Wiedelbach. Hildesheim: Olms, 1997, pp. 1–33.

Brandt, Reinhardt, 'Hermeneutik und Seinslehre bei Hermann Cohen', in *Philosophisches Denken-Politisches Wirken: Hermann Cohen-Kolloquium Marburg 1992*, eds Reinhardt Brandt and Franz Orlik. Hildesheim: Olms, 1993, pp. 37–54.

Brelage, Manfred, *Studien zur Transzendental Philosophie*. Berlin: de Gruyter, 1965.

Cassirer, Ernst, 'Hermann Cohen und die Erneuerung der kantischen Philosophie', *Kant-Studien* 17 (1912), 252–273.

Holzhey, Helmut, 'Cohen and the Marburg School in Context', in *Hermann Cohen's Critical Idealism*, ed. Reinier Munk. Dordrecht: Springer, 2005, pp. 3–41.

Kalmar, Ivan, "The *Völkerpsychologie* of Lazarus and Steinthal and the Modern Concept of Culture', *Journal of the History of Ideas* 48 (1987), 671–690.

Kinkel, Walter, *Hermann Cohen: Eine Einführung in sein Werk*. Stuttgart: Strecker und Schröder, 1924.

Klatzkin, Jakob, *Hermann Cohen*. Zweite erweiterte Auflage. Berlin: Jüdischer Verlag, 1921.

Kluback, William, *The Legacy of Hermann Cohen*. Atlanta, GA: Scholars Press, 1989.

Köhnke, Klaus, '"Unser junger Freud" – Hermann Cohen und die Völkerpsychologie', in *Hermann Cohen und die Erkenntnistheorie*, eds Wolfgang Marx and Ernst Orth. Würzburg: Königshausen & Neumann, 2001, pp. 62–77.

Kühn, Manfred, 'Interpreting Kant Correctly: On the Kant of the Neo-Kantians', in *Neo-Kantianism in Contemporary Philosophy*, eds Rudolf Makkreel and Sebastian Luft. Bloomington, IN: Indiana University Press, 2010, pp. 113–131.

Marck, Siegfried, 'Die Lehre vom erkennenden Subjekt in der Marburger Schule', *Logos* IV (1913), 364–366.

Munk, Reinier, ed., *Hermann Cohen's Critical Idealism*. Dordrecht: Springer, 2005.

Natorp, Paul, 'Kant und die Marburger Schule', *Kant-Studien* 17 (1912), 193–221.

Orth, Ernst Wolfgang, 'Trendelenburg und die Wissenschaft als Kulturfaktum', in *Hermann Cohen und die Erkenntnistheorie*, eds Wolfgang Marx and Ernst Orth. Würzburg: Königshausen & Neumann, 2001, pp. 49–61.

Poma, Andrea, *The Critical Philosophy of Hermann Cohen*. Albany, NY: State University of New York, 1997.

Poma, Andrea, *Yearning for Form and Other Essays on Herman Cohen's Thought*. Dordrecht: Springer, 2006.

Schmidt, Winrich de, *Psychologie und Transzendentalphilosophie: Zur Psychologie Rezeption bei Hermann Cohen und Paul Natorp*. Bonn: Bouvier, 1976.

Schulthess, Peter, 'Einleitung' to Band V of *Hermann Cohen Werke*. Hildesheim: Olms, 2005. V, 7*–46*.

Sieg, Ulrich, 'Hermann Cohen und die Völkerpsychologie', *Aschkenas* XIII (2004), 461–483.

Strawson, P.F., *The Bounds of Sense*. London: Methuen, 1966.

Zank, Michael, *The Idea of Atonement in the Philosophy of Hermann Cohen*. Providence, RI: Brown Judaic Studies, 2000.

Darwin, Charles

Backenköhler, Dirk, 'Only Dreams from an Afternoon Nap? Darwin's Theory of Evolution and the Foundation of Biological Anthropology in Germany 1860–1875', in *The Reception of Charles Darwin in Europe*, eds Eve-Marie Engels and Thomas Glick. London: Continuum, 2008. I, 98–115.

Daum, Andreas, *Wissenschaftspopulisierung im 19. Jahrhundert*. Munich: Oldenbourg, 2002.

Engels, Eve-Marie, *Die Rezeption von Evolutionstheorien im 19. Jahrhundert*. Frankfurt: Suhrkamp, 1995.

Engels, Eve-Marie, and Glick, Thomas F., *The Reception of Charles Darwin in Europe*. London: Continuum, 2008. 4 vols.

Gregario, Mario Di, 'Under Darwins Banner: Ernst Haeckel, Carl Gegenbaur and Evolutionary Morphilogy' in *The Reception of Charles Darwin in Europe*, eds Eve-Marie Engels and Thomas Glick. London: Continuum, 2008. I, 79–97.

Hull, David, 'Darwin's science and Victorian philosophy of science', in *The Cambridge Companion to Darwin*, second edition, eds Jonathan Hodge and Gregory Radick. Cambridge: Cambridge University Press, 2009, pp. 173–196.

Kelly, Alfred, *The Descent of Darwin: The Popularization of Darwinism in Germany 1860–1914*. Chapel Hill, NC: University of North Carolina Press, 1981.

Montgomery, William, 'Germany', in *Comparative Reception of Darwinism*, ed. Thomas F. Glick. Austin, TX: University of Texas Press, 1972, pp. 81–115.

Nyhart, Lynn, *Biology Takes Form: Animal Morphology in German Universities, 1800–1900*. Chicago, IL: University of Chicago Press, 1995.

Richards, Robert, *The Meaning of Evolution*. Chicago, IL: University of Chicago Press, 1992.

Richards, Robert, *The Tragic Sense of Life: Ernst Haeckel and the Struggle over Evolutionary Thought*. Chicago, IL: University of Chicago Press, 2008.

Waters, Kenneth, 'The Arguments in the Origin of Species', *The Cambridge Companion to Darwin*, 2nd edn, eds Jonathan Hodge and Gregory Radick. Cambridge: Cambridge University Press, 2009, pp. 120–146.

Weindling, P.J., 'Darwinism in Germany', *The Darwinian Heritage*, ed. David Kohn. Princeton, NJ: Princeton University Press, 1985, pp. 685–698.

Fichte, Johann Gottlieb

Breazeale, Daniel, ed. 'Introduction'. *Fichte: Early Philosophical Writings*. Ithaca, NY: Cornell University Press, 1988, pp. 307–315.

Fischer, Kuno

Arnoldt, Emil, *Kant nach Kuno Fischers neuer Darstellung*. Königsberg: Beyer, 1882.
Briese, Olaf, 'Im Geflecht der Schulen. Christian Hermann Weißes akademisches Karriere', in *Konkurrenzen: Philosophische Kultur in Deutschland, 1830–1850*. Würzburg: Königshausen & Neumann, 1998, pp. 65–77.
Falckenheim, Hugo, 'Kuno Fischer', *Biographisches Jahrbuch und Deutscher Nekrolog* 12 (1907), 257–272.
Hülsewiesche, Reinhold, *System und Geschichte: Leben und Werke Kuno Fischers*. Bern: Peter Lang, 1989
Windelband, Wilhelm, *Kuno Fischer: Gedächtnisrede bei der Trauerfeier der Universität in der Stadthalle zu Heidelberg am 23 Juli 1907*. Heidelberg: Winter, 1907.

Fries, Jakob Friedrich

Blencke, Erna, 'Zur Geschichte der neuen Fries'ischen Schule', *Archiv für Geschichte der Philosophie* 60 (1978), 199–208.
Bonsiepen, Wolfgang, *Die Begründung einer Naturphilosophie bei Kant, Schelling, Fries und Hegel*. Frankfurt: Klostermann, 1997.
Elsenhans, Theodor, *Fries und Kant, ein Beitrag zur Geschichte und zur systematischen Grundlegung der Erkenntnistheorie*. Giessen: Töpelmann, 1906. 2 vols.
Görland, Albert, *Religionsphilosophie als Wissenschaft aus dem Systemgeiste des kritische Idealismus*. Berlin: de Gruyter, 1922.
Gregory, Frederick, 'Regulative Therapeutics in the German Romantic Era: The Contribution of Jakob Friedrich Fries (1773–1843)', *Clio Medica* XVIII (1983), 179–189.
Gregory, Frederick 'Die Kritik von Fries an Schellings Naturphilosophie', *Sudhoffs Archiv für Geschichte der Medizin* 67 (1983), 145–157.
Gregory, Frederick, 'Extending Kant: The Origins and Nature of Jakob Friedrich Fries's Philosophy of Science', in *The Kantian Legacy in Nineteenth Century Science*, eds. Michael Friedman and Alfred Nordmann. Cambridge, MA: MIT Press, 2006, pp. 81–100.
Henke, Ernst Ludwig, *Jakob Friedrich Fries. Aus seinem handschriftlichen Nachlasse dargestellt*. Leipzig: Brockhaus, 1867.
Henrich, Dieter, 'Kant's Notion of a Deduction and the Methodological Background of the First *Critique*', in *Kant's Transcendental Deductions*, ed. Ekhart Förster. Stanford, CA: Stanford University Press, 1989, pp. 24–46.
Hermann, Kay, *Mathematische Naturphilosophie in der Grundlagediskussion: Jakob Fries und die Wissenschaften*. Göttingen: Vandenhoeck & Ruprecht, 2000.
Hiller, Kurt, 'Die philosophische Rechtslehre des Jakob Friedrich Fries', *Archiv für Geschichte der Philosophie* XXX (1917), 251–269.
Hubmann, Gerald, *Ethische Überzeugung und politisches Handeln: Jakob Friedrich Fries und die deutsche Tradition der Gesinnungsethik*. Heidelberg: Winter, 1997.
Kronfeld, Arthur, 'Geleitworte zum zehnjährigen Bestehen der neue Friesischen Schule', in *Das Wesen der psychiatrischen Erkenntnis*. Berlin: Springer, 1920, pp. 46–65.
Mechler, Walter, *Die Erkenntnislehre bei Fries*. Berlin: Reuther & Reichard, 1911. *Kant-Studien* Ergänzungsheft Nr. 22.
Nelson, Leonard, *Jakob Friedrich Fries und seine jüngsten Kritiker*. Göttingen: Dieterich, 1909.

Nelson, Leonard, ed. *Abhandlungen der Fries'schen Schule. Neue Folge*. Göttingen: Vandenhoeck & Ruprecht, 1904–1937. 6 vols.

Nelson, Leonard, *Gesammelte Schriften in neuen Bänden*. Hamburg: Meiner, 1970. 9 volumes.

Nelson, Leonard, *Geschichte und Kritik der Erkenntnistheorie*. Hamburg: Meiner, 1973.

Otto, Rudolf, *Kant'isch-Fries'sche Religionsphilosophie und ihre Anwendung auf die Theologie*. Tübingen: Mohr, 1909.

Otto, Rudolf, *Das Heilige: Ueber das Irrationale in der Idee des Göttlichen und sein Verhältniß zum Rationalen*. Breslau: Trewandt und Granier, 1917.

Pulte, Helmut, 'Kant, Fries and the Expanding Universe of Science', in *The Kantian Legacy in Nineteenth-Century Science*, eds Michael Friedman and Alfred Nordmann. Cambridge, MA: MIT Press, 2006, pp. 101–122.

Herbart, Johann Friedrich

Asmus, Walter, *Johann Friedrich Herbart. Eine pädagogische Biographie*. Heidelberg: Quelle & Meyer, 1968–1970. 2 volumes.

Asmus, Walter, *Herbart in seiner und in unserer Zeit*. Essen: Neue deutsche Schule Verlagsgesellschaft, 1972.

Dunkel, Howard, article on Herbart in the *Encyclopedia of Philosophy*. New York: MacMillan 1963, III, 481.

Flitner, Willy, *August Ludwig Hülsen und der Bund der freien Männer*. Jena: Diedrich, 1913.

Flügel, Otto, *Herbarts Leben und Lehren*, Zweite Auflage. Leipzig: Teubner, 1912.

Fuchs, Erich, 'Aus dem Tagebuch von Johann Smidt (1794/95), *Fichte-Studien* VII (1995), 173–192.

Garmo, Charles de, *Herbart and the Herbartians*. New York: Scribner, 1896.

Lang, Ossian, *Outlines of Herbart's Pedagogics*. Chicago, IL: Kellogg & Co., 1894.

Weiß, Georg, *Herbart und seine Schule*. Munich: Reinhardt, 1928.

Lange, Friedrich

Bernstein, Eduard, 'Zur Würdigung Friedrich Albert Lange', *Die neue Zeit X* (1891–1892) II, 68–78, 101–109, 132–141.

Ellisen, A.O., *Friedrich Albert Lange. Eine Lebensbeschreibung*. Leipzig: Baedeker, 1894.

Holzhey, Helmut, 'Philosophische Kritik. Zum Verhältnis von Erkenntnistheorie und Sozialphilosophie bei F.A. Lange', in *Friedrich Albert Lange, Leben und Werke*, eds J.H. Knoll and J.H. Schoeps. Duisburg: Walter Braun Verlag, 1975, pp. 207–225.

Plump, Klaus, 'Der Nachlaß F.A. Langes im Stadtarchiv Duisburg', in *Friedrich Albert Lange, Leben und Werke*, eds J.H. Knoll and J.H. Schoeps. Duisberg: Walter Braun Verlag, 1975, pp. 236–267.

Sass, Hans Martin, 'Der Standpunkt des Ideals als kritische Überwindung materialistischer und idealistischer Metaphysik', in *Friedrich Albert Lange, Leben und Werke*, eds J.H. Knoll and J.H. Schoeps. Duisburg: Walter Braun Verlag, 1975, pp. 188–206.

Vorländer, Karl, 'Kant und der Sozialismus', *Kant-Studien* 4 (1900), 361–412.

Weyer, Adam, 'Religion und Sozialismus bei F.A. Lange', in *Friedrich Albert Lange, Leben und Werke*, eds J.H. Knoll and J.H. Schoeps. Duisburg: Walter Braun Verlag, 1975, pp. 226–235.

Liebmann, Otto

Adickes, Erich, 'Liebmann als Erkenntnistheoretiker', *Kant-Studien* 15 (1910), 1–52.

Bauch, Bruno, 'Nachruf auf den Sarge im Namen der Kant-Gesellschaft gesprochenen Worten', *Kant-Studien* 17 (1912), 5–8.

Bauch, Bruno, 'Kritizismus und Naturphilosophie bei Otto Liebmann', *Kant-Studien* 15 (1910), 115–138.

Bauch, Bruno, 'Vorwort des Herausgebers', *Kant und die Epigonen*. Berlin: Reuther & Reichard, 1912, pp. v–xii.

Bauch, Bruno, 'Otto Liebmann', Anhang to *Kant und die Epigonen*. Berlin: Reuther & Reichard, 1912, pp. 223–239.

Eucken, Rudolf, 'Ansprache bei der Bestattung', *Kant-Studien* 17 (1912), 1–5.

Hönigswald, Richard, 'Zu Liebmanns Kritik der Lehre vom psychophysischen Parallelismus', *Kant-Studien* 15 (1910), 94–114.

Kinkel, Walter, 'Das Verhältnis von Philosophie und Mathematik nach Liebmann', *Kant-Studien* 15 (1910), 54–85.

Medicus, Fritz, 'Otto Liebmann als Dichter', *Kant-Studien* 15 (1910), 139–151.

Windelband, Wilhelm, 'Otto Liebmanns Philosophie', *Kant-Studien* 15 (1910), iii–x.

Meyer, Jürgen Bona

Lipps, Theodor, 'Jürgen Bona Meyer', *Biographischer Jahrbuch und Deutscher Nekrolog* II (1898), 397–400.

R.D., 'Meyer, Jürgen Bona', *Allgemeine deutsche Biographie* 55 (1910), 560–563.

Riehl, Alois

Heidelberger, Michael, 'Kantianism and Realism: Alois Riehl (and Moritz Schlick)', in *The Neo-Kantian Legacy in Nineteenth Century Science*, eds Michael Friedman and Alfred Nordmann. Cambridge, MA: MIT Press, 2006, pp. 211–226.

Jaensch, Erich, 'Zum Gedächtnis von Alois Riehl', *Kant-Studien* 30 (1925), i–xxxvi.

Maier, Heinrich, 'Alois Riehl. Gedächtnisrede, gehalten am 24. Januar 1925', *Kant-Studien* 31 (1926), 563–579.

Rickert, Heinrich, 'Alois Riehl', *Logos* XIII (1924/25), 162–185.

Siegel, Carl, *Alois Riehl. Ein Beitrag zur Geschichte des Neukantianismus*. Graz: Leuschner & Lubensky, 1932.

Trendelenburg, Adolf

Bonitz, Hermann, *Erinnerung an Friedrich Adolf Trendelenburg*. Berlin: Dümmler, 1873.

Köhnke, Klaus Christian and Hartung, Gerald, eds, *Friedrich Adolf Trendelenburgs Wirkung*. Eutin: Eutiner Landesbibliothek, 2006.

von Prantl, Karl, *Gedächtnisrede auf Friedrich Adolf Trendelenburg*. Munich: Akademie der Wissenschaften, 1873.

Windelband, Wilhelm

Beiser, Frederick, 'Historicism and Neo-Kantianism', *Studies in History and Philosophy of Science* 39 (2008), 554–564.

Beiser, Frederick, *The German Historicist Tradition*. Oxford: Oxford University Press, 2011, pp. 365–392.

Honigsheim, Paul, 'Zur Hegel Renaissance im Vorkriegsheidelberg', *Hegel-Studien* II (1963), 291–301.

Maher, Chauncey, *The Philosophy of the Pittsburgh School*. London: Taylor & Francis, 2012.

Rickert, Heinrich, *Wilhelm Windelband*. Zweite Auflage. Tübingen: Mohr, 1929.

Zeller, Eduard

Hartung, Gerald, ed., *Eduard Zeller: Philosophie und Wissenschaftsgeschichte im 19. Jahrhundert*. Berlin: de Gruyter, 2010.

Diels, Hermann, *Gedächtnisrede auf Eduard Zeller*. Berlin: Akademie der Wissenschaften, 1908.

Dilthey, Wilhelm, 'Aus Eduard Zellers Jugendjahren', in *Gesammelte Schriften*. Leipzig: Teubner, 1921. IV, 432–450.

Ehlers, Dietrich, ed. *Hermann Diels, Hermann Usener, Eduard Zeller, Briefwechsel*. Berlin: Akademie Verlag, 1992.

Index